Communications in Computer and Information Science 645

Commenced Publication in 2007
Founding and Former Series Editors:
Alfredo Cuzzocrea, Dominik Ślęzak, and Xiaokang Yang

More information about this series at http://www.springer.com/series/7899

Lin Zhang · Xiao Song
Yunjie Wu (Eds.)

Theory, Methodology, Tools and Applications for Modeling and Simulation of Complex Systems

16th Asia Simulation Conference
and SCS Autumn Simulation Multi-Conference
AsiaSim/SCS AutumnSim 2016
Beijing, China, October 8–11, 2016
Proceedings, Part III

Editors
Lin Zhang
Beihang University
Beijing
China

Yunjie Wu
Beihang University
Beijing
China

Xiao Song
Beihang University
Beijing
China

ISSN 1865-0929   ISSN 1865-0937 (electronic)
Communications in Computer and Information Science
ISBN 978-981-10-2668-3   ISBN 978-981-10-2669-0 (eBook)
DOI 10.1007/978-981-10-2669-0

Library of Congress Control Number: 2016946015

Printed on acid-free paper

This Springer imprint is published by Springer Nature
The registered company is Springer Science+Business Media Singapore Pte Ltd.

Preface

AsiaSim/SCS AutumnSim 2016 (the 2016 International Simulation Multi-Conference) was a joint conference of the 16th Asia Simulation Conference and the 2016 Autumn Simulation Multi-Conference. The Asia Simulation Conference (AsiaSim) is an annual international conference started in 1999. In 2011, the Federation of Asian Simulation Societies (ASIASIM) was set up and the AsiaSim became an annual conference of ASIASIM. The SCS Autumn Simulation Multi-Conference (SCS AutumnSim) is one of the premier conferences of the Society for Modeling and Simulation International (SCS), which provides a unique opportunity to learn about emerging M&S applications in many thriving fields. AsiaSim/SCS AutumnSim 2016 was the first conference jointly sponsored by ASIASIM and SCS and organized by the China Simulation Federation (CSF), Science and Technology on Special System Simulation Laboratory (STSSSL), and Beihang University (BUAA). It was also co-sponsored by the China Simulation Federation (CSF), the Japanese Society for Simulation Technology (JSST), the Korea Society for Simulation (KSS), the Society for Simulation and Gaming of Singapore (SSAGSG), the International Association for Mathematics and Computers in Simulation (IMACS), the Chinese Association for Artificial Intelligence (CAAI), China Computer Federation (CCF), the China Electrotechnical Society (CES), the China Graphics Society (CGS), and the China Ordnance Society (COS).

This conference is a big event that provides a unique opportunity to learn about emerging M&S research achievements and applications in many thriving fields, focusing on the theory, methodology, tools and applications for M&S of complex systems; it provides a forum for the latest R&D results in academia and industry.

The papers contained in these proceedings address challenging issues in M&S theory and methodology, model engineering for system of systems, high-performance computing and simulation, M&S for smart city, robot simulations, M&S for intelligent manufacturing, military simulation, as well as cloud technologies in simulation applications.

This year, AsiaSim/SCS AutumnSim received 639 submissions. Submissions came from around 15 countries and regions. After a thorough reviewing process, 267 papers were selected for presentation as full papers, with an acceptance rate of 41.8 %. These papers are published in the proceedings in the four volumes, 643–646. Volume 643 mainly addresses the issues of basics of M&S theory and methodology. Volume 644 discusses M&S for intelligent manufacturing and military simulation methods. In Vol. 645, cloud technologies in simulation applications, simulation and big data techniques are covered. And Vol. 646 presents M&S applications and simulation software.

The high-quality program would not have been possible without the authors who chose AsiaSim/SCS AutumnSim 2016 as a venue for their publications. Also, we would like to take this opportunity to thank the ASIASIM Federation for allowing us to host AsiaSim 2016 in Beijing.

We also thank the members of the Program Committee for their valuable effort in the review of the submitted papers. Finally, we would also like to thank our technical co-sponsors and sponsors. Your contributions and support have helped to make AsiaSim/SCS AutumnSim 2016 a memorable and successful event.

We hope that you enjoy reading and benefit from the proceedings of AsiaSim/SCS AutumnSim 2016.

October 2016

Lin Zhang
Xiao Song
Yunjie Wu

Organization

Sponsors

Federation of Asian Simulation Societies (ASIASIM)
The Society for Modeling & Simulation International (SCS)

Co-Sponsors

China Simulation Federation (CSF)
Japanese Society for Simulation Technology (JSST)
Korea Society for Simulation (KSS)
Society for Simulation and Gaming of Singapore (SSAGSG)
International Association for Mathematics and Computers in Simulation (IMACS)
Chinese Association for Artificial Intelligence (CAAI)
China Computer Federation (CCF)
China Electrotechnical Society (CES)
China Graphics Society (CGS)
China Ordnance Society (COS)

Organizers

China Simulation Federation (CSF)
Science and Technology on Special System Simulation Laboratory (STSSSL)
Beihang University (BUAA)

Honorary Chairs

Chuanyuan Wen, China
Robert M. Howe, USA
Yukio Kagawa, Japan
Sadao Takaba, Japan
Sung-Joo Park, Korea
Tianyuan Xiao(†), China

General Chairs

Bo Hu Li, China
Qinping Zhao, China

Deputy General Chair

Agostino Bruzzone, Italy

General Co-chairs

Satoshi Tanaka, Japan
Jonghyun Kim, Korea
Axel Lehmann, Germany
Zicai Wang, China
Xianxiang Huang, China

Program Committee Chair

Lin Zhang, China

Program Committee Co-chairs

Bernard Zeigler, USA
Tuncer Ören, Canada
Ralph C. Huntsinger, USA
Xiaofeng Hu, China
Soo-Hyun Park, Korea
H.J. Halin, Switzerland
Kaj Juslin, Finland
Roy E. Crosbie, USA

Ming Yang, China
Xiaogang Qiu, China
Satoshi Tanaka, Japan
Jin Liu, China
Min Zhao, China
Shiwei Ma, China
Francesco Longo, Italy
Agostino Bruzzone, Italy

Program Committee

Anxiang Huang, China
Yoonbae Kim, Korea
Yu Yao, China
Fei Xie, USA
Toshiharu Kagawa, Japan
Giuseppe Iazeolla, Italy
Mhamed Itmi, France
Haixiang Lin, Netherlands
Henri Pierreval, France
Hugh HT Liu, Canada
Wolfgang Borutzky, Germany
Jong Sik Lee, Korea
Xiaolin Hu, USA
Yifa Tang, China

Wenhui Fan, China
Bernard Zeigler, USA
Mingduan Tang, China
Long Wang, China
ChaoWang, China
Doo-Kwon Baik, Korea
Shinsuke Tamura, Japan
Pierre Borne, France
Ratan Guha, USA
Reinhold Meisinger, Germany
Richard Fujimoto, USA
Ge Li, China
Jinhai Sun, China
Xinping Xiong, China

Changjian Bi, China
Jianguo Cao, China
Yue Dai, China
Minrui Fei, China
Chen Guo, China
Fengju Kang, China
Guoxiong Li, China
Jin Liu, China
Shiwei Ma, China
Jipeng Wang, China
Zhongjie Wang, China
Hongjun Zhang, China
Qinping Zhao, China
Guomin Zhou, China
Gary S.H. Tan, Singapore
Francesco Longo, Italy
Hong Zhou, China
Shin'ichi Oishi, Japan
Zhenhao Zhou, China
Beike Zhang, China
Alain Cardon, France
Xukun Shen, China
Yangsheng Wang, China
Marzuki Khalid, Malaysia
Sergio Junco, Argentina
Tieqiao Wen, China
Xingsheng Gu, China
Zhijian Song, China
Yue Yang, China

Yongsheng Ding, China
Huimin Fan, China
Ming Chen, China
Javor, Andras, Hungary
Nabendu Chaki, India
Koji Koyamada, Japan
Osamu Ono, Japan
Yunjie Wu, China
Beiwei Guo, China
Ni Li, China
Shixuan Liu, China
Linxuan Zhang, China
Fei Tao, China
Lei Ren, China
Xiao Song, China
Xudong Chai, China
Zonghai Chen, China
Yuhao Cong, China
Guanghong Gong, China
Zhicheng Ji, China
Weidong Jin, China
Bo Hu Li, China
Ma Ping, China
Shaojie Mao, China
Zhong Su, China
Jianping Wu, China
Min Zhao, China
Huizhou Zheng, China

Organization Committee Chair

Yunjie Wu, China

Organization Committee Co-chairs

Shixuan Liu, China
Zaijun Shi, China
Linxuan Zhang, China
Ni Li, China
Fei Tao, China

Beiwei Guo, China
Xiao Song, China
Weijing Wang, China
Lei Ren, China

General Secretaries

Shixuan Liu, China
Xiao Song, China

Special Session Chairs

Ni Li, China
Linxuan Zhang, China

Publication Chairs

Shiwei Ma, China
Xiao Song, China

Publicity Chairs

Fei Tao, China
Baiwei Guo, China

Awards Committee Chairs

Lin Zhang, China
Axel Lehmann, Germany

Awards Committee Co-chair

Yifa Tang, China

Awards Committee Members

Sung-Yong Jang, Korea
Wenhui Fan, China
Xiao Song, China

Contents – Part III

Fractional Calculus with Applications and Simulations

M&S for Energy, Environment and Climate

SBA Virtual Prototyping Engineering Technology

Simulation and Big Data

Cloud Technologies in Simulation Applications

Visualizing the Architectural Structure of a Historical Building by Clustering Its Laser-Scanned Point Cloud

Wang Sheng[1]([⊠]), Kyoko Hasegawa[2], Atsushi Okamoto[3], and Satoshi Tanaka[3]

[1] Graduate School of Information Science and Engineering, Ritsumeikan University, 1-1-1 Nojihigashi, Kusatsu, Shiga, Japan
cm013076@ed.ritsumei.ac.jp
[2] College of Information Science and Engineering, Ritsumeikan University, Kyoto, Japan
[3] History Reasearch Institute, Otemae University, Osaka, Japan

Abstract. A new approach to visualize the laser-scanned point cloud of historical buildings is introduced. It has 2 advanced features: transparent rendering effect and an unsupervised extraction of architectural information. The transparent rendering is conducted using our previously reported rendering tool, Stochastic Point-based Rendering (SPBR). The architectural information extraction is realized with the point cloud clustering method, which considers pre-segmented sub point sets as the primitive units in the feature space for clustering instead of using raw points. This method increases the accuracy and reduces the computational cost of architectural information extraction.

Keywords: Point cloud visualization · Historical building · Point cloud clustering

1 Introduction

The visualization of laser-scanned point clouds has been widely used for create BIMs (Building Information Models), maintain industrial products, preserve cultural properties, etc. [1–3]. However, the general applications can only visualize notably basic features such as the 2D/3D coordinate position, surface normal, and curvature because of the unstructured data format of the input point cloud and poor characteristics of each point. Further-more, the huge data size (more than 10^8 in practical usage) is another bottleneck of advanced visualization based on raw laser-scanned point clouds [4–6].

Based this background, point-based rendering considering a single point as the rendering primitive has become a focus of the research field and has been actively developed. Until now, a laser-scanned point cloud can be rendered, as it is initially acquired or simply interpolated based on the height, color, surface normal, etc. [7,8]. Stochastic point-based rendering (SPBR) was reported in our

© Springer Science+Business Media Singapore 2016
L. Zhang et al. (Eds.): AsiaSim 2016/SCS AutumnSim 2016, Part III, CCIS 645, pp. 3–12, 2016.
DOI: 10.1007/978-981-10-2669-0_1

previous work [9,10]. It features not only high-speed rendering based on a large-scale point cloud but also a new rendering effect that allows the input point cloud to be transparently rendered. SPBR is good at visualizing objects with complicated structures, such as motor engines, human organs, and historical buildings, on which we would like to focus in this paper.

Unlike motor engines and human organs, historical buildings are basically measured using a long-range laser scanner. Hence, the acquired data are commonly unorganized and feature nonuniform density, which makes the feature extraction difficult to apply. However, the visualization of high-level features is strongly demanded. With SPBR, the interior and exterior of historical buildings have been visualized, and the rendering result (see Fig. 5a) shows that the architectural structures can be roughly observed. However, the indication of specific construction parts (walls, floor, ceiling, pillars, beams, etc.) remains unavailable.

As an extension of our previous work, this paper aims to resolve this problem. We use the point cloud segmentation and point cloud clustering methods to extract underling architectural information from the laser-scanned point cloud of human-designed buildings (historical buildings are the main target in this paper). Then, with the extracted results, we use SPBR to visualize the architectural structures of the target building.

The paper consists of 2 parts. In Sect. 2, we discuss the extraction of architectural structures. In Sect. 3, we introduce how the architectural structures are visualized. Section 4 is the conclusion.

2   Extraction of Architectural Information

Before the visualization, the architectural structures must be extracted. The extraction of specified features of the point cloud has attracted much attention when the point cloud concept was introduced, and several point cloud processing methods have been proposed [11,12]. However, it is still a challenging because the nonuniform and unstructured data form prevent researchers from precisely decomposing a point cloud, particularly with a complicated inner or outer structure. The most used point cloud processing methods to extract features from a point cloud or segment point cloud into sub point clouds can be divided to 3 categories: region-based methods [13,14], shape-based methods [15], and feature-based methods [16,17]. All methods have advantages and disadvantages. The region-based methods focus on the local variation of specific features (point distance, surface normal, color, etc.). Shape-based methods such as RANSAC and Hoff transform can extract points on a specific geometric shape. Feature-based methods throw all points into a feature space and cluster the points with similar features. The common principle of all existing methods is that they consider a single point as the most basic unit.

In this paper, a combination of point cloud processing methods is used to extract the architectural structures from the laser-scanned point cloud of a target building. Unlike the existing processes, which directly obtain output information from the input data, a medium layer between the input point cloud and the output result is added, where the most basic unit is a planar point cloud fragment.

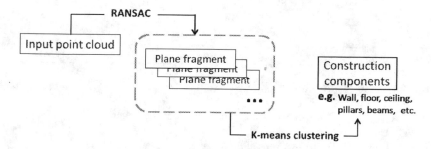

Fig. 1. Flow chart of the architectural structures extraction.

Our process has 2 phases. In the first phase, the input point cloud is segmented to planar fragments and outliers using RANSAC. In the second phase, the K-means clustering method is used to group the segmented result according to the features of each planar fragment instead of a single point. A flow chart of the process is shown in Fig. 1.

2.1 Plane Extraction

The basic construction components such as walls, floor, ceiling, etc., compose the human-designed buildings and can be further decomposed into planar surfaces. RANSAC is used to extract the planar surfaces. However, directly running RANSAC may cause errors that over-extract points that do not belong to the target area because RANSAC is insensitive to the consecutiveness of the point cloud. To solve this problem, a hybrid plane extraction method is used.

The method is a combination of RANSAC, Euclidean clustering, and a process to judge whether the extracted point set is wanted. First, RANSAC is called to extract the initial plane point set. Second, Euclidean clustering is applied to segment the point set into several sub clusters based on the point distance. Third, for each sub cluster, the judging process is called to check whether the sub cluster belongs to a single component; the positive ones are saved, and the negative ones are rejected. The cycle is repeated until no sub planes are obtained from the initial plane point set. A pseudo code to implement the hybrid method is shown in Algorithm 1.

The hybrid method can precisely extract planar fragments from the input point cloud. The shortcoming of RANSAC of over-segmenting unrelated points is improved using the Euclidean clustering and judging process. For human-designed buildings, the laser-scanned point cloud can be deeply decomposed, and the extracted planar fragments can be considered the most basic components, which overturns the usual practice of existing studies which regards the single point as the primitive. An extraction results using the hybrid method is shown in Fig. 2. As shown, the hybrid method successfully segmented the point cloud into sub planar fragments.

Algorithm 1. Pseudo code of the implementation of the plane extraction

Input: *cloud*

    <u>RANSAC</u>(*cloud*): Return a sub point cloud in which all points belong to a plane model in *cloud*.

    <u>Euclidean</u>(*cloud*): Return a vector of sub point cloud from *cloud* which is segmented based on the Euclidean distance.

    <u>PlaneCheck</u>(*cloud*): Return *true* if *cloud* fits the given plane model.

```
1: procedure PLANAR-FRAGMENT EXTRACTION
2:     while cloud.size > threshold do
3:         tmp cloud ← RANSAC(cloud)
4:         cluster[1], ..., cluster[n] ← Euclidean(tmp cloud)
5:         for i = 1 → n do
6:             if PlaneCheck(cluster[i]) = true then
7:                 Store cluster[i]
8:                 cloud ← cloud − cluster[i]
```

Fig. 2. Segmentation results of a laser-scanned point cloud by RANSAC. The red-colored area is the rejected outlier, the other parts are the segmented sub point sets. (Color figure online)

2.2   K-Means Clustering

Segmented planar fragments hold more features and are easier to differentiate from one another than the raw points. K-means clustering, which is a typical method to resolve clustering issues, is used to label the segmented planar fragment. A desirable result of K-means clustering is that all clustered samples are clearly grouped and separated in the feature space. For the laser-scanned point cloud of buildings, the clusters should be the construction components (e.g., walls, floor, ceiling, pillars, beams) which represent the architectural structures of the buildings. Former approaches, which directly cluster the raw points in the point cloud (see Fig. 3a), always obtain ambiguous results, where the samples in the feature space appear messy because of the large-scale number and poor features of the raw points. Biosca, J. M. et al. [16] reported their work for clustering the raw points of a laser-scanned point cloud, but they required strict data acquisition condition or specific supplementary devices.

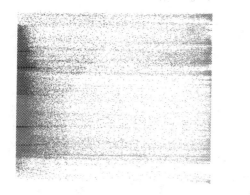

(a) Clustering result with a raw point cloud.

(b) Clustering result with planar fragments.

Fig. 3. A comparison of the K-means clustering results ($K = 5$). The vertical axis refers to the height. The horizontal axis indicates the third components of the surface normal.

As previously mentioned, instead of raw points, we consider the planar fragments as the samples in the feature space of the K-means clustering. First, a two dimensional feature space is constructed, where the x-axis indicates the ratio of the height of the fragment to the max height, the y-axis refers to the third components of the surface normal (Fig. 3b shows the result). Second, K which is the number of clusters to be labeled is determined. k depends on the complexity of the target building, where a proper range is 3 to 6. Third, the points of each labeled cluster are extracted from the input point cloud. A K-means clustering result with planar fragments is shown in Fig. 3b, where the labeled

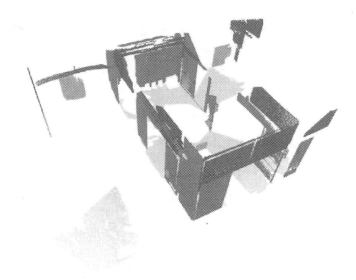

Fig. 4. Extracted construction components. The yellow-colored area denotes the floor, the violet and red areas denote the walls, the blue area is ceiling, and the green colored area is ornament. (Color figure online)

groups of samples in the feature space are clearly separated. Each group refers to a component part (e.g., walls, floor, ceiling, pillars, beams, ornaments, etc.). The corresponding component part can be directly extracted from the input point cloud according to the K-means clustering result. An example of extraction result ($K = 5$) is shown in Fig. 4. As shown, the floor, wall, and ceiling parts were extracted and separated from one another. Further-more, the upper walls which include the beams and parts of the decoration, were also extracted. The K-means clustering was conducted using opencv (http://opencv.org/) and pcl (http://pointclouds.org/).

3   Visualization of Architectural Structures

In this section, we visualize the architectural structures of the target building based on the extracted construction components. We used the advantage of SPBR, which renders objects with the transparent effect to manipulate the transparency (opacity) of component parts of the target building, and we obtained a rendering result with partially enhanced visual effect. In Sect. 3.1, the details regarding SPBR are introduced. In Sects. 3.2, to evaluate our work, a case study is conducted using Nakajima residence, which is a traditional Japanese farmer house.

3.1 Stochastic Point-Based Rendering (SPBR)

The transparent rendering of a large-scale point cloud has been challenging. Even with the latest powerful GPU, real-time rendering remains difficult to achieve because sorting by depth (which is ignored in opaque rendering) along the line of sight, which is directly relevant to the transparent effect, is computationally expensive. Instead, a point projection process based on binomial distribution is implemented in SPBR to skip the sorting issue. The transparency (opacity) is determined based on the number of projected points in the local area. The projected points are stochastically selected, and the relation between the point number and the transparency (opacity) is summarized in formula (1):

$$\alpha = 1 - \left(1 - \frac{s}{S}\right)^{n/L_R} \tag{1}$$

α, S, n are the transparency (opacity), size of any local area, and number of points in the entire area, respectively. s is the default size of a single point. L_R is a variable to control the fineness of the rendering result.

This approach was introduced in details in our previous report on SPBR [9,10]. However, only the global transparency (opacity) was mentioned, and the local transparency (opacity) could not be adjusted. To resolve this problem, we consider the input point cloud as a group of sub point sets. For each sub point set, we suppose that it is an entire point cloud, and its transparency (opacity) is determined using formula (1), but n and S are altered. Hence, we obtain 1 unique transparency (opacity) for every single sub point set. In other words, the local transparency (opacity) can be adjusted by extracting the local area from the input point cloud. The local transparency (opacity) generalization is derived from formula (1) as follows:

$$\alpha_i = 1 - \left(1 - \frac{s}{S_i'}\right)^{n_i/L_R}$$
$$P_{all} = \sum_i P_i \tag{2}$$

α_i is the transparency (opacity) of the sub point set P_i. S_i' is the size of an arbitrary area in P_i. n_i is the number of points in P_i. P_{all} refers to the input point cloud.

In summary, we can assign distinct transparencies to different parts of the input point cloud if such parts are correctly extracted.

3.2 Case Study by Nakajima Residence

The Nakajima residence is a traditional Japanese farmer house that typifies the structure "Tanoji" in old Japan. The visualization of the specific structure is strongly demanded. We measured the house using a terrestrial laser scanner and obtained a point cloud with 30 M points. A rendering result of the raw point

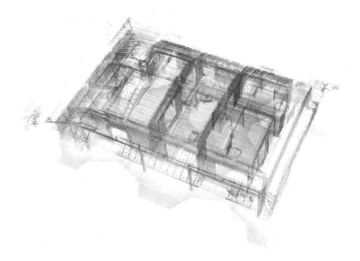

(a) Rendering result with the raw point cloud of Nakajima residence.

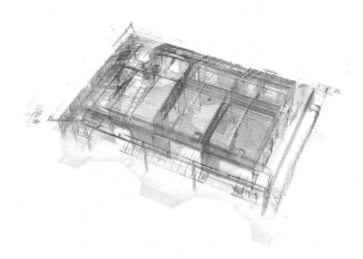

(b) Rendering result with the extracted construction components.

Fig. 5. A comparison of the rendering result using SPBR with 1 global transparency (opacity) and locally adjusted transparencies (opacities). The color hue of the extracted components is changed in (b).

cloud using SPBR is shown in Fig. 5a. Both interior and exterior information is included and transparently visualized. However, the structure features remain indistinct. The rendering result after the architectural feature extraction is displayed in Fig. 5b. As shown, by adjusting rendering parameters (transparency (opacity), color, and particle size) a part of the architectural structure can be clearly observed. The rendering effect can also be customized so that the users can change the parameters depending on their preferences and demands.

4   Conclusion

A new approach to visualize the architectural structures of laser-scanned point clouds of buildings is introduced in this paper. A combination of the point cloud segmentation techniques and K-means clustering method is used to extract the architectural features. Then the processed point cloud is rendered using SPBR, which is our rendering tool for particle based data.

In this paper, planar fragments, which are pre-segmented from the raw point cloud are considered the smallest units instead of the single point. This approach reduces the number of samples in the feature-space of K-means clustering from tens of million to hundreds and increases the accuracy of the architectural structure extractions. The basic construction components in the point cloud, such as walls, floor, ceiling, a part of pillar and beams, can be recognized.

SPBR is the key point and is used to visualize the extracted architectural structures. As an extension of our previous work, where the point cloud was rendered as it was initially acquired, this paper decomposes the raw point cloud and sets various rendering features to the subdivided point sets to separate the foreground and background in the rendering result. The users can customize the rendering effect in accordance with their preferences and demands to obtain the desired rendering result.

In future work, we will focus on extracting more detailed structure information. Further-more, we can only decompose the point cloud into planar fragments until now. Segmenting the point cloud into other basic geometric shapes such as cylinders and spheres is another problem to be solved.

Acknowledgment. The authors would like to thank Rui Xu for the technical assistance. We also thank the cooperation of the history and folk culture museum of Ritto (Shiga, Japan). This work was supported by JSPS KAKENHI Grant Number 16H02826.

References

1. Rusu, R.B., Cousins, S.: 3D is here: point cloud library (PCL). In: 2011 IEEE International Conference on Robotics and Automation (ICRA), pp. 1–4. IEEE (2011)
2. Buckley, S.J., Howell, J.A., Enge, H.D., Kurz, T.H.: Terrestrial laser scanning in geology: data acquisition, processing and accuracy considerations. J. Geol. Soc. **165**(3), 625–638 (2008)

3. Linsen, L.: Point cloud representation. Univ., Fak. für Informatik, Bibliothek (2001)
4. Vosselman, G., Maas, H.G. (eds.): Airborne and Terrestrial Laser Scanning. Whittles Publishing, Dunbeath (2010)
5. Slob, S., Hack, R.: 3D terrestrial laser scanning as a new field measurement and monitoring technique. In: Hack, R., Azzam, R., Charlier, R. (eds.) Engineering Geology for Infrastructure Planning in Europe. LNES, vol. 104, pp. 179–189. Springer, Heidelberg (2004)
6. Wolfgang, B., Vicent, M.B., Marbs, A.: Investigating laser scanner accuracy. Int. Arch. Photogrammetry Remote Sens. Spat. Inf. Sci. **34**(Part 5), 696–701 (2003)
7. Fröhlich, C., Mettenleiter, M., et al.: Terrestrial laser scanning new perspectives in 3D surveying. Int. Arch. Photogrammetry Remote Sens. Spat. Inf. Sci. **36**(Part 8), W2 (2004)
8. Al-Kheder, S., Al-Shawabkeh, Y., et al.: Developing a documentation system for desert palaces in Jordan using 3D laser scanning and digital photogrammetry. J. Archaeol. Sci. **36**(2), 537–546 (2009)
9. Tanaka, S., Hasegawa, K., et al.: Particle-based transparent rendering of implicit surfaces and its application to fused visualization. In: Proceedings of EuroVis 2012 (2012)
10. Tanaka, S., Uemura, M., Hasegawa, K., et al.: Application of stochastic point-based rendering to transparent visualization of large-scale laser-scanned data of 3D cultural assets. In: Pacific Visualization Symposium. IEEE (2014)
11. Hno, R., Chandelier, L.: Point cloud processing. In: 3D Modeling of Buildings, pp. 133–181
12. Vosselman, G.: Advanced point cloud processing. In: Photogrammetric Week, vol. 9 (2009)
13. Pu, S., Vosselman, G.: Automatic extraction of building features from terrestrial laser scanning. Int. Arch. Photogrammetry Remote Sens. Spat. Inf. Sci. **36**(5), 25–27 (2006)
14. Rabbani, T., van den Heuvel, F., Vosselmann, G.: Segmentation of point clouds using smoothness constraint. Int. Arch. Photogrammetry Remote Sens. Spat. Inf. Sci. **36**(5), 248–253 (2006)
15. Schnabel, R., Wahl, R., et al.: Efficient RANSAC for point cloud shape detection. Comput. Graph. Forum **26**(2), 214–226 (2007). Blackwell Publishing Ltd
16. Biosca, J.M., Lerma, J.L.: Unsupervised robust planar segmentation of terrestrial laser scanner point clouds based on fuzzy clustering methods. ISPRS J. Photogrammetry Remote Sens. **63**(1), 84–98 (2008)
17. Rusu, R.B., Holzbach, A., Blodow, N., Beetz, M.: Fast geometric point labeling using conditional random fields. In: IEEE/RSJ International Conference on Intelligent Robots and Systems, IROS 2009, pp. 7–12. IEEE (2009)

Cloud Manufacturing Service Selection Model Based on Adaptive Variable Evaluation Metrics

Jin Cui[1,2], Lei Ren[1,2], and Lin Zhang[1,2(✉)]

[1] School of Automation Science and Electrical Engineering, Beihang University,
Beijing 100191, China
{jincui,renlei}@buaa.edu.cn, johnlin9999@163.com
[2] Engineering Research Center of Complex Product Advanced Manufacturing Systems,
Ministry of Education, Beijing 100191, China

Abstract. Efficient solution for Cloud Manufacturing (CMfg) service optimal-selection plays an increasing critical part in CMfg systems as an ever-growing number of CMfg services are aggregating in a CMfg platform. In most current methods, a set of relatively fixed quality of service (QoS) indicators are adopted to deal with the optimal-selection for different types of CMfg services. However, this often leads to low accuracy and flexibility, especially when cloud users' requirements involve different CMfg services with respective individualized characteristics. This paper presents evaluation metrics pool based CMfg service selection model (CSS-P), a framework of CMfg service selection that introduces an evaluation metrics pool as well as a new service selection mechanism based on adaptive variable evaluation metrics. Adaptive individualized metrics contribute to improving the accuracy and flexibility of CMfg service matching and selection, and better meet the customized needs of cloud users.

Keywords: Cloud Manufacturing · Service-oriented manufacturing · Service selection · Adaptive variable evaluation metrics

1 Introduction

Against the background of the in-depth development of global industrial chain, manufacturing industry is transforming from traditional production-oriented mode to high value-added service-oriented mode [1]. Driven by the rapid development of information technology and advanced manufacturing mode, a new manufacturing paradigm as well as a new integrated technology, Cloud Manufacturing [2–7], is taking its shape gradually. CMfg is a service-oriented net-worked manufacturing model. By providing various manufacturing resources and capabilities as standard manufacturing services, CMfg makes it possible to achieve high utilization and on-demand use of manufacturing resources and capabilities conveniently and efficiently during the whole lifecycle of a product [2]. In addition, reliable and high-quality manufacturing services in CMfg platform will definitely benefit different customers with individualized requirements. Under the centralized management of a CMfg platform, various heterogeneous manufacturing resources and capabilities could be virtualized and encapsulated as CMfg services with

© Springer Science+Business Media Singapore 2016
L. Zhang et al. (Eds.): AsiaSim 2016/SCS AutumnSim 2016, Part III, CCIS 645, pp. 13–19, 2016.
DOI: 10.1007/978-981-10-2669-0_2

standard interfaces, thus different cloud users could request and invoke the customized CMfg services for product design, simulation, and fabrication on demand.

Numerous manufacturing services are aggregating in CMfg platform and becoming accessible to customers with various manufacturing requirements, there raises the concern over CMfg service optimal-selection. As one of the key issues as well as an essential supporting technique for CMfg platform, the CMfg service optimal-selection problem has attracted broad attention. A number of optimal-selection research works on manufacturing resource and manufacturing service have been carried out in the scenarios of advanced manufacturing systems. Existing researches on manufacturing resource and manufacturing service optimal-selection process focus on the decision model and the corresponding solving algorithm. Compared with optimal-selection model, it seems that researchers pay much more attention to high efficient intelligent solving algorithms.

Actually, the challenge to CMfg service optimal-selection lies in that how to design efficient model to meet consumers' customized demands for CMfg services, which is critical to the performance of a CMfg platform as well as to user satisfaction [8]. Current research fruits regarding such models mainly include QoS based model [9, 10], energy-aware resource service scheduling model [11], as well as QoS and energy consumption based service optimal selection model [12]. In practical terms, Tao et al. [13] studied the manufacturing grid resource service scheduling problem by introducing a new concept, trust-QoS. Measurement and evaluation approaches for trust-QoS are given in the context of manufacturing grid system. In order to achieve optimal allocation of the computing resources in the scenario of CMfg environment, Laili et al. [14] proposed a comprehensive optimization model with computation, communication and reliability constraints considered. In [9], Huang et al. presented a service composition selection model based on QoS for CMfg system. Then a chaos control mechanism based optimization algorithm is given to address the proposed optimal-selection model. In addition, Cheng et al. [11] investigated the energy-aware CMfg service scheduling mechanism based on a utility evaluation process. Taking energy consumption, cost, as well as risk for the providers, the consumers, and the operator into consideration, a comprehensive utility model is established for the manufacturing resource service scheduling process.

While these approaches address specific issues successfully in corresponding application scenarios, much more work need to be done when we face the personalized evaluation indices for CMfg service as well as reuse of CMfg service evaluation historical knowledge. The majority of existing CMfg service optimal-selection models usually employ a set of uniform metrics of QoS indicators, e.g., service time, cost and quality grade, for the evaluation process of all different types of CMfg services. However, relatively fixed metrics often leads to an overlook of the difference among different types of CMfg services that belong to different stages (product design phase, simulation phase, production phase, testing phase, etc.) of a product life cycle. For instance, parts processing services require more emphasis on product qualification rate, while simulation services need to focus on simulation accuracy and credibility. In fact, a CMfg platform should discover and select the services based on individualized evaluation indicators. In other words, it is more practical to design CMfg service optimal-selection model by employing variable QoS metrics. Besides, a CMfg platform can be regarded as an ever-growing knowledge base from another perspective. The CMfg platform could accumulate a large amount of historical service transaction data. The abundant knowledge contained in historical service cases has great potential for a CMfg platform to pick up the most suitable QoS indicators for different CMfg services [15], enabling intelligent discovery of adaptive evaluation metrics for specific service. In fact, adaptive individualized metrics contribute to the improvement of accuracy and flexibility of CMfg service matching and selection, which better meet the customized needs of CMfg service consumers. So far, there still lacks a theoretical framework that could support CMfg service optimal-selection based on adaptive variable evaluation metrics.

That is to say, absent from the trend is the adaptive evaluation metrics for CMfg service. Thus, there is a need to develop a framework for CMfg service optimal-selection process with adaptive variable evaluation metrics considered. To address these issues, this paper presents CSS-P, a CMfg service selection framework that introduces an evaluation metrics pool as well as a new service selection mechanism based on adaptive variable evaluation metrics. By reusing the historical data of CMfg service transactions, the CMfg service evaluation metrics pool is able to provide adaptive assessment indices for different CMfg services. Moreover, the operational mechanism of CMfg service evaluation metrics pool is illustrated in detail.

The remainder of the paper is organized as follows. Section 2 is the framework of CMfg service selection based on evaluation metrics pool. Section 3 presents the detailed description of CMfg service evaluation metrics pool as well as its dynamic operational mechanism. Section 4 concludes the work with recommendations for future studies.

2 CSS-P: Framework of CMfg Service Selection Based on Evaluation Metrics Pool

The users submit their manufacturing service requests to the CMfg platform and then publish these requirements to the CMfg task publication center. Through CMfg task decomposition system, the service requests are decomposed into a series of corresponding atomic subtasks which can be finished by certain CMfg services. In general, the basic decomposition structures for CMfg task could be classified into four modes [12], i.e., sequence mode, circular mode, selective mode and parallel mode. More ever, the CMfg task decomposition system converts the subtask requirement into standard description form (Fig. 1).

In the meantime, the manufacturing resource owners, either individuals or enterprises, publish their manufacturing resources to the CMfg platform via CMfg service publication center. The techniques of IoT and the relevant interfaces are utilized to perceive manufacturing resource [6]. Then, the virtual manufacturing resources are encapsulated into CMfg services. The corresponding standard CMfg service information is stored in the CMfg service information center.

In order to provide CMfg services for service users according to their individualized requirements, the CMfg platform intelligently selects services from the CMfg service information center for the subtasks generated in the CMfg task decomposition process. By invoking the similarity matching algorithms, the CMfg service matcher matches the

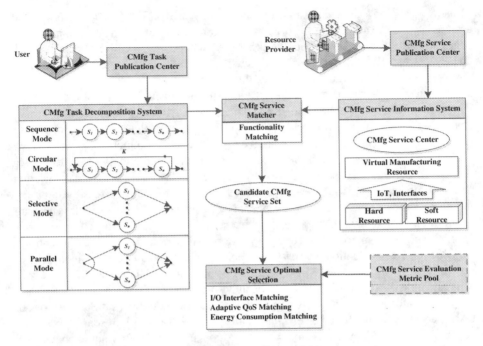

Fig. 1. Frame diagram of CSS-P

requested service information with each published CMfg service extracted from CMfg service information center. After the functionality matching step, each subtask obtains a candidate CMfg service set.

As there may exist a lot of services for a certain subtask according to the functional characteristics matching results, it raises the concern over CMfg service optimal selection. A CMfg service evaluation metric pool is introduced to achieve service optimal-selection according to their adaptive evaluation metric assigned by the pool. The detailed operational mechanism of the CMfg service evaluation metric pool will be presented in Sect. 3. The CMfg service optimal-selection module selects the optimal service through I/O interface matching, adaptive variable QoS matching and energy consumption matching. Note that the individualized assessment indices of each qualified CMfg service in the matching processes are provided by the evaluation metric pool.

3   Operational Mechanism of CMfg Service Evaluation Metrics Pool

For the sake of picking a suitable CMfg service which providing both high quality and low energy consumption service from the candidate CMfg service set for a certain CMfg service requirement, the quantitative evaluation metrics of CMfg service are indispensable. Existing works on resource service assessment, whether QoS based or energy consumption oriented, possess the fixed quantitative assessment indices which neglect the difference among the varied resource services. By utilizing intelligent inference algorithms, the CMfg service evaluation metric pool customizes evaluation metrics for CMfg service according to the accumulated knowledge in the pool as well as the specific demands of the service user. At the same time, new CMfg service types and fresh evaluation metrics are added to the evaluation metric pool constantly through the implementation of machine learning algorithms. The brief working flows of the CMfg service evaluation metric pool are described as follows:

1. The detailed description information of the candidate CMfg service is presented to the CMfg service evaluation metric pool. Next, the system matches the service type of the input CMfg service with the historical service types in the evaluation metric pool. There are two possible options according to the matching result (Fig. 2).

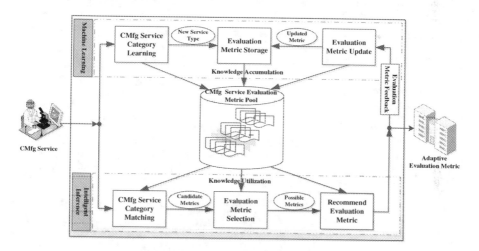

Fig. 2. Operational mechanism of CMfg service evaluation metrics pool

2. If the input CMfg service acquires a matched service type from the CMfg service evaluation metric pool, then the historical assessment indices of the specific type of CMfg service are listed as the candidate metrics of the input service. As one kind of service probably get several quite different indices, the evaluation metric selection process choose the most promising metrics in the light of a statistical analysis of the historical records of the service users, which generating the possible metric set. In addition, the customer of the input CMfg service perhaps pays extra attention to some special aspects of the service. With user's concerns taken into account, the adaptive evaluation metrics are finally identified. In short, the adaptive evaluation metrics for CMfg service take the individuality of the service, the specific requirements of the customer and the solving complexity into consideration comprehensively.

3. Else if the input CMfg service does not match any available information from the CMfg service evaluation metric pool, it indicates that the input service belongs to a totally new CMfg service category which has little information in the evaluation metric pool. In this case, the input CMfg service should be expanded in the CMfg service evaluation metric pool as a new type of service. Meanwhile, a number of general metrics, i.e., service execution time, service cost, are recommended to measure the input CMfg service. And then, the eventually selected metrics which consider the user's concerns are recorded in the evaluation metric pool via the evaluation metric feedback mechanism. Better still, the new CMfg service type and the adaptive metrics are related to each other and could be updated continually.

Along with the constant invoking of the CMfg service evaluation metric pool, new service categories and fresh service evaluation metrics are accumulated and updated continually. By means of machine learning and intelligent inference, the knowledge accumulation and knowledge utilization procedures of the evaluation metric pool play an irreplaceable important role in the process of CMfg service optimal selection.

4   Conclusion and Future Works

As an ever-growing number of CMfg services are gathering in a CMfg platform, efficient solutions for CMfg service optimal-selection play an increasing critical part in a CMfg system. In most current methods a set of relatively fixed QoS indicators are adopted to deal with the optimal-selection for different types of CMfg services. This tends to lead to low accuracy and flexibility especially when cloud users' requirements involve different CMfg services with respective individualized characteristics. To address this problem, this paper proposes a framework for CMfg service optimal-selection based on a service evaluation metrics pool. The adaptive assessment metrics for different types of CMfg services can be identified by using the knowledge and historical service evaluation data in the CMfg service evaluation metrics pool. Historical evaluation knowledge of CMfg service is accumulated constantly and then be used to select the optimal service to meet users' request. The prototype experiment platform of CMfg service evaluation metrics pool is under development.

In our future work, analyzing the relationships between different service evaluation metrics is quite necessary. From the perspective of algorithm design, it could be very interesting and important to develop advanced algorithms for knowledge accumulation and update in CMfg service evaluation metrics pool.

Acknowledgements. The research is supported by the National High-Tech Research and Development Plan of China under grant No. 2015AA042101, the Natural Science Foundation of Beijing under grant No. 4142031, the National Science Foundation of China under grant No. 61572057 and the Fund of State Key Laboratory of Intelligent Manufacturing System Technology in China.

References

1. Ren, L., Zhang, L., Wang, L.H., Tao, F., Chai, X.D.: Cloud manufacturing: key characteristics and applications. Int. J. Comput. Integr. Manuf. (2014). doi:10.1080/0951192X.2014.902105
2. Li, B.H., Zhang, L., Ren, L., Chai, X.D., Tao, F., Luo, Y.L., Wang, Y.Z., Yin, C., Huang, G., Zhao, X.P.: Further discussion on cloud manufacturing. Comput. Integr. Manuf. Syst. **17**(3), 449–457 (2011). doi:10.13196/j.cims.2011.03.3.libh.004
3. Li, B.H., Zhang, L., Ren, L., Chai, X.D., Tao, F., Wang, Y.Z., Yin, C., Huang, P., Zhao, X.P., Zhou, Z.D.: Typical characteristics, technologies and applications of cloud manufacturing. Comput. Integr. Manuf. Syst. **18**(7), 1345–1356 (2012). doi:10.13196/j.cims.2012.07.4.libh. 006
4. Zhang, L., Luo, Y.L., Tao, F., Li, B.H., Ren, L., Zhang, X.S., Guo, H., Cheng, Y., Hu, A.R.: Cloud manufacturing: a new manufacturing paradigm. Enterp. Inf. Syst. (2012). doi: 10.1080/17517575.2012.683812
5. Adamson, G., Wang, L H., Holm, M.: The state of the art of cloud manufacturing and future trends. In: ASME 2013 International Manufacturing Science and Engineering Conference collocated with the 41st North American Manufacturing Research Conference (2013). doi: 10.1115/MSEC2013-1123
6. Ren, L., Zhang, L., Tao, F., Zhao, C., Chai, X.D., Zhao, X.P.: Cloud manufacturing: from concept to practice. Enterp. Inf. Syst. (2013). doi:10.1080/17517575.2013.839055
7. Wu, D.Z., Greer, M.J., Rosen, D.W., Schaefer, D.: Cloud manufacturing: strategic vision and state-of-the-art. J. Manuf. Syst. **32**(4), 564–579 (2013). doi:10.1016/j.jmsy.2013.04.008
8. He, W., Xu, L.D.: A state-of-the-art survey of cloud manufacturing. Int. J. Comput. Integr. Manuf. **28**(3), 239–250 (2015). doi:10.1080/0951192X.2013.874595
9. Huang, B.Q., Li, C.H., Tao, F.: A chaos control optimal algorithm for QoS-based service composition selection in cloud manufacturing system. Enterp. Inf. Syst. **8**(4), 445–463 (2014). doi:10.1080/17517575.2013.792396
10. Cui, J., Ren, L., Zhang, L., Wu, Q.: An optimal allocation method for virtual resource considering variable metrics of cloud manufacturing service. In: ASME 2015 International Manufacturing Science and Engineering Conference (2015). doi: 10.1115/MSEC2015-9245
11. Cheng, Y., Tao, F., Liu, Y.L., Zhao, D.M., Zhang, L., Xu, L.D.: Energy-aware resource service scheduling based on utility evaluation in cloud manufacturing system. In: Proceedings of the Institution of Mechanical Engineers, Part B: Journal of Engineering Manufacture, pp. 1–15 (2013). doi: 10.1177/0954405413492966
12. Xiang, F., Hu, Y.F., Yu, Y.R., Wu, H.C.: QoS and energy consumption aware service composition and optimal-selection based on Pareto group leader algorithm in cloud manufacturing system. Cent. Eur. J. Oper. Res. **22**(4), 663–685 (2013). doi:10.1007/ s10100-013-0293-8
13. Tao, F., Hu, Y.F., Zhou, Z.D.: Application and modeling of resource service trust-QoS evaluation in manufacturing grid system. Int. J. Prod. Res. **47**(6), 1521–1550 (2009). doi: 10.1080/00207540701551927
14. Laili, Y.J., Tao, F., Zhang, L., Sarker, B.R.: A study of optimal allocation of computing resources in cloud manufacturing systems. Int. J. Adv. Manuf. Technol. **63**(5–8), 671–690 (2012). doi:10.1007/s00170-012-3939-0
15. Ren, L., Cui, J., Wei, Y.C., Laili, Y.J., Zhang, L.: Research on the impact of service provider cooperative relationship on cloud manufacturing platform. Int. J. Adv. Manuf. Technol. (2016). doi:10.1007/s00170-016-8345-6

A Dynamic Task Scheduling Method Based on Simulation in Cloud Manufacturing

Longfei Zhou[1,2] and Lin Zhang[1,2(✉)]

[1] School of Automation Science and Electrical Engineering, Beihang University,
Xueyuan Rd. No.37, Haidian District, Beijing, China
zhanglin@buaa.edu.cn
[2] Engineering Research Center of Complex Product Advanced Manufacturing Systems,
Ministry of Education, Xueyuan Rd. No.37, Haidian District, Beijing, China

Abstract. One of the most important issues which need to be focused is multi-tasks scheduling, especially the dynamic task scheduling problem in cloud manufacturing (CMfg) environment. In this paper, the dynamic task scheduling process in CMfg is firstly analyzed. Then a method of dynamic scheduling based on real-time simulation is presented and the system framework of this method is proposed. This framework consists of three layers that are task processing layer, core scheduling layer and resource service layer. Key modules in the core scheduling layer include subtask dispatcher, service scheduler and scheduling scheme simulator. Finally, we discuss the advantages and disadvantages of this simulation-based scheduling method in solving dynamic task scheduling problem in cloud manufacturing environment.

Keywords: Task scheduling · Dynamic process · Cloud Manufacturing · Simulation-based

1 Introduction

Cloud manufacturing [1] has become a catchword in the area of advanced manufacturing technology (AMT) as it provides on-demand access to a pool of manufacturing resources and capabilities via Internet in a service-oriented and dynamically scalable mode [2–5]. The task scheduling problem in CMfg has been the focus of interest of many recent studies due to its relevance to the execution process of manufacturing tasks and the actual production environment. Typical task scheduling problem has been described by many researchers. But the system states of manufacturing resources and service change over time and there are many uncertainties in the practical manufacturing environment [6–9]. Some researchers have considered the simulation-based method to solve the dynamic scheduling problem in typical manufacturing system such as [10–13]. In this paper, the simulation-based scheduling method is used to solve the dynamic task scheduling problem in CMfg. In Sect. 2, we analyzed the dynamic process of task scheduling in cloud manufacturing. In Sect. 3, we proposed a dynamic scheduling method based on simulation in the CMfg environment.

© Springer Science+Business Media Singapore 2016
L. Zhang et al. (Eds.): AsiaSim 2016/SCS AutumnSim 2016, Part III, CCIS 645, pp. 20–24, 2016.
DOI: 10.1007/978-981-10-2669-0_3

2   Dynamic Task Scheduling Process in CMfg

Traditional scheduling methods in cloud manufacturing are always allocating many tasks to a set of available resources in order to achieve a certain optimal objective. However, in this way, the scheduling problem is simply considered as a mathematical optimization problem which is not corresponding to the actual production environment. The executing processes of tasks in CMfg usually go through a longer time than traditional manufacturing system because the manufacturing resources in CMfg are distributed unlike workshop environment. Because tasks arrive at CMfg system all the time and there are chain-like precedence relationships between different subtasks of a task, manufacturing services will be preempted if we still use static scheduling strategies in dynamic CMfg environment. Below we will give a simple example to illustrate the resource preemption problem.

We assume that there are two manufacturing services S1 and S2, and the logistics time between the two services is 1. Service S1 and S2 can perform subtask ST1 and ST2, respectively. Tasks T1 and T2 arrive at the cloud manufacturing systems at time 1 and 2, respectively. And the subtask sequences of task T1 and T2 are shown below.

T1: ST1 - ST2

T2: ST2

If we adopt previous static scheduling strategy, the scheduling result is shown in Fig. 1(a). The subtasks of T1 are scheduled at time 1. Subtask T1ST1 will be executed on service S1 from time 1 to 3, and subtask T1ST2 will be executed on service S2 from time 4 to 6. At time 2, the subtask T2ST2 is scheduled. Because the service S2 has been occupied by T1ST2, subtask T2ST2 can only be executed on service S2 from time 6 to 8. Hence, the total execution time of task T1 and T2 is 7 by this static scheduling strategy.

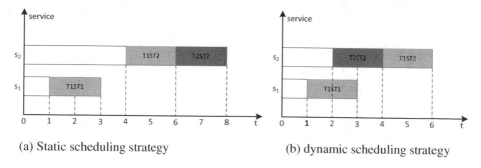

(a) Static scheduling strategy   (b) dynamic scheduling strategy

Fig. 1. Service preemption of dynamic scheduling

In this scheduling scheme, we allocate subtask T1ST2 to S2 at time 1, but the starting executing time of subtask T1ST2 is future time 4. Since the preemption of subtask T1ST2, subtask T2ST2 which arrives at time 2 cannot utilize the optimal service S2. We call this issue in dynamic environment as service preemption.

If we only schedule subtask T1ST1 to service S1 and pend subtask T1ST2 at time 1, subtask T2ST2 can be directly scheduled to service S2 when task T2 arrive at time 2 because the service S2 are not be preempted at this moment. The total execution time of task T1 and T2 is 5(<7) by this scheduling strategy. Therefore, this dynamic scheduling strategy is more applicable to multi-task scheduling problem in dynamic cloud manufacturing environment.

3   Dynamic Scheduling Method Based on Simulation

In this Section, we proposed a dynamic scheduling model which selects subtask dispatching rules and service scheduling strategies dynamically for a next short time period in order to respond to changes of system state. Typically, these resources and services are heterogeneous, distributed and prone to dynamic changes. In order to effectively and quickly find optimal scheduling strategies for tasks which arrive at the CMfg system continuously, we proposed a simulation-based dynamic scheduling model for multi-tasks in CMfg environment. This dynamic scheduling model consists of three layers as shown in Fig. 2. From top to bottom are task processing layer, core scheduling layer and resource service layer.

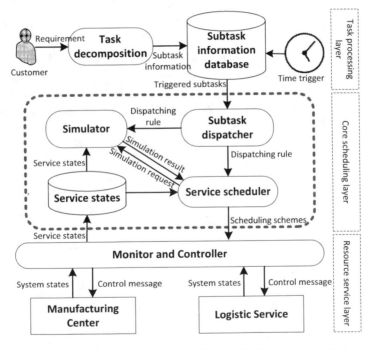

Fig. 2. Framework of dynamic scheduling method based on simulation.

- Task processing layer

   At the task processing layer, customers continuously send manufacturing requirements to the task decomposition module. After decomposing tasks into subtask sequences, task decomposition module sends subtask information to the subtask information database. Subtask information will be stored in the subtask information database as subtask information tables. Subtask information table is shown in Table 1. Time trigger inquires subtask information table periodically and selects those subtasks needed to be scheduled and send their information to the subtask dispatching module.

Table 1. Subtask information table

Task ID	Task type	Subtask ID	Subtask type	Arrival time	Due date	Priority
001	01	00101	02	201506030910	20150615	5
001	01	00102	01	201506030910	20150615	5
001	01	00103	03	201506030910	20150615	5
002	03	00201	01	201506051121	20150611	3
002	03	00202	02	201506051121	20150611	3

- Core scheduling layer

  Core scheduling layer consists of four modules including subtask dispatcher, service scheduler, simulator and service states database. After receiving the information of triggered subtasks, the subtask dispatcher sorts the triggered subtasks according to current subtask dispatching rule and then sends the dispatching rule and triggered subtask information to the simulator. Simultaneously, subtask dispatcher sends the subtask dispatching rule to the service scheduler. Then service scheduler sends a simulation request to the simulator and simulator will simulate the subtask dispatching rules and service scheduling strategies according to current service states information stored in the service states database. After completing the simulation, simulator will return the simulation result to the service scheduler. Afterwards, the service scheduler sends optimal service scheduling scheme to relevant manufacturing centers and manufacturing tasks are executed according to the optimal service scheduling scheme.

- Resource service layer

  At resource service layer, monitor and controller perceive and control the real-time states of manufacturing resources and logistics services. The resource service layer is the basis for tasks dynamic scheduling in cloud manufacturing system.

4   Conclusions and Future Work

We study the dynamic task scheduling process in the cloud manufacturing system and we find that the traditional intelligent optimization algorithms cannot solve the scheduling problem because there is resource preemption problem in the practical manufacturing environment. Then we propose a simulation-based scheduling method to deal with the task scheduling problem in a dynamic CMfg environment and the system framework of this method is presented. This simulation-based method can solve these problems such as changes of system states and uncertainties. However, there are also disadvantages of this method, such as the request of high-speed computational capability and high-speed network transmission. Therefore, the computation complexity of scheduling simulation and the effects of network transmission speed should be researched in the future.

Acknowledgements. The research is supported by the National High-Tech Research and Development Plan of China under Grant No. 2015AA042101, the Natural Science Foundation of Beijing under grant No. 4142031 and the Fund of State Key Laboratory of Intelligent Manufacturing System Technology in China.

References

1. Bohu, L., Lin, Z., Shilong, W., Fei, T., Junwei, C., Xiaodan, J., et al.: Cloud manufacturing: a new service-oriented networked manufacturing model (in Chinese). Comput. Integr. Manuf. Syst. **16**(141), 1–7 (2010)
2. Zhang, L., Luo, Y.L., Tao, F., Li, B.H., Ren, L., Zhang, X.S., et al.: Cloud manufacturing: a new manufacturing paradigm. Enterp. Inf. Syst. **8**, 167–187 (2014)
3. Tao, F., Zhang, L., Venkatesh, V.C., Luo, Y., Cheng, Y.: Cloud manufacturing: a computing and service-oriented manufacturing model. Proc. Inst. Mech. Eng. Part B J. Eng. Manuf. **225**, 1969–1976 (2011)
4. Xu, X.: From cloud computing to cloud manufacturing. Robot. Comput. Integr. Manuf. **28**, 75–86 (2012)
5. Wu, D., Greer, M.J., Rosen, D.W., Schaefer, D.: Cloud manufacturing: Strategic vision and state-of-the-art. J. Manuf. Syst. **32**, 564–579 (2013)
6. Chiu, C., Yih, Y.: A learning-based methodology for dynamic scheduling in distributed manufacturing systems. Int. J. Prod. Res. **33**, 3217–3232 (1995)
7. Cowling, P., Johansson, M.: Using real time information for effective dynamic scheduling. Eur. J. Oper. Res. **139**, 230–244 (2002)
8. Wong, T.N., Leung, C.W., Mak, K.L., Fung, R.Y.K.: Dynamic shopfloor scheduling in multi-agent manufacturing systems. Expert Syst. Appl. **31**, 486–494 (2006)
9. Ouelhadj, D., Petrovic, S.: A survey of dynamic scheduling in manufacturing systems. J. Sched. **12**, 417–431 (2008)
10. Wu, S.-Y.D., Wysk, R.A.: An application of discrete-event simulation to on-line control and scheduling in flexible manufacturing. Int. J. Prod. Res. **27**, 1603–1623 (1989)
11. Min Hee, K., Kim, Y.-D.: Simulation-based real-time scheduling in a flexible manufacturing system. J. Manuf. Syst. **13**, 85–93 (1994)
12. Jeong, K.C., Kim, Y.D.: A real-time scheduling mechanism for a flexible manufacturing system: using simulation and dispatching rules. Int. J. Prod. Res. **36**, 2609–2626 (1998)
13. Chong, C.S., Appa Iyer, S., Gay, R.: Simulation-based scheduling for dynamic discrete manufacturing. In: Simulation Conference 2003, Proceedings of the 2003 Winter, vol. 2, pp. 1465–1473 (2003)

Simulation Based Design of Innovative Quick Response Processes in Cloud Supply Chain Management for "Slow Food" Distribution

Agostino G. Bruzzone[✉], Marina Massei, Francesco Longo, Davide Scalzo, Carlo Martini, Jonathan Villanueva, and Luca Bucchianica

Simulation Team, Genoa, Italy
{agostino.bruzzone,marina.massei,francesco.longo,
davide.scalzo,carlo.martini,jonathan.villanueva,
luca.bucchianica}@simulationteam.com,
http://www.simulationteam.com

Abstract. This paper proposes an innovative business model for making accessible premium quality food worldwide, in respect with its origins and cultural background; the authors present a simulation approach to design the general architecture and the supply chain processes devoted to achieve this result as well as the description of the Supply Chain Architecture. The authors introduced the concept of data consistency for processing reliability of the input over the uncertainty of market demand as well as the influence of stochastic factors. The paper proposes this case study as a good example of using these innovative techniques integrated with simulation.

Keywords: Cloud · Supply Chain Management · Simulation

1 Introduction

The design of a new supply chain is always a very difficult problem considering that is affected by many stochastic elements (e.g. delays in delivery, fluctuations in custom fees, supplier and production reliability, customer satisfaction, demand evolution); therefore when the supply chain addresses new business sectors and markets the problems is even more complex considering the uncertainty related to the capability to create a consistent demand. In this sense the idea to develop a slow food culture, related to premium quality food, within new countries is a very good example for this kind of challenges. Slow food represents indeed the reaction to "fast food" approach and consider critical to develop a culture of food and a respect for high quality alimentary products related to typical traditions of different areas and regions; this concept was introduced probably around middle of '80 in Italy and France and promoted the establishment of networks of producers and restaurateurs respecting the original quality of the food (Portinari 1989, Petrini 2003, 2013).

Most recently the World Expo in Milan was exactly focused on food and importance of guarantee quality and to feed the whole planet (Cull 2015). For instance the cheese market in China was mostly not existing till few years ago and several companies trying

© Springer Science+Business Media Singapore 2016
L. Zhang et al. (Eds.): AsiaSim 2016/SCS AutumnSim 2016, Part III, CCIS 645, pp. 25–34, 2016.
DOI: 10.1007/978-981-10-2669-0_4

to import there goods from France or Italy achieved very bad results (Debuef et al. 2004); therefore the world is evolving and globalization deals also with blending different cultures and diffusing new knowledge on emerging areas. The authors are currently interested in developing processes to distribute high quality food products worldwide and especially in Far East, by delivering not only the goods, but even the cultural background related to them. This process deals with creating kits to be available for customers worldwide by web service and, concurrently, to connect the qualified original producers directly through cloud service. This paper presents a preliminary approach to develop a simulation model of the supply chain management (SCM) reproducing this processes and including information and good flows; therefore in this case it becomes critical to consider that the input data are strongly affected by hypotheses about market reactions. From this point of view it is proposed an innovative approach in characterizing the input not only in terms of values, but also in terms of their confidence band and reliability of the info and sources (Bruzzone et al. 2008, De Felice et al. 2010); these variables are used by the simulator producing results that could estimate the consistency of the results, the experimental error of the models as well as the overall reliability of the output.

2 Cloud Manufacturing (CMfg) for Slow Food SCM

CMfg is a new, production networks-based paradigm that enables to increase readiness and capabilities of the whole network (Tao et al. 2011). The CMfg provides a safe, reliable, high quality, on demand and economic service for the entire production life cycle (Ren et al. 2014).

Being the case study focused on slow so high quality products and not off-the-shelf goods, the authors emphasize the importance of agility for CMfg, requiring an high degree of capability to be adaptive to evolution of market conditions and changes in customer requirements (Hao et al. 2005, Wu et al. 2013, Tao et al. 2014). The enabling factors for Cloud Manufacturing and SCM are summarized in Fig. 1 for our context in consistency with existing research in other areas (Zhang et al. 2010a). The maximum degree of adaptability has to be reached through five forms of flexibility respect the Resource Service Composition (RSC): Task, Flow, Resource Service, Quality of Service (QoS) and Correlation (Zhang et al. 2010b). The purpose of such platform is providing common features to support customers and suppliers to achieve their goals, therefore it is necessary to adopt a proper business model, able to generate added value for all the "actors" involved in order to be widely used for cooperation and collaboration purposes (Bruzzone et al. 2012). The use of a core engine to distribute the orders and to decide delivery process and routing guarantees a continuous improvement (Baruwa et al. 2008, Vonolfen et al. 2011). Existing researches in this sector outline the fact for collaboration it is intended the capability of several actors to work together to gain common results by sharing knowledge and expertise (Parker 2007). When actors share information an Intellectual Property Right (IPR) issue could arises. It mainly focuses on the use and control of background and foreground rights and could be addressed and solved only through effective negotiation among the actors. Starting from these considerations, the authors propose their vision on slow food SCM by using CMfg as a strategic "tool" able to support future globalized food chain with respect of its original high quality characteristics (Li et al. 2010).

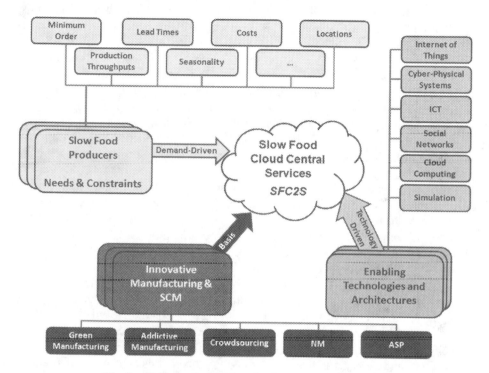

Fig. 1. CMfg applied to slow food cloud central services

3   Case Study: "Eat in Cloud"

The case study proposed in this paper, as anticipated is related to the model of a new business titled "Eat in Cloud". In facts the basic concept of "Eat in Cloud" comes out combining two basic principles: the first is to provide consumers with high quality and certified products immersed within their cultural heritage and the second is to help and facilitate cooperation among SMEs (Small Medium Size Enterprises) active in agricultural business such as Olive Oil Producers, Gourmet artisans (Jüttner et al. 2009). The complexity of this supply chain suggests to adopt M&S as main investigation technique (Busato et al. 2009). Therefore the "Eat in Cloud" goal is to propose itself as a powerful service concurrently to SMEs and consumers, using Internet and its ability to create social dynamic networks and to combine different technologies; most of these products result fresh and strongly affected by logistics processes, so these elements make it evident the necessity to use M&S (Modeling and Simulation) as a tool to reproduce the related processes (Bruzzone, Massei and Bocca 2009); indeed the coordination network in some way is mirroring the concepts in use for "Cloud Computing" with benefits of evolving

Internet of Things (IoT) that provide quick and immediate access to these services as well as to control the related processes creating useful synergies such as catching the proper vector for delivery at a specific destination in respect of transportation constraints (Rodrigue et al. 2006, Rossi et al. 2012). The processes in order to be able to respect time and cost constraints, as well as the handling protocols that guarantee organoleptic characteristics of the food, need to develop effective management algorithms (Sun et al. 2005, Bruzzone et al. 2013, GMA 2011). Obviously the success of this initiative is deeply related to the capability to identify the proper ways to penetrate the region and to create this new market; this deals with the identification of target customers (e.g. customer profile in terms of culture, social status, age) and specific area to address (e.g. most promising countries, provinces, towns); for instance it is crucial to define if it makes sense to start promotion through service to regional restaurants within an area or to address special events or directly the final customers; obviously these alternatives are going concurrently, therefore it should be tuned the effort for each single channel (Bruzzone et al. 2004). Due to these reasons it becomes evident the necessity to collect the large quantity of available data on this framework and to adopt most recent analysis and management techniques for processing these big data.

In similar way, it necessary to proceed to identify and promote the initiative among SME's for their development and growth. Indeed this requires the capability to react dynamically, in full respect of the original and traditional food production processes, to the demand by adopting a quick response delivery service guaranteeing the high quality of the products. Marketing will be also important to guarantee the flows needed for the SCM, therefore the quality of the service obviously relies on the capacity to include in the delivery kits also the value of the food cultural heritage. For instance the delivery of a specific slow food related to the region should include additional info, pictures, video, image, crafts and elements allowing to perceiving properly this good within his cultural framework.

The model proposed by "Eat in Cloud" is based on reliability and collaboration among the cloud service providers and slow food producers; in this way it results possible to advance in creating an efficient logistic and distribution model avoiding wastes and guaranteeing a smart and tailored service for each single consumer and channel (Massei 2006); this approach could lead to improve the whole supply chain and to support evolution of SME (Merkuryev et al. 2008, 2009, Merkuryeva et al. 2011).

4   Logistics Architecture

It is hereafter proposed the preliminary logistics model adopted for investigating this context; the approach is based on a service model coordinated by a Slow Food Cloud Central Services (SFC2S) that regulates orders and deliveries among producers and customers.

In facts based on agreements among food producers and SFC2S, the goods are expected to be stocked in the nearest warehouse available in consistent quantities; in this location the kits are prepared by combining the different elements; the number of kits to be available in the warehouses are estimated based on data fusion predictive analysis. The forecasts consider historical sales, measured trends and market expectations, the values are corrected in consistency with sustainable volumes in terms of logistics costs, capabilities and constraints (Pfohl et al. 2010).

It is proposed an architecture based on a logistics network composed by a set of distributed hub covering different regions to be served both in the customer area and in production sites; therefore it is necessary to evaluate dynamically for each good the trends for country and target customers and to aggregate them in each hub in relation to the logistics network architecture and flows.

As consequences of this analysis the management algorithms are devoted to achieve several main goals including, respect of food protocols, time response with minimum stocks in each warehouse, reduction of unsold goods stocked through pre-assignments, based on preventive analysis, and promotional distribution policies to affect the demand.

A simple representation of the logistics is proposed in the Fig. 2 and considers the different delivery approaches:

– One Step Deliveries, further subdivided into the following elements:
  • Producer → Slow Food Area Hub
  • Slow Food Area Hub → Consumer
– Two Step Deliveries devoted to regulate the following elements:
  • Producer → Slow Food Area Hub
  • Slow Food Area Hub → Customer Regional Hub
  • Customer Regional Hub → Consumers

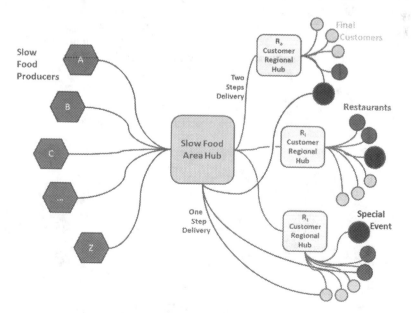

Fig. 2. Slow food supply chain with different delivery approaches

Talking about logistic hubs, we refer to a service like WaaS (Warehouse as a Service), also known as a temporary warehouse service; in this way the platform decreases the fixed costs and guarantees dynamic and scalable services enhancing the agility of the SCM.

5   Modeling the Processes and Evaluating the Data Consistency

As previously said, the "Eat in Cloud" concept is not limited to sales and distribution only, but includes also elements of the production processes as in other industrial context (Macias et al. 2004). As matter of fact, often SME's in agricultural business, are not optimizing their production processes and/or waste their assets; in this context the assets are not limited to primary goods, but include also their production capability, their resources and their know-how.

The general scheme of the delivery process is summarized in the Fig. 2. Therefore the intent of the proposed SFC2S platform is to avoid, or at least mitigate the asset waste, creating and reinforcing the interaction among the productive realities by establishing virtual enterprises able to react dynamically to the demand evolution and to manage new kind of products obtained by combining their primary goods with other ones and/or with additional cultural heritage elements; in this way it is possible not only to maintain, but also to raise the qualitative standards which are the base of our productive vision and to penetrate new market by developing high value goods.

Obviously to estimate the market response requires to develop models not only of the production, but also of the markets; it is also crucial to be able to evaluate the reliability of the SCM as well as the confidence of the estimations and hypothesis provided by the experts on a specific area or region and could support evaluation of the supply chain reliability (Christopher et al. 2004, Sceffi 2005, Sceffi et al. 2005, Longo et al.

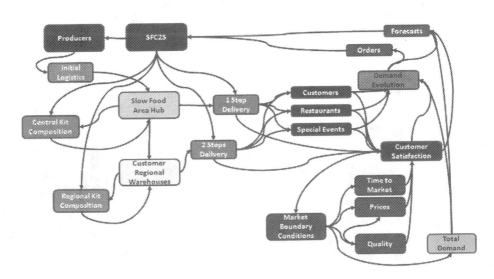

Fig. 3. Interaction among the different entities of the SCM

2008, Falasca et al. 2008, Barroso et al. 2011, Stravos 2012). These assessments could be obtained through analysis on the big data by applying data farming and design of experiments (Montgomery 2000). A representation of the connections among the different entities is proposed in the Fig. 3; the lead times and specific costs affect the customer satisfaction during the simulation therefore also the general market situation is used as a bias for considering the performance of our new cloud services; this approach is an evolution of previous models used to represent fresh food supply chain (De Sensi et al. 2008, Bruzzone et al. 2013). The SFC2S platform will serve as a slow food pool, where each good, defined in terms of quality, quantity and readiness, will be defined by each producer. A common matching algorithm engine will act as core engine for SFC2S platform to suggest and notify new opportunities for possible developments and synergies among goods and producers.

The algorithm should consider the reliability and confidence of the estimations; these parameters and their trends and standard deviations could be computed based on forecasts and orders dynamic evolution; indeed the data consistency could evaluated by the following functions:

$$Ao^j(t,t_0) = \sum_{i=1}^{n^j} H\big(ODD_i^j(t) - t_0\big) \cdot H\big(t_0 + It - ODD_i^j(t)\big) \cdot OS_i^j(t)$$

$$Fo^j(t,t_0,dpt) = Ao^j(t - dpt) + \int_{t_0}^{t_{o+It}} Fs^j(t, t - dpt)dt$$

$$Df^j(t,t_0,dpt) = Ao^j(t_0 + It, t_0) - Fo^j(t,t_0,dpt)$$

$$Da^j(t,t_0,dpt) = Ao^j(t_0 + It, t_0) - Ao^j(t,t_0)$$

$Ao^j(t,t_0)$	Actual Orders for j-th product type at t time expected to be delivered between t_0 and $t_0 + It$
$Fo^j(t, t_0, dpt)$	Future Order Estimator for j-th product type at t-dpt time, expected to be delivered between t_0 and $t_0 + It$
$Fs^j(t,t_0,dpt)$	Forecasts of quantities to be delivered at t time, net from consolidated Orders, for j-th product estimated at t-dpt time
dpt	Temporal anticipation for evaluating future orders
n^j	Number of orders for j-th product type
t	Time
t_0	Beginning of the time interval for order consistency evaluation
It	Time Interval for Order Consistency Evaluation
$ODD_i^j(t)$	Delivery Date of i-th order for j-th product type at t time
$OS_i^j(t)$	Status of i-th order for j-th product type at t time [0 inactive, 1 active]
$H(x)$	Heavyside function
$Df^j(t,t_0,dpt)$	Difference between the real finalized orders within t_0 and $t_0 + It$ and the Forecasts at t-dpt time for j-th product

$Da^j(t,t_0,dpt)$ Difference between the real finalized orders within t_0 and t_0 + It and consolidated orders within the same time interval at t-dpt time

The $Df^j(t,t_0,dpt)$ allows to measure the reliability of the forecasts as soon as dpt goes to zero and t approaches to t_0; these parameters represent a key performance about forecasts; vice versa $Da^j(t,t_0,dpt)$ is a measure of the reliability of the orders provided by the different kinds of customers and allows to measure the related changes as soon as t approaches at t_0.

6 Conclusions

This paper includes a description of a new business approach to develop slow food market in new regions through use of innovative supply chain models inspired to cloud manufacturing (Zhang et al. 2012). Simulation is expected to be used in order to evaluate this new architecture as well as the adopted approach and criteria; this paper proposes a preliminary approach to the problem and it is devoted to create the framework to evaluate the reliability and consistency of the solution, as well as to identify alternative configurations and opportunities to improve the whole SCM performance.

The authors are currently cooperating for using this model in developing new business over Far East with products arriving mostly from South Europe and especially Italy.

Acknowledgment.   The authors are glad to thank Prof.Lin Zhang and his team from the Beihang University for being supportive in the development of this research and for sharing knowledge on CMfg.

References

Barroso, A.P., Machado, V.H., Machado, V.C.: Supply chain resilience using the mapping approach. In: Li, P. (ed.) Supply Chain Management. InTech, Rijeka (2011). http://www.intechopen.com/books/supply-chain-management/supply-chain-resilience-using-themapping-approach

Baruwa, O.T., Piera, M.À.: A derivative Control mechanism for supply chain performance improvement. In: Proceedings of 22nd European Conference on Modelling and Simulation, Campora San Giovanni, September (2008)

Li, B.H., Zhang, L., Wang, S.L., Tao, F., Cao, J.W., Jiang, X.D., Song, X., Chai, X.D.: Cloud manufacturing: a new service-oriented networked manufacturing model. Comput. Integr. Manuf. Syst. **16**(1), 1–8 (2010)

Bruzzone, A.G., Massei, M., Agresta, M., Ferrando, A.: Modelling fresh goods supply chain contamination. In: Proceedings of I3 M, Athens, September (2013)

Bruzzone, A.G., Longo, F.: Simulation based analysis of a manufacturing system devoted to produce hazelnut based products. In: Proceedings of EMSS, Wien, September, pp. 602–609 (2012)

Bruzzone, A.G., Massei, M., Bocca, E.: Fresh food supply chain. In: Merkuryev, Y., Merkuryeva, G., Piera, M.À., Guasch, A. (eds.) Simulation Based Case Studies in Logistic, pp. 127–146. Springer, London (2009)

Bruzzone, A.G., Tremori, A.: Safety & security in retail: modeling value chain dynamics. In: Proceedings of the 2008 Spring Simulation Multiconference, San Diego, USA (2008)

Bruzzone, A.G., Viazzo, S., Longo, F., Papoff, E., Briano, C.: Simulation and virtual reality to modelling retail and store facilities. In: Proceedings of SCSC 2004, San Josè, CA (2004)

Busato, P., Berruto, R.: Use of simulation models to study the dynamic of recall of non-conform perishable produce through the supply chain. In: Proceedings of International European Forum on System Dynamics and Innovation in Food Network, Innsbruck-Igls, Austria (2009)

Christopher, M., Peck, H.: Building the resilient supply chain. Int. J. Logist. Manag. **15**(2), 1–13 (2004)

Cull, N.J.: Editorial: digesting the Milan expo, 2015. Place Branding Public Diplomacy **11**(3), 169–174 (2015)

De Felice, F., Di Bona, G., Falcone, D., Silvestri, A.: New reliability allocation methodology: the integrated factors method. Int. J. Oper. Quant. Manag. **16**(1), 67 (2010). ISSN: 1082-1910

De Sensi, G., Longo, F., Mirabelli, G.: Inventory policies analysis under demand patterns and lead times constraints in a real supply chain. Int. J. Prod. Res. **46**(24), 6997–7016 (2008)

Dubeuf, J.P., Morand-Fehr, P., Rubino, R.: Situation, changes and future of goat industry around the world. Small Ruminant Res. **51**(2), 165–173 (2004)

Grocery Manufactures Association (GMA), Ernst, Young: Capturing Recall Costs Measuring and Recovering the Losses. (2011)

Falasca, M., Zobel, C.W., Cook, D.: A decision support framework to assess supply chain resilience. In: The Proceedings of the 5th International ISCRAM Conference – Washington, DC, USA, May 2008, pp. 596–605 (2008)

Tao, F., Zhang, L., Venkatesh, V.C., Luo, Y., Cheng, Y.: Cloud manufacturing: a computing and service-oriented manufacturing model. In: Proceedings of the Institution of Mechanical Engineers, Part B: Journal of Engineering Manufacture, 22 August 2011, vol. 225 (2011). doi: 10.1177/0954405411405575

Jüttner, U., Ziegenbein, A.: supply chain risk management for small and medium-sized businesses. J. Supply Chain Risk **124**, 199–217 (2009)

Longo, F., Ören, T.: Supply chain vulnerability and resilience: a state of the art overview. In: Proceedings of European Modeling & Simulation Symposium, Campora San Giovanni, Italy (2008)

Hao, Q., Shen, W., Wang, L.: Towards a cooperative distributed manufacturing management framework. Comput. Indus. **56**(1), pp. 71–84 (2005). [14]

Macías, E.J., de la Parte, M.P.: Simulation and optimization of logistic and production systems using discrete and continuous. Simulation **80**(3), 143–152 (2004)

Massei, M.: Logistics and process solution for supply chain of fresh food in retail. In: Proceedings of MAS2006, Bergeggi, October 2006

Merkuryev, Y., Merkuryeva, G., Hatem, J., Desmet, B.: Supply chain simulation in the ECLIPS project. In: Proceedings of the Second Asia International Conference on Modelling and Simulation, Kuala Lumpur, Malaysia, May, pp. 684–690 (2008)

Merkuryev, Y., Merkuryeva, G., Piera, M.A., Guasch, A.: Simulation-based Case Studies in Logistics: Education and Applied Research. Springer, London (2009). 232 p

Merkuryeva, G., Merkuryev, Y., Vanmaele, H.: Simulation-based planning and optimization in multi-echelon supply chains. Simul. Trans. Soc. Model. Simul. Int. **87**(8), 698–713 (2011)

Montgomery, D.C.: Design and Analysis of Experiments. Wiley, New York (2000)

Parker, N.: Intellectual property issues in joint ventures and collaborations. J. Intellect. Property Law Pract. **2**(11), 729–741 (2007)

Petrini, C.: Slow Food Nation. Rizzoli, Milan (2013)

Petrini, C.: Slow Food: The Case for Taste. Columbia University Press, New York (2003)

Pfohl, H.C., Kohler, H., Thomas, D.: State of the art in supply chain risk management research: empirical and conceptual findings and a roadmap for the implementation in practice. J. Logist. Res. **2**(1), 34–44 (2010)

Portinari, F.: The Slow Food Manifesto. Opéra Comique, Paris (1989)

Ren, L., Zhang, L., Wang, L., Tao, F., Chai, X.: Cloud manufacturing: key characteristics and applications. Int. J. Comput. Integr. Manuf. pp. 1–15 (2014)

Rodrigue, J.P., Comitos, C., Slack, B.: The Geography of Transport Systems. Routledge, London (2006)

Rossi, R., Rijpkema, W.A., Van der Vorst, J.: The impact of dual sourcing in food supply chain networks: the case of Egyptian strawberries. In: WICaNeM, Netherlands (2012)

Sceffi, Y.: Building a resilient supply chain. Harvard Bus. Rev. **1**(8), 1 (2005)

Sceffi, Y., Rice, J.: A Supply Chain View of the Resilent Enterprise. MIT Sloan Manag. Rev. **47**(1), 41–48 (2005)

Stravos, T.P.: Supply chain resilience; definition of concept and its formative elements. J. Appl. Bus. Res. **28**(5), 921–930 (2012)

Sun, C., Yu, H.: Supply chain contract under product cost disruption. In: Proceedings of the International Conference on Services Systems and Serivice Management, vol. 1, pp. 708–711 (2005)

Tao, F., Cheng, Y., Da Xu, L., Zhang, L., Li, B.H.: CCIoT-CMfg: cloud computing and internet of things-based cloud manufacturing service system. IEEE Trans. Indus. Inform. **10**(2), 1435–1442 (2014)

Vonolfen, S., Affenzeller, M., Beham, A., Lengauer, E., Wagner, S.: Simulation-based evolution of resupply and routing policies in rich vendor-managed inventory scenarios. Cent. Eur. J. Oper. Res. **19**(4), 23 (2011)

Wu, D., Greer, M.J., Rosen, D.W., Schaefer, D.: Cloud manufacturing: strategic vision and state-of-the-art. J Manuf Syst (2013). http://dx.doi.org/10.1016/j.jmsy.2013.04.008

Zhang, L., Luo, Y.L., Tao, F., Ren, L., Guo, H.: Key technologies for the construction of manufacturing cloud. Comput. Integr. Manuf. Syst. **16**(11), 2510–2520 (2010)

Zhang, L., Guo, H., Tao, F., Luo, Y.L., Si, N.: Flexible management of resource service composition in cloud manufacturing. In: IEEE International Conference on Industrial Engineering & Engineering Management 2010, pp. 2278–2282 (2010b)

Zhang, L., Luo, Y.L., Tao, F., Li, B.H., Ren, L., Zhang, X.S., Guo, H., Cheng, Y., Hu, A.R.: Cloud manufacturing: a new manufacturing paradigm. Enterp. Inf. Syst. 21 May 2012. doi: 10.1080/17517575.2012.683812

Manufacturing Capability Service Modeling, Management and Evaluation for Matching Supply and Demand in Cloud Manufacturing

Ting Yu Lin[1,2,3(✉)], Yingying Xiao[1,2,3], Chen Yang[4],
Xiaoliang Liu[1,2,3], Bo Hu Li[1], Liqin Guo[1,2], and Chi Xing[1,2,3]

[1] Beijing Complex Product Advanced Manufacturing Engineering Research Center, Beijing Simulation Center, Beijing, People's Republic of China
lintingyu2003@sina.com
[2] State Key Laboratory of Intelligent Manufacturing System Technology, Beijing Institute of Electronic System Engineering, Beijing, People's Republic of China
[3] Science and Technology on Space System Simulation Laboratory, Beijing Simulation Center, Beijing, People's Republic of China
[4] HKU-ZIRI Lab for Physical Internet, Department of Industrial and Manufacturing Systems Engineering, The University of Hong Kong, Hong Kong, People's Republic of China

Abstract. Currently, the manufacturing sector faces challenges brought by the global technological revolution and industrial revolution. Cloud manufacturing can be of great help to break the traditional pattern of static enterprise resource configuration through the on-demand provision and consumption of manufacturing capability (MCap), and thus optimize industrial chains and improve competitiveness. Comparing to the traditional e-commerce, matching supply and demand of MCap will require the consideration of complex conditions, such as static and dynamic attributes of MCap services, scalability of domain attributes of heterogeneous MCap services, and other characteristics (e.g., multiple stakeholders and multi-round competition) in the open and dynamic environment of social manufacturing. To address the above demand, we propose meta-models for MCap service description, an approach to the management of MCap services based on the data model "EAV" and the enterprise search platform "Solr", and an approach to the evaluation of MCap services based on the dynamic composition & screening. Finally, those methods have been implemented in a cloud manufacturing platform for an aerospace conglomerate, and the results show their effectiveness.

Keywords: Cloud manufacturing · Manufacturing capability · Supply and demand matching · Service modeling · Service management · Service evaluation

© Springer Science+Business Media Singapore 2016
L. Zhang et al. (Eds.): AsiaSim 2016/SCS AutumnSim 2016, Part III, CCIS 645, pp. 35–48, 2016.
DOI: 10.1007/978-981-10-2669-0_5

1 Introduction

Currently, the manufacturing sector faces challenges brought by the global techno-logical revolution and industrial revolution. Specifically, the deep integration of manufacturing technologies and a new generation of ICTs (Information and Commu-nication Technologies) leads to the important revolution of manufacturing modes, processes, means, eco-systems, etc. These will greatly facilitate and optimize the products and their time to market, quality, cost, service, environment and knowledge. Cloud manufacturing (CMfg) [1–3] provides a new mode and means of intelligent manufacturing based on network, servitization and socialization, and support the establishment of service clouds of manufacturing resources and capabilities, so that users can acquire manufacturing services on demand anytime and anywhere to accomplish various tasks in the full lifecycle of manufacturing.

In the CMfg body of knowledge, manufacturing capability refers to the ability to accomplish some kinds of manufacturing tasks. It is a broad concept of manufacturing resource that contains manufacturing resource, human/intelligence resource, know-how and management. Generally, manufacturing resource refers to the tools or machines that can be servitized and remotely operated (accessed), for example, design and analysis software, 3D printing resource. However, there are also some resources that cannot be easily digitalized and directly handled by users, due to the reasons, such as high cost/too complex to adapt them as web services, the operation of them requiring very professional skills and knowledge, the expensiveness and vulnerability of them. For those resources, owners can only or would rather outsource them as manufacturing capability (MCap) services. In manufacturing clouds, matching supply and demand plays a fundamental role in delivering MCap service, and helps break the traditional pattern of static enterprise resource configuration and thus optimize industrial chains and improve competitiveness.

The core technology of traditional e-commerce is the matching of supply and demand. C2C, B2C and B2B primarily involve finished products, off-the-shelf products, and consumer goods. However, they do not deal with the capability needed in the full lifecycle of products, such as research and development, production and experimenta-tion. This requires new methods of service modeling, management and evaluation.

(1) Modeling of MCap services

Comparing to the finished product, MCap not only have static attributes, which roughly remains stable over a period of time (e.g., machining precision, machinable materials), but also own dynamic attributes, which may change at any time (e.g., availability, productivity, completion time). Besides, different types of MCap services show heterogeneity. For example, they have different attributes in terms of index of equipment, quality of service, etc., which should be extended differently according to the domain demand.

(2) Management of MCap services

The meta-models of different MCap services have some degree of heterogeneity and will evolve to be more specific along with the deeper application of CMfg in industries and manufacturing processes, leading to the formation of common standard sets of attributes and customizable sets of domain attributes. Thus the framework for registration and searching of MCap services should support the heterogeneity and domain scalability.

(3) Management of MCap services

Comparing to the finished product, the evaluation of MCap services involves more factors, such as performance, progress, quality and price. Moreover, this also should consider not only the performance of historical transactions, but also current bids/price. Traditional methods to rate suppliers can provide some clues, but they only use the rating from customers, while the ratings from historical partners and supervisors have not been included in the evaluation framework.

The paper is organized as follows: Sect. 2 reviews related work; Sect. 3 presents the business process of matching supply and demand for MCap; Sects. 4, 5 and 6 propose the methods to model, manage and rate MCap services respectively; Sects. 7 and 8 give out the application example and the conclusion.

2 Related Work

The consultation report of CMfg released by the DLA Piper UK points out that more and more companies provide services that can be offered in the manufacturing cloud, including crowd-sourcing service, 3D printing service, etc. Through the integration with social networks, they can effectively collect the demand for manufactured products and thus reduce the R&D risk for new products and the time to market. Currently, those cloud services have been successfully applied in the manufacture of some parts for Apple's cell phone and will be used gradually to serve the whole area of durable consumer goods.

In China, a specialized CMfg platform developed by the Huazhong University of Science and Technology provides four kinds of service modes for two industries (die and flexible material) according to the characteristics of industrial clusters in Dongguan and Hangzhou. The modes include pure internet-based service mode, providing SaaS service, like sheet metal nesting; online-to-offline service mode (online transaction & offline service), like tailoring of costume and flexible material; offline-to-online service mode (offline submission & online service), like online inspection; pure offline service mode, like mold design and processing.

There is some theoretical work on description/management/evaluation of MCap [4–7] and MCap service [8–14]. Typically, Tao et al. [15] proposed a three-step approach to describe MCap services: first building conceptual models of resource, then building object models of resource, and finally describing the established classes and attributes formally using the ontology language; meanwhile proposed an algorithm to evaluate MCap services based on six QoS parameters: time, cost, reliability, maintainability, trust and function similarity, according to the characteristics of QoS in manufacturing.

Overall, there is substantial work on the matching of supply and demand in CMfg. However, most MCap research and application (1) target one specific type of MCap, for example, machining capability, and seldom consider the generalized meta-models of MCap; (2) cannot support the management and intelligent searching of MCap with scalable attributes, as they only support the matching of MCap supply and demand based on static attributes; (3) cannot be applied in the dynamic sorting and recommendation under the complex condition of multiple participants (including supervisors) and multi-round competition, as they mostly aim to the evaluation of a single business in a single stage.

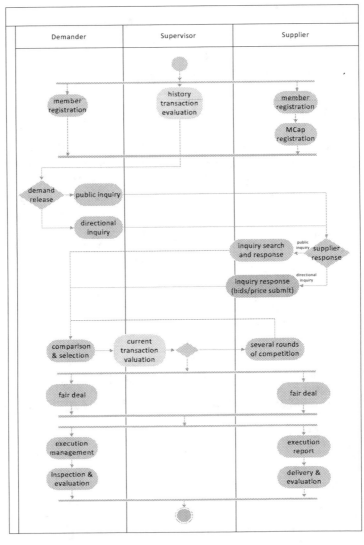

Fig. 1. Process of supply and demand Matching for MCap

3 The Business Process of Supply and Demand Matching for MCap

The supply and demand Matching of MCap supports public inquiry and directional inquiry business model, the business process is shown as the Fig. 1, including "member registration – MCap registration – demand release – supplier response – comparison & selection – fair deal – contract execution – two-way evaluation".

4 MCap Service Modeling

As MCap is a kind of "generalized manufacturing resources", which includes manufacturing resources, human/intellectual resources, professional technical and management. Combining with the characteristics of manufacturing, describe the static and dynamic property of MCap, establish the universal standard property set of MCap service (element) model, at the same time, the standard property set can be extended while the cloud manufacturing has in-depth application in various fields and every stage of the manufacturing process.

4.1 Static Property

The static property of MCap service could be described as six-tuple

$$StaticInfo = <BasicInfo, AptitudeInfo, EquipmentInfo,$$
$$HumanResourceInfo, KnowledgeInfo, HistoryTaskInfo > , \text{ whereby:}$$

BasicInfo =< Name, EnterpriseName, Location, ContactionInfo, PerfProduct, TechnologyInfo, Context, Picture>, represents the basic information includes capability name, Company name, address, contact information, good products, technology route, introduction and pictures.

AptitudeInfo represents the relevant qualification/certification of the company the MCap belong.

EquipmentInfo represents the key equipment supporting for the MCap service, for each type of MCap service, the parameters of the corresponding key equipment are different. Such as, machining equipment includes (brand, model, quantity, rated hours, precision, roughness, machining maximum size, machinable materials) information; Electric equipment includes (brand, model, quantity, rated hours, the processing level, temperature, maximum temperature, infrared \ vacuum function, patch repeat accuracy, patch speed, material type, material capacity, SMT components, X-ray detector (2 d and 3 d), printing speed, printing pressure, printing clearance);

HumanResourceInfo represents the key human resources supporting for the MCap service, includes the list and information of experts, the number of professional and technical personnel at every levels (for research and development design manufacture ability service, the corresponding property can be extended to assistant engineer/ engineer/senior engineer/researcher; for processed manufacturing ability service, the corresponding property can be extended for primary worker/intermediate worker / advanced worker/technician/senior technician), etc.

KnowledgeInfo represents the related intellectual rights supporting for the MCap service, such as patents, copyright, etc.

HistoryTaskInfo represents the transaction records supporting for the MCap service, explaining the details of tender records, total amount of the annual contract, etc.

4.2   Dynamic Property

MCap service is changing with time and market. Based on the features of each attribute, determining the expression to reflect the ability of dynamic characteristics correctly, mainly includes the average completion time, the current working status, availability, quality, cost, etc., could be described as five-tuple:

DynamicInfo =< AverageFinishTime, Status,

AvailableVolume, Quality, Price>

(1) **AverageFinishTime** represents the average completion time for an operation, is defined as the time that the MCap completes the ith manufacturing task.

$$t_i = \frac{D_i}{N_i}$$

Whereby the D_i is the actual task execution time for I, N_i is total output for I. $[t_1, t_2, t_3, \ldots, t_i, \ldots, t_n]$ is the record of the MCap execute manufacturing tasks, the average completion time(dynamic property) of MCap could be analyzed with statistical methods. As time belongs to the metrology characteristic value, generally obey normal distribution $N(\mu, \sigma^2)$, whereby μ is $\bar{t}$, namely the average value of completion time. σ is the standard deviation, the important indicators of MCap characteristics. The smaller the value of σ is, indicating the smaller average completion time fluctuation range is, declaring the level of MCap is stable, controlled well.

(2) **Status** refers to the current Status of the MCap services, such as idle, full-load operation, definition:

$$s\% = \frac{CurrentOutput}{MaximalOutput} * 100\%$$

$s\%$ represents the current state of the MCap, changing with manufacturing execution in real time. *CurrentOutput*represents the current output,*MaximalOutput* represents the maximum output. If $s\% = 0$ %,MCap current state is idle. If $s\% = 100$ %, MCap current state is full-load operation.

(3) **AvailableVolume** represents the number of tasks that the MCap service can do, has certain corresponding relationship with the Status, changing with the order's quantity and time. This article uses graph to express available remaining production capacity for a period of time (as shown in Fig. 2).

The Starting point stand for the current time and the available production capacity, namely *(1−s%), ① indicates that from the current capacity to time t1, utilization of

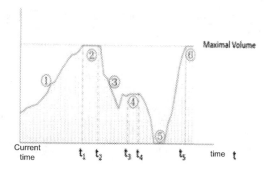

Fig. 2. The relationship of available production capacity and time

MCap decreases, available production capacity increases. ② indicates MCap is idle, ③ indicates from t2 time, the MCap is scheduled, the production activity is in stepping up, ④ shows that the order is stable, ⑤ indicates MCap is fully scheduled, in this period MCap services can't accept orders any more.

Available capacity charts can visually show that MCap utilization, providing reference for the customer to select available MCap service.

(4) **Quality** represents the quality of service for MCap service, generally produced by the customer scoring and the system judging based on the previous production cases and other information comprehensively. In this paper, the quality of service for MCap service is determined by a number of characteristic values, which avoids the problem that the traditional result is too subjective only by the customer scoring. Take the processed manufacturing as an example, the attributes for quality of service can be extended to:

$$\text{Quality} = \{\text{rejection rate, rework/repair rate, delay rate,}$$
$$\text{early completion rate, failure rate, user evaluation}\}$$

where,

Rejection Rate: For part and product, rejection rate is the percentage ration of the number of rejection to the total output in a production activity; for operation, rejection rate refers to the percentage ratio of the operation cause irreparable error to all operations. Scrap is the direct economic loss of the manufacturer, and the high rejection rate indicates the lack of quality assurance in the MCap. Rejection rate = (rejection quantity /total output) * 100 %, so:

$$\overline{R_{rjc}} = \frac{1}{n}\sum_{i=1}^{n} R_{rjc_i}$$

$\overline{R_{rjc}}$ is average rejection rate, R_{rjc_i} is the rejection rate of the ith batch, n is the batch to check.

Rework/repair rate is the ratio of the number of product required rework /repair to the total output for the batch.

$$\overline{R_{rw/rp}} = \frac{1}{n} \sum_{i=1}^{n} R_{rw/rp_i}$$

$\overline{R_{rw/rp}}$ is the average Rework/repair rate, R_{rw/rp_i} is the Rework/repair rate of the ith batch,n is the batch to deliver.

Delay rate is the ratio of the number of delayed batches to the number of total batches.

Early completion rate is the ratio of the number of early completion batches to total batches.

Failure rate is the ratio of the number of failure which is fed back by receiver after delivered within the rated service term to the total output.

$$\overline{R_{fail}} = \frac{1}{n} \sum_{i=1}^{n} R_{fail_i}$$

$\overline{R_{fail}}$ is the average failure rate. R_{fail_i} is the failure rate of the ith products. n is the batch to deliver.

User evaluation is the consumer's subjective scoring evaluation, user evaluation = {not satisfied, not really satisfied, general, some satisfied, satisfied}, respectively corresponding to value $1 \sim 5$.

The above six quality characteristics need to be evaluated comprehensively, and get the comprehensive quality index of manufacturing ability for the users to consult. The normalization of each attribute: namely, every attribute need to be pretreated to a unitary:

$$X_{ik} = \frac{\max_i x_{ik} - x_{ik}}{\max_i x_{ik} - \min_i x_{ik}}, k = 1, 2, 3, 5$$

Indicates, for the failure rate, the smaller the value is, the better. Take use of the above equation on X_{ik}, transfer the small value failure rate to big value, it's more convenient.

$$X_{ik} = \frac{x_{ik} - \min_i x_{ik}}{\max_i x_{ik} - \min_i x_{ik}}, k = 4, 6$$

Indicates, for early completion rate and user evaluation, the bigger the value is, the better. So taking use of the above equation on X_{ik} to pretreat to a unitary is logical.

After finishing, get the matrix $[X] = \begin{bmatrix} X_{11} & X_{12} & \cdots & X_{16} \\ X_{21} & X_{22} & \cdots & X_{26} \\ \vdots & \vdots & & \vdots \\ X_{m1} & X_{m2} & \cdots & X_{m6} \end{bmatrix}$, $X_{ik} \in [0, 1]$

$W = [w_1, w_2, w_3, w_4, w_5, w_6]$ is the weight of every attribute, $[X] * [W]^T$ can get the comprehensive quality index of m alternative MCap.

(5) **Price** is MCap service's offer, changing with market factors, etc. Price is an important reference index during the manufacturing ability selection process, this article use four price feature values to evaluate price objectively: Pminimun is the minimum value of the MCap's price, Pmaximum is the maximum value of the MCap's price, PRminimum and PRmaximum respectively stand for the minimum and maximum values among all similar MCap's price.

5   MCap Service Management

Although it is simple to storage the data of the MCap service based on the relational database and search the key words of its attributes based on the SQL (Structured Query Language), it could not satisfy the scalability demand for the meta model of the MCap service which not only have common standard sets of attributes but also customizable sets of domain attributes. The approach to the management of MCap services based on the data model "EAV"[1] and the enterprise search platform "Solr"[2] could support the registration and efficient search for the meta-models of different MCap services with different number of attributes.

The management platform of MCap services (Fig. 3) includes three modules of:

(1) the Meta-Model-Based Management Module of MCap service: MCap service modeling engineers can firstly build the customized domain MCap service model using XML format, and then MCap service model conversion tool would automatically access the EAV model data interaction interface to persist the different MCap service Entity to the Attribute tables and Value tables in the MCap service library, which can support different data types of number, text, selection and so on.

(2) the Indexing Configuration Module of MCap service: MCap service modeling engineers can configure the searchable attribute sets for different MCap service online, which should be used in Solr server.

(3) the Solr-based Distributed full-text retrieval module: With users' input search statements, the search interactive interface will call the Solr full-text retrieval service to create Solr query instances, and then return the query results in JSON format. MCap service modeling engineers also can monitor the running statements of all the distributed Solr services.

6   MCap Service Evaluation

To address the complex condition of multiple participants (including supervisor) and multi-round competition in open and dynamic social manufacturing, the approach to the evaluation of MCap services based on the dynamic composition & screening is

---

[1] EAV model names Entity - Attribute - Value model, which is used to describe the entities with large number of attributes and different number of attributes. The model has an entity table, and each entity relates to an attribute table, and each attribute table corresponding to a number of value tables (Each type of attribute value corresponds to a value table).

[2] See also http://lucene.apache.org/solr/.

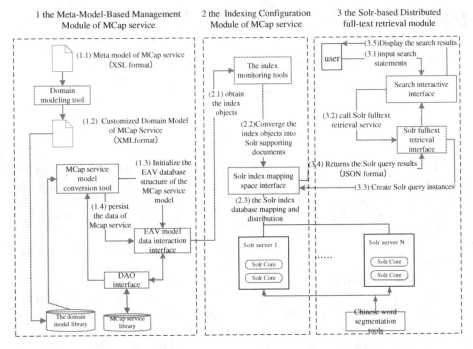

Fig. 3. The business scenario of the optimization model

proposed which takes not only the performance of historical transactions but also current bids/price into account, and considers not only the opinions by the demander and historical partners but also the intention of the suppliers and supervisor, which allows the supervisor to grant a number of bonus point to the leading supplier for reward or to the weak supplier for support. Specific steps are shown as follow:

(1) Bonus point for the supplier on the phase of supplier submitting: bonus point will be given based on the goodness of fit for the non-mandatory demands such as prepayment for cooperation and early completion; and bonus point will be used by the supplier autonomously that the quota of the points is granted by the supervisor.

$$BonusScore = <ProfessionBonus,\ CertificationBonus,$$
$$EarlyCompBonus,\ Prepayment\ Bonus >$$

where,

ProfessionBonus is the bonus point for the supplier's leading profession. No more than 2 points at one time, and no more than quota repeatedly.

CertificationBonus is the bonus point for the supplier's advanced certification in the field of quality. No more than 2 points at one time, and no more than quota repeatedly.

EarlyCompBonus is the bonus point for the supplier's answer fitting the demand of early completion. 2 points when fitting the demand, zero otherwise.

PrepaymentBonus is the bonus point for the supplier's answer fitting the demand of prepayment for cooperation. 2 points when fitting the demand, zero otherwise.

(2) On the phase of supplier response, score of supplier's current bids/price would be determined.

$$ResponseScheScore = <PerformanceScore, QuilityScore,$$
$$ProgressScore, PriceScore >$$

where,

PerformanceScore represents the score of current bids/price on the aspect of performance.

QuilityScore represents the score of current bids/price on the aspect of quality determined by the demander. Comparing between the demand and current bids/price, "Very consistent" was 100 points, "Doincides well" was 75 points, "General consistent" was 50 points, " Does not match" was 25 points, "very inconsistent" was zero.

ProgressScore represents the score of current bids/price on the aspect of progress by automatically comparing the suppliers' response with the expected date of the demander (the more consistent, the higher score; the less consistent, the lower score). (1) If the delivery date in bids/price is in accordance with the expected date of the demander, the score would be 100; (2) If the delivery date delays 1 % of the total time, the score would be 80; (3) If the delivery date delays 1 %-3 % of the total time, the score would be 60; (4) If the delivery date delays 3 %-5 % of the total time, the score would be 40; (5) If the delivery date delays 5 %-10 % of the total time, the score would be 20; (6) If the delivery date delays more than 10 % of the total time, the score would be zero.

PriceScore represents the score of current bids/price on the aspect of price by automatically comparing the suppliers' response (the lower price, the higher score; the higher price, the lower score). (1) If the price is lower than the expected price of the demander, the score would be $75 + \frac{c_{avr} - c_x}{\max(c_{max} - c_{avr}, c_{avr} - c_{min})} \times 25$ between 50 and 100; (2) If the price is higher than the expected price of the demander, the score would be $\frac{c_{avr} - c_x}{\max(c_{max} - c_{avr}, c_{avr} - c_{min})} \times 25$ between 0 and 50; (3) If there is no expected price of the demander, the score would be the same with "1)" (where Cmax is the highest price of the response; Cmin is the lowest price of the response; Cavr is the average price of the response).

(3) On the phase of comparison & selection, score of supplier's historical transactions would be calculated automatically: referring to the traditional e-commerce which uses star rating system to collect the evaluation of consumers, the evaluation of MCap services uses the same way to evaluate the supplier's historical transactions on the aspects of performance, progress, quality and price.

$$HistoryScore = <PerformanceHisScore, QuilityHisScore,$$
$$Progress - HisScore, PriceHisScore >$$

where, the highest rate of each aspect is 5 stars, and the score of each aspect equals to the number of stars multiplied by 20. So the score of each aspect is in the range of [0–100].

(4) The result of the evaluation would be produced by weighted calculation and ranking: the score equals to the weighted sum of the score of the bonus, the current bids/price and the score of the historical transactions on the aspects of performance, progress, quality and price.

$$Score = c_1 \times (0.6PerformanceScore + 0.4PerformanceHisScore) +$$
$$c_2 \times (0.6QuilityScore + 0.4QuilityHisScore) +$$
$$c_3 \times (0.6\Pr ogressScore + 0.4\Pr ogressHisScore) +$$
$$c_4 \times (0.6\Pr iceScore + 0.4\Pr iceHisScore) +$$
$$(ProfessionBonus + CertificationBonus +$$
$$EarlyCompBonus + PrepaymentBonus)$$

where, c1, c2, c3 and c4 are weight, and $c_1 + c_2 + c_3 + c_4 = 1$.

7   Application Examples

The methods of manufacturing capability service modeling, management and evaluation have been implemented in a cloud manufacturing platform for an aerospace conglomerate to support the manufacturing process and component outsourcing. In the manufacturing process outsourcing, there have been forming 14 types of mechanical processing MCap service models (which have been subdivided into 66 distinct classifications), 12 types of experiment (testing) MCap service models (which have been subdivided into 139 distinct classifications), and 3 types of measuring detection MCap service models (which have been subdivided into 30 distinct classifications).

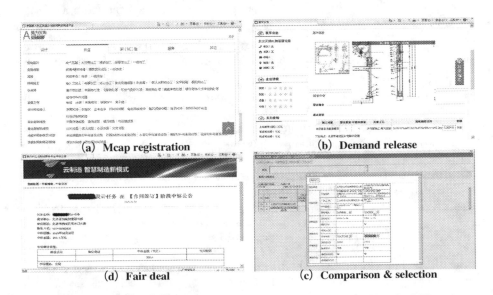

(a) Mcap registration

(b) Demand release

(d) Fair deal

(c) Comparison & selection

Fig. 4. The application screenshots of supply and demand matching for MCap

Based on those MCap services, the application screenshots of supply and demand matching for MCap are shown in Fig. 4. Currently, the cloud manufacturing platform for the aerospace conglomerate has hundreds of enterprises registered, and nearly thousands of manufacturing equipment published. The published MCap services and the released outsourcing missions have been reached to thousands and the signed contract amount have been accumulated more than one billion RMB Yuan.

8 Conclusions and Future Works

The contributions of this paper include:

(1) Generalized meta-models for MCap service description

We have proposed generalized meta-models for modeling Mcap services, that contain elements for both static and dynamic attributes. The meta-models can be used to define common standard attributes, and also allow for the domain extension of attributes. Thus the meta-models can support the modeling of various MCap in the full lifecycle of complex products.

(2) An approach to management of MCap services based on the data model "EAV" and the enterprise search platform "Solr"

Based on "EAV", our proposed approach uses the attribute table and multiple value tables to support dynamic customization of meta-models and the storage of corresponding data. "Solr" helps build the index database for queries and thus improve the effectiveness of batch and multi-attribute queries.

(3) An approach to evaluation of MCap services based on dynamic composition & screening

We have proposed a comprehensive evaluation framework that involves multiple parties (outsourcer, supervisor and service supplier). The framework also takes into account historical performance and current bids, to realize the dynamic evaluation and automatic sorting of intended MCap-service suppliers.

Our future work includes:

(1) Introduction of Big Data technology into the evaluation of manufacturing services, by mining data about the collaborations between suppliers and customers, to provide more support for optimal decisions.

(2) Introduction of advanced planning and scheduling (APS) into the matching of supply and demand to consider the feasibility of plans and comprehensively optimize the period and cost.

Acknowledgements. This work is financially supported by the National 863 Plan (2015AA042101), China.

References

1. Li, B.H., Zhang, L., Wang, S.L., et al.: Cloud manufacturing: a new service-oriented networked manufacturing model. Comput. Integr. Manuf. Syst. **16**(1), 1331–1343 (2010)
2. Iordache, O.: Introduction. In: Iordache, O. (ed.) Modeling Multi-Level Systems. UCS, vol. 8, pp. 1–10. Springer, Heidelberg (2011)
3. Li, B.H., Zhang, L., Ren, L., et al.: Further discussion on cloud manufacturing. Comput. Integr. Manuf. Syst. **17**(3), 449–457 (2011)
4. Yin, S., Yin, C., Liu, F., et al.: Out sourcing resources integration service mode and semantic description in cloud manufacturing environment. Comput. Integr. Manuf. Syst. **17**(3), 525–532 (2011)
5. Ji, E.Q., Duan, X.F.: Research of manufacturing resource model for cloud manufacturing. In: Manufacturing Information in China, vol. 9, pp. 5–8. Academic Edition (2012)
6. Luo, Y.L., Zhang, L., Tao, F., et al.: Key technologies of manufacturing capability modeling in cloud manufacturing mode. Comput. Integr. Manuf. Syst. **18**(7), 1357–1367 (2012)
7. Luo, Y.L., Zhang, L., Tao, F., et al.: Study on the servilization of simulation capability. In: The 23rd European Modeling & Simulation Symposium (EMSS 2011), Rome, Italy (2011)
8. Yin, C., Zhang, Y., Zhong, T.: Optimization model of cloud manufacturing services resource combination for new product development. Comput. Integr. Manuf. Syst. **18**(7), 1368–1378 (2012)
9. Wang, S.L., Song, W.Y., Kang, L., et al.: Manufacturing resource allocation based on cloud manufacturing. Comput. Integr. Manuf. Syst. **18**(7), 1396–1405 (2012)
10. Kesen, S.E., Das, S.K., Gungor, Z.: A genetic algorithm based heuristic for scheduling of virtual manufacturing cells (VMCs). Comput. Oper. Res. **37**(6), 1148–1156 (2010)
11. Ganslandt, T., Mueller, M., Krieglstein, C.F., et al.: A flexible repository for clinical trial data based on an entity-attribute-value model. In: Proceedings of the AMIA Symposium. American Medical Informatics Association, pp. 1064–1070 (1999)
12. Nadkarni, P.M., Marenco, L., Chen, R., et al.: Organization of heterogeneous scientific data using the EAV/CR representation. J. Am. Med. Inf. Assoc. **6**(6), 478–493 (1999)
13. McCandless, M., Hatcher, E., Gospodnetic, O.: Lucene in Action: Covers Apache Lucene 3.0. Manning Publications Co., Cherry Hill (2010)
14. Grainger, T., Potter, T., Seeley, Y.: Solr in Action. Manning, Cherry Hill (2014)
15. Tao, F., Hu, Y.F., Zhang, L.: Optimal configuration theory and method for manufacturing grid resource service. China Machine Press, Beijing (2010)

An Optimal Selection Method of Manufacturing Resources in Cloud Environment

Xiaobin Li[1(✉)], Chao Yin[2], Fei Liu[1,2], and Xu Zhao[2]

[1] School of Economics and Business Administration,
Chongqing University, Chongqing, China
cqlixiaobin@163.com
[2] State Key Laboratory of Mechanical Transmission,
Chongqing University, Chongqing, China

Abstract. Cloud Manufacturing allows geographically separated factories to cooperate for finishing one manufacturing task with less time, less cost, higher quality. The key issue is to achieve the optimal combination of manufacturing resources in cloud. In this paper, the constraint characteristics among manufacturing resources in cloud environment are analyzed, involving the attributes of manufacturing resources and constraints relationship among them. Based on Rough Set theory, an optimal selection method for manufacturing resources in the cloud manufacturing environment is proposed, along with its implementation framework and processing approach. A case study is demonstrated and discussed to validate the proposed method.

Keywords: Cloud manufacturing · Cloud · Constraint characteristics · Optimal selection · Manufacturing resource

1 Introduction

Under the conditions of the economic globalization and the development of information and network, cloud manufacturing, a kind of network manufacturing mode applying the idea and technologies of cloud computing, is becoming one important strategy of the organization management of production for modern manufacturing enterprises all over the world [1–3]. In cloud manufacturing environment, geographically separated manufacturing enterprises, who have some technical expertise and excellent resources, are able to work together to finish a complex, sophisticated manufacturing task with less time, less cost, higher quality. Appling such a manufacturing model, manufacturing enterprises, especially small and medium enterprises, can use advantages from around the world, outsource non-core manufacturing operations to enhance their core competitiveness.

Considering the number of manufacturing resource in cloud is huge, and the constraints among them are many, one of the key technical problem faced by the cloud manufacturing model is optimal combination of manufacturing resources. This paper

© Springer Science+Business Media Singapore 2016
L. Zhang et al. (Eds.): AsiaSim 2016/SCS AutumnSim 2016, Part III, CCIS 645, pp. 49–56, 2016.
DOI: 10.1007/978-981-10-2669-0_6

presents an optimal selection method of manufacturing resources based on Rough Set theory for solving the above technical problem.

The remainder of the paper is organized as follows. In Sect. 2, we review related work in the areas of manufacturing resource optimization from massive literature. Section 3 analyses attributes of manufacturing resources and constraints relationship among them. Based on Rough Set theory, an optimal selection method of manufacturing resources in the cloud manufacturing environment is proposed in Sect. 4, along with its implementation framework and processing approach. Section 5 gives a case for demonstrating the value of the proposed method. Eventually, Conclusions and future research hints are given in Sect. 6.

2   Literature Review

Optimal combination of manufacturing resources is one of enabling technologies for cloud manufacturing. Since cloud manufacturing is still in the theoretical research phase, the related research for such a technology is still little. Aiming to optimal selection and allocation of manufacturing resources in cloud, Yin et al. [4] proposed a decision-target system, containing collaborative time, collaborative quality, collaborative cost, ability of information interaction, safety and security of technique, and built a decision frame model for optimal selection of manufacturing resources. Aiming to optimize the selection index of resources including cost, time, and quality, Wadhwa et al. [5] studied on a multi-goal optimal selection method of collaborative resources. Yin et al. [6] established a service evaluation system in cloud environment, which consists of non-functional attributes of services, such as time, cost, quality, availability of services. With the help of this system, better resources can be selected and composed according to the weight value ranking calculated by the grey related algorithm. Taking cost, management level, service quality, and logistic strategy as the optimal goal, Araz et al. [7] put forward an optimal decision method of collaborative manufacturing partners based on Fuzzy Goal Programming. In order to solve the selection of suppliers in cloud, Zhiying et al. [8] developed a multi-objective supplier selection model, which is determined with simultaneous consideration of the total cost, quality rejection rate, late delivery rate and flexibility rate, and use a specific genetic algorithm to solve the problem. Liou et al. [9] proposes a new hybrid multiple criteria decision-making (MCDM) model, which addresses the dependent relationships among criteria with the aid of the Decision-Making Trial and Evaluation Laboratory (DEMATEL) method to build a relations-structure among criteria. Yu et al. [10] proposes an integrated approach for resource allocation problem in cloud, which combines the voting method and the Lexicographic Goal Programming (LGP) model and takes into account both qualitative and quantitative factors involved in the resource allocation decision process. Lee et al. [11] presents an intelligent data management induced resource allocation system (RAS), which aims at providing effective and timely decision making for resource allocation. Manupati et al. [3] developed a multi objective based Territory Defining Evolutionary Algorithm (TDEA) to implement near optimal process plan selection for multiple jobs in network environment.

3 Attributes of Manufacturing Resources and Constraint Characteristics

3.1 Attributes of Manufacturing Resources in Cloud Manufacturing

In cloud manufacturing environment, the attributes of manufacturing resources, which affect the operation of resources and services, mainly contain *Basic Information ()*, *Status ()*, *Performance ()*, *Cost ()*, *Time ()*, and *Other Attributes ()*.

- *Basic Information ()* presents the essential attribute of manufacturing resources, including name, type, location etc., which are respectively expressed as R_n, R_t, and R_l.
- *Status ()* means the situation of manufacturing resources, such as run or stop, maintenance etc. We denote these status as R_s.
- *Performance ()* represents the properties and functions of manufacturing resources, including Machining accuracy (M_a), Machining efficiency (M_e), Real-time monitoring (R_{tm}), Real-time interaction (R_{ti}), Information security (I_s), and Digital level (D_l) as the performance attribute of manufacturing resources.
- *Costs ()* contains material cost, energy consumption cost, equipment wear cost, machining cost, and logistic cost, etc. In this paper we only take Machining cost (M_c), and Logistic cost (L_c) in account.
- *Time ()* contains Machining time per 100pcs (M_t) and Logistic time (L_t).
- *Other Attributes ()*, such as Technical ability (T_a) and Knowledge accumulation (K_a), etc. should be considered.

3.2 Constraint Characteristic

Constraint characteristic means a set of constraint relationship between attributes and different evaluation indexes of manufacturing resources (shown as in Fig. 1). The relationship will affect execution efficiency, quality and cost of coproduction task in cloud manufacturing environment.

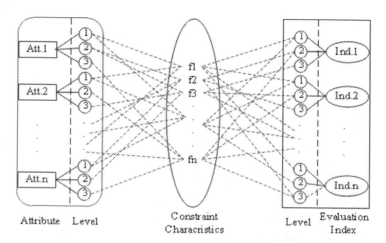

Fig. 1. Constraint relationship between attributes and evaluation indexes

In this paper, constraint characteristic can be described by **function** f.

$$f : AttributeSet \rightarrow EvaluationIndexSet \qquad (1)$$

4   An Optimal Selection Method Based on Rough Set

4.1   Rough Set

Rough Set, a mathematic tool to analyze and process data, to uncover the hidden knowledge, and reveal the potential regulations, was put forwarded by Pawlak [12], a Poland scholar in1982. Now, the Rough Set theory is being widely used in Data Mining (DM), Decision Analysis (DA) and Assistant Decision-making (AD), etc.

In Rough Set theory, information system S is expressed as $S = (U,A)$, in which U is a set of individuals that is nonempty, distinct finite and called universe; A is a nonempty, distinct finite set of attributes. As to attribute $a \in A$, there is a : $U \rightarrow V_a$, in which V_a is called the set of value of attribute a; and the value area of attribute A is expressed as set $V = \cup_{a \in A} V_a$. In this paper, we could use a decision table to describe information system, let $C, D \subseteq A$ be two subsets of attribute set A, and name C, D as attribute A's condition attribute and decision attribute, therefore, an information system S can be expressed as $T = (U, A, C, D)$, and it is called Decision Table.

According to above attributes and constraint characteristics of manufacturing resources in cloud manufacturing, based on rough set theory, we set $C = (R_t, R_l, R_s, M_a, M_e, R_{tm}, R_{ti}, I_s, D_l, M_c, L_c, M_t, L_t, T_a, K_a)$ be the condition attributes, and the decision attributes be $D = (T, Q, C, I, S, E, K)$. Here, Q represents a set of evaluation indexes of manufacturing resources in cloud environment, T means implementation time, Q represents operational quality, C describes service cost, I denotes information interaction ability among manufacturing resources, S represents security and stability of cloud services, E refers to operational environment of manufacturing resources, K means knowledge accumulation ability of manufacturing resources and services.

4.2   An Optimal Selection Method Based on Rough Set

On account of the constraint relationship between attributes and evaluation indexes of manufacturing resources in cloud (Fig. 1), this paper proposes an optimal selection method based on Rough Set theory. The implementation steps for this method are introduced as below:

Step 1:   According condition attributes above, firstly build a decision table of constraint relationship among manufacturing resources. In the decision table, condition attributes represents attributes of manufacturing resources, and decision attributes represents evaluation indexes of manufacturing resources in cloud;

Step 2:   According to the attribute information in the constraint relationship table, we need to establish some quantitative rules for the condition and decision attributes, based on a discretization method named CAIM proposed by Kurgan et al. [13];

Step 3: Getting the quantitative rules by Step 2, we should get all the attributes quantified;

Step 4: Then, we need to import the quantified constraint relationship table of into Rosetta, a Rough Set theory-based software tool, in order to get the result of attribute reduction in Decision Table, and then delete the redundant attribute, and delete the repeated lines, till we get the reduced attribute table;

Step 5: After Step 4, we've got the reduced attribute table, and we are going to reduce the value of the attributes item by item, to extract the rule of optimal selection;

Step 6: Based on the rule of optimal selection, we can build the constraint characteristics model of manufacturing resources;

Step 7: The implementation of optimal selection: firstly, we have to delete and quantify the attributes of candidate manufacturing resources and the evaluation indexes of candidate manufacturing resources, then with the help of restrict functions f, we can find out the right resource to implement manufacturing tasks in cloud.

Step 1 to 6 are the implementation of the extraction of constraint characteristics, and Step 7 is the implementation of optimal selection of manufacturing resources. This process is shown in Fig. 2.

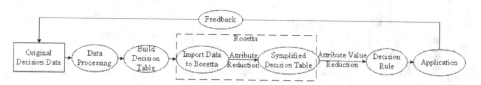

Fig. 2. Implementation process of the optimal selection method

5 Case Studies

In this section, we will introduce the algorithm implementation process and demonstrate its effectiveness by a case about networked collaborative processing task.

Firstly, we established constraint relationship table of candidate manufacturing resources as Table 1.

Then according to the quantitative rules, we transformed constraint relationship table to a quantified decision table that is deal with by Rosetta software. And we got a reduced result of the attributes showed in Table 2.

We analyzed Table 2 item by item to extract the determinant attributes and values with function $f_1 \sim f_5$:

$f_1 : R_{t2}M_{c1}M_{t2}K_{a1} \vee R_{t1}R_{tm1}M_{c1}K_{a1} \vee R_{t1}R_{tm2}M_{t2}K_{a1} \vee R_{t1}R_{tm1}M_{c1}M_{t2} \rightarrow T_1Q_1C_3I_2S_1E_1K_1$

$f_2 : R_{tm3} \rightarrow T_1Q_1C_3I_3S_2E_2K_1$

$f_3 : R_{tm2}M_{c2}M_{t3}K_{a2} \vee R_{t2}R_{tm2}M_{t3}K_{a2} \vee R_{t2}R_{tm2}M_{c2}K_{a2} \vee R_{t2}R_{tm2}M_{c2}M_{t3} \rightarrow T_2Q_2C_2I_2S_3E_1K_2$

$f_4 : M_{c3} \rightarrow T_1Q_1C_1I_1S_1E_1K_1$

$f_5 : K_{a3} \vee R_{tm1}M_{c2}M_{t3}K_{a2} \vee R_{t2}R_{tm1}M_{t3}K_{a2} \vee R_{t2}R_{tm1}M_{c2}K_{a2} \vee R_{t2}R_{tm}M_{c2}M_{t3} \rightarrow T_2Q_2C_3I_1S_1E_3K_3$

Table 1. Constraint relationship table of candidate manufacturing resources

U\A	R_t	R_l	R_s	M_a	M_c	R_{tm}	R_{tj}	L_s	D_l	M_c	L_c	M_t	L_t	T_a	K_a	T	Q	C	I	S	E	K
R1	satisfied	near	stopped	7 grade	297	partial	normal	good	ordinary	16.5	0.8	2.83	3	normal	excellent	complete in advance	better	(*,20)	offline	over 80%	good	high
R2	satisfied	in a city	maintaining	6 grade	298	without	bad	normal	low	18.3	0.45	2.7	0.8	good	excellent	complete in advance	better	(*,20)	traditional below 80%	normal	high
R3	basical	far	running	7 grade	340	partial	normal	bad	ordinary	20	0.43	3.2	1.5	good	regular	complete on schedule	basic	(20,1,25)	offline	public	good	ordinary
R4	satisfied	near	stopped	7 grade	295	real-time	good	good	high	24.5	1	2.76	1	normal	excellent	complete in advance	better	(25,1,*)	online	over 80%	good	high
R5	basical	in a city	running	7 grade	268	real-time	good	good	high	18	0.4	3.2	2	normal	poor	complete on schedule	basic	(*,20)	online	over 80%	weak	low
R6	satisfied	far	maintaining	7 grade	264	partial	normal	bad	ordinary	21	1.5	3.3	11	normal	regular	complete on schedule	basic	(20,1,25)	offline	public	good	ordinary
R7	basical	near	maintained	7 grade	281	real-time	good	good	high	18	0.8	3.3	6	bad	poor	complete on schedule	basic	(*,20)	online	over 80%	weak	low
R8	satisfied	in a city	stopped	6 grade	295	without	bad	normal	low	17.5	0.4	2.75	1.2	good	excellent	complete in advance	better	(*,20)	traditional below 80%	normal	high
R9	basical	far	maintained	7 grade	265	partial	normal	bad	ordinary	21	1.5	3.1	8	normal	regular	complete on schedule	bad	(20,1,25)	offline	public	good	ordinary
R10	satisfied	in a city	stopped	7 grade	298	real-time	good	good	high	25	0.9	2.7	1.5	good	excellent	complete in advance	basic	(25,1,*)	online	over 80%	good	high
R11	satisfied	far	maintaining	6 grade	297	without	bad	good	low	16.3	0.46	2.68	2	normal	excellent	complete in advance	bad	(*,20)	traditional below 80%	normal	high
R12	satisfied	near	stopped	7 grade	295	real-time	normal	good	ordinary	18.4	0.7	2.85	3.4	good	excellent	complete in advance	basic	(*,20)	offline	over 80%	good	high
R13	satisfied	near	stopped	7 grade	304	partial	normal	good	ordinary	17.4	0.75	2.84	3.2	bad	excellent	complete in advance	better	(*,20)	offline	over 80%	good	high
R14	basical	in a city	running	7 grade	284	real-time	good	good	high	18.6	0.4	3.2	2	normal	regular	complete on schedule	basic	(*,20)	online	over 80%	weak	low
R15	satisfied	in a city	stopped	6 grade	296	without	bad	normal	low	16.9	0.45	2.7	1.5	good	excellent	complete in advance	better	(*,20)	traditional below 80%	normal	high
R16	basical	near	maintained	7 grade	284	real-time	good	good	high	16.2	0.7	3.4	5.5	normal	poor	complete on schedule	bad	(*,20)	online	over 80%	weak	low
R17	satisfied	in a city	stopped	7 grade	300	real-time	good	good	high	25.5	0.8	2.75	4.5	good	excellent	complete in advance	basic	(25,1,*)	online	over 80%	good	high

Table 2. Reduced attribute table

U \ A	R_t	R_{tm}	M_c	M_t	K_a	T	Q	C	I	S	E	K
1	1	2	1	2	1	1	1	3	2	1	1	1
2	1	3	1	2	1	1	1	3	3	2	2	1
3	2	2	2	3	2	2	2	2	2	3	1	2
4	1	1	3	2	1	1	1	1	1	1	1	1
5	2	1	2	3	3	2	2	3	1	1	3	3
6	1	2	2	3	2	2	2	2	2	3	1	2
12	1	1	1	2	1	1	1	3	2	1	1	1
14	2	1	2	3	2	2	2	3	1	1	3	3

Table 3. The preferred result of candidate resources

U \ A	Et	Rm	Mc	Mt	Ka
R1	1	1	1	2	1
R2	1	3	1	2	1
R3	1	2	2	3	2
R4	1	1	3	2	1
R5	2	1	1	2	3
R6	2	1	1	3	1

Finally we got the preferred result table. R3 is the best candidate resource shown as Table 3.

6 Conclusions

This paper proposed the concept of constraint characteristics of manufacturing resources in cloud, which can affect the selection of resources and restrict the optimal operation. Then this paper, based on Rough Set theory, proposed an optimal selection method for manufacturing resources in the cloud manufacturing environment, by utilizing Rough Set theory and Rosetta software tool in the operation process of rule extraction, along with its implementation framework and processing approach. Last, this method was applied to a case about networked collaborative processing task and demonstrated the proposed method is valid.

Acknowledgements. This work was supported by the National High-Tech. R&D Program of China (grant No. 2015AA042102).

References

1. Petros, T., Giannoula, F.: Manufacturing strategies and financial performance–the effect of advanced information technology: CAD/CAM systems. Omega **36**(1), 107–121 (2008)
2. Liu, F., Lei, Q., Song, Y.C.: The connotation and research trend of networked manufacturing. Chin. J. Mech. Eng. **39**(8), 1–6 (2003)
3. Manupati, V.K., Thakkar, J.J.: Near optimal process plan selection for multiple jobs in networked based manufacturing using multi-objective evolutionary algorithms. Comput. Ind. Eng. **66**(1), 63–76 (2013)
4. Yin, C., Li, T., Liu, F.: Decision-making framework model for networked outsourcing resources selection. J. Mech. Eng. **26**(1), 53–60 (2010)
5. Wadhwa, V., Ravindran, A.: Vendor selection in outsourcing. Comput. Oper. Res. **34**(12), 3725–3737 (2007)
6. Yin C., Zhang Y., Zhong T.: Optimization model of cloud manufacturing services resource combination for new product development. Comput. Integr. Manuf. Syst. **18**(7), 1368–1378 (2012)
7. Araz, C., Mizrak, O., Ozkarahan, I.: An integrated multicriteria decision-making methodology for outsourcing management. Comput. Oper. Res. **34**(12), 3738–3756 (2007)
8. Zhiying, L., Rittscher, J.: A multi-objective supplier selection model under stochastic demand conditions. Int. J. Prod. Econ. **10**(5), 150–159 (2007)
9. Liou, J.J.H., Chuang, Y.-T.: Developing a hybrid multi-criteria model for selection of outsourcing providers. Expert Syst. Appl. **37**(5), 3755–3761 (2010)
10. Yu, V.F., Hu, K.-J.: An integrated approach for resource allocation in manufacturing plants. Appl. Math. Comput. **245**, 416–426 (2014)
11. Lee, C.K.H., Choy, K.L., et al.: Application of intelligent data management in resource allocation for effective operation of manufacturing systems. J. Manufact. Syst. **33**(3), 412–422 (2014)
12. Pawlak, Z.: Rough set. Int. J. Comput. Inform. Sci. II, 341–356
13. Kurgan, L.A., Cios, K.J.: CAIM discretization algorithm. IEEE Trans. Knowl. Data Eng. **16**(2), 145–153 (2004)

3-Dimensional Classification and Visualization of Clouds Simulated by Cloud-Resolving Atmospheric General Circulation Model

Daisuke Matsuoka$^{(\boxtimes)}$ and Kazuyoshi Oouchi

Japan Agency for Marine-Earth Science and Technology (JAMSTEC),
Yokohama, Japan
{daisuke,k-ouchi}@jamstec.go.jp

Abstract. Cloud-resolving atmospheric general circulation models using large scale supercomputers reproduce realistic behavior of atmospheric field on a global scale. To understand the simulation result for scientists, visualizing individual clouds and their physical characteristics is necessary. In this study, we propose a new feature extraction and classification method of simulated clouds based on their 3-dimensional shape and physical properties. The results of applying the proposed method show the clouds' distribution of a tropical cyclone during its generation, development and disappearance process, and the relation between cloud-forms and precipitation.

Keywords: Visualization · Atmospheric simulation · Cloud · Feature extraction · Classification

1 Introduction

Atmospheric phenomena such as a weather front, heavy rain and tropical cyclone affect the lives of human beings. Understanding these phenomena is important for social issues as well as academic issues. A large number of studies have been conducted in atmospheric and climate science fields by numerical simulations [1]. The conventional global atmospheric models based on primitive equations with hydrostatic approximation are not able to resolve individual clouds. Recently, because of the advances in supercomputing technology, NICAM (Non-hydrostatic Icosahedral Atmospheric Model) [2, 3] was developed for the Earth Simulator. NICAM calculates vertical flow without hydrostatic approximation and is able to reproduce vertical convection and O (10 km) to $O(100$ km) cloud clusters and is used to analyze MJO (Madden-Julian Oscillation) [4], tropical cyclones [5] and other global phenomena.

Generally, clouds have various types strongly related to atmospheric phenomena. To deeply understand such phenomena, understanding individual clouds and their physical properties is necessary. The latest cloud-resolving model can calculate the 3-dimensional (3D) configuration of individual clouds accurately; however, most previous studies for automatic cloud classification are intended at 2-dimensional (2D) simulation using satellite observational data (i.e. [6–9]) and ground based imagery data (i.e. [10, 11])

© Springer Science+Business Media Singapore 2016
L. Zhang et al. (Eds.): AsiaSim 2016/SCS AutumnSim 2016, Part III, CCIS 645, pp. 57–67, 2016.
DOI: 10.1007/978-981-10-2669-0_7

based on the color of clouds. Therefore, they are not adequate for understanding individual clouds, especially their three-dimensional shape and physical properties.

In this study, we try to extract and classify 3D clouds from cloud-resolving simulation data according to their 3D shape and physical properties. The details of the proposed cloud extraction and the classification method and its application results are reported.

2   Data Set

The atmospheric simulation data used in this study is produced by the NICAM. The NICAM was first developed for the Earth Simulator and currently is also carried out on the K computer. The grid model uses an icosahedral grid structure and the horizontal resolution of the computational mesh is approximately 3.5 km. This model employs fully compressible non-hydrostatic equations to obtain statistically equilibrium states and guarantees the conservation of mass and energy. Equations are discretized by finite volume method. One characteristic feature of this model is that it explicitly calculates deep convective circulations without using cumulus parameterizations. For details of the model, please see [2].

The output data includes water vapor (3D), quantities of cloud water (3D), cloud ice (3D), velocity field (3D), precipitation (2D), outgoing long radiation (OLR) (2D). A snapshot image of a simulation result is shown in Fig. 1. 2D distribution of clouds and precipitation are visualized by gray scale color and rainbow color, respectively. Several clouds and rainfall areas are reproduced on the ground as well as on the ocean. Analysis domain in Sect. 3 (for method description and test) and Sect. 4 (for application) are shown in squares with a red solid border.

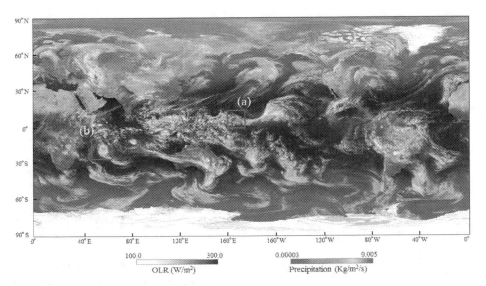

Fig. 1. A snapshot image of simulation results and analysis domain of (a) the Equatorial Pacific (Sect. 3) and (b) the Southern Indian Ocean (Sect. 4).

3 Method

3.1 Concept of Proposed Method

While real clouds have 3D configuration, previous work on cloud classification has not considered vertical distribution, as mentioned in Sect. 1. The general cloud forms have been standardized and published in the International Cloud Atlas by World Meteorological Organization (WMO) [12] as shown in a basic reference for schematic clouds types in Fig. 2(a). In this reference, clouds are roughly classified into ten types such as cirrus, stratus and cumulus based on their altitude and physical properties.

(a)   (b)

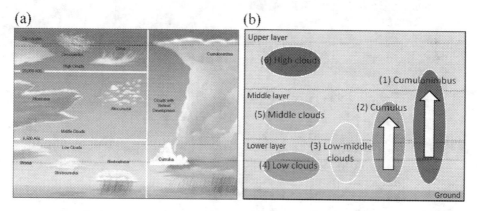

Fig. 2. Classification of clouds. (a) Ten types cloud classification by WMO [12] and (b) a conceptual image of six types cloud classification (proposed method). (Color figure online)

Simulated clouds by numerical model do not correspond to all cloud forms because some cloud forms cannot be reproduced by the current physical scheme and spatial resolution. Hence, this study proposes a new simple and basic 3-dimensional (3D) classification method for simulated clouds based on their altitude and upward flow. The proposed method classifies 3D clouds into the following six types, as shown in Fig. 2 (b): (1) cumulonimbus, (2) cumulus, (3) low-middle clouds, (4) low clouds, (5) middle clouds and (6) high clouds. Compared to the ten type classification by WMO, a couple of cloud forms are lamped together to one group. For example, altostratus and altocumulus are grouped as middle clouds.

3.2 Extraction of Clouds

A cloud is a visible mass of liquid or solid droplets made up of tiny water droplets or ice crystals, usually a mixture of both. In this study, clouds are detected from 3D simulation data on each grid point, where $qc + qi \geq qth$. Here, qc, qi and qth are quantity of cloud water, quantity of cloud ice and the threshold value for cloud detection, respectively. Individual cloud mass is defined by the spatially contiguous grid points that meet the conditions of cloud water and cloud ice. The algorithm is shown below.

```
## Algorithm 1: Extraction of clouds
SET ic to 1
SET cloud[i][j][k] to 0
FOR all grid point[i][j][k]
  IF cloud[i][j][k]=0 THEN
    IF qc[i][j][k]+qi[i][j][k]>qth THEN
      CALL search_cloud(i, j, k, ic);
      cloud_type[ic] = 3456
      ic = ic + 1
    ELSE
      cloud[i][j][k] = -999
    ENDIF
  ENDIF
END FOR

search_cloud(i, j, k, ic){
  IF cloud[i][j][k]=0 THEN
    IF qc[i][j][k]+qi[i][j][k]>qth THEN
      cloud[i][j][k] = ic
      search_cloud(i+1, j  , k  , ic)
      search_cloud(i-1, j  , k  , ic)
      search_cloud(i  , j+1, k  , ic)
      search_cloud(i  , j-1, k  , ic)
      search_cloud(i  , j  , k+1, ic)
      search_cloud(i  , j  , k-1, ic)
    ELSE
      cloud[i][j][k] = -999
    ENDIF
  ENDIF
}
```

Above algorithm explores unexplored grid points to the contiguous six directions (two directions of longitude, latitude and altitude) from seed point in order to indentify identical cloud. This algorithm is a recursive algorithm that repeatedly uses the subroutine `search_cloud()` for exploring neighboring grid points. If the currently explored grid point fulfills the condition of cloud detection, the grid point is grouped with the identical clouds and stored as the candidate for the next seed point. Repeating this recursive process, the algorithm can identify an individual cloud. `cloud[i][j][k]` indicates an existence of a cloud on each grid point (1, 2, 3...: cloud, 0: candidate of cloud, −999: not cloud). An integer value of 1 or more indicates the identification number (`ic`) for individual cloud mass.

Figure 3(a) depicts an extraction result of 3D clouds by using the proposed method (here, qth = 0.0001 kg/kg). However, Fig. 3(b) depicts 2D clouds visualized by OLR (same figure with Fig. 1). While both results roughly correspond with each other, the shapes of the cumulonimbus are slightly different. Cumulonimbus with vertical flow is known to not be able to move upward beyond the boundary of the troposphere, and it spreads widely in a horizontal direction [13]. This spread cloud at the top of cumulonimbus is called an anvil or incus (red dashed line in Fig. 3(a)). While Fig. 3(b) represents the horizontal distribution of an anvil, Fig. 3(a) clearly visualizes 3D configurations of cumulonimbus with an anvil.

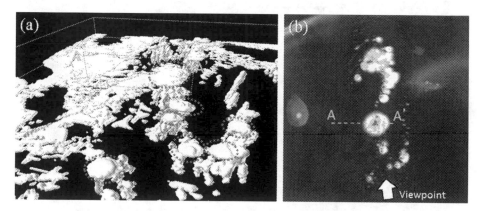

Fig. 3. Visualization results of clouds in (a) 3D (proposed method) and (b) 2D (same as Fig. 1). (Color figure online)

In some cases, the abovementioned algorithm has a problem to be solved. There is a case where vertically developed clouds such as cumulonimbus and cumulus partially connect horizontally distributed clouds such as lower clouds, as shown in Fig. 4(a). Separating these essentially different clouds using an additional physical property is necessary. Figure 4(b) depicts upward flow (vertical component of velocity field) in clouds represented in Fig. 3 (yellow dashed line). While the magnitude of upward flow of the cumulonimbus is greater than 0.2 m/s (anvil cloud is 0.0–0.2 m/s), the same value of the lower cloud is 0.0–0.02 m/s. Therefore, they can be separated using the threshold value of upward flow.

Our proposed cloud extraction method is organized in two steps, cumulonimbus/cumulus extraction (Algorithm 2) and other clouds extraction (Algorithm 1). Algorithm 2 to extract cumulonimbus and cumulus is listed below.

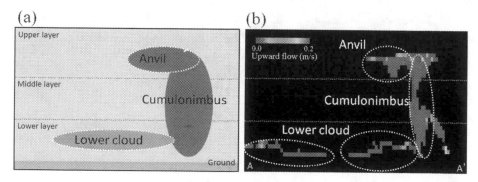

Fig. 4. Handling of connected clouds. Vertical image of (a) cloud form and (b) upward flow.

```
## Algorithm 2: Extraction of cumulus and cumulonimbus
FOR all grid point[i][j][k]
  IF cloud[i][j][k]=0 & alt[k]<7000.0 THEN
    IF qc[i][j][k]+qi[i][j][k]>qth & w[i][j][k]>wth THEN
      CALL search_cloud12(i, j, k, nc);
    ELSE
      cloud[i][j][k] = -999
    ENDIF
  ENDIF
  cloud_type[nc] = 12
  ic = ic + 1
END FOR
IF cloud[i][j][k] != 12 THEN
  SET cloud[i][j][k] to 0
ENDIF

search_cloud12(i, j, k, ic){
  IF cloud[i][j][k]=0 THEN
    IF alt[k]<7000.0 & qc[i][j][k]+qi[i][j][k]>qth
                                          &w[i][j][k]>wth
    || alt[k]>=7000.0 & qc[i][j][k]+qi[i][j][k]>qth THEN
      cloud[i][j][k] = ic
      search_cloud12(i+1, j  , k  , ic)
      search_cloud12(i-1, j  , k  , ic)
      search_cloud12(i  , j+1, k  , ic)
      search_cloud12(i  , j-1, k  , ic)
      search_cloud12(i  , j  , k+1, ic)
      search_cloud12(i  , j  , k-1, ic)
    ELSE
      cloud[i][j][k] = -999
    ENDIF
  ENDIF
}
```

The above listed algorithm is carried out before line 3 in Algorithm 1. The difference between Algorithm 2 and Algorithm 1 is whether the condition of cloud extraction includes threshold value of upward flow (here, *wth* = 0.2 m/s) or not. Furthermore, in order to extract an anvil cloud, when the altitude of an explored grid point is higher than 7000.0, the threshold value *wth* is not included in the condition of cumulonimbus/cumulus detection. The value of cloud_type[ic], the unique ID number of the ic-th cloud, is 12 for cumulonimbus/cumulus and 3456 for other clouds. The separation result of both cloud forms is represented in Fig. 5. Pale red and pale blue clouds indicate cumulonimbus/cumulus and other clouds, respectively. This separation is a preparation for the six type cloud classification as mentioned in Sect. 3.3.

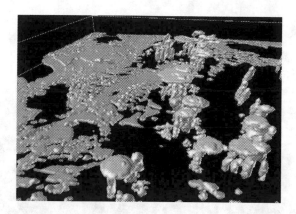

Fig. 5. Separation of cumulonimbus/cumulus and other clouds.

3.3   Classification of Clouds

Detected cumulonimbus and cumulus (cloud_type [ic] = 12) are classified into the following two types based on their altitude: (1) lower to upper layer and (2) lower layer to middle layer, respectively. In the same way, other types of detected clouds (cloud_type [ic] = 3456) are classified into the following four types: (3) lower to middle layer, (4) lower layer, (5) middle layer and (6) upper layer. The algorithm is shown below.

```
## Algorithm 3: Classification of clouds
FOR EACH cloud[ic]
  IF cloud_type[ic] = 12 THEN
    IF 3000.0<alt_min[ic] & 7000.0<=alt_max[ic] THEN
      cloud_type[ic] = 1
    IF alt_min[ic]<3000.0 THEN
      cloud_type[ic] = 2
    ENDIF
  ELSE IF cloud_type = 3456 THEN
    IF 7000.0<=alt_min[ic]
      cloud_type[ic] = 6
    ELSE IF 3000.0<=alt_min[ic] & alt_max[ic]<7000.0 THEN
      cloud_type[ic] = 5
    IF alt_max[ic]<3000.0 THEN
      cloud_type[ic] = 4
    ELSE IF alt_min[ic]<3000.0 & alt_max[ic]<7000.0 THEN
      cloud_type[ic] = 3
    ENDIF
  ENDIF
END FOR
```

The classification results are represented in Fig. 6. Figure 6(a) is a result of using both Algorithms 1 and 2, and Fig. 6(b) is a result of using only Algorithm 1. In both results, extracted clouds are colored by red (cumulonimbus and anvil), orange (cumulus), yellow (low-middle clouds), green (low clouds), cyan (middle clouds) and blue (high clouds), as shown in Fig. 2(b). Compared to Fig. 6(b), cumulonimbus with anvil and cumulus are correctly separated from other clouds in Fig. 6(a).

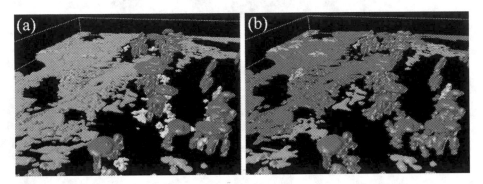

Fig. 6. Classification results (a) using cumulonimbus/cumulus separation (Algorithms 1 and 2) and (b) simple cloud extraction (only Algorithm 1). (Color figure online)

4   Results

The proposed method is applied to visualize tropical cyclones on the Indian Ocean in December 2011 simulated by NICAM (3.5 km mesh). Tropical cyclones are known to have swirling clouds that are vertically developed [14, 15]. Its 2D (horizontal or vertical) structure has been studied; however, its 3D structure is not understood especially from the perspective of an individual cloud form.

Figure 7 displays visualization results of a tropical cyclone using the proposed six type cloud classification during December 1–8, 2011. The color of each cloud is shown in Fig. 2(b). In the initial stage of the tropical cyclone, cumulonimbus and cumulus are developed, and low clouds and low-middle clouds gather around them because of decreasing pressure in the lower atmosphere (Fig. 7(a)–(d)). In the developing stage, such clouds are swirled around the cumulonimbus, and the eye and eye wall (which is a wall of cumulonimbus around the eye) are formed (Fig. 7(e)–(f)). This vortex structure, including swirled clouds, the eye and the eye wall, is called a tropical cyclone. In the fully developed stage, the size and the intensity of the tropical cyclone are developed to the maximum (Fig. 7(g)). In the dissipation stage, the altitude of the eye wall with upward flow becomes lower, and the size of the tropical cyclone also decreases (Fig. 7(h)).

The relationship between cloud form and rainfall in a tropical cyclone in the fully developed stage (Fig. 7(g)) are shown in Fig. 8. Figure 8(a) and (b) depicts 2D distribution of precipitation and cloud form, respectively. Cloud form is represented in the stack in the order of (1) cumulonimbus, (2) cumulus, (3) low-middle clouds, (4) low clouds, (5) middle clouds, and (6) high clouds. The heavy rain region in the vicinity of the eye of the tropical cyclone corresponds to cumulonimbus. Furthermore, we find that spiral-shape rain regions, called rain band inside red dashed line in Fig. 8(a), correspond to the distribution of low-middle clouds.

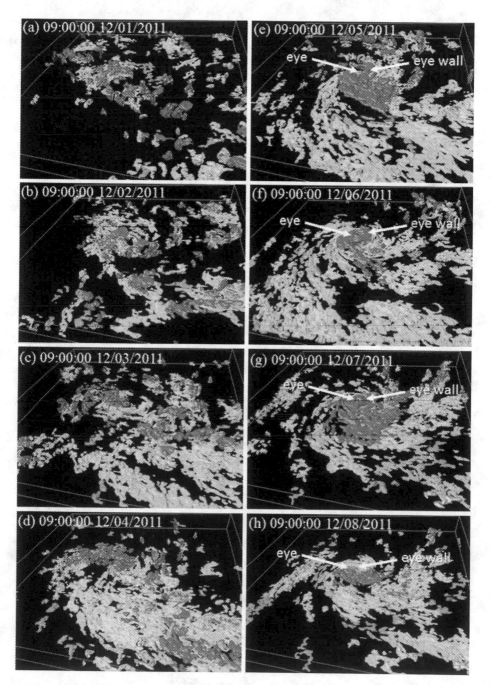

Fig. 7. Visualization results of generation process of tropical cyclone on the Southern Indian Ocean during December 1 to 8, 2011.

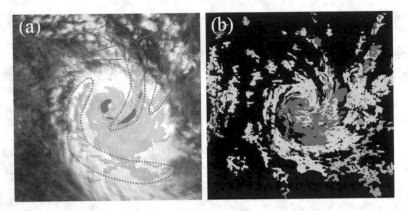

Fig. 8. Relation between (a) rainfall and (b) cloud form. (Color figure online)

5   Summary and Discussion

In this study, we proposed a new extraction and classification method to intuitively understand simulated 3D clouds from cloud-resolving atmospheric simulation data. Extracted clouds are classified into six types using their altitude and vertical flow. As a result, we succeeded in visualizing the 3D structure of an atmospheric event such as a tropical cyclone from the perspective of individual 3D cloud forms. The proposed method is beneficial for understanding atmospheric phenomena. The proposed technique is expected to lead to the analysis of high-resolution atmospheric simulation data.

However, it is noted that all of the threshold values, altitude, qth and wth, are given by user's trial and error, because typical physical values are not strictly defined to general cloud-forms. To determine physically correct threshold values for clouds, extraction and classification is required in future work.

Acknowledgement. We are grateful to Dr. Miyakawa (University of Tokyo), Dr. Nakano (JAMSTEC) and the NICAM team for their data production and model development. This work is supported by KAKENHI (26700010) Grant-in-Aid for Young Scientists (A).

References

1. Ohfuchi, W., Nakamura, H., Yoshioka, M.K., Enomoto, T., Takaya, K., Peng, X., Yamane, S., Nishimura, T., Kurihara, Y., Ninomiya, K.: 10-km Mesh meso-scale resolving simulations of the global atmosphere on the earth simulator–preliminary outcomes of AFES (AGCM for the Earth Simulator). J. Earth Simul. **1**, 8–34 (2004)
2. Tomita, S., Sato, M.: A new dynamical framework of nonhydrostatic global model using the icosahedral grid. Fluid Dyn. Res. **34**(6), 357–400 (2004)
3. Sato, M., Tomita, H., Yashiro, H., Miura, H., Kodama, C., Seiki, T., Noda, A.T., Yamada, Y., Goto, D., Sawada, M., Miyoshi, T., Niwa, Y., Hara, M., Ohno, T., Iga, S., Arakawa, T., Inoue, T., Kubokawa, H.: The Non-hydrostatic icosahedral atmospheric model: description and development. Prog. Earth Planet. Sci. **1**(18), 1–32 (2014)

4. Miura, H., Satoh, M., Nasuno, T., Noda, A.T., Oouchi, K.: A madden-julien oscillation event realistically simulated by a global cloud-resolving model. Science **318**, 1763–1765 (2007)
5. Nakano, M., Sawada, M., Nasuno, T., Satoh, M.: Intraseasonal variability and tropical cyclonenesis in the western north pacific simulated by a global nonhydrostatic atmospheric model. Geophys. Res. Lett. **42**, 565–571 (2015)
6. Karlsson, K.-G.: Development of an operational cloud classification model. Int. J. Remote Sens. **10**, 687–693 (1989)
7. Macías-Macías, M., García-Orellana, C.J., González-Velasco, H., Gallardo-Caballero, R.: ICA and GA feature extraction and selection for cloud classification. In: Singh, S., Singh, M., Apte, C., Perner, P. (eds.) ICAPR 2005. LNCS, vol. 3686, pp. 488–496. Springer, Heidelberg (2005)
8. Zibert, M.I., Derrien, M., Le Gleau, H.: Automatic cloud classification by supervised learning on SEVIRI data using support vector machines method. In: The 2005 EUMETSAT Meteorological Satellite Conference, pp. 188–192 (2006)
9. Kazantzidis, R., Tzoumanikas, P., Bais, A.F., Fotopoulos, S., EconomouU, G.: Equipment and methodologies for cloud detection and classification: a review. Sol. Energy **95**, 392–430 (2012)
10. Heinle, A., Macke, A., Srivastav, A.: Automatic cloud classification of whole sky images. Atmos. Measur. Tech. **3**, 557–567 (2010)
11. Liu, S., Zhang, Z., Mei, X.: Ground-based cloud classification using weighted local binary patterns. J. Appl. Remote Sens. **9**(1), 095062 (2015)
12. The Ten Cloud Types. http://www.weathergamut.com/2011/10/14/cloud-nine/
13. Sinkevich, A.A., Krauss, T.W., Stepanenko, V.D., Dovgalyuk, Y.A., Veremey, N.E., Krov, A.B., Pivovarova, L.V.: Study of dynamics of the cumulonimbus anvil of large vertical extent. Russ. Meteorol. Hydrol. **34**(12), 775–783 (2010)
14. Houze, R.A.: Clouds in tropical cyclones. Mon. Weather Rev. **138**, 293–344 (2010)
15. Oouchi, K., Fudeyasu, H. (eds.): Cyclones: Formation, Triggers and Control. NOVA Publishers, New York (2012)

Modeling Bidirectional Reflectance Factor of Complex Scene Using Iterative MapReduce

Yulun Li[✉], Zhen Yang, Xiaoshan Ma, and Ligang Li

Key Laboratory of Electronics and Information Technology for Complex Aerospace System, National Space Science Center, Chinese Academy of Sciences, Beijing, China
yl_li@nssc.ac.cn

Abstract. Previous Bidirectional Reflectance Factor (BRF) modeling approaches are not sufficient to handle complex scenes, which are radiation-complicated and data-massive. Using iterative MapReduce framework, this paper presents a series of algorithms executable in multiple nodes. Firstly, a virtually scenario is established by 3ds-Max, reconstructable geometry shadow maps method is then employed to count the visibility of patch sets. In addition, endmember variability is accounted for further enhancing simulation fidelity. Finally, an experimental validation is performed. Results by the proposed methods are more coherent with the observation data.

Keywords: Bidirectional reflectance factor · Iterative MapReduce · Reconstructable geometry shadow maps · Endmember variability

1 Introduction and Related Works

The multi-angle aspect has received considerable attention in optical imaging simulation. Traditional Lambertian assumption introduces errors when modeling ground spectrum under arbitrary sensing geometry [1]. Practically, the ***Bidirectional Reflectance Factor (BRF)*** is used to describe that angle-distinct property: note that the apparent reflectance of a hyperspectral pixel can be represented as:

$$f(\theta, \varphi, \lambda) = \frac{dL_p(\theta, \varphi, \lambda)}{dL_r(\theta, \varphi, \lambda)} \tag{1}$$

Where (θ, φ) represent sensing direction, λ is wavelength, dL_p, dL_r are measured radiance of the whole pixel and a reference plate (as a reference).

Despite specific cases, the above factor is estimated using computer simulation methods based on *Linear Mixture Model (LMM)*. A pixel in hyperspectral image is regarded as the combination of different materials (endmembers) with their visible areas from given direction [2]:

© Springer Science+Business Media Singapore 2016
L. Zhang et al. (Eds.): AsiaSim 2016/SCS AutumnSim 2016, Part III, CCIS 645, pp. 68–77, 2016.
DOI: 10.1007/978-981-10-2669-0_8

$$\underline{x_n} = \sum_{i=1}^{m} a_{ni}\underline{s_i} + \underline{\varepsilon_n}$$

$s.t.$

$$\begin{cases} a_{ni} \geq 0 \\ \sum_{i=1}^{m} a_{ni} = 1 \end{cases} \tag{2}$$

Where $\underline{s_i}$ describes directional spectral signature of endmember i, a_{ni} represents abundance values and satisfies positivity/sum-to-one conditions. The additive noise item $\underline{\varepsilon_n}$ is resulted from the shadow effect and the secondary radiation.

Representative work including BRF computation is the *Radiosity Graphics Model (RGM)* proposed by Qin et al. in 2000 [3]. It is deterministic for three-dimensional scene and with the purpose of modeling sparse vegetation's BRF. Validation work has been added from observed data. To the authors' knowledge, famous optical imaging simulation tools rely still on RGM idea, like SENSOR and DIRSIG [4, 5]. Recently, research has been dedicated to the specific application: Carson et al. simulate soil signatures under complex mixture and distribution of particles [6]. Yao et al. evaluate the sub-pixel vegetation structure impact on imaging simulation [7]. Goodenough et al. concern radiance signatures simulation air/water interface [8]. Ma et al. calculate the BRF/BRDF of the upper ocean layer. In addition, the infrared and the polarimetric aspects are also considered, such as study made by Jun et al. and Rehorn et al. [9, 10]. All work above has the same modeling mechanism and only differs from distinct application areas.

Nevertheless, existing BRF modeling approaches prescind two uncertainties: (1)the incomplete radiation of patches; (2) the endmember variability (please see for instance [11] and reference therein). These degrade seriously the fidelity of the simulation process. To explore these problems, a series of algorithms with iterative MapReduce framework is proposed. Section 2 depicts preparation work for programming and experimental validation. Section 3 describes an algorithm series. Simulation and measurement results using synthetic data are presented in Sect. 4. Concluding remarks are finally reported.

2 Preparations

Figure 1a shows a spectrum measuring instrument developed by Hefei Institutes of Physical Science, Chinese Academy of Sciences (CASHIPS). It consists of several black bracket and a spectroradiometer (SVC HR-1024) can rotate on them driven by an electrical engine. Therefore we can record the spectral response from any direction.

Next, a scene containing three geometries with distinct surface properties (i.e., a cone with Lambertian coating, a mirror-reflective cylinder and a wooden cube, as shown in Fig. 1b is established. These three objects are placed on an elliptic dark cloth, which is low reflective and approximately Lambertian. Their geometric parameters are listed in Table 1. The whole scene can be regarded as a synthetic pixel.

(a) Measurement instruments   (b) Geometries

Fig. 1. Experiment elements

Table 1. Geometric parameters of scene's elements

Geometries	Parameters	Values/cm
Cone Cylinder	Bottom diameter	11.7
	Height	21.2
Cube	Length	16
Cloth	Major axis	18.49, 15.52,14.21, 13.99
	Minor axis	13.99
Sensing radius		200
FOV: 8°		

We use 3ds_Max 2015 to numerically generate the above scene as algorithm input, as shown in Fig. 2. It's saved as Obj. document including sets of triangular patches with their vertexes' coordinates/normal vectors given. Material-type (i.e. Spectral reflectance) must be assigned to those patches, which will be detailed in Sect. 4.

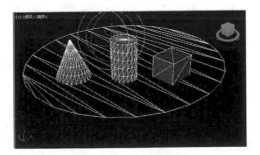

Fig. 2. Obj. model by 3ds_Max 2015

Remark 1: There exist manual errors in geometries. Thus above parameters are estimated by multiple measurements. In addition, zenith angles θ take values at $\pm 45, \pm 30, \pm 15, 0°$ and corresponds to different major axis of cloth by the following formula:

$$\begin{cases} a = \dfrac{r \cdot \sin(\frac{1}{2}FOV)}{\cos(\theta - \frac{1}{2}FOV)} \\ b = r \cdot \tan(\frac{1}{2}FOV) \end{cases} \quad (3)$$

Where a, b represent the major and the minor axis of sensing field, and r, FOV are radius of equipment and the angle of view of spectroradiometer.

3 Algorithms Description

MapReduce framework is employed to develop algorithms [12]. Subsection 3.1 deals with visibility computation for arbitrary incidence or between each two patches. Next, a sampling/adjusting method is introduced based on the Normal Compositional Model in Sect. 3.2.

3.1 Visibility Computation

The reconstructable geometry shadow maps (RGSM) method is used [13]. The main idea is the rasterlization for triangular patches, as shown in Fig. 3a, b. Note that visibility computation from light direction (shadow) or sensing direction (projected area) is the same problem. The coordinate transformation for a certain point d from ground reference to incidence or observed directions can be described as:

$$\begin{bmatrix} s_d \\ t_d \\ r_d \end{bmatrix} = T_v \begin{bmatrix} x_d \\ y_d \\ z_d \end{bmatrix} \quad (4)$$

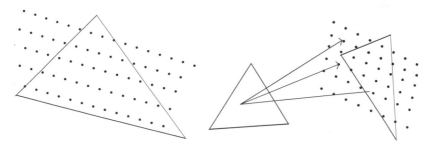

(a) Visibility from arbitrary direction (b) Visibility between each two patches

Fig. 3. A sketch of rasterlization

Where (x_d, y_d, z_d), (s_d, t_d, r_d) represent respectively initial coordinates and these after transformation. The transform matrix T_v is pre-defined.

For a certain direction, we define visibility ratio $F_i(\theta, \varphi)$ attached to a certain patch i :

$$F_i(\theta, \varphi) = \frac{|d_{i\_visible}(\theta, \varphi)|}{|d_i(\theta, \varphi)|} \in [0, 1] \tag{5}$$

The formulas (5) can be understood as a ratio between the number of visible dots and the overall in a patch with rasterlization. *Thus the incomplete radiation is possible to be expressed by this ratio.* The algorithm is described as following:

Algorithm 1: Visibility from arbitrary direction
Map:
Define Map(patch{ }, (s_dot, t_dot))
   %% Rasterlization (parallel light)
   for patch{ }
      if (s_dot, t_dot) interacts after transform then
         compute inversely r by (4)
         patch_visibile=current_min r
         record patch_interacts
      end if
   end for
Return (patch_visible,1)
Return (other_patch_interacts,0)
Reduce:
Define Reduce(patch_ID, 0/1)
   reduce by (5)
Return(patch_ID, F_i)

Similarly, for visibility computation between two patches, we can sum visibility ratios for this kind of selected points to that patch. In this case, each dot in the target patch is a point light source. The visibility from patch j to i is expressed as:

$$F_{ij} = \frac{1}{A_i A_j} \int\limits_{A_i} \int\limits_{A_j} \frac{\cos \theta_i \cos \theta_j}{\pi l^2} dA_i f_{visible} dA_j$$

$$\cong \frac{\cos \theta_i \cos \theta_j}{\pi l^2} \frac{1}{|d_i||d_j|} \sum_{k \in d_i} |d_{kj}| \tag{6}$$

Where areas of patches A_i, A_j can be approximated by overall numbers of dots $|d_i|, |d_j|$ in those surfaces. The item $|d_{kj}|$ represents for a certain dot k, the number of dots visible to it in patch j. The other parameters are assumed to be constant as the classical definition of shape factor [3]. The algorithm is described as following:

Algorithm 2: Visibility between each two patches
rasterlization for target patch as in algorithm 1(normal direction, parallel light)
Map:
Define Map(dots_target_patch{ }, source_patch_ID)
   %% rasterlization (point light)
   for dots_target_patch{ }
       rasterlize the sub-scene bounded by the target and the source patch
       %% hierarchical MapReduce, use algorithm 1
       compute the visibility radio by (5)
       Return (source_patch_ID, visibility radio)
   end for
Reduce:
Define Reduce(source_patch_ID, visibility radio)
   reduce by (6)
Return(source_patch_ID, F_{ij})

With the visibility factors, endmembers' radiance and abundance values s, R from sensing direction (θ, φ) is summed as follows:

$$S_i(\theta, \varphi) = \sum_{j \in patches\_of\_endmember\_i} s_{ij} F_j(\theta, \varphi)$$

$$R_i(\theta, \varphi) = \sum_{j \in patches\_of\_endmember\_i} r_{ij}(\theta, \varphi) \tag{7}$$

$$\cong \sum_{j \in patches\_of\_endmember\_i} [E_0 cos\theta F_j(\theta, \varphi) + \sum_{k \in patches, k \notin j} \rho_k E_0 \cos \theta F_k(\theta, \varphi) F_{ik}]$$

Where for endmember i, the area of each patch j is represented as s_j, and its radiance is r_{ij}. The solar irradiation is E_0, and the reflectivity of patch k is ρ_k, both are assumed to be constant.

Remark 2: The constant assumption in (6) and (7) is not correct. In fact, those values vary and will introduce simulation errors. However, to simulate within satisfied accuracy requires a large amount of computation. Therefore we use a sampling/adjusting algorithm to deal with that problem.

3.2 Sampling/Adjusting

The recently-proposed normal compositional model (NCM) is used. It describes the observation x_i, as a convex combination of vectors, i.e. [14]:

$$\underline{x_n} = \sum_{j=1}^{m} \alpha_r \underline{\varepsilon_r} \tag{8}$$

Where $\varepsilon_j \in R^n$ is a random vector with distribution $N(\mu_j, \Gamma_j)$, namely the spectral vector of endmembers is no longer deterministic but a stochastic distribution. The additive noise term in (2) disappear because it is included into this spectral uncertainty.

NCM seems more practical. We adopt the *Monte Carlo Markov Chain (MCMC) sampling approach* proposed by Zare et al. to adjust endmembers' radiance and abundances distribution. *The intermediate results in (7) are taken as parameter priors* [15]:

$$\mu_j \sim N(\cdot | m, C)$$
$$\alpha_r \sim D(\cdot | 1) \tag{9}$$

Where D is the Dirichlet distribution. The parameters m, C are set using priors we have above obtained. The algorithm is described as follows:

Algorithm 3: Sampling and adjusting radiance and abundance values of endmembers

set reference output x_{n_ref}

each spectral band is assumed independent to others (the spectral curve is record as a set of discredited wavelengths λ)

Map:
Define Map(endmember_abundance{}, endmember_spectral_waveband{})
    MCMC sampling abundance vector by (9)
    MCMC sampling spectral vector for a certain band by (9)
Return(λ , (sampled α_r , sampled $\underline{\varepsilon_r}$))

Reduce:
Define Reduce(λ , (sampled α_r , sampled $\underline{\varepsilon_r}$))

    minimize the difference between sampling generate and reference
    if convergence condition not satisfied then
      do MapReduce recursion
    else
      terminated
    end if
Return(λ , (adjusted α_r , adjusted $\underline{\varepsilon_r}$))

use (8) to model the final reflectance

---

4   Results Discussion

Figure 4a shows four kinds of material spectrum (cone, cylinder, cube and cloth) allocated to patches, it is measured within observation angles 235/0°. These spectral data are overlapped and resampled with each 1.5 nm. Note we can obtain a relatively different result from other directions due to BRF and endmember variability. Here we take those measured data as priors.

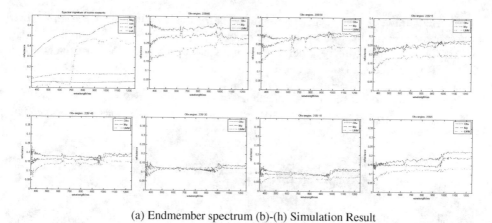

(a) Endmember spectrum (b)-(h) Simulation Result

Fig. 4. Simulation and experimental results (Color figure online)

The Programming environment is listed in Table 2:

Table 2. Simulation environment settings

Computer/OS	Windows 7(64-bits) i5-2410, 2.30 Ghz
Software/Platform	Cygwin 2.5.1
	Eclipse 4.3.2
	Hadoop 0.21
MapReduce mode	single pseudo-distributed
Pseudo node numbers	1
	512
Execution time	27th, April, 2016 nearly 10:30, 1 h
Experimental time	15th, April, 2016 nearly 14:00, 10 min

The observation azimuth angles are considered as 235°, with the zenith angles vary from −45 to +45° at an interval of 15. For each sensor location, we measure three times and take average. Results are visualized in Fig. 4b–h, red curves are observed and reference data, blue curves are algorithms' output using paper's algorithms, and green ones are generated by using LMM under MapReduce, i.e. it's without the sampling/adjusting part.

Both two methods (that presented in this paper and LMM) generate results distinct to observed curve. This is possibly led by: (1) the light source is not strictly parallel, and has a degradation of its luminance quality. In addition, the spectroradiometer is not located at infinity either (When the zenith angle of observation increases, the difference enlarges); (2) only primary and secondary radiation is considered, as a simplification of order 10^{-2}, high orders are neglected as a loss of reflectance (In figures, red curves are usually above others).

In addition, we can see that blue curves are closer to observed reference, compared with green ones. Using novel algorithms, spectrum of materials is not fixed, which can be adjusted through a normal distribution to meet the final result. In fact, various error sources(from measurement, statistical patch properties) are impossible to eliminate. The NCM is a multi-factor, inter-influence from the spirit of large-number or center-limit theory. Thus, correction from part observed data or other measured data is necessary.

Remark 3: The difference among reflectance curves in Fig. 4 is visually obvious. To quantize this difference, tools to describe *cluster distance* J_d in remote sensing area is implemented:

$$J_d = \frac{1}{2} \sum_{i=1}^{C} P_i (\sum_{j=1}^{C} P_j (\frac{1}{N_i N_j} \sum_{x_i \in W_i} \sum_{x_j \in W_j} D(\underline{x_i}, \underline{x_j})))$$

$$= \frac{1}{2} \sum_{i=1}^{3} \sum_{j=1}^{3} (\frac{1}{7*7} \sum_{x_i \in W_i} \sum_{x_j \in W_j} D(\underline{x_i}, \underline{x_j})) \tag{10}$$

$$s.t.$$

$$D(\underline{x_i}, \underline{x_j}) = (\underline{x_i} - \underline{x_j})^T (\underline{x_i} - \underline{x_j})$$

Where $C = 3$ represents three clusters (observed, after adjusted and LMM), it's feasible to use it in simulation results with $N_i = N_j = 7$ experiments. As a result, we have a distance of 0.0478 between observed ones and simulation output, and 0.1103 between observed and LMM.

5   Concluding Remarks

A new modeling approach is proposed, which require either multiple Map-reduce procedures or convergence condition. The results of simulation and experimental validation show the effectiveness. Restricted to resource available, proposed algorithms are obliged to execute in Hadoop single/pseudo-distributed modes. The time performance is for the moment not largely improved. For this reason, future work may include adopting them in fully-distributed clusters towards larger scenes with massive data. The VV&A of optical remote sensing simulator is also an intended study point.

For further application, modeling results can be compared with airborne/spaceborne Albedo products, and the environment condition of camera and plane/satellite platform may be deduced. This is authors' current research direction. Besides, results of optical imaging simulation have the possibility to be merged with Synthetic Aperture Radar(SAR) measurement or SAR simulator output, which can be applied in decision-making processes like target detection, classification and tracking.

References

1. Nag, S., Gatebe, C.K., de Weck, O.: Observing system simulations for small satellite formations estimating bidirectional reflectance. Int. J. Appl. Earth Obs. Geoinf. **43**(4), 102–118 (2015)
2. Small, Christopher, Milesi, Cristina: Multi-scale standardized spectral mixture models. Remote Sensing of Environ. **136**(1), 442–454 (2013)
3. Qin, W.H., Gerstl, S.A.W.: 3-D scene modeling of semidesert vegetation cover and its radiation regime. Remote Sens. Environ. **74**(1), 145–165 (2000)
4. Borner, A., Wiest, L., et al.: SENSOR: a tool for the simulation of hyperspectral remote sensing systems. J. Photogram. Remote Sens. **55**, 299–312 (2001)
5. Arnold, P.S., Brown, S.D., et al.: Hyperspectral simulation of chemical weapon dispersal patterns using DIRSIG. SPIE Conf. **029**, 288–298 (2000)
6. Carson, T., Bachmann, C.M., et al.: Soil signature simulation of complex mixtures and particle size distributions. Opt. Eng. **54**(9), 094103(11 pp.) (2015)
7. Yao, W., et al.: Assessing the impact of sub-pixel vegetation structure on imaging spectroscopy via simulation. Algorithms and Technologies for Multispectral, Hyperspectral and Ultra-spectral Imagery XXI. SPIE Conference
8. Goodenough, A.A., Brown, S.D, Gerace, A.: Advances in simulating radiance signatures for dynamic air/water interfaces. Algorithms and Technologies for Multispectral, Hyperspectral and Ultra-spectral Imagery XXI. SPIE Conference
9. Ma, L., et al.: Monte Carlo simulation of spectral reflectance and BRDF of bubble layer in the upper ocean. Opt. Express **23**(19), 24274–24289 (2015)
10. Li, Y., et al.: Infrared imaging simulation and detection of ship wake. Proc. SPIE **9674**, 96741F(10 pp.) (2015)
11. Zare, A., Ho, K.C.: Endmember variability in hyperspectral analysis. IEEE Sig. Process. **1**, 95–104 (2014)
12. Dean, J., Ghemawat, S.: MapReduce: simplified data processing on large clusters. Comm. ACM **52**(1), 107–113 (2008)
13. Dai, Q.H., Yang, B.G., et al.: Reconstructable geometry shadow maps. In: Proceedings of the Symposium on Interactive 3D Graphics and Games, vol. 4 (2008)
14. Eismann, M.T., Stein, D.: Stochastic mixture modeling. In: Chang, C. (ed.) Hyperspectral Data Exploitation: Theory and Applications. Wiley, New York (2007)
15. Zare, A., Gader, P., Casella, G.: Sampling piecewise convex unmixing and endmember extraction. IEEE Trans. Geosci. Remote Sens. **51**, 1655–1665 (2013)

How to Build a SDN Based IaaS Platform for LSDIS Simulation

Dawei Li$^{(\boxtimes)}$ and Lixin Zhu

Science and Technology on Information Systems Engineering Laboratory,
Nanjing 210007, China
lidw1981@163.com

Abstract. It is a challenging job to carry out effective experiments in
LSDIS with limited resources in laboratory. In this paper, we based on
virtualization technology and software defined network (SDN) architecture, study the mechanism of constructing IaaS platform for LSDIS evaluation and testing environment, proposed virtual resources optimization
mapping algorithm to balance the loads of the hardware, built prototype system and designed some simulation testing use case to verify the
proposed system. The simulation results shows that the proposed approach employs similar performances as physical environment for LSDIS
simulation tasks.

Keywords: SDN · Virtualization · IaaS cloud computing · LSDIS

1 Introduction

Along with the continuous development of cloud computing, network technology
and other IT technology, Information system nowadays is turning to more and
more complex. Connected with large scale networks, subsystems, services, and
other nodes cooperated with each other, we named these information systems
as large scale distributed information systems (short for LSDIS). Though the
function of the system is enhanced, however, system simulation task over LSDIS
becoming a challenge compared with traditional ones [1].

Because of the features of LSDIS, such as wide area distribution, heterogeneity topology, dynamic interactive and incapable centralized control, it is
hard to simulate the status of the system. Even though, the cost of traditional
approaches is higher under the new situation, for example, the complex configuration of hardware and software as well as system parameters, let alone financial
and time costs [2].

IaaS is a pattern of cloud computing, which offers infrastructure as services
to users. Combined with SDN technologies, we can offer IT resources as a service, which offers methodology of building LSDIS simulation platform [3]. The
system provides resources configuration and deployment of the needed environment, which can be used in developing, testing, modeling, evaluation, training of
LSDIS. Compared with traditional simulation platform, it reduce costs of large

© Springer Science+Business Media Singapore 2016
L. Zhang et al. (Eds.): AsiaSim 2016/SCS AutumnSim 2016, Part III, CCIS 645, pp. 78–85, 2016.
DOI: 10.1007/978-981-10-2669-0_9

and complex LSDIS simulations. Because of the advantages mentioned above, study of cloud based simulation system is a hot topic. In simulation field, Li proposed a networked modeling and simulation platform to improves the ability of resources sharing and subtasks [4]. But less concern the runtime resources requirements of LSDIS.

In simulation environment building, literature [5] proposed a botnets simulate system. However, the platform is built only for botnets experiment and manual operation. To improve dynamic abilities, Zhang studied cloud simulation of dynamic running environment in literature [3]. However, the proposed solution does not suitable for simulation tasks of LSDIS but the simulation resources.

In summary, LSDIS simulation platform must organizes all the resources effectively with high-speed network and encapsulated them as a services pool of IssS. In this paper, we focus on the drawbacks of existing solutions of the LSDIS simulation field, proposed a SDN based IaaS platform. The contributions of this paper are: (1) analysed the requirements of constructing LSDIS simulation platform and summarized the common policy; (2) under the principle of IaaS cloud computing, proposed a LSDIS simulation platform with optimal resources mapping; (3) realized a prototype of the platform to verify the results.

2   System Construct

2.1   System Design

The proposed platform are composed of servers, storage, network simulation servers connected by SDN switches. There are three type of networks to handle control, storage and simulation traffics. The physical view of the platform is showed in Fig. 1.

The logic view of proposed platform can be shown as Fig. 2. There are five layers which offer hardware infrastructure, virtualization functions and pool supporting, running environment construction APIs, user interface for configuration and so on. Hardware layer offers physical computing and storage resources. Virtualization layer forms unified pool which offers resources service to upper layers by different APIs.

In environment construction layer, all resources are selected from the resources pool. Then, the system deploys all the resources to virtual machines.

Since network is the special and critical resources of LSDIS. We proposed SDN based Linux container to realize the nodes and links in order to simulated IP network of LSDIS. The network elements can be configured and deployed as real ones. The network of LSDIS are composed of backbone network and access network. See Fig. 3 in detail.

Backbone network is created by lightweight virtualization technology named LXC, more details can be found in [2]. Access network is offered by Quantum. RJ45 interfaces binding to the NICs connect the two network above.

Configuration layer's functions are simulation configuration and management, users can register resources, generate configuration file, dynamic control

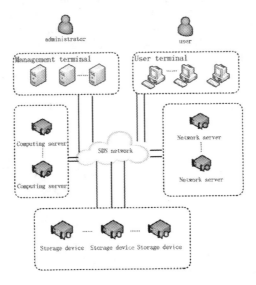

Fig. 1. Physical view of the system

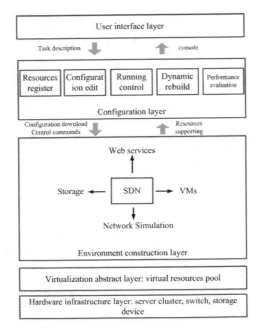

Fig. 2. Logical view of the proposed platform

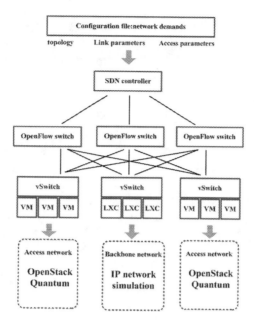

Fig. 3. The network simulation frame

and monitor. When design a simulation, user first search the resources from the pool, then generate a unified configure file and distribute it to environment construction layer, which execute the task. Users can monitor and control the simulation tasks with the help of different APIs. The target of the platform is to put proper resources to right place in order to offer a live environment for LSDIS as in real world.

2.2 Optimal Resources Mapping

LSDIS has a lot of different resources. However, the physical resources of the platform have limit. So that, virtual machines must be applied to proper servers during the simulation. So we proposed a resources scheduler algorithm of the platform.

Suppose we have enough storage in the simulation,which is common in today's laboratories, so that the key resources are computing resource and network resources, let $P = \{P_{Com}, P_{Net}\}$, where $P_{Com} = \{(P^i_{CPU}, P^i_{RAM} | i = 1, \cdots, l_C)\}$, $P_{Net} = \{(P^i_{node} | i = 1, \cdots, l_N)\}$. The resources requirements are $Req = \{R_{Com}, R_{Net}\}$.

We have,

$$R_{Com} = \{(V^i_{CPU}, V^i_{RAM}) | i = 1, \cdots, k_{Com}\}$$

$$R_{Net} = \{(V^i_{node}, D^i_{RAM}) | i = 1, \cdots, k_{Net}\}$$

V^i_{CPU} and V^i_{RAM} are the computing and read only memory demands of virtual resources i, V^i_{node} denote the identity of net node i, D^i denote the throughput of node i. The optimal target is to achieve the highest hardware efficiency of the simulation. As to computing resources, the strategy is mapping the virtual resources, i.e. virtual machines, to the most idle servers first.

Let U_{CPU}^i and U_{RAM}^i are the usage of computing and read only memory of server i, α and β are the usage coefficient, so we get:

$$U_i = \alpha U_{CPU}^i + \beta U_{RAM}^i \tag{1}$$

Sorting the elements of P_C according to U_i and creating U_C, mapping the R_C to U_C.

So we have the average result:

$$\bar{U} = \frac{1}{l_C} \sum_{i=1}^{l_C} U_i \tag{2}$$

When satisfy the Eq. (3), there is an optimal mapping.

$$Opt_C = \min\{\sqrt{\frac{1}{l_C} \sum_{i=1}^{l_C} (U_i - \bar{U})^2}\} \tag{3}$$

The optimal result strict to $R_C \leq U_C$, which is means: there are enough free resources to response the requirement.

Let us considering the network. Since the in-band traffic is higher than outband one in the same situation, the optimistic strategy is to decrease the outband traffics and increase the traffic inner servers. Suppose the network request R_{Net} assign to P_{Net}.

Suppose N^i is the virtual nodes set mapped to P_{Net}^i, $N_B^i \subseteq N^i$ denote the nodes set which have RJ45 interfaces bounded to physical servers. All the outband transmission occurs amount nodes in N_B^i, if U_{ij} is the throughput between node i and node j in simulated network, where $U_{ij} \leq D^i + D^j$. The throughput of nodes in P_N is:

$$T(P_N^{i,j}) = \sum_{i \in N_B^i, j \in N_B^j} U_{i,j} \tag{4}$$

Then, the network optimal mapping is:

$$Opt_N = \min \sum_{i,j \in P_N} T(P_N^{i,j}) \tag{5}$$

3   Simulation Analyses

In this section, we verify the function and performance of the LSDIS simulation platform using several experiments. The prototype system we build has the hardware as follows:IBM3650 M4 installed Intel Xeon E5 serial CPU and 128GB ECC RAM as the computing servers, Lenovo D-30 workstation as the network simulation serves, and some PCs as clients.

3.1   Network Performance Analyses

To find the network performance, we random select some two hops link and configured 100 Mbps bandwidth, use Iperf tools to generate UDP traffics over the links, statistic the packets loss rate of the links and comparinged with physical situation in the same hops, the results are shown in Fig. 4. Physical router we used in experiments is Cisco-1841, in Fig. 4.

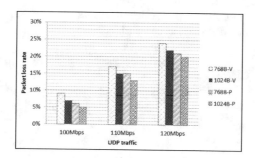

Fig. 4. The PLR(Packets Loss Rate) between UDP traffics

We can see in Fig. 4, when the UDP traffic is down to 90 Mbps, both of the two types of links have lowest packets loss rate. And over 90 Mbps, the packets loss rate increasing, especially the virtual links, because the physical devices have more transmit efficiency.

3.2   Computing Capability

As known to us all, virtual machines have lower performance than native machines, since the virtual layer takes extra resources. In Fig. 5, we determine the performances of the VM deployed Windows XP operation system, with 3 GB DDR RAM and equal native configuration. There are four indexes we used to calculate the performance, which are MFLOPS, PI, KPPS and MIPS, with tools of CPU-Bench v.3.2.0.0. As shown in Fig. 5, the virtual machine's performance is acceptable in LSDIS simulation and testing.

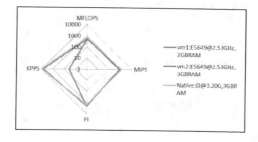

Fig. 5. Comparison the performances of 2 kind of resources

3.3   Application Testing

For studying the total performances of the platform, we deploy a real LSDIS
on prototype system. The tested LSDIS is composed of many different servers,
data collector connected by large scale simulation network. Figure 6 display the
information quality under different traffics. In the testing, the link bandwidth is
limited to 100 Mbps.

As shown in the Fig. 6, when business traffic increase, the performance
decrease. However, when business traffics increased, the simulated system's information quality has rapid decrease than physical environment.

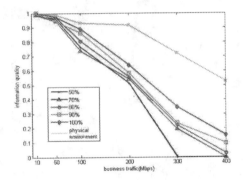

Fig. 6. Application performance of LSDIS

4   Conclusion

In this paper, we proposed a LSDIS simulation platform using IaaS and SDN.
The platform can generate a live running environment of LSDIS according to
the requirement. To verify the performance of the proposed platform, we build a
prototype system and deploy a typical LSDIS, and designed a serious of experiments. The results show that, the proposed platform has same functions as
physical system.

References

1. Gang Z., Kuang, X., Zheng, W.: An emulation environment for vulnerability analysis
   of large-scace distributed system. In: 2009 Eight International Conference on Grid
   and Cooperative Computing, pp. 97–105 (2009)
2. Li, D.: System building method for large-scale IP network simulation and test environment. Command Inform. Syst. Technol. **4**(6), 70–74 (2013)
3. Zhang, Y., Li, B., Chai, X., et al.: Research on virtualization-based cloud simulation
   running environment dynamic building technology. Syst. Eng. Electron. **34**(3), 619–
   624 (2012)

4. Li, B., Chai, X., Hou, B., et al.: Networked modeling & simulation platform based on concept of cloud computing cloud simulation platform. J. Syst. Simul. **21**(17), 5292–5299 (2009)
5. Toward Botnet Mesocosms, 28 December 2008. http://www.usenix.org/enent/
6. Luo, J., Jun, J., Song, A., et al.: Cloud computing: architecture and key technologies. J. Commun. **32**(7), 3–21 (2011)

Fractional Calculus with Applications and Simulations

A Novel Simplified Algorithm for Calculating the Mooring Line Based on Lumped-Mass Method

Zhong-xian Zhu, Yong Yin[✉], and He-long Shen

Navigation College, Dalian Maritime University, Dalian 116026, China
{zzx19861018,bushyin}@163.com, shenhelong@126.com

Abstract. As an important component in Anchor Handling Simulator(AHS), the mooring system's modeling and simulation have great impact on the AHS's physical realism, behavioural realism and operating environment. We built the mooring line's dynamics model based on Lumped-Mass Method (LMM) and used 4th order Runge-Kutta to solve it; However, the huge amounts of calculation in the model's solving seriously hindered its application in AHS. To speed up the model's solving process and realize the real-time simulation, we analysed the variables' variation rates in the governing equation, identified the invariants, fast variables and slow variables, then proposed a novel simplified algorithm by adopting different time steps for their calculation. Experimental results show that, our simplified algorithm can reduce more than 64.5 % of the calculating time on the premise of assuring the accuracy and numerical stability.

Keywords: Anchor handling simulator · Mooring system · Lumped mass method · Dynamics model · Simplified algorithm

1 Introduction

There are various methods in dynamically analysising of the mooring system, including Lumped-Mass Method, Finite Element Method (FEM), Finite Difference Method (FDM), and etc. Among which, LMM [1–4] is a simple and easy to understand method, with definitely physical meaning and was extensively applied in the mooring line's modeling and simulation.

Chai [5] established a three-dimensional lumped-mass formulation of a catenary riser, capable of handling line-seabed interaction, bending and torsional stiffness. Wang Fei [6–8] and Zhu Ke-qiang [9, 10] established the underwater cable's dynamics model based on LMM and investigated the current's drag force, bending and cable-seabed interaction, and also simulated the cable's deployment and retrieval. Hall [11] indicated that the quasi-static model would significantly under-predict the mooring loads and introduced a lumped-mass line model, and validated it against the scale-model test data of the floating offshore wind turbine.

In the lumped-mass model, the mooring line need to be fully discreted in space, and the time step size is usually very limited (within 10 ms) for assuring the accuracy and the numerical stability. This leads into huge amounts of calculation, and brings the severe challenge to real-time simulation.

© Springer Science+Business Media Singapore 2016
L. Zhang et al. (Eds.): AsiaSim 2016/SCS AutumnSim 2016, Part III, CCIS 645, pp. 89–97, 2016.
DOI: 10.1007/978-981-10-2669-0_10

The quest for real-time solving and simulation promoted the development of fast algorithms to accelerate the model's solving process. Generally, if an improved algorithm is 20 %~50 % faster than the original, it can be considered as a significant contribution and can be published in academic journals. Obviously, this improvement is not easy. It requires thorough understanding on the algorithm's connotation, very deep theoretical foundation and strong capability in innovation [12].

2   Lumped-Mass Mooring Line Model

Based on literatures [13, 14], we establish the mooring line's dynamics model using lumped-mass approach. As illustrated in Fig. 1, the line was discreted into $N + 1$ nodes (N segments) over the length numbered by $i = 0$ at the anchor point end and $i = N$ at the upper end. Let s represents the arc length coordinate of the unstretched line measured from the anchor point ($s = 0$) to the upper end (s = S).

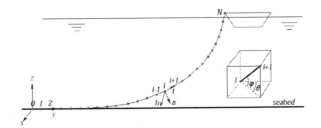

Fig. 1. Coordinate system of the mooring line.

The mass and all the forces of each segment were lumped in equal amounts at its two end points. By invoking the Newton's Second Law for the ith node, we can obtain the governing equation:

$$M_i \ddot{x}_i = \Delta T_i + B_i + G_i + F_{Di} + F_{bfi} + F_{wavei} + F_{bendi} \tag{1}$$

where, $\ddot{x}_i$ is the acceleration; ΔT_i is the tension, the Hooke's law can be adopted to describe its tension-strain relationship; B_i and G_i are the buoyancy and gravity; F_{Di} is the hydrodynamic force (fluid drag) arising from the relative motion of the line and its surrounding fluid, we use the method exploited by Ablow [15] and Huang [2] to calculate it; F_{bfi} is the line-seabed interaction force, and we use Chang Hong-bo's approach [16] to evaluate it; M_i represents the mass matrix, it includes the inertial mass m_i and the added mass M_{ai} in water; F_{wavei} is the second order wave force, we adopt the method exploited in literatures [8, 17]; F_{bendi} is the bending moment force, we use the approach proposed by Wang Fei [6, 7] to describe it.

Although the bending induced force and the second order wave force are very small on a steel line, it cannot be ignored in low-tension and/or lightweight towing cables, fishing nets, fiber lines during deployment and retrieval, etc. To ensure the model's completeness, generality and strong applicability, we insist on taking into account of them.

Combining Eq. (1) and the velocity's definition of $v = dx/dt$, the ordinary differential equations to describe the attitude of a node can be written:

$$\begin{cases} d\dot{x}_i \Big/ dt = M_{ai}^{-1} \cdot F_i \\ dx_i \Big/ dt = \dot{x}_i \end{cases} \qquad (i = 0, 1, 2, \cdots, N) \qquad (2)$$

where F_i represents the right-side of the Eq. (1).

After specifying the boundary conditions at both ends and the initial conditions, Eq. (2) can be solved using classical 4th order Runge-Kutta integration method.

3   Simplified Method

The 4th order Runge-Kutta integrator is five-order accuracy, and was extensively applied in the field of scientific and engineering computation. However, it is conditionally stable. In order to guarantee the stability and accuracy, the time step size is limited in a very small range (usually within 10 ms).

Take a mooring line with a length of 2 000.0 m for example, set the time step size $\Delta t = 2$ ms and the space step size $\Delta s = 10.0$ m. When calculating on a dual-core CPU, there will be 500 iterations in 1 s, and all the 201 nodes will be traversed in each iteration. For each node in each iteration, the 4th order Runge-Kutta will be used, the calculation of the governing equation and the updating of the position will be executed 4 times. This will cause considerable time-consuming.

In spite of large amounts of optimization having done, the real-time calculation can not be assured when the number of discreted nodes is very large and/or the time step size is very small. This seriously hindered the lumped-mass model's application in AHS.

Furthermore, there is more than one line in the mooring system, and the mooring system is not the only component need to be real-timely calculated in the whole large-scale anchor handling simulation scene. To meet the simulation scene's requirement on real-time, the model's solving procedure should be accelerated as much as possible.

Although we set the time step size $\Delta t = 2$ ms, the nodes' positions, attitudes and velocities vary very small even in 100 ms. In Eq. (1), the mass, buoyancy and gravity are position and velocity independent, and can be treated as invariant; The line-seabed interaction force, fluid drag force, second order wave force and bending moment force change very little in a short time (e.g., 100 ms), and can be treated as slow variables; The tension changes considerably even if very slight variation on the spatial attitude due to the very high magnitude (usually 10^{10}) of Young's modulus, and it can be treated as fast variable. The fast variable is the main source of ill-conditioning and diverging in model's solving, and leads to conflict between numerical stability and real-time calculation.

To simplify and speed up the model's solving procedure, we proposed a new approach for the calculation of invariant, slow and fast variables. As illustrated in

Fig. 2, we don't update the invariant unless it was really changed, and apply a very small time step size (e.g., 2 ms) for the fast variables and a large time step size (e.g., 10 ms) for the slow variables.

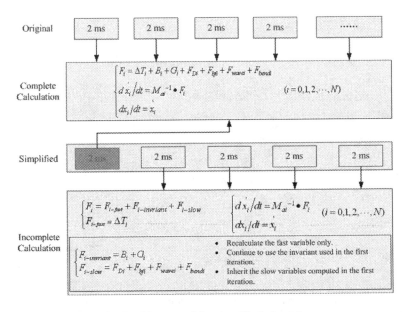

Fig. 2. Diagram of the simplified algorithm

This means that we calculate the entire mooring line 5 times in every 10 ms. Only in the first time, we calculate all the forces through a complete calculation, get the nodes' accelerations, update the positions and velocities. In the rest 4 times, we only re-calculate the fast variable, continue to use the invariant in the first time, inherit the slow variables computed in the first time, and get the nodes' new accelerations and update the positions and velocities.

4   Experimental Results

Take a Jip spar platform operated in 1 018.0 m water depth as a calculating example. The platform's mooring system is consisted of 4 groups (3 lines in each group) of lines distributed regularly in 90° angel interval. Select one of the lines as an example, and its properties (referred to literatures [18, 19]) are shown as in Table 1.

The experimental platform is configured as follows: 2.8 GHz Inter Core2 Duo CPU E7400 with 3.0 GB of RAM, equipped with a NVIDIA GeForce GTS 450 GPU card with 1024 MB of dedicated video memory. Discrete the mooring line into 200 segments, set the fast time step size as 2 ms and slow step size as 10 ms and record the execution time of 500 iterations (1 second in total). The line's steady-state configuration is shown as in Fig. 3. For the purposes of comparison, we exerted a horizontal sinusoidal excitation $x(t) = A \sin\omega t$ at the line's upper end.

Table 1. Properties of the mooring line.

Item	Value
Vertical height from fairleader to sea level h'	106.62 m
Pretension on the line F	13 700.0 kN
Line's diameter D	415.3 mm
Mass per unit length in air m	1100.0 kg/m
Initial line length L	2 000.0 m
Effective elastic stiffness EA	$0.15 * 10^{10}$
Fluid density ρ	1024.0 kg/m³
Drag coefficient in tangent direction C_n	1.50
Drag coefficient in normal direction C_t	0.10

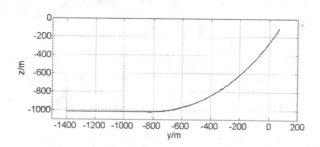

Fig. 3. Configuration of the mooring line.

Figures 4 and 5 are the upper-end's tension. Through comparing with the non-simplified algorithm, the simplified method did not cause obvious loss in accuracy. However, the new method reduced the solving process's time consuming largely. As show in Fig. 6, the calculation time was reduced by 64.5 % than the non-simplified method.

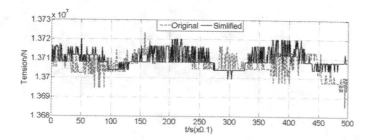

Fig. 4. Tension using simplified method ($A = 0.0$ m, $\omega = 0.0$ rad/s)

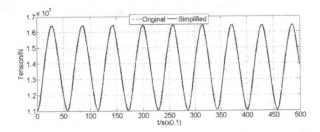

Fig. 5. Tension using simplified method ($A = 5.0$ m, $\omega = 1.1$ rad/s)

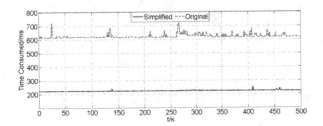

Fig. 6. Time consuming using simplified method

Keep the fast time step size as 2 ms, set the slow time step size as 10 ms, 20 ms and 50 ms, respectively. The larger the slow time step size, the greater degree of simplification. Figures 7 and 8 show that, the greater degree of simplification lead to the larger of the result's oscillating amplitude and more loss in accuracy. But the loss of accuracy is very small and negligible even if the slow time step size reached 50 ms. Figure 9 indicates that, the greater degree of simplification leads into the less time consuming. The calculating time can be reduced as much as 77.0 % than the non-simplified one when the slow time step size is 50 ms.

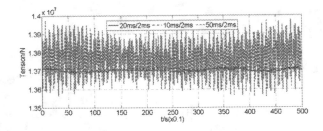

Fig. 7. Tension under varying degrees of simplification ($A = 0.0$ m, $\omega = 0.0$ rad/s)

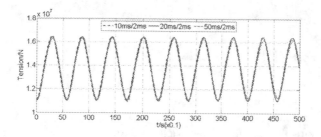

Fig. 8. Tension under varying degrees of simplification ($A = 5.0$ m, $\omega = 1.1$ rad/s)

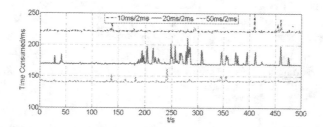

Fig. 9. Time consuming under varying degrees of simplification

The reward of in-significant loss in accuracy is the significant improvement in computing speed. For simulators having critical requirement on real-time, this simplification is necessary and worthwhile.

In the practical application, we can comprehensively coordinate the accuracy, stability and time consuming, and simplify the calculation as much as possible.

Based on the lumped-mass line model and the simplified algorithm, through applying a series of visualization technologies we generated a real-time physical-based anchor handling scene simulation software, and the general visualization effect is shown as in Fig. 10.

Fig. 10. General visualization effect of the AHS

5 Conclusion

The mooring line's lumped-mass model has a high level of accuracy, and can be applied in the mooring system's simulation in AHS. However, the model's solving process is very time-consuming, producing huge amounts of calculation. To meet the AHS's requirement on real-time and accuracy, we introduced the simplified algorithm to speed up the model's solving process.

The highly effective simplified approach can reduce the calculating time largely on the condition of numerical stability, and the processing idea is analogous with the commercial offshore dynamics software OrcaFlex [20].

Our simplified technology has some referring significance for the other areas in ocean engineering involve huge amounts of calculation and/or require real-time calculation, such as underwater towed cables, fishing nets and gears, subsea pipelines, etc.

Acknowledgment. The authors would like to acknowledge the support from the National High Technology Research and Development Program of China ("863" Program) [No. 2015AA016404] and the Fundamental Research Funds for the Central Universities [No. 313204330].

References

1. Walton, T.S., Polachek, H.: Calculation of transient motion of submerged cables. Math. Comput. **14**(69), 27–46 (1960)
2. Huang, S.: Dynamic analysis of three-dimensional marine cables. Ocean Eng. **21**(6), 587–605 (1994)
3. Thomas, D.O.: A numerical investigation of time integration schemes applied to dynamic solution of mooring lines. University of Newcastle upon Tyne (1993)
4. Buckham, B., et al.: Dynamics and control of a towed underwater vehicle system, part I: model development. Ocean Eng. **30**(4), 453–470 (2003)
5. Chai, Y., Varyani, K., Barltrop, N.: Three-dimensional Lump-Mass formulation of a catenary riser with bending, torsion and irregular seabed interaction effect. Ocean Eng. **29**(12), 1503–1525 (2002)
6. Fei, W.: Simulaiton and Control Research of Marine Towed Seismic System. Shanghai Jiao Tong University, Shanghai (2006)
7. Fei, W.: Modeling and simulation of faired cable with anisotropic bending moment and torque. J. Harbin Eng. Univ. **34**(5), 549–554 (2013)
8. Fei, W., Guo-liang, H., Tian-wei, L.: Dynamic study of towed cable in regular waves. Ocean Eng. **24**(1), 92–97 (2006)
9. Bing-ka, Y., et al.: Research of dynamic analysis for submarine pipeline. Ship Sci. Technol. **3**, 102–105 (2013)
10. Yan-jie, Z., et al.: Dynamic modeling and simulation technique of marine cable considering tension and compression bending torsion deformation. Ocean Eng. **32**(1), 112–116 (2014)
11. Hall, M., Goupee, A.: Validation of a lumped-mass mooring line model with DeepCwind semisubmersible model test data. Ocean Eng. **104**, 590–603 (2015)
12. De-yuan, Q.: GPGPU Programming Techniques. China Machine Press, Beijing (2011)
13. Zhongxian, Z., Yong, Y., Helong, S.: Modeling and simulation of the mooring system in anchor handling simulator. J. Simul. Syst. **27**(10), 2285–2290 (2015)

14. Zhongxian, Z., Yong, Y., Helong, S.: Dynamic simulation of mooring system based on lumped mass method. Navig. China **38**(4), 37–41 (2015)

15. Ablow, C., Schechter, S.: Numerical simulation of undersea cable dynamics. Ocean Eng. **10**(6), 443–457 (1983)

16. Hong-bo, C., et al.: Influence of seabed terrain and friction on mooring line. In: The International Workshop on Ship Hydrodynamics 2013, Xi'an (2013). 西安

17. Gang, Z., Yue-zhong, D.: Dynamic analysis of three-dimensional marine cables in regular waves. Ocean Eng. **25**(4), 15–20 (2007)

18. You-gang, T., et al.: Analysis of snap tension of deep water mooring with lumped mass method. J. Tianjin Univ. **42**(8), 695–701 (2009)

19. You-gang, T., Cong, Y., Su-xia, Z.: Analysis of cable shape and cable tension for platforms in deep sea. Ocean Eng. **25**(2), 9–14 (2007)

20. Orcaflex Manual. http://www.orcina.com/SoftwareProducts/OrcaFlex/Documentation.OrcaFlex.pdf (2012)

A New Multi-wing Chaotic System
and Its Fractional-Order Form

Zengqiang Chen[1,2(✉)], Leilei Zhou[1], Jian Ma[1], Zhonglin Wang[1],
and Qing Zhang[2]

[1] Key Laboratory of Intelligent Robotics of Tianjin, College of Computer
and Control Engineering, Nankai University, Tianjin 300353, China
chenzq@nankai.edu.cn
[2] College of Science, Civil Aviation University of China, Tianjin 300300, China

Abstract. This paper presents a new multi-wing chaotic system by adding a piecewise linear function into the simplest memristive chaotic circuit equations. In order to clarify the evolution of the dynamics behavior of this system, phase portraits, Lyapunov exponent spectrum and bifurcation diagram are provided. Moreover, the fractional-order form of the new multi-wing system is constructed by the fractional calculus technique. And the fractional-order multi-wing system is implemented by electronic circuit. The results of circuit experiment are well consistent with the numerical simulations.

Keywords: Fractional-order system · Chaotic system · Memristor · Multi-wing attractors

1 Introduction

Memristor is recognized as the fourth fundamental electronic element, which is postulated by Leon O. Chua [1] in 1971. It took scientists almost 40 years to invent such practical device until a team at Hewlett-Packard Labs announced the successful development of a memristor [2]. Memristor has won its place along with other three existing elements such as the resistor, capacitor and inductor [3, 4], and shared many properties of resistors such as the unit of measurement ohms. The memristor's electrical resistance is not constant but depends on the history of current that had previously flowed through the device. Moreover, memristor shows many special properties, which can be described by a nonlinear constitutive relation [5].

Since the physical model of memristor successfully implemented by HP Company, memristor has captured the attention of the researchers due to its unprecedented behavior. Researchers have demonstrated that the memristor has the potential to be used as a memory switch component and to replace the conventional transistor [6]. The nonvolatile memory applications of memristor can lead to a more dense architecture, and the implementations of the nanoscale component in crossbar arrays allow it to perform either as a latch or logic module [7].

In the last decades, attention has shifted towards exploiting complicated dynamical properties of chaos for technological applications [8–10]. Much effort has been focused on effectively generating chaotic attractors with high complexity, such as a multi-scroll

© Springer Science+Business Media Singapore 2016
L. Zhang et al. (Eds.): AsiaSim 2016/SCS AutumnSim 2016, Part III, CCIS 645, pp. 98–107, 2016.
DOI: 10.1007/978-981-10-2669-0_11

or multi-wing attractor. Besides, fractional derivatives theory has been developing for many years, but it is seldom used in physics. Although multiple nonequivalent definitions of fractional derivatives have been proposed [11], fractional derivatives have no evident geometrical interpretation because of their nonlocal character [12]. Fractional calculus is a classical mathematical concept with a history as long as calculus itself. Its applications to physics and engineering are just a recent subject of interest [13, 14]. And the fractional-order chaotic systems with multi-wing attractor are seldom discussing. Therefore, it is obviously significant to create fractional-order chaotic systems with multi-wing attractors in both theory and engineering applications.

The purpose of this paper is to propose a simpler fractional-order memristive multi-wing chaotic system with simple structure. Firstly, a novel multi-scroll chaotic attractors is generated by adding a piecewise linear function to the simplest memristive circuit. Secondly, phase portraits of the system are provided. The Lyapunov exponent spectrum and bifurcation diagram show that the system has a rich bifurcation properties. Thirdly, the new system is generalized to fractional-order system by using the fractional calculus technique. We make our effort to implement the integer-order and fractional-order memristive multi-wing attractors in an integrated circuit with the appropriate component. The results of the circuits experiment well verify the existence of the proposed multi-wing chaotic attractors.

The paper is organized as follows. In Sect. 2, we briefly introduce this simplest memristive circuit. In Sect. 3, a new multi-wing chaotic system is generated by using a simplest memristor chaotic circuit and a piecewise linear function, then the new system is generalized to fractional-order system by using the fractional calculus technique. In Sect. 4, dynamical behaviors are investigated by analysis of Lyapunov exponents spectrum and bifurcation diagram. In Sect. 5, the new integer-order and fractional-order multi-wing system are implemented by electronic circuit. Finally, in Sect. 6, the experiment results and conclusions are given.

2   The Memristor Structure

The memristor used in this system is a charge-controlled memristor [2, 4]. It is characterized by its incremental memductance function $M(q)$, which describes the charge-dependent rate of the following equations:

$$\begin{cases} V_M = \beta(r^2 - 1)i_M \\ \dot{r} = i_M - \alpha r - i_M r \end{cases} \tag{1}$$

Here, V_M is the voltage across the ends of memristor and i_M indicates the corresponding current, r is an intermediate variable of this memristive model. The simplest chaotic circuit, which is only composed of three elements in series–the inductor, capacitor and a memristor, is shown in Fig. 1.

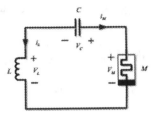

Fig. 1. The memristor-based circuit

From the constitutive relation of a linear capacitor, we can get the following equation:

$$C\frac{dV_C}{dt} = i_L \tag{2}$$

And since

$$V_M = \beta(r^2 - 1)i_M; V_L = L\frac{di_L}{dt}; i_M = -i_L \tag{3}$$

Applying Kirchhoff's Voltage law around the loop circuit in Fig. 1, we can obtain the equation that $V_L + V_C = V_M$, and substituting Eq. (3) into it, then the following equation can be obtained:

$$\frac{di_L}{dt} = -\frac{1}{L}\left[\beta(r^2 - 1)i_L + V_C\right] \tag{4}$$

Substituting i_M into $\frac{dr}{dt} = i_M - \alpha r - i_M r$, and simplifying Eqs. (2) and (4), then we can get:

$$\begin{cases} \frac{dV_C}{dt} = \frac{1}{C}i_L \\ \frac{di_L}{dt} = -\frac{1}{L}[\beta(r^2 - 1)i_L + V_C] \\ \frac{dr}{dt} = (r - 1)i_L - \alpha r \end{cases} \tag{5}$$

Let $V_C = x, i_L = y, r = z, 1/C = a$ and $1/L = b$. Thus, Eq. (5) can be transformed into the following system

$$\begin{cases} \dot{x} = ay \\ \dot{y} = -b[\beta(z^2 - 1)y + x] \\ \dot{z} = (z - 1)y - \alpha z \end{cases} \tag{6}$$

When the parameters are $\alpha = 0.6, \beta = 3/2, a = 1, b = 1/3$ and the initial conditions are $x(0) = 0.1, y(0) = 0, z(0) = 0.1$, the system (6) can display a single-scroll chaotic attractor.

3   The Design of Multi-wing Chaotic System and Its Fractional-Order Form

How to generate multi-wing chaotic attractors from a smooth system remains a technical challenging problem. The first method is based on polynomial transform [15, 16] or Julia process [17] in what annular multi-wing butterfly chaotic attractor are constructed. The second method is generating the grid multi-wing attractors [18, 19] by constructing Heteroclinic loop. The third method is adding a state equation into Lorenz system and designing an appropriate piecewise linear function [20]. Besides, a fully autonomous system is capable of generating a four-wing butterfly attractor by incorporating two state controlled binary switches [21].

Here, the piecewise linear function $f(x) = x - \left[2 \sum\limits_{n=-N}^{M} u(x+2n+1)\right] + 2(M+1)$

is used in the memritive system (6) in order to generate the multi-wing chaotic attractors, where $N, M \in \{0, 1, 2, \cdots\}$ and $u(x+2n+1)$ is an unit-step function. The piecewise linear function $f(x)$ is used for substituting for the state variable x in the right hands of system (6), then a new system can be written as:

$$\begin{cases} \dot{x} = ay \\ \dot{y} = -b[\beta(d^2z^2 - 1)y + f(x)] \\ \dot{z} = (dz - 1)y - \alpha z \end{cases} \tag{7}$$

Set the parameters $\alpha = 0.6, \beta = 3/2, a = 1, b = 1/3$, the system can generate $M+N+2$-wing chaotic attractors. When $M = N = 0$, the double-wing chaotic attractors can be obtained as shown in Fig. 2(a)–(b). When $M = 1, N = 0$, the three-wing chaotic attractors can be obtained as shown in Fig. 2(c)–(d). When $M = 1, N = 1$, the four-wing chaotic attractors can be obtained as shown in Fig. 2(e)–(f). When $M = 2, N = 1$, the five-wing chaotic attractors can be obtained as shown in Fig. 2(g)–(h).

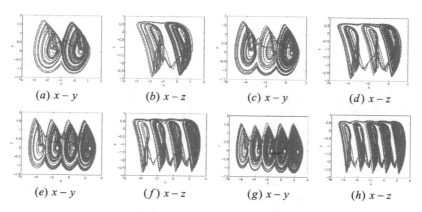

(a) $x - y$ (b) $x - z$ (c) $x - y$ (d) $x - z$

(e) $x - y$ (f) $x - z$ (g) $x - y$ (h) $x - z$

Fig. 2. The phase portrait of multi-wing chaotic attractors in $x - y$ and $x - z$ plane

The definition of fractional derivatives adopted in this paper is the well-known Caputo definition [22], which is given by

$$\frac{d^q f(t)}{dt^q} = \frac{1}{\Gamma(n-\alpha)} \int_0^t \frac{f^{(n)}(\tau)}{(t-\tau)^{\alpha-n+1}} d\tau \tag{8}$$

Where $\Gamma(\cdot)$ is the gamma function and $n-1 \leq q < n$. Considering all the initial conditions to be zero, the Laplace transform of the Caputo definition is

$$L\left\{\frac{d^q f(t)}{dt^q}\right\} = s^q L\{f(t)\} \tag{9}$$

Thus, the fractional integral operator of order q can be represented by the transfer function $F(s) = 1/s^q$ in the frequency domain.

Now, consider a fractional generalization of the system (7), the conventional derivative is replaced by a fractional derivative as follows:

$$\begin{cases} \frac{d^q x}{dt^\alpha} = ay \\ \frac{d^q y}{dt^\beta} = -b[\beta(d^2 z^2 - 1)y + f(x)] \\ \frac{d^q z}{dt^\gamma} = (dz - 1)y - \alpha z \end{cases} \tag{10}$$

Where q is the fractional order, which satisfies $0 < q < 1$. The proposed system (10) is usually defined as a commensurate fractional-order system, i.e., the order q of the three equations is same.

4 Lyapunov Exponent Spectrum and Bifurcation Diagram

Fix $M = N = 1$, $\alpha = 0.6$, $\beta = 3/2$, $b = 1/3$, $d = 1$ and vary parameter a, the Lyapunov exponent spectrums of system (6) and system (7) are shown in Fig. 3. The bifurcation diagrams of the system (6) and the system (7) with variation of a are given in Fig. 4. Obviously, the chaotic regions of the two systems versus parameter a are

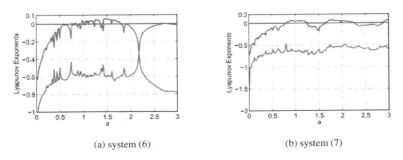

(a) system (6)   (b) system (7)

Fig. 3. Lyapunov exponent spectrum versus $a(a \in [0, 3])$

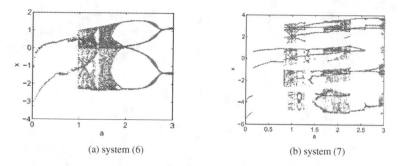

(a) system (6)   (b) system (7)

Fig. 4. Bifurcation diagram versus $a(a \in [0,3])$ with $\alpha = 0.6, \beta = 3/2, b = 1/3, d = 1$.

different. When $a \in [0.96, 1.36] \cup [1.44, 1.82]$, the system (6) is chaotic. When $a \in [0.82, 1.26] \cup [1.7, 2.24] \cup [2.9, 3]$, the system (7) is chaotic.

5 Circuit Implementation

An electronic circuit is designed to realize the multi-wing chaotic system (7), as shown in Fig. 5, where the Fig. 5(a) is the main circuit diagram of system (7) and the Fig. 5(b) is the circuit diagram of the piecewise linear function $f(x)$. The voltages of C_1, C_2 and C_3 are used as the state variables x, y and z, respectively.

The circuit equation of system (7) can be described as:

$$\begin{cases} \frac{dx}{d\tau} = \frac{1}{R_5 C_1} \frac{R_4}{R_1} y \\ \frac{dy}{d\tau} = \frac{1}{R_{12} C_2} \left(\frac{R_{11}}{R_{49}} V_1 - \frac{R_{11}}{R_8} f(x) + \frac{R_{11}}{R_9} y - \frac{R_{11}}{10 R_{10}} y z^2 \right) \\ \frac{dz}{d\tau} = \frac{1}{R_{19} C_3} \left(-\frac{R_{18}}{R_{15}} z - \frac{R_{18}}{R_{16}} y + \frac{R_{18}}{10 R_{17}} yz \right) \end{cases} \tag{11}$$

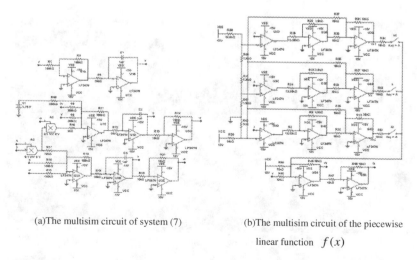

(a)The multisim circuit of system (7)   (b)The multisim circuit of the piecewise
                                                    linear function $f(x)$

Fig. 5. The designed multisim circuit to generate multi-wing chaotic attractors.

Where $f(x)$ is the circuit equation of piecewise linear function, it is implemented in Fig. 5(b) and will be further discussed in the following paragraphs. The value of the integrating resistor R_5, R_{12}, R_{19} is $10\,\text{k}\Omega$, and the value of the feedback resistance R_4, R_{11}, R_{18} is $100\,\text{k}\Omega$.

The parameters α, β, a, b, d of system (7) are changed by adjusting the resistors $R_1, R_8, R_9, R_{10}, R_{15}, R_{17}$. Let $\alpha = 0.6, \beta = 3/2, a = 1, b = 1/3, d = 1$, hence $R_1 = 100\,\text{k}\Omega, R_8 = 300\,\text{k}\Omega, R_9 = 200\,\text{k}\Omega, R_{10} = 2\,\text{k}\Omega, R_{15} = 166\,\text{k}\Omega, R_{17} = 10\,\text{k}\Omega$. All other resistors and capacitors are fixed as labeled in the Fig. 5.

In order to observe the output waveform of the circuit experiment, τ needs to be converted into $\tau_0 t$.

Let $\tau_0 = 10^{-3}$, the equations can be transformed as follows:

$$
\begin{cases}
\frac{dx}{d\tau} = \frac{10^{-3}}{R_5 C_1} \frac{R_4}{R_1} y \\
\frac{dy}{d\tau} = \frac{10^{-3}}{R_{12} C_2} \left(\frac{R_{11}}{R_{49}} V_1 - \frac{R_{11}}{R_8} f(x) + \frac{R_{11}}{R_9} y - \frac{R_{11}}{10R_{10}} yz^2 \right) \\
\frac{dz}{d\tau} = \frac{10^{-3}}{R_{19} C_3} \left(-\frac{R_{18}}{R_{15}} z - \frac{R_{18}}{R_{16}} y + \frac{R_{18}}{10R_{17}} yz \right)
\end{cases}
\tag{12}
$$

In the Fig. 5(b), let $R_2 = R_{24} = R_{28} = 13.5\,\text{k}\Omega$, $R_{38} = 12\,\text{k}\Omega$, $R_{39} = 14\,\text{k}\Omega$, $R_3 = R_{25} = R_{29} = R_{40} = R_{41} = R_{42} = R_{43} = 1\,\text{k}\Omega$ and the other resistors are $10\,\text{k}\Omega$.

Therefore, the case of k closed and k_1, k_2 off in Fig. 5(b) corresponds to $M = N = 0$ in $f(x)$. Let $R_{44} = 75\,\text{k}\Omega$, the $f(x)$ in Eq. (12) is:

$$
f(x) = x + V_k + \frac{R_{46} V_{CC}}{R_{44}} = x - 2u(x+1) + 2
\tag{13}
$$

Then a double-wings chaotic attractor can be obtained, as shown in Fig. 6(a) and (b).

Similarly, $M = 1, N = 0$ corresponds to the case of k, k_1 closed and the k_2 off. Let $R_{44} = 37.5\,\text{k}\Omega$, $f(x)$ can be written as:

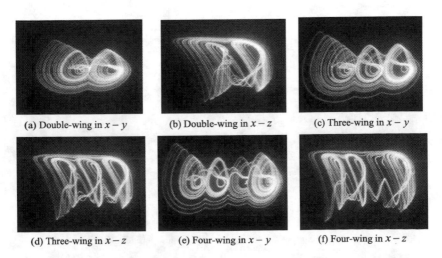

(a) Double-wing in $x - y$ (b) Double-wing in $x - z$ (c) Three-wing in $x - y$

(d) Three-wing in $x - z$ (e) Four-wing in $x - y$ (f) Four-wing in $x - z$

Fig. 6. The chaotic attractors of multi-wing.

$$f(x) = x + V_k + V_{k1} + \frac{R_{46}V_{CC}}{R_{44}} = x - 2u(x+1) - 2u(x+3) + 4 \tag{14}$$

Then, a three-wings chaotic attractor can be obtained, as shown in Fig. 6(c) and (d).

When $M = N = 1$, k, k_1, k_2 are all closed. Let $R_{44} = 37.5\,\text{k}\Omega$, $f(x)$ can be written as:

$$f(x) = x + V_k + V_{k1} + V_{k2} + \frac{R_{46}V_{CC}}{R_{44}} = x - 2u(x-1) - 2u(x+1) - 2u(x+3) + 4 \tag{15}$$

Then a four-wings chaotic attractor can be obtained, as shown in Fig. 6(e) and (f). The results of circuit experiment are well consistent to the results of numerical simulations.

In the literature of the fractional chaos field, time-domain approximation method and the frequency-domain approximation method are two important approximation methods for solving fractional ordinary differential equation. Compared with the time-domain method, the frequency-domain method is more convenient for circuit implementation. So we use the frequency-domain method in this section.

Reference [23] has given the approximations of $1/s^q$ with q equal to the value from 0.1 to 0.9 in step size 0.1 from $\omega = 10^{-2}$ to 10^2 rad/s. Figure 7(a) is the unit circuit of $1/s^q$. When we fix $n = 3, q = 0.1$, the unit circuit of $1/s^{0.1}$ can be realized in Fig. 7(b). The transfer function between in A and B is

$$H(s) = \frac{1/C_1}{s + 1/R_1C_1} + \frac{1/C_2}{s + 1/R_2C_2} + \frac{1/C_3}{s + 1/R_3C_3}$$

$$= \frac{1}{C_0} \frac{(\frac{C_0}{C_1} + \frac{C_0}{C_2} + \frac{C_0}{C_3})\left[s^2 + (\frac{C_2+C_3}{R_1} + \frac{C_1+C_3}{R_2} + \frac{C_2+C_1}{R_3} + \frac{R_1+R_2+R_3}{R_1R_2R_3})/(C_1C_2 + C_1C_3 + C_2C_3)\right]}{(s + 1/R_1C_1)(s + 1/R_2C_2)(s + 1/R_3C_3)}.$$

Where C_0 is a unit parameter, set $C_0 = 1\mu F$, so $H(s) = F(s)/C_0$.

From the Table 1 of [23], we know that the approximation of $1/s^{0.1}$ with error of about 2 dB:

$$\frac{1}{s^{0.1}} \approx \frac{1584.8932(s + 0.1668)(s + 27.83)}{(s + 0.1)(s + 16.68)(s + 2783)} \tag{16}$$

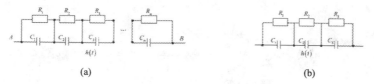

(a)   (b)

Fig. 7. (a) The unit circuit of $1/s^q$. (b) The unit circuit of $1/s^{0.1}$.

By comparing $H(s)$ with Eq. (16), we can obtain the unit circuit of $1/s^{0.1}$ as shown in Fig. 7(b), where $C_1 = 15.72\mu F, C_2 = 0.157\mu F, C_3 = 633.5pF, R_1 = 0.636M\Omega, R_2 = 0.382M\Omega, R_3 = 0.567M\Omega$.

Substituting the integral capacitor C_1, C_2, C_3 with the unit circuit of $1/s^{0.1}$ in the circuit diagram of multi-wing chaotic system shown in Fig. 5, the circuit diagram of the 0.1-order multi-wing system can be obtained. The corresponding results of circuit experiment are shown in Fig. 8.

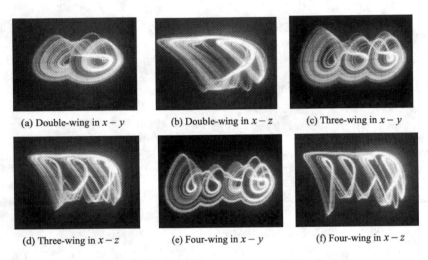

(a) Double-wing in $x - y$ (b) Double-wing in $x - z$ (c) Three-wing in $x - y$

(d) Three-wing in $x - z$ (e) Four-wing in $x - y$ (f) Four-wing in $x - z$

Fig. 8. The multi-wing chaotic attractors of 0.1-order system.

6   Conclusions

This paper presents a new multi-wing chaotic system by using a simplest memristive chaotic circuit and a piecewise linear function, and its dynamics behavior is studied. Moreover, the new system is generalized to fractional-order form by utilizing the fractional calculus technique. The constructed multi-wing attractors has implemented by numerical simulations and circuits experiment. The results verify the existence of the proposed multi-wing chaotic attractors. The implementation of the new fractional-order system is based on frequency-domain approximation method. In the future, we will commit to finding the real fractional circuit to realize the fractional system.

Acknowledgements. This work was supported in part by the Natural Science Foundation of China Under Grants of 61573199 and 61573200, the Tianjin Natural Science Foundation Grant No. 14JCYBJC18700.

References

1. Chua, L.O.: Memristor-the missing circuit element. IEEE Trans. Circuits Syst. **18**, 507–519 (1971)
2. Strukov, D.B., Snider, G.S., Stewart, G.R., Williams, R.S.: The missing memristor found. Nature **453**, 80–83 (2008)
3. Itoh, M., Chua, L.O.: Memristor oscillators. Int. J. Bifurc. Chaos **18**, 3183–3206 (2008)
4. Muthuswamy, B., Chua, L.O.: Simplest chaotic circuit. Int. J. Bifurc. Chaos **20**, 1567–1580 (2010)
5. Chua, L.O., Kang, S.M.: Memristive devices and systems. Proc. IEEE **64**, 209–223 (1976)
6. Snider. G. S.: Architecture and methods for computing with reconfigurable resistor crossbars. U.S. Patent No. 7,203,789 (2007)
7. Rajendran, J., Manem, H., Karri, R., Rose, G. S.: Memristor based programmable threshold logic array. In: International Symposium on Nanoscale Architectures (NANOARCH), pp. 5–10. IEEE/ACM, Anaheim (2010)
8. Yun, H.: A family of multi-wing chaotic attractors and its circuit implementation. Acta Phys. Sin. **63**, 080505 (2014)
9. Celikovsky, S., Chen, G.: On a generalized Lorenz canonical form of chaotic systems. Int. J. Bifurc. Chaos **12**, 1789–1812 (2002)
10. Chen, G., Yu, X.: Chaos Control: Theory and Applications, pp. 201–214. Springer, Berlin (2003)
11. Hilfer, R.: Applications of Fractional Calculus in Physics. World Scientific, Singapore (2000)
12. Podlubny, I.: Geometric and physical interpretation of fractional integration and fractional differentiation. Fractional Calculus Appl. Anal. **4**, 367–386 (2001)
13. Cafagna, D., Grassi, G.: On the simplest fractional-order memristor-based chaotic system. Nonlinear Dyn. **70**, 1185–1197 (2012)
14. Grigorenko, I., Grigorenko, E.: Chaotic dynamics of the fractional Lorenz system. Phys. Rev. Lett. **91**, 034101/1–034101/4 (2003)
15. Miranda, R., Stone, E.: The proto-Lorenz system. Phys. Lett. A **178**, 105–113 (1993)
16. Yu, S., Tang, W.K., Lu, J., Chen, G.: Generating 2n-wing attractors from Lorenz-like systems. Int. J. Circ. Theor. App. **38**, 243–258 (2010)
17. Bouallegue, K., Chaari, A., Toumi, A.: Multi-scroll and multi-wing chaotic attractor generated with Julia process fractal. Chaos Soliton Fract. **44**, 79–85 (2011)
18. Yu, S., Lu, J., Chen, G., Yu, X.: Generating grid multiwing chaotic attractors by constructing Heteroclinic loops into switching systems. IEEE Trans. Circuits-II **58**, 314–318 (2011)
19. Yu, S., Lu, J., Yu, X., Chen, G.: Design and implementation of grid multiwing hyperchaotic Lorenz system family via switching control and constructing super-heteroclinic loops. IEEE Trans. Circuits-I **59**, 1015–1028 (2012)
20. Ming-Wei, L., Xiao-Hua, L., Hua-Qing, L.: A family of four-dimensional multi-wing chaotic system and its circuit implementation. Acta Phys. Sin. **62**, 020512 (2013)
21. Elwakil, A.S., Ozoguz, S., Kennedy, M.P.: A four-wing butterfly attractor from a fully autonomous system. Int. J. Bifurc. Chaos **13**, 3093–3098 (2003)
22. Caputo, M.: Linear models of dissipation whose Q is almost frequency independent-II. Geophys. J. R. Astron. Soc. **13**, 529–539 (1967)
23. Ahmad, W.M., Sprott, J.C.: Chaos in fractional-order autonomous nonlinear systems. Chaos Soliton Fract. **16**, 339–351 (2003)

Design and FEM Simulation of Damped Milling Cutter

Yiqing Yang[✉], Yunfei Wang, and Yu Yu

School of Mechanical Engineering and Automation, Beihang University, Beijing, China
yyiqing@buaa.edu.cn

Abstract. Milling cutter with large length-diameter ratio is usually used in machining complex aerospace parts with deep pockets and thin ribs. Large over-hang causes stiffness reduction of the cutting tool, which is a significant factor leading to machining chatter. Damped milling cutter can effectively suppress the vibration. Three structural designs of damped cutter are proposed, and modal analysis and harmonious analysis are performed by ANSYS. Simulation results show that the milling cutter embedded with two degree-of-freedom passive damper exhibits the best vibration suppression and the magnitude of frequency response is reduced by 63.7 %, which therefore enhances the machining stability.

Keywords: Finite element simulation (FEM) · Milling · Cutter · Passive damper

1 Introduction

High-speed milling is widely used in the industry. For deep pocket milling, long slender cutter has increased its applications. When the length-diameter ratio of cutter is greater than four, it will be easy to occur chatter in machining because of the lack of rigidity. Chatter causes damage to the structure of machine or tool and reduces machining accuracy. The long slender cutter with passive damper is effective in suppressing flexible mode and improving cutting stability.

Passive damper can reduce the vibration of main structure by adding sub-structure on it. In 1928, Ormondroyd proposed single degree-of-freedom (SDOF) passive damper [1]. The original SDOF passive damper is comprised of the mass and springs and Den Hartog firstly proposed the 'fixed point theory' for optimizing this type of damper [2]. Zuo et al. compared the vibration suppression effect of the double SDOF and two degree-of-freedom (two-DOF) passive damper based on H_2 and H_∞ criterions, and found the later had a clear advantage and successfully utilized it to suppress vibration of single-mode structure [3].

There is limited research about the application of passive damper for milling cutter. Yutaka et al. used multiple passive dampers in suppressing milling chatter. The drawback is the external damper, so the part to be machined is restricted [4]. Ziegert et al. designed a milling cutter based on the principle of coulomb friction and the critical depth of stable cut increased by 53 % [5]. The Sandvik Company produced a milling cutter embedded with passive damper which doubled the production efficiency [6].

This paper presents three designs of damped milling cutter, i.e. embedded with friction damper, embedded with SDOF passive damper and embedded with two-DOF

© Springer Science+Business Media Singapore 2016
L. Zhang et al. (Eds.): AsiaSim 2016/SCS AutumnSim 2016, Part III, CCIS 645, pp. 108–113, 2016.
DOI: 10.1007/978-981-10-2669-0_12

passive damper. Finite element analyses of various cutters are implemented. Finally, the performance of various cutters is compared based on modal analysis and harmonic response analysis.

2   Structural Design and FEM Simulation

2.1   Case I: Milling Cutter Embedded with Internal Friction Damper

Based on the principle of coulomb friction, milling cutter with internal friction damper is mainly composed of four parts, i.e. milling cutter bar, cutter holder, cutter plate and damping bars (Fig. 1). There are four guide grooves inside the cutter bar embedded damping bars. When the cutter bar bending deformation occurs, the inner wall of the tool and damping sticks bend at the same time. Because their axes are not coincident, the displacement of the head-end of damper bar will be slightly larger than the displacement of the end of cutter bar and they produce relative displacement. When vibration occurs, vibration energy is dissipated through friction between damping bars and guide grooves.

Fig. 1. The structure of milling cutter with internal friction damper

As the surface quality machined by the cutter without damper is greatly influenced by the first vibration mode (primary mode), the frequency shift of the primary mode is shown in Table 1. It can be found that the natural frequency is 279 Hz before the damper is installed, and it is increased to 283 Hz when the cutter is fitted with damper.

Table 1.   Frequency shift of the primary mode

	Natural frequency (Hz)			
Solid cutter without damper	====	279		
Damped cutter, case I	====	283		
Damped cutter, caseII	====	263	298	
Damped cutter, case III	134	185	256	312
The damper of case III	138	187	276	====

2.2   Case II: Milling Cutter Embedded with SDOF Passive Damper

Internal guide grooves are canceled in the design of milling cutter embedded with SDOF passive damper, and the cavity is set in the bar for installing the SDOF damper (Fig. 2). The SDOF damper uses the principle of energy transfer, transferring the vibrational energy of the cutter bar to damper, and the damper dissipates vibration energy through damper units.

Fig. 2.   The structure of milling cutter embedded with SDOF passive damper

The first and second order natural frequencies are 263 Hz and 298 Hz after the damper is installed. It can be inferred that the first order natural frequency of the undamped milling cutter is influenced by damper. The original first order bending mode (279 Hz) is divided into two bending modes (263 Hz, 298 Hz).

2.3   Case III: Milling Cutter Embedded with Two-DOF Passive Damper

The bar of the cutter is designed as a segmented bar to facilitate loading and unloading of the damper. The assembly schematic diagram of milling cutter embedded with two-DOF passive damper is shown in Fig. 3.

Fig. 3.   The structure of milling cutter embedded with two-DOF passive damper

Before installing the damper, there is just a first order natural frequency of milling cutter bar under 500 Hz and it is 279 Hz. After installing the damper, the third order natural frequency of damper moves closer to the first order natural frequency of the cutter without damper and the damper has an impact on the dynamic characteristics of the cutter. There are four natural frequencies of the damping cutter under 500 Hz and they are 134 Hz, 185 Hz, 256 Hz and 312 Hz respectively. By comparing the frequencies of damping cutter and two-DOF damper, it can be found the first and second order natural frequencies (134 Hz, 185 Hz) of damping cutter are from the first and second order natural frequencies (138 Hz, 187 Hz) of two-DOF passive damper. The third and the fourth natural frequencies (256 Hz, 312 Hz) of damping cutter are splitted from the first order natural frequency (279 Hz) of the solid cutter without damper.

3   Results and Discussion

The vibration modes of the undamped and damped milling cutters (i.e. caseI, case II and case III) are shown in Table 2.

Table 2. The mode shape of four cutters

Cutter type / Mode order	Solid cutter without damper	Damped cutter, case I	Damped cutter, case II	Damped cutter, case III
1st				
2nd				

   In order to measure the vibration reduction performance of the cutters under periodical cutting force, the harmonic analysis is carried out. Assuming that the damping ratio of the cutter bar material is 2 %, a 1N sine force is applied on the cutter plate within a frequency range of 200 Hz–350 Hz. the damper should simultaneously satisfy the optimal conditions of frequency and damping in order to achieve the best damping effect. When the mass ratio is 5 %, the damping ratio of the second order of passive damper should be 2 % for achieving the optimal damping effect. The frequency response function of undamped milling cutter and three models of damping cutter are shown in Fig. 4. The most obvious decrease is the curve of case III and the peak value reduces by 63.7 %.

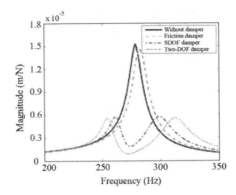

Fig. 4. The compare of harmonic analysis

Bandwidth is the distance of two frequencies whose signal strengths are $1/\sqrt{2}$ of the largest one, thus the bandwidth of three designs of damping cutters can be calculated. The suppressed bandwidth of two-DOF is significantly wider than the suppressed bandwidth of signal freedom damper. In a word, the vibration reduction effect of case III is the most appropriate option (Table 3).

Table 3. Frequency response amplitude and bandwidth for various cutters

	Solid cutter without damper	Damped cutter, case I	Damped cutter, case II	Damped cutter, case III
Amplitude (N/m)	15.80e–06	14.20e–06	5.82e–06	5.74e–06
Bandwidth (Hz)	10	14	65	83

4   Conclusions

Modal analysis shows that passive damper has significant effects on the vibration mode of tool. The amplitude reduction is caused by the first bending mode of the damper. For the cutter embedded with passive damper, the frequency of damper and tool must satisfy the optimal conditions of homology. Harmonic response analysis shows that the vibration amplitude of the primary mode for case I, case II and case III is reduced by 10.2 %, 63.1 % and 63.7 % respectively. The bandwidths of case I, case II and case III are 14 Hz, 65 Hz and 83 Hz.

Acknowledgements. This project is sponsored by the National Science and Technology Program of Machine tools (2014ZX04012013), National Natural Science Foundation of China (Grant 51205013) and Fundamental Research Funds for the Central Universities (YWF-15-JXXY-01).

References

1. Ormondroyd, J.: Theory of the dynamic vibration absorber. Trans. ASME **50**, 9–22 (1928)
2. Den Hartog, J.P.: Mechanical Vibration, 2nd edn. McGraw-Hill Book Company, New York (1940)
3. Zuo, L., Nayfeh, S.A.: Minimax optimization of multi-degree-of-freedom tuned-mass dampers. J. Sound Vib. **272**(3), 893–908 (2004)
4. Nakano, Y., Takahara, H., Kondo, E.: Countermeasure against chatter in end milling operations using multiple dynamic absorbers. J. Sound Vib. **332**(6), 1626–1638 (2013)
5. Madoliat, R., Hayati, S., Ghalebahman, A.G.: Investigation of chatter suppression in slender endmill via a frictional damper. Scientia Iranica **18**(5), 1069–1077 (2011)
6. Richt, C.: The innovative vibration reduction technology of long slender cutting tools. MW Metal Cut. **19**, 024 (2013). (in Chinese)

Particle-Based Two-Way Coupling of Fluids and Solids

Xiaolong Yang[✉], Hao Gu, and Fengju Kang

School of Marine Science and Technology, Northwestern Polytechnical University,
Xi'an, China
yangxl060120@aliyun.com

Abstract. In this paper, we present a novel method to simulating incompressible fluids and solids in real time. To accurately simulate the coupling, both fluids and solids are described by particles, thus the need to define an interface for coupling disparate fluids and solids models is eliminated, and the interaction between them can be achieved naturally without the complex coupling interface. The coupling method is entirely implemented on GPUs using CUDA. The method is tested in the scenario of ship sailing, and the result show the advantages of the method.

Keywords: Two-way coupling · Smoothed Particle Hydrodynamics · CUDA

1 Introduction

Interactive physically based simulation is a rapidly growing research area with an increasing number of applications, e.g. in games and computational surgery. The interaction between fluids and solids is becoming increasingly important in computer graphics. These interaction processes such as ship-wave interaction are physically very complex, thus it is very difficult to achieve realistic simulation. Typically the effect of the solid on the fluid is modeled by taking the solid velocity as a boundary condition for the fluid solve. Conversely, the effect of the fluid on the solid is determined by integrating the fluid pressure along the solid boundary to compute a force on the solid. One of the most popular particle methods for simulating fluid flow coupled to other bodies is SPH (Smoothed Particle Hydrodynamics) [1], which was introduced to the graphics community by Desbrun and Cani [2].

In this paper, we present a unified particle model based on SPH for the simulation of water and ship, which eliminates the need to define an interface for coupling different fluid and solid models. Using this approach, fluids and solids are both represented by particles, each of which has its own attribute values describing its physical properties. Since each particle interacts with its neighboring particles regardless of the state of matter, we achieve a two-way coupled fluid-solid interaction without any further treatment. This proposed technique can be implemented easily and be integrated with the existing SPH fluid solvers.

© Springer Science+Business Media Singapore 2016
L. Zhang et al. (Eds.): AsiaSim 2016/SCS AutumnSim 2016, Part III, CCIS 645, pp. 114–120, 2016.
DOI: 10.1007/978-981-10-2669-0_13

2 Related Work

Relevant to the central theme of this paper, we now briefly review previous works in two categories: SPH and coupling.

Müller [3] derived interparticle forces from SPH and the Navier-Stokes equations to interactively simulate water with free surfaces. However, it is difficult to model strong incompressible fluid. To solve this problem, Becker [4] proposed a Weakly Compressible SPH (WCSPH) method by introducing Tait equation. Alternatively, Solenthaler [5] proposed a Predictive-Corrective Incompressible SPH (PCISPH) method, which corrects pressure of fluid particles iteratively to provide smooth density and pressure distributions. Meanwhile, some SPH-based methods were also proposed to simulate deformable solids. For example, Becker [6] proposed a co-rotational SPH method by introducing the co-rotational idea.

Given SPH based fluid simulation, a variety of methods were proposed to model fluid-fluid and fluid-solid coupling. Müller [7] proposed a technique to model the interaction of multiple SPH fluids that have different physical properties and dynamic phases. Recently, Iwasaki [8] proposed a particle-based model to simulate the melting and freezing of ice objects, and achieved interactive simulation with the help of CUDA. Additionally, Qin [9] proposed to couple blood flow (SPH) and vessel wall (mass-spring model) by employing an improved repulsive boundary condition. Akinci [10] proposed a pressure-based coupling method to simulate the interaction of arbitrarily-complicated rigid objects and fluids, which employed boundary particles to represent rigid objects and effectively avoided the problem due to high pressure ratios. Therefore, it can afford large time steps. However, the method heavily relied on pre-sampled objects and was very hard to be generalized to handle solids with large deformation.

3 Smoothed Particle Hydrodynamics

Fluid behavior is controlled by the Navier-Stokes equations, which comprise two equations. The first equation is momentum equation, which can be formulated by the fundamental Newton's second law:

$$\rho \frac{d\mathbf{v}}{dt} = -\nabla P + \mu \nabla^2 \mathbf{v} + \mathbf{f} \tag{1}$$

where ρ is the fluid's density, $\mathbf{v}$ is the velocity, P is the fluid's pressure, μ is its viscosity coefficient, and $\mathbf{f}$ represents the external force.

The second equation is continuity equation, which can impose mass conservation for fluid.

$$\frac{d\rho}{dt} + \rho(\nabla \cdot \mathbf{v}) = 0 \tag{2}$$

In principle, SPH is a meshless Lagrangian method, it uses particles to discretize the continuum. The particles carry individual properties, which should be smoothed in the volume surrounding each particle node. According to SPH, a scalar quantity A at location r is estimated by a weighted sum of all particles in its local supporting domain:

$$A_s(\mathbf{r}) = \sum_j m_j \frac{A_j}{\rho_j} W(\mathbf{r} - \mathbf{r}_j, h) \tag{3}$$

where m_j is the mass of particle j, $\mathbf{r}_j$ is its position, ρ_j is the density.

The function $W(\mathbf{r}, h)$ is the smoothing kernel with supporting radius h. In the interest of robustness, the kernel is preferred to be smooth and normalized.

The acceleration of all particles can be computed by solving Eqs. 1 and 2 at each time step for every particle using the SPH formulations. Then we employ Leap-Frog scheme to update their velocities and positions.

To avoid strong compressibility, we take the weakly compressible pressure formulation into account, which can guarantee a small density ratio between the current density ρ and the initial density ρ_0

$$P = \frac{\rho_0 c_s^2}{\gamma} \left(\left(\frac{\rho}{\rho_0} \right)^\gamma - 1 \right) \tag{4}$$

with $\gamma = 7$, and c_s is the speed of sound in the fluid.

4   Coupling Simulation

In the standard particle level set algorithm, passive marker particles are seeded on both sides of the fluid interface and advected along the fluid flow. In areas where the grid is unable to fully resolve the level set's behavior, these marker particles will pass from one side of the interface to the other, indicating an error in the level set representation and prompting a local rebuilding of the level set function with the characteristic information present in these particles. Proxy Particle Generation.

After collision detection, we can get the contact polygons and particles. In fact, it is difficult to directly compute the coupling forces, especially when a fluid particle collides

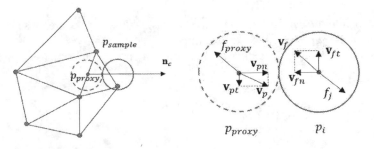

Fig. 1. Proxy particle generation and coupling force analysis

with more than one polygon. To facilitate the coupling force computing, we generate proxy particles dynamically over the solid surface to represent the local region of the solid. Then the coupling interaction is simplified to sphere-sphere collision, this way the forces can be computed efficiently.

As illustrated in Fig. 1, when the solid mesh collides with a fluid particle p_i, a proxy particle p_p is created over the boundary with predefined radius r_0 of the fluid particle. And the mass of the proxy particle m_p can be computed according to its volume and the density of the solid.

To define the position of the proxy particle, we need to estimate the normal of the boundary at the contact position first. We compute the distance d_{ij} from fluid particle p_i to the contacted triangle Tri_j. Then we use d_{ij} to construct a weighting function Eq. 6. By taking the normal $\mathbf{n}_j$ of Tri_j into account, we can get the normal $\mathbf{n}_c$ as

$$\mathbf{n}_c = \frac{\sum_j w_{ij}\mathbf{n}_j}{\| \sum_j w_{ij}\mathbf{n}_j \|} \tag{5}$$

$$w_{ij} = max\left(0, \frac{r_0 - d_{ij}}{r_0}\right) \tag{6}$$

As shown in Fig. 1, we place the proxy particle to be in front of the fluid particle along the direction $-\mathbf{n}_c$. Then we search the nodal points in the neighboring region of the contacted triangles, and denote them as sample points p_j. Thus the velocity of the proxy particle can be obtained by interpolating the corresponding properties of the sampled points. When the coupling is done, the force will be distributed to the sampled points along the opposite direction. For the purpose of simplicity, we adopt $w_j = m_j/d_j^2$ as a weighting function to interpolate the velocity $\mathbf{v}_p$, where d_j is the distance between the proxy particle and the sampled point j, m_j is the mass of the sampled point. Thus the velocity of the proxy particle can be computed by using

$$\mathbf{v}_p = \frac{1}{\sum_j w_j} \sum_j w_j\mathbf{v}_j \tag{7}$$

With the position, mass, velocity, normal of the proxy particle already computed in the aforementioned procedures, we can proceed to compute the coupling force efficiently.

4.1 Coupling Force Computation

To model the normal and tangential boundary conditions, as shown in Fig. 1, we first respectively project the velocities of proxy particles and fluid particles to the normal direction and the tangential direction, then compute $\mathbf{v}_{pn}$, $\mathbf{v}_{pt}$, $\mathbf{v}_{fn}$, and $\mathbf{v}_{ft}$. Here $\mathbf{v}_p$, $\mathbf{v}_f$ respectively denotes the velocities of proxy particle and fluid particle. To get the unknown velocities after collision, we can formulate the following equations

$$m_p \mathbf{v}^*_{pn} + m_f \mathbf{v}^*_{fn} = m_p \mathbf{v}_{pn} + m_f \mathbf{v}_{fn} \tag{8}$$

$$m_p \mathbf{v}^*_{pt} + m_f \mathbf{v}^*_{ft} = m_p \mathbf{v}_{pt} + m_f \mathbf{v}_{ft} \tag{9}$$

Where variables labeled with a single star (*) denote the unknown velocities after collision, m_p and m_f represent the mass of proxy particle and fluid particle.

To model the restitution in normal direction, we introduce Newton's coefficient e as

$$e = -\frac{\mathbf{v}^*_{pn} - \mathbf{v}^*_{fn}}{\mathbf{v}_{pn} - \mathbf{v}_{fn}} \tag{10}$$

Where $e = 0$ means that the collision is perfectly inelastic, while $e = 1$ means the collision is perfectly elastic.

Then we define a variable δ to control the different slip condition.

$$\delta = \frac{\mathbf{v}^*_{pt} - \mathbf{v}^*_{ft}}{\mathbf{v}_{pt} - \mathbf{v}_{ft}} \tag{11}$$

where $\delta = 0$ means no-slip in the collision, while $\delta = 1$ states the collision is free to slip.

By solving Eqs. 8 to 11, we can obtain the velocities of proxy particle and fluid particle. The collision between the two particles is directly controlled by parameters e and δ, and both of their value ranges are $[0, 1]$.

Then we need to compute the coupling forces of proxy particles and then distribute them to the sampled points. Inspired by the idea of direct forcing, we compute the force as

$$\mathbf{f}_p = \frac{\left(\mathbf{v}^*_p - \mathbf{v}_p\right) m_p}{\Delta t} \tag{12}$$

Furthermore, the force distribution of proxy particle can be formulated as

$$\mathbf{f}_j = \frac{w_j}{\sum_j w_j} \mathbf{f}_p \tag{13}$$

where w_j has the same meaning as that in Eq. 7.

5   Implementation

Figure 2 shows the computational procedure of our method. In each render frame, the new positions and velocities are updated based on the results of last frame.

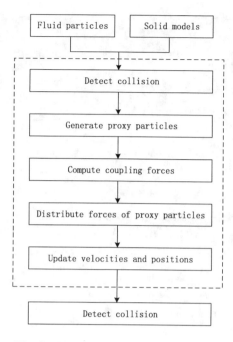

Fig. 2. The pipeline of each update frame

6   Results

We implemented our method on a PC with a Geforce GTX 560 GPU, Intel Core i5 CPU using C++, CUDA and OSG APIs. We demonstrate the advantages of our method via the scenario of ship sailing. Table 1 shows the parameter values using in the experiment.

Table 1. The values of parameters

Properties	Parameters	Values	Unit
Density	ρ_0	1000	kg/m^3
Mass	m_f	0.0002	kg
Speed of sound	c_s	20	m/s
Viscosity	μ	0.2	Pa · s

Figure 3 illustrates the two-way interaction between a ship and water. We used up to 100 k particles for water, and generated about 1400 proxy particles for the ship. The average frame rate was 17.9.

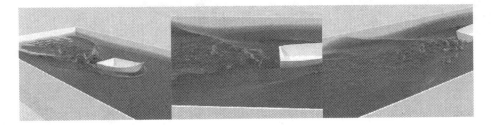

Fig. 3. Simulation scenario of ship sailing

7 Conclusion

To simulate the interactions fluids and solids in real time, a novel two-way coupling method is proposed. By discretizing both fluids and solids to the SPH particles, our method eliminates the need to define an interface for coupling different models, and the two-way fluid-solid interaction can be achieved naturally. Moreover, the SPH can be implemented efficiently with the CUDA techniques, thus the performance of the proposed method can be increased further on GPUs, and we believe that infinite water area can be simulated in real time via SPH method.

References

1. Monaghan, J.J.: Smoothed particle hydrodynamics. Ann. Rev. Astron. Appl. **30**, 543–574 (1992)
2. Destrun, M., Gascuel, M.-P.: Smoothed particles: a new paradigm for animating highly deformable bodies. In: Boulic, R., Hégron, G. (eds.) Computer Animation and Simulation 1996. Eurographics, pp. 61–76. Springer, Wien (1996)
3. Müller, M., Charypar, D., Gross, M.: Particle-based fluid simulation for interactive applications. In: Proceedings of the 2003 ACM SIGGRAPH/Eurographics Symposium on Computer Animation, pp. 154–159 (2003)
4. Becker M., Teschner M.: Weakly compressible SPH for free surface flows. In: Proceedings of the 2007 ACM SIGGRAPH/Eurographics Symposium on Computer Animation, pp. 209–217. ACM (2007)
5. Solenthaler, B., Pajarola, R.: Predictive-corrective incompressible SPH. ACM SIGGRAPH **40**, 1–6 (2009)
6. Becker, M., Ihmsen, M., Teschner, M.: Corotated SPH for deformable solids. In: NPH, pp. 27–34 (2009)
7. Müller, M., Solenthaler, B., Keiser, R., Gross, M.: Particle-based fluid-fluid interaction. In: Proceedings of the 2005 ACM SIGGRAPH/Eurographics Symposium on Computer Animation, pp. 237–244. ACM (2005)
8. Iwasaki, K., Uchida, H., Dobashi, Y., Nishita, T.: Fast particle-based visual simulation of ice melting. Comput. Graph. Forum **29**, 2215–2223 (2010)
9. Qin, J., Pang, W.: Particle-based simulation of blood flow and vessel wall interactions in virtual surgery. In: Proceedings of the 2010 Symposium on Information and Communication Technology, pp. 128–133 (2010)
10. Akinci, N., Ihmsen, M., Akinci, G., Solenthaler, B., Teschner, M.: Versatile rigid-fluid coupling for incompressible SPH. ACM SIGGRAPH **31**(4), 62:1–62:8 (2012)

Simulation Study on Micro-grid Control Based on the Optimal Droop Method

Ming-fang Lu[⊠], Xian-shan Li, and Tie Chen

School of Electrical and New Energy,
China Three Gorges University, Yichang, China
28139164@qq.com

Abstract. The traditional droop control method has adjusting deviation problem when micro-grid switched from parallel operation to isolated operation. So this paper proposed a optimal droop control method, combining the secondary frequency regulation method with droop control, it can solve the problem of large deviation of traditional droop control effectively. The experimental results show that the optimal droop method has increased the stability of frequency and voltage greatly in the process of micro-grid mode switching.

Keywords: Optimal droop method · PQ control · Micro-grid

1 Introduction

As the demand is increasing and the conventional energy sources gradually become exhausted, we have alternative option of renewable energy sources to sustain the growth of power generation in future [1].

Micro-grid as a effective carrier of distributed power can operate on connection and off-grid, and two kinds of isolated net. It is the key problem of the micro-grid operation control to ensure that frequency and voltage is in the acceptable range in the process of operating mode switch whether it's parallel operation mode or island operation mode [2].

When the distributed power generators of the micro-grid adopt droop control strategy, its output can adjust automatically in accordance with the characteristics of P-f and Q-u. It has no master-slave difference, thus it can achieve equivalent control. The advantage of this strategy is easy to help distributed power implement plug and play, at the same time, it can open the interconnection switch of micro grid directly on micro-grid mode switching [3–5]. Then distributed power generators on droop control model will share the imbalance of active power and reactive power of micro grid automatically.

2 Alternating Current Micro-grid Modeling

This paper uses Fig. 1 as example of micro network and introduces the controller design method of Micro-grid. The design does not consider the dynamic response characteristics of distributed power generator itself. That is to say distributed power generators in Fig. 1 are assumed to be ideal dc source, and it be reversed into three-phase ac by converter. After being filtered out higher harmonic by the RLC filter,

© Springer Science+Business Media Singapore 2016
L. Zhang et al. (Eds.): AsiaSim 2016/SCS AutumnSim 2016, Part III, CCIS 645, pp. 121–129, 2016.
DOI: 10.1007/978-981-10-2669-0_14

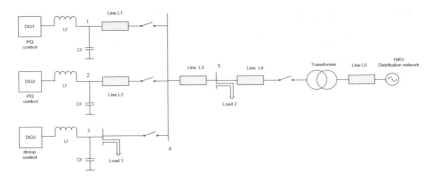

Fig. 1. Micro-grid structure

then it goes through transmission lines, switches, transformer and connects to the power distribution network.

The voltage amplitude and frequency of converter output terminal is determined by the converter control strategy, so the converter control strategy is particularly important in the micro power grid control. Commonly used control method has PQ control, UF control and droop control. DG1 and DG2 in Fig. 1 of micro-grid model adopt **PQ** control method, DG3 adopts the droop control method.

2.1   PQ Controller Design

PQ Control refers to the active power P and reactive power Q output by the converter can be controlled, and it can output according to the set value. PQ Control chart is shown in Fig. 2. It measures current and voltage on the connecting line of converter and power grid, then *dq* transforms the measuring value. It gains direct axis and quadrature axis component of voltage and current from *dq* transformation. Instantaneous power module calculates the active power P and reactive power Q output by converter based on the instantaneous power calculation method of transformation.

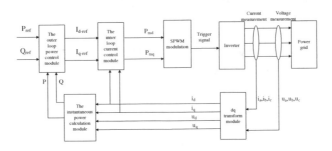

Fig. 2. PQ control structure diagram

The power outer loop control module generates reference value of straight axis component i_{d-ref} and quadrature axis component i_{q-ref} according to the set value of active power P_{ref} and reactive power Q_{ref} as well as the real-time active power P and reactive power Q output by converter of the reference and the output.

The current inner loop control module generates straight axis component P_{md} and quadrature axis component P_{mq} of pulse-width modulation coefficient according to i_{d-ref}, i_{q-ref}, i_d and i_q. Converter driving signal generating module generates the converter driving signal to drive the converter according to P_{md} and P_{mq}, and makes the converter output power close to the set value, so as to realize the PQ control of the converter.

As long as the setting value of active power P_{ref} and reactive power setting value Q_{ref} set up properly, meanwhile no more than the capacity of the converter and the maximum allowable current, the active power P and reactive power Q output by the converter will follow with the set value, thus realize the PQ control. The distributed power generator is not involved in the micro-grid frequency and voltage regulation under the PQ control.

2.2 Droop Controller Design

Droop control can realize the similar adjustment feature with the frequency regulation of traditional power system by controlling the converter. Now droop control method mainly adopted by converter is similar with the conventional regulation of synchronous generator, it uses the active-frequency $(P-f)$ and reactive power-voltage $(Q-f)$ regulating mode.

$P-f$ relation curve is shown in Fig. 3, $Q-V$ relation curve is shown in Fig. 4, structure diagram of droop control is shown in Fig. 5

$$K_{Pf} = (P_1 - P_n)/(f_n - f_1) \qquad (1)$$

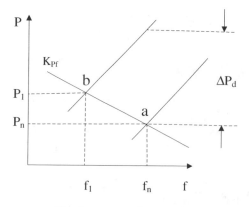

Fig. 3. $P-f$ relation curve

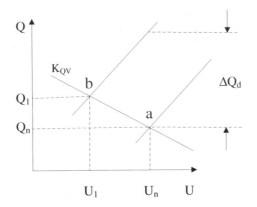

Fig. 4. $Q - V$ relation curve

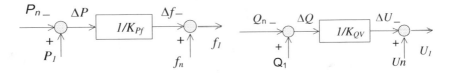

Fig. 5. Structure diagram of droop control

P_n is the active power output of generator at initial stable operation point a, P_1 is the active power output of generator at the new stable operation point b. f_n is the frequency at initial stable operation point a, it's the rated frequency, f_1 is the frequency at the new stable operation point b, K_{Pf} is the droop coefficient.

$$K_{QV} = (Q_1 - Q_n)/(U_n - U_1) \qquad (2)$$

Q_n is the reactive power output of generator at initial stable operation point a, Q_1 is the reactive power output of generator at the new stable operation point b. U_n is the voltage at initial stable operation point a, it's the rated voltage, U_1 is the voltage at the new stable operation point b, K_{QV} is the droop coefficient.

3   Optimal Droop Method

It can be seen that from the droop characteristic curve Figs. 3 and 4 that droop control basing on the principle of frequency adjustment exists adjusting deviation problem, when the deviation is beyond a certain range, the power quality will not conform to the requirements. Therefore it need to optimize the traditional droop control method and reduce to adjust deviation.

The second adjustment of frequency is operated the frequency modulator manually or automatically, and make the frequency characteristic curve of generator move up and down parallel, then it can keep the frequency offset caused by load changes within the scope of permit. So combining this method with droop control, it can effectively reduce the control error. Optimal droop control curve is shown in Fig. 6, Optimal droop control structure diagram is shown in Fig. 7.

$$K_{Pf} = (P_2 - P_n - \Delta P_G)/(f_n - f_2) \tag{3}$$

P_n is the active power output of generator at initial stable operation point a, ΔP_G is the secondary active power generated by the generator directly, P_2 is the active power output of generator at the new stable operation point c. f_n is the frequency at initial stable operation point a, it's the rated frequency, f_2 is the frequency at the new stable operation point c, K_{Pf} is the droop coefficient.

$$K_{QV} = (Q_2 - Q_n - \Delta Q_G)/(U_n - U_2) \tag{4}$$

Q_n is the reactive power output of generator at initial stable operation point a, ΔQ_G is the secondary reactive power generated by the generator directly, Q_2 is the reactive power output of generator at the new stable operation point c. U_n is the voltage at initial stable operation point a, it's the rated voltage, U_2 is the voltage at the new stable operation point c, K_{QV} is the droop coefficient.

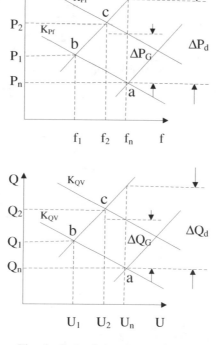

Fig. 6. Optimal droop control curve

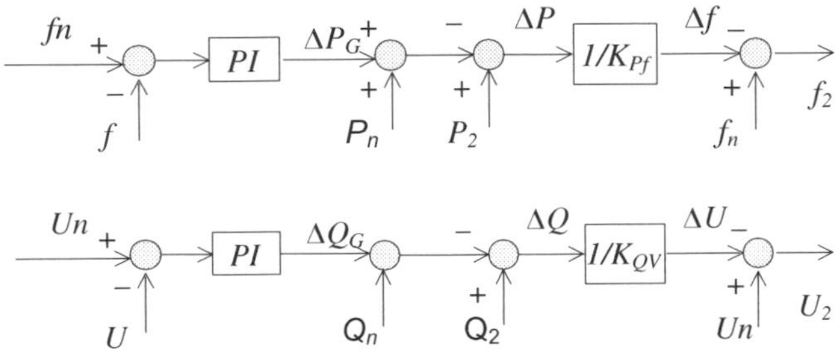

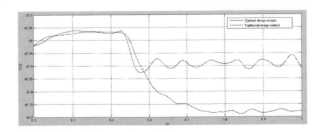

Fig. 7. Optimal droop control structure diagram

If $\Delta P_d = \Delta P_G$, the generating generates the original active power incremental of load power ΔP_d directly, then $\Delta f = 0$. If $\Delta Q_d = \Delta Q_G$, the generating generates the original reactive power incremental of load power ΔQ_d directly, then $\Delta U = 0$.

4   Simulated Analysis

In the micro-grid system as shown in Fig. 1, suppose the reference active power of $DG1$ is $P_{ref1} = 12$ KW, the reference reactive power of $DG1$ is $Q_{ref1} = 0$var, the reference active power of $DG2$ is $P_{ref2} = 12$ KW, the reference active power of $DG2$ is $Q_{ref2} = 0$var. Transmission line $l1$, $l2$, $l3$, $l4$ is 380 V, and the resistance of line is $R = 64.1 \times 10^{-3}\,\Omega$, the reactance of line is $L = 3.22 \times 10^{-5}H$;Transmission line $l5$ is 10 KV, the resistance of line is $R = 0.347\,\Omega$,the reactance of line is $L = 7.5 \times 10^{-4}H$. Load is constant impedance load, $R_{Load1} = 4\,\Omega$, $L_{Load1} = 5 \times 10^{-3}H$; $R_{Load2} = 4\,\Omega$, $L_{Load1} = 5 \times 10^{-3}H$.The dc Voltage is 750 V, the frequency of power grid is 50 HZ.

Micro-grid connected with power grid before 0.5 S, and isolated after 0.5 S. The simulation results are shown from Figs. 8, 9, 10, 11, 12, 13, 14, 15 to 16.

It can be seen from Figs. 8, 9 and 10 that when micro-grid switched from parallel operation to isolated operation, micro-power DG3 raised it's active power ΔP_G and reactive power ΔQ_G directly by Optimal droop control, and it reduced the adjustment deviation of the frequency and voltage, the adjustment deviation is in the permit scope. It can be seen from Figs. 11, 12, 13 to 14 that DG1 and DG2's active power and reactive power are invariable in the process of connection and off-grid due to the PQ

Fig. 8. Frequency of bus 5

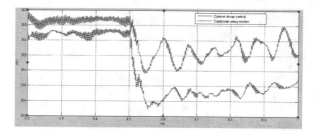

Fig. 9. Voltage of bus 5

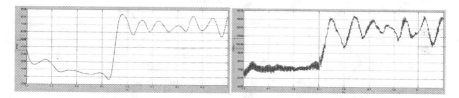

Fig. 10. ΔP_G and ΔQ_G of optimal droop control

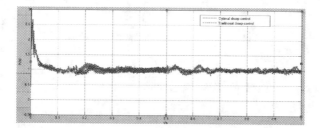

Fig. 11. Active power curve of DG1

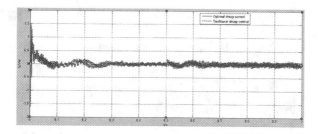

Fig. 12. Reactive power curve of DG1

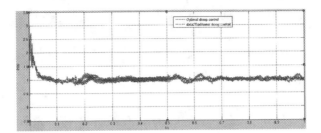

Fig. 13. Active power curve of DG2

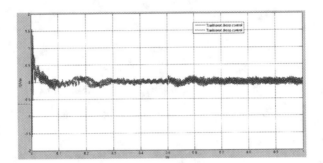

Fig. 14. Reactive power curve of DG2

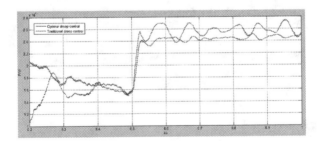

Fig. 15. Active power curve of DG3

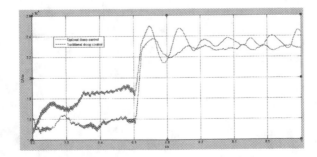

Fig. 16. Reactive power curve of DG3

control method. It can be seen from the Figs. 15 and 16 that the active power and reactive power of DG3 under optimized control are more than traditional droop control when micro-grid switched from parallel operation to isolated operation.

5 Conclusion

As we know the traditional droop control has adjusting deviation, if the adjusting deviation is very large and beyond the allowed range, it will affect the power quality of micro-grid. When we adopt optimal droop control method based on the secondary frequency modulation principle, we can let micro power operate as a frequency modulation unit. When micro-grid switches from parallel operation to isolated operation, the power shortage of micro-grid can be supplied by micro power directly, thus it can reduce the adjusting deviation and improve the stability of voltage and frequency.

References

1. Kaur, A., Kaushal, J., Basak, P.: A review on microgrid central controller. Renew. Sustain. Energy Rev. **55**, 338–345 (2016)
2. Chen, L., Wang, Z.: Research of operation control of micro-grid based on improved droop control. Power Syst. Prot. Control **44**(4), 17–21 (2016)
3. Wang, C.: The Micro Grid Theory of Analysis and Simulation, pp. 141–149. Science Press (2013)
4. Han, H., et al.: Review of power sharing control strategies for islanding operation of AC microgrids. IEEE Trans. Smart Grid **7**(1), 200–215 (2016)
5. Bouzid, A.M., et al.: A survey on control of electric power distributed generation systems for microgrid applications. Renew. Sustain. Energy Rev. **44**, 751–766 (2015)

Finite Element Methods for Semilinear Stochastic Volterra Equation with Multiplicative Noise

Xiaocui Li[✉], Xiaoyuan Yang, and Zeting Liu

Department of Mathematics, Beihang University,
LMIB of the Ministry of Education, Beijing 100191, China
xiaocuili@buaa.edu.cn

Abstract. This paper studies the Galerkin finite element approximations of a class of semilinear stochastic Volterra equation. The discretization in space is done by a standard continuous finite element method. And the discretization in time is achieved via an implicit Euler scheme and a Laplace transform convolution quadrature. We give strong convergence error estimates for both semidiscrete and fully discrete schemes.

Keywords: Stochastic Volterra equation · Finite element method · Euler scheme · Strong convergence · Convolution quadrature

1 Introduction

In this paper we study the finite element approximations of the semilinear stochastic Volterra equation with multiplicative noise

$$\mathrm{d}u + \left(A \int_0^t b(t-s)u(s)\mathrm{d}s \right) \mathrm{d}t = F(u)\mathrm{d}t + G(u)\mathrm{d}W, \ t \in [0,T], \qquad (1)$$

$$u(0) = u_0.$$

The process $\{u(t)\}_{t\in[0,T]}$, defined on a filtered probability space $(\Omega, \mathcal{F}, \mathbb{P}, \{\mathcal{F}_t\}_{t\geq 0})$ with a normal filtration $\{\mathcal{F}_t\}_{t\geq 0}$, takes values in a separable Hilbert space H with inner product $(\cdot,\cdot)$ and norm $\|\cdot\|$. The initial data u_0 is H-valued and $\mathcal{F}_0$-measurable random variable. The process W is a nuclear Q-Wiener process with respect to the filtration with values in some separable Hilbert space U. Let Q be a selfadjoint and positive semidefinite operator with finite trace. The operator $A : \mathcal{D}(A) \subset H \to H$ is an unbounded, densely defined, linear, selfadjoint operator with compact inverse. In Sect. 2 we give a precise formulation of our conditions on F, G, u_0.

Equations of the above type are used to model phenomena in viscoelasticity and heat conduction in materials with memory, cf. the references in [3,5].

This research is supported by the National Natural Science Foundation of China under grant 61271010.

L. Zhang et al. (Eds.): AsiaSim 2016/SCS AutumnSim 2016, Part III, CCIS 645, pp. 130–140, 2016.
DOI: 10.1007/978-981-10-2669-0_15

The numerical methods for deterministic Volterra equations are studied by many authors. The authors [2] study the existence, uniqueness and regularity for a class of semilinear stochastic Volterra equations with multiplicative noise, in the sequel we will continue the work of [2], give the error estimates for semi-discrete case as well as fully discrete case, and obtain error estimates.

The structure of this paper is as follows: In Sect. 2, we introduce basic notations and the main assumptions on F, G, u_0. In Sect. 3, we present the semi-discrete error estimate for the stochastic Volterra equation. In Sect. 4, we derive the fully discrete approximation of the stochastic Volterra equation.

2   Preliminaries

Let U and H be real separable Hilbert spaces with inner product $(\cdot, \cdot)$ and norms $\|\cdot\|_U$ and $\|\cdot\|_H$. $L(U, H)$ denotes the space of bounded linear operators from U to H and $\mathcal{L}_2(U, H)$ the space of Hilbert-Schmidt operators with norm

$$\|T\|^2_{\mathcal{L}_2(U,H)} := \sum_{k=1}^{\infty} \|Te_k\|^2_H < \infty,$$

where $\{e_k\}_{k=1}^{\infty}$ is an orthonormal basis of U.

Let $(\Omega, \mathcal{F}, \mathbf{P})$ be a probability space. We define $L_2(\Omega, H)$ to be the space of H-valued square integrable random variables with norm

$$\|v\|_{L_2(\Omega,H)} = \mathbf{E}(\|v\|^2_H)^{\frac{1}{2}} = \left(\int_{\Omega} \|v(w)\|^2_H d\mathbf{P}(w) \right)^{\frac{1}{2}},$$

where $\mathbf{E}$ stands for expected value. The stochastic process $W(t)$ is a U-valued Q-Wiener process. Let $Q \in \mathcal{L}(U)$ be a selfadjoint, positive semidefinite operator, with $Tr(Q) < \infty$. Furthermore, $W(t)$ has the orthogonal expansion

$$W(t) = \sum_{j=1}^{\infty} \gamma_j^{1/2} \beta_j(t) e_j,$$

where $\{(\gamma_j, e_j)\}_{j=1}^{\infty}$ are the eigenpairs of Q and $\{\beta_j(t)\}_{j=1}^{\infty}$ are real-valued mutually independent standard Brownian motions. Let $L_2^0 = HS(Q^{1/2}(H), H)$ denote the space of Hilbert-Schmidt operators, then for $\psi \in L_2^0$, we have the following Itô's isometry

$$\mathbf{E} \left\| \int_0^t \psi(s) dW(s) \right\|^2_H = \int_0^t \mathbf{E}\|\psi(s)Q^{1/2}\|^2_{\mathcal{L}_2(U,H)} ds. \tag{2}$$

Let $\{\mathcal{T}_h\}$ be a regular family of triangulations of $\mathcal{D}$ with $h_k = \mathrm{diam}(K), h = \max_{K \in \mathcal{T}_h} h_K$, and denote by V_h the space of piecewise linear continuous functions with respect to $\mathcal{T}_h$ which vanishes on $\partial \mathcal{D}$. Hence, $V_h \subset H_0^1(\mathcal{D}) = \dot{H}^1$.

Introducing the "discrete Laplace"

$$A_h : V_h \to V_h, \quad (A_h \psi, \chi) = (\nabla \psi, \nabla \chi), \quad \psi, \chi \in V_h,$$

and we introduce the projection P_h from H onto V_h defined by

$$(P_h v, \chi) = (v, \chi), \quad v \in H, \quad \forall \chi \in V_h. \tag{3}$$

Next we introduce the fractional powers A^s, $s \in \mathbb{R}$, of A as

$$A^s v = \sum_{k=1}^{\infty} \lambda_k^s (v, e_k) e_k, \mathcal{D}(A^s) = \{v \in H : \|A^s v\|^2 = \sum_{k=1}^{\infty} \lambda_k^{2s} (v, e_k)^2 < \infty\},$$

where $\{\lambda_k, e_k\}$ are the eigenpairs of A.

Next we show the main assumptions about the kernel b, F and G.

Assumption 1. *The kernel* $0 \neq b \in L_{loc}^1(\mathbb{R}_+)$, *is 3-monotone; that is,* $b, -\dot{b}$ *are nonnegative, nonincreasing, convex, and* $\lim_{t \to \infty} b(t) = 0$. *Furthermore,*

$$\rho := 1 + \frac{\pi}{2} \sup\{|arg\hat{b}(\lambda)|, Re\lambda > 0\} \in (1,2). \tag{4}$$

Assumption 2. *The Laplace transform* $\hat{b}$ *of* b *can be extended to an analytic function in a sector* $\sum_\theta$ *with* $\theta > \frac{\pi}{2}$ *and* $|\hat{b}^{(k)}(z)| \leq C|z|^{1-\rho-k}$.

Assumption 3. *The nonlinear operator* F *maps* H *into* H *and there exists a constant* C *such that*

$$\|F(x) - F(y)\| \leq C\|x - y\| \quad \forall x, y \in H.$$

Assumption 4. *The nonlinear operator* G *maps* H *into* L_2^0 *and there exists a constant* C *such that*

$$\|G(x) - G(y)\|_{L_2^0} \leq C\|x - y\| \quad \forall x, y \in H.$$

Assumption 5. *Suppose that the initial data* u_0 *is* $\dot{H}^{\frac{1+\epsilon}{\rho}}$ ($\epsilon > 0$ *small enough)-valued* $\mathcal{F}_0$-*measurable with* $u_0 \in L_2(\Omega, \dot{H}^{\frac{1+\epsilon}{\rho}})$.

Under the above conditions, there exists a unique mild solution u (cf. [2]) which satisfies

$$\sup_{t \in [0,T]} \mathbf{E}[\|u(t)\|^p] < \infty, \quad p \in [2, \infty), (\mathbf{E}[\|u(t_1) - u(t_2)\|^p])^{\frac{1}{p}} \leq C|t_1 - t_2|^{1-\frac{\rho}{2}}. \tag{5}$$

There exists a strongly continuous family $\{S(t)\}_{t \geq 0}$ such that $u(t) = S(t)u_0$ is the unique solution of

$$\dot{u}(t) + A \int_0^t b(t-s)u(s)\mathrm{d}s = 0, t > 0, u(0) = u_0. \tag{6}$$

Besides, we have

$$S(t)v = \sum_{k=1}^{+\infty} s_k(t)(v, e_k)e_k, v \in H,$$

where the functions $s_k(t)$ are the solutions of the ordinary differential equations

$$\dot{s}_k(t) + \lambda_k \int_0^t b(t-s)s_k(s)\mathrm{d}s = 0, s_k(0) = 1. \tag{7}$$

with $\{\lambda_k, e_k\}$ being the eigenpairs of A.

3   The Error Estimate for a Spatially Semidiscrete Approximation

In this section we discrete (1) in space by a standard piecewise continuous finite element method. We rewrite the spatially semidiscrete problem in the same form as the original one as

$$\mathrm{d}u_h + \left(A_h \int_0^t b(t-s)u_h(s)\mathrm{d}s \right) \mathrm{d}t = P_h F(u_h)\mathrm{d}t + P_h G(u_h)\mathrm{d}W, u_h(0) = P_h u_0.$$

Similarly to the original problem, the weak solution is given by (cf. [2])

$$u_h(t) = S_h(t)P_h u_0 + \int_0^t S_h(t-s)P_h F(u_h(s))\mathrm{d}s + \int_0^t S_h(t-s)P_h G(u_h(s))\mathrm{d}W,$$

where the resolvent family $\{S_h(t)\}_{t\geq 0}$ can be written explicitly as

$$S_h(t)P_h u_0 = \sum_{k=1}^{+\infty} s_{h,k}(t)(u_0, e_{h,k})e_{h,k}.$$

Here $\{\lambda_{h,k}, e_{h,k}\}$ are the eigenpairs of A_h and $s_{h,k}(t)$ are the solution of ODEs

$$\dot{s}_{h,k}(t) + \lambda_{h,k} \int_0^t b(t-s)s_{h,k}(s)\mathrm{d}s = 0, s_k(0) = 1. \tag{8}$$

The following lemma gives the error estimate for the corresponding deterministic homogeneous problem.

Lemma 1. *Let* $0 \leq v \leq \mu \leq 2$, $F_h(t) = S_h(t)P_h - S(t)$. *Suppose that the convolution kernel b satisfies Assumption 1, then for every $\epsilon > 0$ we have*

$$\|F_h(t)x\| \leq Ch^\mu t^{-\rho\frac{\mu-v}{2}}\|x\|_{v(1+\epsilon)}.$$

Proof. We first note that the case $v = \mu = 0$ is true by the properties of $S(t)$ (cf. [1,2]). Besides, [4, Theorem 2.1] proves the case $v = 0$ and $\mu = 2$.

The proof of the case $v = \mu = 2$ can be found in [7, Proposition 3.3]. The intermediate cases follow by the interpolation technique.

Theorem 1. *Under the Assumptions of Sect. 2 with $\rho \in (1, 2)$, we have*

$$\|u_h(t) - u(t)\|_{L_2(\Omega, H)} \le Ch^{\frac{1}{\rho} - \epsilon},$$

where $\epsilon > 0$ is small enough.

Proof. We have the following equality

$$
\begin{aligned}
u_h(t) &- u(t) \\
&= (S_h(t)P_h - S(t))u_0 + \int_0^t (S_h(t-s)P_hF(u_h(s)) - S(t-s)F(u(s)))\mathrm{d}s \\
&+ \int_0^t (S_h(t-s)P_hG(u_h(s)) - S(t-s)G(u(s)))\mathrm{d}W(s) =: I + II + III. \quad (9)
\end{aligned}
$$

The term I is estimated by Lemma 1 with $\mu = v = \frac{1}{\rho}$ and Assumption 5, which yields

$$\|I\|_{L_2(\Omega, H)} = \|(S_h(t)P_h - S(t))u_0\|_{L_2(\Omega, H)} \le Ch^{\frac{1}{\rho}}\|u_0\|_{L_2(\Omega, \dot{H}^{\frac{1+\epsilon}{\rho}})} \le Ch^{\frac{1}{\rho}}. \quad (10)$$

The term II in (9) is dominated by three additional terms as follows

$$
\begin{aligned}
II &= \int_0^t (S_h(t-s)P_h(F(u_h(s)) - F(u(s))))\mathrm{d}s \\
&+ \int_0^t (S_h(t-s)P_h - S(t-s))(F(u(s)) - F(u(t)))\mathrm{d}s \\
&+ \int_0^t (S_h(t-s)P_h - S(t-s))F(u(t)))\mathrm{d}s =: II_1 + II_2 + II_3.
\end{aligned}
$$

We estimate each term separately. Using the properties of $S(t)$ (cf. [2]), we obtain

$$
\begin{aligned}
\|II_1\|_{L_2(\Omega, H)} &\le \int_0^t \|S_h(t-s)P_h(F(u_h(s)) - F(u(s)))\|_{L_2(\Omega, H)} \,\mathrm{d}s \\
&\le C \int_0^t \|u_h(s) - u(s)\|_{L_2(\Omega, H)} \,\mathrm{d}s. \quad (11)
\end{aligned}
$$

The term II_2 is estimated by applying Lemma 1 with $\mu = \frac{1}{\rho}, v = 0$, Assumption 3 and (5), then we have

$$
\begin{aligned}
\|II_2\|_{L_2(\Omega, H)} &\le \int_0^t \|(S_h(t-s)P_h - S(t-s))(F(u(s)) - F(u(t)))\|_{L_2(\Omega, H)} \,\mathrm{d}s \\
&\le C \int_0^t h^{\frac{1}{\rho}}(t-s)^{-\frac{1}{2}} \|F(u(s)) - F(u(t))\|_{L_2(\Omega, H)} \,\mathrm{d}s \le Ch^{\frac{1}{\rho}}. \quad (12)
\end{aligned}
$$

Finally, the estimate for II_3 is a straightforward application of Lemma 1 with $\mu = \frac{1}{\rho}, v = 0$, Assumption 3 and (5), we get

$$\|II_3\|_{L_2(\Omega, H)} \le \int_0^t \|(S_h(t-s)P_h - S(t-s))F(u(t))\|_{L_2(\Omega, H)} \,\mathrm{d}s \le Ch^{\frac{1}{\rho}}. \quad (13)$$

A combination of the estimates (11)–(13) yields

$$\|II\|_{L_2(\Omega,H)} \leq C \int_0^t \|u_h(s) - u(s)\|_{L_2(\Omega,H)} \, ds + Ch^{\frac{1}{\rho}}. \tag{14}$$

The estimate for term III works in a similar way as for II. We divide III into three parts as usual and estimate each term separately.

$$III = \int_0^t (S_h(t-s)P_h(G(u_h(s)) - G(u(s)))dW(s)$$

$$+ \int_0^t (S_h(t-s)P_h - S(t-s))(G(u(s)) - G(u(t))) \, dW(s)$$

$$+ \int_0^t (S_h(t-s)P_h - S(t-s))G(u(t))dW(s) =: III_1 + III_2 + III_3.$$

For term III_1, by an application of Itô isometry, Using the properties of $S(t)$ (cf. [1,2]), we derive

$$\|III_1\|_{L_2(\Omega,H)} = \left\| \left(\int_0^t \|S_h(t-s)P_h(G(u_h(s)) - G(u(s))\|_{L_2^0}^2 \, ds \right)^{\frac{1}{2}} \right\|_{L_2(\Omega,\mathbb{R})}$$

$$\leq C \left(\int_0^t \|u_h(s) - u(s)\|_{L_2(\Omega,H)}^2 ds \right)^{\frac{1}{2}}. \tag{15}$$

In a similar way as for II_2, we find an estimate for III_2 by using Lemma 1 with $\mu = \frac{1}{\rho}, v = 0$ and Itô isometry. With Assumption 4 and (5), then we have

$$\|III_2\|_{L_2(\Omega,H)} = \left\| \left(\int_0^t \|F_h(t-s)(G(u(s)) - G(u(t))\|_{L_2^0}^2 \, ds \right)^{\frac{1}{2}} \right\|_{L_2(\Omega,\mathbb{R})}$$

$$\leq Ch^{\frac{1}{\rho}} \left(\int_0^t (t-s)^{-1}(t-s)^{2-\rho} ds \right)^{\frac{1}{2}} \leq Ch^{\frac{1}{\rho}}. \tag{16}$$

Finally, for III_3, by making use of Lemma 1 with $\mu = \frac{1}{\rho} - \epsilon (\epsilon > 0$ small enough), $v = 0$, Assumption 4, Itô isometry and (5), then we obtain

$$\|III_3\|_{L_2(\Omega,H)} = \left\| \left(\int_0^t \|F_h(t-s)G(u(t))\|_{L_2^0}^2 \, ds \right)^{\frac{1}{2}} \right\|_{L_2(\Omega,\mathbb{R})} \leq Ch^{\frac{1}{\rho}-\epsilon}. \tag{17}$$

In total, by (15)–(17), we have

$$\|III\|_{L_2(\Omega,H)} \leq C \left(\int_0^t \|u_h(s) - u(s)\|_{L_2(\Omega,H)}^2 ds \right)^{\frac{1}{2}} + Ch^{\frac{1}{\rho}-\epsilon}. \tag{18}$$

Coming back to (9), by (10), (14) and (18), and by Gronwall's lemma, we conclude that

$$\|u_h - u\|_{L_2(\Omega,H)} \leq Ch^{\frac{1}{\rho}-\epsilon},$$

which completes the proof.

4   The Error Estimate for a Fully Discrete Approximation

In this section, we derive strong error estimate for a fully discrete scheme for (1). Time discretization is achieved via a classical implicit Euler scheme and, concerning the convolution in time, via a quadrature rule. Let k be a time step, $\Delta t > 0$ and we set $t_n = n\Delta t = nk$ for any integer $n \geq 0$. We seek for an approximation $u_{n,h}$ of $u(t_n)$ defined by the recurrence

$$u_{n,h} - u_{n-1,h} + \Delta t \left(\sum_{k=1}^{n} \omega_{n-k} A_h u_{k,h} \right)$$
$$= P_h F(u_{n,h})\Delta t + P_h G(u_{n,h})(W^Q(t_n) - W^Q(t_{n-1})), n \geq 1, u_{0,h} = P_h u_0. \quad (19)$$

Next we derive a discrete mild formulation for (19) in the same way as in [7]

$$u_{n,h} = B_{n,h} P_h u_0 + k \sum_{j=0}^{n-1} B_{n-j,h} P_h F(u_{j,h}) + \sum_{j=0}^{n-1} B_{n-j,h} P_h G(u_{j,h}) \Delta W_{j+1}^Q, \quad (20)$$

where the definition of $B_{n,h}$ is the same as in [7]. Next we will need a Hölder type estimate on the resolvent family $\{S(t)\}_{t \geq 0}$.

Lemma 2 ([7]). *If b satisfies Assumption 1, then there is $C > 0$ such that*

$$\left(\sum_{k=1}^{n} \int_{t_{k-1}}^{t_k} \|S(t_n - s) - S(t_n - t_{k-1})x\|^2 \mathrm{d}s \right)^{\frac{1}{2}} \leq C\Delta t^\gamma \|x\|_{s-\frac{1}{\rho}}, \quad n\Delta t = T,$$

for all $\gamma < \frac{\rho s}{2}$ where $0 < s \leq \frac{1}{\rho}$.

The following lemma is the full-discrete error estimate for the corresponding deterministic homogeneous equation.

Lemma 3. *$0 \leq v \leq \mu \leq 2$, Let $F_{n,h}(t_n) = B_{n,h} P_h - S(t_n)$. Then for every $\epsilon > 0$ there exists a constant C such that*

$$\|F_{n,h}(t_n)x\| \leq C(h^\mu t_n^{-\rho \frac{\mu-v}{2}} + k^{\frac{\mu}{2}} t_n^{-\frac{\mu-v}{2}})\|x\|_{v(1+\epsilon)}.$$

Proof. By the properties of $S(t)$ (cf. [1,2]), the case $v = \mu = 0$ is obviously true. In the case of $v = 0, \mu = 2$, we have, by combination of [4, Theorem 3.2] and Lemma 1,

$$\|B_{n,h} P_h x - S(t_n)x\| \leq \|B_{n,h} P_h x - S_h(t_n)x\| + \|S_h(t_n)x - S(t_n)x\|$$
$$\leq Ckt_n^{-1}\|x\| + Ch^2 t_n^{-\rho}\|x\|.$$

For the case $v = 2, \mu = 2$, using [6, Theorem 3.1] and [4, Lemma 3.2], we arrives at the deterministic estimate

$$\|B_{n,h} P_h x - S(t_n)x\| \leq C(h^2 + k) \left(\|x\|_2 + \int_0^t \|\dot{S}(s)x\|_2 \mathrm{d}s + \int_0^t \|\ddot{S}(s)x\| \mathrm{d}s \right) (21)$$

If $x \in \mathcal{D}$, then $u(t) = S(t)x$ is a strong solution of (6). And we know that

$$\int_0^t \|\ddot{S}(s)x\| ds \leq C \left(\int_0^t \|\dot{S}(s)x\|_2 ds + \|x\|_2 \right).$$

By the properties of $S(t)$ (cf. [1,2]), we obtain that

$$\int_0^t \|\dot{S}(s)x\|_2 ds = \int_0^t \|A^{-\epsilon} \dot{S}(s) A^{1+\epsilon} x\| ds \leq C \|x\|_{2+2\epsilon},$$

and then we insert it into (21), which proves the case of $v = 2, \mu = 2$. The intermediate cases follow by the interpolation technique.

Our second main result is the analogue of Theorem 1.

Theorem 2. *Under the Assumptions of Sect. 2 with $\rho \in (1,2)$, there exists a constant C such that*

$$\|u_{n,h} - u(t_n)\|_{L_2(\Omega,H)} \leq C(h^{\frac{1}{\rho}} + k^{\frac{1}{2\rho}}).$$

Proof. Defining $e^n = u_{n,h} - u(t_n)$, we obtain

$$e^n = (B_{n,h} P_h - S(t_n)) u_0 + \left(k \sum_{j=0}^{n-1} B_{n-j,h} P_h F(u_{j,h}) - \int_0^{t_n} S(t_n - s) F(u(s)) ds \right)$$

$$+ \left(\sum_{j=0}^{n-1} B_{n-j,h} G(u_{j,h}) \Delta W_{j+1}^Q - \int_0^{t_n} S(t_n - s) G(u(s)) dW \right) =: e_1 + e_2 + e_3. \tag{22}$$

Note that the terms e_1, e_2 and e_3 are of the same structure as the terms I, II, and III in the proof of Theorem 1, we estimate each term seriatim. For term e_1, we apply Lemma 3 with $\mu = v = \frac{1}{\rho}$ and Assumption 5,

$$\|e_1\|_{L_2(\Omega,H)} = \|(B_{n,h} P_h - S(t_n)) u_0\|_{L_2(\Omega,H)}$$
$$\leq C(h^{\frac{1}{\rho}} + k^{\frac{1}{2\rho}}). \tag{23}$$

Term e_2 can be divided into the following terms,

$$e_2 = \sum_{j=1}^n \int_{t_{j-1}}^{t_j} (B_{n-j+1,h} P_h (F(u_{j-1,h}) - F(u(s)))$$

$$+ (B_{n-j+1,h} P_h - S(t_n - t_{j-1})) F(u(s)) + (S(t_n - t_{j-1}) - S(t_n - s)) F(u(s)) ds$$
$$=: e_{21} + e_{22} + e_{23}.$$

For term e_{21}, by virtue of the property of $B_{n,h}$(cf. [1]), Assumption 3, the triangle inequality and (5), we have

$$\|e_{21}\|_{L_2(\Omega,H)}$$

$$\leq C\sum_{j=1}^{n}\int_{t_{j-1}}^{t_j}\left(\|u(t_{j-1})-u(s)\|_{L_2(\Omega,H)}+\|u_{j-1,h}-u(t_{j-1})\|_{L_2(\Omega,H)}\right)\mathrm{d}s$$

$$\leq C\sum_{j=1}^{n}\int_{t_{j-1}}^{t_j}(s-t_{j-1})^{1-\frac{\rho}{2}}\mathrm{d}s+Ck\sum_{j=1}^{n}\|e^j\|^2\leq Ck^{2-\frac{\rho}{2}}+Ck\sum_{j=1}^{n}\|e^j\|^2.\quad(24)$$

For the estimate of e_{22}, by using Lemma 3 with $\mu=\frac{1}{\rho}$, $v=0$ and (5), we obtain

$$\|e_{22}\|_{L_2(\Omega,H)}\leq\sum_{j=1}^{n}\int_{t_{j-1}}^{t_j}\|(B_{n-j+1,h}P_h-S(t_n-t_{j-1}))F(u(s))\|_{L_2(\Omega,H)}\mathrm{d}s$$

$$\leq C\sum_{j=1}^{n}\int_{t_{j-1}}^{t_j}(h^{\frac{1}{\rho}}((n-j+1)\Delta t)^{-\frac{1}{2}}+k^{\frac{1}{2\rho}}((n-j+1)\Delta t)^{-\frac{1}{2\rho}})\mathrm{d}s$$

$$\leq C(h^{\frac{1}{\rho}}+k^{\frac{1}{2\rho}}).\quad(25)$$

For term e_{23}, by using Lemma 2 with $s=\frac{1}{\rho}$ and (5), we get

$$\|e_{23}\|_{L_2(\Omega,H)}\leq\sum_{j=1}^{n}\int_{t_{j-1}}^{t_j}\|(S(t_n-t_{j-1})-S(t_n-s))F(u(s))\|_{L_2(\Omega,H)}\mathrm{d}s$$

$$\leq Ck^{\gamma}.\quad(26)$$

In total, by (24)–(26), we have

$$\|e_2\|_{L_2(\Omega,H)}\leq Ck^{\frac{1}{2}}+Ck\sum_{j=1}^{n}\|e^j\|^2+C(h^{\frac{1}{\rho}}+k^{\frac{1}{2\rho}})+Ck^{2-\frac{\rho}{2}}.\quad(27)$$

For term e_3, we have

$$e_3=\sum_{j=1}^{n}\int_{t_{j-1}}^{t_j}(B_{n-j+1,h}P_h(G(u_{j-1,h})-G(u(s))))$$

$$+(B_{n-j+1,h}P_h-S(t_n-t_{j-1}))G(u(s))+(S(t_n-t_{j-1})-S(t_n-s))G(u(s)))\mathrm{d}W$$

$$=:e_{31}+e_{32}+e_{33}.$$

We now estimate each term e_{31}, e_{32} and e_{33}. For term e_{31}, similarly to the estimate of the previous case e_{21}, by making use of the property of $B_{n,h}$ (cf. [1]), Assumption 4, the triangle inequality and (5), we obtain

$$\|e_{31}\|_{L_2(\Omega,H)}=\|(\sum_{j=1}^{n}\int_{t_{j-1}}^{t_j}\|B_{n-j+1,h}P_h(G(u_{j-1,h})-G(u(s)))\|_{L_2^0}^2\mathrm{d}s)^{\frac{1}{2}}\|_{L_2(\Omega,\mathbb{R})}$$

$$\leq C\|(\sum_{j=1}^{n}\int_{t_{j-1}}^{t_j}\|u_{j-1,h}-u(s)\|^2\mathrm{d}s)^{\frac{1}{2}}\|_{L_2(\Omega,\mathbb{R})}\leq Ck^{2-\frac{\rho}{2}}+Ck\sum_{j=1}^{n}\|e^j\|^2.\quad(28)$$

For the estimate of e_{32}, by using Lemma 3 with $\mu = v = \frac{1}{\rho}$, Assumption 4 and (5), we obtain

$$\|e_{32}\|_{L_2(\Omega,H)} = \|(\sum_{j=1}^{n} \int_{t_{j-1}}^{t_j} \|(B_{n-j+1,h}P_h - S(t_n - t_{j-1}))G(u(s))\|_{L_2^0}^2 ds)^{\frac{1}{2}}\|_{L_2(\Omega,\mathbb{R})}$$

$$\leq C(h^{\frac{1}{\rho}} + k^{\frac{1}{2\rho}}). \tag{29}$$

For term e_{33}, by using Lemma 2 with $s = \frac{1}{\rho}$, Assumption 4 and (5), we have

$$\|e_{33}\|_{L_2(\Omega,H)} = \|(\sum_{j=1}^{n} \int_{t_{j-1}}^{t_j} \|(S(t_n - t_{j-1}) - S(t_n - s))G(u(s))\|_{L_2^0}^2 ds)^{\frac{1}{2}}\|_{L_2(\Omega,\mathbb{R})}$$

$$\leq Ck. \tag{30}$$

By (28), (29) and (30), we have

$$\|e_3\|_{L_2(\Omega,H)} \leq Ck^{\frac{1}{2}} + Ck \sum_{j=1}^{n} \|e^j\|^2 + C(h^{\frac{1}{\rho}} + k^{\frac{1}{2\rho}}) + Ck + Ck^{2-\frac{\rho}{2}}. \tag{31}$$

Coming back to (22), by (23), (27), and (31) we conclude that

$$\|e^n\|_{L_2(\Omega,H)} \leq C(h^{\frac{1}{\rho}} + k^{\frac{1}{2\rho}}) + Ck^{\frac{1}{2}} + Ck \sum_{j=1}^{n} \|e^j\|^2 + Ck + Ck^{2-\frac{\rho}{2}}.$$

By using the discrete Gronwall's lemma, we get

$$\|u_{n,h} - u(t_n)\|_{L_2(\Omega,H)} \leq C(h^{\frac{1}{\rho}} + k^{\frac{1}{2\rho}}),$$

which completes the proof.

References

1. Kovács, M., Printems, J.: Weak convergence of a fully discrete approximation of a linear stochastic evolution equation with a positive-type memory term. J. Math. Anal. Appl. **413**, 939–952 (2014)
2. Baeumer, B., Geissert, M., Kovács, M.: Existence, uniqueness and regularity for a class of semilinear stochastic Volterra equations with multiplicative noise. J. Differ. Equ. **258**, 535–554 (2015)
3. Clément, P., Da Prato, G., Prüss, J.: White noise perturbation of the equations of linear parabolic viscoelasticity. Rendiconti Dellistituto Di Matematica Delluniversita Di Trieste **29**, 207–220 (1997)
4. Lubich, C., Sloan, I., Thomée, V.: Nonsmooth data error estimates for approximations of an evolution equation with a positive-type memory term. Math. Comp. **65**, 1–17 (1996)

5. MacCamy, R.C.: An integro-differential equation with application to heat flow. Quart. Appl. Math. **35**, 1–19 (1977)
6. McLean, W., Thomée, V.: Numerical solution of an evolution equation with a positive-type memory term. J. Aust. Math. Soc. Ser. B **35**, 23–70 (1993)
7. Kovács, M., Printems, J.: Strong order of convergence of a fully discrete approximation of a linear stochastic Volterra type evolution equation. Math. Comp. **83**, 2325–2346 (2012)

M&S for Energy, Environment and Climate

Simulation on the Characteristics of Pneumatic Booster Valve with Energy Recovery

Fan Yang[1,2(✉)], Kotaro Tadano[2], Gangyan Li[1], Toshiharu Kagawa[2], and Jiehong Peng[2]

[1] School of Mechanical and Electronic Engineering,
Wuhan University of Technology, Wuhan, China
yang_fan@whut.edu.cn
[2] Precision and Intelligence Laboratory,
Tokyo Institute of Technology, Yokohama, Japan

Abstract. In this study, we proposed a new booster valve with energy recovery (BVER) for improving the energy-efficiency. The principle of the BVER was introduced first by comparing with the traditional boost valve. We established the mathematics model of BVER which included the tank pressure response, and then Matlab/Simulink software was used for modeling and simulation. Last, air power was introduced to assess the energy-efficiency of booster valves, and the energy efficiency of booster valve was verified by experiment. The study shows that the boost ratio of BVER increases 15–25 % and the energy-efficiency increases 5–10 % according to different supply pressure. The BVER has biggest boost ratio when the recovery chamber and boost chamber diameter ratio is 1.3–1.5, and the pressure fluctuation is small than 1 % when tank volume is larger than 10 L. This study proves that BVER has better performance for its high boost ratio, stable pressure output and high energy efficiency, it provides a good reference for booster valve's design and energy saving.

Keywords: Pneumatic booster valve · Energy recovery · Air power · Energy efficiency · Matlab/Simulink

1 Introduction

Pneumatic systems are widely used in industry for cleanness, simple structure and low maintenance cost. The electric consumption by air compressors have up to 20 % of total electric consumption every year [1], so it has come to our focus to decrease the energy consumption by pneumatic systems. A study by Yukio [2] showed that the supply pressure decreased by every 0.1 MPa, the electric consumption reduces by 8 %. For this reason more and more factories save energy by decreasing the supply pressure, however, they face a problem that the pressure is too low to drive a heavy load or a machine that need a high one, so, the booster valves were widely demanded for locally pressure boost.

Booster valves can be categorized as symmetrical and asymmetrical type. The structure of symmetrical booster valve is simple and it can boost double in each cycle. Asymmetrical booster valve can get large boost ratio but its structure is complex and

© Springer Science+Business Media Singapore 2016
L. Zhang et al. (Eds.): AsiaSim 2016/SCS AutumnSim 2016, Part III, CCIS 645, pp. 143–153, 2016.
DOI: 10.1007/978-981-10-2669-0_16

inefficient [3]. In order to improve the performance of booster valve, Wang [4] mentioned that large dead volume may lead draw and vent useless and suggested that the dead volume should be 3–8 % of chamber volume. Mathematic model of asymmetrical booster valve was proposed in literature [5], it proved that piston mass and section ratio has little affection on the output pressure. An EEU boost valve was proposed for energy saving in [6–8], and it could use expansion power for pushing piston to the end. However, it is complicated to judge the piston position and the expansion energy is not enough to drive the piston with low supply pressure. Then the existing problems can be summarized as follows: it is waste of energy for the pressure air exhausting directly to atmosphere. The mathematic models in previous work didn't consider the tank, and the output pressure of booster valve was confused with tank pressure. Finally, there wasn't systematically evaluation of energy efficient of booster valve.

The purpose of this study was to propose a booster valve that can recover the high pressure for a second use, and the analytical model would consider the tank together. The efficiency of the boost valve will be analyzed based on this model. And this study suggests that BVER has better performance compared with traditional products, it has high boost ratio, high energy efficiency and little pressure fluctuation.

2 Principle of Booster Valve

Pneumatic booster valve can transfer low pressure to high pressure for the piston area difference based on Pascal's law [9]. A typical booster valve used for comparison is SMC's VBA20A, its high pressure air in drive chamber exhaust directly to the atmosphere, air power are squandered in long running time by this way. To overcome this defect, a new booster valve with energy recovery was proposed as in Fig. 1.

When the booster valve starts to work, the piston pretends to be located at the left end and the solenoid valve with two-position seven-port is in the position as shown in Fig. 1. In this state, the air source directly connects with booster chamber B, another

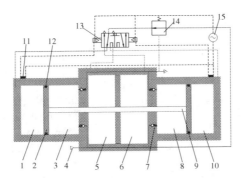

1. Drive chamber A 2.Piston 3.Boost Chamber A 4.Air source 5.Recovery chamber A 6. Recovery chamber B 7. Check Valve 8.Boost chamber B 9.Piston rod 10.Drive chamber B 11.Magnatic switch 12. Magnetic ring 13.Two-position seven-port solenoid valve 14. Regulator 15. Controller

Fig. 1. The structure schematic diagram of BVER

branch of air source connects with driver chamber A by passing a regulator and a solenoid valve. With air flow into these two chambers, the air pressure rises and generates thrust to drive the piston moving to right. Because of the piston's moving, volume of booster chamber A becomes smaller and smaller, as a result, pressure in this chamber will become much higher until it is higher than the pressure in the tank, then the check valve opens and the air in boost chamber begins to exhaust to the tank. Meanwhile, when the piston moves to right, the air in driver chamber B is recycled by recovery chamber A and used to work by pushing piston, the low pressure in recovery chamber A discharged to atmosphere directly. When the piston move to right end, a magnetic plus signal will be generated, and the solenoid valve will change its state after the controller detect the plus. The discharge chambers and charge chambers exchanged with each other, so the piston can reciprocate and discharge high-pressure air two times in each cycle. High pressure gas in drive chamber flows into recovery chamber which helps to recover energy each stroke.

3   Mathematic Model of Booster Valve

In order to analyze the characteristics of booster valve, the ideal gas state equation, energy conservation and kinematics equation will be used, to facility the model, the following assumptions are valid: (1) The air in the system is considered to be ideal gas, and it meets ideal gas state equation; (2) There is no leakage in the system, including the pistons and fittings; (3) Initial temperature in booster valve chambers is equal to atmosphere, and the air source temperature is same as atmosphere temperature.

3.1   Flow-Rate Characteristics Equation

The flow-rate characteristics equation of pneumatic components was first proposed by Sanville [10] and then standardized by ISO6358 [11]. But when we use this equation for numerical simulation, there will be negative number and then complex number in solve process; this will lead to divergence or error in simulation. To overcome this problem, Kassa [12] proposed an improved flow-rate characteristics as Eq. (1). The laminar model was used to instead the subsonic flow model when the pressure ratio is 0.995–0.999.

$$G = \begin{cases} k_1 p_1 \left(1 - \frac{p_2}{p_1}\right) \sqrt{\frac{T_0}{T_1}} & \frac{p_2}{p_1} \geq 0.999 \\ C p \rho_0 \sqrt{\frac{T_0}{T_1}} \left(1 - \left(\frac{\frac{p_2}{p_1} - b}{1 - b}\right)^2\right)^{0.5} & b < \frac{p_2}{p_1} < 0.999 \\ C p_1 \rho_0 \sqrt{\frac{T_0}{T_1}} & \frac{p_2}{p_1} \leq b \end{cases} \quad (1)$$

Liner gain k_1 is expressed as follows:

$$k_1 = 1000C\rho_0\sqrt{1 - \left(\frac{0.999 - b}{1 - b}\right)^2} \tag{2}$$

Where G is mass flow rate, [kg/s]; C is sonic conductance, [m³/(s·Pa)]; b is critical pressure ratio; p_1 is upstream pressure, [Pa]; T_1 is upstream temperature, [K].

3.2   Gas State Equation

The gas in each chamber always meets the gas state equation when the piston move right or left. When gas state equation is deviated to time and then the pressure response in each chamber can be illustrated as follows:

$$V_d\frac{dp_d}{dt} = -G_d R T_d + p_d S_d u + \frac{p_d V_d}{T_d}\frac{dT_d}{dt} \tag{3}$$

$$V_c\frac{dp_c}{dt} = G_c R T_c - p_c S_c u + \frac{p_c V_c}{T_c}\frac{dT_c}{dt} \tag{4}$$

Where S stands for piston area, [m²]; V is chamber volume, [m³]; u is the velocity of piston, [m/s]; Subscripts d, c stand for discharge and charge chamber separately.

3.3   Energy Conservation Equation

There is mass flow out or into the chambers, then each chamber can be treated as variable quality system, the inner energy, enthalpy, work and heat output or input the system meet the energy conservation. Handle energy conservation equation the same as gas state equation, and then the temperature response in chamber can be obtained as follows:

$$m_d C_v\frac{dT_d}{dt} = -R T_d G_d + p_d S_d u + h S_{hd}(T_a - T_d) \tag{5}$$

$$m_c C_v\frac{dT_c}{dt} = C_v G_c(T_a - T_c) + R T_a G_c - p_c S_c u + h S_{hc}(T_a - T_c) \tag{6}$$

In these equations, C_v is specify heat ratio in constant volume, [J/(kg·K)]; h is heat transfer coefficient, [W/(m²·K)]; S_h is heat transfer area, [m²]; Subscripts a stands for atmosphere state.

3.4   Kinematic Equation

According to the second law of Newton, the kinematic equation of piston is:

$$M\frac{du}{dt} = (p_{da} - p_{db})S_{da} + (p_{ra} - p_{rb})S_{ra} + (p_{bb} - p_{ba})S_{ba} - F_f \tag{7}$$

The friction of piston is so complex that several of friction models have been studied in [13], and the often used models are Coulomb friction, viscous model and Stribeck model. Here we use Coulomb friction and viscous model as a mixed model for its relatively well accuracy and easy setting, so the friction force is

$$F_f = cu + \begin{cases} F_{sf} & u = 0 \\ F_{df} sign(u) & u \neq 0 \end{cases} \tag{8}$$

3.5 Pressure Response in the Tank

Tank is used with booster valve simultaneously for restraining output pressure fluctuation. So the output flow is decided by the pressure in the tank, and the pressure in the tank depends on the flow output and input the tank. When pressure inside the tank increases, then flow into the tank reduces and out flow increases, and vice versa. Thus, the pressure inside tank will be balanced, and the opening of check valve depends on the feedback pressure, so the pressure fluctuation can be reduced.

Tank has a large heat-exchange area that it can change heat with surroundings sufficiently, so it was treated as isothermal, and then the pressure response in the tank is:

$$\frac{dp_t}{dt} = \frac{RT_a}{V_t}(G_{in} - G_{out}) \tag{9}$$

G_{in} is the air flow into the tank.

$$G_{in} = p_b f(p_{boost} - p_{tank}) \rho_0 \sqrt{\frac{T_0}{T_b}} \varphi\left(\frac{p_t}{p_b}\right) \tag{10}$$

And G_{out} is the air flow out of the tank.

$$G_{out} = p_t C_{th} \rho_0 \sqrt{\frac{T_0}{T_a}} \varphi\left(\frac{p_a}{p_t}\right) \tag{11}$$

4   Simulation and Experiment Analysis

4.1   Modeling the Simulation Model

The mathematic model in preceding section will be transformed to Simulink in order to compare the characteristics of VBA and BVER. As we know, there are four chambers and six chambers for VBA and BVER separately. Three control equations will be used to illustrate the characteristics of each chamber, and then the numbers of control equations will up to 14 and 20 for VBA and BVER. A heavy work should be done in order to model the booster valves. To minimize the amount of work, the chambers are classified as charge chambers and discharge chambers, the Eqs. (1), (4), (7) were used for discharged chambers and Eqs. (1), (5), (8) were used for charge chambers. Then five standard subsystems were modeled first as shown in Fig. 2, the parameters of chambers can be redefined in each subsystem. All of these subsystems can be called repeatedly.

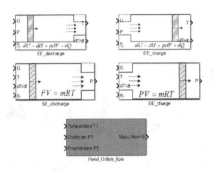

Fig. 2. The standard subsystem used for booster valve modeling

By using these stand subsystems, Simulink model of VBA and BVER can be established much easier, the variable step solver of Dormand-Prince was used to solve the differential equation above, then the pressure response of booster valve can be solved.

4.2   Boost Ratio of Booster Valve

Boost ratio reflects the performance of booster valve, it helps to decrease the supply pressure and save energy. Analysis indicates that boost ratio of BVER is affected by coefficient of regulator, supply pressure and the area ratio of recovery chamber to boost chamber.

Influence of regulator coefficient. Figure 3 shows the output pressure of VBA and BVER with different regulator coefficient. It suggested that BVER's boost ratio increased up to 20 % compared with VBA.

Influence of supply pressure. Pressure response inside the tank are shown in Fig. 4 when supply pressure change from 200 kPa to 500 kPa. The output pressure of BVER is much higher than VBA. So it can further reduce the supply pressure with BVER, it will helps to save energy.

Influence of diameter ratio. The boost ratio of BVER is also affected by diameter ratio of recovery chamber and boost chamber. The change of boost ratio is shown in Fig. 5. It increases firstly and reduces afterward with the increase of diameter ratio, and it reaches the largest boost ratio for BVER when the diameter ratio equal to 1.3 to 1.5. So BVER studied in this paper has largest boost ratio when recovery chamber diameter equals to 100 mm.

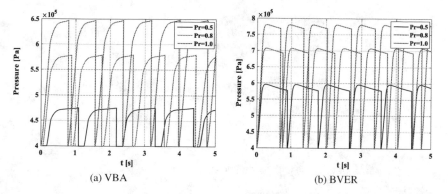

(a) VBA   (b) BVER

Fig. 3. Pressure response curves with different Pr

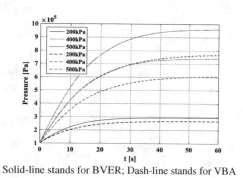

Solid-line stands for BVER; Dash-line stands for VBA

Fig. 4. Pressure response in the tank with different supply pressure

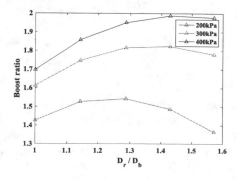

Fig. 5. The boost ratio with different pressure and diameter ratio

4.3   Pressure Fluctuation of Booster Valve

Booster valve is always used with air tank to obtain stable pressure output. For the opening of tank is fixed in application, the pressure fluctuation in the tank only depends

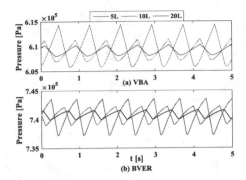

Fig. 6. The pressure fluctuation in the tank

on the tank volume. The pressure fluctuation inside the tank is illustrated in Fig. 6, it decreases when tank volume increases. When the tank volume is bigger than 10 L, then the fluctuation is smaller than 1 % and can be neglected.

4.4   Energy Efficient Analysis of Booster Valve

BVER can recover energy exhaust from drive chamber for secondary using each cycle. Therefore, it has much higher energy-efficiency than VBA which exhausts the power to atmosphere directly. Base on the assumption (3), air power [14, 15] of BVER can be expressed simply as Eq. (12).

$$P = p_a Q_a \ln \frac{p_s}{p_a} \tag{12}$$

The efficient of booster valve is ratio of output to input energy. According to Eq. 12, the energy input to booster valve is

$$E = \int_0^t p_a Q_a \ln \frac{p_s}{p_a} dt = p_a (V_{bb} + V_{da}) \ln \frac{p_s}{p_a} \tag{13}$$

Where V_{bb} and V_{da} are the volume of drive and boost chamber. Equation (13) suggests that input energy only depends on supply pressure on the condition that the volume is constant. Then the input energy is constant in each cycle with constant supply pressure. So, we just need to compare the energy output of VBA and BVER. The air power of VBA and BVER are shown in Fig. 7, it is obviously that the peak value and average valve of BVER are greater than VBA, it means that BVER has more energy output.

To measure the air power output from the tank [16], the test schematic diagram is design as Fig. 8.

The test and simulation results are shown in Fig. 9. The simulation results has a little time delay than experiment results, and this is the isothermal model of tank whose pressure response is slower which lead to the deviation for pressure response in

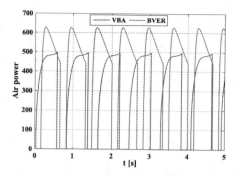

Fig. 7. The air power of VBA and BVER

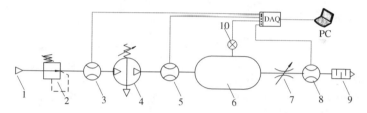

1-Air source 2-Regulator 3- Air power meter 4-Booster valve 5-Flow meter 6- Air tank
7-Throttle valve 8-Air power meter 9.Silencer 10. Pressure sensor

Fig. 8. The schematic diagram of booster valve test

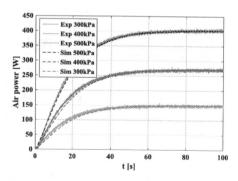

Fig. 9. The air power output from the tank

isothermal tank [17]. So it is a good consistent of experiment and simulation. Then several measurement results were summarized in Fig. 10, and the energy efficient of BVER is 5–10 % higher than VBA according to different supply pressure. So it will help to save energy in long time running.

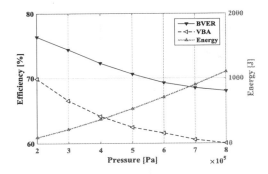

Fig. 10. The efficiency of VBA and BVER

5   Conclusion

A new type booster valve with energy recovery was proposed in this paper, its characteristics of boost ratio, pressure fluctuation and energy efficient were studied systematically. The mathematic model was verified by experiment, and it proved that BVER has much better performance compared with traditional booster valve. Through this analysis we can conclude that:

(1) BVER has much higher boost ratio than VBA, the boost ratio increases up to 15–25 %;
(2) BVER can obtain its largest boost ratio when diameter ratio of recovery chamber to boost chamber ratio equals to 1.3–1.5;
(3) The output pressure is stable when air tank is larger than 10 L, and the pressure fluctuation is less than 1 percent;
(4) BVER has average 8 percent higher efficiency than VBA, and it can recover energy to save energy in each stroke.

This study proposed a reference for booster valve design and energy saving. A further work should be done to analyze the relationship of characteristics response and structure parameters, and it will propose an optimization scheme for design of booster valve.

References

1. Dragan, S., Ivana, I., Slobodan, D.: Energy efficiency-the innovation ways for smart energy, the future towards modern utilities, pp. 151–174 (2012)
2. Terashima, Y., Kawakami, Y., Kawai, S.: An approach for energy conservation in pneumatic systems. In: Proceedings of Japan Fluid Power System Society, pp. 157–163 (2000) (in Japanese)
3. Liu, Z.: Design and experimental research into air driven gas booster. Dalian Maritime University (2010) (in Chinese)

4. Peter, B.: Pneumatic Drivers—System Design. Modeling and Control. Springer, New York (2007)
5. Wang, H., Xiong, W., Wang, X.: Research on the static characteristics of air driven gas booster. In: Proceedings of the 7th JFPS International Symposium on Fluid Power, Toyama, (2008)
6. Li, Z., Zhao, Y., Li, L.: Mathematical modeling of compression processes in air-driven boosters. Appl. Thermal Eng. **27**, 1516–1521 (2007)
7. Yan, S., Jia, G., Cai, M., Xu, W.: Study on the dynamics of local pressure boosting pneumatic system. Math. Prob. Eng. **2015**, 1–11 (2015)
8. Yan, S., Cai, M.: Dimensionless study on output flow characteristics of expansion energy used pneumatic pressure booster. J. Dyn. Syst. Measur. Cont. **135**, 1–8 (2013)
9. Saidur, R., Rahim, N.A., Hasanuzzaman, M.: A review on compressed-air energy use and energy savings. Renew. Sustain. Energy Rev. **14**, 1135–1153 (2010)
10. Sanville, F.E.: A new method of specifying the flow capacity of pneumatic fluid power valves. In: Proceedings of the 2nd Fluid Power Symposium, Guildford, pp 37–47 (1971)
11. ISO 6358-1 Pneumatic fluid power-Determination of flow-rate characteristics of components using compressible fluids (2013)
12. Kaasa, G.-O., Chapple, P.J., Lie, B.: Modeling of an electro-pneumatic cylinder actuator for nonlinear and adaptive control, with application to clutch actuation in heavy-duty trucks. In: Proceedings of the 3rd FPNI - Ph.D. Symposium, Terrassa (2004)
13. Paul, G.H., Garret, E.O.: Modelling and identification of industrial pneumatic drive system. Int. J. Adv. Manuf. Technol. **58**, 1075–1086 (2012)
14. Cai, M., Kawashima, K., Kagawa, T.: Power assessment of flowing compressed air. J. Fluid Eng. **128**, 402–405 (2006)
15. Cai, M., Kagawa, T.: Energy consumption assessment and energy loss analysis in pneumatic system. Chin. J. Mech. Eng. **43**, 69–74 (2007)
16. Cai, M., Kagawa, T.: Design and application of air power meter in compressed air system. In: Proceedings EcoDesign, Tokyo (2001)
17. Kagawa, T., Cai, M.: Measurement and Control of Compressible Fluid. Japan Industrial Publishing, Tokyo (2010)

Stability Simulation Analysis of a Hybrid Wind-Battery System

Jun Sun[1], Lijian Sheng[1], Yong Sun[2], Zhenkai Zhou[3], and Rong Fu[3(✉)]

[1] State Grid Electric Power Research Institute, Nanjing 210061, Jiangsu Province, China
[2] Jingsu Posts and Telecommunications Planning and Designing Institute Co. LTD., Nanjing 210006, Jiangsu Province, China
[3] College of Automation, Nanjing University of Posts and Telecommunications, Nanjing 210023, Jiangsu Province, China
furong@njupt.edu.cn

Abstract. This paper focuses on the control of a hybrid wind-battery system. The mathematical model of dynamic behavior of the hybrid wind-battery system is established. We figure out there is inter-area low frequency oscillation caused by wind power fluctuation, and propose an approach for obtaining the sensitivities between eigenvalue changes and wind power fluctuation. Then a lithium-ion based battery energy storage model is designed to limit the damping active power associated with inter-area low frequency oscillation to reduce the electrical power oscillation, increase the damping and reinforce the dynamic stability of the systems. A simulation of small signal stability and forced power oscillation stability in two-area power system also shows the necessity of the hybrid wind-battery system.

Keywords: Wind farm · Battery storage · Eigenvalue sensitivity · Oscillation stability

1 Introduction

With the increase in the proportion of wind turbines in the power system, uncertainty and intermittency of the wind bring challenge to the safe and stable operation of the power system. Therefore, the concept of wind co-generation storage systems is proposed. Wind co-generation storage systems, effectively, are made up of wind power system and energy storage system. In [1], carrying out the research of wind co-generation storage systems is important theoretical and practical value to solve problems of development of wind power generation, and improve the uncertainty of wind power.

However, with the large-scale development of wind power, wind power characteristics increasingly negative impact on the grid significantly. Low frequency oscillation is an important factor on affecting the power system dynamic security. On the glorious trend of wind power, the paper verifies that the gust is a kind of resonant forced disturbance source [2]. Several published papers have discussed how to analysis the forced power oscillation of the power grid on DFIG-based wind farms [3, 4]. It is reported that

L. Zhang et al. (Eds.): AsiaSim 2016/SCS AutumnSim 2016, Part III, CCIS 645, pp. 154–163, 2016.
DOI: 10.1007/978-981-10-2669-0_17

when the disturbance frequency of wind signal is close to the natural oscillation frequency of the system, it will cause the system resonance. Power system forced power oscillation theory has been used to explain the disturbance caused by wind power oscillation. Simulation analysis of Machine two-zone system and New England 39-bus system contribute to a better understanding of forced power oscillation caused by the periodic load disturbances.

For the control of wind turbines, the following articles give many different strategies. In [5], eigenvalue sensitivity with respect to machine and control parameters is performed to assess their impacts on system stability. In [6], with studying the maximum power point tracking mode and the maximum power point tracking mode with additional virtual inertia control, the proposed power injection model of double-fed wind turbine can be better analyze small signal stability of power system. Furthermore, in [7], the designed hybrid PID plus fuzzy logic controller (FLC) damping controller has the best damping characteristics to improve the stability performance of the DFIG-based offshore wind farm. In [8], DFIG's wide-area damping controller designed in terms of pole placement technology can effectively suppress the low frequency oscillation of the interconnected power systems.

Energy storage system (ESS) can solve intermittent wind power problems when the wind farms combine to the grid. Advantage of fast response and high short-term power throughput capacity of the battery energy storage system (BESS) contributes to a new power frequency modulation technology [9]. Among the many kinds of storage batteries, lithium-ion batteries, especially all solid-state lithium-ion batteries, become the first choice because of its many advantages, but the material and cost is the constraint of large-scale use [10]. In [11], double-closed-loop active disturbance rejection control is proposed in accordance with the advantages of BESS, however, the control strategy is mainly applied voltage symmetrical case. In [12], an advanced control strategy is designed to effectively stabilize the short-term fluctuations in wind power. In [13], it is aimed at the application characteristics of load shifting of energy storage system to put forward an active balance control strategy with the target of the maximize use of battery capacity. Before studying the performance of a practical power system, a multi-machine power system should be studied.

In this paper, the mathematical model of dynamic behavior of the hybrid wind-battery system is established firstly. And then inter-area low frequency oscillation caused by wind power fluctuation is investigated and approach for obtaining the sensitivities between eigenvalue changes and wind power fluctuation is proposed. On this base, a lithium-ion based battery energy storage model is designed to limit the oscillation. Finally a simulation of small signal stability and forced power oscillation stability in two-area power system in Matlab/Simulink shows the necessity of the hybrid wind-battery system.

2 Hybrid Wind-Battery System

In a hybrid wind-battery system, a wind farm and a battery energy storage system (BESS) are linked to a point of common coupling. As the wind turbine mechanical output can be affected by various factors, such as wind speed. When a wind farm connected to a multi-machine power system, it is easily caused low-frequency oscillatory. The battery energy storage system is used to solve the problem of stability. The schematic diagram of hybrid wind-battery system is shown in Fig. 1.

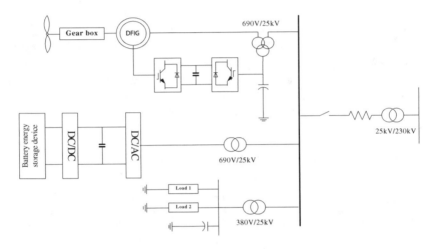

Fig. 1. Schematic diagram of hybrid wind-battery system

2.1 DFIG Based Wind Farm

The DFIG based wind generator model can be divided into six parts: wind speed model, aerodynamic model, pitch angle control model, mechanical drive model, DFIG model and control system. As the running of the model is very complex, so we need to do assume that:

– Ignore the stator and rotor currents harmonic component;
– Ignore the effects of the motor core hysteresis, eddy current loss and magnetic saturation;
– Parameter of the rotor side converted to the stator side;
– The positive directions of physical quantities are selected according to the motor practice.

   The equivalent circuit diagram of DFIG is shown in Fig. 2.

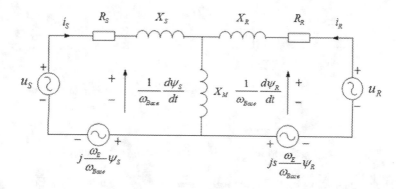

Fig. 2. DFIG equivalent circuit diagram

where subscript 's' stands for stator, subscript 'r' stands for rotor, Ψ is the flux, R is the resistance, X is the reactance, I is the current, U is the voltage and ω_{Base} is the base value for the rotate speed of the grid.

The voltage of DFIG in synchronous reference frame described with the following equations:

$$\begin{cases} u_{DS} = R_S i_{DS} - \dfrac{\omega_E}{\omega_{base}}\psi_{QS} + \dfrac{1}{\omega_{base}}\dfrac{d\psi_{DS}}{dt} \\[2mm] u_{QS} = R_S i_{QS} + \dfrac{\omega_E}{\omega_{base}}\psi_{DS} + \dfrac{1}{\omega_{base}}\dfrac{d\psi_{QS}}{dt} \\[2mm] u_{DR} = R_R i_{DR} - \dfrac{1}{\omega_{base}}\dfrac{d\theta_R}{dt}\psi_{QR} + \dfrac{1}{\omega_{base}}\dfrac{d\psi_{DR}}{dt} \\[2mm] u_{QR} = R_R i_{QR} + \dfrac{1}{\omega_{base}}\dfrac{d\theta_R}{dt}\psi_{DR} + \dfrac{1}{\omega_{base}}\dfrac{d\psi_{QR}}{dt} \end{cases} \tag{1}$$

Where ω_E is the stator electric speed and rotor angle θ_R is the rotor speed for the time integral of the electromagnetic field.

2.2 Battery Energy Storage Model

As shown in Fig. 1, the battery energy storage model includes a battery model, DC/DC converter and DC/AC inverter.

Here we used lithium-ion battery as the storage device. As shown in Fig. 3, the battery model consists of a voltage controlled voltage source in series with constant resistances and capacitor. The voltage controlled voltage source is used to represent the non-linear relationship between the state-of-charge (SOC) and the open circuit voltage of the battery.

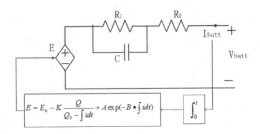

Fig. 3. Lithium-ion battery equivalent circuit diagram

The mathematical model of the lithium-ion battery is described by Eq. (2) as follow:

$$E = E_0 - K\frac{Q}{Q_0 - \int idt} + A\exp(-B \cdot \int idt) \qquad (2)$$

Where,

E = no-load voltage (V)

E_0 = battery constant voltage (V)

K = polarization voltage (V)

Q = battery capacity (Ah)

Q_0 = initial battery capacity (Ah)

$\int idt$ = actual battery charge (Ah)

A = exponential zone amplitude (V)

B = exponential zone time constant inverse $(Ah)^{-1}$

As the model was not intended to simulate long term behavior in which a self-discharge resistance would be meaningful, the battery model does not include this resistance. Moreover, the effect of temperature on the battery performance has not been accounted because the battery is expected to operate in a relatively narrow range of temperature conditions. We can get K, A and B from the data from the actual 3.4 V/3Ah lithium-ion battery charging and discharging curves. In order to meet the demand of power, we make a battery group through series-parallel connection of the single battery model. The parameters of the battery group are shown in Table 1.

Table 1. Li-Ion battery group parameters

Parameter	Value	Unit
Q	200	Ah
E_0	3.4	V
R_1	0.0004	Ω
R_2	0.00023	Ω
C	2000	uF
K	0.07	V

3   Oscillatory Stability Problem Description

Many large weakly interconnected power systems have the problem of inter-area oscillations. With large wind farms connected to the grid, the wind speed fluctuation causes low frequency oscillations and forced power oscillations. It is necessary to reduce the electrical power oscillation, increase the damping and reinforce the dynamic stability of the systems.

As the wind turbine output power changes with the fluctuation of wind speed, the grid will continue to suffer the interference of the wind power source. The change of wind speed is random in a certain time and space, but from the long statistical results, there is a distribution in the change of wind speed. In principle, the wind speed model can be divided into four parts: average wind (v_{wa}), gust wind (v_{wg}), ramp wind (v_{wr}), noise wind (v_{wn}). As v_{wg} can be described as the following equations:

$$v_{wg} = \begin{cases} 0, t \leq T_{1G} \\ v_{\cos}, T_{1G} \leq t < T_{1G} + T_G \\ 0, t \geq T_{1G} + T_G \end{cases}$$

$$v_{\cos} = (v_{wg}\text{max}/2)\{1 - \cos 2\pi[(t/T_G) - (T_{1G}/T_G)]\}$$

(3)

Where T_G is the period, T_{1G} is the start time; $v_{wg\text{max}}$ is the maximum value of the gust wind speed.

The continuous cyclical wind speed disturbances can lead to forced power oscillations of power system.

Here we put a large wind farm into a two-area four-machine system. As shown in Fig. 4, the system consists of two similar areas connected by two transmission lines. Each area consists of two generating units, each having a rating of 900 MVA and 20 kV. In Area 1, a wind farm with rated capacity of 230 MW is connected to the system. We use the Lyapunov linearization method to obtain the system state equation:

$$\dot{X} = AX$$

(4)

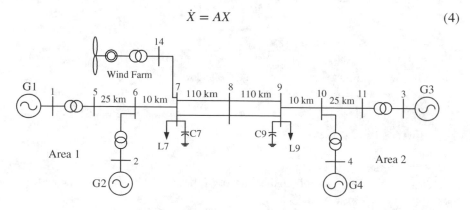

Fig. 4. Two-area four-machine system

Where, A is the state matrix of the system, and the eigenvalues of A reflect the stability about the system.

(1) A real eigenvalue corresponds to a non-oscillation mode. Negative real eigenvalue represents decay mode, and positive real eigenvalue represents aperiodic instability.
(2) Complex eigenvalues always exist as conjugate pair, in the form of,

$$\lambda = \alpha \pm j\omega \tag{5}$$

Each pair of conjugate complex eigenvalues corresponds to an electromechanical oscillation mode. The real part of the complex eigenvalues denotes the damping effect of the oscillation mode, while the imaginary part reflects the oscillation frequency. The oscillation frequency f is:

$$f = \frac{\omega}{2\pi} \tag{6}$$

And damping ratio ζ is:

$$\zeta = \frac{-\alpha}{\sqrt{\alpha^2 + \omega^2}} \tag{7}$$

It can be seen from the Table 2, with the wind farm connected the system, the damping ratio of the local oscillation mode 1 (Area 1) and inter-area oscillation mode increases from 8.31 % to 10.06 %, and the damping ratio of inter-area oscillation mode increases significantly from 3.77 % to 10.09 %.

Table 2. Eigenvalue analysis of electromechanical modes

Mode	Eigenvalues	f/Hz	ζ/%
Without wind farm			
Local (Area 1)	$-0.5665 \pm 6.7940i$	1.0813	8.31
Local (Area 2)	$-0.5572 \pm 6.6015i$	1.0507	8.41
Inter-area	$-0.1295 \pm 3.4272i$	0.5455	3.77
With wind farm (230 MW)			
Local (Area 1)	$-0.6742 \pm 6.6701i$	1.0616	10.06
Local (Area 2)	$-0.5744 \pm 6.5425i$	1.0413	8.75
Inter-area	$-0.2513 \pm 2.4291i$	0.3866	10.29

4   Control of the Bess

DC/DC converter is used to enable a constant output voltage from the BESS. DC/AC inverter plays an important role in the control of the BESS. It interfaces the batteries to the utility, regulates the battery charging/discharging.

The double loop control mode is used in the DC/AC inverter. The external power control loop provides active and reactive power command to achieve the desired system response. In order to face different condition, instantaneous power method and average power method are both used. As instantaneous power method may have an impact on the power quality, this paper uses the average power method for control. Besides, the synchronizing scheme ensures the d-axis of dq frame is aligned with the grid voltage vector. So the q-axis voltage (u_q) is equal to zero. The power calculation is shown as:

$$P = u_d i_d, Q = u_d i_q \qquad (8)$$

The control loop is shown in Fig. 5, proportional-integral (*PI*) control is used to get reference input i_{d_ref}, i_{q_ref} for the current loop from the difference between P, Q and P_{ref}, Q_{ref}. Then we compare current reference value with actual value (i_d and i_q) through *PI* controller, so can get the reference voltage. In this paper, feed-forward control value ($-L\omega i_q$ and $-L\omega i_d$) is added in the internal current loop regulation, so that the impact of grid voltage (U_d and U_q) on the system would reduce. After decoupling operation, we can get control value of the DC/AC inverter (U_{d_ref} and U_{q_ref}).

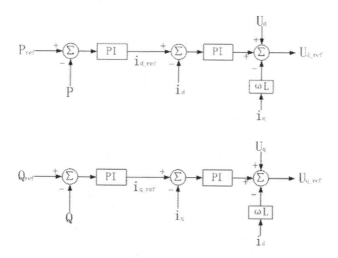

Fig. 5. *PQ* controller of DC/AC inverter

5   Case Study

In this case study, the system in Fig. 4 is used to analysis the forced power oscillation caused by wind farm. Here, a 5 % step change is introduced in the voltage reference of Machine G_1 in area 1 at t = 5.0 s. Here we set T_G in Eq. (3) to 1/0.3866, so the wind frequency is equal to the oscillation frequency of inter-area. The transmission voltage, current and power of the two tie-lines is shown in Fig. 6.

We also did a same simulation with gust wind but can't cause forced power oscillation. The result is shown in Fig. 7.

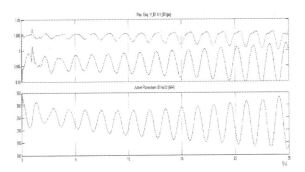

Fig. 6. Forced power oscillation diagram

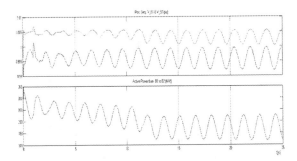

Fig. 7. Without forced power oscillation diagram

Here we can see that forced power oscillation can cause larger power oscillation of the system. In 25 s, the amplitude of power oscillation in Fig. 6 is almost twice over it in Fig. 7, and is growing larger. Therefore, it is necessary to solve the stability problem caused by forced power oscillation.

6   Conclusion

Result of mathematical analysis and simulation of two-area four-machine system shows that the wind turbine's access is likely to excite the low frequency oscillation and forced power oscillations of AC system. The main factor causing the phenomenon is that the frequency of wind fluctuation is close to the oscillation frequency of an area. Therefore, a hybrid wind-battery system is needed to reduce the electrical power oscillation, and increase the damping and reinforce the dynamic stability of system by appropriate control strategy of DC/AC inverter of the battery system.

References

1. Ye, H., Song, Y., Liu, Y.: Forced power oscillation response analysis and oscillation type discrimination. Proc. CSEE **33**(34), 197–204 (2013). (in Chinese)
2. Elkington, K., Ghandhari, M.: Non-linear power oscillation damping controllers for doubly fed induction generators in wind farms. IET Renew. Power Gener. **7**(2), 172–179 (2013)
3. Zhang, Z., Hu, Z., Hu, M.: Delay-dependent stability analysis and robust damping control of power system with wind power integration. Proc. CSEE **32**(34), 8–16 (2012)
4. Wang, L., Truong, D.: Stability enhancement of DFIG-based offshore wind farm fed to a multi-machine system using a STATCON. IEEE Trans. Power Syst. **28**(3), 2882–2889 (2013)
5. Yang, L., Xu, Z., Østergaard, J.: Oscillatory stability and eigenvalue sensitivity analysis of a DFIG wind turbine system. IEEE Trans. Energy Convers. **26**(1), 328–339 (2011)
6. Zeni, L., Rudolph, A.J., Münster-Swendsen, J.: Virtual inertia for variable speed wind turbines. Wind Energy **16**(8), 1225–1239 (2013)
7. Aissaoui, A.G., Tahour, A., Abid, M.: Power control of wind turbine based on fuzzy controllers. Energy Procedia **42**(42), 163–172 (2013)
8. Rahim, A.H.M.A., Alam, M.A., Kandlawala, M.F.: Dynamic performance improvement of an isolated wind turbine induction generator. Comput. Electr. Eng. **35**(4), 594–607 (2009)
9. Xu, G., Xu, L., Morrow, D.J.: Wind turbines with energy storage for power smoothing and FRT enhancement. Power Energy Soc. Gen. Meet. IEEE **5**(22), 1–7 (2011)
10. Mandic, G., Nasiri, A., Ghotbi, E.: Lithium-ion capacitor energy storage integrated with variable speed wind turbines for power smoothing. IEEE J. Emerg. Sel. Top. Power Electron. **1**(4), 287–295 (2013)
11. Zheng, T.W., Feng, L., Xiao, X.Y.: Double-closed-loop active disturbance rejection control design for the charging/discharging of lithium-battery energy storage system. Electric Mach. Control **17**(11), 20–27 (2013)
12. Vigueras-Rodríguez, A., Sørensen, P., Cutululis, N.A.: Wind model for low frequency power fluctuations in offshore wind farms. Wind Energy **13**(5), 471–482 (2009)
13. Chen, M., Zhigang, L.U., Liu, Y.: Research on optimal peak load shifting strategy of battery energy storage system operated in constant power mode. Power Syst. Technol. **36**(9), 232–237 (2012)

The Application of Spark-Based Gaussian Mixture Model for Farm Environmental Data Analysis

Honglin Pang[1,2], Li Deng[1,2(✉)], Ling Wang[1,2], and Minrui Fei[1,2]

[1] School of Mechatronics Engineering and Automation, Shanghai University,
Shanghai 200072, People's Republic of China
[2] Shanghai Key Laboratory of Power Station Automation Technology,
Shanghai 200072, People's Republic of China
martinphl@163.com, {dengli,wangling}@shu.edu.cn,
mrfei@staff.shu.edu.cn

Abstract. For fully taking into account the feature of environmental data set the Gaussian mixture model (GMM) is combined with the Dirichlet Process (DP) to solve the problem of specifying the initial cluster number. The Gibbs sampling algorithm is also used as the substitute of the Expectation Maximization algorithm to estimate the parameter of the model with Dirichlet Process. The clustering process is implemented under the framework of Spark so as to deal with farm environmental data set stored in distributed computer cluster. Experiment results with external criterion show that the improved clustering method has a better ability in data anomaly detection compared with other common cluster methods. Farm environmental data anomaly detection is implemented by the improved clustering method.

Keywords: Gaussian Mixture Model · Dirichlet Process · Gibbs sampling · Spark · Anomaly detection

1 Introduction

With the development of agricultural technology, the solution including the greenhouse intelligent monitoring system and agricultural expert knowledge database accumulated a large amount of data, machine learning can guide the production of agriculture in an effective way. Many successful application rely on machine learning, such as the establishment of forecasting model of crop yield [1], environmental anomaly detection [2], plant variety characteristic division [3] and so on.

At present, the common unsupervised methods, such as density based DBSCAN which is sensitive to user set parameters and different density datasets need to set different scanning radius and cluster points [4], FCM clustering improved by hierarchical clustering can only find data clusters in globularity and the effect is not ideal [5]; on the other hand, with the expansion of the agricultural production and the distribution storage of dataset, the defect of low ability of single computer operation faced with large dataset is getting serious day by day.

© Springer Science+Business Media Singapore 2016
L. Zhang et al. (Eds.): AsiaSim 2016/SCS AutumnSim 2016, Part III, CCIS 645, pp. 164–173, 2016.
DOI: 10.1007/978-981-10-2669-0_18

Aimed at the above problems, we introduce Gaussian mixture model (GMM) to approximately model the feature distribution of data set. As a generative probabilistic model known as common machine learning model, GMM performs well in image segmentation and background of target extraction [5]. We first introduce the Dirichlet processs (DP) into GMM to solve the problem of specifying the initial cluster number, DP has been widely applied in clustering and topic modeling, label extraction etc. Such as Fox [6] using the cluster property of Dirichlet process to determine the number of targets in maneuvering target tracking; Orbanz [7] introduced DP into Markov model, and use Gibbs sampling to imply the automatic generation for the number of image segmentation regions.

In this paper, An improved GMM clustering method implemented under the framework of Spark is proposed. The prior and posterior distribution of the model is analyzed according to the environmental dataset. We use Gibbs sampling method to estimate the parameter of the model. The validity of the distributed clustering method has been deployed on Spark and verified via multi-method comparison.

2 Dataset and Pre-processing

The farm environmental dataset comprises about forty thousand, and each of the samples consists of 55 attributes, including some environmental index such as temperature, related humidity (RH), CO2 and photosynthetic active radiation (PAR) sum and some information about the state of equipment in the greenhouse. According to the information of the suitable growth environmental indexes for tomato given by the agriculture expert that works for the greenhouse, temperature, related humidity and CO2 are chosen as the main attributes of the dataset for analysis. Suitable growth environmental indexes are shown in Table 1.

Table 1. Suitable growth environmental indexes

	Daytime	Night
Temperature (°C)	18 ~ 30	10 ~ 18
RH (%)	80 ~ 95	
CO_2 (ppm)	Larger than 300	Larger than 400

Since the daytime changes along with the season, in order to make use of the suitable indexes in Table 1 for anomaly data detection, we calculate the time of sunrise and sunset with date and latitude and longitude coordinates so as to distinguish daytime from night.

Actually, the environmental data is affected by many factors during sampling process, the dataset exists missing values and needs data cleaning. Referring to the common way of dealing with the incomplete dataset, we use the interpolation method to fill the missing data. For example, dataset exists 90 pieces of loss record between 23:10:00 December 10 and 6:55:00 December 11. Since the sampling period of dataset is 5 min, the situation belongs to the interval data missing so the linear interpolation method is used to complement the data here, part of the data after completion are shown in Table 2.

Table 2. Three dimentional dataset after data cleaning

Temperature (°C)	RH(%)	CO$_2$ (ppm)	Date
...	...	...	...
15.30	90.81	430.23	10-12-2014 23:10:00
15.30	91	428.55	10-12-2014 23:15:00
15.23	91.09	426.87	10-12-2014 23:20:00
...	...	...	...
11.64	99.22	282.39	11-12-2014 06:45:00
11.57	99.31	280.71	11-12-2014 06:50:00
11.47	100	279.03	11-12-2014 06:55:00
...	...	...	...

3 Model

3.1 Dirichlet Process Gaussian Mixture Model

Since GMM can smoothly approximate density distribution of any shape, we use GMM to describe the environmental dataset. GMM is a kind of generative probabilistic model and finite mixture model. The data points are generated by K Gaussian distributions, each Gaussian distribution has its own mean μ_j and covariance matrix Σ_j, and the proportion of the data point numbers in each Gaussian distribution is decided by the prior distribution $\tau = (\tau, \ldots, \tau_K)$.

However, the weakness of GMM is that the original cluster number must be given before the process of parameter estimation. By designating the prior distribution τ of GMM as DP, Dirichlet Process Gaussian mixture model (DPGMM) can be seen as a combination for the extension of finite mixture model.

Dirichlet process (DP) [4] is a distribution seen as an extension of a Dirichlet distribution with infinite dimension. The construction of the DP used here is the Chinese restaurant process (CRP).

Visualize a Chinese restaurant with potential infinite number of tables. Consider the data points to cluster as clients to the table in the restaurant, and assigning data to the cluster can be imagined like clients sit around table. The CRP works in the following way, the first client will sit at the first table, and the nth client will sit at:

$$table\ k \quad with\ probability \quad \frac{n_k}{\alpha_0 + n - 1}, 1 \leq k \leq K \tag{1a}$$

$$new\ table\ k + 1 \quad with\ probability \quad \frac{\alpha_0}{\alpha_0 + n - 1} \tag{1b}$$

where n_k is the number of clients sat at the table k, and K is the number of all the tables (clusters). Equation (1b) guarantees that there exists always a little probability to generate a new cluster. Clients can be reallocated after the first allocation is carried out.

The CRP method to solve the DPGMM is used with a potentially infinite number of components (clusters). The farm environmental data to cluster are represented as draws from a Gaussian distribution whose parameters $\theta_{z_i}(\mu_{z_i}, \Sigma_{z_i})$ are independent with each other and the base distribution G_0 is generated by a Gaussian-inverse-Wishart distribution. The mean vector is μ_{z_i} whose subscript correspond to a cluster with index z_i (i.e. $z_i = j$ indicates that ith data is assigned to jth cluster). The covariance matrix is Σ_{z_i}. Formally, to cluster n farm environmental data points $X = \{x_1, \ldots, x_n\}$, where each data points x_i is formed by d dimensional attributes $x_i = (c_{i1}, \ldots, c_{id})$.

3.2 Model Probability Distribution

The Distribution of DPGMM that models our problem can be hierarchically expressed as:

$$x_i = (c_{i_1}, \ldots, c_{i_d})|\mu_i, z_i, \Sigma_i^{-1} \sim N(\mu_{z_i}, \Sigma_{z_i}), i = 1, \ldots, n \tag{2}$$

$$\mu_{z_i} = (\mu_{z_i1}, \ldots, \mu_{z_id})|\Sigma_{z_i}^{-1} \sim N(\varepsilon_0, (\gamma_0\Sigma_{z_i}^{-1})^{-1}), 1 \leq z_i \leq K \tag{3}$$

$$\Sigma_{z_i}^{-1} \sim W(\lambda_0, \beta_0), 1 \leq z_i \leq K \tag{4}$$

$$z_i \sim Multi(\Pi), i = 1, \ldots, n \tag{5}$$

$$\Pi = (\pi_1, \ldots, \pi_{K+1}) \sim DP(G_0, \alpha_0) \tag{6}$$

where $\varepsilon_0, \lambda_0, \gamma_0, \beta_0, \alpha_0$ are the hyper-parameters that will be discussed in Sect. 3.4. DP denotes Dirichlet Process, N and W denote Normal and Wishart distributions, respectively. The Gaussian and Wishart distributions that generate the parameters of the Gaussian distribution in Eq. (2) of each cluster (prior distribution in Bayesian statistics) are given respectively by Eqs. (3) and (4), where the number of clusters is K that can vary depending on the observed data. The distribution of Eqs. (3) and (4) are chosen to be the conjugate prior distribution of the parameter in Eq. (2) in order to reduce the calculation work of Gibbs Sampling.

The distribution of Eq. (5) models the cluster selection of sample data. It corresponds to sample from multinomial distribution. These π s governed by the distribution in Eq. (6) are the priors of mixture model. These draws from a DP were calculated based on Eqs. (1a) and (1b) where π_{K+1} corresponds to the probability of allocating the data point to a new cluster.

The conditional posterior distributions for the means μ_{z_i} and the precision $\Sigma_{z_i}^{-1}$ are given by Eqs. (7) and (8). The parameter $\varepsilon_{z_i}^*, \gamma_{z_i}^*, \Sigma_{z_i}^{-1}$ in Eq. (7) are given respectively by Eqs. (8), (9) and (10). The $n_{z_i}n_{z_i}$ is the summation number of the data in the z_iz_i th cluster. The parameter $\beta_{z_i}^*$ in Eq. (8) is given by Eq. (12).

$$\mu_{z_i}|x_i, z_i, \Sigma_{z_i}^{-1} \sim N(\varepsilon_{z_i}^*, (\gamma_{z_i}^*\Sigma_{z_i}^{-1})^{-1}), 1 \leq z_i \leq K \tag{7}$$

$$\varepsilon_{z_i}^* = \frac{\gamma_0\varepsilon_0 + n_{z_i}\bar{x}_{z_i}}{\gamma_0 + n_{z_i}} \tag{8}$$

$$\gamma_{z_i}^* = \gamma_0 + n_{z_i} \tag{9}$$

$$\Sigma_{z_i}^{-1} | x_i, z_i \sim W(\lambda_0 + n_{z_i}, \beta_{z_i}^*), 1 \leq z_i \leq K \tag{10}$$

$$\bar{x}_{z_i} = \frac{\sum_{i=1}^{n} x_{z_i}}{n_{z_i}} \tag{11}$$

$$\beta_{z_i}^* = \beta_0 + (\sum_{i=1}^{n} (x_{z_i} - \bar{x}_{z_i})(x_{z_i} - \bar{x}_{z_i})^T) + \frac{\gamma_0 n_{z_i}}{\gamma_0 + n_{z_i}} (\varepsilon_{z_i} - \bar{x}_{z_i})(\varepsilon_{z_i} - \bar{x}_{z_i})^T \tag{12}$$

4 DPGMM Clustering for Environmental Dataset on Spark

4.1 Clustering Process Based on Gibbs Sampling and Spark

We use Gibbs sampling to approach iteratively the probability of reallocating the farm environmental data x_i to a new cluster z_i'. The reallocating posterior distribution $(\pi_1, \ldots, \pi_{K+1})$ from Eq. (6) was computed for each iteration and ith farm environmental data point in the following way:

$$\pi_k = P(z_i = k | Z_{-i}, X) = \frac{1}{c} \frac{n_k}{\alpha_0 + n - 1} P(x_i | z_i = k), 1 \leq k \leq K \tag{13}$$

$$\pi_{K+1} = P(z_i = K + 1 | Z_{-i}, X) = \frac{1}{c} \frac{\alpha_0}{\alpha_0 + n - 1} P(x_i | z_i = K + 1) \tag{14}$$

where k is the label of the cluster in which point x_i is reallocated and $z_i = K + 1$ indicates creating a new cluster. c is a normalization factor that guarantees that probabilities sum to one. Z_{-i} denotes all the indexes Z excluding index z_i. The marginal probabilities $P(x_i | z_i = k)$ is the likelihood of the data point x_i, given that the index of the cluster to which the point x_i is reallocated is the k. Computing this marginal is not straightforward. We computed it analytically, integrating the parameter $\theta_{z_i}(\mu_{z_i}, \Sigma_{z_i})$ in the following way:

$$P(x_i | z_i = k) = \int_{\theta_k} F(x_i | \theta_k) G(\theta_k) d\theta_k \tag{15}$$

$$P(x_i | z_i = K + 1) = \int_{\theta_{K+1}} F(x_i | \theta_{K+1}) G_0(\theta_{K+1}) d\theta_{K+1} \tag{16}$$

where $F(x_i | \theta_k)$ in Eq. (15) corresponds to the probability mass function of x_i in the Gaussian-Wishart distribution with parameter $\theta_{z_i}(\mu_{z_i}, \Sigma_{z_i})$ in the latest iteration. $G(\theta_k)$ denotes the posterior Gaussian-Wishart distribution given respectively by Eq. (7) and

Eq. (10) based on G_0 and all the observations x_{-i} (except x_i). Equation (15) corresponds to the probability of allocating the data point to a cluster that already exists in the mixture model. Equation (16) corresponds to the probability of allocating the data point to a new cluster that is not included in the model. $F(x_i|\theta_{K+1})$ in Eq. (16) denotes the posterior distribution in Eq. (2). $G_0(\theta_{K+1})$ in Eq. (16) denotes the prior Gaussian-Wishart distribution given respectively by Eqs. (3) and (4).

According to the analysis of model, we use DP to determine the component of GMM. Gibbs sampling used to estimate parameters of DPGMM is considered as the simulation of data assignment through DP. In order to analyze environmental dataset stored in computer cluster, we applied the DPGMM clustering algorithm in cluster with Spark framework. The application process of DPGMM clustering based on Gibbs sampling and Spark for the farm environmental data is given as follows:

1: Initial value to $\varepsilon_0, \lambda_0, \gamma_0, \beta_0, \alpha_0$

2: Initial assignment of data points X=$(x_1, \ldots, x_n)$ to cluster $Z^{(0)} = (z_1^{(0)}, ..., z_n^{(0)})$ using Eq. (1a) and Eq. (1b)

3: **while** stop condition for α_0 is not achieved **do**

4:   I=1

5:   **while** stop condition for Z is not achieved **do**

6:     **for** i =1 to n **do**

7:       Reallocating points x_i into cluster $z_i^{(I)}$ based on $z_i^{(I-1)}$ using distribution given by Eq. (13) and Eq. (14)

8:     **end for**

9:     Updating $k^{(I)}$ according to the number of clusters in $Z^{(I)}$

10:    I=I+1

11: **end while**

12: Re-computing α_0 according to Eq. (17) using $k^{(0)}, ..., k^{(I)}$

13: **end while**

In line1, the hyper-parameters $\varepsilon_0, \lambda_0, \gamma_0, \beta_0$ are initialized with informative prior

In line1, the hyper-parameters $\varepsilon_0, \lambda_0, \gamma_0, \beta_0$ are initialized with informative prior and precision hyper-parameter α_0 is initialized with constant value for non-informative prior. The prior rules is given in Sect. 3.4.

Step2 Model initialization: initialize the DPGMM according to the line 2 from the Gibbs sampling above.

In line 7, the reallocation process is implemented under Spark framework, the reallocation process of the Gibbs sampling above can be expressed in detail below: firstly, in the iteration I, we achieve the $\theta_{z_i}^{(I-1)}(\mu_{z_i}^{(I-1)}, \Sigma_{z_i}^{(I-1)})$ to get the present model based on $z_i^{(I-1)}$ which is implemented via mapToPair function in Spark; The mapToPair function split the data line into the form of key-value pair. The value represents the latent variable $z_i^{(I-1)}$ while key represents the data attributes and data sampling time. Then, we scan all the key-value pair through mapToPair function for twice to calculate separately the $\theta_{z_i}^{(I-1)}(\mu_{z_i}^{(I-1)}, \Sigma_{z_i}^{(I-1)})$. Secondly, we scan all data line in mapToPair function to update each cluster number $n_{z_i}^{(I)}$ and the parameters $\varepsilon_{z_i}^{(I)}, \gamma_{z_i}^{(I)}, \beta_{z_i}^{(I)}, \bar{x}_{z_i}^{(I)}$ in the posterior distribution so as to calculate $\theta_{z_i}^{(I)}(\mu_{z_i}^{(I)}, \Sigma_{z_i}^{(I)})$ for the $k^{(I)}$ Gaussian clusters in the next iteration; finally, we reallocate each point x_i to the existed cluster or a new one based on the model with parameter $\theta_{z_i}^{(I-1)}(\mu_{z_i}^{(I-1)}, \Sigma_{z_i}^{(I-1)})$ according to the probability distribution function calculated by Eqs. (13) and (14). The reallocating process is implemented by mapToPair and updateStateByKey function in Spark; mapToPair split the data line and updateStateByKey function update the latent variable $z_i^{(I)}$ according to the sampling result of Eq. (5) of which the parameter Π is generated from Eqs. (13) and (14). After reallocation, some cluster with empty data point will be deleted during the process of updating $k^{(I)}$ in line 9. The stop condition for the iteration in line 5 of Gibbs sampling process appears when a continuous number of values from Z are constant during reallocations, or when a maximum number of iterations is reached.

5 Experiments

5.1 Experimental Environment

In order to verify the application performance of the proposed distributed algorithm and analyze the environmental data set, we deploy the distributed experimental environment with Spark. The computer cluster consists of 3 computers, the architecture of Spark cluster is based on Hadoop framework, the file system is still HDFS, but we replace the MapReduce framework with Spark due to its high effectiveness of iteration. The software and hardware information about the cluster is shown in Table 3.

Table 3. Cluster information of software and hardware

Node	MartinMaster	MartinPoint1	MartinPoint2
Processor	AMD FX(tm) 8300 Eight@3.30 GHz	Pentium(R) Dual E5300@2.60 GHz	Pentium(R) Dual E2180@2.00 GHz
Memory	16G DDR3	4G DDR3	6G DDR2
Storage	2 TB	1 TB	1 TB
OS	Ubuntu14.05 (desktop edt)		
JDK	Jdk1.8.0_45		
Hadoop	Hadoop-2.6.0		
Scala Spark	Scala-2.11.7 Spark-1.5.2		

The name of each node of the cluster is shown in the first line of Table 1. Node MartinMaster is considered as both master and slave. The other two node (MartinPoint1 and MartinPoint2) are just regarded as slave that receive jobs assigned from master and execute task. We decide to build platform under Ubuntu OS in order to reduce the workload. The underlying of Hadoop and Spark are separately implemented by Java and

Scala. We chose software edition with reference to the official announcements. After deploying JDK and Scala, we configure the Secure Shell for each node and exchange the security password between master and slave. Finally we edit the configuration file of Hadoop and Spark and copy both of them to the other slaves.

The DPGMM model is implemented in Java with all experiments performed over the farm environmental dataset. The clusters obtained with the DPGMM are compared with other well-known clustering methods using external criteria.

5.2   Experimental Results and Analysis

In the follow experiments, we test the performance of the proposed method on the environmental dataset, then, the anomaly detection result of DPPGMM is given and analyzed. According to the optimum environmental indicator for growth of tomato given by the agricultural expert. We chose temperature, related humidity and CO_2 as the attributes of the dataset for analysis. In the application our specific choice for the hyper-parameters of DPGMM is $\varepsilon_0 = [18.43, 86.66, 395.84]^T$, $\gamma_0 = [2.99, 8.35, 57.83]^T$, $\lambda_0 = 3$, $\beta_0 = I_{3 \times 3}$, $\alpha_0 = 0.001$. The hyper-parameters mean ε_0 and relative precision γ_0 are computed throughout the whole environmental dataset. The learning rate is fixed to $\alpha_0 = 0.001$ with non-informative prior which means the cluster raise in a low rate. The max iteration number of Gibbs sampling is 10000. The initial cluster number of K-means and FCM is set to 11 in order to keep consistent with the cluster number in DPGMM result.

F-measure index is used to measure the clustering performance based on external criteria. Different criteria such as Recall (Re), the Precision (Pr) and the F-measure are used for evaluation.

To raise the quality of evaluation, F-measure (F) given by (17) is used to estimate the precision of the algorithm.

$$F = 2 * \frac{Re * Pr}{Re + Pr} \tag{17}$$

The values F ranges from 0 to 1 and value close to 1 better than that close to 0. The evaluation results for the considered 3 methods and using the above criteria are displayed in Table 4. The result of the DPGMM clustering is given in Table 5.

As shown in Table 4, the optimal evaluation in each row are highlighted in bold. From Table 4, the result of FCM obtain the optimal evaluation in Recall which means

Table 4. Comparison between the F-measure, Precision, and Recall values for each clustering method

Evaluation	K-means	FCM	DPGMM
Precision	0.8915	0.8978	**0.9675**
Recall	0.8457	**0.9105**	0.9054
F-Measure	0.8680	0.9041	**0.9354**

Table 5. DPGMM clustering result

Label	SumNum	Proportion	AbnormalNum	Abnormality
0	2527	0.055322	2327	A
1	13333	0.291891	1567	N
2	15071	0.32994	2109	N
3	7749	0.169644	1357	N
5	3961	0.086716	810	A
6	104	0.002277	0	N
7	2824	0.061824	173	N
8	1	2.19E-05	1	A
9	31	6.79E-04	0	N
10	1	2.19E-05	1	A
12	76	0.001664	0	N

the recall number of abnormal points under FCM achieve the minimum. But DPGMM get better performance in precision, considering both precision and recall, DPGMM obtain the optimal in F-measure.

As shown in Table 5, the result of DPGMM finally forms 11 clusters. The cluster label is not continuous since the empty cluster is deleted in the iteration process. The number of abnormal data of each cluster is recorded in column 'AbnormalNum'. 4 clusters are judged as abnormal according to value 'A' which means abnormal in column 'Abnormality' while 'N' means normal. The data number of the rest 7 clusters account for 79 % of the total which means 21 % data is judged as abnormal data. The percentage of sum normal data can be obtained from column 'proportion'.

The result of DPGMM and anomaly detection for DPGMM result are shown in 3 dimension via Matlab in Fig. 1(a) and (b), The three coordinates separately represent the attributes of temperature, related humidity and CO_2. 11 different clusters are marked with different color according to cluster label in Fig. 1(a). The abnormality of dataset can be directly observed in Fig. 1 (b). All the blue points in Fig. 1 (b) belongs to one of the clusters with 'N' in Table 4 while the color of abnormal points are brown. Experimental result shows the well performance of DPGMM clustering in data analysis and imply that DPGMM is the best among the 3 clustering method in anomaly detection.

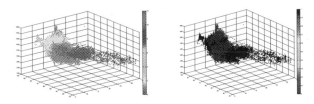

Fig. 1. (a). DPGMM clustering result (b). Anomaly detection for DPGMM clustering result (Color figure online)

6 Conclusions

In this paper, we have proposed an improved GMM clustering method and implemented under the framework of Spark which is used for farm environmental data anomaly detection. The Gibbs sampling method implements the parameter estimation process of the model. The validity of the distributed clustering method has been deployed on Spark and verified via multi method comparison. The experiment shows that DPGMM method obtain the optimal evaluation based on external criteria and the result of farm environmental data anomaly detection is given according to the suitable growth environmental indexes for tomato given by agriculture expert.

Acknowledgments. This work is supported by the Key Project of Science and Technology Commission of Shanghai Municipality under Grant No. 14DZ1206302. National Natural Science Foundation of China (Grant No. 61304031), and Innovation Program of Shanghai Municipal Education Commission (14YZ007). This work was also supported by Shanghai College Young Teachers' Training Plan (No. B37010913003). The authors would like to thank editors and anonymous reviewers for their valuable comments and suggestions to improve this paper.

References

1. Ananthara, M.G., Arunkumar, T., Hemavathy, R.: CRY — an improved crop yield prediction model using bee hive clustering approach for agricultural data sets. In: International Conference on Pattern Recognition, Informatics and Mobile Engineering, pp. 473–478 (2013)
2. Cleverly, J., Eamus, D., Gorsel, E.V., et al.: Productivity and evapotranspiration of two contrasting semiarid ecosystems following the 2011 carbon land sink anomaly. Agric. For. Meteorol. **220**, 151–159 (2016)
3. Dieleman, H.: Urban agriculture in Mexico City; balancing between ecological, economic, social and symbolic value. J. Clean. Produc. (2016)
4. Dudik, J.M., Kurosu, A., Coyle, J.L., et al.: A comparative analysis of DBSCAN, K-means, and quadratic variation algorithms for automatic identification of swallows from swallowing accelerometry signals. Comput. Biol. Med. **59**, 10–18 (2015)
5. Sansegundo, R., Cordoba, R., Ferreiros, J., et al.: Frequency features and GMM-UBM approach for Gait-based person identification using smartphone inertial signals. Pattern Recogn. Lett. **73**, 60–67 (2016)
6. Fox, E.B., Choi, D.S., Willsky, A.S.: Nonparametric Bayesian methods for large scale multi-target tracking. In: 1977 11th Asilomar Conference on Circuits, Systems and Computers 1977, Conference Record, pp. 2009–2013 (2006)
7. Orbanz, P., Buhmann, J.M.: Nonparametric Bayesian image segmentation. Int. J. Comput. Vis. **77**(1–3), 25–45 (2008)
8. Ahmadi, S., Yeh, C.H., Papageorgiou, E.I., et al.: An FCM-FAHP approach for managing readiness-relevant activities for ERP implementation. Comput. Indus. Eng. **88**, 501–517 (2015)

Multisensor Information Fusion Scheme Based on Intelligent Particle Filter

Chuang Zhang[1(✉)] and Chen Guo[2]

[1] Navigation College, Dalian Maritime University, Dalian 116026, China
zhchuangdmu@163.com
[2] School of Information Science and Technology, Dalian Maritime University, Dalian 116026, China
dmuguoc@126.com

Abstract. For the sake of solve the low-quality particles and degeneration in the process of particle filter, Multisensor information fusion based on intelligent particle filter scheme is proposed. The process is divided into two steps, On the one hand, Multi-sensor data is sent to the appropriate particle filter calculation module in order to optimize the particle distribution for the purpose updating the proposed distribution density. On the other hand, By incorporating the algorithm into the likelihood model structured by multi-sensor data, meanwhile, the low-weight particles will be modified into high-weight ones according to genetic operators and the posterior distribution will be more effectively estimated, thus high-quality particles can be obtained. Ultimately, a more precise estimate value will be achieved. A simulation experiment shows the effectiveness of the algorithm.

Keywords: Genetic operators · Intelligent Particle Filter · Information fusion

1 Introduction

Multisensor information fusion schemes have been extensively applied to target tracking, surveillance, communication, navigation, signal and image processing. Centralised fusion and distributed fusion constitute the information fusion methods. Optimum state estimate has provided by centralised fusion (CF) and Partial measurement information. Plenty of work are concentrated on the CF query and some fusion schemes [1–4] have been put forward according to Gaussian filters. On the basis of Gaussian assumption, these fusion schemes are only suitable for linear systems. Lately, particle filters (PFs) have reflect the good capability for the solution of nonlinear, non Gauss systems, and have made great achievements in industry [5, 6]. Yet, particle filter algorithm is difficult to select the appropriate importance sampling density, which leads to the problem of poor performance, low quality and serious particle degradation.

Some amended PFs have been put forward in order to overcome these shortcoming. Eric Wan et al. [7, 8] proposed unscented particle filter (UPF) scheme for alleviating the particle impoverishment based on sequential importance sampling. They have shown that the UPF result in more accurate, meanwhile it produces preferable estimates of the

© Springer Science+Business Media Singapore 2016
L. Zhang et al. (Eds.): AsiaSim 2016/SCS AutumnSim 2016, Part III, CCIS 645, pp. 174–182, 2016.
DOI: 10.1007/978-981-10-2669-0_19

states covariance. However, more particles, lower realtime. Another way to approach the general filtering question apply to local importance sampling [9], this method chooses importance density function as priori density and neglects the influence of the latest measurement information of the system. This strategy can, however, fail if the condition of the non-normalized likelihood function exceeds the preset threshold and new particle is generated and new measurement information is added. Li xue et al. [10] have introduced an adaptive unscented particle filtering algorithm by adopting the concept of unscented transform in particle filtering. When likelihood distribution lie in the trailer of transition prior distribution or observation model has a high precision, due to the normalized weights are small and become invalid samples, lower sampling rate is likely to the failure of the particle filter.

As genetic algorithm (GA) has common feature with PF, lots of experts merge GA into particle filter. In [11], The crossover and mutation were apply to enhance PF. The coding process enhance complicacy of particle filter before resampling. Besides the probability of a crossover and mutation operator to change, the weights of high-weight particles may be cut down. Kwok et al. put down evolutionary PF, Kwok et al. [12] put forward an evolving PF. The amended PF has a disadvantage of depending on the resampled particles mainly, meanwhile has a weak basis for enhancing particle variousness. S. M. K. Heris [13] solved the multiobjective optimization problem with GA for the sake of the impoverishment question in PF. But this scheme may bear the huge calculating cost since, a multiobjective majorization should be disposed during each iteration. Thus, the article establish multisensor information fusion scheme based on intelligent particle filter to tackle this problem.

The process is divided into two steps, On the one hand, Multi-sensor data is sent to the appropriate particle filter calculation module in order to optimize the particle distribution for the purpose updating the proposed distribution density. On the other hand, By incorporating the algorithm into the likelihood model structured by multi-sensor data, meanwhile, the low-weight particles will be amended into high-weight ones according to genetic operators and the posterior distribution will be more effectively estimated, thus high-quality particles can be obtained. Ultimately, a more precise estimate value will be achieved.

2   Two-Stage Multisensor Information Fusion Scheme Based on Intelligent Particle Filter

2.1   Standard PF(SPF)

Taking into account the multisensory nonlinear discrete system [14]:

$$\begin{cases} x_t = f_t(x_{t-1}) + v_{t-1} \\ z_t^{(m)} = h_t^{(m)}(x_t) + w_t^{(m)} \end{cases} \tag{1}$$

where m is sensor index and t is time index, $m = 1,2,\ldots,M$, $z_t^{(m)}$ is measurement vector and x_t is state vector. v_{t-1} is process noise and $w_t^{(m)}$ is measurement noise, both are zero-mean and independent respectively. $f(\cdot)$ and $h(\cdot)$ are state transition equation and observation equation. Our goal expects to gain estimate x_t according to usable measurements $z_{1:t} := \{z_\tau\}_{\tau=1}^t$, where $z_\tau := \{z_\tau^{(m)}\}_{m=1}^M$.

In PF, the posterior probability density $p(x_t|z_{1:t}) = \sum_{i=1}^N \omega_t^i \delta(x_t - x_t^i)$. According to multisensory measurements, the integrated likelihood $p(z_t|x_t)$ can be divided into $\prod_{m=1}^M p(z_t^{(m)}|x_t)$. Within every filtration period, the weight ω_t^i satisfy the following formula

$$\omega_t^i \propto \frac{p(x_t^i|x_{t-1}^i) \prod_{m=1}^M p(z_t^{(m)}|x_t^i)}{q(x_t^i|x_{t-1}^i, z_t)} \tag{2}$$

where proposal density (PD) is define as $q(x_t^i|x_{t-1}^i, z_t)$ and applied to produce the particle x_t^i and estimate $q(x_t^i|x_{t-1}^i, z_t)$. In general, PD is defined as transition density $p(x_t^i|x_{t-1}^i)$, meanwhile the calculated weight expressed the shorthand notation $\omega_t^i \propto \prod_{m=1}^M p(z_t^{(m)}|x_t^i)$.

2.2   PF-Based Two-Stage CF (PF-TSCF)

Every barber knows that Multisensor information enhance the evaluation precision availably. Nevertheless, likelihood model has applied to multisensor information usually, yet neglected the process of importance sampling. Therefore, within the PF framework, two-stage fusion method is put forward, shown in Fig. 1. On the one hand, multisensor information is transferred to the data process stage step by step in order to optimising the particle distribution in state space to update the PD. A total of M modules in data process stage and PF_n indicate the nth module. On the other hand, Intelligent particle filter module is marked as IPF_M + 1, where the multisensor data is returned to design the likelihood function $\prod_{m=1}^M p(z_t^{(m)}|x_t)$. The ultimate estimate $\hat{x}_t$ is obtained by IPF_M + 1.

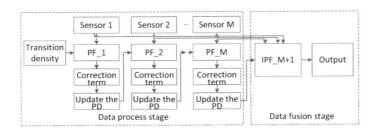

Fig. 1. Put forward the two-stage fusion method

Clearly, M basic PF modules and one IPF module are demanded in every filtering period. The PD is defined as $q_n(x_t|x_{t-1}^i, z_t)$, $n \in \{1, 2, \cdots, M+1\}$. We accept the mean in [15] to ensure $q_n(x_t|x_{t-1}^i, z_t)$, that is achieved through the updated system equation:

$$x_t = f(x_{t-1}) + c_n(z_t) + v_{t-1} \tag{3}$$

$$q_n(x_t|x_{t-1}^i, z_t) := p_v(x_t - f(x_{t-1}^i) - c_n(z_t)) \tag{4}$$

Here, $c_n(z_t)$ is defined as amend term and is firstly equal to zero vector and renewed due to the arise of n. Supposed $c_1(z_t) = 0$ in PF_1 implies $q_1(x_t|x_{t-1}^i, z_t) = p(x_t|x_{t-1}^i)$, afterward we apply the first sensor information to indicate the likelihood $p(z_t^{(1)}|x_t)$ and then get the $\hat{x}_{t,1}$ by circulating PF_1. Supposed $c_2(z_t) = \hat{x}_{t,1} - f(\hat{x}_{t-1})$ in PF_2 and indicate $q_2(x_t|x_{t-1}^i, z_t)$, afterward we apply the second sensor information to indicate the likelihood $p(z_t^{(2)}|x_t)$ and get the $\hat{x}_{t,2}$, which will applied to gain $q_3(x_t|x_{t-1}^i, z_t)$ and ordinal recursion in order. Data process stage terminates on condition that the whole sensor information have been utilized. Hence, the $\hat{x}_{t,n}$, $n \in \{1, 2, \cdots, M\}$ are sole interim outcomes applied to make the PD as effective as possible.

2.3 Intelligent Particle Filter (IPF)

Mutation and crossover have applied in the put forward IPF in order to alleviate the particle impoverishment [16]. But make some modifications in these two operators so that fulfill the characteristics of PF. In crossover operator, information of the high-weight particles is applied to amend the low-weight ones. The low-weight particles will be altered into high-weight ones, afterward the variousness will be enhanced by two operators.

Supposed that particles have defined as $\{x_t^i, \tilde{\omega}_t^i\}$ ($i = 1, 2, \cdots, N$), thereinto, $\tilde{\omega}_t^i$ indicates the normalized particle weight. A method must be framed so that isolate the low-weight particles from high-weight, and it can be formulated as

$$x_t^i \in \begin{cases} C_L, & \tilde{\omega}_t^i \le W_T \\ C_H, & \tilde{\omega}_t^i > W_T \end{cases} \tag{5}$$

where C_H and C_L are datasets which include the high- and low-weight particles. W_T is a criticality value applied to isolating. Low-weight particles are defined as weights smaller than W_T and preserved in C_L in Eq. (5). High-weight particles are defined as weights higher than W_T and preserved in C_H. W_T is decided by the effective sample size N_{eff}, and follow these steps.

(1) Calculate N_{eff}

$$N_{eff} = \left[1 \bigg/ \sum_{i=1}^{N} (\tilde{\omega}_t^i)^2 \right] \tag{6}$$

$[\bullet]$ means the rounding symbol.

(2) Arranged in descending order of particle weights and preserve them in $\tilde{W}$,

$$\tilde{W} = \left[\tilde{\omega}_t^1, \tilde{\omega}_t^2, \cdots, \tilde{\omega}_t^N\right] \tag{7}$$

(3) W_T is the N_{eff}th particle weight,

$$W_T = \tilde{W}(N_{eff}) \tag{8}$$

It implements crossover operator after separating the particles. With respect to the simplicity and state x_t^i is encoded, low-weight particles has chosen to alter the arithmetic crossover. Supposed x_{tL}^l and x_{tH}^j mean the particle root in C_L and C_H, individually, and x_{tS}^l defines the altered low-weight particle. Arithmetic crossover operator can be formulated as

$$x_{tS}^l = \alpha x_{tL}^l + (1 - \alpha)x_{tH}^j \tag{9}$$

where $l = 1, 2, \cdots, N_L$ and $j = 1, 2, \cdots, N_H$. N_L and N_H mean particle count from C_L and C_H, individually. Each x_{tS}^l, x_{tH}^j is randomly chosen from C_H. $\alpha \in [0, 1]$ is a parameter that decides how much information from x_{tL}^l is converted to x_{tS}^l. The greater α is, the more information will be converted from x_{tL}^l to x_{tS}^l. When $\alpha = 1$, $x_{tL}^l = x_{tS}^l$ means no crossover happening.

To improve the particles variousness, a mutation method is devised.

$$x_{tM}^l = \begin{cases} 2x_{tH}^j - x_{tS}^l, & r_l \le p_M \\ x_{tS}^l, & r_l > p_M \end{cases} \tag{10}$$

In which r_l is the stochastic variable for x_{tS}^l. It follows the uniform distribution of [0,1]. p_M means the mutation probability, which is preset. In the condition of $p_M = 0$, mutation will not be happened. α and p_M should be various in different systems in application.

2.4 Two-Stage Multisensor Information Fusion Scheme Based on IPF

One cycle scheme is as shown below
First stage: Supposed n = 1 $c_n(z_t) = 0$;
    for n = 1:M
On the basis of Eq. (5), indicate the PD $q_n(x_t|x_{t-1}^i, z_t)$ and get particle x_t^i from it, calculate the normalised weight by $\omega_t^i \propto p(x_t^i|x_{t-1}^i)p(z_t^{(n)}|x_t^i)/q_n(x_t^i|x_{t-1}^i, z_t)$, obtain the estimate $\hat{x}_{t,n} = \sum_{i=1}^{N} \omega_t^i x_t^i$, let $c_{n+1}(z_t) = \hat{x}_{t,n} - f(\hat{x}_{t-1})$ and n: = n + 1.
    End for

Second stage:

(1) Define the PD $q(x_t|x^i_{t-1}, z_t) = q_{M+1}(x_t|x^i_{t-1}, z_t)$ and known $c_{M+1}(z_t)$, calculate the weight on the basis of (3), Sample from the distribution $p(x_t|x^i_{t-1})$ and then get particle x^i_t.

(2) Compute the normalized weights of whole particles by utilizing Eq. (2) and indicate particles as $\{x^i_t, \tilde{\omega}^i_t\}$.

(3) Calculate the state $\hat{x}_t$ through **MMSE**, which can be denoted as

$$\hat{x}_t = \sum_{i=1}^N x^i_t \tilde{\omega}^i_t \tag{11}$$

(4) The particle will be classified into low-weight particle $x^l_{tL}(l = 1, 2, \cdots, N_L)$ and high-weight particle $x^j_{tH}(j = 1, 2, \cdots, N_H)$ and afterward preserve in C_L and C_H, individually.

(5) Perform the mutation and crossover operators on the basis of (9) and (10) to get particles x^l_{tM}.

(6) Estimate and normalize the weights of x^l_{tM} and x^j_{tH}.

(7) Implement the resampling step.

3   Simulation Studies

In this section, practical ship tests are applied to evaluate the proposed algorithm according to Fig. 2. Three filters were used to evaluate the state sequence x_t, including unscented Kalman filter based on CF (UKF_CF), Standard PF based on CF (SPF_CF) and IPF-based two-stage CF (IPF_TSCF). The measurement system applied to experiments consists of SINS, GPS receiver and LOG.

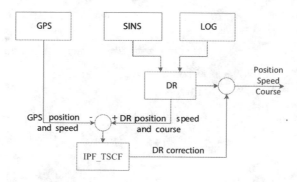

Fig. 2. Flow chart of integrated navigation system

The experimental outline of integrated navigation system is divided into two parts. Firstly, acquire the original data of multisensors. Secondly, simulate by the original data of multisensors according to IPF_TSCFs.

In Fig. 3, latitude error within the −20 m ~ 100 m, −20 m ~ 90 m and −10 m ~ 70 m in UKF_CF, and SPF_CF and IPF_TSCF individually. In Fig. 4, longitude error within the −70 m ~ 50 m, −70 m ~ 50 m and −60 m ~ 40 m in UKF_CF, and SPF_CF and IPF_TSCF individually.

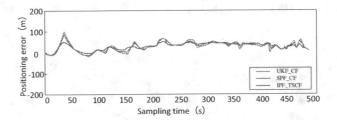

Fig. 3. Variance curve of latitude error

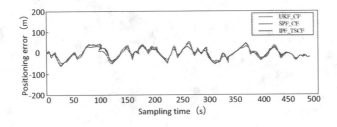

Fig. 4. Variance curve of longitude error

The error curve can also be seen clearly, in the initial stage and during the steering UKF_CF and SPF_CF positioning errors are larger; but in the whole system positioning error is smaller and stable basically using IPF_TSCF.

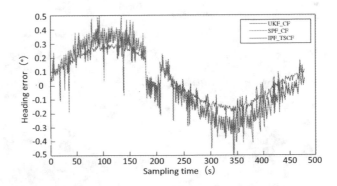

Fig. 5. Variance curve of heading error (Color figure online)

In Fig. 5, the blue line, red line, black line are heading error estimation results of UKF_CF and SPF_CF and IPF_TSCF, respectively. From the figure, both UKF_CF and SPF_CF heading error can be up to ±0.5 °. But heading error is ±0.3 ° in IPF_TSCF. Thus this method obtains a better estimation of ship's heading.

From Figs. 6 and 7, the fluctuation of the velocity curve is relatively large using UKF_CF and SPF_CF, during the early period of acceleration movement and ship steering, there are some fluctuation for speed, but on the whole the speed is relatively stable.

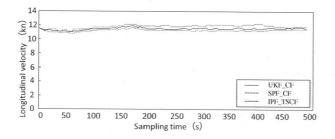

Fig. 6. Fusion curve of longitudinal velocity

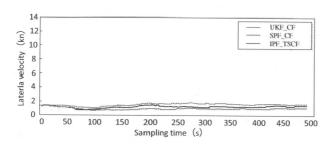

Fig. 7. Fusion curve of lateral velocity

4 Conclusions and Discussion

A two-stage multisensor data fusion method based on intelligent particle filter is put forward according to the PF method. Multisensor information has been renew the PD in order, sensor data will be brought into the importance sampling, that in order to enhanced evaluation precision. A genetic operators has been devised in IPF_TSCF. According to method, the low-weight particles will altered to the high-weight and the particle impoverishment is lessened ultimately. Mutation occurs on the altered particle on a basis of given probability. By using two operators the particle variousness will be improved. The validity of IPF_TSCF was tested and verified by using experiment examples. The experimental result shows that the capability of IPF_TSCF for SINS/GPS/LOG integration are fulfilling.

Whereas, there are many usability improvements that should be made on IPF_TSCF. Burden of computing of PFs is a common and important question. To decrease the computational loads of IPF_TSCF could be another area of study.

Acknowledgements. This work was supported by the National Nature Science Foundation of China (Nos. 51579024, 61374114) and the Fundamental Research Funds for the Central Universities (DMU no. 3132016311, 3132016005).

References

1. Goh, S.T., Abdelkhalik, O., Zekavat, S.A.A.: Weighted measurement fusion Kalman filter implementation for UAV navigation. Aerosp. Sci. Technol. **28**(1), 315–323 (2013)
2. Wang, Y., Tang, X., Cui, Q.: Dynamic appearance model for particle filter based visual tracking. Pattern Recogn. **45**(12), 4510–4523 (2012)
3. Erdem, E., Dubuisson, S., Bloch, I.: Fragments based tracking with adaptive cue integration. Comput. Vis. Image Underst. **116**(7), 827–841 (2012)
4. Vural, R.A., Yildirim, T., Kadioglu, T., Basargan, A.: Performance evaluation of evolutionary algorithms for optimal filter design. IEEE Trans. Evol. Comput. **16**(1), 135–147 (2012)
5. Das, S., Kale, A., Vaswani, N.: Particle filter with a mode tracker for visual tracking across illumination changes. IEEE Trans. Image Process. **21**(4), 2340–2346 (2012)
6. Yin, S., Zhu, X.: Intelligent particle filter and its application to fault detection of nonlinear system. IEEE Trans. Indus. Electron. **62**(6), 3852–3861 (2015)
7. Dini, D.H., Mandic, D.P., Julier, S.J.: A widely linear complex unscented Kalman filter. IEEE Sig. Process. Lett. **18**(11), 623–626 (2011)
8. Johansen, A.M., Doucet, A.: A note on auxiliary particle filters. Stat. Prob. Lett. **78**(12), 1498–1504 (2008)
9. Torma, P., Szepesvári, C.: Local importance sampling: a novel technique to enhance particle filtering. J. Multimedia **1**(1), 32–43 (2006)
10. Xue, L., Gao, S., Zhao, Y.: Weight adaptive adjustment unscented particle filtering and its application in integrated navigation. J. Chin. Inert. Technol. **20**(4), 459–463 (2012)
11. Higuchi, T.: Monte Carlo filter using the genetic algorithm operators. J. Stat. Comput. Simul. **59**(1), 1–23 (1997)
12. Kwok, N.M., Fang, G., Zhou, W.: Evolutionary particle filter: re-sampling from the genetic algorithm perspective. In: IEEE/RSJ International Conference on IROS, Sydney, Australia, pp. 155–174 (2005)
13. Heris, S.M.K., Khaloozadeh, H.: Non-dominated sorting genetic filter a multi-objective evolutionary particle filter. In: Proceedings of Iranian Conference Intelligent System, pp. 1–6 (2014)
14. Hu, Z., Liu, X., Hu, Y.: Particle filter based on the lifting scheme of observations. IET Radar Sonar Navig. **9**(1), 48–54 (2015)
15. Zuo, J.Y., Jia, Y.N., Zhang, Y.Z., Lian, W.: Adaptive iterated particle filter. Electron. Lett. **49**(12), 742–743 (2013)
16. Yin, S., Zhu, X.: Intelligent particle filter and its application to fault detection of nonlinear system. IEEE Trans. Indus. Electron. **62**(6), 3852–3861 (2015)

A Mode Converter for Large-Aspect-Ratio TE$_{10}$ Mode to Standardized TE$_{10}$ Mode in a Rectangular Waveguide

Jun Ma[1,2(✉)], Guang-xing Du[2], Hong-gang Wang[2],
Fan-zheng Zeng[2], and Bao-liang Qian[2]

[1] Northwest Institute of Nuclear Technology, Pingyu Road, Xi'an 710024, China
[2] College of Optoelectric Science and Engineering, National University of Defense Technology,
Deya Road 109, Changsha 410073, China
majun_steed@163.com

Abstract. A novel kind of microwave mode converter, transforming the large-aspect-ratio TE$_{10}$ mode into the standardized TE$_{10}$ mode in a rectangular waveguide, is designed in this paper. It's designed with syntonic slotted waveguide antenna arrays theory and optimized by software via finite element method. A case, transforming TE$_{10}$ mode with across Section 160 mm * 10 mm into the TE$_{10}$ mode in the standardized waveguide BJ120 (19.050 mm * 9.525 mm) at 12.5 GHz, has been presented. The conversion efficiency reaches 99.5 % at 12.5 GHz, and exceeds 90 % over 12.19–12.81 GHz. The band of interest can be expanded to 11.67–13.34 GHz, almost 2.7 times, by embedding three different coupling plates. It can be used to connect the high-power microwave (HPM) generator with sheet electron beams (SEB) and a traditional horn antenna. With one more coaxial-to-waveguide transducer, it can also be used to cool-test some instruments correlative to HPM generator driven by SEB.

Keywords: Mode converter · Cool test · Sheet electron beam · High-power microwave

1 Introduction

With the rapid progress of applications of high-power microwave (HPM), higher performances of HPM generators, such as higher power, longer pulse and quicker repetition, have been desired. However, the traditional HPM generators based on cylindrical or annular election beam have barged up against the bottleneck and the breakthrough can hardly be got. HPM generators driven by sheet election beam (SEB), is promising to breach the bottlenecks on the way of increasing power, as a result of low current density, high beams-wave interaction, fine structure compactness and good convenience to adjust injection impedance and power [1–6]. Since SEB with large-aspect-ratio rectangular structure is quite different from traditionally cylindrical or doughnut-shaped ones, it is hard to employ traditional antenna on HPM generators driven by SEB. It is necessary to design new antennas with large-aspect-ratio rectangular structure or mode converter transforming the microwave mode with large-aspect-ratio rectangular structure into the traditional one.

© Springer Science+Business Media Singapore 2016
L. Zhang et al. (Eds.): AsiaSim 2016/SCS AutumnSim 2016, Part III, CCIS 645, pp. 183–189, 2016.
DOI: 10.1007/978-981-10-2669-0_20

In the field of HPM, it is a routine to cool test the new-designed instruments before hot testing and applications. It is necessary to validate the feasibility and obtain some performances during the cool testing, because of the high costs, intricacies and indeterminateness of HPM platform. Signal generators, oscillographs, dynamometers and vector network analyzer are commonly used when cool testing some microwave instruments, whose normative coaxial ports might not meet the ports of instruments, being tested. A mode converter is needed to connect both sides and transform the TEM mode into operating mode of instruments being tested. The large-aspect-ratio TE_{10} mode is one of the operating modes of instruments in HPM system with SEB. A mode converter, transforming the TEM mode in the normalized coaxial line into the large-aspect-ratio TE_{10} mode, is needed when cool testing. High purity of operating mode and high suppression of parasitic modes are required to ensure the reliability and high conversion efficiency and broadband are needed at the same time to reduce the measuring error.

A coaxial-to-waveguide transducer can effectively transform the TEM mode into the TE_{10} mode, but it has to operate in the single-mode regime, otherwise the parasitical modes would reduce the efficiency and purity. Unfortunately, as the large-aspect-ratio rectangular structure belongs to over-mode structure, this scheme would not be competent. A standardized TE_{10} mode can be got through a coaxial-to-waveguide transducer and be expanded to a large-aspect-ratio one by an H-plane intergradation structure. However, in order to ensure the efficiency and purity, the axial length of H-plane intergradation structure has to be long enough which will increase the cost and decrease the compactness.

To sum up, it is an important work to design a mode converter that can transform the large-aspect-ratio TE_{10} mode into the TEM mode in the standardized coaxial line and the TE_{10} mode in the standardized waveguide, but the traditional schemes are helpless [7–9]. Some new ideas are desired to complete this two mode conversions while keeping compact. That is what we proposed in this paper. The syntonic slots array is employed to change the large-aspect-ratio TE_{10} mode into the standardized one. With one more coaxial-to-waveguide transducer, The TEM mode in the standardized coaxial line can be easily got for cool testing.

2 Design of Mode Converter

2.1 Theory Analysis

The mode converter is shown in Fig. 1. The large-aspect-ratio TE_{10} mode is injected into the input waveguide and enters the launch waveguide through the slotted on the coupling plate. The launch waveguide is one standardized rectangular wav with one port obturated. The microwave output from the other port in the form of standardized TE_{10} mode, which can be directly injected to the traditional horn antenna to efficiently radiate.

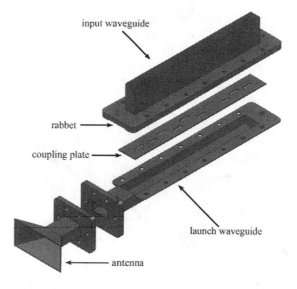

Fig. 1. The structure of mode converter with a horn antenna

If the horn antenna is replaced with a coaxial-to-waveguide transducer, shown in Fig. 2, it can be used to transform the TEM mode into the large-aspect-ratio TE_{10} mode when cool testing some microwave instrument. The TEM mode in the standardized coaxial line is transformed into the TE_{10} mode by the coaxial-to-waveguide transducer. Then the TE_{10} mode is imported into the end-obturated launch waveguide and form a standing wave. Finally, the energy of standing waves will be

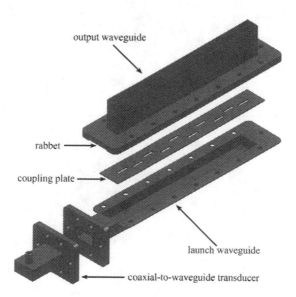

Fig. 2. The structure of mode converter with a coaxial-to-waveguide transducer

radioed into the output waveguide through the syntonic slots array and form the large-aspect-ratio TE_{10} mode. The electrical fields are shown in Fig. 3.

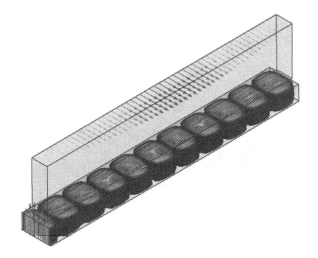

Fig. 3. Electrical fields of mode conversion

The following presents how to design the syntonic slots array. The center of every slot locates on the antinodes of stationary wave and is interlaced along the axis, making the transverse current strong enough and in phase. The length of every slot is around half of the waveguide wavelength of TE10 mode in the launch waveguide. Offsets to the axis of every slot, x_n, are decided in Eq. (1)

$$\frac{g_n}{Y_0} = 2.09 \frac{\lambda_g}{\lambda_0} \frac{a}{b} \cos^2 \frac{\pi \lambda_0}{2 \lambda_g} \sin^2 \frac{\pi x_n}{a} \tag{1}$$

where Y_0 is the admittance of launch cavity, g_n is the normalized conductance of nth slot [10]. Since the power is in direct proportion to the conductivity, they are the same in number when both normalized. The large-aspect-ratio TE_{10} mode is equally separated into n sections, and the power of every section can be calculated by Eq. (2), and the normalized conductivity of every section can be calculated by Eq. (3).

$$P_k = \int_0^b dy \int_{\frac{a}{n}(k-1)}^{\frac{a}{n}k} \mathbf{S} \cdot \mathbf{e}_z dx$$

$$= \frac{ab}{4\eta_e} E_m^2 \sqrt{1 - (\frac{\lambda}{2a})} \left\{ \frac{1}{n} + \frac{1}{2\pi} \left[\sin(\frac{k-1}{n}2\pi) - \sin(\frac{k}{n}2\pi) \right] \right\} \tag{2}$$

Where vacuum impedance $\eta_e \approx 377\Omega$, and E_m is the maximum of electrical field, $\mathbf{S}$ is the Poynting vector, and $\mathbf{e}_z$ is the unit direction vector.

$$g_n = P_k \bigg/ \sum_{k=1}^{n} P_k$$
$$= \frac{1}{n} + \frac{1}{2\pi}\left[\sin(\frac{k-1}{n}2\pi) - \sin(\frac{k}{n}2\pi)\right] \tag{3}$$

2.2 Simulation and Optimization

A mode converter operating at 12.5 GHz has been simulated and optimized, which can transform TE_{10} mode with across Section 160 mm * 10 mm into the TE_{10} mode in the standardized waveguide BJ120 (19.050 mm *9.525 mm).The energy conversion efficiency reaches 99.5 % at 12.5 GHz and exceeds 90 % over the frequency ranges 12.16-12.81 GHz, shown in Fig. 4.

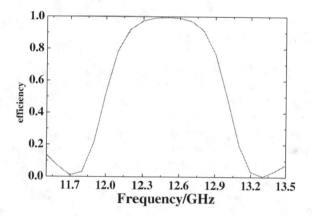

Fig. 4. Energy conversion efficiency of mode converter

3 Expandation of the Bandwidths

For the syntonic slots array, the more slots comprised, the better efficiency can be achieved, but the narrower bandwidth at the same time [11]. A scheme has been introduced to solve the inconsistency between efficiency and bandwidth. The syntonic slots array on broad wall of waveguide is peeled off and distributes onto the coupling plate. Almost all the parts influencing the frequency character are centralized to the coupling plate. The coupling plates operating at different center frequency can be achieved by redesigning the sizes and positions of slots. Bandwidth can be shifted by substituting different coupling plates. Theoretically, the bandwidth can be expanded as broad as that of the launch waveguide with enough coupling plates. In fact, two more coupling plates can expand the band broad enough. Another two coupling plates aimed at 12 GHz and 13 GHz have been designed. Their performances are shown in Fig. 5.

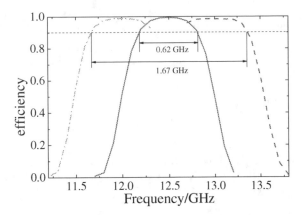

Fig. 5. Energy conversion efficiency with different coupling plates

Two more coupling plates can expand the band from 12.14–12.82 GHz to 11.60–13.42 GHz, almost 2.7 times. Coupling plates are inexpensive and easy-installed, but can evidently expand the bandwidth. However, as the coupling plate is peeled off, the broad wall is amputated, as well as the current, which will influence the transmission of TE_{10} mode. Proper length of coupling plate can locate the edge on the right position where axial current is zero, which can reduce this problem. Measures, such as embedding coupling plate into the rabbet, and mechanical extrusion, are also taken to increase electrical contact at the same time.

4 Conclusions and Future Work

In conclusion, based on the slotted waveguide antenna array theory, we have investigated a mode converter, which can transform the large-aspect-ratio rectangular TE_{10} mode into the TE_{10} mode in a standardized rectangular waveguide. The conversion efficiency reaches 99.5 % at 12.5 GHz, and exceeds 90 % over the frequency ranges 12.19–12.81 GHz. The band of interest can be expanded to 11.67–13.34 GHz, almost 2.7 times, by embedding three different coupling plates. It can be used to connect the HPM generator with SEB and a traditional horn antenna. With one more coaxial-to-waveguide transducer, it can be used when cool testing some instruments correlative to HPM generator driven by SEB. It is excellent that this mode converter takes only a few of wavelengthes along the axis to achieve results above. It will be interesting in the field of HPM with SEB.

The large-aspect-ratio TE_{10} mode is just one of the most common modes with SEB. There are still lots of work to do when we try to improve the radiation performances of HPM with SEB. Such as, how to convert large-aspect-ratio TM_{11} mode, another common mode with SEB, into standardized TE_{10} mode or other modes which is suit to radio.

References

1. Guangxing, D., Bao-liang, Q.: Propagation of intense relativistic sheet electron beam in periodic cusped magnetic fields. High Power Laser Part. Beams **22**(10), 2425–2431 (2010)
2. Jun, M., Honggang, W., Guangxing, D., Baoliang, Q.: Preliminary design of TM_{11}-TE_{10} mode converter in rectangular waveguide. High Power Laser Part. Beams **26**(6), 063004 (2014)
3. Guo, G., Wei, Y., Yue, L., et al.: A research of W-band folded waveguide traveling wave tube with elliptical sheet electron beam. Phys. Plasmas **19**(9), 093117-1–093117-7 (2012)
4. Shin, Y.-M., Baig, A., Barnett, L.R., et al.: System design analysis of a 0.22-THz sheet-beam traveling-wave tube amplifier. IEEE Trans. Electr. Devices **59**(1), 234–240 (2012)
5. Panda, P.C., Srivastava, V., Vohra, A., et al.: Analysis of sheet electron beam transport under uniform magnetic field. IEEE Trans. Plasma Sci. **41**(3), 461–469 (2013)
6. Hou, Y., Xu, J., Wang, S., Lu, Z.G., Wei, Y.Y., Gong, Y.B.: Study of high efficiency novel folded waveguide traveling-wave tube with sheet electron beam. Progr. Electromagnet. Res. **141**, 431–441 (2013)
7. Liu, Q.X., Yuan, C.W.: A new kind of coaxial TEM-circular TE_{11} mode converter. High Power Laser Part. Beams **16**(11), 1421–1424 (2004)
8. Niu, X.J., Li, H.F., Xie, Z.L.: Analysis of high-power millimeter wave circular waveguides TM_{01}-TE_{11} mode converter. High Power Laser Part. Beams **14**(1), 90–94 (2002)
9. Qiang, Z., Chengwei, Y., Lie, L., et al.: TM 01–TE11 mode converter of tri-bend circular waveguide. High Power Laser Part. Beams **20**(7), 1173–1176 (2008)
10. Wanzheng, L.: Antenna theory and techniques, University of Electronic Science and Technology of Xi'an Press (2004)
11. Richardson, P., Yee, H.Y.: Design and analysis of slotted waveguide antenna arrays. Microwave J. **31**, 105–129 (1988)

Application of Stochastic Control Theory to Biophysics of Fish Migration Around a Weir Equipped with Fishways

Hidekazu Yoshioka[1(✉)], Yuta Yaegashi[2], Koichi Unami[2], and Masayuki Fujihara[2]

[1] Faculty of Life and Environmental Science, Shimane University, Matsue, Japan
yoshih@life.shimane-u.ac.jp
[2] Graduate School of Agriculture, Kyoto University, Kyoto, Japan
Yaegashi.yuta.54s@st.kyoto-u.ac.jp,
unami@adm.kais.kyoto-u.ac.jp,
fujihara@kais.kyoto-u.ac.jp

Abstract. A weir installed along a river cross-section potentially serves as a physical barrier that prevents fishes from migrating toward upstream. Many rivers in the world encounter this severe and ubiquitous ecological issue. The objective of this paper is to present a biophysical application of stochastic control theory to upstream fish migration in river reaches where movements of individual fishes are considered as horizontally 2-D controlled processes. Identifying the biological and ecological objective function to be maximized with the dynamic programming principle leads to a 2-D nonlinear elliptic equation referred to as the Hamilton-Jacobi-Bellman Equation (HJBE). Solving the HJBE leads to an optimal swimming velocity field of individual fishes in water flows. Utilizing appropriate differential equations associated with the HJBE enables us to efficiently and consistently compute attraction ability of fishways installed at a weir from a statistical viewpoint. An application of the present mathematical model to upstream migration of juvenile *Plecoglossus altivelis* (Ayu) around a recently renovated weir in Hii River, San-in area, Japan is carried out in order to assess attraction ability of its associated fishways.

Keywords: Fish migration · Stochastic control theory · Hamilton-Jacobi-Bellman equation · Spatially-distributed statistics · Finite element approximation

1 Introduction

River environment has severely been modified because of human activities, such as constructions of dams and weirs for stable water supply, hydropower generation, and flood and sediment controls. These hydraulic structures are usually installed along river cross-sections and potentially serve as physical barriers that critically affect fish migration in rivers; many of which are important aquatic species from ecological, economical, and cultural viewpoints [1, 2]. Fragmentations of habitats and migration

© Springer Science+Business Media Singapore 2016
L. Zhang et al. (Eds.): AsiaSim 2016/SCS AutumnSim 2016, Part III, CCIS 645, pp. 190–200, 2016.
DOI: 10.1007/978-981-10-2669-0_21

routes of the fishes would lead to structural regime shifts of river ecosystems and possibly their population extinction [3, 4]. Restoring the degraded river environment is currently an urgent topic in ecological research areas where assessing attraction ability and passage efficiency of fishways that are associated with weirs plays an indispensable role [5, 6].

Numerical computation with a mathematical model for movement of individual fishes in river flows has been an effective means for assessing attraction ability and passage efficiency of fishways [7, 8]. Most of such mathematical models are mechanistic where an individual fish is considered as an active particle that has certain preferred swimming velocity *a priori* specified before computation [7, 9]. However, it is more reasonable to consider that the swimming behavior is a result of dynamic decision-making processes during migration, which therefore should not be specified *a priori*. In addition, the decision-making processes would not be deterministic but rather stochastic because of a variety of internal and external factors that are uncertain in general; the former include complex biological phenomena and the latter include environmental conditions related to hydrodynamics.

The authors have recently asserted that stochastic control theory leads to a mathematical model of fish migration where the swimming velocity is dynamically decided during migration processes under stochastic environment [10–12]. In this model, computation of swimming behavior of fishes reduces to solving a Hamilton-Jacobi-Bellman Equation (HJBE): a nonlinear elliptic equation. Mathematical properties of the HJBE have been analyzed in detail [10–12], while its applicability to real problems has not been focused on so far. This is the motivation of writing this paper.

The objectives of this paper are to apply stochastic control theory to mathematical modelling of biophysics of fish migration around weirs equipped with fishways and to provide its numerical implementation example. The rest of this paper is organized as follows. Section 2 presents the mathematical model used in this paper. Section 3 shows its application to numerical assessment of attraction ability of fishways that are associated with an existing weir. Section 4 provides conclusions of this paper.

2   Mathematical Model

2.1   Stochastic Differential Equation

Horizontal position of an individual fish is considered as a 2-D continuous stochastic process $\mathbf{X}_t$ in a river reach Ω with the boundary $\partial\Omega$ where $t \geq 0$ is the time. $\mathbf{X}_t$ is a controlled stochastic process where swimming velocity $\mathbf{u} = \mathbf{u}_t$ of the fish is a control variable. It is assumed that $\mathbf{u}$ is a Markov control [13] and thus expressed as $\mathbf{u} = \mathbf{u}(\mathbf{X}_t)$. The boundary $\partial\Omega$ contains the absorbing boundary $\partial\Omega_A$ and the reflecting boundary $\partial\Omega_R$ with $\partial\Omega = \partial\Omega_A \cup \partial\Omega_R$ and $\partial\Omega_A \cap \partial\Omega_R = \emptyset$. The fish can pass through $\partial\Omega_A$ while cannot do though $\partial\Omega_R$. A horizontally 2-D steady flow field $\mathbf{V} = \mathbf{V}(\mathbf{x})$ is given at each $\mathbf{x} \in \Omega \cup \partial\Omega$. The absorbing boundary $\partial\Omega_A$ consists of the upstream boundary $\partial\Omega_{AU}$ with $\mathbf{V} \cdot \mathbf{n} < 0$ and the downstream boundary $\partial\Omega_{AD}$ with $\mathbf{V} \cdot \mathbf{n} > 0$ where $\mathbf{n}$ is the outward boundary normal vector. The boundaries $\partial\Omega_{AU}$ and $\partial\Omega_{AD}$ represent the downstream cross-section of the domain Ω and the outlets or inlets of fishways installed at a weir along the upstream cross-section. The reflecting boundary $\partial\Omega_R$ consists of the wall boundary $\partial\Omega_{RW}$ with $\mathbf{V}\cdot\mathbf{n}=0$ and the non-permeable upstream boundary $\partial\Omega_{RN}$ with $\mathbf{V}\cdot\mathbf{n}<0$. The boundaries $\partial\Omega_{RW}$ and $\partial\Omega_{RN}$ represent sidewalls and weirs of the river reach Ω, respectively. The governing equation of $\mathbf{X}_t$ in Ω is given as the Itô's SDE

$$d\mathbf{X}_t = (\mathbf{V}(t,\mathbf{X}_t) - \mathbf{u}_t)dt + b(t,\mathbf{X}_t)d\mathbf{B}_t \tag{1}$$

where $\mathbf{B}_t$ is the 2-D standard Brownian motion [13] and the 2-D positive-definite matrix b modulates stochastic swimming behavior of the fish. The positive direction of $\mathbf{u}$ is taken opposite to that of $\mathbf{V}$ to focus on upstream migration. The process $\mathbf{X}_t$ and the control $\mathbf{u}_t$ are adapted to a natural filtration generated by $\mathbf{B}_t$ and the admissible set of $\mathbf{u}$ is given as $\mathcal{U} = L^\infty([0,+\infty); U)$ with the range $U = \{|\mathbf{u}| \le u^{(M)}\}$ where $u^{(M)}$ is the maximum swimming speed of the fish. The infinitesimal generator $A^\mathbf{u}$ associated with the stochastic process $\mathbf{X}_t$ is expressed for generic $\psi = \psi(\mathbf{x})$ as

$$A^\mathbf{u}\psi = \sum_{i=1}^{2}(V_i - u_i)\frac{\partial\psi}{\partial x_i} + \sum_{i,j=1}^{2}D_{i,j}\frac{\partial^2\psi}{\partial x_i \partial x_j} \tag{2}$$

with $D_{i,j} = \frac{1}{2}\sum_{k=1}^{2}b_{i,k}b_{k,j}$. Yoshioka et al. [10–12] considered an HJBE associated with a 1-D stochastic process model assuming unbounded $u^{(M)}$ and found that to well-pose the problem requires a regularization of the drift nonlinear term, which is equivalent to artificially truncating the swimming speed [10]. Boundedness of $u^{(M)}$ is therefore a reasonable assumption from both mathematical and biophysical viewpoints.

2.2   Hamilton-Jacobi-Bellman Equation

The objective function $\phi(\mathbf{X},\mathbf{u})$ to be maximized through the migration process of the fish is formulated. The objective function considering physiological energy consumption of swimming and profit of the upstream migration is formulated as [10]

$$\phi(\mathbf{X},\mathbf{u}) = -\int_0^\tau f(|\mathbf{u}_t|)dt + \chi_{\{X_\tau \in \partial\Omega_{AU} \cup \partial\Omega_{RN}\}}P \tag{3}$$

where f is a non-negative and strictly increasing function of $|\mathbf{u}|$, χ_S represents the indicator function for the set S: $\chi_S = 1$ for $\mathbf{x} \in S$ and $\chi_S = 0$ otherwise, $P > 0$ represents the ecological profit that the fish believes to receive when it arrives at the "inflow" boundary $\partial\Omega_{AU} \cup \partial\Omega_{RN}$, and τ is the first hitting time defined as

$$\tau = \inf\{t \ge 0 : X_0 = x \in \Omega, X_t \in \partial\Omega_{AU} \cup \partial\Omega_{RN}\} \tag{4}$$

The value function, which is a maximized objective function, is expressed as

$$\Phi(\mathbf{x}) = \sup_{\mathbf{u} \in \mathcal{U}} E[\phi(\mathbf{X}, \mathbf{u})] = E[\phi(\mathbf{X}, \mathbf{u}^*)] \tag{5}$$

where $E[\cdot]$ represents the expectation and $\mathbf{u}^*$ is the optimal swimming velocity. The dynamic programming principle [14] then leads to the HJBE

$$A^{\mathbf{u}^*} \Phi - f(|\mathbf{u}^*|) = 0 \text{ in } \Omega \tag{6}$$

where the optimal swimming velocity $\mathbf{u}^*$ is expressed with the gradient $\nabla\Phi$ as

$$\mathbf{u}^* = -\frac{\nabla\Phi}{|\nabla\Phi|} \min\left\{u^{(M)}, g(|\nabla\Phi|)\right\} \tag{7}$$

where g is the inverse of f' and $\mathbf{u}^* = 0$ when $|\nabla\Phi| = 0$. The gradient $\nabla\Phi$ thus determines both the direction and magnitude of the optimal swimming velocity $\mathbf{u}^*$. The boundary conditions appropriate for the HJBE (6) are

$$\Phi = P \text{ on } \partial\Omega_{\text{AU}} \cup \partial\Omega_{\text{RN}}, \ \Phi = 0 \text{ on } \partial\Omega_{\text{AD}}, \text{ and} \tag{8}$$

$$\sum_{i,j=1}^{2} D_{ij} \frac{\partial\Phi}{\partial x_j} n_j = 0 \text{ on } \partial\Omega_{\text{RW}} \tag{9}$$

2.3   Spatially-Distributed Statistics

Once the optimal swimming velocity $\mathbf{u}^*$ in the domain Ω is obtained through solving the HJBE (6), a variety of spatially-distributed statistics [15] can be evaluated with solving appropriate linear elliptic equations associated with the SDE (1) without resorting to application of a Monte-Carlo type numerical method, which is one of the most advantageous points of using the present mathematical formulation from the viewpoint of computational efficiency. An important such statistics is the k th ($k = 0, 1, 2\ldots$) statistical moment $M_k(\mathbf{x})$ of the first hitting time of a fish from a point $\mathbf{x} \in \Omega$ to the upstream absorbing boundary $\partial\Omega_{\text{AU}}$. M_k is governed by [15]

$$A^{\mathbf{u}^*} M_k + k M_{k-1} = 0 \text{ in } \Omega \text{ for } k \geq 1 \tag{10}$$

where $M_0 = 1$ in Ω. The boundary conditions for M_k are specified as

$$M_k = 0 \text{ on } \partial\Omega_{\text{AU}} \text{ and} \tag{11}$$

$$\sum_{i,j=1}^{2} D_{ij} \frac{\partial M_k}{\partial x_j} n_j = 0 \text{ otherwise,} \tag{12}$$

so that the fishes that escape from the domain Ω through the downstream absorbing boundary $\partial\Omega_{\text{AD}}$ is excluded from computation of the statistics.

3 Application

3.1 Study Area

The study area for the model application is Hii River, San-in area, Japan where *Plecoglossus altivelis* (Ayu) inhabits, which is one of the most common diadromous migratory fish species in Japan. The total length of the mainstream and the catchment area of Hii River are 153 (km) and 2,070 (km^2), respectively [16]. Hydrological characteristics of the river are described in Sato et al. [17]. Population of *P. altivelis* in the river is thought to have been considerably decreasing because of constructing physical barriers and excessive predation pressure from some waterfowls [18]. The downstream reach of the river has the two downstream brackish lakes referred to as Lake Shinji and Lake Nakaumi from upstream where many endemic aquatic species inhabit. Life history of *P. altivelis* is summarized in Yaegashi et al. [18]. They spawn at a downstream reach of the river during autumn and hatched larvae descend to Lake Shinji. The larvae grow up to juveniles with feeding on zooplankton until the next spring. The juveniles then ascend toward the middle reach of the river; however, there exist several huge weirs with the height of several meters, which potentially serve as severe physical barriers. One of them is Yoshii Weir focused on in this paper.

Yoshii Weir is installed at a midstream reach of Hii River for the purpose to control channel erosion (Fig. 1(a)). The weir has the width of 80 (m) and the height of 3 (m). Our field survey during June 2015 found that the mainstream of Hii River had a number of weirs and Yoshii Weir was the second highest one among them. Figure 1(b) shows two fishways that associate with Yoshii Weir. Originally, the weir had only the pool-type fishway. Fluid transport capacity, passage efficiency, and attraction ability of the fishway were thought to be degraded by the sediment deposition. In 2013, the downstream part of the pool-type fishway was renovated to mitigate severe sediment deposition problems. A nature-like fishway was installed at the same time to further improve passage efficiency of Yoshii Weir. Currently, Hii River Fishery Cooperatives, who manage fishery resources in the middle and upstream reaches of Hii River, are

Fig. 1. A satellite photo around Yoshii Weir (left panel) and a photo of the pool-type and nature-like fishway taken from downstream (right panel).

concerned with attraction ability and passage efficiency of the renovated Yoshi Weir. Ecological assessment of the two fishways is therefore an urgent issue.

3.2   Identification of the Cost Function f

The cost function f for juvenile $P.$ $altivelis$, which is the core of the present mathematical model, is identified following Yoshioka et al. [12]. A longitudinally 1-D counterpart of the HJBE is considered where the domain is the interval $\Omega = (0, L)$ with the length of L. The flow velocity along the channel is $V = const > 0$ and the stochastic fluctuations in the migration process are ignored. Assuming that the profit to be gained at the upstream-end $x = 0$ is sufficiently large, the optimal swimming speed $u^* \geq 0$ of individuals toward upstream becomes a constant in Ω. The optimal swimming speed u^* is assumed to be parameterized with the flow speed V as

$$u^* = -\alpha V^2/2 + 2V \text{ for } 0 \leq V \leq u_{max} = 2\alpha^{-1} \tag{13}$$

with $\alpha > 0$. Equation (13) is a concave parabola whose vertex exists on the line $u^* = V$. The cost function f then satisfies the differential equation [12]

$$f(u^*) = f'(u^*)(u^* - V) \text{ for } 0 \leq u^* \leq u_{max} \tag{14}$$

Substituting (13) into (14) and solving (14) for f yields

$$f(u) = C[h(u)]^2 \text{ with } h(u) = \alpha^{-1}\left(2 - \sqrt{4 - 2\alpha u}\right) \text{ for } 0 \leq u \leq u_{max} \tag{15}$$

where $C = u_{max}^{-2}$ is the integration constant chosen to make f be dimensionless.

Here an experimentally observed longitudinal upstream swimming speed of individual juvenile $P.$ $altivelis$ [19, 20] along an experimental flume subject to a given flow speed $V(<u^*)$ is identified as a realization of $u^* = u^*(V)$ as shown in Fig. 2. A standard nonlinear least square method between the theoretical (13) and experimental $V-u^*$ relationships gives the identified parameter value $\alpha = 1.71$ (-) with $u_{max} = 1.17$ (m/s) subject to the reasonably high correlation coefficient of 0.80. The identified cost function (15) is utilized for the model application in this paper.

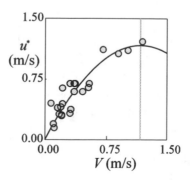

Fig. 2. Experimental [19, 20] and identified $V-u^*$ relationships for juvenile $P.$ $altivelis$.

3.3   Computational Conditions

A computational domain, which corresponds to the downstream reach of Yoshii Weir, is generated with a satellite image extracted from Google Earth (Google Inc., Mountain View, Calif.). The free software Voro (available at http://www.yss-aya.com/voro.html) is used to discretize the domain into 57,443 triangular elements with 113,609 nodes in an unstructured manner. The steady flow velocity $\mathbf{V}$ is computed with the horizontally 2-D shallow water model whose accuracy has already been verified through applications to benchmark and experimental problems [21]. The friction slope terms in the momentum equations are formulated with the conventional Manning's equation and are semi-implicitly discretized in time with an operator-splitting technique to deal with the flows with small depths and high flow speed. The HJBE and the governing Eq. (10) of the mean first hitting time M_1 is numerically solved with a 2-D Petrov-Galerkin finite element scheme [22] whose accuracy and unconditional stability in space has already been verified for simpler HJBEs. A 1-D counterpart of the scheme has also been verified from a theoretical viewpoint and its convergence rate and unconditional stability have been found [23].

The Manning's roughness coefficient is set as 0.040 (s/m$^{1/3}$) over Ω. The downstream cross-section of Ω is considered as the downstream boundary $\partial\Omega_{\mathrm{AD}}$. The entrance of the pool-type fishway and the top of the nature-like fishway where the individual fishes possibly arrive at are set as the upstream boundary $\partial\Omega_{\mathrm{AU}}$. The body of Yoshii Weir is set as the non-passable upstream boundary $\partial\Omega_{\mathrm{RN}}$ and the remaining parts of $\partial\Omega$ as the wall boundary $\partial\Omega_{\mathrm{RW}}$. The inflow discharge per unit width is 0.25 (m^2/s) along $\partial\Omega_{\mathrm{RN}}$ and 0.50 (m^2/s) along $\partial\Omega_{\mathrm{AU}}$, so that the total inflow discharge is 22 (m^3/s), which is near the ordinary flow discharge of the river reach. The profit P is set as $P = 2,000$ (s). Preliminary numerical computations implied that the optimal swimming velocity $\mathbf{u}^*$ does not significantly depend on P such that $P > 1,000$ (s). A theoretical analysis shows that the 1-D model has a similar property [23]. This paper thus considers attraction ability of juvenile $P.$ $altivelis$ subject to sufficiently high profit to be possibly gained. The dispersivity matrix $D = \left[D_{i,j}\right]$ is set to be isotropic as $D = D_0 I$ where $D_0 > 0$ and I is the 2-D identity matrix. The order of D_0 would be $O(10^{-2})$ (m^2/s) assuming an analogy with passive solute transport in horizontally 2-D flows with $|\mathbf{V}| = O(10^{-1}) - O(10^0)$ (m/s). The parameter D_0 is thus set as 0.05 (m^2/s). Numerical solution to the HJBE is computed with a Picard iteration method.

3.4   Computational Results

Figure 3(a) presents the computed flow velocity field and water depth with the shallow water model, which qualitatively agree with field observation results carried out during 2015. Figure 3(b) shows the computed optimal swimming velocity field and the mean first hitting time M_1 of the individual fishes. Figure 3(b) shows that the computed M_1 has a sharp transition along a downstream cross-section of the weir. The computed M_1 in the upstream area of the cross-section is significantly higher than that in the downstream area, indicating that the juvenile $P.$ $altivelis$ once attracted by the flow from the weir would remain just in its downstream for a long time. On the other hand,

(a)

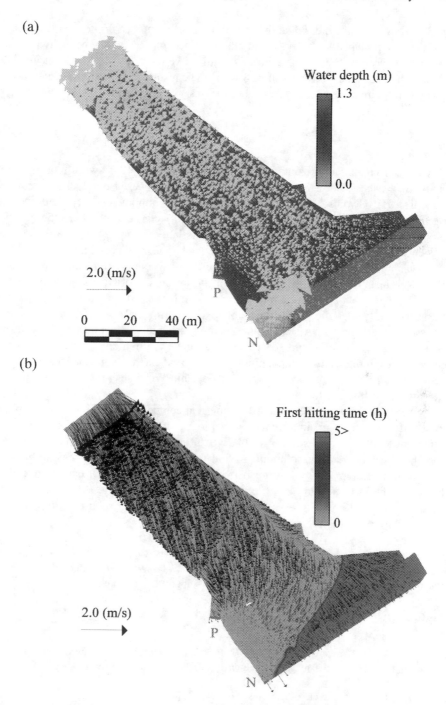

Fig. 3. (a): Computed flow velocity vectors and water depth and (b): computed optimal swimming velocity vectors and the mean first hitting time to the fishways. "P" and "N" represent the entrance of the pool-type fishway and the top of the nature-like fishway, respectively.

Fig. 3(b) shows that the individual fishes at the downstream area of the cross-section of the transition possibly be able to find the entrance of the pool-type fishway with non-zero probability. The flow speed in the nature-like fishway is too high for juvenile *P. altivelis* to ascend: exceeding almost 3 (m/s). The results suggest that the nature-like fishway can be improved to serve as a better passage for juvenile *P. altivelis*.

4   Conclusions

This paper formulated a horizontally 2-D mathematical model for swimming behavior of individual fishes in downstream river reaches of weirs based on stochastic control theory. The HJBE whose solution gives an optimal swimming velocity field and the governing PDEs of the spatially-distributed statistics were derived where the optimal swimming velocity field serves as an input for the latter.

Focusing on juvenile *P. altivelis* as a target fish species, the presented mathematical model was applied to assessing attraction ability of fishways of recently renovated Yoshii Weir installed along a cross-section of the midstream of Hii River, San-in area, Japan. The cost function and the maximum swimming speed for juvenile *P. altivelis* were successfully identified from the published experimental results of their laboratorial swimming behavior. A stable finite element scheme was applied to numerically solving the HJBE, which could successfully compute the numerical solutions for the application example. The computational results indicated long-time residence of juvenile *P. altivelis* at just downstream of Yoshii Weir where predators such as waterfowls possibly find the fishes easily.

Future research will address detailed numerical comparison of the attraction ability of Yoshii Fishway before and after the renovation. Mathematical analysis of the HJBE in the context of viscosity solutions [14] will also be performed in order to deeper comprehend behaviors of its solutions, to find links between mathematics and biology of real fish migration, and to develop better numerical schemes that can approximate solutions to the HJBE. Field observations of migration of juvenile *P. altivelis* will be carried out during the spring season of 2016 whose results will be used for validation and improvement of the present mathematical model.

Acknowledgements. We thank officers in Hii-River Fishery Cooperatives for their valuable comments and providing data. The River Fund No. 27-1263-020 in charge of The River Foundation and JSPS Research Grant No.15H06417 support this research.

References

1. Nishizawa, E., Kurokawa, T., Yabe, M.: Policies and resident's willingness to pay for restoring the ecosystem damaged by alien fish in Lake Biwa. Japan Environ. Sci. Policy **9**(5), 448–456 (2006)
2. Smith, C.L.: The life cycle of fisheries. Fisheries **11**(4), 20–25 (1986)
3. Fagan, W.F.: Connectivity, fragmentation, and extinction risk in dendritic metapopulations. Ecology **83**(12), 3243–3249 (2002)

4. Fuller, M.R., Doyle, M.W., Strayer, D.L.: Causes and consequences of habitat fragmentation in river networks. Ann. N. Y. Acad. Sci. **1355**(1), 31–51 (2015)
5. Brevé, N.W., Buijse, A.D., Kroes, M.J., Wanningen, H., Vriese, F.T.: Supporting decision-making for improving longitudinal connectivity for diadromous and potamodromous fishes in complex catchments. Sci. Total Environ. **496**, 206–218 (2014)
6. Bentley, K.T., Schindler, D.E., Armstrong, J.B., Cline, T.J., Brooks, G.T.: Inter-tributary movements by resident salmonids across a boreal riverscape. PLoS ONE **10**(9), e0136985 (2015)
7. Arenas, A., Politano, M., Weber, L., Timko, M.: Analysis of movements and behavior of smolts swimming in hydropower reservoirs. Ecol. Model. **312**, 292–307 (2015)
8. Gao, Z., Andersson, H.I., Dai, H., Jiang, F., Zhao, L.: A new Eulerian-Lagrangian agent method to model fish paths in a vertical slot fishway. Ecol. Eng. **88**, 217–225 (2016)
9. Scheibe, T.D., Richmond, M.C.: Fish individual-based numerical simulator (FINS): a particle-based model of juvenile salmonid movement and dissolved gas exposure history in the Columbia River basin. Ecol. Model. **147**(3), 233–252 (2002)
10. Yoshioka, H., Unami, K., Fujihara, M.: Mathematical and numerical analyses on a Hamilton-Jacobi-Bellman equation governing ascending behaviour of fishes. RIMS Kôkyûroku **1946**, 250–260 (2015)
11. Yoshioka, H., Shirai, T.: On analytical viscosity solution to a 1-D Hamilton-Jacobi-Bellman equation for upstream migration of individual fishes in rivers. In: Proceedings of EMAC 2015, p. 52 (2015)
12. Yoshioka, H., Yaegashi, Y., Unami, K., Fujihara, M.: Identifying the cost function for upstream migration of individual fishes in 1-D open channels based on an optimal control theory. J. JSCE. Ser. B1 **72**(4), I_1147–I_1152 (2016)
13. Øksendal, B.: Stochastic Differential Equations. Springer, Berlin (2003)
14. Fleming, W.H., Soner, H.M.: Controlled Markov Processes and Viscosity Solutions. Springer Science & Business Media, New York (2006)
15. Yoshioka, H.: Mathematical and numerical approaches for transport phenomena in surface water networks. Doctor's thesis for Graduation of Graduate School of Agriculture, Kyoto University, Japan (2016)
16. MLIT: Hydrological characteristics of Hii River. http://www.mlit.go.jp/river/toukei_chousa/kasen/jiten/nihon_kawa/87072/87072-1.html. Last Accessed 25 June 2016
17. Sato, H., Takeda, I., Somura, H.: Secular changes of statistical hydrologic data in Hii river basin. J. JSCE. Ser. B1 **68**(4), 1387–1392 (2012)
18. Yaegashi, Y., Yoshioka, H., Unami, K., Fujihara, M.: Numerical simulation of a hamilton-jacobi-bellman equation for optimal management strategy of released Plecoglossus Altivelis in river systems. In: Ohn, S.Y., Chi, S.D. (eds.) AsiaSim 2015. CCIS, vol. 603, pp. 91–101. Springer, Heidelberg (2016). doi:10.1007/978-981-10-2158-9_8
19. Takashima, N., Nakamura, S.: Experimental study on the behaviour of Ayu in fishladder. In: Proceedings of Japanese Conference on Hydraulics, vol. 28, pp. 353–358 (1984) (in Japanese)
20. Onitsuka, K., Akiyama, J., Matsuda, K., Noguchi, S., Takeuchi, H.: Influence of sidewall on swimming behavior of isolated Ayu. Plecoglossus Altivelis Altivelis. J. JSCE. Ser. B1 **68**(4), I_661–I_666 (2012)
21. Yoshioka, H., Unami, K., Fujihara, M.: A finite element/volume method model of the depth averaged horizontally 2-D shallow water equations. Int. J. Numer. Methods Fluids **75**(1), 23–41 (2014)

22. Takagi, K.: A regime-switching diffusion process model for advection-dispersion-deposition phenomena in surface water flows. Master's thesis for Graduation of Graduate School of Agriculture, Kyoto University, Japan (2016)
23. Yoshioka, H., Unami, K., Fujihara, M.: Mathematical analysis on a conforming finite element scheme for advection-dispersion-decay equations on connected graphs. J. JSCE Ser. A2 **70**(2), I_265–I_274 (2014)

A Comprehensive Optimization for the Trade-off of Energy Saving and System Performance in Controller Design

Yijie Zhang, Min Zheng[✉], and Ke Zhang

School of Mechatronic Engineering and Automation, Shanghai University,
Shanghai 200072, China
zhengmin203@shu.edu.cn

Abstract. This paper is trying to achieve the comprehensive optimization for energy consumption and system performance in PI control of ball-beam system while meeting the requirements of performance firstly. For this purpose, the expression of performance evaluation, energy evaluation and comprehensive evaluation are given firstly, and then discretizing the mathematical model of the controlled object ball-beam system and the difference equations of the ball-beam system are obtained thereafter, numerical results demonstrate the trade-off between the tracking performance and the control energy and to find the proper choices of P and PI controller parameters.

Keywords: PI control · Energy consumption · System performance · Ball-beam system · Genetic algorithm

1 Introduction

The world's energy consumption is mainly on fossil fuels nowadays. As a kind of non-renewable energy resource, fossil fuels have limited reserves. So that fossil fuels will eventually be exhausted one day. The large use of fossil fuels brings human beings two serious problems. One problem is environmental pollution, the other is climatic change. Though the transform of energy structure is on the way, it is also a tough task with a long way to go. What's more, the renewable energy sources will also bring various problems the same as fossil fuels. So, whatever the structure of the energy, whatever the advantage or disadvantage the energies may have, the effective use of energy will always be an aim people pursuing. Facing the energy crisis and the energy problems at the present times, how to use energy effectively becomes a more and more concerned topic.

This paper concerns the energy saving problem in PI control. PI control is a mature technique which generally be used in the industry. Of course the performance of PI is good enough for industrial requirements, but the energy consumption has been put few attention. As the high scale in the industry the PI control has occupied, the energy consumption of PI control should not be neglected. In fact, the PI control parameters which could be satisfied with the performance requirements have more than one group. Different groups have different energy costs. There could be a

© Springer Science+Business Media Singapore 2016
L. Zhang et al. (Eds.): AsiaSim 2016/SCS AutumnSim 2016, Part III, CCIS 645, pp. 201–209, 2016.
DOI: 10.1007/978-981-10-2669-0_22

trade-off on system performance and energy consumption, with the precondition that the system performance should be satisfied [1–11].

The optimization for PI control gives PI control new vitality in a time of artificial intelligence. The energy consumption problems PI control facing will also occur on the artificial intelligence. This means the idea of this paper may also be useful for the comprehensive optimization of system performance and energy consumption on artificial intelligence.

In this paper, the ball-beam system is introduced firstly, then the method of comprehensive optimization is given, at the last the simulation on MATLAB is presented.

2   Ball-Beam System

Ball-beam system is a convenient study plat for basic experiment and study. It is exploited for learning and studying automatic control theory and other basic control course. Ball-beam system is a non-linear system that there are non-linear relationships between the driver guide motion of motor spindle and the elevation of the rail, as well as transmission of the gear and the guide rail. Ball-beam system is also an instability system that the position of the ball is unknown even the elevation of the rail is settled. When the elevation of the rail is settled, the ball will roll to the bottom of the rail by certain acceleration.

The modeling of non-linear instability system and the design of controller have many tough problems to overcome. As the ball-beam system has the important dynamic characteristics behaved in the non-linear instability system [12–16], it is an effective experiment tool to solve those problems (Fig. 1).

Fig. 1. Ball-beam system

Ball-beam system is consist of a V shape rail, a stainless steel ball, connecting rod, DC servo motor and gear retarding mechanism. The V shape rail is made up by a stainless steel bar and a linear displacement resistor. The ball is played as a contact brush of linear displacement resistor when it rolls on the rail. As the voltage is put on the resistor's both ends, the position of the ball can be known by measuring the output voltage of the stainless steel bar. One end of the V shape rail is led by DC servo motor while the other end is settled. The angle between the V shape rail and horizontal line can be known by measuring the rotational angle of big angle and having simply geometric calculation. The position of the ball on the V shape rail is controlled by the rotation of the DC servo motor which can be controlled by designing a feedback control system [16]. Positioning the ball on the given position at any time is the main goal which is a tough and complex task because the only execution unit rail and its rotation is a non-linear instability unit.

As the precise mathematical model of ball-beam system is very complex, it is replaced by the simplified mathematical model of ball-beam system which is enough for the use of feedback control system. In fact, it is approximately impossible to build the mathematical model which can describe ball-beam system completely. In order to build the model conveniently, the mathematical model of ball-beam system is decomposed into three parts: machinery model, angle model and motor model. The machinery model connects the position of the ball on the rail x(t) and the angle between the rail and the horizontal line $\phi(t)$, the angle model connects the angle $\phi(t)$ and the rotational angle of the motor $\theta(t)$. The motor model connects the input voltage of motor control system u(t) and $\theta(t)$ which is obtained from position sensor.

2.1   Machinery Model [12]

The force let the ball roll on the rail is the resultant force of two forces, the component force which gravity gives on the rail parallel direction and the component force of friction. The process the ball rolls on the rail is approximated to a process that a mass point rolls on a smooth surface without friction. According to newton theorem, the kinetic equation which describes the process that the ball rolls on the rail is,

$$M\ddot{y}(t) = Mg\,sin\phi(t) \tag{1}$$

Where y(t) is the position of the ball on the rail, M is the mass of the ball, g is the gravitational acceleration of the ball, $\phi(t)$ is the angle between the rail and the horizontal line. Assume $\phi(t)$ is very small, (1) can be linearized as,

$$\ddot{y}(t) = g\phi(t) \tag{2}$$

Make Laplace transformation for (2), then the transfer function of the machinery model can be written as,

$$\frac{Y(s)}{\phi(s)} = \frac{g}{s^2} \tag{3}$$

2.2   Angle Model

The angle between the rail and horizontal line $\phi(t)$ is led by the rotational angle of the DC servo motor. The relationship between $\phi(t)$ and $\theta(t)$ is non-linear, and it is also influenced by the reduction ratio between the big gear and the small gear. Approximately,

$$\frac{\phi(s)}{\theta(s)} = \frac{\phi(t)}{\theta(t)} = \frac{R}{L} \tag{4}$$

Where, R is the radius of the motor plate, L is the length of the rail.

2.3 Motor Model

As the Motor is the only power source of ball-beam system, the output of the motor both control the angle of the rail directly and influence the position of the ball on the rail. Thus, the modeling of DC servo motor is necessary and the task of the DC servo motor is controlling the angle of the rail to coordinate with the reference position.

Because the motor of the ball-beam system is controlled by IPM 100 control card, the response speed of the motor is very fast, and the time constant of motor rotation θ(t) to voltage u(t) is very small. So the model of the motor can be approximated as a pure gain K.

Then, the whole system can be approximated as a cascaded system with three parts: the machinery part, the angle conversion part and the DC motor part. This is showed in Fig. 2.

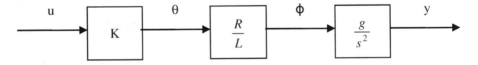

Fig. 2. Ball-beam system block diagram

The transfer function of the whole system therefore can be written as

$$\frac{Y(s)}{U(s)} = \frac{KRg/L}{s^2} \tag{5}$$

Where is simplified as 1.

It has to be emphasized that a lot of approximation has been made during the modeling process. Firstly, the motor dynamics have been ignored to a pure gain. Secondly, the motor dynamics and the ball dynamics are coupled, and this fact is ignored too. However, these approximations do not affect the validity of the results.

3 The Comprehensive Optimization of PI in Ball-Beam System

As the purpose of this paper is to study the comprehensive optimization for energy consumption and system performance in feedback control of PI control, the evaluation of performance and energy consumption should be given firstly. This paper uses the expressions in [1], and makes some changes from the original expressions as,

$$E_y = \sum_{k=1}^{t} (r(k) - y(k))^2 \tag{6}$$

$$E_u = \sum_{k=1}^{t} u(k)^2 \tag{7}$$

$$u(k) = k_p e(k) + k_i \sum_{j=0}^{k} e(j)T \tag{8}$$

Where, E_y is the performance evaluation, E_u is the energy evaluation, T is the sampling period. The comprehensive evaluation is the sum of the two evaluations. That is,

$$E_s = E_y + E_u \tag{9}$$

The goal of this paper is to find the minimum E_s while guaranteeing the requirements of the performance.

The block diagram of negative feedback control loop is shown in Fig. 3.

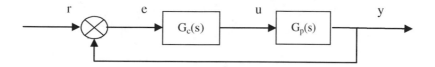

Fig. 3. Negative feedback control loop block diagram

Where $G_c(s)$ is the transfer function of controller, $G_p(s)$ is the transfer function of ball-beam system, r is the reference input, e is error, u is the output of controller, y is the output of the loop. The expressions of $G_c(s)$ and $G_p(s)$ are,

$$G_c(s) = \frac{U(s)}{E(s)} = k_p + \frac{k_i}{s} \tag{10}$$

$$G_p(s) = \frac{C}{s^2} \tag{11}$$

Make z-transform to the Laplace's expression of ball-beam system, then transfer the z-transform expression into difference equation which could be used in MATLAB directly.

$$G_p(s) = \frac{C}{s^2} \Rightarrow g_p(t) = c \cdot t \tag{12}$$

Using nT instead of t,

$$g(nT) = CnT \tag{13}$$

Make z-transform to (13),

$$G(z) = \sum_{n=0}^{\infty} CnT \cdot z^{-n} = \frac{CTz}{(z-1)^2} = \frac{Y(z)}{U(z)} \tag{14}$$

That is,

$$\frac{CTz}{z^2 - 2z + 1} = \frac{Y(z)}{U(z)} \tag{15}$$

Both numerator and denominator are divided by z2,

$$\frac{CTz^{-1}}{1 - 2z^{-1} + z^{-2}} = \frac{Y(z)}{U(z)} \tag{16}$$

Then, we have,

$$CTz^{-1}U(z) = Y(z) - 2z^{-1}Y(z) + z^{-2}Y(z) \tag{17}$$

Change (17) into difference equation,

$$CTu(k-1) = y(k) - 2y(k-1) + y(k-2) \tag{18}$$

So,

$$y(k) = 2y(k-1) - y(k-2) + CTu(k-1) \tag{19}$$

The difference equations of negative feedback control loop in Fig. 3 is obtained as,

$$\begin{cases} e(k) = r(k) - y(k) \\ u(k) = k_p e(k) + k_i \sum_{j=0}^{k} e(j) \\ y(k) = 2y(k-1) - y(k-2) + CTu(k-1) \end{cases} \tag{20}$$

In this paper, we use the following controller form of incremental PI controller.

$$\begin{cases} e(k) = r(k) - y(k) \\ \Delta u(k) = k_p(e(k) - e(k-1)) + k_i \cdot e(k) \\ y(k+1) = 2y(k) - y(k-1) + CTu(k) \end{cases} \tag{21}$$

This difference equations can be used in MATLAB directly.

4 Simulation

The genetic algorithm is used in this paper to search for the minimum. The genetic algorithm is based on the genetic algorithm optimization toolbox(GAOT), and some changes have been made to adjust the ball-beam system.

Using genetic algorithm to search the minimum in MATLAB, the K_p and K_i which make E_s to the minimum is the goal value. The initial values are given as: $r = 10$, $y(1) = 0$, $y(2) = 0$, $e(1) = 0$, the recycle starts from $k = 2$ to ensure the subscript to be positive.

Figure 4 shows the relationships between the value K_p, K_i and the value E_s, where x-axis is the value of K_p, y-axis is the value of K_i, z-axis is the value of E_s. It can be concluded from Fig. 4 that E_s will be smallest when the value of K_p is around 0.5, and the bigger the value of K_i is, the bigger the value of E_s is. The whole functional image is like a dustpan.

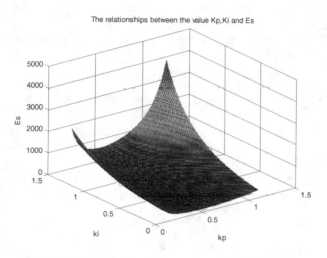

Fig. 4. The relationships between the value K_p, K_i and E_s

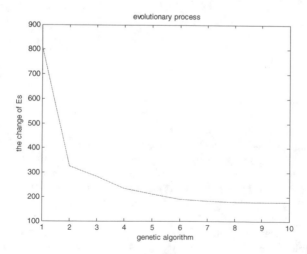

Fig. 5. Genetic iterative process

Figure 5 is the genetic iterative process, abscissa is the number of iterations, and ordinate is the value of E_s. As the function image is simple, the number of iterations is only 10.

The final result of the search of genetic algorithm is: $x = 0.55706$ for K_p, $y = 0.011441$ for K_i, $z = 169.3842$ for E_s. It can be known from the results that K_p is very small and K_i is nearly 0. The results have matter with simplification and approximation of ball-beam system, which make the number of iterations to be 10. In fact, the results indicate that the method this paper proposed makes the comprehensive optimization of system performance and energy consumption comes true.

The mathematical model will be different when the control object is different, which will let the final value of K_p, K_i and the number of iteration become widely different from the ones this paper get.

5   Conclusion

The purpose of this paper is to achieve the PI comprehensive optimization of system performance and energy consumption. For this purpose the expression of performance evaluation, the energy evaluation and comprehensive evaluation are given firstly. Then the mathematical model of ball-beam system is transferred into difference equation through discretization. At the end of this paper, the best combination of K_p and K_i are founded by using genetic algorithm.

Acknowledgements. This work is supported by Shanghai Key Laboratory of Power Station Technology, the Project-sponsored by SRF for ROCS, SEM, and Shanghai Science Technology Commission No. 14ZR1414800, 14JC1402200.

References

1. Li, K., Wu, Y.L., Li, S.Y., Xi, Y.G.: Energy saving and system performance - an art of trade-off for controller design. In: IEEE 2013 International Conference on Systems, Man, and Cybernetics (SMC), vol. 806, pp. 4737–4742 (2013). doi:10.1109/SMC
2. International Energy Agency: World Energy Outlook 2005. IEA, London (2005)
3. The Climate Group: Profits Up, Carbon Down, The Climate Group (2005). www.the climategroup.org/what-we-do/publications/carbon-downprofits-up-new-edition/
4. Freudenberg, J.S., Looze, D.P.: Right half plane zeros and poles and design tradeoffs in feedback systems. IEEE Trans. Autom. Control **30**, 555–565 (1985)
5. Bellman, R.E.: Dynamic Programming. Princeton University Press, Princeton (1957)
6. Fleming, W., Rishel, R.: Deterministic and Stochastic Optimal Control. Springer, Heidelberg (1975)
7. Chen, J., Ren, Z., Hara, S., Qiu, L.: Best tracking and regulation performance under control energy constraint. IEEE Trans. Autom. Control **48**, 1320–1336 (2003)
8. Cloostermand, M.B.G., Hetel, L., Van DeWouwa, N., Heemels, W.P.M.H.: Controller synthesis for networked control systems. Automatica **46**(10), 1584–1594 (2010)
9. Dorf, R.C., Bishop, R.H.: Modern Control Systems, 10th edn. Addison-Wesley, Boston (2004)

10. Kwakernaak, H., Sivan, R.: Linear Optimal Control Systems, 1st edn. Wiley-Interscience, Hoboken (1972)
11. Garcia, C.E., Prett, D.M., Morari, M.: Model predictive control: theory and practice. Automatica **25**(3), 335–348 (1989)
12. Pang, Y.X., Jin, D., Meng, X.D.: Modeling, simulation and controller design of ball-beam system. Eng. J. Wuhan Univ. **38**(6), 142–146 (2005)
13. Ogata, K.T.: Modern Control Engineering, 3rd edn. Electronic Industry Press, Beijing (2000)
14. Salvatore, S., Esposito, E., Miller, J.: Ball & beam control system. IEEE Trans. Autom. Control **30**(3), 376–388 (2002)
15. Mark, R.M.: Robust Control. Academic Press, New York (1986)
16. Qiu, L., Zhou, K.M.: Feedback Control. Prentice Hall, Upper Saddle River (2005)

Electromagnetic Wave Propagation Simulation in Horizontally Inhomogeneous Evaporation Duct

Yang Shi, Yinxin Yang$^{(\boxtimes)}$, and Kunde Yang

School of Marine Science and Technology,
Northwestern Polytechnical University, Xi'an, China
yxyang@nwpu.edu.cn

Abstract. The evaporation duct forms above the ocean and has an important impacts on electromagnetic wave propagation. In this paper, the electromagnetic wave propagation in horizontally inhomogeneous evaporation duct is investigated based on the advanced propagation model. Two inhomogeneous cases are investigated and compared with the homogeneous case. The result shows that path loss is higher than that in the homogeneous case when the evaporation duct height at the receiver is lower than that at the transmitter. It is also concluded that the horizontal inhomogeneity has a significant influence when the frequency of electromagnetic wave is lower than 13 GHz.

Keywords: Electromagnetic wave propagation · Advanced propagation model · Evaporation duct · Horizontally inhomogeneous

1 Introduction

Humidity decreases rapidly above the ocean surface, resulting in a leaky wave guide. The electromagnetic wave propagation bends towards the ocean surface in this guide. It is known as the evaporation duct, which has an important effects on electromagnetic propagation above the ocean. The evaporation duct almost exists all over the world's ocean and usually affects the low-altitude radar and communication systems [1, 2].

Many propagation models were developed to study electromagnetic wave propagation in troposphere. There are the ray optics model, parabolic equation model [3–5], waveguide mode model, [6] and hybrid model [7]. The advanced propagation model (APM) is a hybrid model and it combines radio optics model and terrain parabolic equation model. The terrain and rough sea surface effects are considered in this model and it was adopted by the U.S. navy in the advanced refractive effects prediction system (AREPS). However, there are still large error between model and experimental results [2]. The inhomogeneous evaporation duct environment is believed to be a significant factor accounting for these errors, but the relevant research was seldom reported.

In this paper, the effects of horizontally inhomogeneous evaporation duct on electromagnetic propagation are investigated. The rest of the paper is structured as follows. The evaporation duct model and the propagation model are introduced in Sect. 2. The electromagnetic wave propagation in inhomogeneous evaporation duct is investigated in Sect. 3. The conclusions are introduced in Sect. 4.

© Springer Science+Business Media Singapore 2016

L. Zhang et al. (Eds.): AsiaSim 2016/SCS AutumnSim 2016, Part III, CCIS 645, pp. 210–216, 2016.

DOI: 10.1007/978-981-10-2669-0_23

2   Simulation Models

2.1   Evaporation Duct Model

The propagation of microwave in the atmosphere depends on gradient of the refractivity index of air. The refractive index is the ratio of the speed of microwave in a vacuum (c) to that in the material (v), i.e.,

$$n = \frac{c}{v}. \tag{1}$$

As n nearly equals 1 in the troposphere (about 1.0003), the refractive index is represented by a quantity N:

$$N = (n - 1) \times 10^6. \tag{2}$$

The refractivity N can be calculated by the following empirical equation (frequency: 1 GHz–100 GHz):

$$N = \frac{77.6P}{T} - 5.6\frac{e}{T} + 3.75 \times 10^5 \frac{e}{T^2}, \tag{3}$$

where T(K) is atmospheric temperature, P(hPa) is atmospheric pressure, e(hPa) is water vapor pressure, and the constants have been determined empirically. Modified refractivity takes earth's curvature into consideration and it is defined as:

$$M = 77.6\frac{P}{T} - 5.6\frac{e}{T} + 375000\frac{e}{T^2} + 0.157z, \tag{4}$$

where z(m) is the altitude above sea level, and more details can be found in Babin' s research [8, 9].

The vertical gradient of M determines the refraction types in the troposphere. When the evaporation duct happens, the microwave bends downward and reflects from the sea surface. The evaporation duct height (EDH) is the position where the

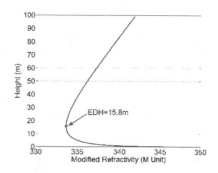

Fig. 1.   The evaporation duct modified refractivity profile (EDH = 15.8 m, pressure: 1022.2 hPa, wind speed: 8 m/s, sea surface temperature: 20°C, air temperature: 20°C, relative humidity: 65 %).

minimum M is located. In this paper, the Naval Postgraduate School (NPS) model [10] is used to calculate the EDH. As it is shown in Fig. 1, the EDH is 15.8 m.

2.2 Propagation Model

The parabolic equation (PE) method are widely used in simulating the electromagnetic wave propagation. The standard parabolic equation can be obtained from the Helmholtz equation in the following form:

$$\frac{\partial^2 u(x,z)}{\partial z^2} + 2ik_0 \frac{\partial u(x,z)}{\partial x} + k_0^2[m^2(x,z) - 1]u(x,z) = 0, \tag{5}$$

where u is the electric field for horizontal polarization, k_0 is the free space wave number, x is the range, z is the height, and m is the modified refractive index.

$u(x_k, z)$ is the complex scalar component of the field at the height z and in the range x_k. Then, $u(x_{k+1}, z)$ could be obtained by the Fourier split-step solution as:

$$u(x_{k+1}, z) = \exp(i\frac{k_0}{2}(m^2 - 1)\delta x) \times F^{-1}\left\{ \exp(-i\frac{p^2\delta x}{2k_0})F\{u(x_k, z)\} \right\}, \tag{6}$$

F[•] is the Fourier transform and F^{-1}[•] is the Fourier inverse transform. δx is the range increment and p is the transform variable. More information about Fourier split-step PE solution can be found in Ref. [11, 12].

3 Simulation and Discussion

The simulation conditions are shown in the Table 1. The EDH is 15 m (Fig. 1) and the frequency is 10.5 GHz. The electromagnetic wave propagation in homogeneous evaporation duct is shown in Fig. 2. The evaporation duct is like a waveguide and the path loss is low in the evaporation duct. For example, when the receiving antenna is 5 m, the path loss at 60 km is about 140 dB. The path loss at 200 km is about 150 dB, about 10 dB higher than that at 50 km. However, if the receiving antenna is outside the evaporation duct, the path loss is about 20 dB higher than in the evaporation duct.

Table 1. Simulation conditions.

Transmitter	
Frequency	10.5 GHz
Elevation angle	0°
Transmitting antenna height	6 m
Range	0–200 km
Height	0–100 m
Polarization	Horizontal

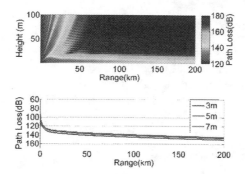

Fig. 2. Electromagnetic wave propagation in evaporation duct (the homogeneous case).

The two inhomogeneous cases are then calculated. The EDH decreases on the propagation path in one case and increases in the other. Figure 3 shows the modified refractivity profiles.

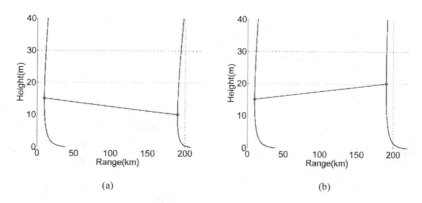

(a)   (b)

Fig. 3. Two Inhomogeneous cases (a) EDH: 15 m-10 m and (b) EDH: 15 m–20 m.

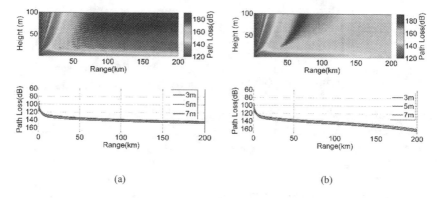

(a)   (b)

Fig. 4. The microwave propagation in the inhomogeneous case (a) EDH: 15 m–20 m (b) EDH: 15 m–10 m.

The microwave can be trapped in both cases. However, the impacts are quite different. The path loss is lower in the second case and the trapping capacity of evaporation duct is stronger. The reasons are as follows. When the EDH increases along the propagation path (15 m–20 m), the trapping capacity of the evaporation duct becomes stronger. As a result of the refractivity, the microwave which departures from the evaporation duct returns back to the duct. The path loss is reduced in the evaporation duct. When the EDH decreases along the propagation path (15 m–10 m), the trapping capacity of the duct becomes weaker. As a result, the microwave can't be trapped and leaves the evaporation duct.

Figure 5(a) compares the of path loss at 3 m in the homogeneous case and in the inhomogeneous cases In the first case, the path loss at 200 km is about 1 dB lower than that in the homogeneous case. While in the second case (EDH: 15 m-10 m), the path loss is about 13 dB higher than that in the homogeneous case. The difference is about 14 dB between the two inhomogeneous cases. In Fig. 5 (b), the path loss at 200 km is shown both in homogeneous and inhomogeneous cases. When the receiving antenna height is less than 5 m, the path loss (EDH: 15 m-20 m) is the lowest, about 1 dB lower than that in the homogeneous case. However, the path loss (EDH: 15 m-10 m) is about 10 dB higher than that in the homogeneous case. When the receiving antenna height is higher than 20 m, the path loss in the second case is the lowest, about 10 dB-20 dB lower than the other cases. The reason is that the microwave leaks from the evaporation duct in the second case (Fig. 4).

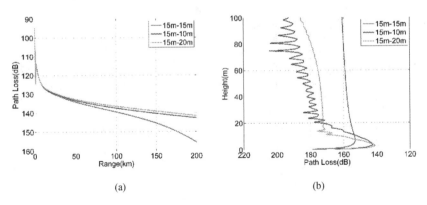

Fig. 5. The microwave propagation path loss evaporation duct (a) receiving antenna height: 3 m (b) in homogeneous and inhomogeneous evaporation duct

The horizontally inhomogeneous evaporation duct also has different impacts on electromagnetic propagation at different frequencies. The evaporation duct information and the other transmitting information are shown in the Table 1. The frequency range is from 3 GHz to 15 GHz. The path losses (200 km, 3 m) at different frequencies are shown in Fig. 6. The result shows that the horizontal inhomogeneity of evaporation duct has a larger impact on the low frequency microwave. For example, when the frequency is higher than 14 GHz, the both two cases only cause a small impact (less than 5 dB). As the frequency increases, the impact continues to reduce. However, when the frequency is 5 GHz, the first case (EDH: 15 m–20 m) causes an increase of 32 dB compared with the homogeneous case. In the second case (EDH: 15 m–10 m), the path loss reduces about 39 dB compared with the homogeneous case.

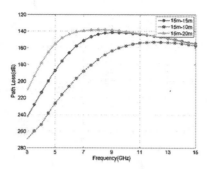

Fig. 6. The microwave path losses of different frequencies (at 3 m and 200 km).

4   Conclusions

In this paper, the impacts of horizontally inhomogeneous evaporation duct on electromagnetic wave propagation are studied. The horizontal inhomogeneity of evaporation duct has an important impact on microwave propagation above the ocean. The following conclusions are obtained.

(1) When the EDH at receiver is lower than at transmitter, the horizontal inhomogeneity of evaporation duct causes a significant impact on microwave propagation near the sea surface. The path loss is higher in this case than in the homogeneous case. While in the opposite case, the impact of inhomogeneous evaporation duct is slight.

(2) The horizontally inhomogeneous evaporation duct has different influences on microwave propagation at different frequencies. In general, the microwave propagation at low frequency is affected more seriously by horizontal inhomogeneity of evaporation duct.

References

1. Anderson, K.D.: 94-GHz propagation in the evaporation duct. IEEE Trans. Antennas Propag. **38**(5), 746–753 (1990)
2. Woods, G.S., Ruxton, A., Huddlestone-Holmes, C., Gigan, G.: High-capacity, long-range, over ocean microwave link using the evaporation duct. IEEE J. Oceanic Eng. **34**(3), 323–330 (2009)
3. Barrios, A.E.: A terrain parabolic equation model for propagation in the troposphere. IEEE Trans. Antennas Propag. **42**(1), 90–98 (1994)
4. Kuttler, J.R., Dockery, G.D.: Theoretical description of the parabolic approximation/Fourier split-step method of representing electromagnetic propagation in the troposphere. Radio Sci. **26**(2), 381–393 (1991)
5. Donohue, D.J., Kuttler, J.R.: Propagation modeling over terrain using the parabolic wave equation. IEEE Trans. Antennas Propag. **48**(2), 260–277 (2000)

6. Budden, K.G.: The Wave-Guide Mode Theory of Wave Propagation. Logos Press, Wicklow (1961)
7. Hitney, H.V.: Hybrid ray optics and parabolic equation methods for radar propagation modeling. In: Radar 1992, International Conference, IET, pp. 58–61 (1992)
8. Babin, S.M., Young, G.S., Carton, J.A.: A new model of the oceanic evaporation duct. J. Appl. Meteorol. **36**(3), 193–204 (1997)
9. Babin, S.M., Dockery, G.D.: LKB-based evaporation duct model comparison with buoy data. J. Appl. Meteorol. **41**(4), 434–446 (2002)
10. Frederickson, P.A., Davidson, K.L., Goroch, A.K.: Operational evaporation duct model for MORIAH. Naval Postgraduate School Report Draft version 1.2 (2000)
11. Dockery, G.D.: Modeling electromagnetic wave propagation in the troposphere using the parabolic equation. IEEE Trans. Antennas Propag. **36**(10), 1464–1470 (1988)
12. Barrios, A.E., Patterson, W.L.: Advanced propagation model (APM) ver.1.3.1 computer software configuration item (CSCI) documents (2002)

Seasonal Effects of Sound Speed Profile on Mid-Range Acoustic Propagations Modes: Reliable Acoustic Path and Bottom Bounce

Peng Xiao, Yixin Yang[✉], Long Yang, and Yang Shi

School of Marine Science and Technology,
Northwestern Polytechnical University, Fremont, China
yxyang@nwpu.edu.cn

Abstract. The detection of objects for tens of kilometers' distance is difficult in the deep sea. For the purpose, Reliable acoustic path (RAP) and bottom bounce (BB) propagation modes are studied and utilized frequently in recent years. In this paper, the seasonal effects of sound speed profile (SSP) on these two modes are simulated and analyzed. From the simulation, it is concluded that the changes of SSP in different seasons have little influence on the transmission loss (TL) on RAP if the receiver depth is below the critical depth of summer, and the BB mode is insensitive to the SSP change, too. The simulations can help us to have a better use of these two propagation modes.

Keywords: Sound speed profile · Season effect · Reliable acoustic path · RAP · Bottom bounce · BB · Acoustic propagation

1 Introduction

Sound exhibits efficient propagation features in the water, and it is also used as the most important tool for detecting and communicating applications in the ocean, especially for the military use [1]. Since World War I, the underwater acoustic equipment, sonar, has been used to detect submarines. However, till now the sonar technologies still face a lot of challenges. The main difficulty comes from the great uncertainties that underwater environment works on the sound propagation [2, 3]. The sound propagation is greatly influenced by the sound speed field and seabed properties in the ocean, and it is a key factor to improve sonar performances to get hold of the laws that sound propagation obeys under various conditions.

Another challenge for sonar technologies is to detect objects on Mid-range (10 km–50 km) in the deep ocean. The sound has a feature that it propagates to the lower speed area, thus in the deep ocean with a canonical speed profile, sound rays will bend downward after leaving a source close to the sea surface. This leads to a shadow zone area 10 km–50 km away from the source. To detect objects on this range, more propagation modes is needed, such as reliable acoustic path (RAP) mode [4, 5] and the bottom bounce (BB) mode. The RAP conditions occur when the receiver is placed at the large depth where the sound speed exceeds the maximum sound velocity in the vicinity of the

© Springer Science+Business Media Singapore 2016
L. Zhang et al. (Eds.): AsiaSim 2016/SCS AutumnSim 2016, Part III, CCIS 645, pp. 217–222, 2016.
DOI: 10.1007/978-981-10-2669-0_24

surface. The depth where this occurs is referred as the critical depth. The concept of RAP has been proposed for many decades, but till recent years it began to be analyzed and applied. The RAP provides a high signal-to noise ratio environment because (i) the direct path between source and receiver, insensitive to surface and bottom reflections and (ii) ambient noise lower than the average ambient noise in the deep ocean [4]. At the same time, the bottom bounce (BB) mode uses the reflected signals by the bottom to detect objects. In the bottom bounce mode, sound energy is directed towards the bottom, and these paths combine to produce an increase in the received signal and reduce the extent of the shadow zone. With these two method at hand, opportunities have been brought to detect the objects on the Mid-range. We need to know the effect that under-water environment worked on the these two mode. In this paper, the seasonal effects of sound speed profile is mainly discussed.

2   Simulation Models

Figure 1 shows the sound speed profile of a deep location in Philippine Sea (20°40′N, 128°50′E) obtained from the WOA09 dataset: Fig. 1(a) is a mean sound speed profile of a year, and Fig. 2(b) shows the upper 500 m sound speed profiles of February, May, August and November. The profiles illustrate that the seasonal changes are obvious in the upper water of the deep ocean (within 200 m depth). A mixed layer appears in winter and vanishes in summer. In February, the surface temperature is lowest in the year, so there is a thick mixed layer about 120 m; in May, the surface temperature and sound speed begin to rise, and the mixed layer vanishes; in August, the surface temperature is highest, and the surface speed shows a very strong positive gradient; and in November, the surface temperature is cold again, the mixed layer begins to appear. The sound speed shows a seasonal cycle resulting from the annual variation of wind stirring and heat flux. Since the sound propagation is greatly influenced by the profile, the sound field will be different in different seasons, for both RAP mode and BB mode.

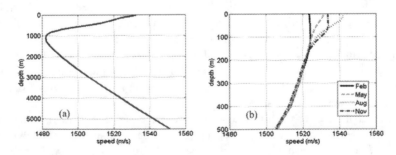

Fig. 1. (a) The mean SSP for a year; (b) The upper 500-m SSP in four different months.

It should be noticed that the RAP is the direct path between receiver and source, so it has no interactions with the bottom. However, the BB mode mainly uses the bottom reflected signal, thus the bottom conditions are also very important for BB propagation. In this report, except for the modeling of the real situation, the seismo-acoustic model

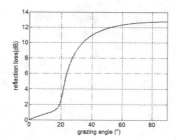

Fig. 2. Bottom reflection loss as function of incident grazing angle. The loss is calculated for a bottom sound speed of 1600 m/s, density 1.5 g/cm3 and the bottom absorption of 0.5 dB per wavelength. The water sound speed is 1500 m/s and the density is 1 g/cm3.

is simple, assuming the bottom to be a homogenous fluid with sound speed 1600 m/s, density of 1.5 g/cm^3 and bottom absorption of 0.5 dB per wavelength. These parameters results in a frequency independent bottom reflection loss in Fig. 2. The following simulations are based on the acoustic-field calculation model, Ramgeo, which is a well-spread Fortran code based on the parabolic equation (PE) method [6]. Ramgeo uses the split-step Pade solution allowing large range steps and is the most efficient PE algorithm that has been developed. The simulation frequency is 200 Hz.

3   Simulation and Discussion

3.1   Seasonal Effects of Sound Speed Profile on RAP

The sound fields are plotted in Fig. 3 for four different months. The source depth is 50 m in Fig. 3(a), (b), (c) and (d), and 200 m in Fig. 3(e), (f), (g) and (h). The seasonal profiles mainly affect the critical depth, or in other words, they change the working area of RAP. The critical depths are about 4000 m, 4500 m, 5000 m and 4500 m in February, May, August and November respectively. The change of the profiles result in that the turning

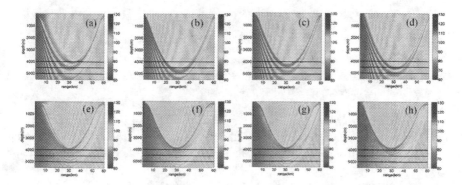

Fig. 3. Sound field calculated by PE model. February: panel (a) and (e); May: panel (b) and (d); August: panel (c) and (g); November: panel (d) and (h). The upper four panels are for the 50-m depth source, and the lower four panels are for the 200-m depth source.

depth are different too, especially for the 50-m source case: The turning depth is the smallest in February (4000 m), and the largest in August (4500 m). If the receiver is located at a 4000 m depth which is the RAP area in winter, it will be in the shadow zone in summer. So the transmission loss will suffer a great reduction from winter to summer at this depth. However, if the receiver depth is set at a 5000 m depth, which is below the critical depth all the year round, the transmission loss will change very little. For the 200-m source, the seasonal-changed speed profiles have very small effects on the propagation. This is because that the acoustic rays bend downwards soon after leaving the source, and the speed below the source location is the most important factor for the sound propagation; since the season change has very small effects on the speed profile below 200-m source, very small influence will be worked on the RAP propagation, too.

The above discussions are more obvious in the following Figs. 4 and 5. Figure 4 are the transmission loss curve for different seasons. The source depth is 50 m and the receivers are at the depth of 4000 m, 4500 m and 5000 m. It can be seen in the figures that the TL received at 4000 m changes most and TL received at 5000 m is more stable.

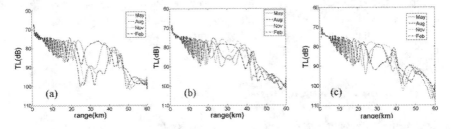

Fig. 4. Transmission loss curves of different months for the 50-m depth source. (a) receive depth: 4000 m; (b) receive depth: 4500 m; (c) receive depth: 5000 m.

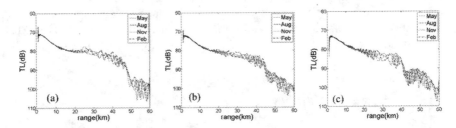

Fig. 5. Transmission loss curves of different months for the 200-m depth source. (a) receive depth: 4000 m; (b) receive depth: 4500 m; (c) receive depth: 5000 m.

Figure 5 are the transmission loss curves similar to Fig. 4 but the source depth is 200 m. The curves change very little for different months, and it shows that the sound speed changes result from the seasons change have very small effect on the propagations of relative deep sources.

From the above simulations, we can know that when we use the RAP, the receivers are better to be set at a depth that below the critical depth of summer. This trick can help to avoid the effect of the season change. However, if the depth of source is deeper than the depth that season change influences, the change of TLs will be small, too.

3.2 Seasonal Effects of Sound Speed Profile on BB

Next we will analyze the seasonal effects of sound speed on BB mode. The transmission curves are plotted in Figs. 6 and 7. Figure 6 are the curves of four different months of which source depth is 50 m, and the receiver depth are 50 m in (a) and 200 m in (b) respectively. Within 20 km, the TLs change very much due to the mixed layer's existence: the TL is the smallest in February because the mixed layer forms a surface duct for the sound, and the part of sound energy trapped in the mixed layer can propagate in the duct for a relative long distance [7, 8]. In Fig. 6(b), although the receiver depth is deeper than the mixed layer lower boundary, the sound energy will have a leakage from the surface duct. Thus the TL is still smaller that other months. In August, since the mixed layer vanishes, the energy will propagate near the surface for a very short range. Within the range between 20 km to 50 km, the energy of BB is dominant. From the figures we can see that although the change of SSP makes the interference patterns different in four months, the envelope of the curves are similar, which means that the change of SSP in different seasons will have relative small influence on the BB energy.

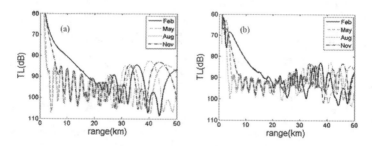

Fig. 6. The transmission loss curves in four different months with 50-m source depth. (a) receiver depth: 50 m; (b) receiver depth: 200 m.

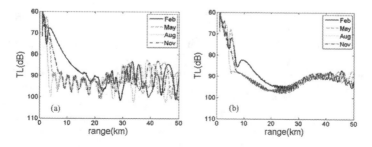

Fig. 7. The transmission loss curves in four different months with 200-m source depth. (a) receiver depth: 50 m; (b) receiver depth: 200 m.

Figure 7 shows the TL curves with a 200-m source depth. Similar to 50-m source case, we can see in the figure that the changed SSPs mainly influence the transmission loss within 20 km, but have little affect on the BB energy.

According to the above simulations, it is reasonable to give the conclusion that the BB propagation mode is insensitive to the season-changed SSP. Actually, when the BB mode is utilized, more attention should be focused on the sea bottom parameters such as bottom composition and the bottom roughness. Besides, the frequency and grazing angle that rays strike the bottom are also main factors.

4   Conclusions

We study the seasonal effects of sound speed profile on RAP mode and BB mode, and some conclusions can be generated from the simulations:

(a) The seasonal profiles mainly affect the critical depth and the working area of RAP. If the receiver depth is set at a depth which is below the critical depth all the year round, the change of seasonal SSP has very little influence on the RAP transmission loss;

(b) If the depth of source is deeper than the depth that season change influences, the change of TLs will be small, too;

(c) BB propagation mode is insensitive to the season-changed SSP.

These conclusions help us to have a better use of these two propagation modes for detecting objects and some other applications.

References

1. Jensen, F.B., et al.: Computational Ocean Acoustic, 2nd edn. Springer, New York (2011)
2. Colosi, J.A., Brown, M.G.: Efficient numerical simulation of stochastic internal-wave-induced sound-speed perturbation fields. J. Acoust. Soc. Am. **103**, 2232–2235 (1998)
3. Beron-Vera, F.J., et al.: Ray dynamics in a long-range acoustic propagation experiment. J. Acoust. Soc. Am. **114**, 1226–1242 (2003)
4. Duan, R., et al.: A reliable acoustic path: physical properties and a source localization method. Chin. Phys. B **21**, 276–289 (2012)
5. Rui, D., et al.: Moving source localization with a single hydrophone using multipath time delays in the deep ocean. J. Acoust. Soc. Am. **136**, 159–165 (2014)
6. Collins, M.D.: A split-step Padé solution for the parabolic equation method. J. Acoust. Soc. Am. **93**, 1736–1742 (1993)
7. Duan, R., et al.: Investigation of long-range sound propagation in surface ducts. Chin. Phys. B **22**, 124301 (2013)
8. Duan, R., et al.: A study of the mixed layer of the South China Sea based on the multiple linear regression. Acta Oceanol. Sinica **31**, 19–31 (2012)

A Centralized Cubature Information Filter Algorithm for Real Time Orbit Determination by Multiple Handheld Terminals

Zhaoming Li[1(✉)], Wenge Yang[2], Dan Ding[2], and Shuyan Ni[2]

[1] Company of Postgraduate Management, Academy of Equipment,
Beijing 101416, China
lizhaomingzbxy@163.com
[2] Department of Optical and Electrical Equipment,
Academy of Equipment, Beijing 101416, China

Abstract. A centralized cubature information filter algorithm by multi-handheld terminals is proposed to improve the real time orbit determination precision. First, nonlinear state and measurement equation of orbit determination is given. Then, cubature transformation is embedded in extended information filter to obtain cubature information filter, the equivalent expression of pseudo measurement matrix is obtained by using the statistical linear error propagation method, and the multi-source observation information fusion process is expressed as accumulation form of local information matrix contribution and information state contribution. Finally, the simulation results verify the effectiveness of the proposed algorithm.

Keywords: Centralized cubature information filter · Orbit determination · Handheld terminal

1 Introduction

It mainly depends on the large ground TT&C equipment to determine the satellite orbit state in real time for space target surveillance [1]. However, due to the equipment is complexity and has no mobility, it is necessary to study to use the mobile handheld terminal to realize the real time orbit determination. The measurement elements mainly include range, velocity and angle, velocity measurement device uses Doppler principle, it is simple and has less error sources, which is convenient to make into handheld products. The handheld terminal uses ground control points combined with inertial navigation to realize its high precision positioning, it avoids to use large measurement antenna, and get rid of the dependence on traditional ground station. Due to its light weight and mobility, it can constitute a real time orbit determination system with a portable data processing computer for more flexible application.

Satellite real time orbit determination is essentially a nonlinear filter problem, the common used methods are Extended Kalman filter [2] (EKF) and Unsented Kalman filter [3, 4] (UKF). EKF uses first order Taylor expansion of nonlinear function, and reduces the filter estimation precision. UKF adopts Sigma points [5] to approximate

© Springer Science+Business Media Singapore 2016
L. Zhang et al. (Eds.): AsiaSim 2016/SCS AutumnSim 2016, Part III, CCIS 645, pp. 223–232, 2016.
DOI: 10.1007/978-981-10-2669-0_25

nonlinear function, effectively improved the precision of nonlinear estimation, but the selection of parameters has no clear theoretical basis, and when the variable dimension is greater than 3, there exists negative weight, which will affects the stability of the estimates directly. Arasaratnam [6, 7] proposes Cubature kalman filter (CKF), which uses spherical radial principle, and adopts a set of equally weighted cubature points to realize the nonlinear approximation of Bayesian integral, and has a high filtering accuracy. Compared with UKF, CKF has strict mathematical proof, and reduces the amount of calculation, which has been widely used in many fields. Research now mainly focus on ground radar, measurement elements mainly include range, velocity, azimuth and elevation. Single handheld terminal has only velocity, and it is a weak observation system. So we consider to use multiple handheld terminals to constitute a centralized filter.

2 State and Measurement Equation of Orbit Determination

2.1 State Equation

The satellite orbit dynamics equation with J_2 perturbation in Earth Fixed Coordinate system is as follows [8]:

$$
\begin{cases}
\dot{x} = v_x \\
\dot{y} = v_y \\
\dot{z} = v_z \\
\dot{v}_x = \frac{\mu x}{r^3}\left[J_2\left(\frac{R_e}{r}\right)\left(7.5\frac{z^2}{r^2} - 1.5\right) - 1\right] + \omega_e^2 x + 2\omega_e \cdot v_y + a_x \\
\dot{v}_y = \frac{\mu y}{r^3}\left[J_2\left(\frac{R_e}{r}\right)\left(7.5\frac{z^2}{r^2} - 1.5\right) - 1\right] + \omega_e^2 y - 2\omega_e \cdot v_x + a_y \\
\dot{v}_z = \frac{\mu z}{r^3}\left[J_2\left(\frac{R_e}{r}\right)\left(7.5\frac{z^2}{r^2} - 4.5\right) - 1\right] + a_z \\
r = \sqrt{x^2 + y^2 + z^2}
\end{cases}
\tag{1}
$$

Where, J_2 denotes harmonic coefficient, R_e denotes the radius of earth, ω_e denotes earth angular velocity, $\boldsymbol{a} = \begin{bmatrix} a_x & a_y & a_z \end{bmatrix}^{\mathrm{T}}$ denotes the sum of other disturbing force, which can be equivalent to zero mean white Gaussian noise.

State equation is need to be discretized when calculated by computer, the traditional Euler method has only first order accuracy, the discretization error growing over time may reduce filtering estimation accuracy. So we use Euler prediction-correction method instead of Euler method to obtain the discrete form of formula (1) as follows:

$$
X_k = f(X_{k-1}) + w_{k-1}
\tag{2}
$$

Where, $X_k = \begin{bmatrix} x_k & y_k & y_k & v_{x,k} & v_{y,k} & v_{z,k} \end{bmatrix}^{\mathrm{T}}$ denotes the orbit state at k, w_k denotes system noise.

2.2 Measurement Equation

Measurement equation is defined in the horizontal coordinate system of handheld terminal, the transformation matrix from Earth Fixed Coordinate system to horizon coordinate system is as follows:

$$M = \begin{bmatrix} -\sin\lambda & \cos\lambda & 0 \\ -\sin\varphi\cos\lambda & -\sin\varphi\sin\lambda & \cos\varphi \\ \cos\varphi\cos\lambda & \cos\varphi\sin\lambda & \sin\varphi \end{bmatrix} \tag{3}$$

Where, λ denotes the geocentric longitude, φ denotes the geocentric latitude. The satellite orbit state $\boldsymbol{\rho}_i = \begin{bmatrix} \rho_{x,i} & \rho_{y,i} & \rho_{z,i} & \dot{\rho}_{x,i} & \dot{\rho}_{y,i} & \dot{\rho}_{z,i} \end{bmatrix}^{\mathrm{T}}$ is defined in horizon coordinate system of the ith handheld terminal, and we obtain:

$$\begin{bmatrix} \rho_{x,i} \\ \rho_{y,i} \\ \rho_{z,i} \end{bmatrix} = M \cdot \begin{bmatrix} x - x_{c,i} \\ y - y_{c,i} \\ z - z_{c,i} \end{bmatrix}, \begin{bmatrix} \dot{\rho}_{x,i} \\ \dot{\rho}_{y,i} \\ \dot{\rho}_{z,i} \end{bmatrix} = M \cdot \begin{bmatrix} \dot{x} \\ \dot{y} \\ \dot{z} \end{bmatrix} \tag{4}$$

Where, $\begin{pmatrix} x_{c,i} & y_{c,i} & z_{c,i} \end{pmatrix}$ denotes geocentric coordinate of the ith terminal, and we achieve the relationship between the velocity measurement $\dot{r}_i$ and orbit state as follows:

$$\begin{aligned} \dot{r}_i &= \frac{(\rho_{x,i}\dot{\rho}_{x,i} + \rho_{y,i}\dot{\rho}_{y,i} + \rho_{z,i}\dot{\rho}_{z,i})}{\sqrt{\rho_{x,i}^2 + \rho_{y,i}^2 + \rho_{z,i}^2}} \\ &= \frac{(x - x_{c,i})\dot{x} + (y - y_{c,i})\dot{y} + (z - z_{c,i})\dot{z}}{\sqrt{(x - x_{c,i})^2 + (y - y_{c,i})^2 + (z - z_{c,i})^2}} \end{aligned} \tag{5}$$

3 Centralized Cubature Information Filter Algorithm

The following discrete nonlinear dynamic systems is considered:

$$\begin{cases} x_k = f(x_{k-1}) + w_{k-1} \\ z_{i,k} = h_i(x_k) + v_{i,k} \end{cases} \tag{6}$$

Where, $x_k \in \mathbf{R}^{n_x}$ denotes the state vector, $y_{i,k} \in \mathbf{R}^{n_y}$ denotes measurement vector, system noise w_{k-1} and measurement noise $v_{i,k}$ are independent, and meet $w_{k-1} \sim (0, Q_{k-1})$, $v_{i,k} \sim (0, R_{i,k})$.

3.1 Extended Information Filter

Information filter is a mathematically equivalent expression of Kalman filter, and has higher computational efficiency in information fusion. Likewise, Extended Information filter (EIF) is the information representation of EKF. $Y_{k-1}^+ = (P_{k-1}^+)^{-1}$ is defined as information matrix, $\hat{y}_{k-1}^+ = Y_{k-1}^+ \hat{x}_{k-1}^+$ is defined as information state, and the update equations of EIF is as follows:

$$\hat{x}_k^- = f(\hat{x}_{k-1}^+) \tag{7}$$

$$Y_k^- = \left[F_{k-1}(Y_{k-1}^+)^{-1} F_{k-1}^{\mathrm{T}} + Q_{k-1} \right]^{-1} \tag{8}$$

$$\hat{y}_k^- = Y_k^- \hat{x}_k^- \tag{9}$$

$$Y_k^+ = Y_k^- + I_{i,k} \tag{10}$$

$$\hat{y}_k^+ = \hat{y}_k^- + i_{i,k} \tag{11}$$

Where, $I_{i,k} = H_{i,k}^{\mathrm{T}} R_{i,k}^{-1} H_{i,k}$ denotes information matrix contribution, $i_{i,k} = H_{i,k}^{\mathrm{T}} R_{i,k}^{-1}$ $(\varepsilon_{i,k} + H_{i,k}\hat{x}_k^-)$ denotes information state contribution, $\varepsilon_{i,k} = z_{i,k} - h_i(\hat{x}_k^-)$ denotes filter innovation, $F_{k-1} = \partial f / \partial x|_{\hat{x}_{k-1}}$ and $H_{i,k} = \partial h_i / \partial x|_{\hat{x}_k^-}$ denote the Jacobi matrix of nonlinear function, respectively.

3.2   Cubature Transformation

EIF has a low filtering accuracy for strongly nonlinear system, however, CKF uses spherical radial principle, adopts a set of equally weighted cubature points to realize the nonlinear approximation of Bayesian integral [6], and has a high filtering accuracy, thus we need to embed CKF into EIF to achieve CIF. The core step to achieve Bayesian filtering of nonlinear system under Gaussian domain is to calculate Gaussian weighted integral. In n-rectangular coordinate system, the following vector function integral is considered:

$$I(g) = \int_{\mathbf{R}^n} g(x)e^{-x^{\mathrm{T}}x} dx \tag{12}$$

In order to transform the domain of integration from rectangular coordinate system to spherical-radial coordinate system, let $x = ry$, where y denotes the direction vector, and meet $y^{\mathrm{T}}y = 1$, $r \in [0, \infty)$ denotes the sphere radius, and constitute the surface of the unit sphere $U_n = \{y \in R^n | y^{\mathrm{T}}y = 1\}$. It can be seen that $x^{\mathrm{T}}x = y^{\mathrm{T}}rry = r^2$, and meet the differential relation as follows:

$$dx = r^{n-1} dr d\sigma(y) \tag{13}$$

Where, $\sigma(\cdot)$ denotes the domain of integration of direction vector y corresponding to the sphere surface. Then formula (12) can be converted into the following spherical-radial coordinate integral:

$$I(g) = \int_0^\infty \int_{U_n} g(ry) r^{n-1} e^{-r^2} d\sigma(y) dr \tag{14}$$

Therefore, formula (14) can be decomposed into spherical integral $S(r)$ and radial integral R respectively as follows:

$$S(r) = \int_{U_n} g(ry) d\sigma(y) \tag{15}$$

$$R = \int_0^\infty S(r) r^{n-1} e^{-r^2} dr \tag{16}$$

The three order cubature rule is adopted as the integral weight function is Gaussian probability density function $N(x; \mu, P)$, the following numerical approximation is obtained:

$$\int_{R^n} g(x) N(x; \mu, P) dx \approx \frac{1}{2n} \sum_{i=1}^{2n} g(\sqrt{P} \xi_i + \mu) \tag{17}$$

$$\xi_i = \sqrt{n} [1]_i, i = 1, 2, \cdots, 2n \tag{18}$$

Where, the cubature points ξ_i are mutual orthogonal point set, $[1]_i$ denotes the ith column of the following matrix. $\sqrt{P}$ denotes the lower triangular matrix through Cholesky decomposition of P. It can be seen from formula (17) that, Cubature transformation adopts result of numerical integral of 2n equally weighted points to approximate Gaussian weighted integral.

$$[1]_i = \left[\begin{pmatrix} 1 \\ 0 \\ \vdots \\ 0 \end{pmatrix} \cdots \begin{pmatrix} 0 \\ 0 \\ \vdots \\ 1 \end{pmatrix} \begin{pmatrix} -1 \\ 0 \\ \vdots \\ 0 \end{pmatrix} \cdots \begin{pmatrix} 0 \\ 0 \\ \vdots \\ -1 \end{pmatrix} \right]_i \tag{19}$$

3.3 Centralized Cubature Information Filter

The equivalent expression of cross covariance matrix $P_{i,xy}$ is obtained using the statistical linear error propagation method as follows:

$$P_{i,xz} = E\left[(x_k - \hat{x}_k^-)(z_{i,k} - \hat{z}_{i,k}^-)^\mathrm{T} \right] \approx E\left[(x_k - \hat{x}_{i,k}^-)(x_k - \hat{x}_k^-)^\mathrm{T} H_{i,k}^\mathrm{T} \right] = P_k^- H_{i,k}^\mathrm{T} \tag{20}$$

Then, $\tilde{H}_{i,k} = P_{i,xz}^T Y_k^-$ is defined as the pseudo measurement matrix to achieve the follows:

$$I_{i,k} = \tilde{H}_{i,k}^T R_{i,k}^{-1} \tilde{H}_{i,k} = Y_k^- P_{i,xz} R_{i,k}^{-1} P_{i,xz}^T Y_k^- \tag{21}$$

$$i_{i,k} = \tilde{H}_{i,k}^T R_{i,k}^{-1} \left(\varepsilon_{i,k} + \tilde{H}_{i,k} \hat{x}_k^- \right) = Y_k^- P_{i,xz} R_{i,k}^{-1} \left[\varepsilon_{i,k} + P_{i,xz}^T Y_k^- \hat{x}_k^- \right] \tag{22}$$

The following variable and the matrix are defined according to the centralized filtering:

$$z_k = \begin{bmatrix} z_{1,k} \\ z_{2,k} \\ \vdots \\ z_{n,k} \end{bmatrix}, \tilde{H}_k = \begin{bmatrix} \tilde{H}_{1,k} \\ \tilde{H}_{2,k} \\ \vdots \\ \tilde{H}_{n,k} \end{bmatrix}, \varepsilon_k = \begin{bmatrix} \varepsilon_{1,k} \\ \varepsilon_{2,k} \\ \vdots \\ \varepsilon_{n,k} \end{bmatrix}, R_k = \begin{bmatrix} R_{1,k} & & & \\ & R_{2,k} & & \\ & & \ddots & \\ & & & R_{n,k} \end{bmatrix} \tag{23}$$

The centralized information matrix contribution I_k and state contribution i_k are defined as follows:

$$
\begin{aligned}
I_k &= \tilde{H}_k^T R_k^{-1} \tilde{H}_k \\
&= \tilde{H}_{1,k}^T R_{1,k}^{-1} \tilde{H}_{1,k} + \tilde{H}_{2,k}^T R_{2,k}^{-1} \tilde{H}_{2,k} + \cdots + \tilde{H}_{n,k}^T R_{n,k}^{-1} \tilde{H}_{n,k} \\
&= I_{1,k} + I_{2,k} + \cdots + I_{n,k} = \sum_{i=1}^{n} I_{i,k}
\end{aligned} \tag{24}
$$

$$
\begin{aligned}
i_k &= H_k^T R_k^{-1} \left(\varepsilon_k + H_k \hat{x}_k^- \right) \\
&= H_{1,k}^T R_{1,k}^{-1} \left(\varepsilon_1 + H_{1,k} \hat{x}_k^- \right) + H_{1,k}^T R_{1,k}^{-1} \left(\varepsilon_1 + H_{1,k} \hat{x}_k^- \right) \\
&\quad + \cdots + H_{1,k}^T R_{1,k}^{-1} \left(\varepsilon_1 + H_{1,k} \hat{x}_k^- \right) \\
&= i_{1,k} + i_{2,k} + \cdots + i_{n,k} = \sum_{i=1}^{n} i_{i,k}
\end{aligned} \tag{25}
$$

It can be seen that the centralized information matrix contribution I_k and state contribution i_k are equal to the sum of local information matrix contribution $I_{i,k}$ and local information state contribution $i_{i,k}$. Based on the above analysis, the centralized CIF is summarized as follows:

Step 1: Initialization

$$\hat{x}_0^+ = E(x_0), P_0^+ = E\left[(x_0 - \hat{x}_0^+)(x_0 - \hat{x}_0^+)^T \right] \tag{26}$$

Circulate $k = 1, 2, \cdots$, complete the following steps.

Step 2: Time Update

$$P_{k-1}^{+} = S_{k-1}^{+}(S_{k-1}^{+})^{\mathrm{T}} \tag{27}$$

$$\hat{x}_{k-1}^{(i)} = \hat{x}_{k-1}^{+} + S_{k-1}^{+}\xi^{(i)} \tag{28}$$

$$\hat{x}_{k}^{-} = \frac{1}{2n_x}\sum_{i=1}^{2n_x} X_{k}^{(i)} = \frac{1}{2n_x}\sum_{i=1}^{2n_x} f(\hat{x}_{k-1}^{(i)}) \tag{29}$$

$$P_{k}^{-} = \frac{1}{2n_x}\sum_{i=1}^{2n_x} X_{k}^{(i)}(X_{k}^{(i)})^{\mathrm{T}} - \hat{x}_{k}^{-}(\hat{x}_{k}^{-})^{\mathrm{T}} + Q_{k-1} \tag{30}$$

$$Y_{k}^{-} = (P_{k}^{-})^{-1} \tag{31}$$

$$y_{k}^{-} = Y_{k}^{-}\hat{x}_{k}^{-} \tag{32}$$

Step 3: Measurement Update

$$P_{k}^{-} = S_{k}^{-}(S_{k}^{-})^{\mathrm{T}} \tag{33}$$

$$\hat{x}_{k}^{(i)} = \hat{x}_{k}^{-} + S_{k}^{-}\xi^{(i)} \tag{34}$$

Receive $z_{i,k}$ from other terminals, and calculate the local information matrix contribution and the local information state contribution

$$\hat{z}_{i,k} = \frac{1}{2n_x}\sum_{j=1}^{2n_x} Z_{i,k}^{(j)} = \frac{1}{2n_x}\sum_{j=1}^{2n_x} h_{i,k}(\hat{x}_{k}^{(j)}) \tag{35}$$

$$P_{i,xz} = \frac{1}{2n_x}\sum_{j=1}^{2n_x} \hat{x}_{k}^{(j)}(Z_{i,k}^{(j)})^{\mathrm{T}} - \hat{x}_{k}^{-}(\hat{z}_{i,k})^{\mathrm{T}} \tag{36}$$

$$\varepsilon_{i,k} = z_{i,k} - h_{i,k}(\hat{x}_{k}^{-}) \tag{37}$$

$$I_{i,k} = \tilde{H}_{i,k}^{\mathrm{T}}R_{i,k}^{-1}\tilde{H}_{i,k} = Y_{k}^{-}P_{i,xz}R_{i,k}^{-1}P_{i,xz}^{\mathrm{T}}Y_{k}^{-} \tag{38}$$

$$i_{i,k} = \tilde{H}_{i,k}^{\mathrm{T}}R_{i,k}^{-1}(\varepsilon_{i,k} + \tilde{H}_{i,k}\hat{x}_{k}^{-}) = Y_{k}^{-}P_{i,xz}R_{i,k}^{-1}\left[\varepsilon_{i,k} + P_{i,xz}^{\mathrm{T}}Y_{k}^{-}\hat{x}_{k}^{-}\right] \tag{39}$$

Local information is fused to obtain centralized global information

$$I_{k} = \sum_{i=1}^{n} I_{i,k} \tag{40}$$

$$i_k = \sum_{i=1}^{n} i_{i,k} \tag{41}$$

Step 4: State Update

$$Y_k^+ = Y_k^- + I_k \tag{42}$$

$$\hat{y}_k^+ = \hat{y}_k^- + i_k \tag{43}$$

$$P_k^+ = (Y_k^+)^{-1} \tag{44}$$

$$\hat{x}_k^+ = (Y_k^+)^{-1}\hat{y}_k^+ \tag{45}$$

4 Simulation

STK is a professional software in space simulation. In order to get reliable simulation data, HPOP algorithm in STK is used to generate the nominal orbit. The Access module is used to analyze satellite transit, and generate simulation velocity data. Orbital epoch is 1 Jul 2015 16:00:00, and the orbit elements are as follows:

$$a = 6778.137 \text{ km}, \ e = 0, \ i = 97.035°, \ \Omega = 279.066°, \ \omega = 0°, \ f = 0°$$

The longitude and latitude of six handheld terminals are (107.993°, 25.766°), (117.27°, 27.512°), (111.179°, 25.968°), (115.089°, 25.048°), (111.213°, 23.583°), (114.541°, 27.839°), respectively. The visible time from handheld terminals to the satellite is 1 Jul 2015 16:03:30 (UTCG) to 1 Jul 2015 16:10:00 (UTCG), 390 s in total. Assume that velocity precision is 0.1 m/s. In order to study the influence of number of terminals on orbit determination precision, consider the following 5 conditions: case 1 include 2 terminals, case 2 include 3 terminals, case 3 include 4 terminals, case 4 include 5 terminals, and case 5 include 6 terminals.

The initial value of filter:

$$\hat{x}_0^+ = [-3032370 \quad 5879052 \quad 1576819 \quad 2112 \quad -915 \quad 7394]^T$$

The initial covariance matrix:

$$P_0^+ = diag(10^6 \quad 10^6 \quad 10^6 \quad 10^2 \quad 10^2 \quad 10^2)$$

State noise covariance matrix:

$$Q = diag(0.001^2 \quad 0.001^2 \quad 0.001^2 \quad 0.00001^2 \quad 0.00001^2 \quad 0.00001^2)$$

The real time orbit determination precision is evaluated using position RMSE and velocity RMSE, as defined:

$$
E = \sqrt{\frac{\sum\limits_{c=1}^{N}\left[(r_{x,c}^{i} - \hat{r}_{x,c}^{i})^{2} + (r_{y,c}^{i} - \hat{r}_{y,c}^{i})^{2} + (r_{z,c}^{i} - \hat{r}_{z,c}^{i})^{2}\right]}{N}}
\tag{46}
$$

Where, N denotes the number of Monte Carlo simulation, and velocity RMSE has the similar definition.

First, single terminal for orbit determination is simulated, filter period $T = 1.0$ s, running 200 Monte Carlo simulation, the simulation results are shown in Fig. 1. As can be seen from the results, when there is only velocity data, single terminal orbit determination is a weak observation system, and filter calculation is not convergence. In order to verify the performance of the proposed algorithm, communication topology among terminals is shown in Fig. 2 and the simulation results are shown in Fig. 3. Average position RMSE and velocity RMSE during 150 s–250 s is shown in Table 1. As can be seen from the results, we achieve that the more terminals take part in orbit determination, the higher accuracy and the faster convergence speed is achieved.

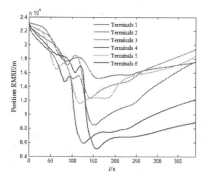

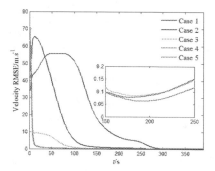

Fig. 1. Position RMSE of single terminal

Fig. 2. Communication topology among terminals

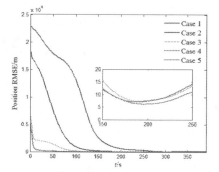

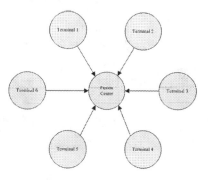

Fig. 3. Communication topology among radars

Table 1. Average position RMSE and velocity RMSE during 150 s–250 s

Case	Position RMSE/m	Velocity RMSE/m.s^{-1}
1	876.297	8.383
2	65.429	0.629
3	9.682	0.102
4	9.260	0.098
5	8.098	0.080

5   Conclusion

A centralized cubature information filter algorithm by multi-handheld terminals is proposed to improve the real-time orbit determination precision. Cubature transformation is embedded in EKF to obtain cubature information filter, the equivalent expression of pseudo measurement matrix is obtained by using the statistical linear error propagation method, and the multi-source observation information fusion process is expressed as accumulation form of local information matrix and information contribution state. The simulation results show that: (1) Multiple handheld terminals centralized cubature information filter algorithm can effectively realize the real time satellite orbit determination. (2) the more terminals take part in orbit determination, the higher accuracy and the faster convergence speed is achieved.

References

1. Liu, Y., Zhu, J.B., Hu, Z.H., et al.: Sliding polynomial method for determining trajectory by use of rate data. J. Ballistics **20**(2), 75–76 (2008)
2. Psiaki, M.L.: Backward-smoothing extended Kalman filter. J. Guidance Cont. Dyn. **28**(5), 885–894 (2005)
3. Julier, S.J., Uhlmann, J.K., Durrant, H.F.: A new method for nonlinear transformation of means and covariances in filters and estimators. IEEE Trans. Autom. Cont. **45**(3), 477–482 (2000)
4. Julier, S.J.: The scaled unscented transformation. In: Proceedings of the American Control Conference, pp. 4555–4559 (2002)
5. Lee, D.K., Alfriend, K.T.: Sigma point filtering for sequential orbit estimation and prediction. J. Spacecraft Rockets **44**(2), 388–398 (2007)
6. Arasaratnam, I., Haykin, S.: Cubature Kalman filters. IEEE Trans. Autom. Cont. **54**(6), 1254–1269 (2009)
7. Arasaratnam, I., Haykin, S.: Cubature Kalman smoothers. Automatica **47**(10), 2245–2250 (2010)
8. Zhao, M.H., Wu, B., Shi, M., et al.: Satellite autonomous orbit determination using magnetometers and radar altimeter. J. Astronaut. **25**(4), 412–415 (2004)

Research on Detecting Abnormal Energy Consumption in Energy Management System

Li Shi, Ying Zuo, and Fei Tao[✉]

School of Automation Science and Electrical Engineering,
Beihang University, Beijing, China
ftao@buaa.edu.cn

Abstract. Energy management system is an important means to realize energy saving emission reduction (ESER). Meanwhile, because of people's bad habit of using energy, the abnormal energy consumption occur frequently. In order to solve this problem, a convenient energy management system, which can detect the abnormal energy, is designed. In this progress, it first builds a unified energy-using model and realizes a fast sensing and access to a large amount of energy equipment, and then a visual monitoring platform of energy consumption is established. Finally, a prototype application system that can detect the abnormal energy is developed by using C# and R programming language. Experiments result indicates that the proposed method can effectively find the phenomenon of energy waste and improve energy efficiency.

Keywords: Energy management system · Data acquisition · Abnormal energy

1 Introduction

Energy is the basic guarantee of economic development. At the same time, the rapid economic growth also led to the increasingly serious energy crisis and environmental degradation. In such circumstances, implementing energy saving and emission reduction (ESER) has become an important trend in the world. Energy management system is an effective way to realize ESER. It can collect and manage the energy data, monitor and analyze the use of energy, optimize the structure of energy, find out the energy-saving space, and improve the transparency, planning, efficiency, security of energy and so on. Therefore, the construction of energy management system is very necessary.

At the present, current research trends in EMS are focused on various scopes. With the increase of smart cities, smart and green building, a very hot research trend is based on optimizing the energy consumption keeping a high level of well-being for the occupants [1, 2]. However, in the current process of constructing energy management system, there still exist some disadvantages that hinder the promotion of energy management system and the further mining of energy-saving potential. These problems include mainly: (1) different systems have different energy consumption models, how to build a unified energy consumption model; (2) there are a large number of energy equipment in the system, how to realize the fast and convenient sensing and monitoring of the energy equipment; (3) many energy management systems just stay in the stage of

© Springer Science+Business Media Singapore 2016
L. Zhang et al. (Eds.): AsiaSim 2016/SCS AutumnSim 2016, Part III, CCIS 645, pp. 233–244, 2016.
DOI: 10.1007/978-981-10-2669-0_26

collection, monitoring and management of energy, but lack of intelligent analysis to data [3], which causes abnormal energy consumption occur frequently. Therefore, in this paper, the main research goal is to construct a convenient and easy-to-use energy management system to collect, monitor, and analyze the consumption of energy, above the system, a model of detecting abnormal energy can be established to find out the phenomenon of energy waste and regularize the behavior of using energy to improve the energy efficiency.

2   System Design

2.1   Design of the System Framework

In order to detect the abnormal energy and taps the energy saving potential, it needs to build the energy management system. By analyzing the energy demand of buildings industries, it is found that their focus is that in the condition of ensuring people comfortable, as far as to reduce the consumption of energy, improve energy efficiency and ensure the safety of energy. Therefore, it can establish the following system architecture according to the above requirements, which are divided into five layers and each layer is independent of each other, so the system is easy to expand (Fig. 1).

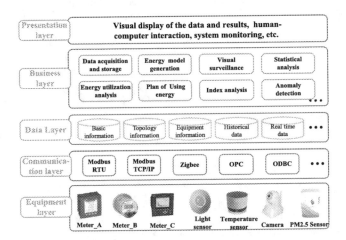

Fig. 1. Architecture of energy management system.

Equipment layer is located at the bottom in the system, it is the most basic layer of the whole system and is the direct data source in the system. It mainly includes the smart meter, Ethernet gateway, ZigBee sensor, ZigBee gateway, temperature and humidity sensor, camera, etc. It is mainly responsible for collecting and monitoring energy consumption information, etc.

Communication layer is the bridge between the system and the external physical world, and it is mainly to connect external sensor to obtain data through a variety of communication protocols, the protocols mainly includes Modbus RTU, Modbus TCP/IP, OPC, ZigBee, etc.

Data layer is a very important layer in the system. It manages the system energy model and stores all kinds of energy consumption data in the system. It mainly includes the database of system basic information, system topology, equipment information, alarm record, historical data and real-time data, etc.

Business layer is the core of the whole system. It is divided into two parts, the background business layer is mainly related to the system configuration and energy consumption model, etc. The front-end is mainly to carry on the related logic analysis according to the user needs, it includes visual surveillance, statistical analysis, using-energy planning, index analysis, safety analysis and anomaly detection, etc.

Presentation layer is the upper layer of the system. It directly interacts with the users and displays relevant analysis results.

2.2 Description and Construction of Energy Model

In order to analyze the energy consumption of the system, the first step is to establish corresponding energy model. Energy consumption model [4] mainly describe a system energy consumption type, energy consumption structure and properties, etc. Through the model, users can clearly understand when and where how much energy the system consume. In order to describe the system energy consumption model, it can be divided into three parts: the first part is mainly to describe the model of energy consumption nodes, the second part is to describe the system structure and the third part is to map between the model of energy consumption nodes and the system structure. Through the three parts, a complex system energy model can be clearly described.

Step1:   Physical model of energy consumption node is mainly to describe the attributes of energy equipment in the system, the related attributes of energy consumption equipment are divided into static and dynamic attributes. Static attributes refer to the basic properties of energy consuming equipment, such as device name, device interface, etc. Dynamic attributes mainly refer to the operating parameters of equipment in the running process, the model is described as the following Fig. 2.

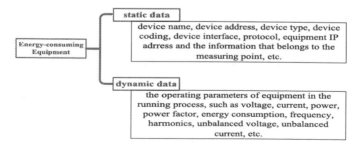

Fig. 2. Physical model of energy consumption node

Step2: Description of system organization structure model. In order to describe the model clearly and dynamically, the software design mainly describes the concept model based on tree structure model. It can facilitate the user to change and expand according to the subsequent dynamic change. As shown in Fig. 3.

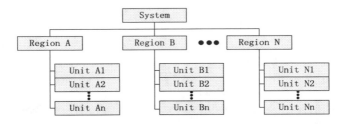

Fig. 3. System organization structure model

Step3: Mapping between the energy consumption nodes model and the system organization structure model. In this mapping, the relationships are not just one to one, there may be relationships of one to many and many to many, the corresponding relations need to be build according to the actual situation. It can set up the corresponding relationship based on the primary key and foreign key in the database. As shown in Fig. 3, the unit B1 in the system can be based on the actual situation map to lighting, socket, air conditioning energy consumption, etc.

2.3 Fast and Convenient Access to Energy Consumption Equipment

In the process of constructing energy management system, the most basic is to carry out the data acquisition. Data acquisition is the host computer collect sensor data with various communication protocol through the Ethernet, then store the data in data server. Because the categories of field equipment are different, and the system's topology change with the time, so a dynamic data acquisition system needs to be established. It can be divided into three parts:

Step1: Entity class design of the metering device. In order to collect sensor data, the key is to design the entity class of metering device according to its attributes and functions, then it needs to create a concrete object and realize mapping between the real equipment and entity class. In this progress, the data communication is the most

Table 1. Frame format of Modbus RTU (send)

Sending data	Byte	Example
Slave address	One byte	01
Function code	One byte	03
First address of Reg.	Two byte	00 01
Number of Reg.	Two byte	00 04
CRC	Two byte	15 C9

important, the main communication protocols are Modbus RTU, Modbus TCP/IP, Zigbee, OPC, etc. To use the Modbus protocol, the most important thing is to understand the principle, encoding, structure, transaction processing mechanism of the protocol [5], the protocol frame format is shown in Table 1.

In the construction process of the entity class, the key is to design the member properties and member functions of the entity class. The member have: device basic properties, communication parameters, running parameters, register information, interface command and so on, the member functions have the connection, transmission and reception of communication, protocol conversion, data check, data storage and display, etc. as shown in Fig. 4.

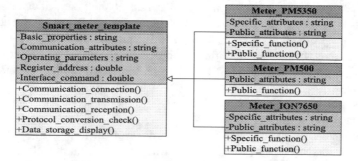

Fig. 4. Entity class inheritance of metering device

Step2: Model inheritance and protocol configuration. In order to collect the energy consumption information, it is necessary to configure the equipment, but if you make a protocol configuration for each type of equipment, it takes much time and effort. For different types of metering equipment, the basic structure is the same, only the differences are the communication protocols and registers. Therefore, the entity class of a certain type of equipment can be built according to the related attributes and functions, other types of devices can inherit the entity class, rewrite the corresponding different registers to complete the protocol configuration, finally it can realize one to one mapping between the entity class and real equipment. In this way, the system can collect energy consumption information in large scale with in less time. The process of modeling and generalization in UML is shown in Fig. 4, the Meter_PM500, Meter_5350 and Meter_ION7650 three types of smart meters are inherited from the total template of smart meter.

Step3: Real-time data acquisition based on multi threads. In order to achieve real-time data acquisition of a large number of devices, it is necessary to use multi threads technology and creates a thread for each area device to perform the task of real-time data acquisition. Using multiple threads, energy data can be collected in parallel, so it can improve the efficiency of computing resources.

2.4 Detecting Abnormal Energy Consumption

In the process of daily energy consumption, due to various reasons, such as their own habits, there are always non-standard places of using energy, which would lead to energy waste and reduce the efficiency of energy. Therefore, it needs to conduct data mining and analyze the behavior of using energy to find out abnormal energy consumption phenomenon, and standardize and improve the habits of using energy to improve the energy efficiency.

In order to detect the abnormal energy consumption, the key is to find out the rules of data or abnormal fluctuation data. There are several methods: anomaly detection method based on time window, anomaly detection method based on model prediction, anomaly detection method based on nearest neighbor similarity, anomaly detection method based on segmentation and so on, each of these methods has its own advantages and disadvantages [6–8], so it needs to select the appropriate method according to the specific problems. Under the condition of the running laws of energy consumption changing dynamically, the anomaly detection method based on the prediction model used widely.

Because the energy consumption are affected by different factors in different periods, operation laws of energy consumption data are not the same, the energy consumption have linear and nonlinear characteristics. So in order to obtain the energy operation rules, a model that contains both linear modeling ability and nonlinear modeling ability need to be built. In terms of linear modeling in time series, the most widely used model is the ARIMA model. In terms of nonlinear modeling, there be many approaches, BP neural network has good performance, so the combination of ARIMA time series model and BP neural network model are mainly used to model and analyze.

2.4.1 Procedure of Detecting Abnormal Energy Consumption

In order to detect the abnormal energy consumption, the key is to obtain the rules of data, then discriminate the abnormal point according to the abnormal fluctuation data. It is divided into three steps, the specific process as shown in Fig. 5.

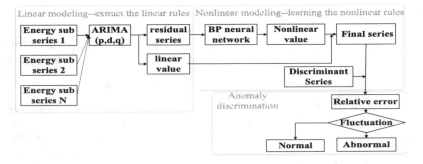

Fig. 5. The procedure of detecting abnormal consumption

Step1: Linear modeling and analysis of energy consumption data. The energy consumption data have a certain operation rules in the case that the energy consumption model does not change greatly, it mainly uses the ARIMA (p, d, q) time series to model. Through the progress, the liner rules and the residual sequence can be got.

Step2: In this progress, the main purpose is to mine the nonlinear operation laws in residual data. It mainly use the actual data as the input of the neural network, the residual series as the output of the network to train the neural network, then correct the residual series, finally it add the linear data to get the final rules.

Step3: Determining abnormal energy consumption. It gets the relative error based on the original value of the energy consumption and the model value of energy running rules, then it can determine whether the error is abnormal or not according to the fluctuation.

2.4.2   Linear Modeling Based on ARIMA Time Series

ARIMA (p, d, q) model is non-stationary time series model, its full name is called auto regressive integrated moving average model. The series model mainly contains three parameters: the order of auto regressive P, the order of moving average Q, the order of difference D, and two basic time series model: auto regressive model AR (P) and moving average model MA (q), the general mathematical expression are:

$$\Delta^d X_t = \sum_{i=1}^{p} \varphi_i \Delta^d X_{t-i} + \varepsilon_t + \sum_{j=1}^{q} \theta_j \varepsilon_{t-j} + \theta \tag{1}$$

The process of modeling is as follows: it is divided into five steps, the specific process steps as shown below:

Step 1: Determining energy consumption series are stable or not. Only the energy consumption series are smooth sequence, the subsequent is meaningful. It mainly uses the ADF unit root testing method to test the series are stable or not.

Step 2: In this progress, it is mainly to transform the non-stationary series into stationary time series, after the treatment of d order difference, a stationary time series can be got.

Steps 3: Parameter estimation of ARIMA Model. The process is mainly to estimate the parameters of P and Q according to the auto correlation function (ACF) and partial auto correlation function (PACF) [9].

Step 4: Model optimization. This progress is mainly to optimize the parameters through the AIC, SC standard, it makes the model become more optimal.

Step 5: Model checking. Because this progress is to smooth the series and deal with stable series, the series residuals should mostly belong to white noise sequence, if it is not, the model need to be remodeled until the residuals mostly meet the conditions.

2.4.3   Nonlinear Modeling Based on BP Neural Network

In the progress of nonlinear modeling of energy consumption data, the BP neural network [10] are mainly used. BP neural network is mainly based on the simulation of the brain neurons, it has a very powerful nonlinear mapping ability and is a multi-layer neural network. It is mainly divided into three-layer network structure: input layer, hidden layer and output layer, and its learning mechanism are error back propagation algorithm. It uses the original data of energy consumption as the input of the network, and the residual data that contain the nonlinear law as the output of the network, then adjust the weights of the neural network to make the final total error reach a minimum through a large number of training samples, finally it can realize the nonlinear mapping.

3   Results and Discussion

3.1   Development of Prototype System

In order to monitor and analyze the use of energy and tap the potential of energy saving, we develop a prototype system based on the above system framework of energy management system. It uses the Oracle as the database of system, and uses the SocanCode software to generate three-layer architecture model of database, the C sharp and R language are used to develop the system. In the aspect of graph visualization, it uses the tool of DevExpress to display a variety of data. In the aspect of circuit monitoring, it mainly adopts the Microsoft Visio plug-in for second development, the functions are as shown in the figure of system architecture. The monitoring center of energy consumption are shown in Fig. 6(left), users can grasp all energy information through it. In Fig. 6(right), it shows the function of system circuit monitoring, if there is any problem in system, users can handle it in time through it. In Fig. 7, it shows the function of detecting abnormal energy consumption, through it, users can find out the phenomenon of abnormal using energy of each region.

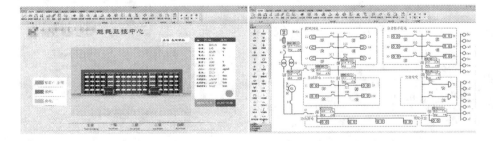

Fig. 6. Monitoring center of energy consumption

3.2   Experimental Analysis

Experimental data: in order to verify the accuracy of the model, eight weeks of energy consumption data are simulated. The energy consumption data of Monday to Friday are higher and obey the normal distribution, the energy consumption data of Saturday and

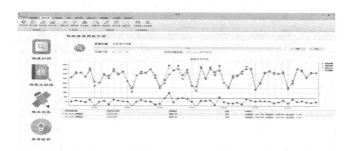

Fig. 7. Detecting abnormal energy consumption

Sunday are lower, so it conforms to the actual situation. At the same time, it adds the abnormal interference in the fourth and fifth weeks, the experimental data are shown in Fig. 9 (The blue curve).

3.2.1   Linear Modeling Based on ARIMA (P, D, Q) Model

According to the above steps of ARIMA modeling, first, it needs to test the stability of the sequence. From the energy consumption data in Fig. 9 (The blue curve), it can be seen that the average of energy consumption data are change over time and have a fixed period. After testing the original sequence using ADF method, it is found that the sequence is non-stationary, so it needs to be smoothed to be a stable sequence.

After smoothing the energy consumption data, the follow up step is mainly to determine the parameter of model. According to the relevant principle, the autocorrelation function and the partial autocorrelation function of energy consumption data are draw out, as shown in Fig. 8. It can be seen that the auto correlation of energy have 21 order truncation property and the partial autocorrelation have 11 order truncation property, so the model ARIMA (11,1,21) can be initially determined. Then by analyzing, the ARIMA (11, 1, 21) is the best model based on the SC and AIC criteria.

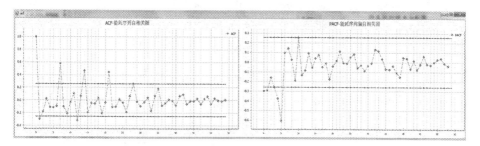

Fig. 8. Diagram of ACF and PACF

3.2.2   Residual Error Correction

After linear modeling, then it needs to extract the nonlinear laws of energy consumption data. The nonlinear laws are mainly embodied in the residual data, in this progress, the BP neural network are mainly used and build three-layer network structure. It uses the actual energy consumption data as the input of the neural network and the residuals data as the output of the network to train the neural network to learn the nonlinear laws, and then the residuals can be corrected according to the neural network.

The nodes of input layer are set N = 7 and the output layer nodes L = 1, the hidden layer nodes M are mainly determined by the experience, it are set M = 10 according to the experiments, the target error of neural network is 10e-5, the learning rate is 0.01, the maximum iterations is 2000, the transfer function is Sigmoid function. The final revised results are shown in Table 2.

Table 2. The final revised results

Week	Mon.	Tue.	Wed.	Thu.	Fri.	Sat.	Sun.
1	2639	3101	3115	2711	3436	2208	2018
2	2900	2818	3271	2963	3285	2280	1523
3	2797	3036	3110	3591	2892	1718	1945
4	2984	3567	3609	2626	3277	1812	1537
5	3525	2388	3620	3362	3356	2098	1590
6	2802	2838	3392	3549	3541	1272	2011
7	3083	3402	3229	3135	3091	1546	1982
8	3535	3423	2725	3356	3211	1577	1995

3.2.3   Abnormal Energy Detection

After extracting the linear rules and learning the nonlinear rules of energy consumption data through the ARIMA model and BP neural network, then the abnormal energy consumption can be judged. Because the abnormal consumption point and other normal points are different, the normal energy points follow the overall operation rules and are in the range of normal, but the abnormal energy points are not in conformity with the operation rules and over the range of normal fluctuation. Therefore, it can judge the abnormal energy consumption according to the relative rate of error, as shown in Fig. 9. The blue curve represents the original data, the red is the value of energy running rules, and the green is fluctuation data.

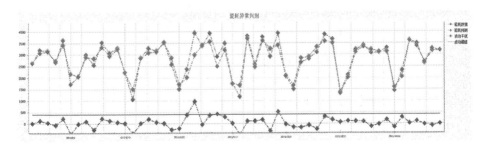

Fig. 9. Anomaly detection curve

From the graph, the energy consumption data are almost in normal range and most of the energy consumption data follow the overall operation rules, the fluctuation of data in an acceptable range. However, there are some exceptions, from the chart, it can be seen that the twenty-second and thirty-third points are obviously larger anomaly and the relative error rate is over the acceptable range. In fact, it can be seen from the chart that the first three weeks of energy data are very smooth and follow the corresponding operating rules, but in the four weeks, there exists obvious abnormal fluctuations, which can be seen from the fluctuation curve, there are reasons to determine the existence of abnormal energy consumption. Then the historical energy data and video monitoring can be seen to do further discriminate and find the cause of abnormal energy consumption.

4   Conclusions and Future Work

Abnormal energy consumption is a major cause of energy waste, so it needs to detect the abnormal energy consumption to improve the energy efficiency. In this progress, the key is to build an energy management system to collect, manage, monitor, and analyze the energy data. In this paper, in the progress of system design, the following conclusions can be drawn:

In the progress of constructing energy management system, the purpose is mainly to improve the transparency, planning, efficiency and safety of energy. It constructs an energy management system based on five-layer network architecture and builds a unified dynamic model of energy consumption. It can realize the large scale and fast data acquisition, visual monitoring of energy consumption, multi dimension analysis of energy consumption data and anomaly detection of energy, etc.

In the progress of detecting abnormal energy consumption, the energy series are divided into many sub series, then for each sub series, the abnormal energy consumption can be judged based on ARIMA model and BP neural network. Because the ARIMA model has strong linear modeling capabilities and BP neural network has strong nonlinear learning ability. The two can effectively extract the overall operating rules of energy consumption data and get abnormal interference in various periods, and then the abnormal points can be determined according to fluctuation conditions. Through the analysis of experiment, the performance is excellent.

In the future, we need to continue to develop the energy management system and improve the energy efficiency through data-driven technology.

Acknowledgements. The authors acknowledge the financial support from the 863 Program project in China (2013AA041302,2015AA042100), the Science & Technology Ministry Innovation Method Program (2015IM040700), and the Fundamental Research Funds for the Central Universities in China.

References

1. Peña, M., Biscarri, F., Guerrero, J.I.: Rule-based system to detect energy efficiency anomalies in smart buildings, a data mining approach. Expert Syst. Appl. **56**(1), 242–255 (2016)
2. Tao, F., Zuo, Y., Xu, L.D., Lv, L., Zhang, L.: Internet of things and bom-based life cycle assessment of energy-saving and emission-reduction of products. IEEE Trans. Ind. Inf. **10**(2), 1252–1261 (2014)

3. Kim, H., Stumpf, A., Kim, W.: Analysis of an energy efficient building design through data mining approach. Autom. Constr. **20**(1), 37–43 (2011)
4. Harishn, V.S.K.V., Kumar, A.: A review on modeling and simulation of building energy systems. Renew. Sustain. Energy Rev. **56**, 1272–1292 (2016)
5. Goldenberg, N., Wool, A.: Accurate modeling of Modbus TCP for intrusion detection in SCADA systems. Int. J. Crit. Infrastruct. Prot. **6**(2), 63–75 (2013)
6. Li, X., Bowers, C.P., Schnier, T.: Classification of energy consumption in buildings with outlier detection. IEEE Trans. Ind. Electron. **57**(11), 3639–3644 (2010)
7. Iglewicz, B., Hoaglin, D.C.: How to Detect and Handle Outliers. American Society for Quality, Milwaukee (1993)
8. Capozzoli, A., Lauro, F., Khan, I.: Fault detection analysis using data mining techniques for a cluster of smart office buildings. Expert Syst. Appl. **42**(9), 4324–4338 (2015)
9. Gairaa, K., Khellaf, A., Messlema, Y.: Estimation of the daily global solar radiation based on Box-Jenkins and ANN models: a combined approach. Renew. Sustain. Energy Rev. **57**, 238–249 (2016)
10. Krishnaiah, T., Srinivasa, S., Madhumurthy, K.: Neural network approach for modelling global solar radiation. J. Appl. Sci. Res. **3**(10), 1105–1111 (2007)

Study on Temperature Distribution with CFD Simulations of an Air-Conditioned Room

Ping Fang[1,2], Tingzhang Liu[1,2(✉)], Kai Liu[1,2], and Jianfei Zhao[1,2]

[1] Shanghai Key Laboratory of Power Station Automation Technology,
Shanghai, China
[2] School of Mechanical Engineering and Automation,
Shanghai University, Shanghai, China
848561236@qq.com, Liutzhcom@163.com

Abstract. Accurate thermal load prediction is beneficial for minimizing cost and energy consumption of buildings. Indoor thermal comfort and the air quality greatly influence the health and work efficiency of building occupants. For energy efficiency and thermal comfort is significantly impacted by the choice of an appropriate reference air temperature, indoor air temperature distribution analysis is very important. In this study, the temperature distribution of an air conditioned room was calculated by FLUENT under different air supply parameters, and the calculated temperatures agreed well with the measured data in both cooling and heating modes of simulations. Then, proper simulation models was determined and used to seek the characteristic point that can represent the room reference air temperature directly. The outlet point of the air conditioner was verified to be the approximation of the characteristic point in the tested room. This provides a convenient approach to obtain the reference temperature used to predict real-time thermal load which is the key factor of building energy performance improving.

Keywords: Temperature distribution · CFD simulation · Air-conditioned · Reference air temperature · FLUENT · Building energy

1 Introduction

With the development of building environmental assessment rating systems and their following modifications since 1990 [1], studies on building energy performance and energy efficient have accumulated and are abundant now. Among these studies, some focused on the modeling methodology of the energy consumption or energy performance [2, 3], some addressed the life cycle energy analysis [4, 5], some chose to predict the thermal loads of the buildings or rooms [6, 7], and some tried to find a nonuniform indoor environment to meet the demand for both energy efficiency and thermal comfort [8]. It is expected that building energy simulation results will be significantly impacted by the choice of an appropriate reference air temperature for the prediction of thermal load in an air-conditioned room and the calculation of heat transfer through construction materials. Therefore, it has become necessary to include temperature distribution in energy simulations [9].

© Springer Science+Business Media Singapore 2016
L. Zhang et al. (Eds.): AsiaSim 2016/SCS AutumnSim 2016, Part III, CCIS 645, pp. 245–252, 2016.
DOI: 10.1007/978-981-10-2669-0_27

In a case study, Javad Taghinia et al. [10] investigated the flow structure around an human body subjected to a displacement ventilation system through the computational fluid dynamics (CFD). Their model results showed a good compromise between accuracy and robustness in predicting the airflow and temperature fields in an indoor environment. Zhang et al. [9] proposed an acceptably fast simulation method that couples the contribution ratio of indoor climate (CRI) with the network model to implement an energy simulation that incorporates a temperature distribution. The CRI-coupled method achieves a precision as high as that of CFD and a calculation speed as fast as that of the network model. Mba et al. [11] used ANN model for the prediction of hourly air temperature and relative humidity in a building as a basic study of reducing energy consumption for air conditioning. Their results showed that ANN can be used for modeling indoor air temperature and is superior to the classical methods on the speed of calculations. Zhang et al. [12] applied CFD to investigate indoor convective heat transfer and adjusted the wall Prandtl number in CFD simulations to obtain correct temperature profiles and convective heat transfer coefficients for near-wall modeling. The adjusted temperature wall function is able to solve accurately indoor convective heat transfer with a moderate grid number while the standard temperature wall function with the default wall Prandtl number is inappropriate.

In this study, the temperature distribution model and simulation methods will be introduced first. Then, actual temperature measuring experiments under different conditions carried out in an air-conditioned office room and the corresponding simulation process will be explained in detail. Finally, by comparing measured data and simulated data, a reasonable simulation model is determined and used to seek the characteristic point that can represent the room reference air temperature.

2 Temperature Distribution Model and Simulation Methods

2.1 The Mathematical Model

The governing equations of fluid flow represent mathematical statements of the conservation laws. The air flow is assumed to be incompressible in this study for it has very low velocity and the change in pressure is very small [13]. The governing equations for the three-dimensional flow are as follows.

Continuity conservation equation:

$$\frac{\partial \rho}{\partial t} + \nabla \cdot (\rho V) = 0 \tag{1}$$

Where ρ is the air density and V is a velocity vector in Cartesian space.

Energy conservation equations:

$$\frac{\partial(\rho T)}{\partial t} + div(\rho V T) = div(\Gamma \, gradT) + S_T \tag{2}$$

Where Γ is diffusion coefficient, T is temperature and ST is source item.

N-S equation (momentum conservation equation):

$$\begin{cases} \dfrac{\partial(\rho u)}{\partial t} + \nabla \cdot (\rho u \mathbf{V}) = -\dfrac{\partial p}{\partial x} + \dfrac{\partial \tau_{xx}}{\partial x} + \dfrac{\partial \tau_{yx}}{\partial y} + \dfrac{\partial \tau_{zx}}{\partial z} + \rho f_x \\[2mm] \dfrac{\partial(\rho v)}{\partial t} + \nabla \cdot (\rho v \mathbf{V}) = -\dfrac{\partial p}{\partial y} + \dfrac{\partial \tau_{xy}}{\partial x} + \dfrac{\partial \tau_{yy}}{\partial y} + \dfrac{\partial \tau_{zy}}{\partial z} + \rho f_y \\[2mm] \dfrac{\partial(\rho w)}{\partial t} + \nabla \cdot (\rho w \mathbf{V}) = -\dfrac{\partial p}{\partial z} + \dfrac{\partial \tau_{xz}}{\partial x} + \dfrac{\partial \tau_{yz}}{\partial y} + \dfrac{\partial \tau_{zz}}{\partial z} + \rho f_z \end{cases} \tag{3}$$

Where the u, v and w are velocity components of x, y and z, and they are functions of both space and time t. The sign τ_{ij} denotes a stress in the j direction exerted on a plane perpendicular to the i axis. The body force per unit mass acting on the fluid element is denoted by f_i. p denotes pressure.

The k-ε turbulence model is the most widely used model for its applicability to wide-ranging flow problems and its lower computational requirement. In case of the k-ε turbulence models, two additional transport equations are needed to solve the turbulent viscosity as a function of k and ε. The modelled transport equations for k and ε are given as follows:

$$\frac{\partial(\rho k)}{\partial t} + div(\rho \mathbf{V} k) = div(\Gamma_k grad k) + S_k \tag{4}$$

$$\frac{\partial(\rho \varepsilon)}{\partial t} + div(\rho \mathbf{V} \varepsilon) = div(\Gamma_\varepsilon grad \varepsilon) + S_\varepsilon \tag{5}$$

2.2 Simulation Methods

The simulation of the temperature distribution of an air-conditioned office room can be divided into three steps: the pre-processing, the calculation and the post-processing.

To provide the three-dimensional mesh model of the room, the CAD file generated by using the software SolidWorks as the geometry model is imported into ICEM CFD. ICEM CFD is the major tool for performing the pre-processing work.

A general-purpose commercial CFD code known as FLUENT was applied to calculate the temperature distribution in this study. FLUENT software provides abundant physical models. It adopts finite volume method, which divides computational domain into a series of control volumes. The discrete equation is derived from the integral equation of the control volume. Finite volume method provides three numerical algorithms, while any other commercial CFD software can only provide one of them: Segregated Solver, Coupled Explicit Solver and Coupled Implicit Solver. FLUENT has the facility to add user-defined scalars and functions, which allow the user to control the way in which the solver is applied to the system modelled.

To get a complete 360° view of the air temperature of the office room, a CFD & Numerical Simulation Visualization Software called Tecplot 360 is applied to do post-processing.

3   Temperature Experiments and Simulations

3.1   Temperature Experiments

A case study of an air-conditioned office room with floor air conditioner was carried out to verify CFD model. The experiments led by the air conditioner were conducted under two working modes, namely, the cooling mode in summer and the heating mode in winter. The operating conditions of the two modes are presented in Table 1.

The office room is in a building faced south and located in Shanghai. The experiments were carried out with 31 temperature sensors inside the room and one outside. The room is shown as Fig. 1. The long oval table is located at the central of floor with eight chairs lined on the two sides. The window faces the south and the floor air conditioner is beside the window against the southwest corner. There are two bookshelves against the east wall next to the south wall. The door is in the west wall. It is a room plot derived from Tecplot 360, so it shows the air, i.e. the computational domain with all the physical objects such as the wall and the cabinets hidden. The sensors are presented by 32 points distributed in the room. The six black points in the working area are verification points. They are distributed on four chairs, the central of the table and the outlet of the air conditioner. These locations marked with white and grey points are used to provide boundary conditions for the simulation model. And the isolated white point outside the room is used to collect the outdoor temperature.

Table 1. Summary of operating conditions of air conditioner

Mode	Velocity (m/s)	Inlet angle	Setting temperature (°C)
Cooling	2.15	45°, 0°	15, 16
Heating	3.3	0°, −45°	26, 28

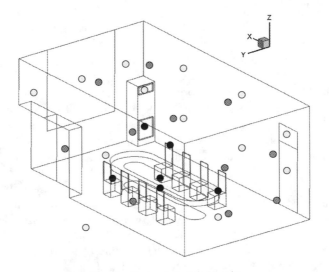

Fig. 1. Computational domain

In the experiments, the simultaneous multiple-point temperature measurements were obtained, collected, sorted and saved with a set of sensors, circuit and computer software.

3.2   The CFD Simulations

The CFD simulation process consists of three parts. First, SolidWorks is used to create 3D geometry model of the office room. Second, the 3D model is imported into the ICEM CFD to do the meshing work. Then, the mesh file is imported into the FLUENT to carry out the simulation. Finally, the data file is exported and can be loaded into the Tecplot 360 to analyze the temperature of the air flow.

The simulation models are modified repeatedly according to the comparison of calculation results and measurements. In accordance with different operating conditions presented in Table 1, turbulent models or other parameters in the simulations varies. To begin with, the empirical parameters are adopted to implement the simulation. According to the comparison results, the unsatisfied models are modified. First, the turbulent parameters are changed. Then, the standard k-epsilon model is replaced by the RNG k-epsilon model. All the simulations consider steady state air flow.

4   Results and Discussion

4.1   Simulation Model Verification

The model modification process is presented in Tables 2 and 3. AE is the acronym of Absolute Error. Table 2 shows the simulation results under the condition of a setting temperature of 26°C and inlet flow angle of –45°. The turbulent empirical parameters using the specification method of intensity and viscosity ratio is 5 % and 10, respectively. But the absolute errors of the actual data and simulated results reached 4.57°C of the four verification points. Based on Eqs. (4) and (5), the precise values of turbulent kinetic energy and turbulent dissipation rate are calculated and set in FLUENT. As shown in the table, with the calculated parameters, the absolute error is obviously decreased. And the modified simulation model with the calculated turbulence parameters has better performance as well under the other working conditions.

On the basis of changed turbulence parameters, an appropriate turbulent model was chosen to further enhance the accuracy of the model. Table 3 shows the simulation results under the condition of a setting temperature of 28°C and 0° inlet flow angle. The

Table 2. Comparison of model modification on turbulence parameters

Location		Table central	Chair A	Chair B	Chair C	Chair D
26°C, –45°	Measured (°C)	20.85	24.86	25.36	20.50	24.52
Empirical parameters	Simulated (°C)	25.43	27.69	26.34	24.93	25.67
	AE	4.57	2.83	0.98	4.43	1.15
Calculated parameters	Simulated (°C)	23.70	23.27	22.20	22.64	25.16
	AE	2.84	1.60	3.16	2.14	0.64

Table 3. Comparison of model modification on turbulence models

Location		Table central	Chair A	Chair B	Chair C	Chair D
28°C, 0°	Measured (°C)	13.68	13.40	18.54	15.46	18.58
Standard	Simulated (°C)	17.12	16.24	15.96	16.42	18.22
	AE	3.44	2.84	2.57	0.97	0.36
RNG	Simulated (°C)	16.58	16.37	15.60	16.07	17.51
	AE	2.90	2.96	2.93	0.61	1.08

standard k-epsilon model was replaced by the RNG k-epsilon model. The maximum absolute error decreased from 3.44°C to 2.96°C. Hence, the RNG k-epsilon model reveals a better performance.

To clearly illustrate the simulation results, the cooling mode calculated data and their comparisons with the corresponding measurements are given in Tables 4 and 5, including four different working conditions with five verification points. In the table or figure captions below, the symbols 15°C and 16°C are the two target temperatures set in the air conditioner; the symbols 0° and 45° are the two inlet flow angles. RE is the acronym of Relative Error. Tables 4 and 5 show that the relative errors are small and the maximum value is 7.75 % that can be indicated in Chair D under condition 16°C and 0°with the max absolute error 1.57°C of all.

An evaluation criterion called root mean square error (RMSE) is utilized to compare the performance of simulation model. It is computed to find the square error of the simulation results compared to actual values and to find the square root of the summation value. The RMSE value of the steady simulation results is displayed in Table 6. Table 6 shows that the simulated results obtained high accuracy.

Table 4. Simulation results of 15°C, 45°

Location	Measurement (°C)	Simulation result (°C)	RE
Table central	20.60	19.45	5.61 %
Chair A	19.81	19.38	2.19 %
Chair B	20.04	19.69	1.74 %
Chair C	20.19	19.54	3.26 %
Chair D	19.18	19.35	0.86 %
Outlet	19.69	19.73	0.23 %

Table 5. Simulation results of 16°C, 0°

Location	Measurement (°C)	Simulation Result (°C)	RE
Table central	22.68	21.77	4.01 %
Chair A	21.53	21.78	1.17 %
Chair B	21.44	21.78	1.57 %
Chair C	21.66	21.75	0.44 %
Chair D	20.19	21.76	7.75 %
Outlet	21.21	21.84	2.94 %

Table 6. RMSE of simulation results

Specific condition	15°C, 0°	15°C, 45°	16°C, 0°	16°C, 45°
RMSE	0.60	0.59	0.80	0.67

4.2 Characteristic Point Research of Temperature

For the errors are within acceptance limits, the present model could be used to search the characteristic point that can represent the room reference air temperature. The outlet temperature of the air conditioner is supposed to be the approximation. Therefore, the steady temperature of the outlet is discussed below. Table 7 shows the comparison of the outlet temperature and the average temperature of the five points distributed in the working area. In Table 7, M and S are abbreviations of two types of data, i.e., measured data and simulated data. $|\Delta T|$ is the absolute error of the average temperature and outlet temperature. From the measured data of $|\Delta T|$, 0.22°C, 0.27°C, 0.29°C and 0.34°C come from four different conditions, it can be seen clearly that the absolute errors are small. The simulated type, 0.11°C, 0.25°C, 0.07°C and 0.29°C are within 0.3°C which is even better. Thus, it can conclude that, the outlet point could be regarded as the characteristic point and its temperature could represent the room reference air temperature.

Table 7. Temperature comparison of the outlet and the working area

Specific condition	15°C, 0°		15°C, 45°		16°C, 0°		16°C, 45°	
Data type	M	S	M	S	M	S	M	S
Average (°C)	18.94	18.96	19.96	19.48	21.5	21.77	20.36	19.83
Outlet (°C)	18.72	19.07	19.69	19.73	21.21	21.84	20.02	20.12
$|\Delta T|$ (°C)	0.22	0.11	0.27	0.25	0.29	0.07	0.34	0.29

5 Conclusion

In the steady simulation, the max relative error is 7.75 % and the max absolute error is 1.57°C of all the working conditions. The RMSE index shows that the simulated results obtained high accuracy compared with measured values. Thus it is verified that the present temperature distribution simulation model is useful and reasonable for steady state situation.

Based on the present simulation model, the temperature comparison table of the outlet and the working area indicates that the absolute errors are satisfying in both measured data and simulated results under four working conditions.

Consequently, the FLUENT simulation model provides a good basis for developing a real-time building energy performance management system in future study. In practice, people may apply the simulation model to calculate a reference air temperature for early predictions of cooling or heating load of a room during the building design process or the energy design of air conditioner.

Acknowledgment. Thanks to the supports by National Natural Science Foundation (NNSF) of China under Grant 61273190 and Shanghai Natural Science Foundation under Grant 13ZR1417000.

References

1. Castellano, J., Ribera, A., Ciurana, J.: Integrated system approach to evaluate social, environmental and economics impacts of buildings for users of housings. Energy Build. **123**, 106–118 (2016)
2. Stefanovic, A., Gordic, D.: Modeling methodology of the heating energy consumption and the potential reductions due to thermal improvements of staggered block buildings. Energy Build. **125**, 244–253 (2016)
3. Khayatian, F., Sarto, L., Dall'O', G.: Application of neural networks for evaluating energy performance certificates of residential buildings. Energy Build. **125**, 45–54 (2016)
4. Chastas, P., Theodosiou, T., Bikas, D.: Embodied energy in residential buildings-towards the nearly zero energy building: a literature review. Build. Environ. **105**, 267–282 (2016)
5. Bunning, M.E., Crawford, R.H.: Directionally selective shading control in maritime sub-tropical and temperate climates: life cycle energy implications for office buildings. Build. Environ. **104**, 275–285 (2016)
6. Yuna, K., Lucka, R., Magoa, P.J., Chob, H.: Building hourly thermal load prediction using an indexed ARX model. Energy Build. **54**, 225–233 (2012)
7. Chou, J.-S., Bui, D.-K.: Modeling heating and cooling loads by artificial intelligence for energy-efficient building design. Energy Build. **82**, 437–446 (2014)
8. Li, H., Lee, W.L., Jia, J.: Applying a novel extra-low temperature dedicated outdoor air system in office buildings for energy efficiency and thermal comfort. Energy Convers. Manag. **121**, 162–173 (2016)
9. Zhang, W., Hiyama, K., Kato, S., Ishida, Y.: Building energy simulation considering spatial temperature distribution for nonuniform indoor environment. Build. Environ. **63**, 89–96 (2013)
10. Taghinia, J., Rahman, Md. M. Siikonen, T.: Numerical simulation of airflow and temperature fields around an occupant in indoor environment. Energy Build. **104**,199–207 (2015)
11. Mba, L., Meukam, P., Kemajou, A.: Application of artificial neural network for predicting hourly indoor air temperature and relative humidity in modern building in humid region. Energy Build. **121**, 32–42 (2016)
12. Zhang, T. (Tim), Zhou, H., Wang, S.: An adjustment to the standard temperature wall function for CFD modeling of indoor convective heat transfer. Build. Environ. **68**, 159–169 (2013)
13. Nada, S.A., El-Batsh, H.M., Elattar, H.F., Ali, N.M.: CFD investigation of airflow pattern, temperature distribution and thermal comfort of UFAD system for theater buildings applications. J. Build. Eng. **6**, 274–300 (2016)

Power System Simulation
of Ocean-Wave Device

He Guo[1], Yuying Zhou[2(✉)], and Li Liu[1]

[1] School of Automation Science and Electrical Engineering,
Beihang University, Beijing, China
[2] China Shipbuilding Systems Engineering Research Institute,
Beijing, China
zhouyy_bj@139.com

Abstract. In the field of wave power, using the inertial device for energy acquisition is the novelty of marine energy generation technology. Aiming at a new inertial wave energy collection device, this paper has analyzed its working principle and established a set of electrical system structure applicable for the field of wave power, which has an important significance for the wave power generation field. Inertial collection device can convert wave energy to mechanical energy by using the Procession effect of gyroscope. Based on the output performance analysis of gyroscope device, power system design can be finished in MATLAB, which is built with Buck-Boost voltage circuit topology containing permanent-magnet synchronous generator (PMSG). The basic components and operation principle are given. Finally, the paper has accomplished united simulation of the mathematical model acquisition device and the electrical model, which has tested and verified that power system design can meet the design requirements of power. The simulation results provide data support for the follow-up design of power control.

Keywords: Inertial wave power generation · MATLAB · Power system simulation · United simulation

1 Introduction

Global energy crisis has become increasingly prominent due to the rapid development of economy and society. Nowadays, all countries in the world attach great importance to the study of new and high-efficient marine power generation device. It has great significance for solving the global energy crisis to research on sea wave power energy generation device [1].

The inertial wave power device has the obvious advantages compared with the existing wave power generation device. In the first place, due to the structural characteristics of the inertial wave device, the key components of gyroscope system, transmission system, generator etc. are placed in a sealed casing, which achieves isolation from sea, and ensures safety and reliability of components; secondly, because of the characteristics of tightness, no movable component will contact with seawater direct which reduces the requirements standard of the device material, greatly reduces the cost and the design difficulty, and improves the survival ability of the device itself.

© Springer Science+Business Media Singapore 2016
L. Zhang et al. (Eds.): AsiaSim 2016/SCS AutumnSim 2016, Part III, CCIS 645, pp. 253–264, 2016.
DOI: 10.1007/978-981-10-2669-0_28

Design of the device makes itself able to adapt to the changeful marine environment. The fixed mooring mode of the device is conducive to layout and recovery, and also it is environment-friendly, maintaining the stability of the marine environment; finally, orientation stability of gyroscope can stabilize irregular interfere which is favorable both for accuracy and practical efficiency of the final device. Therefore, research on inertial wave generation has important significance for wave energy power generation, gyroscope technology application field and wave power control field etc.

The objective of this paper is to design a electrical system for a new type of inertial wave energy acquisition device, which is based on physical characteristics and output characteristics of the device. The paper has analyzed the principle of wave power generation system and the specific function of each unit, and built simulation model of the wave power system, based on permanent magnet synchronous generator using MATLAB. Finally, the simulation results verify the correctness of the design parameters.

2 Model Principle and Analysis

2.1 Inertial Acquisition Unit Model Analysis

2.1.1 Wave Power Principle

Hyperion power generation devices use different media for energy conversion. And according to the kind of media can be broadly divided into: "Duck", Pendulous, Oscillating water column, and Oscillating-buoy wave power device [2]. All ocean-wave power devices contain two stage energy-conversion sections. First, it can convert the ocean energy to the kinetic energy of acquisition part. In the second stage, generator rotor will be forced by transmission gear, which converts the kinetic energy to electrical power for the load [3] (Fig. 1).

Fig. 1. Energy conversion

However, the existing acquisition device has obvious disadvantages of design in virtue of exposed in sea. Although this design is convenient to absorb energy from the ocean directly, the reliability of the device is greatly reduced and the maintenance cost is increased due to the variability of marine conditions and the corrosion of marine organisms. Recently, foreign researchers put forward a new energy conversion device design ideas, that is, inertial wave energy power generation technology with high reliability and stability, which can effectively overcome the shortcomings above [4].

2.1.2 Inertial Ocean Energy Acquisition Device

Gyro instrument is used for navigation, and with the development of science and technology, it has been widely used in aviation and aerospace industry [5]. Application of gyro instrument is quite extensive. It occupied an important position in the modernization of national defense construction and national economic construction.

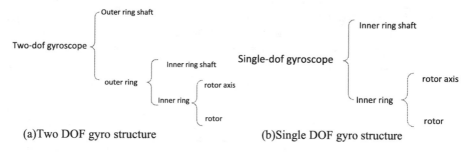

(a)Two DOF gyro structure   (b)Single DOF gyro structure

Fig. 2. Two kinds of gyroscope structure

Gyroscope can be divided into two kinds according to the rotational degrees-of-freedom (DOF): two DOF gyro and single DOF gyro [6] (Fig. 2).

Gyroscope has two important characteristics: orientation stability and precession. And inertial wave acquisition device mainly uses the precession of gyroscope, namely, when external torque acts on outer ring shaft with rotor rotating at a high speed, the gyroscope will rotate around the inner axis. The rotational angular velocity direction is perpendicular to external torque. The precession direction can be judged by the right hand rule. Considering the advantage of gyroscope,we can add gyroscope system into original acquisition device to improve its performance, using its inertia characteristics to achieve conversion of marine mechanical energy. This is called gyroscopic ocean-wave power generator (GOWPG) [7].

2.1.3   Gyroscope System Model

When the wave arrives, the wave will act the moment of force on the device which will lead to motion of precession. The gyroscope can output moment, precession moment, which can be connected to shaft of generator through transport mechanism. To facilitate connection to electrical system, the paper setup three output terminals, precession angular velocity, precession torque, and the average mechanical power (Fig. 3).

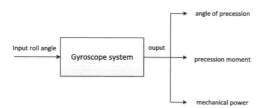

Fig. 3. Gyroscope system model

2.2   Generating System Principle and Model

2.2.1   Integrated System Design

In this paper, the design of the overall structure is mainly composed of the gyro system, synchronous generator, none-controlled rectifier bridge, DC-DC converter and the load. The magneto synchronous generator will make use of the energy gathered by gyroscope.

The Three Phase Bridge will convert alternating current to direct current which can be adjusted by DC-DC converter. The main function of the converter is to adjust the equivalent load of Load circuit, so as to realize the optimization of the output power of the system. Adding the DC-DC converter can pave the way for the power control in the future (Fig. 4).

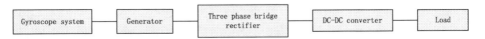

| Gyroscope system | Generator | Three phase bridge rectifier | DC–DC converter | Load |

Fig. 4. Integrated system composition

2.2.2 Generator Model

Permanent magnet synchronous generator has the advantages of simple structure, low cost and reliable operation, which can increase the air gap magnetic density, reduce the volume of the motor and improve the power quality. At present, the application field of permanent magnet synchronous generator in China is very wide, such as the small-sized and medium-sized wind power generator. And with the improvement of high performance permanent magnet material manufacturing process, large capacity wind power generation system is also inclined to use permanent magnet synchronous generator (Fig. 5).

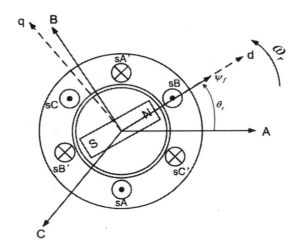

Fig. 5. Generator d-q axis coordinate system

The d axis of the synchronous rotating coordinate system is directed to the pole axis of the rotor, and the q axis is ahead of the d axis at 90° [8]. In the d − q coordinate system, according to the motor practice, the electrical equation of the permanent magnet synchronous generator is as followed [9]:

$$\frac{d}{d_t}i_d = \frac{1}{L_d}u_d - \frac{R}{L_d}i_d + \frac{L_q}{L_d}p\omega_r i_q \tag{1}$$

$$\frac{d}{d_t}i_q = \frac{1}{L_d}u_q - \frac{R}{L_q}i_q - \frac{L_d}{L_q}p\omega_r i_d - \frac{\lambda p\omega_r}{L_q} \tag{2}$$

Mechanical equation in the permanent magnet synchronous generator is written to:

$$T_e = 1.5p[\lambda i_q + (L_d - L_q)i_d i_q] \tag{3}$$

This paper uses the permanent magnet generator model in the Simulink and set the parameter, in which three-phase load circuit is designed and the parameters of the generator set is verified. The correctness can be tested and verified by detecting load output power (Fig. 6).

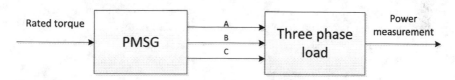

Fig. 6. Generator parameter validation

2.2.3 Rectifier Model Analysis

The diode circuit is added between the AC power supply and the DC load, and the switching of the AC to DC is realized by using the single conduction characteristic of the diode. In this paper, the use of load tracking power control requires the DC circuit environment. Therefore, the use of three-phase bridge rectifier circuit can ensure the output of three-phase alternating current into DC power, which can be used by the future design (Fig. 7).

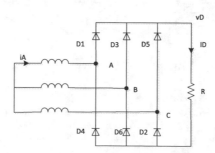

Fig. 7. Three phase bridge structure diagram

In the three-phase bridge rectifier circuit, two diodes conduct at any moment which are connected with the highest voltage, and make the other diodes withstand the pressure to turn off (Fig. 8).

Three phase bridge rectifier can output the high average DC, and the pulse is smaller, easy to filter. Output current is 120° pulse width, positive and negative said alternating current, no DC component, which is widely used in uncontrolled rectifier.

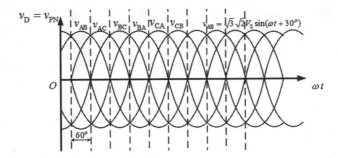

Fig. 8. Output voltage of rectifier bridge

This design adopts the conduction angle whose value is zero, and in a power cycle, output voltage consists by six same pulse of the same width, that is, sixty degree [10].

$$
V_D = \frac{1}{\pi/3} \int_{30°}^{90°} v_{AB} d(\omega t)
$$

$$
= \frac{1}{\pi/3} \int_{30°}^{90°} \sqrt{3} \cdot \sqrt{2} V_S \sin(\omega t + 30°) d(\omega t) = 2.34 V_S
$$

(4)

In the design process, because the circuit contains a number of electric capacity and inductors, it is necessary to verify the correctness of each part step by step. The simulation can be designed as follows (Fig. 9):

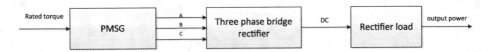

Fig. 9. Rectifier bridge parameter validation

2.2.4 DC/DC Converter Model
In this paper, the Buck-Boost converter is used, which has the advantages of small input and output current ripple (Fig. 10).

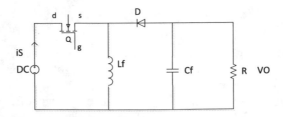

Fig. 10. Lifting voltage circuit

The work situation of converter can be divided into three kinds of states. First, Q tube conducts and D tube blocks. We can define duty ratio as D_y. The circuit structure can be equivalent to the following (Fig. 11):

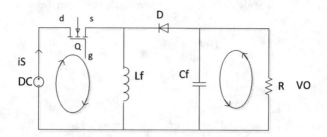

Fig. 11. D tube blocks

At this point the input voltage charges the inductor with output voltage of filter essentially unchanged. The relationship of circuit can be calculated as:

$$L_f \frac{di_{Lf}}{dt} = V_{in} \tag{5}$$

$$\Delta i_{Lf(+)} = \frac{V_{in}}{L_f} T_{ON} = \frac{V_{in}}{L_f} D_y T_S \tag{6}$$

In the second situation, Q tube cuts off and D tube conducts. The circuit structure can be equivalent to the following (Fig. 12):

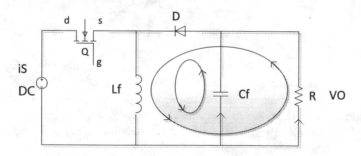

Fig. 12. Q tube blocks

At this point the inductor will release the energy stored at the last stage to the load R and capacitance C. And if the moment energy release finishes is before the period point, the circuit will gain the third working situation.

$$L_f \frac{di_{Lf}}{dt} = -V_o \tag{7}$$

$$\Delta i_{Lf(-)} = \frac{V_o}{L_f}(T_S - T_{ON}) = \frac{V_o}{L_f}(1 - D_y)T_S \tag{8}$$

The relationship between values of voltage can be calculated using $\Delta i_{Lf(+)} = \Delta i_{Lf(-)}$:

$$\frac{V_{in}}{L_f}D_y T_S = \frac{V_o}{L_f}(1 - D_y)T_S \tag{9}$$

$$V_o = \frac{\alpha}{1-\alpha}V_{in} \tag{10}$$

If the power loss is not considered, the output current can be written as [11]:

$$I_o = \frac{1-\alpha}{\alpha}I_{in} \tag{11}$$

When the inductor current is interrupted, there is the third kind of working situation as follows (Fig. 13):

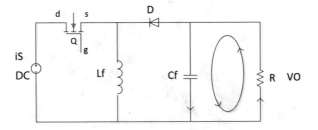

Fig. 13. Inductive energy depletion

It will broaden the range of application of the circuit, enhance the ability to adjust the circuit, and pave the way for the optimization of the circuit to add the DC-DC converter to the existing circuit. At this point, the switching device input pulse frequency is set as 1000 Hz, and duty cycle as 50 %, that means DC-DC converter won't play the role of transforming voltage, so that the simulation results will verify the value validity of capacitance and inductance in the Buck-Boost voltage circuit.

3   Simulation and Discussion

3.1   Gyroscope System Simulation and Discussion

The output angular velocity, torque and mechanical power output are obtained by simulation based on the existing gyroscope system. All output parameters have been processed after standard one treatment (Figs. 14, 15 and 16).

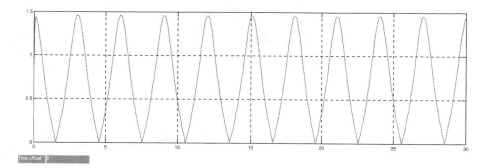

Fig. 14. Gyro precession angular velocity

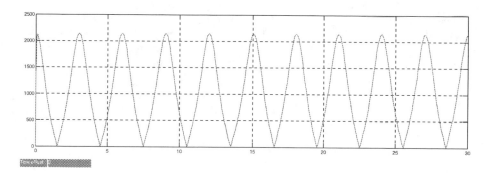

Fig. 15. Gyro output torque

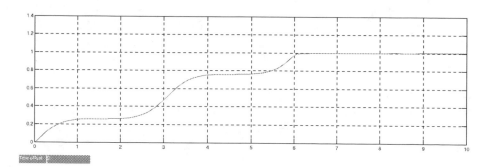

Fig. 16. Gyroscope output mechanical power

It can be found and analyzed by the simulation graph above that the output angular velocity and torque of the gyroscope are periodic, with oscillation characteristics, and it has rapid response speed. Gyroscope precession angular velocity response time is 0.3 s, and precession torque response time is 0.1 s. The output mechanical power of the gyroscope system can meet the design targets and the stable value of the output power quickly.

3.2   Power Generation System Simulation and Discussion

3.2.1   None Controlled Rectifier Bridge Circuit Simulation

In the previous part, the correctness of the generator model parameters has been verified. After adding the rectifier into the circuit, due to the existence of nonlinear devices such as inductor, it required further verification to ensure the feasibility of the parameters of the inductor current. In order to make the output power of the load meet the design goal, it is necessary to match the load with the front parameters. The peak value of the output voltage of the generator is 69 V, so that the effective value of the output DC voltage of the rectifier bridge can be calculated as:

$$V_D = \frac{3}{\pi} V_{\max} = 67 \text{ V} \tag{12}$$

The measured current from output detection mechanism is 16 A, which can be used to calculate the load resistance, which is 67 V/16 A = 4.18 Ω, finally get the load power to achieve the design goal, reasonable parameters. In this paper, the output characteristic of the electric system has been changed after standard one treatment (Fig. 17).

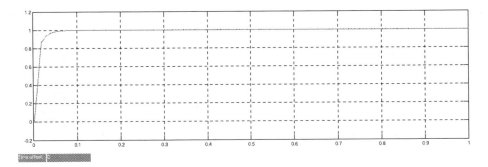

Fig. 17. Output power of load

3.2.2   Buck-Boost Circuit Simulation

From the model built in MATLAB using the circuit structure in former section, the output voltage of load is observed as follows (Fig. 18):

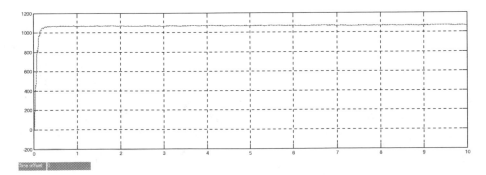

Fig. 18. Output voltage of load

From the result can we find that, the load voltage has reached eighty percent of the set value in 0.2 s, which means a good response. Due to value of the duty ratio set as 50 %, the output of the DC-DC circuit doesn't alter the voltage from rectifier bridge. In this situation, we can judge the feasibility of the value of inductance and capacitance by response speed. Obviously the parameters are advisable and reasonable. By using the PWM control technology, the duty cycle of the control system is changed to change the load of the circuit, which realizes the matching between the load and the output of the generator, and finally maximizes the utilization of electric energy. Therefore, adding the lifting voltage circuit provides the basis for follow-up power control technology research.

3.3   Whole System Simulation

Since the correctness of each part of the system is verified in the above, the input of the generator is changed to the torque output end of the gyroscope system. The whole system is as follows (Fig. 19):

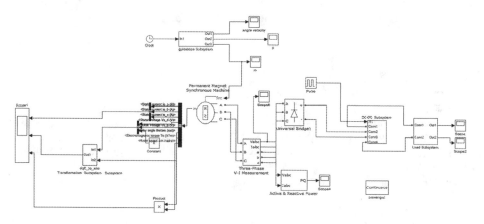

Fig. 19. Simulink model of integrated system

The average output power of the observed load is shown in the following Fig. 20:

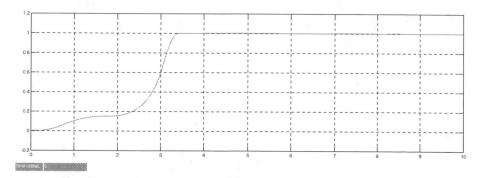

Fig. 20. Final results of load power

The result shows that, the ultimate load power has reached the requirement of design, and verified for correctness of the inertial waves acquisition device based on the power system, and finally achieve the design goals.

4 Conclusions and Future Work

This paper expounds the principle of gyro precession and concluded the advantages of the new wave power device based on gyroscope structure by compare with existing device. In view of the model of a kind of inertia ocean-wave power device, the output characteristic of the model in MATLAB is obtained. Then the structure of power system is designed based on the characteristics of the design goals and generator output design. Principle components analysis is used to calculate the parameters, and the paper has built gyroscope, permanent magnet synchronous generator, DC-DC converter circuit module in MATLAB. The correctness of the component parameters is verified by the simulation results of each part of the system. Finally the paper has completed the joint simulation of whole system and output power can meet the design requirements, which provides data support for the follow-up system structure optimization and the join of the Buck-Boost circuit paves the way for future power control technology.

References

1. Falcão, A.F.D.O.: Wave energy utilization: a review of the technologies. Renew. Sustain. Energy Rev. **14**(3), 899–918 (2010)
2. Robertson, B.R.D., Hiles, C.E., Buckham, B.J.: Characterizing the near shore wave energy resource on the west coast of Vancouver Island, Canada. In: IEEE/RSJ International Conference on Intelligent Robots & Systems, pp. 665–678 (2014)
3. Liu, J., Sandhu, G.: Spin current generator for STT-MRAM or other spintronics applications: US, US 8885398, pp. 113–127 (2014)
4. Pollack, J., Wille, H.: Ocean energy conversion: US, US 8740583 B2 (2014)
5. Fell, C., Fox, C.H.J.: Gyroscope: US, US 6343509 B1 (2002)
6. Rozelle, D.M.: Self calibrating gyroscope system: US, US 20100063763 A1, pp. 207–215 (2010)
7. Bracco, G., Giorcelli, E., Mattiazzo, G.: ISWEC: a gyroscopic mechanism for wave power exploitation. Mech. Mach. Theory **46**(10), 1411–1424 (2011)
8. Mantere, J., Mechler, G., Shen, J.: Synchronous generator: WO, WO 2003073591 A1 (2003)
9. Bhende, C.N., Mishra, S., Malla, S.G.: Permanent magnet synchronous generator-based standalone wind energy supply system. IEEE Trans. Sustain. Energy **2**(4), 361–373 (2011)
10. Park, S.-C.: DC-DC converter and organic light emitting display using the same: US, US 8581897 (2013)
11. Ismail, E.H., Sabzali, A.J., Al-Saffar, M.A.: Buck–boost-type unity power factor rectifier with extended voltage conversion ratio. IEEE Trans. Ind. Electron. **55**(3), 1123–1132 (2008)

Multi-agent-based Simulation for Policy Evaluation of Carbon Emissions

Meirong Zhou, Ming Zhou[✉], Yanchun Pan, Zhimin Chen, and Jun Zeng

College of Management, Shenzhen University,
Shenzhen, People's Republic of China
1953275607@qq.com, {mzhou,panyc,chenzm}@szu.edu.cn,
zengjun19881202@126.com

Abstract. To effectively control air pollution, China has established regional carbon emissions trading markets based on cap and trade in seven pilot provinces and cities. Government agencies that manage the market want to know that whether the policies of carbon emissions are effective and appropriate. Under cap and trade, the emissions trading system, made up of the government, emissions exchange and participating enterprises, is nonlinear, dynamic, uncertain, and decision-decentralized. Also, there exist interactive influences among participants and multiple decision objectives in the emissions trading system. So, this research applied a multi-agent modeling and simulation approach to build such a simulation model for the regional emissions trading system, and then analyzed the policies related to total emissions control, emission quotas allocation, emission quotas auction, and excessive emission fines.

Keywords: Policy evaluation · Cap and trade · Emissions trading system · Multi-agent modeling and simulation · Analysis of variance

1 Introduction

Due to over-developed human activities, unrestricted greenhouse gas emissions have been a primary cause for the global warming that caused significant environmental changes (Zhang et al. 2011; IPCC 2007). Over the years, there have been some positive progresses in coping with climate change.

In China, the government has committed to cut its CO2 emissions (Yi et al. 2011), and is aggressively pushing for a compulsory carbon emission reduction program (EN 2010). In 2011, Beijing, Guangdong, Shanghai, Tianjin, Chongqing, Hubei and Shenzhen were determined as the first carbon emissions trading pilot provinces and cities. Unified national carbon emissions trading market will run in 2016, and the quotas are allocated by the state. On November 12, 2014, the Chinese government promised in the sino-us joint statement on climate change: China plans to make carbon dioxide emissions reach peak around 2030, and will try to reach peak at an early date.

There has been a rich body of literature related to the study of cap and trade application or emissions trading system. Many are qualitative studies that used a descriptive approach to discuss the risks and allocating initial emission allowance to

© Springer Science+Business Media Singapore 2016
L. Zhang et al. (Eds.): AsiaSim 2016/SCS AutumnSim 2016, Part III, CCIS 645, pp. 265–272, 2016.
DOI: 10.1007/978-981-10-2669-0_29

generating companies (Yi et al. 2011; Wei et al. 2012; James and Chen 2012) and the design of mechanism for carbon-credit trade (Robert et al. 2012). Some papers focused on optimization issues related to the carbon-credit resource planning from a production system perspective (Chen et al. 2013). Mathematical programming models (e.g. LP, NLP, MIP) in particular have been developed to optimizing resource decisions for single manufacturer (Kockar et al. 2009; Wang et al. 2012; Chang et al. 2012). These studies demonstrated that cap and trade conditions generate significant impact on the resource selection and allocation of enterprise, and analytical models can be effective in identifying decision trade-offs that lead to optimal solutions.

However, there is little literature using multi-agent modeling and simulation to study the carbon emissions reduction, and there is less literature using multi-agent modeling and simulation to study the complex system made up of the government, emissions exchange and numerous participating enterprises at present. The purpose of this research is to apply a multi-agent modeling and simulation approach to build such a simulation model for the regional emissions trading system, and then to analyze the policies of total emissions control, emission quotas allocation, emission quotas auction, and excessive emission fines. The rest of the paper is organized as follows. In Sect. 2, we propose a conceptual modeling framework that captures essential characteristics of a regional emissions trading system including enterprise agent function design, government agent function design, exchange agent function design and interaction among agents. Section 3 presents the results of the experimental results, and discuss their managerial implication. Finally, Sect. 4 concludes the study. It is noted that due to the limit of space the descriptions presented in this paper are a little abstract.

2   Conceptual Modeling of the Emissions Trading System Model

An emissions trading system must perform a number of functions to ensure the control and operation of the market (Robert et al. 2012), e.g. total quantity control, emission quotas allocation, monitoring-reporting-verification (MRV), auction mechanism, market transaction, reserve mechanism, entrance mechanism, offset mechanism, penalty

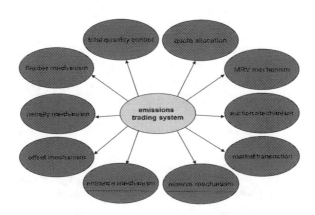

Fig. 1. Functions of an emissions trading system

mechanism, flexible mechanism, etc. During the conceptual design stage, we focused on four main tasks: (1) enterprise agent function design, (2) government agent function design, (3) exchange agent function design and (4) interaction among agents. The functions of emissions trading system in our model is shown in Fig. 1.

2.1   Enterprise Agent Function Design

The functions of an enterprise agent based on real world, are shown in Fig. 2.

An enterprise agent has the following functions: to satisfy the insufficient quotas, to manage the surplus quotas, to view the account information, to update the account information, and so on. If emission quotas of an enterprise agent is insufficient, the enterprise agent has three approaches to satisfy its insufficient quotas: to purchase quotas, to do self-purification or to be fined. And, if emission quotas of an enterprise agent is surplus, the enterprise agent has two approaches to manage its surplus quotas: to sell quotas or to hold quotas. The detailed functions, attributes and logic of an enterprise agent is omitted here due to the limit of space.

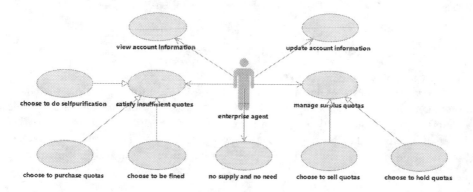

Fig. 2. Functions of an enterprise agent

2.2   Government Agent Function Design

The functions of the government agent based on real world, are shown in Fig. 3.

The government agent has the following functions: to control the total emission quantity, to allocate the emission quotas, to release the reserves, to repurchase the emission quotas, to hold an auction, to allow an enter, to check the emissions, to collect the emission quotas, to make a fine, and so on. The government agent will determine

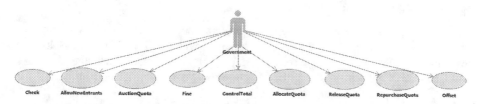

Fig. 3. Functions of the government agent

the regional total carbon emissions (that is to determine the budget emission quotas) according to the grandfather principle and the baseline principle (Aihman et al. 2005; Sterner et al. 2006). Then, it allocates free emission quotas to the enterprises under the principle of no more than total carbon emissions determined. When the government agent allocates free emission quotas to the enterprises, it will take into consideration the budget emission quotas, the costs of self-purification, the output values, the amount of standard coal of per ten thousand yuan GDP, the auction ratio of emission quotas reserved, the government reserve ratio of emission quotas reserved, the ratio of emission quotas reserved for new entrants. Both this free emission quota allocation scheme is beneficial to the survival of the fittest of enterprises, and it appropriately takes care of those enterprises that have the large amount of standard coal of ten thousand yuan GDP. The government agent has a set of its own reserve mechanism. Once the market situation triggers the government reserve mechanism, the government agent will accordingly release or repurchase emission quotas. At the stipulated time, the government agent will check an enterprise agent's emissions, and then collect its emission quotas. When an enterprise agent does not meet the emission reduction requirements, the government agent will fine it. The detailed functions, attributes and logic of the government agent is omitted here due to the limit of space.

2.3 Exchange Agent Function Design

The functions of the exchange agent based on real world, are shown in Fig. 4.

The government agent has the following functions: to promote a deal, to create a account for an enterprise, to update the enterprise account information, to delete the enterprise account information, to release the market information, to update the market information, to delete the market information, and so on. The detailed functions, attributes and logic of the exchange agent is omitted here due to the limit of space.

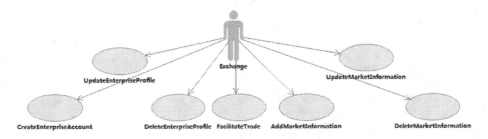

Fig. 4. Functions of the exchange agent

2.4 Interaction Among Agents

The emissions trading system made up of the government, the carbon emissions exchange and numerous controlled enterprises, has many levels, and each level has its own structure, such as the area, the government, the carbon emissions exchange, the indus-tries, and many enterprises. There are interactions between individual and individual. For example, the enterprise agents selling emission quotas and purchasing emission quotas will trade with one another in the market, and the exchange agent will promote a deal between buyers and sellers. When the market situation triggers the government agent to release the reserves, the government agent will release the government reserves in the carbon emissions trading market. When the market situation triggers the government to repurchase the emission quotas, the government agent will repurchase the emission quotas in the carbon emissions trading market. When there is a new controlled enterprise to join the emissions trading system, the government agent will allocate free emission quotas to it. When the government agent hold an emission quota auction, the enterprise agents can give their purchase intention to the government agent. The government agent will allocates free emission quotas to each enterprise agent, and each enterprise agent give the summary of its annual output value and carbon emission quantity to the government agent, and so on. All kinds of interactions between individual overlay, and that are just as a complex vast network. And each individual in the vast network will be directly or indirectly affected by other individuals or affect other individuals, which may be said "one change makes all change". The details are omitted here due to the limit of space.

For more details on how the multi-agent-based model is structured and the agents, please see the paper of Zhou et al. (2015).

3 Simulation and Discussion

The baseline model was implemented with ANYLOGIC©. It contains 300 agents, of which 1/3 are metal-processing/equipment manufacturers, 1/3 plastics manufacturers and 1/3 telecommunication manufacturers. We have a detailed analysis and verification about the logic, conceptual model, simulation model construction, operation process and output results of this complex simulation model. The model was also showed to the partners from Shenzhen Emission Exchange and several participating enterprises, and we received positive feedback. Also, we have done the sensitivity analysis. The details are omitted here due to the limit of space.

The purpose of this research is to analyze the policies of total emissions control, emission quotas allocation, emission quotas auction, and excessive emission fines, as shown in Table 1. X_1 represents the policy of total emission control, X_2 represents the policy of carbon emission auction, X_3 represents the policy of self-purification, X_4 represents the policy of excessive emission fines.

Where P1 is the emission quota average price of last three days of released auction notice, P2 the regional average self-purification cost of last year, P3 is auction reserve price, P4 is the buyer's expected price, and max (P1/2, P2) is the greater value between P1/2 and P2.

According to the policy settings, we have designed a 24 factorial experiment, and conducted a total of 16 simulated combinations. Each simulation experiment was repeated 50 times. The simulation model used in the study was in days' time units and the length of each replication was set 72 months. This study selects the total actual annual emissions as the statistical output indicator, and the result of multi-factor analysis of variance is as shown in Table 2.

Table 1. Policies and its proposals

Policy	Proposal	
	Proposal 1	Proposal 2
X_1	X_{11}: Denote that the regional emission quota budget is based on historical emission method.	X_{12}: Denote that the regional emission quota budget is based on carbon emission intensity method.
X_2	X_{21}: Denote the auction reserve price according to the auction method shown in Fig. 5	X_{22}: Denote the auction reserve price according to the auction method shown in Fig. 6
X_3	X_{31}: Denote that the government planning regional carbon emission intensity declines 4 % annually	X_{32}: Denote that the government planning regional carbon emission intensity declines 5.59 % annually (according to Shenzhen City)
X_4	X_{41}: Denote Fines = excessive emissions * 3 times of the market average price. (The market average price is based on the past six months)	X_{42}: Denote Fines = excessive emission * 3 times of the market average price. In addition, the excessive emissions are subtracted from next annual emission quotas.

Table 2 shows that the policy variables X_1, X_3, $X_1 * X_2$, $X_1 * X_3$, and $X_2 * X_3$ have significant impacts on the total actual annual emissions, when the significant level is 0.05. While the interactions of other policy variables are not significant, when the significant level is 0.05. As an example to compare the difference between experimental levels of the policy variable X_1 on the total actual annual emissions, we show the results of paired samples t test in the Table 3.

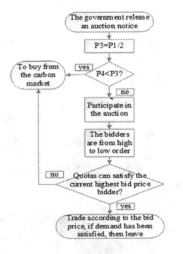

Fig. 5. Auction policy 1

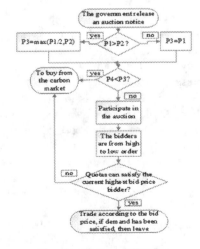

Fig. 6. Auction policy 2

Table 2. Multi-factor analysis of variance

Source	III type of sum of squares	df	Mean square	F	Sig.
Calibration model	235035042773722.53	15	15669002851581.502	167.091	.000
Intercept	205413860857468032	1	205413860857468032	2190490	.000
X1	42964775882115.600	1	42964775882115.600	458.167	.000
X2	297628626993.727	1	297628626993.727	3.174	.075
X3	173440554012755.94	1	173440554012755.94	1849.53	.000
X4	46360752272.133	1	46360752272.133	.494	.482
X1 * X2	401512242926.267	1	401512242926.267	4.282	.039
X1 * X3	17264956275625.582	1	17264956275625.582	184.110	.000
X1 * X4	12685118611.442	1	12685118611.442	.135	.713
X2 * X3	408674841782.019	1	408674841782.019	4.358	.037
X2 * X4	3276745914.575	1	3276745914.575	.035	.852
X3 * X4	2286679933.946	1	2286679933.946	.024	.876
X1 * X2 * X3	61790308135.596	1	61790308135.596	.659	.417
X1 * X2 * X4	7485325661.331	1	7485325661.331	.080	.778
X1 * X3 * X4	79301445.836	1	79301445.836	.001	.977
X2 * X3 * X4	2461135414.184	1	2461135414.184	.026	.871
X1 * X2 * X3 * X4	120515524123.092	1	120515524123.092	1.285	.257
Error	73519812729723.280	784	93775271338.933		
Total	205722415712971552	800			
Calibrated total	308554855503445.80	799			

[a]R Square = .762 (Adjusted R Square = .757)
Independent: the total actual annual emissions (unit: ton)

Table 3. Paired samples t test

Paired differences					t	df	Sig. (2-tailed)
Mean	Std. deviation	Std. error mean	95 % Confidence interval of the difference				
			Lower	Upper			
463491	406180	20309	423565	503417	22.8	399	.000

total actual annual emissions1 - total actual annual emissions2

From Table 3, for the policy variable X_1 (the policy of total emission control), its proposal 2 (the regional emission quota budget is based on relative quota method) has greater impact on the total actual annual emissions compared with its proposal 1 (the regional emission quota budget is based on historical method), because the mean of total annual actual emissions is smaller at this time.

4   Conclusions and Future Work

This research aims at applying a multi-agent modeling and simulation approach to build such a simulation model for the regional emissions trading system, and then to analyze the policies of total emissions control, emission quotas allocation, emission quotas auction, and excessive emission fines. The individual decision behavior is simulated through a group of agents, each representing an independent participating enterprise. Cap and trade restrictions and related risk conditions were applied and controlled by system agents. In this paper, we have selected the total actual annual emissions as the statistical output indicator, and evaluated how the relevant polices of carbon emission reduction affect it. In the future, we will select more variable as the statistical output indicators, and evaluated how the relevant polices of carbon emission reduction affect them.

Acknowledgement. This research is partially funded by the Natural Science Foundation of China (NSFC) under grant codes 71572114, 71272089 and 71472126.

References

James, B., Chen, Y.: Allocation and leakage in regional cap-and-trade markets for CO2. Resour. Energy Econ. **34**(4), 647–668 (2012)

Wei, C., Ni, J.L., Du, L.M.: Regional allocation of carbon dioxide abatement in China. China Econ. Rev. **23**(3), 552–565 (2012)

EN (Enigin News). China Set to Use Iron Hand to Force Energy Efficiency (2010). http://www.enigin.com/about/enigin-plc/news/-/enigin-news

Kockar, I., Conejo, A.J., McDonald, J.R.: Influence of the emissions trading scheme on generation scheduling. Electr. Power Energy Syst. **31**(9), 465–473 (2009)

IPCC. Climate Change 2007: The Physical Science Basis, pp. 1–18. Cambridge University Press, UK (2007). http://www.ipcc.ch/pdf/assessment-report/ar4/wg1/ar4-wg1-spm.pdf

Aihman, M., Zetterberg, L.: Options for emission allowance allocation under the Eu emissions trading directive. Mitig. Adapt. Strat. Glob. Change **10**(4), 597–645 (2005)

Robert, M., Flachsland, C., Jakob, M.: Sectoral linking of carbon markets: a trade-theory analysis. Resour. Energy Econ. **34**(4), 585–606 (2012)

Wang, M.X., Wang, M.R., Wang, S.Y.: Optimal investment and uncertainty on China's carbon emission abatement. Energy Policy **41**(2), 871–877 (2012)

Zhou, M., Zhou, M., Pan, Y., Chen, Z.: Modeling a regional emission trade market via computer simulation. Conf. Summer Comput. Simul. **47**(10), 35–40 (2015)

Zhang, Q., Min, X., Chen, Y.: Reflection on the development of low-carbon cities from the perspective of systems engineering. Syst. Eng. **29**(1), 1–7 (2011)

Sterner, T., Isaksson, L.H.: Refunded emission payments theory, distribution of costs, and Swedish experience of NOx abatement. Ecol. Econ. **57**(1), 93–106 (2006)

Yi, W.J., Zou, L.L., Guo, J., Wang, K., Wei, Y.M.: How can China reach its CO2 intensity reduction targets by 2020? a regional allocation based on equity and development. Energy Policy **39**(5), 2407–2415 (2011)

Chen, X., Benjaafar, S., Elomri, A.: The carbon-constrained EOQ. Oper. Res. Lett. **41**(2), 172–179 (2013)

Unit Commitment with Wind Power and Pumped Hydro Energy Storage

Qun Niu[(⊠)], Dandan Hua, Letian Zhang, and Chao Wang

Shanghai Key Laboratory of Power Station Automation Technology,
School of Mechatronic Engineering and Automation, Shanghai University,
Shanghai 200072, China
comelycc@hotmail.com

Abstract. Pumped hydro energy storage (PHES) can relieve the variability and fluctuation of wind energy in power system. Introducing PHES and wind power into unit commitment (UC) has great significance in the control and operation of power systems, which as well as brings great challenge. In this paper, two harmony search methods called ACHS and NPAHS-M are applied to UC-Wind-PHES problems. Numerical experiments have been done on a power system with one PHES station, one wind power unit and ten thermal units. Comparison results show that ACHS and NPAHS-M can provide higher accuracy and better convergence speed, and the utilization of PHES contributes to the improvement of cost saving and system robustness.

Keywords: Unit commitment · Pumped hydro energy storage · Wind power · Harmony search

1 Introduction

Unit commitment (UC) has great significance in the control and operation of power systems, which is a large scale, nonlinear, mixed-integer optimization problem. Conventional UC aims at scheduling thermal generating units to meet the load demand for minimizing the operation cost while satisfying a number of constraints [1]. More recently, renewable energy sources are becoming an important portion of power systems due to the rising fossil fuel costs and concerns about environmental impact of burning fossil fuels. Among renewable energies, wind power is ever-increasing since it is clean, indigenous, economic and fast to deploy [2]. However, the intermittent and stochastic characteristic of wind power has huge impact on the stable dispatch of UC problems. In order to mitigate the undesirable effects, such as variability and uncertainty of wind power, a joint coordination with pumped hydro energy storage (PHES) is adopted to deal with UC with wind power [3].

PHES can rapidly ramp and convert between pumping and generating conditions, which provides flexibility for energy deviations [4]. The utilization of PHES units can save costs by reducing the dependency on thermal units, while guaranteeing the safe and stable operation of the system. Introducing wind power and PHES into UC is now becoming a hot tendency that obtains large scale popularization. However, PHES systems must consider the stream-flow equations, which bring complexity of

© Springer Science+Business Media Singapore 2016
L. Zhang et al. (Eds.): AsiaSim 2016/SCS AutumnSim 2016, Part III, CCIS 645, pp. 273–281, 2016.
DOI: 10.1007/978-981-10-2669-0_30

system scheduling. Zhou et al. [5] focused on constructing UC model that coordinate hydro and thermal power generation to support secure and economic wind power integration. Brown et al. [6] analyzed the economic benefits of a small island system with inclusion of pumped storage, which has abundant available wind power. Wu et al. [7] proposed a robust optimization model to accommodate wind output uncertainty in Taiwan Power System. Since UC-Wind-PHES is a nonlinear, multi-constrained, NP-hard optimization problem, it is essential to explore new technologies to solve these problems.

Harmony search (HS) is a meta-heuristic algorithm based on mimicking the improvisation process of music players, which has been widely applied for engineering optimization fields with continuous design variables [8]. In this paper, two improved harmony search algorithms called ACHS and NPAHS-M are extended to solve the UC-Wind-PHES problems due to their advantage of simple concept, few parameters and easy implementation. Incorporating arithmetic crossover operation, ACHS vastly improves the accuracy and convergence speed [15]. NPAHS-M shows high robustness and exploration ability with new pitch adjustment rule [13]. Compared with LR (lagrangian relaxation), GA (Genetic algorithm) and HS, ACHS and NPAHS-M can greatly improve the population diversity, as well as enhance the globally search capabilities.

2　UC-Wind-PHES Formulation

Introducing wind power and PHES into UC model makes a significant difference to the conventional UC model. The objective function of conventional UC optimization is to minimize the operating costs of thermal units over the given time horizon. As wind power and PHES are zero fuel cost clean sources, the new objective function only calculates the cost of the thermal units.

2.1　Objective Function

The new objective function can be formulated as:

$$\min\ CFuel = \sum_{t=1}^{T} \sum_{i=1}^{N} \left[Fuel(P_{i,t}) + Start_{i,t}(1 - U_{i,t}) \right] \cdot U_{i,t} \tag{1}$$

Where $CFuel$ is the total operating cost; $U_{i,t}$ is the status of unit i at period t, 1 means online while 0 means offline; T is the operating period; N is the number of available thermal units; $Fuel(P_{i,t})$ is the fuel cost function of a thermal unit and $Start_{i,t}$ is the start-up cost of unit i, which are defined as followed:

$$Fuel(P_{i,t}) = a_i + b_i \times P_{i,t} + c_i \times P_{i,t}^2 \tag{2}$$

$$Start_{i,t} = \begin{cases} h\cos t_i & T_{i,down} \le T_{i,off} \le T_{i,down} + T_{i,cold} \\ c\cos t_i & T_{i,off} > T_{i,down} + T_{i,down} \end{cases} \tag{3}$$

Where a_i, b_i, c_i are the cost function coefficients of unit i; $T_{i,cold}$, $T_{i,off}$ and $T_{i,down}$ represent the cold start time, continuous shutdown time and minimum down time of unit i at period t separately; $P_{i,t}$ is the output power of unit i at period t; $h \cos t_i$ is hot start-up cost, while $c \cos t_i$ is the cold start-up cost.

2.2 Constraints

(1) Power balance: L_t, $P_{w,t}$ and Ph_t are predicted load demand, wind power output and output power of PHES in time t.

$$\sum_{i=1}^{N} P_{i,t} + Ph_t + P_{w,t} = L_t \qquad (4)$$

(2) Spinning reserves: P_i^{max} is the maximum output power of unit i; R_t is defined as 10 % of the load.

$$\sum_{i=1}^{N} P_i^{max} + Ph_t + P_{w,t} \geq L_t + R_t \qquad (5)$$

$$R_t = 10\% \times L_t \qquad (6)$$

(3) Generation limits: P_i^{min} is the minimum output power of unit i.

$$P_i^{min} \leq P_{i,t} \leq P_i^{max} \qquad (7)$$

(4) Minimum up and downtime limits: $T_{i,on}$ is the continuously on time; $T_{i,up}$ is the minimum up time of unit i.

$$U_{i,t} = \begin{cases} 1, & if \ T_{i,on} < T_{i,up} \\ 0, & if \ T_{i,off} < T_{i,down} \end{cases} \qquad (8)$$

(5) Pumped storage output limits: P_p^{min} / P_g^{min} and P_p^{max} / P_g^{max} are the minimum and maximum pumping/generating power limit of PHES.

$$P_p^{min} \leq P_{p,t} \leq P_p^{max} \qquad (9)$$

$$P_g^{min} \leq P_{g,t} \leq P_g^{max} \qquad (10)$$

(6) Water dynamic balance limits and reservoir limits: $E_{a,max}$, E_a^0 and E_a^1 are maximum limits, initial and end condition of the upper reservoirs; η is charging is efficiency; σ is variation of equivalent electricity of upper reservoir.

$$0 \leq E_a^0 - \sum\nolimits_{t=0}^{t} P_{g,t} + \eta \sum\nolimits_{t=0}^{t} P_{p,t} \leq E_{a,\max} \tag{11}$$

$$\left| E_a^1 - E_a^0 \right| \leq \sigma \tag{12}$$

3 Improved HS for UC-Wind-PHES

Harmony Search is a novel meta-heuristic algorithm developed by Geem et al. (2001) using the musical process concept of searching for a perfect state of harmony [9]. The harmony quality is enhanced practice after practice, which is analogous to find the optimality in optimization problems iteration by iteration.

There have been variants of conventional HS, such as improved harmony search (IHS) [10], modified harmony search (MHS) [12] and global best harmony search GHS [11], which have been successfully applied to solve nonlinear, non-convex, large-scaled and combinatorial optimization problems. NPAHS-M highly enhances convergence speed and optimal solution with a new pitch adjustment rule [14]. Combined the searching ability of HS with exploitation of crossover operation, ACHS provides a better search direction as well as improves the diversity of the new population [12]. NPAHS-M and ACHS remain the characteristic of simplicity, which are both improved solvers for optimization problems. NPAHS-M and ACHS are extended to UC problem with wind power and PHES, which are shown as follows:

- **Step 1**: Initialize the optimization problem and algorithm parameters.
- **Step 2**: Initialize the state and output power of PHES unit. HM-h-state is determined by the improved methods in [14], while output power of PHES unit HM-h-power is generated randomly. PHES can only work on one status at time t, such as pumping, idle, or generating mode; 1 means generating energy, −1 means pumping energy, while 0 is on idle mode. $P_w^{\min}/P_w^{\max}$ and $L^{\min}/L^{\max}$ are relatively lower/higher outputs of wind power and load demand.

$$HM - h - State_{s,t} = PS_t = \begin{cases} 1, & if \ L_t > L^{\max} \ \& \ P_w < P_w^{\min} \\ -1, & if \ L_t < L^{\min} \ \& \ P_w > P_w^{\max} \\ 0, & others \end{cases} \tag{13}$$

$$HM - h - Power_t = Ph_t = (Ph_{\min} + rand * (Ph_{\max} - Ph_{\min})) * PS_t \tag{14}$$

- **Step 3**: Initialize the state and output power of thermal units. In this step, HM-State and HM-Power are randomly generated solutions. 1 means the thermal units is committed while 0 means the thermal units is uncommitted.

$$HM - State_{s,i*t} = U_{i,t} = \begin{cases} 1 & if \ rand \leq 0.5 \\ 0 & if \ rand > 0.5 \end{cases} \tag{15}$$

$$HM - Power_{s,i*t} = P_{i,t} = \left(P_{i,\min} + rand * \left(P_{i,\max} - P_{i,\min}\right)\right) * U_{i,t} \qquad (16)$$

- **Step 4**: Adjust the initial values of HM-h-power, HM-State and HM-Power to satisfy power balance constraints, spinning reserves constraints, UC constraints, wind power constraints and PEHS constraints. Calculate the objective values of all the solutions that meet the constraints and choose the optimal one.
- **Step 5**: Improvise the new solution using ACHS and NPAHS-M. The details of improvising state and power by ACHS and NPAHS-M can be found in [13, 15], while the main modification of generating h-Power is shown in Fig. 1.
- **Step 6:** Check for stopping criteria. Otherwise, repeat step 4.

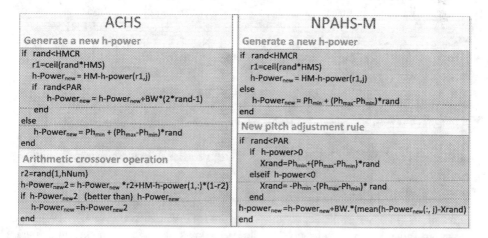

Fig. 1. Main modification of improvising in ACHS and NPAHS-M

4 Simulation and Discussion

4.1 Experiment Parameters

The optimization methods are conducted on a system including one PHES station, one wind power unit and ten thermal units. It should be noted that the prediction output of wind power is mainly certain expected from [15]. The load demand and parameters of ten thermal units are derived from [1]. The parameters of PHES station is collected from [3]. The control parameters ACHS and NPAHS-M algorithms are adopted from [13, 15]. The numbers of maximum fitness evaluations FES are all set as 12000.

4.2   Simulation Results

A series of simulations are carried out on a PC with 2.6 GHz Pentium Dual-Core CPU and 4 G RAM. All the programs in this paper were independently run 30 times in MTLAB R2008b for an overall presentation.

In this paper, LR, GA, HS ACHS and NPAHS-M are adopted to solve UC-Wind-PHES, UC-Wind and conventional UC. Table 1 shows that the economic benefits of ACHS and NPAHS-M are superior to LR, GA and HS for conventional UC problems. Moreover, ACHS and NPAHS-M can clearly provide better results than other existing methods, such as EP (Evolutionary Programming) [16], SA (Simulated Annealing) [17] and IPSO (Quantum-inspired Particle Swarm Optimization) [18]. Results in Table 2 indicate that ACHS and NPAHS-M are stable and capable for both UC-Wind-PHES and UC-Wind problems. Obviously in Table 2, NPAHS-M is a robust method in obtaining improved solution, which outperforms other methods for most of the examined systems. The best total running cost of UC-Wind-PHES using NPAHS-M is $527,416, while UC-Wind using NPAHS-M is $528,724. Therefore, $1,208 can be saved one day with the introduction of PHES in 10-unit system. The results also show that the performance of UC-Wind-PHES is better than other models since PHES can improve the operation of the economy by reduce the thermal power output fluctuations.

The best scheduling result of 10-unit system considering wind power and PHES using NPAHS-M can be seen in Table 3, including the power output plan of thermal units, wind farm, and PHES. Due to the strict construct requirement of PHES station, the efficiency for charge-discharge is about 80 %. In hour 1–3, 23, 24, the output of PHES was negative which means PHES was on pumping status and the total consumption is 130.3 MWh; in hour 10, 12, 20, 21, the output of PHES was positive which means PHES was on generating status and the generation is 104.3 MWh. As shown in Table 3, the utilization of the PHES allows an increase in the wind park economic profit, since wind energy can be stored in off-peak hours and be preferentially delivered to the power system during peak hours.

Figure 2 reveals that ACHS and NPAHS-M converge to a faster rate than conventional HS. Meanwhile, NPAHS-M can vastly improve the solution quality for UC-Wind-PHES problems. Figure 3 shows that during the dispatching period the base load units (unit 1 and unit 2) are always committed, while other intermediate units (units 3, 4, 5, 6, and 7) and peak load units (units 8, 9, and 10) are picked to be started up for meeting the timing-varying load. During low electricity demand and high wind output periods, PHES unit works on generating which pumps water into a reservoir. During high load demand and low wind output periods, PHES unit discharges the

Table 1. Total cost of the conventional 10-unit system

	EP [16]	SA [17]	IPSO [18]	LR	GA	HS	ACHS	NPAHS-M
Best	564,551	565,828	563,954	568,274	568,014	567,797	563,977	563,977
Ave	565,352	565,988	564,162	569,455	569,286	568,459	564,007	563,981
Worst	566,231	566,260	564,579	571,998	570,585	569,286	564,123	564,018

Table 2. Comparison of different methods for UC-Wind-PHES and UC-Wind system

	UC-Wind			UC-Wind-PHES		
	Best	Ave	Worst	Best	Ave	Worst
LR	538,867	539,559	540,652	534,989	535,231	535,540
GA	532,700	533,215	533,761	531,952	532,873	533,452
HS	538,168	539,297	540,286	537,160	538,695	540,162
ACHS	528,963	529,692	529,773	528,188	529,044	529,631
NPAHS-M	528,724	528,955	529,214	527,416	528,225	528,844

Table 3. Best scheduling of thermal units with wind power and PHES

Hour	1	2	3	4	5	6	7	8	9	10	P_{wind}	P_{hydro}
1	455	239.3	0	0	0	0	0	0	0	0	44	−38.3
2	455	255.9	0	0	0	0	0	0	0	0	70.2	−31.1
3	455	350	0	0	0	0	0	0	0	0	76	−31
4	455	388	0	0	25	0	0	0	0	0	82	0
5	455	436	0	0	25	0	0	0	0	0	84	0
6	455	406	0	130	25	0	0	0	0	0	84	0
7	455	440	0	130	25	0	0	0	0	0	100	0
8	455	360	130	130	25	0	0	0	0	0	100	0
9	455	455	130	130	32	20	0	0	0	0	78	0
10	455	455	130	130	112	20.2	25	0	0	0	64	8.8
11	455	455	130	130	135	20	25	0	0	0	100	0
12	455	455	130	130	143	20.1	25	10	0	0	92	39.9
13	455	455	130	130	101	20	25	0	0	0	84	0
14	455	455	130	130	30	20	0	0	0	0	80	0
15	455	382	130	130	25	0	0	0	0	0	78	0
16	455	281	127	130	25	0	0	0	0	0	32	0
17	455	259	127	130	·25	0	0	0	0	0	4	0
18	455	352	130	130	25	0	0	0	0	0	8	0
19	455	450	130	130	25	0	0	0	0	0	10	0
20	455	455	130	130	140	20.2	25	0	0	0	5	39.8
21	455	455	130	130	63	20.2	25	0	0	0	6	15.8
22	455	442	102	0	0	20	25	0	0	0	56	0
23	455	364.2	0	0	0	0	0	0	0	0	82	−1.2
24	455	321.7	0	0	0	0	0	0	0	0	52	−28.7

stored water that lead to a heavily money saving of fuel cost and start-up cost every day. It is obviously that UC-Wind-PHES saves considerable cost for reason that the peak load units (unit 8, unit 9, and unit 10) with high operation cost are replaced with wind power and PHES.

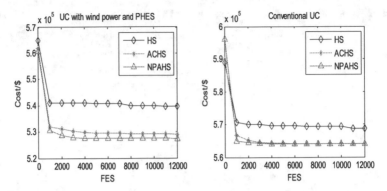

Fig. 2. Convergence curves of different HS versions

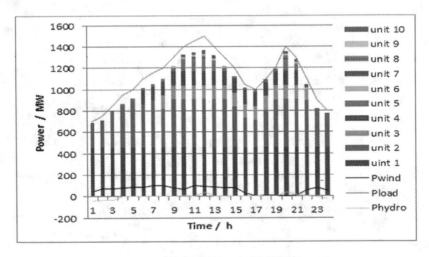

Fig. 3. Outputs of UC-Wind-PHES system

5 Conclusion

This paper has been successfully applied ACHS and NPAHS-M to solve UC-Wind-PHES problem which consists of conventional thermal units, renewable energy and energy storage facility. The comparison results show that ACHS and NPAHS-M have high potential effectiveness and strong searching ability, which are better than LR, GA and HS. Meanwhile, NPAHS-M outperforms ACHS in terms of numerical results in most of the examined systems. Moreover, UC-Wind-PHES is much better than the UC-Wind with the competitive superiority of its robustness in system security and its high economic efficiency. In the future, new strategies for large wind parks and large water storage hydro facilities need to be developed due to the increase of wind-energy penetration in power systems.

Acknowledgments. This work is supported by the National Natural Science Foundation of China (61273040).

References

1. Ongsakul, W., Petcharaks, N.: Unit commitment by enhanced adaptive Lagrangian relaxation. IEEE Trans. Power Syst. **19**(1), 620–628 (2004)
2. Pinto, M.S., Miranda, V., Saavedra, O.R.: Risk and unit commitment decisions in scenarios of wind power uncertainty. Renew. Energy **97**, 550–558 (2016)
3. Ming, Z., Kun, Z., Liang, W.: Study on unit commitment problem considering wind power and pumped hydro energy storage. Int. J. Electr. Power Energy Syst. **63**, 91–96 (2014)
4. Rehman, S.K., Al-Hadhrami, L.M., Alam, M.M.: Pumped hydro energy storage system: a technological review. Renew. Sustain. Energy Rev. **44**, 586–598 (2015)
5. Zhou, B., Geng, G., Jiang, Q.: Hydro-Thermal-Wind coordination in Day-Ahead unit commitment. IEEE Trans. Power Syst. (2016, Impress)
6. Brown, P.D., Lopes, J., Matos, M.A.: Optimization of pumped storage capacity in an isolated power system with large renewable penetration. IEEE Trans. Power Syst. **23**(2), 523–531 (2008)
7. Wu, Y.K., Chang, G.W., Hsiao, B.Y., Chang, L.T.: Providing frequency support of hydro-pumped storage to taiwan power system with wind power integration. Smart Grid Renew. Energy **7**(04), 131 (2016)
8. Lee, K.S., Geem, Z.W.: A new meta-heuristic algorithm for continuous engineering optimization: harmony search theory and practice. Comput. Methods Appl. Mech. Eng. **194**(36), 3902–3933 (2005)
9. Geem, Z.W., Kim, J.H., Loganathan, G.V.: A new heuristic optimization algorithm: harmony Search. Simulation **76**, 60–68 (2001)
10. Mahdavi, M., Fesanghary, M., Damangir, E.: An improved harmony search algorithm for solving optimization problems. Appl. Math. Comput. **188**(2), 1567–1579 (2007)
11. Omran, M.G.H., Mahdavi, M.: Global-best harmony search. Appl. Math. Comput. **198**(2), 643–656 (2008)
12. Mun, S., Cho, Y.H.: Modified harmony search optimization for constrained design problems. Expert Sys. Appl. **39**(1), 419–423 (2012)
13. Niu, Q., Zhang, L., Zhang, H.: Impact of wind power penetration on unit commitment. In: Li, K., Xue, Y., Cui, S., Niu, Q. (eds.) LSMS/ICSEE 2014, Part III. CCIS, vol. 463, pp. 388–397. Springer, Heidelberg (2014)
14. Nazari, M.E., Ardehali, M.M., Jafari, S.: Pumped-storage unit commitment with considerations for energy demand, economics, and environmental constraints. Energy **35**(10), 4092–4101 (2010)
15. Niu, Q., Zhang, H., Li, K.: An efficient harmony search with new pitch adjustment for dynamic economic dispatch. Energy **65**, 25–43 (2014)
16. Juste, K.A., Kita, H., Tanaka, E.: An evolutionary programming solution to the unit commitment problem. IEEE Trans. Power Syst. **14**(4), 1452–1459 (1999)
17. Simopoulos, D.N., Kavatza, S.D., Vournas, C.D.: Unit commitment by an enhanced simulated annealing algorithm. IEEE Trans. Power Syst. **21**(1), 68–76 (2006)
18. Jeong, Y.W., Park, J.B., Jang, S.H.: A new quantum-inspired binary PSO: application to unit commitment problems for power systems. IEEE Trans. Power Syst. **25**(3), 1486–1495 (2010)

Simulation Investigation of Novel Waveguide Phase Shifters for High Power Applications

Yi-Ming Yang[1(✉)], Cheng-Wei Yuan[2], and Zhang Qiang[2]

[1] Northwest Institute of Nuclear Technology, Xian 710024, China
yymkko@aliyun.com
[2] College of Optoelectronic Science and Engineering,
National University of Defense Technology, Changsha 410073, China

Abstract. High-power phase shifter that can adjust the transmit phase of high-power microwave (HPM) on-line is of great interest. It has an extensive application in mode converter, high power array antenna and other fields. However, the traditional phase shifters cannot satisfy the power capacity requirement. There is a pressing need to come up with new alternative phase shifters. In this paper, three kinds of waveguide phase shifters are investigated. To increase the power capacity, no dielectric is introduced, and they are all mechanical phase shifters. The first one named waveguide-inserting-fin phase shifter. The inserting-fin changes the transmission constant of the microwave. 360° phase shift can be obtained by adjusting the length of the inserting metal fin. The advantage of this phase shifter is that the microwave propagation keeps on the same direction but with longer longitudinal length. The second one named narrow side slot-waveguide phase shifter. It is designed based on 3 dB power divider of waveguide Slot Bridge. The difference is using adjustable metal choke plunger at the terminal position of the power divider. Then, it can realize 360° phase shift by adjusting the choke plunger position. The last one named folded rectangular waveguide phase shifter. It includes E-bend phase shifter and H-bend phase shifter. The output phase is changed by adjusting the position of the bend waveguide. The advantage of this phase shifter is that it can achieve 360 phase degree with smaller size. All the phase shifters are with high transmission efficiency over 99 % and high power capacity over 50 MW in the vacuum.

Keywords: Phase shifter · High-power microwave (HPM) · Transmission efficiency · Power capacity

1 Introduction

High-power phase shifter that can on-line adjust the transmit phase of high-power microwave (HPM) is of great interest [1–7]. It has an extensive application in mode converter, high power array antenna and others. Ferrite phase shifter [8] and PIN diode phase shifter [9] are the two well-developed phase shifters that can be applied in above mentioned fields. However, they cannot be applied directly for high-power applications because ferrite and semiconductor has limited power handling capacity

© Springer Science+Business Media Singapore 2016
L. Zhang et al. (Eds.): AsiaSim 2016/SCS AutumnSim 2016, Part III, CCIS 645, pp. 282–289, 2016.
DOI: 10.1007/978-981-10-2669-0_31

[10, 11]. In view of such limitation, it is a pressing need to come up with novel phase shifters for high-power applications.

In this paper, three kinds of waveguide phase shifters are investigated. To increase the power capacity, no dielectric is introduced, and they are all mechanical phase shifters. The first one named waveguide-inserting-fin phase shifter. The inserting-fin changes the transmission constant of the microwave. 360° phase shift can be obtained by adjusting the length of the inserting metal fin. The advantage of this phase shifter is that the microwave propagation keeps on the same direction but with longer longitudinal length. The second one named narrow side slot-waveguide phase shifter. It is designed based on 3 dB power divider of waveguide Slot Bridge. The difference is using adjustable metal choke plunger at the terminal position of the power divider. Then, it can realize 360° phase shift by adjusting the choke plunger position. The last one named folded rectangular waveguide phase shifter. It includes E-bend phase shifter and H-bend phase shifter. The output phase is changed by adjusting the position of the bend waveguide. The advantage of this phase shifter is that it can achieve 360 phase degree with smaller size. All the phase shifters are with high transmission efficiency over 99 % and high power capacity over 50 MW in the vacuum.

2   Waveguide-Inserting-Fin Phase Shifter

Figure 1 is the scheme of the waveguide-inserting-fin phase shifter. The rectangular waveguide is divided to four regions by metal fin 1 and fin 2 in the middle of the waveguide perpendicular to the broad wall, the input TE10 mode microwave in region 1 then changes to two TE10 mode in region 2 and region 3, respectively. And the two TE10 modes finally combined again to TE10 mode in region 4. It is known that the transmission constant in region 2 and region 3 is different from that in region 1 and region 4 [12]. Fin 1 is fixed to the waveguide, and fin 2 can be sliding in and out into fin 1 to change the transmission length L of the two TE10 modes, resulting in the phase shift of the microwave. The convex 1 and 2 are used to diminish the reflections.

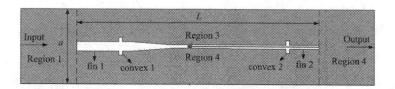

Fig. 1. Scheme of the Waveguide-inserting-fin phase shifter

As an example, a phase shift operates at frequency 9.5 GHz is designed. The wide side dimension a is 40 mm, the narrow side dimension b is 20 mm, thickness of fin 1 and 2 is 5 mm and 1 mm, respectively. The dimensions of the convex 1 and 2 are optimized.

Figure 2 displays the electric field distribution inside the waveguide-inserting-fin phase shifter. It shows the microwave propagation process. Besides, it can be seen that there is no obvious electric field enhancement during the adjustment of the dimension of the wide side, the maximum field is 3.226 kV/m during the adjustment when the inject power is 1 W. It is known that the breakdown electric field is about 30 kV/cm in the normal condition, however, according to Kilpatrick criterion [13] in the vacuum condition $f = 1.643E2e-8.5/E$, where f is the frequency (MHz); E is the corresponding breakdown electric field (MV/m), so the breakdown electric field is about 80.178 MV/m for microwave at 9.5 GHz in the vacuum. Then it can be obtained that a waveguide-inserting-fin phase shifter has a power capacity larger than 864.8 kW and 617.8 MW in the atmosphere and vacuum, respectively.

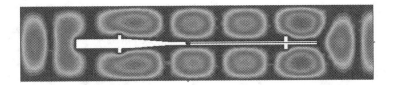

Fig. 2. Electric field distribution inside the Waveguide-inserting-fin phase shifter

Figure 3 presents the phase shift and transmission coefficient versus the transmission length L changed by sliding fin 2. From the simulation results by electromagnetism software, the transmission efficiency keeps over 99 % when the phase shift reaches 360. The phase shift reaches 4.1 deg per millimeter. The fin 2 need to slide about 50 mm to achieve 360 phase shift, and the whole length of this phase shift structure need about 200 mm. The advantage of this phase shifter is that the microwave propagation keeps on the same direction but with longer longitudinal length.

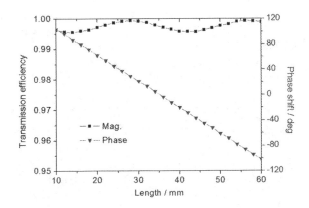

Fig. 3. Phase shift and transmission efficiency versus the transmission length L

3   Narrow Side Slot-Waveguide Phase Shifter

Figure 4 is the structure of the narrow side slot-waveguide phase shifter. The structure is similar to the 3 dB power divider of the waveguide slot bridge and the operate mechanism is also similar. The microwave is in TE10 mode in port 1, and transforms to TE20 mode in the region of narrow side slot. **By** designing the length L of the narrow side slot and the wide side dimension of the slot region a, the power can be equally divided to port 2 and port 3. Different from the power divider, here we use the choke plunger at the terminal position of the power divider. Then, the microwaves in port 2 and 3 are reflected to port 4. Optimizing the dimension L and a can obtain high transmission efficiency in port 4. Moreover, the output phase in port 4 can be changed by adjusting the length ΔL. It can realize 360° phase shift by adjusting the choke plunger position.

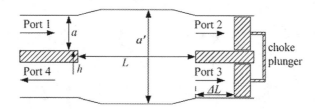

Fig. 4. Scheme of the narrow side slot-waveguide phase shifter

Taking 14.25 GHz microwave as an example, a narrow side slot-waveguide phase shifter is designed. The wide side dimension and narrow side dimension of port 1, port 2, port 3 and port 4 is 15.8 mm and 10 mm, respectively. The length L of the slot is 24.14 mm, the wide side dimension a' is 30.6 mm, the wall thickness h is 2 mm.

Figure 5 displays the electric field distribution inside the narrow side slot-waveguide phase shifter. It also shows the microwave propagation process. The maximum field is 5.501 kV/m during the adjustment of ΔL when the inject power is 1 W. As calculated above in Sect.2, it can be obtained that the breakdown threshold for Ku band 14.25 GHz in the vacuum is 97.3 MV/m. Then, such a narrow side slot-waveguide phase shifter has a power capacity larger than 297.4 KW and 312.8 MW in the atmosphere and vacuum, respectively.

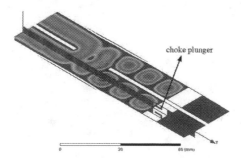

Fig. 5. Electric field distribution inside the narrow side slot-waveguide phase shifter

Figure 6 presents the phase shift and transmission coefficient versus the length ΔL adjusted by the choke plunger. From the simulation results by electromagnetism software, the transmission efficiency keeps over 99 % when the phase shift reaches 360. The phase shift reaches 23.12 deg per millimeter. The choke plunger need to slide about

15.6 mm to achieve 360 phase shift, and the whole length of this phase shift structure need about 70 mm. The advantage of this phase shifter is that this kind phase shifter has high power handling capacity with relatively small size. And it is easy to be realized in engineering. The choke plunger can be drive by stepper motor.

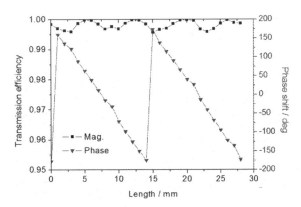

Fig. 6. Phase shift and transmission efficiency versus the transmission length L

4   Folded Rectangular Waveguide Phase Shifter

Folded rectangular waveguide phase shifter includes E-bend phase shifter and H-bend phase shifter. As the name suggests, E-bend folded rectangular waveguide phase shifter means the phase shifter is bent in the field E plane while H-bend folded rectangular waveguide phase shifter is bent in H plane. Figure 7(a) and (b) is the structure of the E-bend and H-bend folded rectangular waveguide phase shifter, respectively. This structure can easily achieve high transmission efficiency. The phase shift is realized by changing the distance of the microwave. And the distance is adjusted by changing the bend structure position.

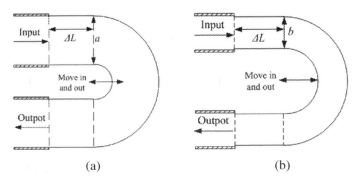

(a)   (b)

Fig. 7. Scheme of the folded rectangular waveguide phase shifter: (a) is the H-bend folded rectangular waveguide phase shifter; (b) is the E-bend folded rectangular waveguide phase shifter

An H-bend folded rectangular waveguide phase shifter is designed for X-band 9.5 GHz high power applications. The cross section dimension of the rectangular waveguide is 23 mm × 15 mm. for the same application, an E-bend folded rectangular waveguide phase shifter is also designed, and its cross section dimension is 30 mm × 15 mm.

Figure 8 displays the electric field distribution in side folded rectangular waveguide phase shifter. It is easy to understand that there is no electric field enhancement in this kind phase shifter, either E-bend or H-bend. The maximum field is less than 2.686 kV/m during the adjustment of the bend structure position when the inject power is 1 W. As calculated above in Sect. 2, it can be obtained that such a narrow side slot-waveguide phase shifter has a power capacity larger than 1.25 MW and 891 MW in the atmosphere and vacuum, respectively.

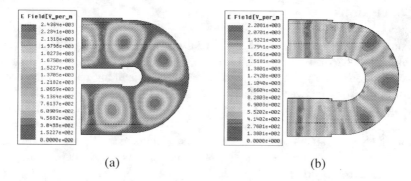

(a)   (b)

Fig. 8. Electric field distribution inside the folded rectangular waveguide phase shifter: (a) is the H-bend folded rectangular waveguide phase shifter; (b) is the E-bend folded rectangular waveguide phase shifter

Figure 9 presents the phase shift and transmission coefficient versus the bend structure position ΔL for H-bend folded rectangular waveguide phase shifter. From the simulation results by electromagnetism software, the transmission efficiency of both phase shifters keeps over 99 % when the phase shift reaches 360. For H-bend phase

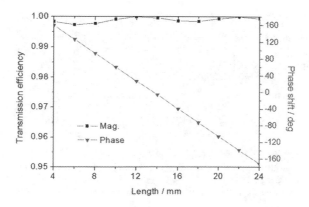

Fig. 9. Phase shift and transmission efficiency versus the transmission length L

shifter, the phase shift reaches 16.7 deg per millimeter, and the bend structure needs to move about 22 mm to obtain 360 phase shift. The whole length of the phase shifter is about 70 mm. For E-bend phase shifter, the phase shift reaches 19.5 deg per millimeter, and the bend structure needs to move about 18.5 mm to obtain 360 phase shift. The whole length of the phase shifter is about 60 mm. compared to the other two kind phase shifters discussed above, the advantages of the folded rectangular waveguide phase shifter are that it is easy to obtain high power handling capacity and high transmission efficiency, moreover, it achieve 360 phase shift with smaller size. However, it may hard to realize in engineering while it needs to work in vacuum environment to pursue high power handling capacity.

5   Conclusions

Phase shifter, as a key device of array antenna used to adjust the output phase of HPM, is urgently needed to be investigated since the common phase shifter can not satisfy the HPM applications. Up to now, there are few references about high power phase shifter for on-line adjusting the transmit phase of HPM. In this paper, three kinds of phase shifters that adjust the output phase of HPM are put forward. The inserting-fin changes the transmission constant of the microwave. $360°$ phase shift can be obtained by adjusting the length of the inserting metal fin. The advantage of this phase shifter is that the microwave propagation keeps on the same direction but with longer longitudinal length. The narrow side slot-waveguide phase shifter realize $360°$ phase shift by adjusting the choke plunger position. The folded rectangular waveguide phase shifter achieve phase shift by adjusting the position of the bend waveguide. The advantage of this phase shifter is that it can achieve 360 phase degree with smaller size. All the phase shifters are with high transmission efficiency over 99 % and high power capacity over 50 MW in the vacuum. Researchers can choose a phase shifter according to their applications.

References

1. Xiao, R.Z., Chen, C.H., Song, W., et al.: RF phase control in a high-power high-efficiency klystron-like relativistic backward wave oscillator. J. Appl. Phys. **110**, 013301 (2011)
2. Yang, Y.M., Cheng, C.W., Qian, B.L.: A novel phase shifter for Ku-band high power microwave applications. IEEE Trans. Plasma Sci. **42**(1), 51–54 (2014)
3. Li, X.Q., Liu, Q.X., Zhang, J.Q., Zhao, L., Zhang, Z.Q.: The high-power radial line helical circular array antenna: theory and development. In: ICMMT, p. 671 (2010)
4. Li, X.Q., Liu, Q.X., Wu, X.J., Zhao, L., Zhang, J.Q., Zhang, Z.Q.: A GW level high-power radial line helical array antenna. IEEE Trans. Antennas Propag. **56**(9), 2943–2948 (2008)
5. Yang, Y.M., Yuan, C.W., Qian, B.L.: Beam steering antenna for high power microwave application. High Power Laser Part. Beams **25**, 2648–2652 (2013)
6. Zhang, J., Zhong, H.H., Jin, Z., Shu, T., Cao, S., Zhou, S.: Studies on efficient operation of an X-band oversized slow-wave HPM generator in low magnetic field. IEEE Trans. Plasma Sci. **37**, 1552–1557 (2009)

7. Fan, Y.W., Zhong, H.H., Yang, H.W., Li, Z.Q., Shu, T., Zhang, J., Wang, Y., Luo, L.: Analysis and improvement of an X-band magnetically insulated transmission line oscillator. J. Appl. Phys. **12**, 3304 (2008)

8. Erker, E.G., Nagra, A.S., Liu, Y., Periaswamy, P., Taylor, T.R., Speck, J., York, R.A.: Monolithic Ka-band phase shifter using voltage tunable BaSrTiO3 parallel plate capacitors. IEEE Microwave Guided Wave Lett. **10**(1), 10–12 (2000)

9. Malczewski, A., Eshelman, S., Pillans, B., Ehmke, J., Goldsmith, C.L.: X-band RF MEMS phase shifters for phased array applications. IEEE Microwave Guided Wave Lett. **9**(12), 517–519 (1999)

10. Wilhelm, H., Aulock, V.: Handbook of Microwave Ferrite Materials. Academic Press, New York and London (1965)

11. Amitay, N., Glance, B.: Switching performance of a 12 GHz p-i-n phase shifter/driver module for satellite communication phased array. IEEE Trans. Commun. **29**(1), 46–50 (1981)

12. Collin, R.E.: Field Theory of Guided Waves. McGraw-Hill, New York (1960)

13. Jameson, R.A.: High brightness RF linear accelerators. In: NATO Advanced Study Institute on High-Brightness Accelerators Conference, Pitlochry, p. 497 (1986)

UHF Near-Field Coupling of Patch Antenna: Analysis, Simulation and Experiment

Liquan Wang[✉], Xudong Pang, Qingqing Yuan, and Weihua Zhu

Shanghai Electro-Mechanical Engineering Institute, Shanghai, China
liq_wang@163.com

Abstract. A method employing aperture-field integration (AI) is used to analyze UHF near-field coupling effect of a pair of patch antennae, and coupling degree and amplitude-phase consistency were also examined using software HFSS. Analyses and simulations indicate that signals received by receiving patch antenna are linearly related to those of submitting patch antenna, which can be applied in hard-ware-in-the-loop simulation, if the couple antennae satisfy near-field condition. However, mutual coupling effect introduced by other antennae in the system distorts signals transmission between the couple antenna, therefore further research is needed to solve this disadvantage.

Keywords: Near-field coupling · Aperture-field integration · Coupling degree

1 Introduction

Nowadays, two methods, spatial radiation and cable injection, are generally used for radio frequency (RF) hard-ware-in-the-loop (HWIL) simulations. However, with the development of multi-band multiplexing, HWIL simulations based on UHF near-field coupling are gradually becoming popular. Near-field coupling can bridge the frequency bands which are hardly realized by spatial radiation method. Moreover, no extra cable interfaces need to be added on device under test (DUT) as cable injection method required for signal injection. Therefore, near-field coupling method gradually becomes a useful supplementation and enhancement in the field of RF HWIL simulation.

Normally, near-field coupling consists of two types. One is coupling between a pair of antennae, and the other is mutual coupling effect between all antennae within test environment [1]. Coupling between a pair of antennae can be applied in RF HWIL simulation for signal transmission, but mutual coupling leads to signal distortion due to complex coupling effects introduced by all antennae in the test environment [2].

This paper firstly discussed near-field zone between patch antennae. Then aperture-field integration (AI) was employed to analyze UHF near-field coupling effect, coupling degree and amplitude-phase consistency among patch antennae. Finally, the feasibility of realizing RF HWIL simulations by applying near-field coupling method was examined.

© Springer Science+Business Media Singapore 2016
L. Zhang et al. (Eds.): AsiaSim 2016/SCS AutumnSim 2016, Part III, CCIS 645, pp. 290–299, 2016.
DOI: 10.1007/978-981-10-2669-0_32

2   Analysis on Near-Field Region

Space around an antenna can be divided as near-field region, radiating near-field region and far-field region as shown in Fig. 1. Here, near-field region will be mainly discussed.

A generic illustration of near-field region is shown in Fig. 1. D is the diameter of an antenna. r is the range between the middle of the antenna O and far-field point B, and R is the range between the edge of the antenna A and far-field point B. θ is the angle between vectors OA and OB. λ is the wavelength of the signal transmitted by the antenna. According to Fig. 1, the range R can be described as [3]

$$R = \left(r^2 + \left(\frac{D}{2} \right)^2 - rD\cos\theta \right)^{1/2}$$

$$= r - \frac{D\cos\theta}{2} + \frac{D^2}{8r}\sin^2\theta + \frac{D^3}{16r^2}\sin^2\theta\cos\theta + \dots \tag{1}$$

If a receiving antenna is placed in radiating near-field region or far-field region, it usually satisfies $r \gg D$, and Eq. (1) can be simplified as shown in Eq. (2).

$$R = r - \frac{D\cos\theta}{2} + \frac{D^2}{8r}\sin^2\theta \tag{2}$$

According to Eq. (2), far-field region should satisfy [2].

$$r \geq \frac{2D^2}{\lambda} \tag{3}$$

The forth term of Eq. (1), neglected in Eq. (2), is used to define near-field region. Equation (3) shows a condition normally used to define near-field region [3].

$$\frac{2\pi}{\lambda}\left(\frac{D^3}{16r^2}\sin^2\theta\cos\theta \right) > \frac{\pi}{8} \tag{4}$$

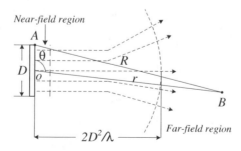

Fig. 1. A generic illustration of near-field region

According to Eq. (4), near-field region satisfy

$$r < 0.62\sqrt{\frac{D^3}{\lambda}} \tag{5}$$

Near-field region is very close to the transmitting antenna as shown in Fig. 1. In this region, inducted field is much greater than radiating field and decays sharply with the increasing of the distance between the antennae. There is less electromagnetic propagation and directional diagram in the region.

3 Analysis on Near-Field Coupling

As illustrated in Fig. 2, coupling degrees of two antennae at different locations are analyzed by fixing one patch antenna and moving the other around radius R. The length and width of patch antennae are 'a' and 'b', respectively.

Figure 2 can be simplified as illustrated in Fig. 3. According to Fig. 3, it gives

$$r^2 - s^2 = (r - s)(r + s) = -x^2 + 2rx\sin\theta \tag{6}$$

Equation (6) can be re-written as

$$\Delta r \approx -\frac{x^2}{2r} + x\sin\theta \tag{7}$$

Where $\Delta r = r - s$ and $s + r \approx 2r$.

According to Eq. (7), the phase difference between signals received by receiving antenna is

$$\Delta\varphi = \frac{2\pi\Delta r}{\lambda} = -\frac{\pi}{r\lambda}x^2 + \frac{2\pi x}{\lambda}\sin\theta \tag{8}$$

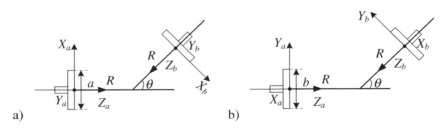

Fig. 2. Models of patch antenna, (a) E model, (b) H model

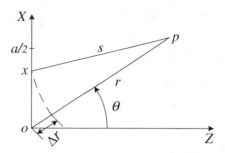

Fig. 3. Range difference in aperture field

If aperture field distribution is E1(x), near-field radiation can be expressed as [4]:

$$D_1(r) = \int_{-\infty}^{+\infty} E_1(x) \exp\left(-j\frac{\pi}{r\lambda}x^2\right) \exp\left(j\frac{2\pi x \sin \theta}{\lambda}\right) dx \qquad (9)$$

Equation (9) shows near-field radiation in x-z plane, and near-field radiation in y-z plane can be expressed as similar as Eq. (9) according to Fig. 2. Therefore, combined near-field radiation field distribution can be expressed as:

$$E(r, \theta, \varphi) = A \cdot D_1(r)D_2(r) \qquad (10)$$

where

$$\begin{cases} D_1(r) = \int_{-a/2}^{a/2} E_1(x) \exp[-j(\pi x^2/r\lambda - k_1 x)]dx \\ D_2(r) = \int_{-b/2}^{b/2} E_2(y) \exp[-j(\pi y^2/r\lambda - k_2 y)]dy \end{cases} \qquad (11)$$

where, a and b are the length and width of patch antennae, respectively. In the Eq. (11), $E_1(x)$ is equal to zero if absolute value of x is greater than $a/2$. Similarly, $E_2(y)$ is equal to zero if absolute value of y is greater than $b/2$.

In an antenna system consists of a pair of patch antennae in near-field region, the power received by the transmitting antenna can be expressed as [5]

$$P_{TR} = \frac{1}{16P_T} \left| \int_{-a/2}^{a/2} \int_{-b/2}^{b/2} (\vec{E}(r, \theta, \phi) \cdot \vec{J})dxdy \right|^2 \qquad (12)$$

where, P_{TR} is the power received by a transmitting antenna, and P_T is the transmitting power from the transmitting antenna. $E(r,\theta,\Phi)$ is the near-field radiation field distribution from receiving antenna. S is the aperture of the receiving antenna. J is the equivalent current density at the aperture of the receiving antenna [6].

In near-field region, the transmission loss between transmitting and receiving antennae can be ignored as discussed in Sect. 2, therefore the power received by the receiving antenna can be written as

$$P_{RR} = P_T - \frac{1}{16P_T} \left| \int_{-a/2}^{a/2} \int_{-b/2}^{b/2} (\vec{E}(r,\theta,\phi) \cdot \vec{J}) dx dy \right|^2 \qquad (13)$$

Where, P_{RR} is the power received by the receiving antenna.
According to Eq. (13), coupling degree ε can be expressed as:

$$\varepsilon = \frac{P_{RR}}{P_T} = 1 - \frac{1}{16P_{TA}^2} \left| \int_{-a/2}^{a/2} \int_{-b/2}^{b/2} (\vec{E}(r,\theta,\phi) \cdot \vec{J}) dx dy \right|^2 \qquad (14)$$

4   Simulations on Near-Field Coupling

The essential principal of near-field coupling has been discussed above. During the simulation of patch antennae along with related near-field coupling effect, software HFSS was used to carry out the calculations and simulations. The schematic of UHF near-field coupling simulation is illustrated in Fig. 4. It consists of three transmitting antennae, T_1, T_2, T_3, and another three receiving antennae, R_1, R_2, R_3. Simulations were carried out at frequencies from 800 MHz–850 MHz.

The simulation results of coupling degree at different frequencies (800 MHz and 850 MHz) are shown in Fig. 5 and Fig. 6, respectively. The ranges between transmitting and receiving antennae are 5 mm, 10 mm, 15 mm, and 20 mm, respectively. It indicates that the coupling degree decreases with the increasing of the range between transmitting and receiving antennae.

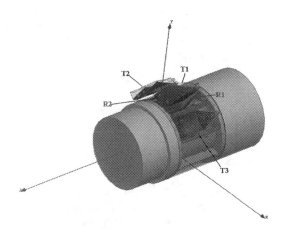

Fig. 4. Schematic of UHF near-field coupling simulation

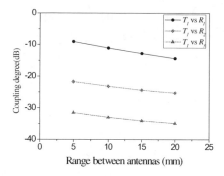

Fig. 5. Simulation results of coupling degree at frequency of 800 MHz

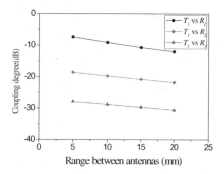

Fig. 6. Simulation results of coupling degree at frequency of 850 MHz

According to the simulation results as shown in Figs. 5 and 6, it indicates that the better near-field effect can be achieved the shorter range between transmitting and receiving antennae is set. Given there must be a gap between transmitting and receiving antennae in order to protect both antennae, the range between transmitting and receiving antennae was set 5 mm for further simulation. Figures 7 and 8 illustrate the simulation results of amplitude-phase consistency between transmitting and receiving antennae.

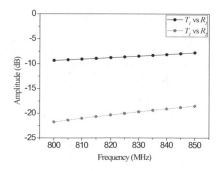

Fig. 7. Amplitude differences between transmitting and receiving antennae

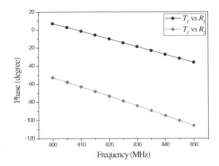

Fig. 8. Phase differences between transmitting and receiving antennae

It includes amplitude-phase consistency measurements between antennae T_1 to R_1, and antennae T_1 to R_2. Simulations results show clearly that signals received by receiving patch antenna are linearly related to those of submitting patch antenna. However, mutual coupling effect also occurs in the system although it is comparatively weaker than that between a pair of antennae, and it is probably to distort signals transmission between the couple antenna.

5   Experiment Results

Coupling degree and amplitude-phase consistency of a couple antennae working in near-field region were characterized in a universal test-fixture from 300 MHz to 1 GHz using an Agilent E5061A series network analyzer as shown in Fig. 9. Figure 10 is the picture of measurement set-up for a couple antennae working in near-field region.

According to the measurement set-up as shown in Fig. 10, phase delay between transmitting and receiving antennae is given

$$\Delta\varphi(f) = -360° \cdot \Delta f \cdot \tau_{gr} \qquad (15)$$

Where Δf is the sweep frequency range, τ_{gr} is the delay time introduced by antennae and cable.

Measure phase delay between transmitting and receiving antennae is shown in Fig. 11, it indicates that signals received by receiving patch antenna are linearly related to those of submitting patch antenna.

Coupling degree and amplitude-phase consistency of a couple antennae working in near-field region at frequency of 800 MHz were also characterized. It was realized by changing the delay time τ_{gr} as shown in Fig. 9. Figures 12 and 13 are measured power and phase characteristics of a couple antennae in near-field region at 800 MHz. They also show high amplitude-phase consistency between a pair of transmitting and receiving antennae.

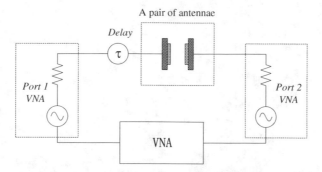

Fig. 9. Schematic of the measurement set-up for a pair of antennae in near-field region

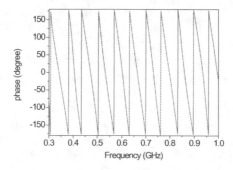

Fig. 10. A picture of measurement set-up for a pair of antennae in near-field region

Fig. 11. Measured phase characteristics of a couple antennae in near-field region

Experiment results indicate that signals received by receiving patch antenna are linearly related to those of submitting patch antenna when the couple antennae work in near-field region, therefore it might be a useful supplementation and enhancement of RF HWIL simulation.

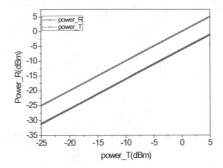

Fig. 12. Measured power characteristics of a couple antennae in near-field region

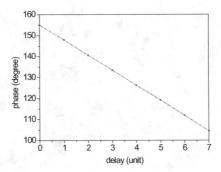

Fig. 13. Measured phase characteristics of a couple antennae in near-field region

6 Conclusion

UHF near-field coupling degree and amplitude-phase consistency among patch antennae have been discussed in this paper. Both simulation and measurement results indicate that signals received by receiving patch antenna are linearly related to those of submitting patch antenna when the couple antennae satisfy near-field condition, therefore it can be applied in hard-ware-in-the-loop simulation and become a useful supplementation and enhancement. However, Simulation results indicate that mutual coupling effect between different submitting antennae might distort signals transmission between the couple antenna, therefore further research is needed to solve this disadvantage.

References

1. Byun, J., Lee, B., Haraekiewicz, F.J.: FDTD analysis of mutual coupling between microstrip patch antennas on curved surfaces. IEEE Int. Symp. **2**(3), 886–889 (1999)
2. Guo, Y.-X., Luk, K.M., Leung, K.W.: Mutual coupling between rectangular dielectric resonant antennas by FDTD. IEE Microwaves Antennas and Propagation **146**(4), 292–294 (1999)
3. Lin, C.-L., Nie, Z.-P.: Antenna Engineering Handbook. Electronic Industry Press (2002)
4. Millar, R.F.: An approximate theory of the diffraction of electromagnetic wave by an aperture in a plane screen. In: Proceedings. 152(R). IEEE (1955)
5. Pace, J.: Asymptotic formulas for coupling between two antennas in the Fresnel region. IEEE Trans. Antennas Propag. **17**(3), 285–291 (1969)
6. Jedlicka, R.P., Poe, M., Carver, K.: Measured mutual coupling between microstrip antennas. IEEE Antennas Propag. **29**(l), 147–149 (1981)

Simulation and Analysis of a New Electromagnetic Wave Concentrator with Reduced Parameter Sets

Xudong Pang[1(✉)], Yi Tian[1], Liquan Wang[1], Weihua Zhu[1], and Shouzheng Zhu[2]

[1] Shanghai Institute of Electro-Mechanical Engineering, Shanghai, China
pxd210@163.com
[2] School of Information Science and Technology,
East China Normal University, Shanghai, China

Abstract. In this paper, a new model of electromagnetic wave concentrator with reduced parameter sets is proposed based on the concentrator with ideal parameter sets. The contrastive simulation work demonstrates that the reduced model also maintains the scattering magnifying function of the concentrator and in the meantime its media parameters are distinctly simplified which can obviously decrease the practical fabrication difficulties. The lossy conditions of the metamaterial media are further analyzed. The parameter-reduced model of wave concentrator apparently benefits the implementation of the metamaterial, which can be practically used as electromagnetic delusion devices and decoy aircrafts in military actions.

Keywords: Transformation electromagnetics · Reduced parameters · Wave concentrator · Scattering characteristics

1 Introduction

Transformation electromagnetics [1, 2] has become a hotspot in the research area of electromagnetics in recent years, and its basic theory is the coordinate transformation method which is based on the form invariance of Maxwell's equations under different coordinates. The method of coordinate transformation provides us a new way to manipulate electromagnetic wave and reshape its propagation in a controlled manner. Combined with metamaterials [1, 2], several new devices can be designed including the invisibility cloaks [3]. With the development of different types of coordinate transformations, a series of new transformation-electromagnetics devices are also derived, such as electromagnetic wave concentrators, wave expanders and wave rotators [4–8].

Reference [8] describes a schematic classification for the coordinate transformation devices with the folding transformations, in which the scattering magnifying functions of electromagnetic wave concentrator are also studied in a measurable way. But the wave concentrator models in Ref. [8] all uses the ideal parameter sets which leads to very complex components of the required metamaterials.

© Springer Science+Business Media Singapore 2016
L. Zhang et al. (Eds.): AsiaSim 2016/SCS AutumnSim 2016, Part III, CCIS 645, pp. 300–307, 2016.
DOI: 10.1007/978-981-10-2669-0_33

Scholars have made efforts to simplify the media parameter [3]. In this paper, a new model of electromagnetic wave concentrator with reduced parameter sets is proposed based on the concentrator with ideal parameter sets [3]. The contrastive simulation work demonstrates that the reduced model also maintains the scattering magnifying function of the concentrator and in the meantime its media parameters are distinctly reduced which can obviously decrease the practical fabrication difficulties. The effect of media loss is further analyzed which can even enhance the scattering magnifying function of the concentrator. The parameter-reduced model of concentrator apparently benefits the implementation of the metamaterial, which can be practically used in electromagnetic delusion applications.

2 Comparison Between Ideal Parameter Model and Simplified Parameter Model

Electromagnetic wave concentrator is a kind of folded coordinate transformation [4–8]. The simulation model of the wave concentrator in Fig. 1(a) uses the two dimensional cylindrical shape [4] where the inner radius is $r = a$ while the outer radius is $r = b$. The expressions of the material parameters along r, θ and z of the wave concentrator with both ideal and simplified material parameter sets are listed in Table 1 [8, 9]. The magnification β equals to s/a, where s is a variable in the folded coordinate transformation [8].

From Table 1 can be seen that the ideal parameter sets along the three directions (r, θ, z) are all gradient and non-uniform, which results in great practical fabrication difficulties of the metamaterial. The reduced parameter sets are listed in Table 1 as a comparison. When the magnification β is a constant, the material parameters along θ

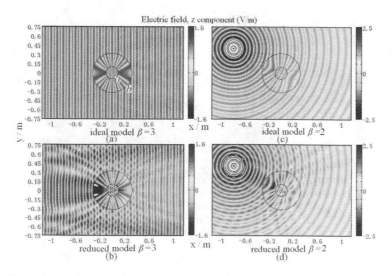

Fig. 1. Comparison of the simulation results between ideal parameter model and reduced parameter model: (a) the $\beta = 3$ ideal model; (b) the $\beta = 3$ reduced model; (c) the $\beta = 2$ ideal model; (d) the $\beta = 2$ reduced model

Table 1. A contrast between ideal parameter sets and reduced parameter sets

Ideal parameter sets	Reduced parameter sets
$\varepsilon_r = \frac{(b-s)r-b(a-s)}{(b-s)r}$	$\varepsilon_r = \left[\frac{(b-s)r-b(a-s)}{(b-s)r}\right]^2 \left(\frac{b-s}{b-a}\right)$
$\varepsilon_\theta = \frac{(b-s)r}{(b-s)r-b(a-s)} = \frac{1}{\varepsilon_r}$	$\varepsilon_\theta = \frac{b-s}{b-a}$
$\varepsilon_z = \frac{(b-s)r-b(a-s)}{(b-s)r} \times \left(\frac{b-s}{b-a}\right)^2 = \varepsilon_r \times \left(\frac{b-s}{b-a}\right)^2$	$\varepsilon_z = \frac{b-s}{b-a}$

and z directions are constants in reduced parameter sets and only the material parameter along r direction remains un-uniform. Compared with the ideal parameter model, the complexity of the simplified metamaterial media is dramatically reduced.

Next, an electromagnetic wave concentrator with the size of $a = 0.1$ m $b = 0.32$ m is simulated by using ideal parameter sets and reduced parameter sets, the results of which are analyzed and compared in Fig. 1.

The electric field distributions of z component are simulated in Fig. 1 where two magnifications ($\beta = 3$ and $\beta = 2$) of the concentrators are both investigated. First, in the case of $\beta = 3$ and hence s $= 0.3$ m, a TE plane wave at the frequency of $f = 3$ GHz illuminates from left to right and Fig. 1(a) is the simulation result of the ideal parameter model while the Fig. 1(b) is the simulation result of the reduced parameter model. Then, in the case of $\beta = 2$ and hence s $= 0.2$ m, the two models of the ideal parameter model and the reduced parameter model are both illuminated by an $f = 2.5$ GHz cylindrical wave at (-0.8 m, 0.4 m), the simulation results of which are shown in Fig. 1 (c) and Fig. 1(d) respectively. As can be seen from Fig. 1, the scattering effect caused by the reduced parameter model is weak, and its result is close to that of an ideal parameter model and its basic function of beam focusing is not deteriorated.

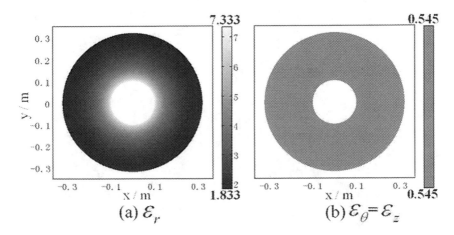

Fig. 2. Material parameters distributions along r, θ and z directions of the parameter-reduced electromagnetic wave concentrator ($\beta = 2$)

Figure 2 shows the material parameters distributions along r, θ and z directions of the $\beta = 2$ parameter-reduced electromagnetic wave concentrator, the model of which is used in Fig. 1(d). From Fig. 2 can be seen that the electromagnetic wave concentrator with reduced parameter sets has no singularity problem in metamaterial media parameter and hence can be feasible to be realized by the method in Ref. [3]. Compared with the ideal parameter model, the basic performance of the reduced model does not significantly decrease. So the parameter-reduced model of the wave concentrator is recommended in practical applications.

3   Scattering Magnifying Function

The former research shows that: (1) electromagnetic wave concentrator with ideal parameter sets has a magnifying function to the scattering cross-section (RCS) of the embedded object; (2) its magnification degree depends on β [8].

In the following part, a validation to the scattering magnifying function of electromagnetic wave concentrator with reduced parameter sets is performed with numeric simulations and quantitative calculations. The method used here is to embed a two-dimensional object model in the core inside the wave expander in Fig. 1(d), and then study the scattering pattern using the FEM solver. Here a two-dimensional simulation model using the geometric cross-section of the F117A fighter [10] is chosen as the embedded object, which is a two-dimensional conformal shrinking model of the practical aircraft. The size of the embedded model is: wingspan $w = 0.12$ m, body length $h = 0.18$ m. Here the metal boundary is applied to the embedded F117-shaped object. The size of the wave expander here is $a = 0.1$ m, $b = 0.32$ m and an $f = 3$ GHz cylinder wave is used as the wave source with a distance $d = 0.894$ m away. For a two-dimensional model, the RCS of the object is actually the scattering width of its cross-section. [11] So a quantitative calculation for the scattering width value of each two-dimensional F117-shaped model is made according to its simulation result. The Huygens principle is required here to convert the near field data from the FEM solver into the far field data which will be used to calculate the scattering width value. The formula used here is: $\sigma = 2\pi r |E^s(\varphi)|^2 / |E^i|^2$ [8]

The validation to the scattering magnifying function of the electromagnetic wave concentrator with $\beta = 2$ is carried out through simulations with a cylinder wave illuminated at $(-0.8$ m, 0.4 m$)$, as shown in Fig. 3(a)–(d). Figure 3(a) is the simulation result of the original size model ($w = 0.12$ m, $h = 0.18$ m); Fig. 3(b) is the simulation result of a conformal model with double original size ($w_2 = 0.24$ m, $h_2 = 0.36$ m); In Fig. 3(c), the embedded model with original size is placed in the core inside the $\beta = 2$ wave concentrator with ideal parameter sets; In Fig. 3(d), the embedded model with original size is placed in the core inside the $\beta = 2$ wave concentrator with reduced parameter sets. The scattering width values of the F117-shaped models in Fig. 3(a)–(d) under plane wave illuminations are shown in Fig. 4(a)–(d) accordingly, where the y-axis represents the results of scattering width value with a same range of 0–2.5 m for further comparison.

As can be seen from Figs. 3 to 4 that the RCS in Fig (d) is slightly larger than the RCS in Fig (b–c) due to the additional scattering effect brought by the reduced model,

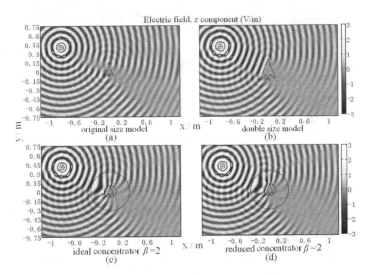

Fig. 3. Verifications for the scattering magnifying function of the $\beta = 2$ wave concentrator: (a) original size model; (b) double size model; (c) ideal concentrator with the original size embedded model inside; (d) reduced concentrator with the original size embedded model inside

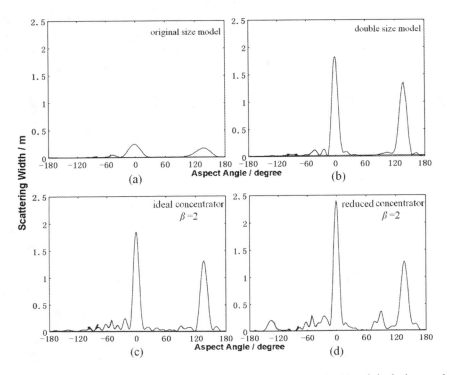

Fig. 4. Calculation results of the scattering width values in Fig. 3: (a) original size model; (b) double size model; (c) ideal concentrator with the original size embedded model inside; (d) reduced concentrator with the original size embedded model inside

both of which are obviously larger than the RCS in Fig (a). In a real case, a stealth aircraft is often coated with absorbing materials to reduce its RCS, so a simulation for an absorbing boundary condition of the aircraft model is also carried out with the same conclusion drawn.

The results in Figs. 3 and 4 are consistent with the result obtained by other scholars using the method of illusion electromagnetics [12]. The work in Fig. 4 shows that the reduced model not only maintains the scattering magnifying function, but also slightly enhances of the scattering magnifying function of the wave concentrator. It seems that the additional scattering brought by the reduced model do not bring any negative effect to the scattering magnifying function, but on the contrary can be used to increase the RCS of the device, so the overall scattering characteristics are gently improved. In the meantime its media parameters are distinctly reduced which can obviously decrease the practical fabrication difficulties. In practical applications, the wave concentrator with reduced parameter sets is strongly recommend instead of the original ideal model, which can be used in electromagnetic delusion applications such as electromagnetic interfere, camouflage and decoy crafts in military actions.

4   Analysis on Lossy Conditions

In real applications the metamaterials used to construct such a device as the wave concentrator are always lossy [2, 3, 5], so here the effect of loss on the scattering performance of the wave concentrator with reduced parameter sets is studied.

The electric field distributions of the $a = 0.1$ m, $b = 0.32$ m, $\beta = 3$ parameter-reduced concentrator under TE wave illumination with electric loss tangents (tgδ) of 0, 0.05, 0.1 and 0.15 are shown in panels (a), (b), (c) and (d) of Fig. 5 accordingly, from which can be seen that the performance of the wave expander in the back scattering region is deteriorated by the increasing loss tangents while the performance in the forward scattering region remains undisturbed. From the above simulations and discussions, we can conclude that the effect of loss on the scattering performance of the parameter-reduced wave concentrator increase with the value of electric loss tangents.

A further research on lossy conditions is made in Fig. 6, where the $a = 0.1$ m, $b = 0.32$ m, $\beta = 3$ parameter-reduced concentrators are illuminated by a 3 GHz cylinder wave. Figure 6(a) shows the simulation result of the reduced concentrator with tg$\delta = 0$ while Fig. 6(b) shows the simulation result of the reduced concentrator with tg$\delta = 0.2$, from which can be seen that a high media loss has an obvious effect on the scattering performance of the parameter-reduced concentrator. Figure 6(c) shows the overall scattering result of the tg$\delta = 0$ reduced concentrator with the F117-shaped embedded model ($w = 0.12$ m, $h = 0.18$ m) inside while Fig. 6(d) shows the overall scattering result of the tg$\delta = 0.2$ reduced concentrator with the F117-shaped embedded model ($w = 0.12$ m, $h = 0.18$ m) inside, from which can be seen that the lossy conditions of the metamaterial media bring little effect to the scattering magnifying performance, and can even enhance the scattering magnifying function of the reduced wave concentrator.

A conclusion can be drawn from the research above that the lossy conditions of the metamaterial media bring little effect to the scattering magnifying performance, and can even enhance the scattering magnifying function of the parameter-reduced wave

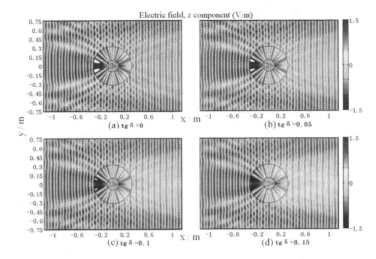

Fig. 5. The electric field distributions of the $\beta = 3$ parameter-reduced concentrator with different electric loss tangents: (a) tgδ = 0; (b) tgδ = 0.05; (c) tgδ = 0.1; (d) tgδ = 0.15

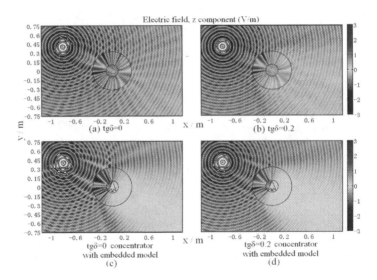

Fig. 6. Different simulation results of the $\beta = 3$ parameter-reduced concentrators: (a) the tgδ = 0 concentrator; (b) the tgδ = 0.2 concentrator; (c) the tgδ = 0 concentrator with embedded model inside; (d) the tgδ = 0.2 concentrator with embedded model inside

concentrator. In practical applications, the parameter-reduced wave concentrator with lossy media condition is much more possible to fabricate and the media loss can bring a positive effect to the scattering magnifying performance of the concentrator.

5   Conclusions

In this paper, a new model of electromagnetic wave concentrator with reduced parameter sets is proposed and the effect of its media loss is analyzed, which can benefit the practical implementation of the required metamaterial media and enhance the scattering magnifying function of the electromagnetic wave concentrator.

References

1. Pendry, J.B., Schurig, D., Smith, D.R.: Controlling electromagnetic fields. Science **312** (5781), 1780–1782 (2006)
2. Chen, H., Chan, C.T., Shen, P.: Transformation optics and metamaterials. Nat. Mater. **9**, 387–396 (2010)
3. Schurig, D., Mock, J.J., Justice, B.J., et al.: Metamaterial electromagnetic cloak at microwave frequencies. Science **314**(5801), 977–980 (2006)
4. Zhang, K., Wu, Q., Fu, J.-H., et al.: Cylindrical electromagnetic concentrator with only axial constitutive parameter spatially variant. J. Opt. Soc. Am. B **28**(6), 1573–1577 (2011)
5. Yang, J.-J., Huang, M., Yang, C., et al.: Metamaterial electromagnetic concentrators with arbitrary geometries. Opt. Express **17**(22), 19656–19661 (2009)
6. Li, W., Guan, J., Wang, W.: Homogeneous-materials-constructed electromagnetic field concentrators with adjustable concentrating ratio. J. Phys. D Appl. Phys. **44**(12), 125401 (2011)
7. Li, T., Huang, M., Yang, J., et al.: Three dimensional electromagnetic concentrators with homogeneous material parameters. Progress Electromagn. Res. M **18**, 119–130 (2011)
8. 庞旭东, 朱守正 电磁波集中器散射放大功能的应用与分析[J]. 电子与信息学报 **35**(2), 468–473 (2013). Pang, X., Zhu S.: The application and analysis of scattering magnifying function of electromagnetic wave concentrator. J. Electron. Inf. Technol. **35**(2), 468–473 (2013)
9. Yang, J.J., Huang, M., Mao, F.C., Cai, G.H., Lan, Y.Z.: Electromagnetic reciprocal cloak with only axial material parameter spatially variant. Int. J. Antennas Propag. 9 (2012). 153086
10. Zadeh, H.G., Dehrizi, H.G., Haddadnia, J.: Identification of F117 fighter with image processing by using labview. In: IEEE International Conference on Computational Intelligence and Computing Research (ICCIC), Coimbatore, 28–29 December 2010, pp. 1–4 (2010)
11. Gente, R., Jansen, C., Geise, R., et al.: Scaled bistatic radar cross section measurements of aircraft with a fiber-coupled THz time-domain spectrometer. IEEE Trans. Terahertz Sci. Technol. **2**(4), 424–431 (2012)
12. Lai, Y., Ng, J., Chen, H.-Y., et al.: Illusion optics: the optical transformation of an object into another object. Phys. Rev. Lett. **102**(25), 253902 (2009)

Research on Fault Diagnosis Method for Over-Discharge of Power Lithium Battery

Yu Wang[1], Chao Wu[1], and Xingsheng Gu[2(✉)]

[1] Department of Electrical Engineering,
Luoyang Institute of Science and Technology, Luoyang, China
[2] Key Laboratory of Advanced Control and Optimization for Chemical Processes,
Ministry of Education, East China University of Science and Technology, Shanghai, China
xsgu@ecust.edu.cn

Abstract. A series of abusive experiments were carried out to understand the over-discharge performance of power LiFePO4 batteries in the paper. The batteries respectively experienced the long- and short-term over-discharge process at different degree. Parameters such as internal temperature, cell voltage, current and AC impedance were monitored and recorded for analysis. Tested cells failed in the recharge process after over-discharge. After the experiments, this paper connects over-discharge fault symptoms with internal mechanism, and a reliable and timely over-discharge diagnosis approach is established to guarantee the safety of battery applications. Eventually, the disassembly examination and electrochemical analysis indicate the effectiveness of the diagnosis approach.

Keywords: LiFePO4 batteries · Over-discharge · Abuse · Fault diagnosis

1 Introduction

With the outbreak of the energy crisis and the human environmental consciousness growing, new energy has become a popular topic. Thanks to their inherent benefits of high power and energy density, long lifespan, low maintenance cost and environmental protection, lithium-ion batteries have caught more and more attentions of scholars and engineers. With the wide application of lithium-ion batteries in various fields, however, the recent frequently-happened accidents lead to people's concerns about the safety performance of the battery, especially the electric vehicles: major laptop manufacturers recalled their batteries frequently due to impurities incorporated during the manufacturing process of the batteries; The five fire accidents occurred in six months for Tesla Model S electric cars and they were directly related to the battery module; A BYD electric taxi for a quick charge in Hong Kong stared a fire, resulting from the cell interface contact resistance [1, 2]. Therefore, fault diagnosis and prediction have a very important significance in the field of battery and new energy.

As is known to all, the safety performance of lithium-ion batteries depends greatly on the operation mode and the environment. Battery abuse — thermal abuse (low or high temperature), mechanical abuse (acupuncture or impact) and electronic abuse (over-charge or over-discharge) — will greatly reduce the service life of battery or even cause an accident.

L. Zhang et al. (Eds.): AsiaSim 2016/SCS AutumnSim 2016, Part III, CCIS 645, pp. 308–314, 2016.
DOI: 10.1007/978-981-10-2669-0_34

An accurate and fast fault diagnosis system is achieved through fully understanding the failure mechanism and abuses of lithium-ion batteries. In fact, the diagnosis is to make predictions and decisions through combining fault symptoms and fault mechanism.

Different from the mechanisms of overcharge or cycles at elevate temperature, slight over-discharge does not directly induce the exothermic side reaction; Even if it is up above 0 V, over-discharge won't directly lead to thermal runaway. But over-discharge does damage the electrode and current-collector. For example, it will lead to an irreversible solid-state amorphization process of the electrode. Generally speaking, copper current collector is used as current collector at the anode of the lithium-ion battery. When the anode potential is low (i.e. over-discharge leads to a low voltage), copper current-collector begins to be oxidized and dissociated into copper-ions. The metals would be involved in the exothermic reaction. Simultaneously, there exists a potential risk of micro short circuit caused by deposition or penetrating diaphragm. These phenomena are likely to eventually trigger thermal runaway of the lithium-ion batteries.

In this paper, a study of the fault for lithium-ion batteries, especially for LiFePo4 batteries in the state of over-discharge is carried out. Over-discharge experiments in various degrees are designed to understand the failure mechanism and effect of over-discharge for the battery, extract the fault symptoms, and establish the fault diagnosis and early warning system.

2   Experiments and Analysis

In this paper, we choose the LiFePO4 batteries with the nominal capacity of 40 Ah and the nominal upper and lower limit voltage of 2.5 V and 3.65 V. Cell volume is 46 mm * 116 mm * 180 mm and energy density is 152 Wh/L. LiFePo4 batteries with its good thermal stability and cost-effective have occupied a larger share in China's electric vehicle power battery market, so the study is more representative. Considering of its security, the top of the batteries has vent and the interior of the batteries buries the thermocouple for the measurement of internal temperature.

In order to thoroughly study the fault phenomenon and symptoms of power lithium batteries over-discharging, we must carry out a series of deeply over-discharge experiments rather than only studying the long-term data. After each section of new battery pre-charge and pre-discharge, it charges fully by the method of the constant current and constant voltage which can be called as 100 % SOC. Namely, it first charges up to 3.65 V at 1C constant current, then charges at 3.65 V constant voltage until the current reduce to C/25. Battery discharges to the different voltage or fixed SOC at the 1C rate later. We have observed the process of over-discharge to 0 V, 110 % SOC and 120 % SOC over-discharge in the paper. Over-discharge with 110 % SOC is that the battery discharges for 1.1 h at the 1C rate after it is filled 100 % SOC. Unlike other fault mode, even if it happened to over-discharge fault, the battery itself does not appear visual symptoms such as leak or obvious deformation. By the measurement of the temperature, the internal temperature of the battery can reach $100°$, which is not enough to cause more serious accidents.

The 0 V over-discharge process shown in Fig. 1 can be divided into 4 phases. The 3.3 V–1.5 V discharge process in which internal temperature rises linearly (temperature change rate is about 0.4 degrees/min) is called the stable phase. Rising temperature in the phase is mainly caused by ohmic heat generated by the constant current discharge. If no fault occurs, the battery temperature will achieve the thermal equilibrium of 45°. However, once the voltage drops to 1.5 V, the batteries will enter the acceleration phase in which the change rate of temperature, voltage and internal resistance will rise significantly. When the voltage drops to 0 V, the temperature change rate reaches its peak value, which is close to 20 degrees/sec. The change rate of the internal resistance, the curve of which appears obvious inflection point when the voltages are 3 V (voltage platform end), 1.5 V and 0 V respectively, is more sensitive. The internal resistance reaches their maximum values later than the temperature about 5S that needed attention. The change of the internal resistance on the surface is likely caused by rapid rising temperature. After over-discharge, batteries enter the static phase in which the internal temperature of the batteries returned to 20° and internal resistance also tends to be stable (but still higher a lot than the initial internal resistance). In order to better show the symptoms of power lithium batteries in the process of over-discharge, the temperature and the change rate of internal resistance are shown in the Fig. 2.

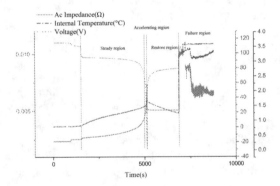

Fig. 1. Voltage-temperature profiles of tested cell during over-discharge test

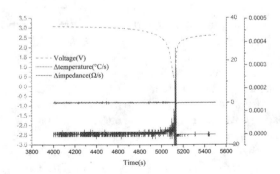

Fig. 2. Detailed voltage-temperature variation profiles of cell during over-discharge test

The cell voltage of over-discharge 120 % will be stabilized around −0.5 V. Even the continuous extraction of the current, the voltage will not continue to reduce. Since the internal temperature of the battery is stabilized at 110° and the shell temperature is about 60°, thermal runaway is not directly caused. There are no signs of gases release or obvious shells expansion in the whole process and the internal resistance of the battery will add 2 orders of magnitude (the typical value is ~10 mohm before the failure of the battery, and the normal internal resistance of new power battery is ~0.6 mohm). The change rate of internal resistance of the battery may be one of the important evidences for fault diagnosis of the power batteries.

3   Cooper Decomposition Symptoms and Measures

In the application of lithium-ion power batteries, most of the electronic equipments can set the upper limit of charge and the lower limit of discharge for the lithium-ion battery pack in order to prevent the batteries from entering the state of over-charge and over-discharge. Once any cell voltage exceeds the pre-set threshold, the protection circuit will disconnect the load. Although it is simple and effective, the mechanism always has some problems. On the one hand, it can be seen from the long-term and deeply over-discharge experiments above that the batteries can still work over a longer voltage range even if voltage of the batteries is lower than the lower limit of the recommended voltage given by the lithium battery manufacturers. Considering that the large-scale series battery modules may appear the condition of imbalance, weak cell may reach the lower limit voltage in the range of the normal module capacity. At this time, the alarm signal is not only no necessary, but also affects the user experience. Meanwhile, this mechanism is unable to deal with the over-discharge caused by the internal battery fault and self-discharge: if the batteries are stored for a long time after fully discharge or the batteries have the condition of slight short circuit, over-discharge may be caused for a short period of time. Therefore, even if the anode may be slightly affected, a better strategy is to allow the over-discharged lithium-ion batteries to recharge, and to measure the damage extent of the battery and make diagnosis in the process of charge [9].

For over-discharge of the batteries example, it can be considered that the battery failure or accident often occurred in the recharge process of the over-discharge batteries although over-discharge slightly of the batteries cannot cause serious damages. Through we had carried out cycle experiments of 100 % SOC charge and 120 % SOC over-discharge at the different rate for our lithium-ion battery, we found that apparent charge and discharge failure of the battery always occurred in the charge process of over-discharged in which the batteries go along with rapid temperature rising, sudden changing of the internal resistance and abnormal decreasing of the battery voltage. According to the diagnosis, we can combine with the known data to give the real-time probability of the battery failure in the process of charge and to verify our diagnosis algorithm through dissection tests.

The highest temperature T_{Ref} of the discharge process and the biggest change rate ΔR_{Ref} of the internal resistance can serve as the reference. The highest temperature T_{Max} in the process of recharge and internal resistance variation ΔR_{Max} are the input of the diagnosis system and the battery failure probability is the output of the diagnosis system. T_{Ref} and ΔR_{Ref} can be updated in each discharge cycle according to the working conditions. According to the historical data, probability distribution function $f(x)$ and $g(x)$ of $T = T_{Max} - T_{Ref}$ and $R = \Delta R_{Max} - \Delta R_{Ref}$ can be obtained. According to the statistical information of the over-discharge faults and the weight information of temperature and internal resistance in the process of over-discharge, fault probability diagnosis of the over-discharge battery can be obtained by (1)–(3).

$$P_1 = \int_{-\infty}^{T} f(x)dx \tag{1}$$

$$P_2 = \int_{-\infty}^{R} g(x)dx \tag{2}$$

$$P = \alpha_1 P_1 + \alpha_2 P_2 \tag{3}$$

Where P1 and P2 are the failure probability estimation of the temperature and the internal resistance change respectively, and α_1 and α_2 are the weight obtained by the

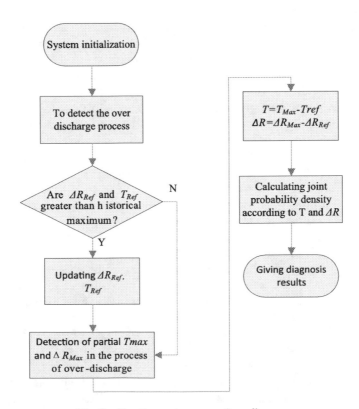

Fig. 3. The diagnosis process flow diagram

experiments. The diagnosis process is shown in Fig. 3. Based on this process, two over-discharged cells at different degradation degree were analyzed and dismantled. Fault probabilities are 26.7 % and 47.3 % respectively, and the dismantle result of anode damage in Fig. 4 primitively proved that our diagnostic method is effective.

Fig. 4. Anode samples from different diagnosis probability

It must be noted that the temperature is internal temperature of the batteries rather than the shell temperature with the characteristic of insensitivity in the experiments. If the shell temperature is used, we need to modify the weight values of temperature changes in the fault algorithm.

4   Conclusions

This paper elaborates the capacity fade of a commercial LiFePo4 battery under the state of over-discharge. The voltage, AC impedance and internal temperature in the whole process are recorded for subsequent analysis. And the symptoms of the fault, such as abnormal rising temperature or the change of internal resistance, are found for the diagnosis. Thus the applications of the power battery can be guaranteed, especially in terms of the safety of electric vehicles.

In the repeated over-discharge experiments, the battery has experienced the acceleration of capacity decay, the rate of which depends on the discharge cut-off voltage. Over-discharge process goes along with the copper current collector dissolution and the irreversible solid amorphization process, which are proved in the disassembly experiment.

The security of the lithium-ion battery system, especially the large-scale series-parallel system has been one of the factors of the application of lithium batteries. Over-discharge is one of the common factors leading to battery out of work. To fully understand its internal mechanism, to observe its symptoms — this is very helpful to establish a complete and reliable fault diagnosis system. In addition, the researches related to the topic will be carried out continuously, including: (1) the accurate estimation algorithm of internal temperature and internal resistance; (2) the extraction method of the optimization feature.

References

1. Bowkett, M.: Design and implementation of an optimal battery management system for hybrid electric vehicles. In: 19th International Conference on Automation and Computing (ICAC), 13–14 September 2013, London, England (2013)
2. Rezvanizaniani, S.M., Liu, Z.C., Chen, Y., Lee, J.: Review and recent advances in battery health monitoring and prognostics technologies for electric vehicle (EV) safety and mobility. J. Power Sources **256**, 110–124 (2014)
3. Aurbach, D., Zinigrad, E., Cohen, Y., Teller, H.: A short review of failure mechanisms of lithium metal and lithiated graphite anodes in liquid electrolyte solutions. Solid State Ionics **148**, 405–416 (2002)
4. Liu, P., Wang, J., Hicks-Garner, J., Sherman, E.: Aging mechanisms of LiFePO4 batteries deduced by electrochemical and structural analyses. J. Electrochem. Soc. **157**(4), 499–507 (2010)
5. Nick, W., Wei, H., Michael, O., Michael, P.: Reliability and failure analysis of lithium ion batteries for electronic systems. In: 13th International Conference on Electronic Packaging Technology and High Density Packaging, August 13–August 16, 2012, Guilin, China (2012)
6. Kaypmaz, T.C., Tuncay, R.N.: An advanced cell model for diagnosing faults in operation of Li-ion Polymer batteries. In: 7th IEEE Vehicle Power and Propulsion Conference, VPPC 2011, 6–9 September 2011, Chicago, USA (2011)
7. Widodo, A., Shim, M.C., Caesarendra, W., Yang, B.S.: Intelligent prognostics for battery health monitoring based on sample entropy. Expert Syst. Appl. **38**, 11763–11769 (2011)
8. Maleki, H., Howard, J.N.: Effects of over discharge on performance and thermal stability of a Li-ion cell. J. Power Sources **160**, 1395–1402 (2006)
9. Xu, S., Sun, D., Yang, S.: A new power lithium battery fault diagnosis system. Manuf. Autom. **36**(2), 20–23 (2014)

Fault Diagnosis Approach for Lithium-ion Battery in Energy Storage Power Station and Its Simulation

Gang Hong[1], Bin Wang[1], and Chao Wu[2(✉)]

[1] Beihai Power Supply Bureau, Guangxi Power Grid Co., Ltd., Beihai, China
[2] Department of Electrical Engineering,
Luoyang Institute of Science and Technology, Luoyang, China
shiningi@163.com

Abstract. In this paper, we propose a fault diagnosis system for lithium-ion battery used in energy storage power station with fully understanding the failure mechanism inside the battery. The system is established based on fuzzy logic. In order to establish the knowledge database, a serial of abusive experiments such as overcharge, over-discharge and low-temperature and several problems such as connection which may commonly occur during battery operations, are considered. Fault symptoms in form of parameter variation are extracted and analyzed for formation of the fault database. Finally, a fuzzy logic based diagnosis system is developed, which is used for detection and isolation of different fault modes. The system provides clear meaning for internal mechanisms for lithium-ion batteries and is practical in application of energy storage power station.

Keywords: Fault diagnosis · Lithium-ion battery · Expert system · Simulation · Fuzzy logic

1 Introduction

As lithium-ion battery plays a more and more important role in wide applications due to its environmental friendliness, high power and energy density, a new topic related to its safety issue has been focused in recent years. Several accidents were during battery operation and caught increasing public concern. Although lithium-ion battery is regarded as long service-life device, problems from several factors indeed degrade its performance, or result in severe failure. So applications with lithium-ion battery have to provide an effective approach to guarantee their reliability and safety. In one hand, researches on electrode material and manufacture process are developed to provide cells with higher specifics; in the other hand, the management during operation is required to guarantee the performance and safety, which will be the main topic in this paper.

Fault diagnosis is a critical technique for battery application to detect successive performance degradation or abrupt fault during operation [1, 2]. More and more researches reported different kinds of diagnosis approaches. Post-mortem analyses such as SEM and XRD are effective ways for quantification of the physical distortion in a failed lithium-ion battery [3]. Intelligent diagnosis systems such as fuzzy logic and neural network are also applied for battery [4, 5]. Other researches focus on one single

© Springer Science+Business Media Singapore 2016
L. Zhang et al. (Eds.): AsiaSim 2016/SCS AutumnSim 2016, Part III, CCIS 645, pp. 315–323, 2016.
DOI: 10.1007/978-981-10-2669-0_35

fault mode like overcharge or high temperature, and use electrochemical way to describe the fault. Several optimization algorithms like Kalman filter or observer are utilized for parameter estimation which indicates occurrence of fault [5]. These methods, however, have their limitations either because they can hardly be applied in situ or they fail to give a physical meaning for diagnosed faults. To our knowledge, the fault diagnosis approach connects external characteristics with chemical process are rare.

Lithium-ion battery is a complex electrochemical system, whose performance may not be easily represented with only one parameter. Well understanding the internal mechanisms connected with fault symptoms during battery fault process helps to establish a complete and accurate diagnosis system. In this paper, we first introduce the common fault modes during applications along with their chemical mechanism; then a serial of abusive tests according to these fault modes are performed to extract the electrical parameter variation during each fault respectively; finally a fuzzy diagnosis system is established based on obtained knowledge database.

2 Fault Analysis of Power Battery and Experiments

2.1 Fault Analysis of Lithium-ion Battery

Knowledge of internal structure of lithium-ion battery helps us understand the internal mechanism of battery fault. In ideal case, only ion intercalation and deintercalation at both electrodes occur which do not result in irreversible capacity fade of battery. However, side reactions and other mechanisms always take place along with intercalation process and may be aggravated by abusive operation or terrible environment, such as thermal abuse (elevated temperature, low temperature), electrical abuse (overcharge, over-discharge, high-current rate) and mechanical abuse (nail penetration, crash). These processes destroy the equilibrium state and induce irreversible consumption of lithium inventory or active material.

However, during real applications, these internal mechanisms can not be detected directly. What we can obtain during battery operation is the measurements from sensors such as voltage, current and temperature. A bridge between internal chemical mechanisms and external electrical symptoms should be established for fault diagnosis of lithium-ion battery, as to say, we need to detect the fault in form of measurable electrical parameters.

2.2 Fault Modes

In this paper, we focus on the following fault modes which commonly occur during applications of lithium-ion battery, especially for energy storage power station:

(1) Overcharge

Overcharge is supposed to be extremely harmful to battery because it directly induces additional energy into individual cell. As a consequence of overcharge, crystalline structure of both electrodes may be affected. Oxide at cathode and electrolyte may be decomposed and generate oxygen. Lithium may be plated at anode in case of deep overcharge. Exothermic side reaction between lithium and oxygen will occur, which will cause loss of lithium inventory and active material [6]. Worst yet, if the cell cannot release heat to environment at a rate higher than or equal to the rate of heat generation, it will undergo thermal runaway.

(2) Over-discharge

Over-discharge will rarely result in direct damage to lithium-ion battery. However, degradation on both electrodes especially on anode can be detected during recharge phase. In the worst case, a thermal runaway is also possible. Electrochemically irreversible solid-state amorphization occurs in case of deep over-discharge process which damages the host structure [7]. Once discharged below 1.5 V, crack of active material at anode and anodic dissolution of the current collector are the main problems. The dissolved copper may migrate through and penetrate the separator, resulting in a potential internal short.

(3) Low temperature charging

Low temperature discharging is supposed to cause less capacity loss, however, lithium plating dominates the process at the anode during low temperature charging. Lithium plating occurs when the graphite potential is reduced below 0 V vs. Li/Li^+ or lithium-ion diffusion in the graphite particle is limited. Both conditions are aggravated with decreasing temperature. Furthermore, there may be metallic lithium dendrite resulting in an internal short circuit [8, 9]. This is the reason why electric vehicle (EV) or power station has difficulties in start in winter.

(4) Connection problem

Connection fault is different from all the faults mentioned above. It does not present the internal chemical property change of lithium-ion battery but the external one. However, it's a typical fault mode during battery operation so we'd like to integrate it into our diagnosis system. The electrical behaviors of connection fault are similar with internal resistance increase; however the contact resistance variation resulting from vibration or connection loosening is highly unstable while the battery capacity is hardly affected [10]. The fault mainly occurs in EV or situation where frequency vibration occurs.

2.3 Experimental Setup

After understanding the internal mechanisms of mentioned faults, the abusive experiments for all the fault modes are planned. Here we don't include the connection fault because it's a mechanical fault and do not involve in any chemical ageing process.

The commercial prismatic lithium-ion phosphate cells with initial capacity 40 Ah are selected for study. The cells are operated and conditioned by Arbin BT2000 battery test system. Normal cycles for the battery include charge/discharge from 2.5 V to 3.65 V. Different abusive cycles are arranged for corresponding fault modes. FUDS test which simulates the dynamic condition is carried out every 10 cycles and current parameter of tested cell is extracted. All tests will end when a visible symptom occurs or the capacity of tested cell decrease to 60 % of its nominal value. The extracted data are collected for further analysis and integration.

3   Fault Diagnosis System for Lithium-Ion Battery

The basic idea of the fault diagnosis system lies in that we try to find a meaningful description for fault modes of lithium-ion battery in form of measurable parameter variations. As to say, a mathematical or electrical representation for battery is required.

3.1   Model of Lithium-ion Battery

During cycles of lithium-ion battery, the real-time data from sensors such as voltage, current and temperature will be obtained. Usually these parameters can not be directly used as indicators for degradation or fault of a battery. Some parameters such as resistance or SOC, which are related with internal chemical process, are required. In this paper, we use Randles equivalent circuit model (ECM) to represent the behavior of a lithium-ion battery, which is shown in Fig. 1. In this model, the voltage source stands for open circuit voltage (OCV), resistor Rs represents the total serial resistance, and parallel RC network describes the charge transfer and other similar process.

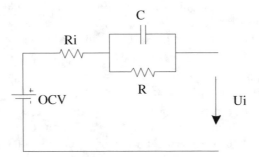

Fig. 1. Equivalent circuit model of lithium-ion battery

According to Kichhoff's lay, we establish the equations for this model which will be used in the following section. The target parameters are U which is the voltage across the battery and Uc which is the voltage across the RC parallel unit. The equations are listed below:

$$\begin{cases} U_c((k + 1)T) = \exp(-\dfrac{T}{RC}) * U_c(kT) + (1 - \exp(-\dfrac{T}{RC}))R * I(KT) \\ U(KT) = -U_c(KT) - I(KT)R_i + E \end{cases}$$

3.2   Fault Feature Extraction

Feature extraction is the key feature for establishing a diagnosis system and it may directly affect diagnosis decisions. They must be able to describe the relationship between fault modes and symptoms mentioned above with clear physical meaning. In our system, the features are extracted from the real-time curves (which is simulated with FUDS condition in this paper), and the variations of parameter in the equivalent circuit model are treated as diagnosis basis.

3.3   Extended Kalman Filter for Parameter Identification

A parameter extraction approach for dynamic condition is always preferred due to real condition of battery applications [11]. Kalman filter (KF) induces state space to filter theory, and describes signal process with white noise through state equations. It estimates parameters and states of dynamic system using digital filter with LMS (least mean square). Extended Kalman filter (EKF) is the extended version for KF which is used for nonlinear system. Since lithium-ion battery is a highly nonlinear system during operation, EKF is extremely suitable for this situation. The process of parameter estimation for lithium-ion batteries is shown in Fig. 2.

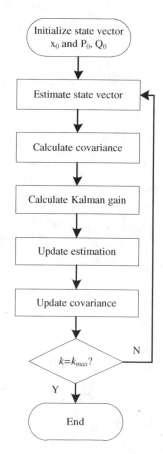

Fig. 2. Process of extended Kalman filter

For nonlinear system, the state transition function $f(x_k, u_k)$ and measurement function $g(x_k, u_k)$ will be linearized by first order Taylor expansion:

$$\begin{cases} f(x_k, u_k) \approx f(\hat{x}_k, u_k) + \dfrac{\partial f(x_k, u_k)}{\partial x_k}\Big|_{x_k = \hat{x}_k} (x_k - \hat{x}_k) \\ h(x_k, u_k) \approx h(\hat{x}_k, u_k) + \dfrac{\partial h(x_k, u_k)}{\partial x_k}\Big|_{x_k = \hat{x}_k} (x_k - \hat{x}_k) \end{cases}$$

In these equations x_k is the system state vector, u_k is the input vector, $\hat{x}_k$ is the estimated value for x_k, and state equations for nonlinear system can be established.

Back to the battery model, the input state vector is set as $x = (U;\ Ro;\ Rp;\ tau;\ Ip)$.

One fresh cell is taken for validation of the accuracy of EKF. The cell is operated under FUDS condition and its current and voltage are recorded regularly. Estimation results are shown in Fig. 3. The estimated voltage curve in this figure agrees well with the measured one, which indicates the accuracy of our parameter estimation.

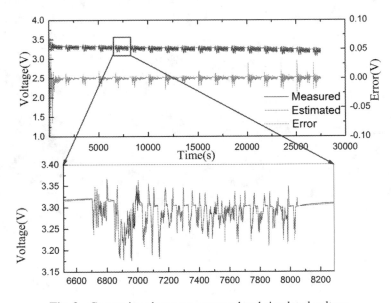

Fig. 3. Comparison between measured and simulated voltage

4   Simulation and Experiment Validation

After all the parameters are derived, they can be used as indicators for diagnostic basis of individual fault. Refined parameter variation as symptoms are shown as Rs variation; Rp variation and Cp variation. Considering that the battery is a complex system and the variations may have some overlaps, fuzzy representation is an appropriate way for representation of all fault modes which are shown in Table 1.

Table 1. Relationship between fault modes and parameter variation

	ΔRs	ΔRp	ΔCp	ΔCap
NCT	ZR	ZR	ZR	ZR
ODT	PS	NS	PM	NS
OCT	PM	PM	NB	NL
LTT	PM	PB	PB	NM
CP	NM-PM	ZR	ZR	ZR

The experiment results are acceptable for diagnosis system because symptoms from different fault modes are distinguishable so that the faults are easy to be isolated. Moreover, the distinguishable symptoms are meaningful and reasonable because they reflect different mechanisms inside lithium-ion batteries respectively. For example, low temperature slows the diffusion and intercalation process, so the polarization phenomena are aggravated; over-discharge may have the same effect for the deposited copper at anode may prevent ions from intercalation into graphite.

Finally, we can establish the diagnosis system based on parameter variation. The diagnosis process of proposed system is shown in Fig. 4. After conditioning, the signals from sensors are transmitted for parameter estimation, which extracts fault features through EKF. The extracted features are compared with those in fault database and help to make decisions [12, 13]. We achieve the system in Matlab with help of fuzzy toolbox (shown in Fig. 5) and Fig. 6 provides the probability of a tested cell to an over-discharge fault.

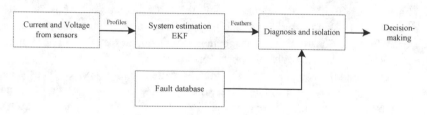

Fig. 4. Block diagram of proposed system

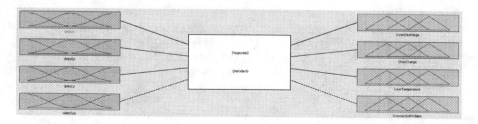

Fig. 5. Fuzzy diagnosis system

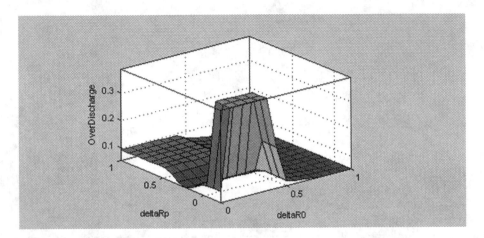

Fig. 6. Over-discharge fault probability diagnosis based on simulation

5   Conclusion

It is important for lithium-ion battery applications to declare a "state of safety" as well as traditional SOC and SOH, which is related with performance degradation, module inhomogenity and individual battery fault.

In this paper, a diagnosis system for lithium-ion battery during applications is established based on EKF after fully understanding the fault mechanism. Abusive tests are performed to extract key features for each fault mode and establish a fault database in a measureable way. Four typical fault mechanisms result in different fault symptoms and they can be isolated through parameter variations.

However, due to the complexity of lithium-ion battery, more work could be done to improve our work. More fault modes should be added to complete the fault database. As the number of fault modes increases, the difficulty for fault isolation increases and the mutual relationship among different faults must be considered.

References

1. Troltzsch, U., Kanoun, O., Trankler, H.S.: Characterizing aging effects of lithium ion batteries by impedance spectroscopy. Electrocihimica Acta **51**, 1664–1672 (2004)
2. Wang, S.L., Shang, L.P., Li, Z.F., Deng, H., Ma, Y.L.: Lithium-ion battery security guaranteeing method study based on the state of charge estimation. Int. J. Electrochem. Sci. **10**(6), 5130–5151 (2015)
3. Yufit, V., Shearing, P., Hamilton, R.W., Lee, P.D., Wu, M., Brandon, N.P.: Investigation of lithium-ion polymer battery cell failure using X-ray computed tomography. Electrochem. Commun. **13**, 608–610 (2011)
4. Liu, W.J.: Research and implementation of failure diagnosis expert system for battery pack. Master dissertation, Hunan University (2005)
5. Sidhu, A., Izadian, A., Anwar, S.: Adaptive nonlinear model-based fault diagnosis of Li-ion batteries. IEEE Trans. Ind. Electron. **62**(2), 1002–1011 (2015)

6. Belov, D., Yang, M.H.: Investigation of the kinetic mechanism in overcharge process for Li-ion battery. Solid State Ionics **179**, 1816–1821 (2008)
7. Maleki, H., Howard, J.N.: Effects of overdischarge on performance and thermal stability of a Li-ion cell. J. Power Sources **160**, 1395–1402 (2006)
8. Kaypmaz, T.C., Uzun, V, Tuncay, R.N.: Analysis of over charge & over discharge characteristics and failure detection of Li-ion polymer batteries. Presented at the 4th International Conference on Automotive Technologies, 13–14 November 2008, Istanbul, Turkey (2008)
9. Petzl, M., Kasper, M., Danzer, M.A.: Lithium plating in a commercial lithium-ion battery - a low temperature aging study. J. Power Sources **275**, 799–807 (2015)
10. Zheng, Y.J., Han, X.B., Lu, L.G., Li, J.Q., Ouyang, M.G.: Lithium ion battery pack power fade fault identification based on Shannon entropy in electric vehicles. J. Power Sources **223**, 136–146 (2013)
11. Hua, C., Youn, B.D., Chung, J.: A multiscale framework with extended Kalman filter for lithium-ion battery SOC and capacity estimation. Appl. Energy **92**, 694–704 (2012)
12. Widodo, A., Shim, M.C., Caesarendra, W., Yang, B.S.: Intelligent prognostics for battery health monitoring based on sample entropy. Expert Syst. Appl. **38**, 11763–11769 (2011)
13. Lee, S., Kim, J., Lee, J.: The state and parameter estimation of an Li-ion battery using a new OCV–SOC concept. Presented at IEEE Power Electronics Specialists Conference, pp. 2799–2803 (2007)

Research on the RF Simulation Technology Based on High Frequency Hybrid Method

Guijie Diao[✉], Hong Ni, Yuehui Qi, and Junjie Lu

Beijing Electromechanical Engineering Institute, Beijing, China
dgjl002@163.com

Abstract. A radio frequency (RF) simulation technique based on high frequency hybrid method is proposed for complex target. Firstly, the radar cross section (RCS) of the target is obtained by vector addition of facets scattering field and wedges scattering field that are calculated respectively by physical optics (PO) method and physical theory of diffraction (PTD). Then, scattering centers of the target are extracted based on multi scattering center theory, and the radar echo signal is simulated through radio frequency simulation system (RFSS). This technique could improve the fidelity of radar signal simulation and the confidence of RF simulation test. At last, simulation results validate the technique.

Keywords: Radio frequency simulation · Scattering center · Radar scattering section · Physical optics · Radar echo signal simulation

1 Introduction

The basic function of radio frequency simulation system (RFSS) is to simulate the complex electromagnetic (EM) environment and the scattering signature of target as real as possible for radar detection. In many radio frequency (RF) simulation technologies, simulation for radar echo signal is one of the key techniques, and it is very important for RF simulation [1].

Generally, radar cross section (RCS) statistical model is adopted for radar echo signal simulation. With development of modern radar, the requirement for target scattering signature simulation is higher. So, the simulation precision of target and the confidence of RF simulation test are limited because of RCS statistical model.

A RF simulation technique based on high frequency hybrid method is proposed for complex target. Firstly, the RCS of the target is obtained by vector addition of facets scattering field and wedges scattering field that are calculated respectively by physical optics (PO) method and physical theory of diffraction (PTD). Then, the scattering centers are extracted based on multi-scattering center theory, and the radar echo signal is simulated through RFSS. Finally, simulation results are presented.

L. Zhang et al. (Eds.): AsiaSim 2016/SCS AutumnSim 2016, Part III, CCIS 645, pp. 324–332, 2016.
DOI: 10.1007/978-981-10-2669-0_36

2   Simulation System

The composition of RFSS is shown in Fig. 1. The RFSS can simulate multiple features of the target including time-feature, frequency-feature, space-feature, power- future and polarization-future. Radar target RF echo signal is simulated by RFSS according to the received radar RF signal and the scattering signature of target. And, the RF echo is radiated to anechoic chamber through antenna array system. Then, it is received by radar for target detection and recognition. Usually, RCS statistical model is adopted to simulate the RF echo. But, this method is difficult to simulate real scattering signature of the target. Adopting the EM numerical method to obtain the scattering signature will enhance the reality of simulations.

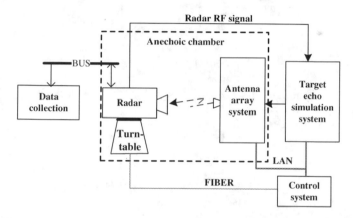

Fig. 1. Composition of RFSS

3   Radar Echo Signal Model

Supposing that the radar transmitted signal is a linear frequency modulation (LFM) signal:

$$s_t(t) = \exp(j2\pi f_c t)p(t) \tag{1}$$

Here, f_c is the carrier frequency.
In Eq. (1) $p(t)$ is the LFM item, that can be expressed by

$$p(t) = \exp(j\pi k_r t^2)\mathrm{rect}(\frac{t}{T_p}) \tag{2}$$

where,

$$\text{rect}(\frac{t}{T_p}) = \begin{cases} 1 & |t| < T_p \\ 0 & \text{else} \end{cases} \tag{3}$$

with T_p and k_r being the chirp duration and rate, respectively.

Based on multi scattering center theory, the radar echo signal of volume distributive target is as follows:

$$\begin{aligned} s_r(t) &= \sum_m \sigma_m s_t(t - t_m) \\ &= \sum_m \sigma_m p(t - t_m) \exp(-j2\pi f_c t_m) \exp(j2\pi f_c t) \\ &= \exp(j2\pi f_c t) \sum_m \sigma_m p(t - t_m) \exp(-j\frac{4\pi R_m}{\lambda}) \\ &= \exp(j2\pi f_c t) p(t) * h(t) \end{aligned} \tag{4}$$

After frequency mixing processing, the signal model is as follows

$$s_r(t) = p(t) * h(t) \tag{5}$$

where,

$$h(t) = \exp(j2\pi f_c t) \sum_m \sigma_m \exp(-j\frac{4\pi R_m}{\lambda}) \delta(t - t_m) \tag{6}$$

$$\sigma_m = |\sigma_m| \exp(j\phi_m) \tag{7}$$

$$t_m = \frac{2R_m}{c} \tag{8}$$

Here, $h(t)$ is the system function; σ_m is the backscattering coefficient of the mth scattering center; R_m is the distance between the scattering center to radar; ϕ_m is the phase of σ_m; $\delta(t - t_m)$ is the unit impulse function.

According to Eqs. (5) to (7), the radar echo signal system function of the target is expressed by the superposition of a series of unit impulse functions, that represent the amplitude modulation (AM) and phase modulation (PM) by the scattering centers, as well as the time-delay derived from R_m.

4 EM Scattering Field Calculation

The high frequency EM scattering signature of isolated complex target can be expressed by facets scattering field and wedges scattering field that are calculated respectively by physical optics (PO) method [4] and physical theory of diffraction (PTD) [5].

4.1 EM Scattering Field Calculation for Facets

Through integration and approximation of the induction field on facet surfaces, the RCS of facets can be solved by PO method. Under the condition of far field, the square root formula of polygon facet RCS is described by [6]:

$$\sqrt{\sigma} = -\frac{\mathbf{n} \cdot (\mathbf{e}_r \times \mathbf{h}_r)}{\sqrt{\pi T}} e^{-jk\mathbf{r}_0 \cdot \mathbf{W}} \sum_{m=1}^{M} (\mathbf{p} \cdot \mathbf{a}_m) e^{-jk\mathbf{r}_m \cdot \mathbf{W}} \cdot \frac{\sin\left[\frac{1}{2}(k\mathbf{a}_m \cdot \mathbf{W})\right]}{k\mathbf{a}_m \cdot \mathbf{W}} \tag{9}$$

in which $\mathbf{W} = \mathbf{i} - \mathbf{s}$, with $\mathbf{i}$ and $\mathbf{s}$ being unit vectors of incidence direction and observing direction respectively; $\mathbf{a}_m$ is the position vector describing margin center of the mth facet; T is the projected length of $\mathbf{W}$ on the facet surface; $\mathbf{p} = \mathbf{n} \times \mathbf{W}/|\mathbf{n} \times \mathbf{W}|$, representing the unit vector perpendicular to $\mathbf{W}$; M is the number of the facet edges; k is the wave number.

4.2 EM Scattering Field Calculation for Wedges

Ufimtsev presented the PTD to solve the edge discontinuity problem concerning EM scattering calculation [7]. The EM scattering field can be expressed by the summation of the facet PO contribution and the wedge diffraction contribution. The wedge diffraction contribution will be extracted using exact solution of two-dimension chopping. So the wedge diffraction contribution can be obtained by subtracting the PO contribution from the exact solution.

For the wedge with length of L, according to PTD, the square root formula of wedge RCS in far field condition is described by

$$\sqrt{\sigma_{\text{edge}}} = \frac{L}{\sqrt{\pi}} e^{-jkr} \frac{[(\mathbf{e}_i \cdot \mathbf{t})(\mathbf{e}_s \cdot \mathbf{t})f + (\mathbf{h}_i \cdot \mathbf{t})(\mathbf{h}_s \cdot \mathbf{t})g]}{\sin^2 \beta} \cdot \frac{\sin[kL\cos\beta]}{kL\cos\beta} e^{-jk\mathbf{k}_i \cdot \mathbf{R}} \tag{10}$$

where, $\mathbf{R}$ is the position vector pointing to the wedge center from original point; $\mathbf{e}_s$ and $\mathbf{h}_s$ are the unit polarization vectors of the scattering field; $\mathbf{e}_i$ and $\mathbf{h}_i$ are the unit polarization vectors of the incidence field; f and g are coefficient of physical diffraction, that can be calculated according to reference [5].

5 Simulation Procedure for Radar Echo Signal

Based on multi scattering center theory, the time-domain radar echo signal can be expressed by,

$$s_{\text{echo}}(t) = \sum_m \sigma_m \cdot \text{rect}(\frac{t - t_m}{T_p}) \cdot \exp\left\{j2\pi\left[f_c(t - t_m) + \frac{1}{2}\gamma(t - t_m)^2\right]\right\} \tag{11}$$

In practical use, in order to decrease the computation and improve the real-time, several adjacent scattering centers can be equal to a strong scattering center [8].

The composition of the radar target echo simulation system is shown in Fig. 2. Radar echo signal is simulated through the radar target echo simulation system. Firstly, according to the distribution of scattering centers and the radar resolution, uniform range zones are divided, ensuring that the interval between the adjacent zones is smaller than radar resolution. Then, the base band radar echo signal of each zone is calculated by vector superposition of all the strong scattering centers distributed in the zone. At last, the RF radar echo signal is acquired through digital quadrature modulation and up-conversion. The realization of different range zones includes two parts: (1) coarse delay, in order to simulate whole delay of the target illuminating by radar, realized by DRFM; (2) precision delay, using to simulate the micro-delay among different range zones, composed by cables with different length.

The RF simulation procedure for the complex target based on high frequency hybrid method is shown in Fig. 3. The steps are follows:

Step1, modeling 3D geometry of the complex target, and dividing facets according to EM parameters;

Step2, hidden processing in accordance with the radar line of sight (RLOS), getting the position of illuminating facet and the information of normal vector;

Step3, obtaining the RCS of the target through vector supposition of facet EM scattering field and wedge EM scattering field that are calculated by PO method and PTD respectively;

Step4, extracting the scattering centers, and calculating the system function;

Step5, calculating the base-band radar echo signal by convolution;

Step6, simulating the RF radar echo signal through the radar target signature simulation system

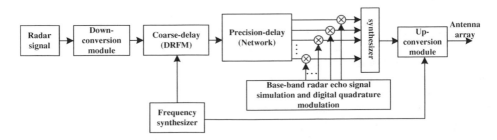

Fig. 2. Composition of radar target echo simulation system

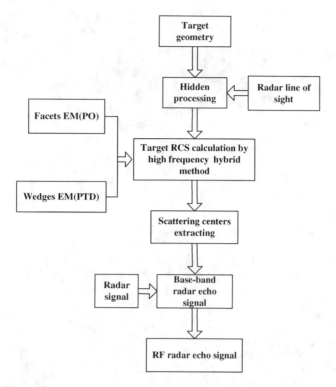

Fig. 3. RF simulation procedure for complex target based on high frequency hybrid method

6 Simulation Results

6.1 RCS Calculation Result

We choose a ship as the target, whose size is 138 m(length) × 15.2 m(width). The RCS is calculated by high frequency hybrid method, and the carrier frequency is 10 GHz. The azimuth angle and grazing angle for RLOS to ship are defined by θ and ϕ. When $\theta = 0°$ and $\phi = 0°$, the RLOS directly face to the head of the ship.

The angle-dependent RCS of Perry is shown in Fig. 4, that $\theta \in (0°, 180°)$ and $\phi \in (0°, 60°)$. From Fig. 4, the RCS fluctuate obviously with angular variation: when $\theta = 90°$ and $\phi = 0°$, the RCS is increased sharply and it is up to 90 dBsm, because in this situation, the radar wave illuminates the side-face of Perry vertically; when the large scattering section is not face to RLOS, the RCS is smaller relatively.

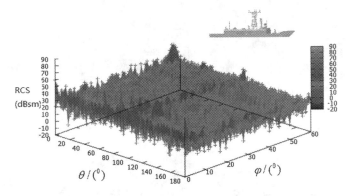

Fig. 4. RCS calculation result for Perry

6.2 Radar Echo Signal Simulation Results

The radar echo signal simulation results are shown in Fig. 5, when $\theta = 0°$ and $\phi = 10°$. Figure 5(a) is the wide-band RCS, when the frequency band is chosen from

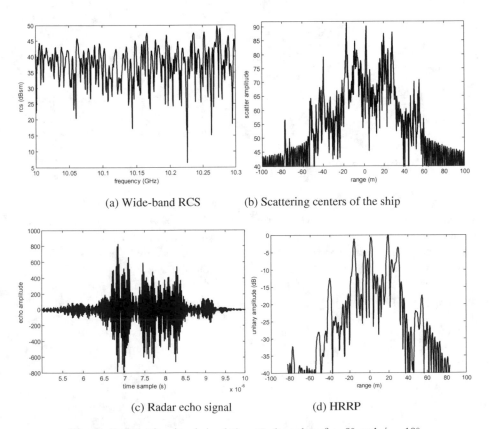

(a) Wide-band RCS   (b) Scattering centers of the ship

(c) Radar echo signal   (d) HRRP

Fig. 5. Radar echo signal simulation results, when $\theta = 0°$ and $\phi = 10°$

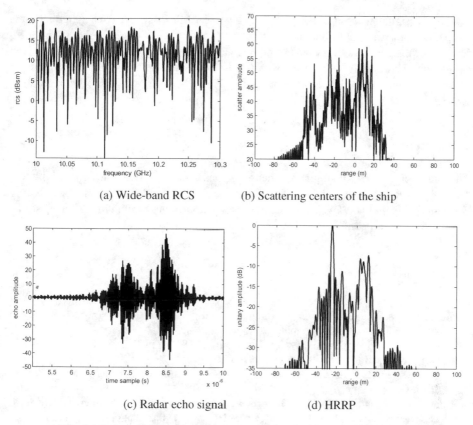

(a) Wide-band RCS   (b) Scattering centers of the ship

(c) Radar echo signal   (d) HRRP

Fig. 6. Radar echo signal simulation results, when $\theta = 60°$ and $\phi = 30°$

10 GHz to 10 GHZ + 300 MHz. It is observed that the RCS is large, and it is ranged from 40 dBsm to 50 dBsm, when the RLOS face to the head of the ship. Figure 5(b) illustrates the distribution of the scattering centers, it shows that many dense and strong scattering centers are produced from the antenna and the ship island located in the middle of the ship. Figure 5(c) shows the radar echo signal when the radar band width is 60 MHz and the carrier frequency is 10 GHz. Figure 5(d) is the pulse compression result, demonstrating the high resolution range profile (HRRP). Comparing Fig. 5(b) and (d), it can be seen that the scattering centers in Fig. 5(b) synthesize to several strong scattering centers shown in Fig. 5(d), due to the lower resolution. But the principals of distribution in Fig. 5(b) and (d) are consistent.

The radar echo signal simulation results are shown in Fig. 6, when $\theta = 60°$ and $\phi = 30°$. Figure 6(a) is the wide-band RCS, when the frequency band is chosen from 10 GHz to 10 GHZ + 300 MHz. It is observed that the RCS is ranged from 10 dBsm to 20 dBsm. Comparing with Fig. 5(a), the scattering intensity decreased. Figure 6(b) illustrates the distribution of the scattering centers. The distribution is more concentrated compared with Fig. 5(b), because of the change of RLOS. Figure 6(c) shows the radar echo signal when the radar band width is 60 MHz and the carrier frequency is 10 GHz. Comparing Fig. 6(c) and Fig. 5(c), the amplitude of the echo is reduced, because of the decrease of the scattering intensity. Figure 6(d) is the pulse compression result demonstrating the HRRP. It also can be seen that the scattering centers synthesize to several strong scattering centers compared Fig. 6(b) with (d), due to the resolution reduction.

7 Conclusions

This paper presents a RF simulation technique based on high frequency hybrid method for complex target. The EM scattering signature of the complex target is calculated by combination of PO and PTD. It is significant for improving the fidelity of radar signal simulation and the confidence of radio frequency simulation test.

References

1. Gu, Z., Yu, L.: Target characteristic simulation and implementation in array RF simulation system. Fire Control Radar Technol. **42**(3), 52–56 (2013)
2. Yuan, D., Yuan, S.-X., Zhao, M., et al.: Key techniques for RF guided simulation system. Fire Control Command Control **40**(1), 108–117 (2015)
3. Jaime, X., Qiao, Z.: Filtered back projection inversion of turntable ISAR data. In: Proceedings of SPIE, vol. 8051, pp. 1–9 (2011)
4. Knot: A tool for predicting the radar cross section of an arbitrary trihedral corner. In: IEEE Proceeding of Southeastcon 1981 Conference, Huntsville, Alabama, pp. 17–20 (1981)
5. Zheng, R.-Y.: Radar Cross Section and Stealth Technique, pp. 120–125. National Deference Industry Press, Beijing (1988)
6. Qin, D.H., Wang, B.F., Lin, T.J.: Improvement of edges diffraction computing in GRECO. Chin. J. Aeronaut. **17**(2), 93–98 (2004)
7. Ufimtsev, P.Y.: Method of edge waves in the physical theory of diffraction. Air Force System Command, Document IN NO. FTD-HC-23-259-71 (1971)
8. Jun, L.-Z.: Radio frequency simulation technology and its application for wide-band radar targets. Aerosp. Shanghai **29**(3), 59–63 (2012)
9. Heng, L.-Z., Hai, P.-M.: Method of target and clutter signal simulation for MMW seeker. J. Syst. Simul. **19**(12), 2723–2726 (2007)

Analysis of the Simulation Fidelity in Millimeter Wave Simulation System

Jing Ma[1]($\boxtimes$), Congjun Jin[1], Bin Shi[1], and Dong Chen[2]

[1] Science and Technology on Space System Simulation Laboratory,
Beijing Simulation Center, Beijing 100854, China
Phd.jingma@gmail.com
[2] China Academy of Space Technology,
Institute of Telecommunication Satellite, Beijing 100094, China

Abstract. The simulation for Millimeter Wave (MMW) target is that using the method of HWIL to simulate the target and environment in MMW within the intercepted processing of radar guidance missile. The target and environment simulation in millimeter wave includes two aspects: space property and electromagnetism property. Space property indicates the position of target to seeker and the changing of position. Electromagnetism property indicates the amplitude, glint, Doppler shift, distance/angular spread and polarization of echo wave. In MMW target simulation, MMW detection can improve the capability of distance and angular resolving. The point-object simulation has been no longer satisfied the detection precision for MMW seeker. Therefore, extended target which simulates the target as the aggregation of Scattering Centers (SC) whose amplitudes and phases adjusted by the line of sight is needed for MMW simulation. By far, One-point Target, which presents a target, can be simulated accurately by Triad of Antenna (TOA) on the array in the chamber. This paper will analyze the fidelity of extended target simulated by TOA producing SC. Then, give the scheme of simulation precision remedy.

Keywords: Simulation fidelity millimeter · Wave simulation system · RF simulation

1 Millimeter Wave Simulation System

Millimeter Wave Simulation System (MMWSS), shown as Fig. 1, is composed of chamber, target array and feed controller, MMS signal producer, computer and interface, the database of target and environment model, monitor and display system, and calibration system. In the processing of MMW target simulation, the database of target and environment model calculates the space and electromagnetism property of target, then the array simulates electric radiation for seeker detection [1].

© Springer Science+Business Media Singapore 2016
L. Zhang et al. (Eds.): AsiaSim 2016/SCS AutumnSim 2016, Part III, CCIS 645, pp. 333–343, 2016.
DOI: 10.1007/978-981-10-2669-0_37

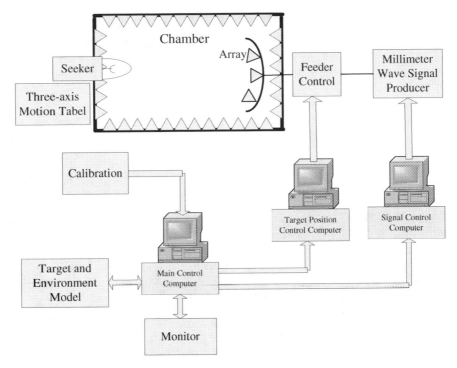

Fig. 1. MMWSS

2   The Modeling and Simulation of MMW Extended Target

When the seeker has highly distance resolution, the target is considered as distance extended target because the size of target exceeds distance resolution of seeker. The target is considered as angle extended target because the angle of target exceeds angle resolution of seeker detection [2, 3]. Up to now, the target can be seen as a distance-angle extended one when the seeker owns the power of MMW detection. The extended target is firstly modeled as geometry model shown as Fig. 2.

Secondly, the grid model, as Fig. 3 shown, is built by separating the geometry model to grids. In succession, the electromagnetic dispersion model is built based on geometrical optics, geometrical theory of diffraction, physical optics and physical theory of diffraction. Several SC in different distance units are chosen to represent the extended target [4]. The chosen SC is shown in Fig. 4.

In MMWSS, geometry model, grid model, electromagnetic dispersion model and chosen SC is calculated by target and environment database. Amplitude-phase control strategy is transferred to signal producer system and feeder control [5]. The same TOA in array simulate the electric characters of SC. In feed circuits, a SC is controlled by one circuit and four circuits consist of one TOA.

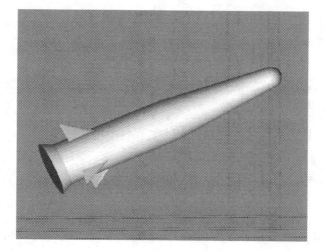

Fig. 2. Geometry model

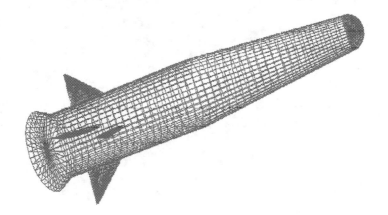

Fig. 3. Grid model

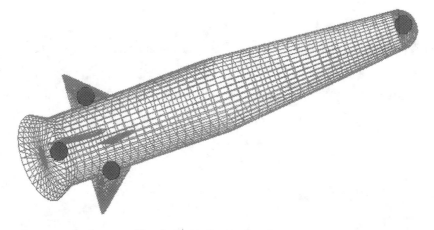

Fig. 4. Scattering centers chosen

3 Analysis of the Fidelity of Target Simulation

According to the radar angle measuring principle, the direction of target observed by radar is the gradient direction of the phases wave-front formed by scattering electromagnetic waves on antenna aperture surface. When using TOA array to simulate the echo wave of target, the electromagnetic fields generated by each antenna in TOA will be superposed on the receiving antenna aperture surface. In following section, we will discuss the MMWSS simulate target effectively?

3.1 One-Point Target

For radiation-type MMWSS, the size of chamber is able to meet the far-field radiation conditions for TOA. For simple calculation, the curvature of array is not taken into account. So the polarization directions of three antennas of TOA are same. Due to each antenna on TOA can be seen as a Source Point (SP), suppose the electric amplitude on antenna is E_i and the phase is β_i (i = 1,2,3). Based on superposition theory, electromagnetic fields generated on the receiving antenna aperture surface is

$$E(x, y, z) = \sum_{i=1}^{3} \frac{E_i}{R_i} e^{j\beta_i} e^{-jkR_i} \tag{1}$$

Seen as the same polarization direction in (1), the difference on direction for E_1, E_2 and E_3 can be neglected.

Therefore

$$R_i = \sqrt{(x_i - x)^2 + (y_i - y)^2 + (z_i - z)^2} \tag{2}$$

(x_i, y_i, z_i) is the coordinate for the ith antenna on TOA. (x, y, z) is the coordinate on receiving antenna aperture surface.

Let

$$A_i = \frac{E_i}{R_i} \tag{3}$$

Superposed electromagnetic field on the receiving antenna aperture surface is

$$
\begin{aligned}
E(x, y, z) &= \sum_{i=1}^{3} A_i e^{j(\beta_i - kR_i)} = \sum_{i=1}^{3} A_i [\cos(\beta_i - kR_i) + j\sin(\beta_i - kR_i)] \\
&= \sum_{i=1}^{3} A_i \cos(\beta_i - kR_i) + j \sum_{i=1}^{3} A_i \sin(\beta_i - kR_i)
\end{aligned}
\tag{4}
$$

Then

$$|E(x,y,z)| = \sqrt{\left[\sum_{i=1}^{3} A_i \cos(\beta_i - kR_i)\right]^2 + \left[\sum_{i=1}^{3} A_i \sin(\beta_i - kR_i)\right]^2} \quad (5)$$

After simplification,

$$|E(x,y,z)| = \sqrt{A_1^2 + A_2^2 + A_3^2 + 2A_1A_2 \cos \varphi_{12} + 2A_1A_3 \cos \varphi_{13} + 2A_2A_3 \cos \varphi_{23}} \quad (6)$$

$$\beta(x,y,z) = a\tan\left[\frac{A_1 \sin(\beta_1 - kR_1) + A_2 \sin(\beta_2 - kR_2) + A_3 \sin(\beta_3 - kR_3)}{A_1 \cos(\beta_1 - kR_1) + A_2 \cos(\beta_2 - kR_2) + A_3 \cos(\beta_3 - kR_3)}\right] \quad (7)$$

In the above equation, $\varphi_{12} = (\beta_2 - \beta_1) - k(R_2 - R_1)$, $\varphi_{13} = (\beta_3 - \beta_1) - k(R_3 - R_1)$, $\varphi_{23} = (\beta_3 - \beta_2) - k(R_3 - R_2)$.

According to above deduction, if the space between each two antenna on TOA is 24mrad and the wavelength is 3 mm, the superposed electromagnetic fields on the receiving antenna aperture surface, the size of which is 0.4 m, are shown in Fig. 5 for electric field intensity and Fig. 6 for phase. In the figure, "Array Simulation" denotes the result generated by TOA and "Theory" denotes the result generated by SP, which is the real electromagnetic field radiated from target in the space.

In Fig. 5, the electric field intensity of TOA is three times larger than which of SP. Through the normalization, the electric field intensity of TOA will be basically the same as which of SP. The error distribution of the electric field intensity is shown in Fig. 7, in which the average of error is -3.3×10^{-3} and variance is 2.1×10^{-3}.

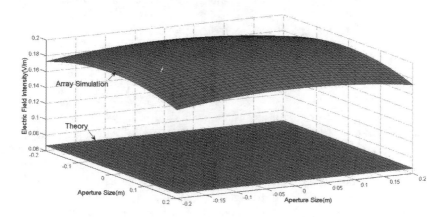

Fig. 5. Electric field intensity distribution of TOA and SP

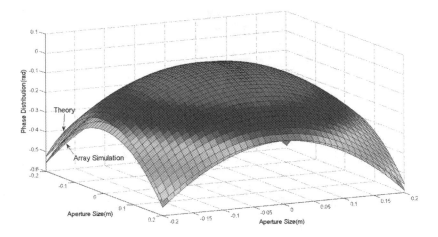

Fig. 6. Phase distribution of TOA and SP

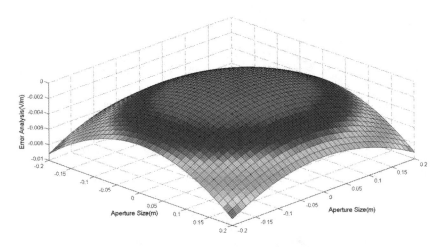

Fig. 7. Error distribution of electric filed intensity for TOA and SP

The error distribution of phase for electromagnetic field is shown in Fig. 8, in which the average of error is 4.82×10^{-5} and variance is 2.63×10^{-2}.

Because angle measurement of radar is based on the gradient direction of the phases wave-front formed by scattering electromagnetic waves on antenna aperture surface, Fig. 9 is the direction of gradient and normal direction of phase wave-front when observing from target to seeker. In the figure, comparing the trend of the black arrows and red arrows denoting the gradient directions of SP and TOA respectively, they are consistent. Meanwhile, the normal of both are in the same direction pointing at the target.

Thus, the electric field intensity and phase distribution simulated with TOA on the seeker's aperture are basically consistent with that of a SP generating. So the One-point target can be well simulated on the TOA array.

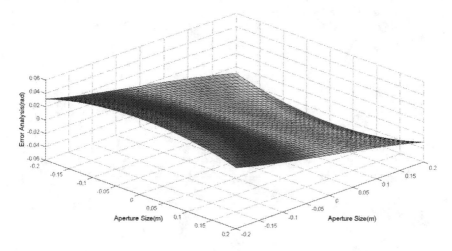

Fig. 8. Error distribution of phase for TOA and SP

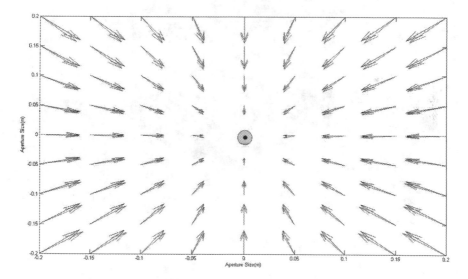

Fig. 9. Gradient and normal of the phases wave-front

3.2 Simulation of Extended Target

Here we use two TOA on array to simulate the extended target with two SC. Each TOA generates a SC. According to the derivation in the One-point target simulation, the synthetic electric field intensity on the seeker's aperture is $|E_k(x,y,z)|$ and the phase is $\beta_k(x,y,z)$ (k = 1,2). $|E_k(x,y,z)|$ and $\beta_k(x,y,z)$ obey Eq. (6) and (7). Thus the synthetic electric field intensity of two TOA is

$$E(x,y,z) = |E_1(x,y,z)|\exp[j\beta_1(x,y,z)] + |E_2(x,y,z)|\exp[j\beta_2(x,y,z)] \quad (8)$$

So

$$|E(x,y,z)|$$
$$= \sqrt{|E(x,y,z)|^2 + |E(x,y,z)|^2 + 2|E_1(x,y,z)||E_2(x,y,z)|\cos[\beta_1(x,y,z) - \beta_2(x,y,z)]}$$
$$(9)$$

$$\beta(x,y,z) = a\tan\frac{E_1(x,y,z)\sin\beta_1(x,y,z) + E_2(x,y,z)\sin\beta_2(x,y,z)}{E_1(x,y,z)\cos\beta_1(x,y,z) + E_2(x,y,z)\cos\beta_2(x,y,z)} \quad (10)$$

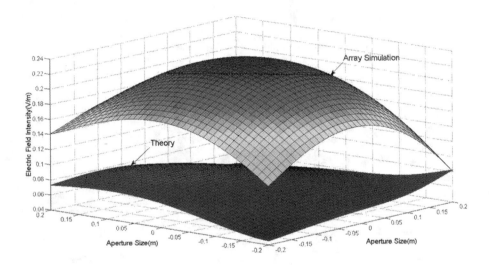

Fig. 10. Electric field intensity distribution of TOA and extended target

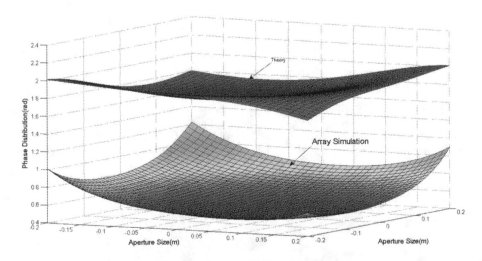

Fig. 11. Phase distribution of TOA and extended target

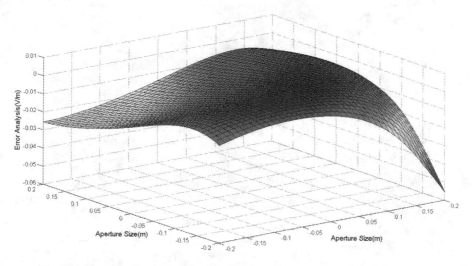

Fig. 12. Error distribution of electric filed intensity for TOA and extended target

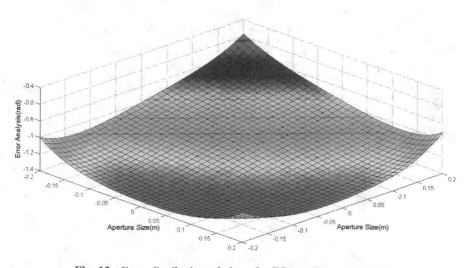

Fig. 13. Error distribution of phase for TOA and extended target

Based on the above inference, the two SC are separated from each other with 10mrad in azimuth and −10mrad in elevation. The distribution of intensity and phase of the synthetic electric field are shown in Figs. 10 and 11. "Array Simulation" denotes the result generated by TOA and "Theory" denotes the result generated by SP, which is the real electromagnetic field radiated from extended target with two SC in the space.

The error distribution of electric field intensity and phase are shown in Figs. 12 and 13. The average error of electric field intensity is -7×10^{-3}, twice as which of One-point, and variance is 8.6×10^{-3}, 4 times as which of One-point. The average

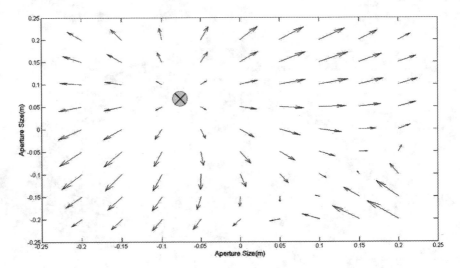

Fig. 14. Gradient and normal of the phases wave-front for extended target

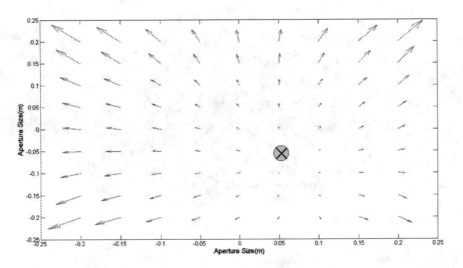

Fig. 15. Gradient and normal of the phases wave-front for TOA

error of phase is −1.1537, up to 20000 times larger than which of One-point, and variance is 0.1539, almost 6 times larger than which of One-point.

We can see clearly from Figs. 14 and 15, the gradient and normal of the Phases Wave-front for TOA and extended target respectively, that the direction gradient and normal are totally different. In that way, TOA array cannot satisfy the precision of extended target simulation.

In sum, the far-filed correction is absolutely necessary for extended target simulation, the processing of which is shown in Fig. 16 错误!未找到引用源.

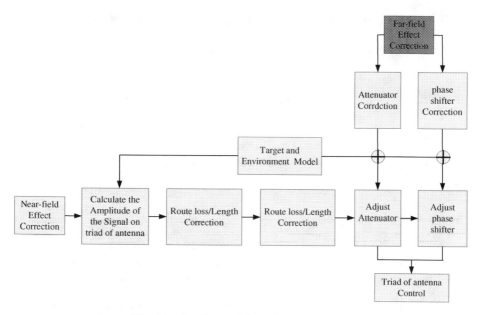

Fig. 16. Amplitude-phase control processing

4 Conclusion

This paper analyzes target simulation in MMWSS making use of TOA array and give the conclusion that the far-field correction is needed because TOA array can simulate One-point target effectively but un-effectively for extended target.

References

1. Zhao, H.: Analysis on credibility of radar seeker hardware-in-loop simulation systems. Ship Electron. Eng. **35**(4), 90–92 (2015)
2. Li, H., Zhou, J., Gong, S., Ben, D.: Modeling and analysis of errors on array hardware-in-loop RF simulation systems. J. Syst. Simul. **35**(6), 77–81 (2013)
3. Xi, Y., Zhang, J., Gao, W., Liu, Y.: Low cost HILS system of radar seeker and application. Fire Control Radar Technol. **39**(1), 12–15 (2010)
4. Wei, H-l, Wang, Z-m, Liu, Z-z, Li, Z-w: Problems and principles of simulation fidelity evaluation. J. Syst. Simul. **12**(1), 14–19 (2000)
5. Duan, S-z, Ma, X-l, Liu, L.: Radar EW test simulation control model and verification. Comput. Simul. **23**(4), 46–49 (2006)

Vessel Routing for Sweeping of Marine Litter in a Port Area

Maurits C.M. van Tol, Mark B. Duinkerken$^{(\boxtimes)}$, Gabriel Lodewijks, and Rudy R. Negenborn

Department of Maritime and Transport Technology,
Delft University of Technology, Delft, The Netherlands
m.b.duinkerken@tudelft.nl

Abstract. Marine litter in port areas has a huge negative environmental impact and poses a risk to vessels. Therefore port authorities are using special vessels for sweeping. Nowadays, these vessels are usually only deployed after complaints on excessive amounts of marine litter. In this paper an innovative routing method is proposed to sweep marine litter in a port area proactively. The routing method is formulated as a mixed-integer programming (MIP) model. In order to test the sweeping model a dynamic model is developed that predicts the locations in the port area where marine litter will accumulate depending on factors like supply, physical dimensions of port compartments and wind directions. To benchmark the performance of the sweeping model simulations are performed comparing the routing method with other more intuitive policies. It is concluded that using the sweeping policy lower litter levels can be achieved at lower costs.

Keywords: Inventory routing problem · Mixed integer programming · Discrete event simulation · Marine litter

1 Introduction

Marine litter is any persistent, manufactured or processed solid material that is discarded, disposed of or abandoned in the marine and coastal environment [1]. This human-created waste is deliberately or accidentally released in the marine environment. It is estimated that between 6.4 million to 7 billion tonnes of litter enters the oceans each year [2]. Marine litter includes a wide range of materials, but plastics account by far for the most predominant share (60 to 80 % [3]). Plastic litter forms a serious environmental threat to marine animals. They are affected in various ways by plastic litter, such as entanglement and ingestion [4].

A huge portion of marine debris originates from land based sources and end up in rivers and canals. Since seaports usually are strategically situated with an inland waterway connection, it is not surprising that seaports have to deal with marine litter. Besides the negative environmental impact, marine litter also

© Springer Science+Business Media Singapore 2016
L. Zhang et al. (Eds.): AsiaSim 2016/SCS AutumnSim 2016, Part III, CCIS 645, pp. 344–355, 2016.
DOI: 10.1007/978-981-10-2669-0_38

poses risks to vessels in port areas. Incidents with marine litter are reported wherein propellers, anchors and rudders were fouled or intake pipes and valves were blocked [5].

The objectives of port authorities with respect to marine litter, the condition of marine litter in a port area and the availability of cleaning vessels determine which sweeping policy is suitable to fulfil these objectives. Concerning the condition of marine litter in a port area two extremes can be distinguished. One extreme is the condition wherein marine litter is present everywhere in very large amounts. The other extreme is the condition wherein marine litter is not a day-to-day problem and sweeping of marine litter one day in the year, for example, is fulfilling needs. This research considers the condition of marine litter in-between these two extremes, whereby the number of cleaning vessels is limited and the objective of sweeping marine litter is to avert excessive amounts of marine litter and accompanying complaints. In this way the risk posed to vessels and the negative environmental impact of marine litter is reduced. Nowadays, these vessels are usually only deployed after complaints on excessive amounts of marine litter.

Because the number of cleaning vessels is considered limited, minimization of the distance travelled is demanded. For minimization of the distance travelled, the distribution of the marine litter over the water surface is of importance. A prediction model for the location and accumulation of marine litter in a port area could be used as input for sweeping of marine litter. Various earlier research has been performed with respect to the spatial distribution of marine litter, e.g. [6–8]. According to [7], many factors can influence the spatial distribution of marine litter. Factors are mentioned like wind, wave-action and tides. Research considering the spatial distribution of marine litter has in common that accumulation sites (or hot spots) are present. At these sites, the marine litter tends to accumulate. A prediction model could make use of, for example, meteorological data, tides forecasts and visual inspection by drones.

Given that the locations of marine litter are dispersed, a cleaning vessel must address multiple locations over a certain time span. To avert excessive amounts of marine litter at these locations while minimizing the distance travelled a routing method may be used. This routing method deploys the vessel along the geographically dispersed hot spots in the port area while making use of information with respect to the spatial distribution of marine litter. The main contribution of this paper is the proposal of a routing method that averts excessive amounts of marine litter (and accompanying complaints) while minimizing the distance travelled, given a number of vessels. This routing method makes use of input from a prediction model considering the location and accumulation of marine litter.

This paper is organized as follows. In Sect. 2 a literature review is given. In Sect. 3 a prediction model for litter accumulation and a MIP model for the routing of sweeping vessels are proposed. In Sect. 4 both models are applied to a case in a simulation study. Section 5 contains the conclusions and recommendations for future research.

2   Overview of Existing Literature

2.1   Spatial Distribution of Marine Litter

Cleassens et al. performed a research to investigate the occurrence and distribution of microplastics [9]. Measurements of the concentration of microplastics in the marine sediments of three coastal seaports in Belgium were performed. From measurements it appeared that partially enclosed port areas (i.e. port compartments) exhibit the highest abundance of microplastics. This could be partially related to the geometry of the port compartments [9]. The water movement depends on various factors, such as geometric factors like port shape [10], entrance geometry [11] and internal structures [12], but also non-geometric factors like tides and the density of water [13]. In [13] it is stated that one or more vertical vortices (i.e. circulations) occur in the port compartments. This is caused by the river flowing by and therefore is called the flow effect. According to [9] microplastics could get trapped into these vortices, instead of flushing out of the port. This is an explanation for the measured high abundance of microplastics in the port compartments.

2.2   Marine Litter Sweeping as an Inventory Routing Problem

A cleaning vessel must address multiple locations over a certain time span. Due to the continuous supply of marine litter by rivers, the amount of litter accumulates at the hot spots over time. For our case, we consider an Inventory Routing Problem [14] as a collection problem rather than a delivery problem [15]. In the collection version of an IRP problem goods are produced at the customers. To prevent reaching maximum inventory level goods are collected at the customers and brought to a central facility. In other words, a hot spot can be seen as a producing customer. The consideration of the IRP as a collection problem corresponds to the situation wherein marine litter is collected by means of a cleaning vessel and brought to a central facility. The limited storage capacity at the customers is represented by setting a boundary value for the amount of marine litter per hot spot. In the end, the IRP is able to take into account a routing aspect and the accumulation of marine litter together for deploying cleaning vessels along hot spots in the port area. Because of the uncertainty in the accumulation process the concept of stochastic IRP [16, 17] becomes relevant.

3   Modelling of Litter Accumulation and Sweeping

Two different models are presented in this paper. The first model predicts the amount of marine litter that will accumulate in the different hot spots of the port area. This is a dynamic model that can be used to simulate the litter distribution over a longer period of time. The Marine Litter Sweeping model (MLS-model) is a mathematical model that determines the optimal routing for sweeping vessels.

3.1 Prediction Model for Accumulation of Litter

A basic prediction model for the location and accumulation of marine litter is developed. Partially enclosed port areas (i.e. port compartments) exhibit the highest abundance of microplastics. Therefore the prediction model assumes that the hot spots are situated in the port compartments (see Fig. 1). The hot spots are regarded as nodes in a network.

Fig. 1. Assigned nodes in port or Rotterdam

For the accumulation rate per node a tree structure is assumed, consisting of a main waterway and dead end branches. The port compartments are situated in the branches. The accumulation of marine litter in a port compartment depends on the supply of marine litter via main waterway. A fraction of the marine litter that is present in the main waterway flows into a port compartment. The fraction of marine litter that flows into a port compartment depends on the entrance width of the port compartment, mutual situation of port compartments along the main waterway and wind direction. It is also assumed that the marine litter that flows into a port compartment does not flow back into the main waterway. The realizations for the supply of marine litter are generated random numbers for a Weibull distribution. The realizations for the wind direction are generated random numbers for a discrete distribution with four possible outcomes (North, East, South, West).

3.2 Marine Litter Sweeping Model

In this section the Marine Litter Sweeping (MLS) model is proposed. Consider a directed graph $G = (N, E)$ that consists of the set of nodes $N = \{1, 2, \ldots, n\}$ and the set of edges $E = \{(i, j): i, j \in N, i \neq j\}$. Node 1 represents the central facility and the nodes of $N' = N \backslash \{1\}$ represent the geographically dispersed hot spots. In this graph vessels remove marine litter at the nodes and transport it to the central facility. The elements c_{ij} of distance matrix C provide the distance associated with traversing edge $(i, j) \in E$. The planning horizon is defined as length h and is divided in discrete periods $t \in T = \{0, 1, \ldots, h\}$. The first period $t = 0$ only serves the purpose of initialization of the model, while the periods in

$T' = T \backslash \{0\}$ represent the 'actual' planning horizon. The set of vessels is denoted with $k \in V = \{1, 2, \ldots, g\}$. The capacity of the vessel is denoted with q, the average vessel speed is denoted with v and the average sweeping rate of the vessel is denoted with e. The average sweeping rate is the average rate at which the cleaning vessel removes marine litter from the water. The accumulation of marine litter during period $t \in T$ of node i is denoted with ξ_i^t. The initial amount of marine litter of node i is denoted with m_i^0 and the amount of marine litter at the end of period t is denoted with m_i^t. The available (working) time per period per vessel is denoted with w. A boundary value for the amount of marine litter per node is set by $m_{thres,i}$. Each scenario s has a certain probability p_s. The set of scenarios is denoted with $S = \{1, 2, \ldots, d\}$.

Objective Function. The objective function (1) minimizes of the sum of the transport cost and the expected penalty cost. The transport cost are the cost associated with travelling between the nodes, whereby a travelling cost p_t is incurred per distance unit. To avert excessive amounts of marine litter at nodes, marine litter should be removed timely at the hot spots. To determine which amounts of marine litter are excessive, a marine litter threshold is set per node. The situation wherein the amount of marine litter at a node is below this threshold is considered acceptable, while it is considered undesirable if the amount of marine litter at a node exceeds this threshold. This is reflected in the objective function by imposing a penalty cost if a marine litter threshold is exceeded. The relative importance of the penalty cost in the objective function is set by a weight p_c. If the marine litter threshold is exceeded, also the degree of this exceedance is of importance. The higher the exceedance, the higher the urgency to remove marine litter at this location. This is reflected in the objective function by imposing a penalty cost that increases linear with the surplus of marine litter. Please note that the penalty cost are fictive cost and are only present in the model to form an incentive to sweep marine litter. The desired efficacy of the model can fine tuned by adjusting the transport cost, penalty cost and marine litter threshold parameters.

Constraints. Constraints (2) define the amount of marine litter at the nodes. Constraints (3) impose that the marine litter retrieved by a vessel does not exceed the vessel capacity. Above that, they impose that if one or multiple nodes are served ($x_i^{kt} > 0$) by a vessel, the central facility must be visited by that vessel. Constraints (4) impose that if a node is served by a vessel ($x_i^{kt} > 0$), the node is visited by that vessel ($z_i^{kt} = 1$). The constraint allows for the amount of marine litter removed to be larger than the threshold. Constraints (5) impose that the time required to execute the routes and serve the nodes does not exceed the available time for each vessel. Constraints (6) and (7) are routing constraints. The first set of constraints imposes that if a node is visited, one edge must be traversed to arrive at that node. The latter set of constraints imposes that one edge must be traversed to leave the node if it is visited.

$$\min \sum_{t=1}^{h}\sum_{k=1}^{g}\sum_{i=1}^{n}\sum_{j=1,j\neq i}^{n} p_t c_{ij} y_{ij}^{kt} +$$

$$\sum_{s=1}^{d}\sum_{t=1}^{h}\sum_{i=1}^{n} p_s p_c \max\{0, m_i^{t(s)} - m_{thres,i}\} \tag{1}$$

subjected to:

$$m_i^{t(s)} = m_i^{t-1(s)} - \sum_{k=1}^{g} x_i^{kt(s)} + \xi_i^{t(s)}$$

$$\forall i \in N', t \in T', s \in S \tag{2}$$

$$\sum_{i=2}^{n} x_i^{kt(s)} \leq q z_1^{kt} \quad \forall k \in V, t \in T', s \in S \tag{3}$$

$$x_i^{kt(s)} \leq q z_i^{kt} \quad \forall i \in N', k \in V, t \in T', s \in S \tag{4}$$

$$\sum_{i=2}^{n} \frac{x_i^{kt(s)}}{e} + \sum_{i=1}^{n}\sum_{j=1,j\neq i}^{n} \frac{y_{ij}^{kt} c_{ij}}{v} \leq w$$

$$\forall t \in T', k \in V, s \in S \tag{5}$$

$$\sum_{i=1,i\neq j}^{n} y_{ij}^{kt} = z_j^{kt} \quad \forall j \in N, k \in V, t \in T' \tag{6}$$

$$\sum_{j=1,j\neq i}^{n} y_{ij}^{kt} = z_i^{kt} \quad \forall i \in N, k \in V, t \in T' \tag{7}$$

$$u_i^{kt} - u_j^{kt} + q y_{ij}^{kt} \leq q - x_j^{kt(s)}$$

$$\forall i \in N', j \in N', j \neq i, k \in V, t \in T', s \in S \tag{8}$$

$$x_i^{kt(s)} \geq 0 \quad \forall i \in N',, k \in V, t \in T', s \in S \tag{9}$$

$$x_i^{kt(s)} \leq m_i^{t-1(s)} \quad \forall i \in N', k \in V, t \in T', s \in S \tag{10}$$

$$y_{ij}^{kt} \in \{0,1\} \quad \forall i \in N, j \in N, j \neq i, k \in V, t \in T' \tag{11}$$

$$z_i^{kt} \in \{0,1\} \quad \forall i \in N, k \in V, t \in T' \tag{12}$$

$$m_i^{t(s)} \geq 0 \quad \forall i \in N', t \in T, s \in S \tag{13}$$

$$x_i^{kt(s)} \leq u_i^{kt} \leq q \quad \forall i \in N', k \in V, t \in T', s \in S \tag{14}$$

Constraints (8) also are routing constraints. These are subtour elimination constraints. To knowledge of the author, a reformulation of the classical subtour elimination constraints for the TSP as proposed by [18] (often referred to as DFJ) is used throughout literature considering the IRP. However, it is known that this formulation results in a relative large number of constraints. Therefore, a reformulation of the subtour elimination for the TSP (often referred to as MTZ) as formulated by [19] is proposed. At the cost of introducing continuous variables,

Table 1. Decision variables

$x_i^{kt(s)}$	amount of marine litter removed of node
y_{ij}^{kt}	edge is traversed or not by vessel
z_i^{kt}	node is visited or not by vessel
$m_i^{t(s)}$	amount of marine litter at node
u_i^{kt}	dummy variable

the number of constraints is reduced with respect to the MTZ formulation. The MTZ formulation is extended to the VRP by [20]. This formulation is extended to suit the specific needs of an IRP, as shown in Constraints (8). Constraints (14) define the introduced continuous variables.

All decision variables are listed in Table 1. Constraints (9) to (14) define the decision variables. Constraints (9) and (10) consider the amount of marine litter removed. The first set of constraints are incorporated because the amount of marine litter removed at a node may not become negative. The latter set is incorporated because the accumulation of marine litter is not an instantaneous process. So the actual amount of marine litter present depends on the time of arrival during a period. To limit that vessels are assigned to remove more marine litter than is actually present, these conservative constraints are used. Constraints (13) define that the amount of marine litter at the nodes may not become negative. Constraints (14) define the introduced continuous variables for the subtour elimination constraints.

3.3   Simulation of Sweeping Policies

To benchmark the performance of the MLS model in the long-term, simulations are performed. In the simulation discrete periods are distinguished. A period is assumed to be one day. We consider three sweeping policies: MLS, on demand (OD), and fixed routes (FR).

MLS Policy. For the MLS model a rolling horizon simulation is proposed. After initialization the main loop is repeated until a termination condition is met. In Sect. 3.1 a model is described to predict the accumulation of marine litter. In the main loop, first a prediction is made for the coming h periods with this model. The prediction forms input for the MLS model. Subsequently, the MIP as presented in Sect. 3.2 is used to derive a routing scheme for the coming h periods. Next, only the solution determined for period t_{sim} is executed. Finally, one complete time step of the simulation is finished. All described steps are repeated until the termination condition is met.

On Demand Policy. During the on demand policy marine litter only is removed at a node after the marine litter threshold is exceeded at that node.

This reflects a reactive policy wherein marine litter only is removed after complaints on excessive amounts of marine litter. In other words, if the threshold is exceeded it is assumed that a complaint is received. If the threshold is exceeded, the corresponding nodes are added to a queue. The nodes are added to this queue in random order to model the arrival of complaints during a day. If the queue is not empty, the first g nodes from the queue are assigned to g vessels based on first-come-first-serve (FCFS). After a node is assigned to a vessel, that node is removed from the queue. For these nodes the maximum amount of marine litter that can be removed at that node is determined. Hereto the limiting factor of three aspects is considered: time, vessel capacity and marine litter present. For the factor time the available time and the time required to travel back to the central facility is considered. Subsequently the nodes are visited and the determined maximum amount of marine litter is removed. The vessels that are not assigned to a node will stay at the central facility. Next, it is registered when a vessel finishes its task. For the vessel that finishes first, it is determined whether the nearest node (with respect to current position) from the queue can be served. Hereto, the remaining time for each vessel is checked. The remaining time must at least be two times larger than the time required to travel to the node and back to the central facility. These steps are also executed for the vessels that finish serving their assigned node after the first vessel did. If the remaining time is not sufficient, the vessel is returned to the central facility. Once returned, the vessel will stay at the central facility for the remainder of the period.

Fixed Routes Policy. The third policy is the fixed routes (FR). Like the MLS policy, the FR policy proactively sweeps marine litter. Hereto the FR policy makes use of predetermined fixed routes, which are based on clustering. To each cluster of nodes one vessel is assigned. For each cluster a shortest TSP route is determined. A vessel travels its route every period of the simulation, whereby the route is alternately travelled clockwise and anticlockwise. Based on the length of the route, a limit is set on the time a vessel may spend on serving a node. A time limit is derived by subtracting the time required to travel a route from the available time and equally distributing the remainder over the nodes in the cluster. If all the marine litter at a node is removed and the time limit is not reached, the remainder is used to equally raise the time limit of the nodes in the cluster that are not served yet. Every period the time limit will be reset to its original value. To cluster the nodes, use is made of k-means clustering (also known as Lloyds algorithm or Voronoi iteration).

4   Case Study: Port of Rotterdam

The proposed model is evaluated by applying it in a case study on the port of Rotterdam. The results presented in this section are determined using an Intel Core i5-4200M 2.50 GHz processor and 3 GB DDR3 available working memory. A solution for the MIP model is constructed using CPLEX. The solution process is stopped if a feasible integer solution is found which is proven to be within 5 % of optimality.

Table 2. Parameters applied for MLS policy

n	10	w	8 h
h	3 days	p_c	35 €/kg
v	12 km/h	p_t	50 €/km
e	10 kg/h	d	1
m_i^0	0 kg	p_s	1

In the case study the input from the prediction model for the MLS model is considered deterministic $(d = 1)$. Hereby it is assumed that the prediction of marine litter accumulation is equal to the realization. In other words, the accumulation of marine litter during the near future (up and to the length of the planning horizon) is known with certainty. In this experiment multiple replication simulation runs are performed, with each a different random seed for generating random numbers for the supply of marine litter and the wind direction. The parameters applied are listed in Table 2. In this case study 10 nodes are considered, as shown in Fig. 1.

To gain insight into the performance of the three policies Fig. 2 is shown. The plots show the remaining amount of marine litter in the system for different policies, which is the total accumulated marine litter minus the total removed marine litter. The plots also show the amount of marine litter accumulated per day and the sum of the marine litter thresholds. In the figure it can be seen that the remaining amount of marine litter in the system reaches a steady state condition for the MLS and OD policy after a start up period of around 20 days. For the FR policy the remaining amount of marine litter is nearly equal to the accumulation. In other words, marine litter is usually removed soon (the next day) after accumulation. An explanation for the start up period and the different levels of remaining marine litter are the marine litter thresholds. For this amount of marine litter (nearly) no incentive is present to be removed in case of the MLS and OD policy. This causes the start up period and different levels of remaining marine litter.

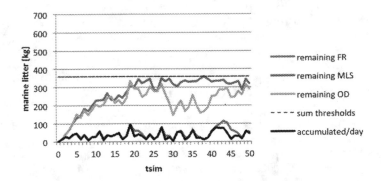

Fig. 2. Amounts of marine litter over time

Table 3. Statistics benchmark (10 replications)

policy	travelled [km/day]		removed [kg/day]		remaining [kg]		complaints [1/day]		exceedance [kg]	
	μ	σ	μ	σ	μ	σ	μ	σ	μ	σ
FR	37.6	0	120	5.32	234	32.9	1.88	0.15	111	28.4
MLS	16.8	0.45	120	5.01	366	26.4	1.83	0.52	38.6	18.1
OD	11.9	0.83	120	4.65	348	36.7	3.06	0.27	110	30.4

For the simulations a duration of 120 days is applied; while for the performance evaluation only the results of the last 100 days (after the start up period) are considered. The minimum number of vessels for feasible operation is taken as starting point for the comparison. To determine whether a configuration is feasible (i.e. able to maintain the remaining amount of marine litter in the system stable), δ is defined as the marine litter in the system at the end of last day minus the marine litter in the system at the start of day 21. By assuming that δ is normally distributed, a 95 % confidence interval for the mean of δ can be determined. If the lower- and upper bound are small (<1 %) compared to the total accumulation over 120 days, the configuration is considered feasible. Based on this analysis, it is determined that 4 vessels are required for the FR policy and 2 vessels for the MLS and OD policy, with the same properties for all vessels.

Statistics of the replication runs are listed in Table 3. In this table five performance indicators are listed: number of kilometres travelled per day, number of kilograms marine litter removed per day, remaining amount of marine litter in the system, number of complaints per day and exceedance of the marine litter threshold. Every day the number of complaints is determined once, whereby at maximum one complaint is registered per node per day. In Sect. 3.2 it is described that the higher the exceedance of the marine litter threshold, the higher the urgency to remove marine litter at this location. Since exceeding the marine litter threshold is considered equivalent to receiving a complaint, the exceedance is a measure for the urgency of a complaint.

From Table 3 it can be seen that both the MLS and the FR policy succeed similarly in preventing complaints on excessive amounts of marine litter by proactively sweeping marine litter. On average the number of complaints reduced by around 40 %. However, if the exceedance is considered, it can be seen that on average the urgency of the complaints is around 65 % lower for the MLS policy compared to FR and OD policy. The table also shows that while applying the FR policy, on average a large distance is travelled compared to the other policies. The average distance travelled is around 55 % lower for the MLS policy and around 70 % lower for the OD policy. If the amount of marine litter removed per day is considered, on average the same amount is removed. This expected because only feasible configurations are considered.

Lastly, if the remaining amount of marine litter is considered, it can be seen that on average the number of kilograms marine litter present in the water is around 50 % higher for the OD and MLS policy. An explanation for this difference is the incorporation of marine litter thresholds in the OD and MLS policy. As described in Sect. 3.2, the situation wherein the amount of marine litter at a node is below a threshold is considered acceptable, while it is undesirable if the amount of marine litter at a node is above this threshold. For the amounts of marine litter below these thresholds, (nearly) no incentive is present to be removed in case of the MLS and OD policy. This can also be seen in Fig. 2. This causes the average number of kilograms marine litter is close to the sum of the marine litter thresholds (360 kg) for the MLS and OD policy. Thus, these policies succeed on average in maintaining the remaining amount of marine litter close to an acceptable level, while the FR policy on average realizes a lower remaining amount of marine litter than strictly necessary.

5   Conclusions and Future Research

Port authorities would like to avert excessive amounts of marine litter with a limited number of cleaning vessels. In this paper an innovative routing method is proposed to sweep marine litter in a port area proactively. This routing method makes use of input from a prediction model considering the location and accumulation of marine litter. To benchmark the performance of the routing method, simulations are performed.

In a case study the performance is compared with the performance of two other sweeping polices. An advantage of developed routing method is that excessive amounts of marine litter and accompanying complaints are averted while the complaints are less urgent and less distance is travelled in comparison with a fixed routes sweeping policy. In perspective of the objective of this research, the benchmark shows that qualitative good predictions for the location and accumulation of marine litter is of added value for sweeping of marine litter in a port area.

For future research it is recommended to further study the spatial distribution of marine litter in a port area. In this model it is assumed that the marine litter that flows into a port compartment does not flow back into the main waterway. It is expected, however, that some marine litter will flow back into the main waterway and will subsequently be discharged into sea. This 'leaking' of marine litter should be added to the prediction model.

References

1. Marine Litter: An analytical overview. United Nations Environment Programme (2005)
2. Cheshire, A., Adler, E.: UNEP/IOC Guidelines on Survey and Monitoring of Marine Litter (2009)
3. Gregory, M.R., Ryan, P.G.: Pelagic plastics and other seaborne persistent synthetic debris: a review of southern hemisphere perspectives. In: Coe, J.M., Rogers, D.B. (eds.) Marine Debris. Springer Series on Environmental Management, pp. 49–66. Springer, New York (1997)

4. Derraik, J.G.B.: The pollution of the marine environment by plastic debris: a review. Mar. Pollut. Bull. **44**(9), 842–852 (2002)
5. Mouat, J., Lozano, R.L., Bateson, H.: Economic Impacts of Marine Litter. KIMO (Kommunenes Internasjonale Miljøorganisasjon), (2010)
6. Hinojosa, I.A., Rivadeneira, M.M., Thiel, M.: Temporal and spatial distribution of floating objects in coastal waters of central-southern Chile and Patagonian fjords. Cont. Shelf Res. **31**(3), 172–186 (2011)
7. Browne, M.A., Galloway, T.S., Thompson, R.C.: Spatial patterns of plastic debris along estuarine shorelines. Environ. Sci. Technol. **44**(9), 3404–3409 (2010)
8. Dameron, O.J., Parke, M., Albins, M.A., Brainard, R.: Marine debris accumulation in the Northwestern Hawaiian Islands: an examination of rates and processes. Mar. Pollut. Bull. **54**(4), 423–433 (2007)
9. Claessens, M., De Meester, S., Van Landuyt, L., De Clerck, K., Janssen, C.R.: Occurrence and distribution of microplastics in marine sediments along the Belgian coast. Mar. Pollut. Bull. **62**(10), 2199–2204 (2011)
10. Jiang, J.X., Falconer, R.A.: On the tidal exchange characteristics of model rectangular harbours. Proc. Inst. Civ. Eng. Part 2 Res. Theory **75**(3), 475–489 (1983)
11. Yin, J., Falconer, R.A., Chen, Y., Probert, S.D.: Water and sediment movements in harbours. Appl. Energy **67**(3), 341–352 (2000)
12. Jung, K.H., Chang, K.A., Huang, E.T.: Two-dimensional flow characteristics of wave interactions with a free-rolling rectangular structure. Ocean Eng. **32**(1), 1–20 (2005)
13. Stoschek, O., Zimmermann, C.: Water exchange and sedimentation in an estuarine tidal harbor using three-dimensional simulation. J. Waterw. Port Coast. Ocean Eng. **132**(5), 410–414 (2006)
14. Coelho, L.C., Laporte, G.: Thirty years of inventory routing. Transp. Sci. **48**(1), 1–19 (2013)
15. Andersson, H., Hoff, A., Christiansen, M., Hasle, G., Lokketangen, A.: Industrial aspects and literature survey: combined inventory management and routing. Comput. Oper. Res. **37**(9), 1515–1536 (2010)
16. Birge, J.R., Louveaux, F.: Introduction to Stochastic Programming. Springer, New York (2011)
17. Solyali, O., Cordeau, J.F., Laporte, G.: Robust inventory routing under demand uncertainty. Transp. Sci. **46**(3), 327–340 (2012)
18. Dantzig, G., Fulkerson, R., Johnson, S.: Solution of a large-scale traveling-salesman problem. J. Oper. Res. Soc. Am. **2**(4), 393–410 (1954)
19. Miller, C.E., Tucker, A.W., Zemlin, R.A.: Integer programming formulation of traveling salesman problems. J. ACM **7**(4), 326–329 (1960)
20. Desrochers, M., Laporte, G.: Improvements and extensions to the Miller-Tucker-Zemlin subtour elimination constraints. Oper. Res. Lett. **10**(1), 27–36 (1991)

A Comparison and Validation of Atmosphere CO_2 Concentration OCO-2-Based Observations and TCCON-Based Observations

Jun Meng, Gangyi Ding[✉], Laiyang Liu, and Rui Zhang

School of Software, Beijing Institute of Technology, Beijing, China
{mengjun,dgy,mail,zhang_rui}@bit.edu.cn

Abstract. This paper's work collected the OCO-2 observation data and four TCCON observation sites' data at the same time (2014.9–2015.8). Through the design of a data's space matching method of latitude and longitude, the complicated netcdf files were processed. We extracted simplified data set from netcdf files and dumped them to the common format files. In the latter part of this paper, we compared the spatial and temporal variation characteristics of atmospheric CO_2 concentration data which verified the uncertainty and rationality of the satellite observations and the ground observations.

Keywords: CO_2 concentration · netcdf file processing · OCO-2 · TCCON · Data matching

1 Introduction

Although the ground-based observation's data accuracy is higher, it is restricted by the number of observation sites. In contrast, although the satellite-based observation is not limited by geographical conditions, the data accuracy is lower. It is significant to compare and verify the atmosphere CO_2 concentration OCO-2-based observations and TCCON-based observations. This paper's work collected the OCO-2-based observation data and four TCCON observation sites' data at the same time (2014.9–2015.8). Through the design of a data's space matching method of latitude and longitude, the complicated netcdf files were processed. We extracted simplified data set from netcdf files and dumped them to the common format files. Finally, we compared the spatial and temporal variation characteristics of atmospheric CO_2 concentration data which verified the uncertainty and rationality of the satellite observations and the ground observations. It also provided a new data support for the study of atmospheric CO_2 concentration.

In January 2009, Japan successfully launched the GOSAT satellite which was specifically for greenhouse gases CO_2 and CH_4 detection. At present, the research progress on CO_2 concentration GOSAT-based observations is very fast. Liping Lei and others had compared the CO_2 concentration GOSAT-based with the CO_2 concentration which simulated by GEOS-Chem model, and they also analyzed and evaluate the error of the retrieved results; the data retrieval accuracy of GOSAT and TCCON were verified by Miao Zhang et al. However, the research progress on OCO-2-based observation was

© Springer Science+Business Media Singapore 2016
L. Zhang et al. (Eds.): AsiaSim 2016/SCS AutumnSim 2016, Part III, CCIS 645, pp. 356–363, 2016.
DOI: 10.1007/978-981-10-2669-0_39

relatively slow. In order to accelerate the progress of related research work, it was necessary to compare and verify the atmosphere CO$_2$ concentration OCO-2-based observations and TCCON-based observations.

In this paper, the main contributions were as follows:

- A method for data's space matching of latitude and longitude was designed.
- The complicated netcdf files were processed. We extracted simplified data set from netcdf files and dumped the simplified data set to the common format files.
- We compared the two kinds of spatial and temporal variation characteristics of atmospheric CO$_2$ concentration data, which verified the uncertainty and rationality of the satellite observation and the ground observation.

2   Data Collections

2.1   Data Sources

The Total Carbon Column Observing Network (TCCON) is a network of ground-based Fourier Transform Spectrometers that record spectra of the sun in the near-infrared. From these spectra, accurate and precise column-averaged abundances of atmospheric constituents including CO$_2$, CH$_4$, N$_2$O, HF, CO, H$_2$O, and HDO, are retrieved. In this paper, the retrieval algorithm of CO$_2$ dry air mixture ratio was provided by Washenfelder et al. Although most TCCON site had been running for a long time, and got a large amount of data, but since the OCO-2 satellite was launched in July 2014, in order to ensure that sufficient data sets can be obtained for the comparative study, so the observation sites need to be screened. In this paper, the CO$_2$ concentration data (from September 2014 to August 2015) of four TCCON ground observation sites were collected. The sites distribution map was as shown below:

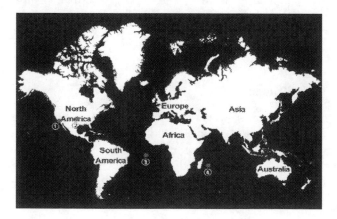

Fig. 1.   A distribution map of four sites

As shown in Fig. 1, the location of observation site1 is Pasadena, CA, USA (34.136N, 118.127W); the location of observation site2 is Lamont, OK, USA (36.604N, 97.486W);

the location of observation site3 is Ascension Island (7.9165S, 14.3325W); the location of observation site4 is Reunion Island (20.901S, 55.485E).

At the same time, the OCO-2 observation data (from September 2014 to August 2015) provided by NASA were collected, and the data product's version was OCO-2 Lite Product v7.

2.2 Data Matching

On the spatial scale, the data obtained by the OCO-2 had a lot of blank zone in the space. This may be caused by the influence of sensor's observation mode or the influence of cloud. In order to obtain an appropriate comparison data sets, we put each ground observation site as the center of the circle, and set 3° as the land surface distance radius. Due to the collection of observation sites were in different geographic locations, the 1° longitude corresponding to land surface distance and the 1° latitude corresponding to land surface distance were probably not equal. In order to guarantee the four ground-based observation sites' sampling range equal as far as possible, it needed to make the following treatment: Because the earth is an almost standard ellipsoid, if we assume that the earth is a perfect sphere, then its radius is the average radius of the earth (about 6371.393 km). If the meridian at 0° as a datum, we can calculate the land surface distance between any two points according to the latitude and longitude of them. Known two points' latitude and longitude, the approximate formula for calculating the land surface distance of two points is as follows. Assuming point A (latitude α_1, longitude β_1) and point B (latitude α_2, longitude β_2):

$$\Delta = 111.199\sqrt{\left(\alpha_1 - \alpha_2\right)^2 + \left(\beta_1 - \beta_2\right)^2 \cos^2\left(\left(\alpha_1 + \alpha_2\right)/2\right)} \tag{1}$$

In the formula (1), the Δ is the land surface distance between point A and point B. In this paper, the value of the data range is $\Delta/111.199 \leq 3$.

3 Data Processing

3.1 Data Storage Structures

The format of the netcdf data set is not fixed, and it is defined by the user according to the requirements. A netcdf data set contains (dimensions, variables and attributes) three kinds of description types, and each type is assigned a name and an ID which together describe a data set. The structure of a netcdf file includes the following objects (Table 1):

- Dimensions: A dimension corresponds to an independent variable in the function. A dimension has a name and scope, and its length is basically limited. A netcdf file can only has one dimension with infinite length.
- Variables: Variables correspond to the real physical data. Every variable is a single value function, and time as its independent variable.
- Attributes: Attributes describe the physical meaning of the variables and dimensions.

Table 1. The structure of netcdf file

Objects	Description
Dimensions	Dimension information of variables
Variables	Store the actual data
Attributes	Auxiliary information attribute

3.2 Data Processing Method

The netcdf files store a large number of independent data. Its data structure is relatively complex, and all associated data cannot be directly display. In order to facilitate the data post-processing, we need to extract the relevant data set and dump them to a common file (.txt). A brief process for single data file processing:

1. Choose the file which will be read and access to the file path and file name.
2. Read data in the file.
3. Set the dump file name.
4. Get the dump file ID.
5. Save simplified data set into the dump file.
6. Close the dump file.

If there are multiple files that need to be processed at the same time, it needs to traverse the directory where the file is located at first. Then, we get the total number of files which to be processed and use the loop algorithm process them:

1. Access to all files in the folder.
2. Get the number of files.
3. Control the loop times and process files.

4 Comparison and Verification

Based on MATLAB R2015a and netcdf library, we implemented data processing described herein above, and completed 22141108 sets of data's validation work on the PC (Intel (R) Core (TM) i5-3470 CPU @ 3.20 GHz (3200 MHz), 8 GB of memory, Seagate ST1000DM hard drives).

4.1 Data Comparisons

In order to compare the common points and the characteristics of the data obtained from two methods, the data analysis of four observation sites were carried out.

Figure 2 are four line charts of the average values by OCO-2-based observations and TCCON-based observations (2014.9–2015.8), and the Table 2 shows its corresponding statistical results. In the Table 2, the 'Site1' stands for Pasadena. The 'Site2' stands for Lamont. The 'Site3' stands for Ascension Island. The 'Site4' stands for Reunion Island. The 'AVG' is short for average value. The 'OCO-2 AC' is short for average concentration of OCO-2. The 'TCCON AC' is short for average concentration of TCCON. The 'OCO-2 SE' is short for standard error of OCO-2. The 'TCCON SE' is short for standard error of TCCON. The 'CC' is short for correlation coefficient of OCO-2's data and TCCON's data. The 'Total' is short for total number of matching points.

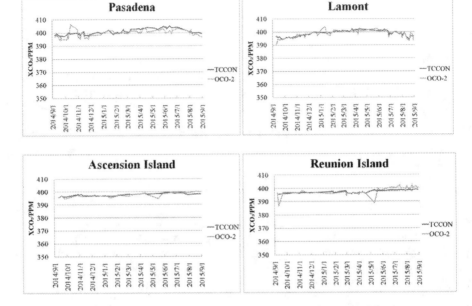

(a) Pasadena (b) Lamont (c) Ascension Island (d) Reunion Island

Fig. 2. Four line charts of the average values by OCO-2-based observations and TCCON-based observations (2014.9–2015.8).

Table 2. A data statistics table of two kinds of observation results (2014.9–2015.8)

Site	OCO-2 AC (ppm)	TCCON AC (ppm)	Error (ppm)	OCO-2 SE (ppm)	TCCON SE (ppm)	CC	Total
Site1	399.4898	400.8793	−1.3895	2.4901	2.2015	0.7013	89786
Site2	398.4750	398.7774	−0.3024	2.7555	2.2532	0.8401	85373
Site3	397.7043	397.9425	−0.2382	1.4977	0.9957	0.7095	20835
Site4	397.6372	397.4954	0.1418	3.0696	1.0398	0.5636	27480
AVG	398.3266	398.7737	−0.4471	2.4532	1.6225	0.7036	

From the negative average value of the error can be seen that the OCO-2 products underestimated CO_2 concentration, and this underestimation may be caused by the multiple scattering of aerosols, the multiple scattering of cloud and the polarization effect of radiation transmission.

From the average value of the correlation coefficient can be seen that the two kinds of data were moderately correlated. The correlation coefficient of Reunion Island observation was low, and the standard error of the data was high, but the two kind's data of Ascension Island observation - which was in the islands also - were relatively stable. This may be due to the island had lack of green plants or had lack of complex landform, so it easily affected by climate, air current and ocean current. Since its self-adjustment ability was very weak, its location and its external environment were the main factors affecting CO$_2$ concentration changing.

From the average value of the standard error can be seen that the accuracy of the ground observation sites' concentration were higher, but the accuracy of the satellites observation' concentration were lower. At the same time, the results also show that the accuracy of OCO-2's retrieved concentration was slightly lower than the accuracy of GOSAT's retrieved concentration [2]. This may lead to the retrieval algorithm required constant progress.

4.2   The Overall Trend Analysis

In order to further verify the spatial and temporal variation characteristics of the data obtained from the two methods, the time series comparison of the data from four observation sites were carried out.

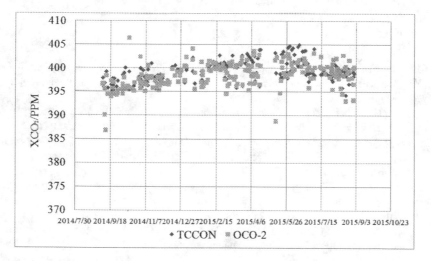

Fig. 3. A comparison of time series between the average values of the data observed by OCO-2 and by TCCON (2014.9–2015.8)

As shown in Fig. 3, by comparison of four observation sites' data and matching the data time series, it can be seen that the observation data of satellite and the observation data of ground were consistent with the seasonal changing. The high monthly average concentration of the two kinds of data appeared in May and June, and the low monthly average concentration appeared in August and September. The results were also verified the phenomena and the causes of the concentration's seasonal variation Because in the winter and spring, green plants' leaves withered, photosynthesis was weak and the winter heating may cause the accumulation of CO_2 concentration, thus caused a higher value in May and June. However, in summer and autumn, due to the relatively lush green plants, the carbon sequestration capacity of photosynthesis significantly increased that caused a lower value in August and September.

5   Conclusions

OCO-2-based observation could objectively capture the atmospheric CO_2 concentration in real time, but it was limited by the sensor and the retrieval algorithm, so that the accuracy compared with the ground observation had a greater error. The error may be caused by the multiple scattering of aerosol, the multiple scattering of cloud, and the polarization effect of radiation transmission; The retrieval data of OCO-2-based observation was lower than by TCCON observation; The island's self-regulating ability of CO_2 concentration changing was very weak, so that its location and its external environment were the main factors affecting CO_2 concentration changing.

At the end of this paper, it was proved that the OCO-2-based observation data and the TCCON-based observation data had a consistent seasonal cycle and the green plants might be the main factors of this phenomenon.

References

1. Chen, X., Liu, Y., Cai, Z.N.: Review of radiative transfer model in retrieval of atmospheric CO_2 from satellite shortwave infrared measurements. Remote Sens. Technol. Appl **30**(5), 825–834 (2015)
2. Lei, L.P., Guan, X.H., Zeng, Z.C.: A comparison of atmospheric CO_2 concentration GOSAT-based observations and model simulations. Sci. China Earth Sci. **1**(44), 61–71 (2014)
3. Zhou, M.Q., Zhang, X.Y., Wang, P.C., Wang, S.P., Guo, L.L., Hu, L.Q.: XCO_2 satellite retrieval experiments in short-wave infrared spectrum and ground-based validation. Sci. China Earth Sci. **58**, 1191–1197 (2015)
4. Zhang, M., Zhang, X.Y., Liu, Y.X.: Study on the validation of atmospheric CO_2 from satellite hyper spectral remote sensing. Progressus Inquisitiones De Mutatione Climatis **10**(6), 427–432 (2014)
5. Zhang, X.Y., Zhou, M.Q., Wang, W.H., Li, X.J.: Progress of global satellite remote sensing of atmospheric compositions and its' applications. Sci. Technol. Rev. **33**(17), 13–22 (2015)
6. Ru, F., Lei, L.P., Hou, S.S., Zeng, Z.C., Guan, X.H.: Evaluation of retrieval errors of greenhouse gas concentrations from GOSAT. Remote Sens. Inf. **1**(28), 65–70 (2013)
7. Xiang, L., Gao, Q.X., Zhou, S.Q., Chen, Y.L.: Comparisons of CO_2 emission from fuel combustion among major countries and regions. Adv. Clim. Change Res. **5**(5), 278–284 (2008)
8. Bai, W.G., Zhang, X.Y., Zhang, P.: Temporal and spatial distribution of tropospheric CO_2 over China based on satellite observations. Chin. Sci. Bull. **55**(31), 3612–3618 (2010)
9. IPCC. Climate change 2007: synthesis report. Cambridge University Press, Cambridge (2007)
10. Wunch, D., Toon, G.C., Blavier, J.-F.L., Washenfelder, R.A., Notholt, J., Connor, B.J., Griffith, D.W.T., Sherlock, V., Wennberg, P.O.: The total carbon column observing network. Phil. Trans. R. Soc. A **369**, 2087–2112 (2011). doi:10.1098/rsta.2010.0240

11. Reuter, M., Bovensmann, H., Buchwitz, M., et al.: Retrieval of atmospheric CO_2 with enhanced accuracy and precision from SCIAMACHY: validation with FTS measurements and comparison with model results. J. Geophys. Res. Atmos. **116**(D04301), 1–13 (2011). doi: 10.1029/2010JD015047
12. Reuter, M., Bovensmann, H., Buchwitz, M., et al.: Algorithm Theoretical Basis Document (ATBD) Bremen optimal estimation DOAS (BESD) version 1 (2011). Accessed 10 Apr 2014
13. Reuter, M., Buchwitz, M., Schneising, O., et al.: A method for improved SCIAMACHY CO_2 retrieval in the presence of optically thin clouds. Atmos. Meas. Tech. **3**, 209–232 (2010)
14. Morino, I., Uchino, O., Moue, M., et al.: Preliminary validation of column-averaged volume mixing ratios of carbon dioxide and methane retrieved from GOSAT short-wavelength infrared spectra. Atmos. Meas. Tech. **4**(6), 1061–1076 (2011)
15. Aumann, H.H., Gregorich, D., Gaiser, S., Chahine, M.: Application of atmospheric infrared sounder data (AIRS) to climate research. In: Proceedings of the SPIE International Society for Optical Engineering, vol. 5570, pp. 202–208 (2004)

SBA Virtual Prototyping Engineering Technology

Design of the Reusable Boosted Vehicle's (RBV) Control Allocation in the Reentry Process

Wanmeng Zhou[1], Hua Wang[1(✉)], Jiangtao Xu[2], Naigang Cui[3], Shuai Guo[1], and Guojin Tang[1]

[1] College of Aerospace Science and Engineering,
National University of Defense Technology, Chang Sha 410073, China
wanghua@nudt.edu.cn
[2] School of Aeronautic and Architecture, Harbin Engineering University,
Harbin 150001, China
[3] School of Astronautics, Harbin Institute of Technology,
Harbin 150001, China

Abstract. This thesis is committed to the design of the reusable boosted vehicle's (RBV) control system in the reentry process. By choosing the proper control allocation strategy, six of freedom nonlinear model of RBV was controlled to fly in accordance with expected flight instructions. This paper presented two-grade control allocation scheme: the primary allocation distributed the expected moment to the different actuators; the secondary allocation further assigned the allocated moment to eight separated rudders, in which the exterior point penalty function method was adapted. This new scheme can limit rudders' deflection angle and deflection velocity, and cost the minimum rudder system energy. Finally, the result shows the entire system combined with the controller and control allocations can precisely meet the control requirements.

Keywords: RBV · Hybrid actuators · Two-grade control allocation · Exterior point penalty function method

1 Introduction

Reusable launch vehicle is required to achieve such a flight frequency, nearly 50 to 100 times a year, for reducing the high prime cost [1]. The vehicle maintenance and the complex thermal protection also lead to the failure of original prospects for sharply reducing the launch and management costs [2]. To rectify this issue, a large amount of researchers have studied about the reusable launch vehicle [3–7]. The reusable boosted vehicle (RBV), as a represent for partial reusable launch vehicle, has invaluable potentials in future launching techniques [8].

In fact, during the entire reentry process, the parameters' nonlinearity in RBV flight dynamic model become more obvious because of the changing atmosphere density, unstable environment temperature, varied Mach number and attitude angles, and other uncertain factors. Reaction control system (RCS) can be utilized upper the sub orbit where the rarefied atmosphere should reduce the operation efficiency of rudder control

© Springer Science+Business Media Singapore 2016
L. Zhang et al. (Eds.): AsiaSim 2016/SCS AutumnSim 2016, Part III, CCIS 645, pp. 367–378, 2016.
DOI: 10.1007/978-981-10-2669-0_40

system [9]. To maximum the effective load, the propellant of RCS is limited; therefore, RCS is unnecessary in service all the flight especially when the rudder efficiency is sufficient for independent control.

In this paper, the hybrid actuator control sequence was designed according to rudders' proper start time. On the basis of the control sequence, the expected moments were allocated to RCS and other rudders. The remainder of this paper is organized as below: In second section, the rudders' start condition was determined and then the hybrid control sequence was designed. In third section, the secondary control allocation was discussed in detail. In the next section, RBV was controlled by designed controllers combined with two-grade control allocation strategy and the simulation result was analyzed. Finally, there was a conclusion for the study.

2   Hybrid Control Sequence Design

Hybrid control sequence is designed based on changing atmosphere density. The low density in upper atmosphere reduces the rudders efficiency, while in lower atmosphere rudders are more suitable for attitude control. In this paper, RBV has two sets of actuators: RCS and rudders. The RCS is adapted upper the sub orbit; when the atmosphere density is sufficient, the attitude is controlled only by rudders; the two-grade control allocation scheme is adapted during the transition section. The primary allocation assigns the expected moments for RCS and rudders. The secondary allocation divides the total expected moments of rudders into separate rudder to optimize the actuators' energy cost.

Under the control conditions, the start conditions are determined based on the flight envelope, shown as Fig. 1. The RBV reached its highest point at 152 s and then entered into reentry process.

In light of the reference trajectory and dynamics characteristics of RBV, the entire trimming rudders deflection angle is calculated. When the angle is in the range of the rudder deflection limitations, from −30° to +30°, the rudder can complete the flight trimming and attitude control, vice versa. The trimming condition is given by

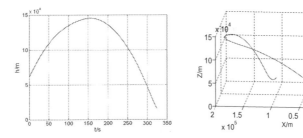

Fig. 1. RBV reference trajectory diagrams represent the expected process of the vehicle. The left diagram illustrates the time history of the height of the vehicle, while the right diagram illustrates the three-dimension trajectory.

$$m_{z0} + m_z^{\alpha}\alpha + m_z^{\delta_z}\delta_z = 0 \tag{1}$$

where m_{z0} is the asymmetric moment coefficient; m_z^{α} is the attack angle moment coefficient; $m_z^{\delta_z}$ is the rudder deflection moment coefficient; δ_z is the rudder deflection angle; α is the attack angle. The trimming rudder deflection angle is given by

$$\delta_z = -(m_{z0} + m_z^{\alpha}\alpha)/m_z^{\delta_z} \tag{2}$$

The offered interpolation table of the static stable moment coefficient is adapted to interpolate the above coefficients. By substituting coefficients and the attack angle of the reference flight into Eq. (2), we can obtain the entire trimming deflection angles and the dynamic pressure, shown as Figs. 2 and 3.

The results in Fig. 3 shows the deflection angle is in the limitation after 205 s. The limitation of deflection angle is only necessary condition for attitude control, the rudder efficient must be considered simultaneously. Typically, operation efficiency of rudders is desirable when the dynamics pressure is more than 1500 Pa [10]. Figure 4 indicates that the dynamics pressure reach the 1500 Pa until 300 s at the height of 46.95 km. Thus, all the rudders should work independently after 300 s. The start time of rudders is set to be 295 s with dynamic pressure of 590 Pa. The hybrid control subsequence is listed in Table 1.

The control allocation coefficient is calculated through the dynamic pressure which is critical for the rudder efficiency. The method is expressed as

$$\begin{cases} Mcd = kMc \\ Mcrcs = (1-k)Mc \end{cases} \tag{3}$$

where Mcd is rudders total moment; $Mcrcs$ is the total moment of RCS; Mc is the expected moment; the allocation coefficient k is given by

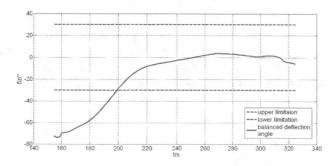

Fig. 2. The solid line represents the balanced deflection angle changing along with the reentry process, while the dashed lines represent the upper and lower limitations of the effective deflection angles.

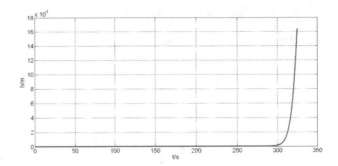

Fig. 3. The dynamical pressure changes sharply at 300 s, when the flight vehicle is in the reentry process.

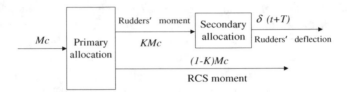

Fig. 4. Schematic diagram of the control allocation consists of two-level allocations: the primary allocation for different actuators and the secondary allocation for the rudders' deflection angles.

Table 1. Hybrid control subsequence schedule.

Time (s)	Height (km)	Dynamic Pressure (Pa)	Actuator
152–295	145–54.15	0.2067–590	RCS
295–300	54.15–46.95	590–1500	RCS, Rudders
300–325	46.95–14.92	1500–164150	Rudders

$$k = \frac{q - 590}{1500 - 590}, \quad q = \frac{1}{2}\rho v^2 \tag{4}$$

where t refers to the time, q refers to dynamic pressure, and v refers to the velocity. When the dynamic pressure is 1500 Pa, the rudder efficient is sufficient, and therefore RCS is closed and the allocation coefficient k is 1; when the dynamic pressure is 590 Pa, the rudder efficient is too low, rudders are closed and the allocation coefficient k is 0. The control allocation scheme is illustrated in Fig. 4.

3   Secondary Control Allocation

The main control allocation strategy includes: the matrix related method (like pseudo-inverse control allocation), the directive method (like area search method, bin search method), optimal method [11]. These three kinds of methods have different characters. Matrix related method has high calculative efficiency but the allocation results of all the rudders cannot be fully effective [11, 12], while directive and optimal methods have high computational cost and poor real-time performance [13]. As the computers performance improves, the defect of high computational and time cost is remedied. Considering about angle constraints and limited deflection energy, we adapted the exterior point penalty function method to calculate the secondary control allocation. This method belonging to the optimal method can offer an effective way to guarantee the optimized allocation and fault-tolerance. When some rudders of the assignment fail, the allocation coefficient is changed instead of the control parameters, which enforces the stability of the control system.

Reconfigurable control is achieved by separated rudders. It has significant meanings for improving the redundancy that the rudders can compensate for any others' breaking down. The deflection angles and equivalent moments for rudders are shown in Fig. 5.

Modern flight control projects the expected moment or acceleration to the body coordinate system axes, and then the control allocation module assigns the moment components into different rudders [14]. Expected moments or angular accelerations are inputs and the deflection angles of each rudder are outputs. Control allocation is the process to determine the rudders' deflection angles according to the given inputs. The results are not unique, so the penalty function is introduced to find the optimization.

Exterior point penalty function method transforms the optimization problem from constrained into unconstrained by amplifying the penalty factor to approach the boundary of constraint conditions [15]. The optimization model is described as:

$$\begin{aligned} &\min f(\boldsymbol{\delta}) \\ &s.t. g_i(\boldsymbol{\delta}) \leq 0 \\ h_j(\boldsymbol{\delta}) = 0 (&i = 1, 2, \cdots, 8, j = 1, 2, 3) \end{aligned} \tag{5}$$

where $h_j(\delta)$ is the equality constraint, $g_i(\delta)$ is the inequality constraint, expressed as

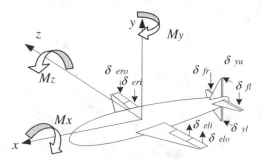

Fig. 5. The directions of moment are determined according to the rudders' deflection. The RBV is equipped with eight rudders, and the deflection angles are expressed as angles of right interior aileron δ_{eri}, left interior aileron δ_{eli}, right exterior aileron δ_{ero}, left exterior aileron δ_{elo}, right elevator δ_{fr}, left elevator δ_{fl}, upper yaw rudder δ_{yu}, and lower yaw rudder δ_{yl}, which compose the vector $\boldsymbol{\delta}$.

$$\begin{bmatrix} M_{cx} \\ M_{cy} \\ M_{cz} \end{bmatrix} = \begin{bmatrix} M_x^{\delta_x}\delta_x \\ M_y^{\delta_y}\delta_y \\ M_z^{\delta_z}\delta_z \end{bmatrix} + \begin{bmatrix} M_{rcsx} \\ M_{rcsy} \\ M_{rcsz} \end{bmatrix} \tag{6}$$

$$\delta_{\min} \le \delta(t) \le \delta_{\max}$$
$$v_{\min} \le \frac{\delta(t) - \delta(t-T)}{T} \le v_{\max}$$

where M_c is the excepted moment; M_{rcs} is the RCS moment; M^δ is the rudder moment coefficient; T is the sample time. The control rudder moment can be expressed by each rudders moment, which is given by

$$\begin{bmatrix} M_x^{\delta_x}\delta_x \\ M_y^{\delta_y}\delta_y \\ M_z^{\delta_z}\delta_z \end{bmatrix} = \frac{1}{2} \begin{bmatrix} M_x^{\delta_x} & 0 & 0 \\ 0 & M_y^{\delta_y} & 0 \\ 0 & 0 & M_z^{\delta_z} \end{bmatrix} \mathbf{Q}\delta \tag{7}$$

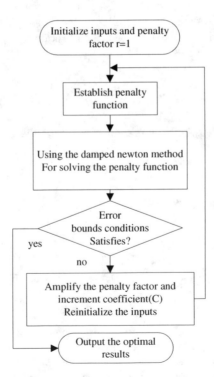

Fig. 6. The exterior point penalty function algorithm is utilized to obtain the satisfied rudders' reflection angles.

where $\mathbf{Q}$ is the assignment matrix, which is based on the assignment and the deflection angles of rudders.

The penalty function is expressed as

$$\phi(\delta, r) = f(\delta) + r \sum_{i=1}^{m} \max[0, g_i(\delta)]^2 + r \sum_{j=1}^{l} h_j(\delta)^2 \qquad (8)$$

where $f(\delta) = \| \delta \|_2$, r is penalty factor, and the latter two terms in the right equation are penalty terms. The specific algorithm is described as (Fig. 6):

a. Set the initial inputs $\delta_i(t)(i = 1, 2, \cdots, n)$ and the initial penalty factor r, where n is the number of rudder pairs;
b. Establish the penalty terms which are derived from equality and inequality constraints;
c. Iterate to solve the no constraints optimization problem by Newton method;
d. Decide whether the results submit to the stop condition. If not, the penalty factor is amplified in the next iteration. The deflection angles $\delta_i(t - T)$ are revalued by the optimized results $\delta_i(t)$;
e. Stop the iteration until the error limitation is satisfied.

4 RBV Control System Simulation

According to the flight dynamics and control theory [16], RBV's six degree of freedom model was established. Several aspects about the model were listed here: (1) Virtual equivalent rudders are deemed to be the first order inertia link. The inputs are expected moment signals, and the outputs are equivalent moments of rudders and RCS; (2) all the aerodynamic parameters in the time varying system are obtained by interpolation; (3) the control allocation link includes primary allocation, secondary allocation, and the

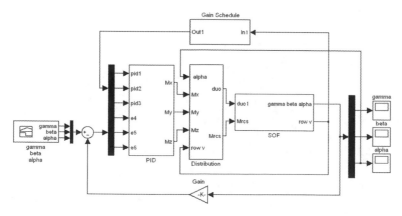

Fig. 7. Combined simulation model consists of expected attitude angles, PID gain scheduling controller, two-level control distribution, and the controlled object.

equivalent rudders calculation. The primary allocation calculates the expected moment of rudders and RCS. The secondary allocation produces eight deflection signals. The equivalent rudders are determined by the equivalent rudders calculation link. Finally, RBV's nonlinear model combined with the control module, the allocation module and the gain scheduling module was simulated in 5 s. The total system is shown in Fig. 7.

The linear model of RBV is established here in the light of the following hypotheses: (1) the first-order derivatives of parameters in horizontal and vertical non-turbulent motions are minor, and the products of themselves and other minor quantities are ignored; (2) deviations in the RBV structure parameters have no influence on the turbulent motion; (3) trigonometric function of minor angles can be expressed as $\sin \theta \approx \theta$, $\cos \theta \approx 1$; (4) parameters of motion, aerodynamics, structures and guidance in undisturbed motion are constant.

In the reentry process, the dynamics equations of RBV are given by

$$
\begin{cases}
m\dfrac{d\Delta v}{dt} = R_x^v \Delta v + R_x^\alpha \Delta \alpha - mg \cos \theta \Delta \theta \\[2mm]
mv\dfrac{d\Delta \theta}{dt} = R_y^v \Delta v + R_y^\alpha \Delta \alpha + mg \sin \theta \Delta \theta + R_y^{\delta_z} \Delta \delta_z \\[2mm]
-mv\dfrac{d\Delta \psi_v}{dt} = R_z^\beta \Delta \beta + R_y \Delta \gamma_v + R_z^{\delta_y} \Delta \delta_y - (1 + \cos \theta) mg \sin \theta \Delta \psi_v + \sin \theta R_y \Delta \psi_v \\[2mm]
J_x \dfrac{d\Delta \omega_{x_b}}{dt} = M_x^\beta \Delta \beta + M_x^{\omega_x} \Delta \omega_{x_b} + M_x^{\omega_y} \Delta \omega_{y_b} + M_x^{\delta_x} \Delta \delta_x + M_x^{\delta_y} \Delta \delta_y \\[2mm]
J_y \dfrac{d\Delta \omega_{y_b}}{dt} = M_y^\beta \Delta \beta + M_y^{\omega_y} \Delta \omega_{y_b} + M_y^{\omega_x} \Delta \omega_b + M_y^{\dot\beta} \Delta \dot\beta + M_y^{\delta_y} \Delta \delta_y \\[2mm]
J_z \dfrac{d\Delta \omega_{z_b}}{dt} = M_z^v \Delta v + M_z^{\omega_z} \Delta \omega_{z_b} + M_z^\alpha \Delta \alpha + M_z^{\dot\alpha} \Delta \dot\alpha + M_z^{\delta_z} \Delta \delta_z
\end{cases}
\tag{9}
$$

The kinematics equations of RBV are

$$
\begin{cases}
\dfrac{d\Delta x}{dt} = \cos \theta \Delta v - v \sin \theta \Delta \theta \\[2mm]
\dfrac{d\Delta y}{dt} = \sin \theta \Delta v + v \cos \theta \Delta \theta \\[2mm]
\dfrac{d\Delta z}{dt} = -v \Delta \psi_v \\[2mm]
\dfrac{d\Delta \vartheta}{dt} = \Delta \omega_{z_b}, \dfrac{d\Delta \psi}{dt} = \Delta \omega_{y_b}, \dfrac{d\Delta \gamma}{dt} = \Delta \omega_{x_b}
\end{cases}
\tag{10}
$$

The complement relationship between the angles is

$$
\begin{cases}
\Delta \alpha = \Delta \vartheta - \Delta \theta \\
\Delta \beta = \Delta \psi - \Delta \psi_v + \Delta \gamma \alpha \\
\Delta \gamma_v = \Delta \gamma - \Delta \psi \alpha
\end{cases}
\tag{11}
$$

Table 2. Simulation initial specifics.

Physical parameters	Symbols	Initial values
Initial time/s	t	295
Position/km	(x, y, z)	(125.46, 528.65, 0.789)
Velocity/m/s	v	1365.1
Pitch/rad	ϑ	4.4055
Roll/rad	γ	0
Yaw/rad	ψ	0
Trajectory pitch/rad	θ	3.7269
Velocity deflection/rad	ψ_v	0.263×10^{-3}
Angular velocity/rad/s	$\omega_x = \omega_y = \omega_z$	0
Mass/kg	m	30500
Moment of inertia/kg.m²	$J(J_x, J_y, J_z)$	$(9 \times 10^4, 9.39 \times 10^5, 9.23 \times 10^5)$

where ϑ, ψ, γ are the pitch angle, the yaw angle, and the roll angle respectively; θ, ψ_v are the trajectory pitch and the velocity deflection respectively; α, β, γ_v are the attack angle, the sideslip angle, and the velocity pitch; m, J_x, J_y, J_z are the mass and the body-axis moments of inertia; R_x^v, R_x^α, R_y, R_y^α, $R_y^{\delta_z}$, R_y^v, R_z^β, $R_z^{\delta_y}$ are the aerodynamics force derivatives in three control channels; M_x^β, $M_x^{\omega_x}$, $M_x^{\omega_y}$, $M_x^{\delta_x}$, $M_x^{\delta_y}$, M_y^β, $M_y^{\omega_y}$, $M_y^{\omega_x}$, $M_y^{\dot\beta}$, $M_y^{\delta_y}$, $M_z^{\omega_z}$, M_z^v, M_z^α, $M_z^{\dot\alpha}$, $M_z^{\delta_z}$ are the aerodynamics moment derivatives in three control channels.

According to the RBV's configuration, the allocation matrix $\mathbf{Q}$ is

$$\mathbf{Q} = \begin{bmatrix} -1.5 & 1.5 & -1 & 1 & -1 & 1 & 1 & -1 \\ 0 & 0 & 0 & 0 & 0 & 0 & 1 & 1 \\ 0.5 & 0.5 & 0.5 & 0.5 & 1 & 1 & 0 & 0 \end{bmatrix} \qquad (12)$$

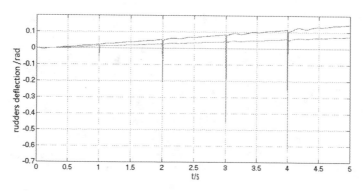

Fig. 8. The upper two dashed lines represent the elevator rudders' deflection angles δ_{fr} and δ_{fl}. The middle two dashed lines represent the yaw rudders' deflection angles δ_{yu} and δ_{yl}. The lower two dashed lines represent the aileron rudders' deflection angles δ_{eri}, δ_{ero}, δ_{eli}, δ_{elo}, respectively.

The limitations of rudders' deflection angles and deflection velocities are

$$\delta_{max} = -\delta_{min} = 0.5233 rad(30°)$$
$$v_{max} = -v_{min} = 1.3956 rad \cdot s^{-1}(80° \cdot s^{-1})$$

(13)

Other simulation specifics are listed in Table 2.

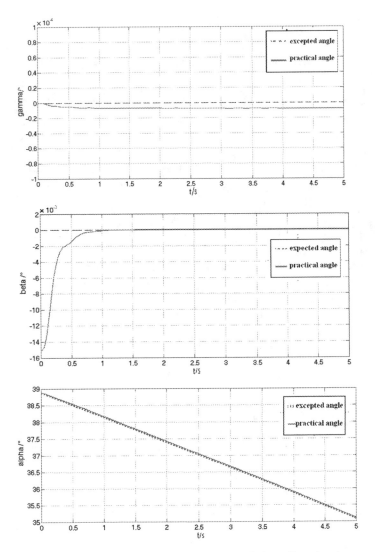

Fig. 9. The first figure represents the simulation results of the roll angle; the second figure represents the sideslip angle result; the third one represents the attack angle result. The solid line means the practical simulation angles, while the dashed line means the desired results.

The rudders deflection angles are shown in Fig. 8. The expected signal is the unflat transition of the six data points from 295 s to 300 s, and therefore the catastrophe happens at the fraction. The catastrophe can lead to the sudden switch of the rudders which can be settled down by holders.

The roll angle, sideslip angle, and attack angle within 5 s are shown in Fig. 9. The expected values in the first two control channels are zero. From the results shown in these figures, we can conclude that the practical angles are mainly coincident. Therefore, the control allocation strategy is verified.

5 Conclusion

The two-grade control allocation strategy is proposed in this paper. In the primary allocation, the normalization is utilized to assign the expected moments in hybrid control actuators, while the exterior point penalty function method is adapted in the secondary allocation to further allocate the rudders' expected moments. The control strategy considers the constraints of rudders' deflection angle, deflection velocity, and the optimal energy target. It breaks through the limitations of original control strategies which have no constraints or optimal energy target.

Acknowledgments. This study was co-supported by the 973 Program (No. 2013CB733100) and the National Natural Science Foundation of China (No. 11272346 and No. 11472301).

References

1. Josephd, D., Kenneth, R., Robert, A.: AREA: Affordable Responsive Spacelift-the U.S. Air Force's Next Generation Launch System. In: AIAA Space 2005, pp. 1–6. AIAA Press, California (2005)
2. Cai, M.R.: New developments about reusable space back and forth transportation systems. Aerospace Control. 4(22), 21–25 (2004). (in Chinese)
3. Andrew, M.C., Dana, G.A.: Go horizontal: a responsible, evolvable, feasible space launch roadmap. In: Space 2004 Conference and Exhibit, 2004-6004, pp. 1–7. AIAA, San Diego (2005)
4. Yu, J.Q., Luo, G.C., et al.: Surface-to-air missile autopilot design using LQG/LTR gain scheduling method. Chin. J. Aeronaut. 24(3), 279–286 (2011)
5. Mcurdy, R.D., Roche, M.J.: Structure sizing of a horizontal take-off launch vehicle with an air collection and enrichment system. In: 40th AIAA/ASME/SAE/ASEE Joint Propulsion Conference and Exhibit, pp. 1–11. AIAA, Fort Lauder dale (2004)
6. Xu, J.T., Cui, N.G., Chen, Y.Y., et al.: Research on control allocation based on improved fixed-point for reusable boosted vehicle. Chin. J. Aeronaut. 12(33), 2269–2276 (2012). (in Chinese)
7. Yu, L., Andrea, S., Stephen, Y.: Model-predictive dynamic control allocation scheme for reentry vehicles. J. Guid. Control Dyn. 30(1), 100–111 (2007)
8. Carlo, T., Laurent, B., Thomas, F., et al.: RLV candidates for European future launchers preparatory programmer. Act Astronaut 65, 40–46 (2009)

9. Xu, J.T., Cui, N.G., et al.: Coordinated gain scheduling reusable booster vehicle attitude controller design. Opt. Precis. Eng. **3**(14), 15–17 (2005). (in Chinese)
10. Han, P.X.: Study on the Navigation Guidance and Control of Reusable Boost Vehicle. Harbin Institute of Technology, Harbin (2011). (in Chinese)
11. Ma, J.J., Li, W.Q., Li, P., et al.: Status and Future of Control Allocation for Aerospace Vehicle. Flight Dyn. **3**(27), 1–5 (2009). (in Chinese)
12. Ma, C.,Wang, L.X.: Flying-wing aircraft control allocation. In: 47th AIAA Aerospace Sciences Meeting, pp. 1–22. AIAA Press, California (2009). (in Chinese)
13. Zhang, Y., Chen, Z.J., Wei, C.: New algorithm for robust control allocation of UAV based on generalized inverse. Acta Aeronautica et Astronautica Sinica **29**, S199–S203 (2008). (in Chinese)
14. Chen, Y., Dong, X.M., Xue, J.P., et al.: Constrained adaptive control allocation for multi-effector flight control system. Syst. Eng. Electron. **33**(5), 1118–1122 (2011). (in Chinese)
15. Sun, J.M., V, Y.C.: Optimization of Mechanical Design, pp. 162–165. Mechanical Industry Press, Beijing (2012). (in Chinese)
16. Qin, X.F., Lin, R.X., Zhao, Y.N.: Missile Flight Mechanics, pp. 14–22, 36–48, 160–244. Beijing Institute of Technology Press, Beijing (2011). (in Chinese)

Benchmarking the Star-CCM+ Compressible Flow Solver by Simulating Typical Compressible Flow Problems: A Case Study and Comparison

Tianmeng Wang[✉], Hua Wang, and Guojin Tang

College of Aerospace Science and Engineering, National University of Defense Technology, Changsha 410073, HuNan, China
wangtianmeng126@163.com

Abstract. Star-CCM+ is a new generation CFD solver which has been widely used in fluid mechanics, engineering, aviation, shipbuilding and aerospace. Better application of software requires sufficient level of understanding of what exactly is happening and how. However, there are few researches done on benchmarking work. As such, the assessment work plays a critical role both in the development and the application of Star-CCM+. The aim of this paper is to testify the accuracy of the compressible flow solver in Star-CCM+ by simulating compressible flow in a condition that is inviscid and steady. The paper describes the process of assessment itself and shows that compressible flow solver in Star-CCM+ is capable of simulating steady and inviscid compressible case in high accuracy, results of which is better than that of other CFD software.

Keywords: Flow problem simulation · CFD · Star-CCM+ application

1 Introduction

So far, the application of CFD technology has surpassed the conventional fluid mechanics, fluid engineering, aviation, shipbuilding and aerospace, but extends to chemical, nuclear power, metallurgy, and construction areas [4]. Star-CCM+ is a new generation CFD solver, which CD-adapco company uses the most advanced numerical techniques continuum mechanics. It uses a CD-adapco's latest original mesh generation technology, which have abilities like: complex data input, surface treatment, the surface division, automatic volume mesh generation. Star-CCM+ provides the most comprehensive engineering physics simulation in a single integrated package. More than just a CFD solver, Star-CCM+ is also a complete engineering process. It can solve problems that involve flow (liquid or solid), heat and pressure. What's more, it provides a set of integrated components that combine to produce a powerful software package and can meet the demand of a variety of shapes.

The basic idea of Star-CCM+ is that it uses computing grid to divide flow field that is divided into discrete control volumes. Also it uses the equation that will be solved to make integral on each control volume, so it is possible to form algebraic equations with

© Springer Science+Business Media Singapore 2016
L. Zhang et al. (Eds.): AsiaSim 2016/SCS AutumnSim 2016, Part III, CCIS 645, pp. 379–391, 2016.
DOI: 10.1007/978-981-10-2669-0_41

many discrete variables like speed, pressure, temperature and so on. Then discrete nonlinear equations are converted into linear ones to obtain a new variable value.

Although Star-CCM+ has been widely used, there are few data to show how good performance the compressible flow solver in Star-CCM+ can give. So the main aim of this project is to test the compressible flow solver in Star-CCM+, by running simulation on a diamond airfoil to get the result and compare them with analytical solutions and other available numerical results.

There are normally two kinds of flow: the incompressible flow and the compressible flow. The former means that during the flow, the change of density can be neglected while the latter is the one that cannot neglect such influence. When Mach number is larger than 0.3, the flow can be considered as compressible flow.

Most of the problems of incompressible flow and compressible flow both have two unknown factors: the pressure and velocity [8]. By using the basic principles of continuity and linearity momentum conservation equations, the pressure and velocity of incompressible flow can be obtained. Apart from the pressure and velocity of compressible flow remain unknown, density and temperature also become unknown factors [6]. This implies the need to address two additional equations: state of gas equation and energy conversation equation. At the same time, there are two types of reference when it comes to such types of dynamics problems: Lagrange and Euler. Lagrange method follows a specific particle or set of particles of fixed identity. Euler reference coordinate system is that it does not move with particles to different places, but it is a fixed line or control the volume that the fluid can flow through [7]. Because compressible flow is related with a wide range of areas and there will be many potential problems, these two frames are both needed for more in-depth analysis of the problem.

In this paper, Diamond airfoil is a major object in simulation and other two compressible flow cases such as compression wedge and Prandtl–Meyer expansion fan problem are also simulated to guarantee the conclusion is reliable. Diamond airfoil is shown in Sect. 4 and the other is shown in Sect. 5. Moreover, the comparison is conducted between simulation results of the solver and theoretical results in three cases. Also, Star-CCM+ is compared with other CFD software like sonicFoam and RhoCentrolFoam.

2   Numerical Method

In CFD fields, the discretization of the Navier-Stokes equations is very important. The discretization of Navier-Stokes equations can have many different kinds, such as forward difference scheme, backward difference scheme, finite volume method etc. Star-CCM+ uses a finite volume method. This is a very rapid development of the discrete method in recent years, which is characterized by high efficiency [3].

Finite volume method is closely related to the finite difference method, and a finite volume method is usually interpreted as a direct finite difference approximation differential equations. However, the finite volume method is derived from the law of conservation. Take first-order accurate method for linear equations as an example.

In the one-dimensional space, finite volume method is based on subdividing the spatial domain to the time interval ("finite volume", also known as grid cells) and track the integral of q approximately on each volume [4]. At each time step, value will be updated by using an approximate interval the magnetic flux through the endpoint.

Suppose the ith grid cell is

$$c_i = (x_{i-1/2}, x_{i+1/2}).$$ (1)

As shown in Fig. 1, the value Q_i^n will approximate the average value over the ith interval at time t_n:

$$Q_i^n \approx \frac{1}{\Delta x}\int_{x_{i-1/2}}^{x_{i+1/2}} q(x, t_n)dx \equiv \frac{1}{\Delta x}\int_{c_i} q(x, t_n)dx.$$ (2)

$$Q_i^n \approx \frac{1}{\Delta x}\int_{x_{i-1/2}}^{x_{i+1/2}} q(x, t_n)dx \equiv \frac{1}{\Delta x}\int_{c_i} q(x, t_n)dx.$$ (3)

Where $\Delta x = x_{i+1/2} - x_{i-1/2}$ is the length of the cell

The integral form of the conservation law is given below:

$$\frac{d}{dt}\int_{c_i} q(x, t)dx = f(q(x_{i-1/2}, t)) - f(q(x_{i+1/2}, t)).$$ (4)

It is known that Q_i^n is the average at time t_n, the next step is to approximate Q_i^{n+1} at time t_{n+1}. Suppose each time step is that $\Delta t = t_{n+1} - t_n$, so

$$\int_{c_i} q(x, t_{n+1})dx - \int_{c_i} q(x, t_n)dx = \\ \int_{t_n}^{t_{n+1}} f(q(x_{i-1/2}, t))dt - \int_{t_n}^{t_{n+1}} f(q(x_{i+1/2}, t))dt.$$ (5)

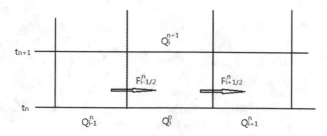

Fig. 1. Updating the cell average Q_i^n by fluxed at the cell edge

Rearrange it and use Δx to divide it and we can get

$$
\begin{aligned}
&\frac{1}{\Delta x} \int_{c_i} q(x, t_{n+1}) dx \\
&= \frac{1}{\Delta x} \int_{c_i} q(x, t_n) dx - \frac{1}{\Delta x} [\int_{t_n}^{t_{n+1}} f(q(x_{i-1/2}, t)) dt - \int_{t_n}^{t_{n+1}} f(q(x_{i+1/2}, t)) dt].
\end{aligned}
\tag{6}
$$

From the above we know how the average of the cell q is updated in one time step. However we cannot tackle with Eq. (7) directly because it need exact solution. So we must try to study a new form of numerical method

$$
Q_i^{n+1} = Q_i^n - \frac{\Delta t}{\Delta x} (F_{i+1/2}^n - F_{i-1/2}^n).
\tag{7}
$$

Where $F_{i-1/2}^n$ is some approximation to the average flux $x = x_{i-1/2}$

$$
F_{i-1/2}^n \approx \frac{1}{\Delta t} \int_{t_n}^{t_{n+1}} f(q(x_{i-1/2}, t)) dt.
\tag{8}
$$

It is reasonable to first suppose that we obtain $F_{i-1/2}^n$ based only on the values Q_{i-1}^n and Q_i^n, the cell averages on either side of this interface. The formula of this form will be used

$$
F_{i-1/2}^n = F(Q_{i-1}^n, Q_i^n).
\tag{9}
$$

Where F is some numerical flux function. So Eq. (7) becomes

$$
Q_i^{n+1} = Q_i^n - \frac{\Delta t}{\Delta x} [F(Q_i^n, Q_{i+1}^n) - F(Q_{i-1}^n, Q_i^n)].
\tag{10}
$$

so we can get

$$
\frac{Q_i^{n+1} - Q_i^n}{\Delta t} + \frac{F_{i+1/2}^n - F_{i-1/2}^n}{\Delta x} = 0 F_{i-1/2}^n = F(Q_{i-1}^n, Q_i^n).
\tag{11}
$$

Many methods can be equally well viewed as finite difference approximations to this equation or as finite volume methods. Second order accuracy can be achieved by making a better approximation to the integral in Eq. (7) [4]. One approximation is to first approximate q at the midpoint in time, $t_{n+1/2} = t_n + \frac{1}{2}\Delta t$, and evaluate the flux at this point. The Richtmyer method [4] is of this form with

$$
\frac{Q_i^{n+1} - Q_i^n}{\Delta t} + \frac{F_{i+1/2}^n - F_{i-1/2}^n}{\Delta x} = 0.
\tag{12}
$$

$$
\frac{Q_i^{n+1} - Q_i^n}{\Delta t} + \frac{F_{i+1/2}^n - F_{i-1/2}^n}{\Delta x} = 0.
\tag{13}
$$

Where

$$Q_{i-1/2}^{n+1/2} = \frac{1}{2}(Q_{i-1}^n + Q_i^n) - \frac{\Delta t}{2\Delta x}[f(Q_i^n - f(Q_{i-1}^n))].$$ (14)

3 Analytic Theory

Equations below can be used to calculate the analytic data to make comparisons with the result gotten by Star-CCM+, which will testify the accuracy of Star-CCM+.

3.1 Mass Conservation

Consider a body of fluid whose mass density is $\rho(x, t)$. The total mass of the body is given by

$$m(t) = \int_{V(t)} \rho(x, t) dV.$$ (15)

the mass conservation equation is

$$\frac{\partial \rho}{\partial t} + \frac{\partial}{\partial x_j}(\rho u_j) = 0.$$ (16)

3.2 Momentum Conversation

The conservation equation for the momentum of a body is a balance between the time rate of change of the momentum of the body and the resultant force acting on the body,

$$\int_V [\frac{\partial \rho u_i}{\partial t} + \frac{\partial}{\partial x_j}(\rho u_i u_j)] dV = F_i.$$ (17)

The vector total force F_i consists of the sum of all the forces acting on the body. This total force can be partitioned into a surface force and a body force,

$$F_i(x, t) = \oint_S \sum_{ij} n_j dS + \int_V \rho f_i dV.$$ (18)

Where, $\sum_{ij} n_j dS$ is the surface force exerted across an element of area dS, and f is the body force per unit mass.

In integral form over the material boundary, the balance equation can be written as

$$\int_V [\frac{\partial \rho u_i}{\partial t} + \frac{\partial}{\partial x_j}(\rho u_i u_j) - \frac{\partial}{\partial x_j}\sum_{ij} - \rho f_i]dV = 0. \tag{19}$$

the corresponding differential form can be written as

$$\rho \frac{Du_i}{Dt} = \frac{\partial(\rho u_i)}{\partial t} + \frac{\partial(u_i \rho u_j)}{\partial x_j} = \frac{\partial}{\partial x_j}\sum_{ij} + \rho f_i. \tag{20}$$

3.3 Energy Conservation

For the conservation equation of total energy, it includes kinetic energy and the body energy from the inside. There is a balance between the time rate of change of total energy and the energy from outside that is collected to the body by work and the heat. Using Reynolds transport theorem, this balance statement can be written as

$$\int_V [\frac{\partial(\rho E)}{\partial t} + \frac{\partial}{\partial x_j}(\rho E u_j)]dV$$
$$= \oint_S u_i \sum_{ij} n_j dS + \int_V \rho u_i f_i dV - \oint_S q_j n_j dS. \tag{21}$$

where the total energy ρE is

$$\rho E = \rho(e + \frac{u_i u_j}{2}). \tag{22}$$

with the internal energy ρE and $\rho(e + \frac{u_i u_j}{2})$ the kinetic energy.

3.4 Oblique Shockwave Theory

Making use of the continuity equation and the fact that the tangential velocity component doesn't change when it comes through shock, it can ultimately derive trigonometric relations θ-β-M of the equation, and it shows that θ is the function of M_1, β, γ.

$$\tan \theta = 2 \cot \beta \frac{M_1^2 \sin^2 \beta - 1}{M_1^2(\gamma + \cos 2\beta) + 2}. \tag{23}$$

The rise in pressure, density, and temperature after an oblique shock can be calculated as follows:

$$\frac{p_2}{p_1} = 1 + \frac{2\gamma}{\gamma + 1}(M_1^2 \sin^2 \beta - 1). \tag{24}$$

$$\frac{\rho_2}{\rho_1} = \frac{(\gamma + 1)M_1^2 \sin^2 \beta}{(\gamma - 1)M_1^2 \sin^2 \beta + 2}. \tag{25}$$

$$\frac{T_2}{T_1} = \frac{p_2}{p_1}\frac{\rho_1}{\rho_2}. \tag{26}$$

$$M_2 = \frac{1}{\sin(\beta - \theta)}\sqrt{\frac{1 + \frac{\gamma-1}{2}M_1^2 \sin^2 \beta}{\gamma M_1^2 \sin^2 \beta - \frac{\gamma-1}{2}}}. \tag{27}$$

3.5 Expansion Fan Theory

The expansion fan consists of infinite number of expansion waves or Mach lines [2]. The first Mach line in an angle is related to the direction of flow, and the last Mach line, at an angle $\mu_1 = \arctan(\frac{1}{M_1})$, is related to the final direction of flow. Since the flow into a small angle $\mu_2 = \arctan(\frac{1}{M_2})$, and the change of each expansion wave is small, so the whole process is isentropic [1]. Finally, static properties are ultimately a function of Mach number and can be related to the initial flow conditions as follows,

$$\frac{T_2}{T_1} = \left(\frac{1 + \frac{\gamma-1}{2}M_1^2}{1 + \frac{\gamma-1}{2}M_2^2}\right)$$

$$\frac{P_2}{P_1} = \left(\frac{1 + \frac{\gamma-1}{2}M_1^2}{1 + \frac{\gamma-1}{2}M_2^2}\right)^{\gamma/(\gamma-1)} \tag{28}$$

$$\frac{\rho_2}{\rho_1} = \left(\frac{1 + \frac{\gamma-1}{2}M_1^2}{1 + \frac{\gamma-1}{2}M_2^2}\right)^{1/(\gamma-1)}.$$

The Mach number after the turn (M_2) is related to the initial Mach number (M_1) and the turn angle (θ) by,

$$\theta = v(M_2) - v(M_1). \tag{29}$$

where $v(M)$ is the Prandtl–Meyer function.

$$v(M) = \int \frac{\sqrt{M^2 - 1}}{1 + \frac{\gamma-1}{2}M^2}\frac{dM}{M}$$

$$= \sqrt{\frac{\gamma + 1}{\gamma - 1}} \cdot \arctan\sqrt{\frac{\gamma - 1}{\gamma + 1}(M^2 - 1)} - \arctan\sqrt{M^2 - 1}. \tag{30}$$

By convention, $v(1) = 0$. Therefore, if given initial Mach number M_1, $v(M_1)$ can be calculated. By using the turning angle, the value of $v(M_2)$ can be obtained. So Mach number M_2 and other flow properties can be found from the value of $v(M_2)$.

4 Diamond Airfoil

4.1 Introduction of Diamond Airfoil

In this case, supersonic stream flows over a diamond airfoil that is to be simulated on Star-CCM+.

Here θ_w is the wedge angle of the airfoil, α the angle of attack, and the free stream flow properties are those with 1 subscript. There are three inlet boundary conditions which are Mach number, pressure and temperature. Inlet Mach number is 3.0, pressure is set to 100 000 pa and temperature is 270 K. The wedge angle is 10° and angle of attack is 15°.

4.2 Simulation in Star-CCM+

When supersonic stream flows through a diamond airfoil, both the shock wave and expansion fan will appear near the wall of airfoil. So this is a problem that includes shock wave problem and expansion fan problem. According to shock wave theory and Prandtl–Meyer expansion fan theory [10], the flow situation in different regions can be predicted. In order to make a qualitative analysis of the flow around the airfoil, the body is divided into six regions which are shown in Fig. 2.

From Fig. 2 we can see, the flow fields between area I and II, area II and III, area IV and V, area V and VI are all expansion fans. When it flows through expansion fan, Mach number will increase while pressure and temperature will decrease.

The physical model for the diamond airfoil simulation is three-dimensional, steady, non-viscid flow, gradient, gas, ideal air, coupling fluid and coupling energy. Also, in order to cut down the running time, three-dimensional model is converted to a two-dimensional one.

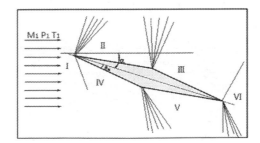

Fig. 2. Diamond airfoil with flow field regions

Table 1. Comparison with analytic solution, sonicFoam and rhoCentral.

Region	Analytical		Star-CCM+		SonicFoam		RhoCentral	
	M_2	P/P_1	M_2	P/P_1	M_2	P/P_1	M_2	P/P_1
II	3.27	0.67	3.272	0.668	3.28	0.65	3.27	0.66
III	4.78	0.09	4.774	0.091	4.78	0.086	4.80	0.087
IV	1.73	4.88	1.714	4.926	1.88	4.85	1.71	4.86
V	2.48	1.51	2.479	1.525	2.47	1.33	2.46	1.56

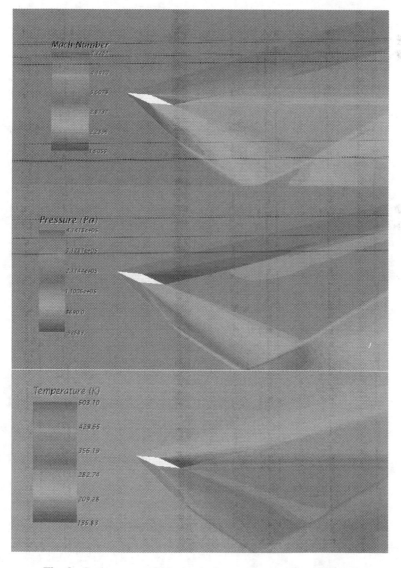

Fig. 3. Scalar scene of Mach number, pressure and temperature

4.3   Result and Discussion

Table 1 is a comparison of analytic solution with Star-CCM+, sonicFoam and rhoCentral in different regions (data of analytic solution, sonicFoam and rhoCentral are from [1]). And pictures in Fig. 3 are scalar scenes of Mach number, pressure, temperature.

Table 1 shows that results given by Star-CCM+ is very close to analytical data, and when compared with other CFD software namely sonicFoam and rhoCentral, results from Star-CCM+ are better. From Fig. 3 it can be concluded that when gas flows through expansion fan, Mach number will increase and pressure and temperature will both decrease. Properties in shock wave case are on the contrary.

5   Other Compressible Flow Cases

5.1   Compression Wedges

An oblique shock wave is inclined with respect to the incident upstream flow direction. When supersonic flow encounters a corner, it will effectively flows into itself and compression will happen. For the given Mach number M_1 and corner angle θ, angle oblique shock angle β and downstream Mach number M_2 can be calculated. M_2 is always less than M_1. Discontinuous change also occurs in the pressure, density and temperature, and all this will lead to increased downstream oblique shock wave parameters [9].

The problem is to observe gas flowing over a wedge whose angel is 15°. To get a better observation, the inlet Mach number $M_1 = [1.65, 1.75, 2.0, 2.25, 2.5, 3.0, 3.5]$ and inlet pressure $P_1 = 100$ kPa, temperature $T_1 = 270$ K. Geometry of the wedge is shown in Figs. 4 and 5.

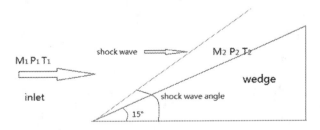

Fig. 4. Configuration of wedge

Comparison between simulation results and analytical results is shown as follow:

5.2   Prandtl–Meyer Expansion Fan Problem

A Prandtl–Meyer expansion fan is a centered expansion process that occurs when a supersonic flow turns around a convex corner [10]. A uniform supersonic gas flows

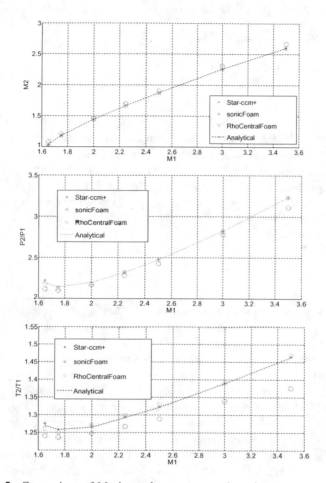

Fig. 5. Comparison of Mach number, pressure ratio and temperature ratio

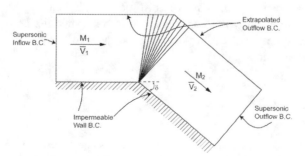

Fig. 6. Configuration of flow region

Table 2. Comparison between the analytical data and simulation results

	Analytic data	Star-CCM+ result
M_2	2.383	2.3846
P_2/P_1	0.5471	0.5478
ρ_2/ρ_1	0.6500	0.6507
V_2/V_1	1.0931	1.0943

along a sudden divergence. When it comes through the corner, it changes its direction by forming expansion fan which is isentropic and smooth. The expansion fan radiates away from the corner, with uniform flow isolated from two regions, as shown in the Fig. 6 (picture is from [5]). The primary variables are $M_1 = 2$ and $\delta = 10°$ (Table 2).

From the result it can be concluded that Star-CCM+ performs better than sonic-Foam and RhoCentralFoam and Star-CCM+ is trustful to simulate compressible flow on condition of inviscid and steady flow.

6   Conclusion

It can be seen that simulation result from Star-CCM+ is very similar to the analytic information, which is better than RhoCentrolFoam and sonicFoam. This paper provides an evidence in one objective that compressible flow solver in Star-CCM+ can simulate steady and inviscid compressible flow in high accuracy, highlighting better performance of Star-CCM+ than other CFD software mentioned above.

As far as I am aware, the size and quality of mesh, the geometry of physical model and boundary condition all play important roles in the process of simulation. In another word, accurate result can be got when suitable conditions are set. When the size of mesh is large, the result derived from it may be coarse but it saves a lot of time running the simulation. Accurate results can be got by creating smaller size mesh but at the same time it also takes a lot of time to run. A good way to tackle this problem is to use mesh refinement method. Take shock wave wedge for example. The mesh near the shock wave should be generated with smaller size because information near the shock wave is very important. However, the mesh far from the model is not as important as that near the shock wave, so it is a waste of time to such areas.

The conclusion given by this paper is not sufficient when it comes to unsteady or transient compressible flow, so I hope more efforts will to be made on benchmarking Star-CCM+ in the future.

References

1. Marcantoni, L.F.G., Tamagno, J.P.T., Elaskar, S.A.: High Speed Flow Simulation Using Openfoam. Asociación Argentina de Mecánica Computacional **XXXI**, 2939–2959 (2012)
2. Gatski, T.B., Bonnet, J.-P.: Compressibility, Turbulence and High Speed Flow, 2nd edn. Elsevier Science Publications, Oxford (2013)

3. Chung, T.J.: Computational Fluid Dynamics. Cambridge University Press, New York (2014)
4. LeVeque, R.: Finite Volume Methods for Hyperbolic Problems. Cambridge University Press, Cambridge (2002)
5. Habchi, S., Bayyuk, S.: Prandtl-Meyer expansion fan. In: AIAA CFD Verification Project, Shock waves, 16 (2010)
6. Batchelor, G.K.: An Introduction to Fluid Dynamics. Cambridge University Press, New York (1967)
7. Osthuizen, P.H., Carscallen, W.E.: Introduction to Compressible Flow, 2nd edn. CRC Press, Boca Raton (2013)
8. Acheson, D.J.: Elementary Fluid Dynamics. Oxford Applied Mathematics and Computing Science Series. Oxford University Press, Oxford (1990)
9. Anderson Jr., J.D.: Fundamentals of Aerodynamics. McGraw-Hill Series in Aeronautical and Aerospace Engineering, 3rd edn. The McGraw Companies Inc., New York (2001)
10. Shapiro, A.H.: The Dynamics and Thermodynamics of Compressible Fluid Flow, vol. 1. Ronald Press, New York (1953)

Modelling and Simulation of Risk Control in Active Distribution Network

Wei Li[1(✉)], Shouzhen Zhu[1], Xiaomin Bai[2], and Weijie Dong[2]

[1] Department of Electrical Engineering, Tsinghua University, Beijing, China
baovr@163.com
[2] China Electric Power Research Institute, Beijing, China

Abstract. More and more distributed generation have accessed to the power distribution network, which brings great risks to the operation security. In this paper, according to the characteristics of the distribution network, the three-phase risk control model is established based on many controllable equipment in active distribution network, and then the original nonlinear non-convex programming problem is converted into a convex feasible domain by the second-order cone relaxation technique. Finally, the improved IEEE34 nodes case study is illustrated to verify feasibility and validity of the proposed method.

Keywords: Active distribution network (ADN) · Distributed generation (DG) · Risk control · Second-order cone programming (SOCP)

1 Introduction

One of the critical functions of intelligent distribution network in the future is the safe and reliable acceptance of distributed generation (DG) such as wind power and solar power. The development of DG not only can optimize the energy structure, promote energy conservation and emissions reduction, and also can achieve sustainable economic development. In recent years, with large number applications of DG in distribution network, energy storage system (ESS), static VAR compensation (SVC), capacitors bank (CB) and other equipment are increasingly employed day by day. The traditional distribution network is gradually evolved into active distribution network (ADN) with thousands of adjustable and controllable resources.

The high penetration of DG in ADN, on the one hand, can improve power supply reliability by continuing to provide electricity for customers when a failure occurs in the network; the other hand, would change the structure and power flow of distribution network. The traditional radial distribution network will be converted into a multi-power system and the operation and control will be full of risk. A large number of distributed power connected to grid may cause voltage fluctuation, partial over-voltage, line overload or even power outages, which seriously affect the operation security. This severely restricts the ability of ADN to absorb renewable energy power generation, and wastes power grid resources and renewable energy. Therefore, there is a necessity to control the risk in ADN effectively. Unlike transmission network, distribution network lines are no longer a three-phase cycle overall transposition, and the

L. Zhang et al. (Eds.): AsiaSim 2016/SCS AutumnSim 2016, Part III, CCIS 645, pp. 392–401, 2016.
DOI: 10.1007/978-981-10-2669-0_42

three-phase load unbalance is widespread phenomenon at customer side. So the establishment of three-phase model for distribution power flow calculation, optimal scheduling, analysis and decision has gradually become the mainstream research. In addition, the line resistance and reactance are almost close in distribution network, and the active and reactive power have stronger coupling. This makes it very difficult to directly apply the traditional decision based on active and reactive decoupling theory into ADN. So, it is full of challenges based on the three-phase active and reactive power coupling model to solve the problems such as bi-directional flow, overvoltage, abandon of wind power or solar power, branch congestion, line loss, and so on.

In addition to generators and other continuous controllable means, there are also discrete control variables such as CB, SVC and on-load tap changer (OLTC) of transformers in ADN. The nature of this risk optimization problem has become a mixed integer non-convex nonlinear programming problem. The joint method of interior-point and penalty function proposed in [1] was employed to process the discrete variables, which converted the mixed integer programming problem into a continuous problem, but this algorithm only makes sure the local optimal solution. With the rise of the second-order cone programming (SOCP), a deep research was studied in [2, 3] for distribution network reactive power optimization problem in second-order cone relaxation accuracy, application scope and its feasibility. If the SOCP problems is equivalence with the original problem, SOCP algorithm can obtain the global optimal solution of the problem. Considering the continuous and discrete variables at the same time and in order to reduce the operation risk in ADN, this paper establishes a three-phase distribution network optimization model. Combining with second order cone relaxation techniques (SOCR), the three-phase power flow equation is trans-formed into a second-order cone problem which can effectively solve the mixed integer optimization problem. In the end, the improved IEEE 34 nodes case study verifies the feasibility and validity of the proposed method.

2 Three-Phase Model of ADN

2.1 Distflow for ADN

As for the radial ADN shown in Fig. 1, the optimization power flow model of Distflow [4] is demonstrated below.

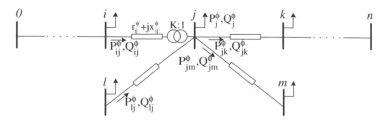

Fig. 1. One line diagram of radial distribution network

For any node j in the network, there is

$$\begin{cases} \sum_{k \in v(j)} P_{jk}^{\varphi} = \sum_{i \in u(j)} \left[P_{ij}^{\varphi} - r_{ij}^{\varphi} \frac{\left(P_{ij}^{\varphi}\right)^2 + \left(Q_{ij}^{\varphi}\right)^2}{\left(V_i^{\varphi}\right)^2} \right] + P_j^{\varphi} \\ \sum_{k \in v(j)} Q_{jk}^{\varphi} = \sum_{i \in u(j)} \left[Q_{ij}^{\varphi} - x_{ij}^{\varphi} \frac{\left(P_{ij}^{\varphi}\right)^2 + \left(Q_{ij}^{\varphi}\right)^2}{\left(V_i^{\varphi}\right)^2} \right] + Q_j^{\varphi} \\ P_j^{\varphi} = P_{j,DG}^{\varphi} + P_{j,discha}^{\varphi} - P_{j,cha}^{\varphi} - P_{j.d}^{\varphi} \\ Q_j^{\varphi} = Q_{j,DG}^{\varphi} + Q_{j.SVC}^{\varphi} + Q_{j,CB}^{\varphi} - Q_{j,d}^{\varphi} \end{cases} \quad (1)$$

For any feeder ij in the network, there is

$$\left(V_j^{\varphi} / K \right)^2 = \left(V_i^{\varphi}\right)^2 - 2\left(r_{ij}^{\varphi} P_{ij}^{\varphi} + x_{ij}^{\varphi} Q_{ij}^{\varphi} \right) + \left[\left(r_{ij}^{\varphi}\right)^2 + \left(x_{ij}^{\varphi}\right)^2 \right] \frac{\left(P_{ij}^{\varphi}\right)^2 + \left(Q_{ij}^{\varphi}\right)^2}{\left(V_i^{\varphi}\right)^2} \quad (2)$$

In (1) and (2), $\varphi \in \{A, B, C\}$ is the set of three-model of A, B and C; $u(j)$ denotes the node set of all the head node of the feeders ending in node j; $v(j)$ denotes the node set of all the end node of the feeders beginning with node j; V_j^{φ} is the voltage amplitude of node j; P_{ij}^{φ} and Q_{ij}^{φ} denote the three-phase active power and reactive power at head point of line ij, respectively; P_j^{φ} and Q_j^{φ} denote the active power injection and reactive power injection at node j, respectively; $P_{j,DG}^{\varphi}$, $P_{j,discha}^{\varphi}$, $P_{j,cha}^{\varphi}$ and $P_{j.d}^{\varphi}$ denote the active power of DG, discharge power of ESS, charge power of ESS and load active power at node j, respectively; $Q_{j,DG}^{\varphi}$, $Q_{j.SVC}^{\varphi}$, $Q_{j,CB}^{\varphi}$ and $Q_{j,d}^{\varphi}$ denote the reactive power of DG, continuous compensation power of SVC, discrete compensation power of CB and load reactive power at node j, respectively; r_{ij}^{φ} and x_{ij}^{φ} are the reactance and resistance of feeders considering self-impedance and mutual impedance in three-phase; K is the ratio of OLTC.

2.2   Constraints

OLTC of Transformer. The model of OLTC is shown as follows.

$$\begin{cases} t_{j,OLTC}^{\varphi} = \alpha_{j,OLTC}^{\varphi,0} \cdot 2^0 + \alpha_{j,OLTC}^{\varphi,1} \cdot 2^1 \\ \alpha_{j,OLTC}^{\varphi,p} \left(\alpha_{j,OLTC}^{\varphi,p} - 1 \right) = 0 \\ 0 \leq \alpha_{j,OLTC}^{\varphi,p} \leq 1 \end{cases} \quad (3)$$

In (3), $\alpha_{j,OLTC}^{\varphi,p}$ is a real number between 0 and 1, and through the constraint $\alpha_{j,OLTC}^{\varphi,p} \left(\alpha_{j,OLTC}^{\varphi,p} - 1 \right) = 0$ it is controlled as 0–1 variable. Then the position variable of OLTC $t_{j,OLTC}^{\varphi}$ converts to integer variable. In this paper, there are four positions, namely $t_{j,OLTC}^{\varphi} \in \{0, 1, 2, 3\}$.

CB. CB is an important reactive power compensation equipment in distribution network, with its switch operation status as discrete variable in nature, and therefore binary encoding and supplement constraint are employed to achieve discrete data serialization. Limited by the manufacture technology and service life of CB, the number of operation within a scheduling period is strictly limited, and each time switching operation is grouped. So the operation of the CB should meet the following constraint.

$$
\begin{cases}
Q_{j,CB}^{\varphi} = tap_{j,CB}^{\varphi} Q_{j,CB,step}^{\varphi} \\
tap_{j,CB}^{\varphi} = \alpha_{j,CB}^{\varphi,0} \cdot 2^0 + \alpha_{j,CB}^{\varphi,1} \cdot 2^1 \\
\alpha_{j,CB}^{\varphi,p} \left(\alpha_{j,CB}^{\varphi,p} - 1 \right) = 0 \\
0 \leq \alpha_{j,CB}^{\varphi,p} \leq 1
\end{cases}
\tag{4}
$$

In (4), $Q_{j,CB}^{\varphi}$ is the reactive compensation capacity for each phase at node j; $Q_{j,CB,step}^{\varphi}$ is the step compensation for each phase; $\alpha_{j,CB}^{\varphi,p}$ is a real number between 0 and 1. In this paper, there are four positions, namely $tap_{j,CB}^{\varphi} \in \{0, 1, 2, 3\}$.

DG. The model of DG is shown as follows.

$$
\begin{cases}
0 \leq P_{j,DG}^{\varphi} \leq \bar{P}_{j,DG}^{\varphi} \\
Q_{j,DG}^{\varphi} = P_{j,DG}^{\varphi} \tan \varphi'
\end{cases}
\tag{5}
$$

In (5), $P_{j,DG}^{\varphi}$ and $P_{j,DG}^{\varphi}$ are active power and reactive power of DG, respectively; φ' denotes the power factor angle; $\bar{P}_{j,DG}^{\varphi}$ denotes the rated active power of DG. The steady state model of DG adopts PQ type, and DG is set in constant power factor operation mode.

ESS. The model of ESS is shown as follows.

$$
\begin{cases}
0 \leq P_{j,cha}^{\varphi} \leq \bar{P}_{j,cha}^{\varphi} C_{j,cha}^{\varphi} \\
0 \leq P_{j,discha}^{\varphi} \leq \bar{P}_{j,discha}^{\varphi} C_{j,discha}^{\varphi} \\
C_{j,cha}^{\varphi} + C_{j,discha}^{\varphi} \leq 1, \ C_{j,cha}^{\varphi} \in \{0, 1\}, \ C_{j,discha}^{\varphi} \in \{0, 1\}
\end{cases}
\tag{6}
$$

$$
\begin{cases}
P_{j,cha}^{A} = P_{j,cha}^{B} = P_{j,cha}^{C} \\
P_{j,discha}^{A} = P_{j,discha}^{B} = P_{j,discha}^{C}
\end{cases}
\tag{7}
$$

In (6), $\bar{P}_{j,cha}^{\varphi}$ and $\bar{P}_{j,discha}^{\varphi}$ are the charge and discharge power upper limit respectively. Considering this doesn't appear in ESS at any time while charging and discharging, the 0–1 variables $C_{j,cha}^{\varphi}$ and $C_{j,discha}^{\varphi}$ are introduced, and $C_{j,cha}^{\varphi} + C_{j,discha}^{\varphi} \leq 1$. This constraint guarantee at any time ESS can only be in one of the three states:

charging, discharging or standby. For simplification this paper set three phases with the same constraint and three-phase linkage, as shown in (7).

SVC. SVC is a three-phase independent continuous adjustable reactive power device, the capacity constraint is as follows:

$$\underline{Q}^{\varphi}_{j.SVC} \le Q^{\varphi}_{j.SVC} \le \overline{Q}^{\varphi}_{j.SVC} \tag{8}$$

In (8), $\underline{Q}^{\varphi}_{j.SVC}$ and $\overline{Q}^{\varphi}_{j.SVC}$ denote the lower and upper limit of each phase, respectively.

2.3   Objective Function

The purpose of optimization is to keep the whole operation risk to a minimum. This paper sets the node overvoltage and line overload as the risk evaluation index.

$$f_{Risk} = \sum_{\varphi=A}^{C} \sum_{i=1}^{N} \sum_{j\in v(i)} \left(I^{\varphi}_{ij}\right)^2 - \left(I^{\varphi}_{ij,0}\right)^2 + (U^{\varphi}_i)^2 - \left(U^{\varphi}_{i,0}\right)^2 \tag{9}$$

In (9), $I^{\varphi}_{ij,0}$ is the rated current of line ij to make sure the distribution security; $U^{\varphi}_{i,0}$ is the rated voltage of node i; f_{Risk} is the objective function.

Due to the lines in distribution network are generally short, this paper only consider the RMS value of voltage or current regardless of the voltage phase angle difference, and the linear relationship between them is as follows:

$$U^{\varphi}_i = \sqrt{\left(r^{\varphi}_{ij}\right)^2 + \left(x^{\varphi}_{ij}\right)^2} I^{\varphi}_{ij} \tag{10}$$

So (9) can be simplified as:

$$f_{Risk} = \sum_{\varphi=A}^{C} \sum_{i=1}^{N} \sum_{j\in v(i)} \left(1 + \left(r^{\varphi}_{ij}\right)^2 + \left(x^{\varphi}_{ij}\right)^2\right) \left(\left(I^{\varphi}_{ij}\right)^2 - \left(I^{\varphi}_{ij,0}\right)^2\right) \tag{11}$$

3   SOCP Model

The standard form of second-order cone programming (SOCP) is shown as follows:

$$\min_{x_i}\left\{c^T x \middle| Ax = b, x_i \in K, i = 1, 2, \ldots, N\right\} \tag{12}$$

Where, the variable $x \in R_N$, the constant coefficient $b \in R_M$, $c \in R_N$ and $A_{M \times N} \in R_{M \times N}$; K is the second-order cone as follows:

$$K = \left\{ x_i \in R_N \middle| y^2 \geq \sum_{i=1}^{N} x_i^2, y \geq 0 \right\} \tag{13}$$

SOCP is essentially a convex programming with excellent features of optimal solution and calculation efficiency. The optimal result can be easily calculated by existing algorithm packages and solving process can be done in polynomial time.

According to the characteristics of the SOCP, the power flow equations are relaxed by SOCR. Set $\tilde{I}_{ij}^{\varphi} = \left(I_{ij}^{\varphi} \right)^2$, $\tilde{U}_{ij}^{\varphi} = \left(U_{ij}^{\varphi} \right)^2$, and replace the voltage amplitude quadratic terms with $\tilde{U}_{ij}^{\varphi}$ in (1) and (2), then get the following equations:

$$\begin{cases} \sum_{i \in u(j)} \left(P_{ij}^{\varphi} - r_{ij}^{\varphi} \tilde{I}_{ij}^{\varphi} \right) = \sum_{k \in v(j)} P_{jk}^{\varphi} + P_j^{\varphi} \\ \sum_{i \in u(j)} \left(Q_{ij}^{\varphi} - x_{ij}^{\varphi} \tilde{I}_{ij}^{\varphi} \right) = \sum_{k \in v(j)} Q_{jk}^{\varphi} + Q_j^{\varphi} \\ P_j^{\varphi} = P_{j,DG}^{\varphi} + P_{j,disch}^{\varphi} - P_{j,ch}^{\varphi} - P_{j,d}^{\varphi} \\ Q_j^{\varphi} = Q_{j,DG}^{\varphi} + Q_{j,SVC}^{\varphi} + Q_{j,CB}^{\varphi} - Q_{j,d}^{\varphi} \\ \tilde{U}_j^{\varphi} = \tilde{U}_i^{\varphi} - 2\left(r_{ij}^{\varphi} P_{ij}^{\varphi} + x_{ij}^{\varphi} Q_{ij}^{\varphi} \right) + \left[\left(r_{ij}^{\varphi} \right)^2 + \left(x_{ij}^{\varphi} \right)^2 \right] \tilde{I}_{ij}^{\varphi} \end{cases} \tag{14}$$

$$\tilde{U}_i^{\varphi} = \frac{\left(P_{ij}^{\varphi} \right)^2 + \left(Q_{ij}^{\varphi} \right)^2}{\tilde{I}_{ij}^{\varphi}} \tag{15}$$

After the modification, the original Distflow power flow equation has become a system of linear equations (14) and a concise form quadratic equation (15). Then (15) can be relaxed to standard second-order cone form as follows:

$$\left\| \left[2P_{ij}^{\varphi} \quad 2Q_{ij}^{\varphi} \quad \tilde{I}_{ij}^{\varphi} - \tilde{U}_{ij}^{\varphi} \right]^T \right\|_2 \leq \tilde{I}_{ij}^{\varphi} + \tilde{U}_{ij}^{\varphi} \tag{16}$$

For the optimization model proposed above, without considering discrete control variables such as OLTC, ESS, CB and SVC, the objective function and all of the equality constraints are linear; the inequality constraints except (16) are also linear. While the mathematical from of (16) can be abstracted as $\sqrt{x_1^2 + x_2^2 + x_3^2} \leq x_4^2$, which satisfies the definition of second-order cone. That means the problem is a SOCP problem. The explanation in [2, 5] demonstrates SOCP is a convex programming with excellent mathematical properties.

The relaxation process is shown in Fig. 2. The original non-convex feasible domain $C_{original}$ is relaxed to a second-order cone convex feasible domain C_{SOC}, then the

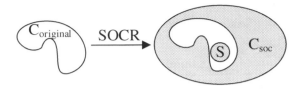

Fig. 2. Schematic figure of second-order cone relaxation

Distflow power flow is converted to convex form. Since the introduction of SOCR, the optimal solution S obtained in C_{SOC} is a lower bound solution to the original problem, and if S is the point in $C_{original}$, the SOCP relaxation is strict and S is the optimal solution to the original problem.

4   Case Study

4.1   Simulation Platform

In order to verify the effect of this method, YALMIP [6] based on MATLAB is developed for the risk optimization program. YALMIP is a modeling language for advanced modeling and solution of convex and nonconvex optimization problems. It is implemented as a free toolbox for MATLAB.

YALMIP was initially indented for SDP and LMIs (hence the now obsolete name Yet Another LMI Parser), but has evolved substantially over these years. The most recent release supports linear programming (LP), quadratic programming (QP), second order cone programming (SOCP), semidefinite programming, determinant maximization, mixed integer programming, posynomial geometric programming, semidefinite programs with bilinear matrix inequalities (BMI), and multiparametric linear and quadratic programming. To solve these problems, around 20 solvers are interfaced. This includes both freeware solvers such as SeDuMi and SDPT3, and commercial solvers as the PENNON solvers, LMILAB and CPLEX. Due to a ·flexible solver interface and internal format, adding new solvers, and even new problem classes, can often be done with modest effort. The main motivation for using YALMIP is rapid algorithm development. The language is consistent with standard MATLAB syntax, thus making it extremely simple to use for anyone familiar with MATLAB. Another benefit of YALMIP is that it implements a large amount of modeling tricks, allowing the user to concentrate on the high-level model, while YALMIP takes care of the low-level modeling to obtain as efficient and numerically sound models as possible.

4.2   Test System

Based on the IEEE 34 nodes three-phase radial distribution network in [7], DG, SVC, CB and ESS are added to form the study case in this paper, as shown in Fig. 3. Table 1 shows the line number and the corresponding node number. Taking into account that PV is the main type in ADN, this paper also selects PV as the grid-connected generation, and in

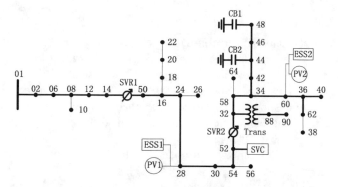

Fig. 3. Modified IEEE 34 nodes test feeder system

Table 1. Line number between nodes

Line no.	From node	To node	Line no.	From node	To node	Line no.	From node	To node
L1	01	02	L2	02	06	L3	06	08
L4	08	10	L5	08	12	L6	12	14
L7	14	50	L8	16	18	L9	16	24
L10	18	20	L11	20	22	L12	24	26
L13	24	28	L14	28	30	L15	30	54
L16	32	58	L17	34	60	L18	34	42
L19	36	40	L20	36	62	L21	42	44
L22	44	46	L23	46	48	L24	50	16
L25	32	88	L26	54	56	L27	54	52
L28	58	64	L29	58	34	L30	60	36
L31	62	38	L32	88	90			

order to suppress the influence of fluctuation to network, a certain volume of ESS is mounted at the same spot. This test system is an actual radial network with heavy load, long feeder and unbalanced load. The total load is set 20.7 + j0.73MVA in this paper. At node 28 and 60, solar power PV1 and PV2 with 0.8 MW are attached respectively, the power factor is set as $\cos \varphi' = 0.95$, three phases can be controllable independently. The total discharge power of ESS is 300 kW, 100 kW per phase, 93.81 % charge-discharge efficiency. At node 52, SVC is attached with compensation range (−100–250) kvar. Node 44 and 48 connect two groups of CB respectively, and in each scheduling cycle at most 4 operations are permitted. Each phase has four groups of 25 kvar, namely each phase compensation has a total of (0–100) at five states.

4.3   Results

In the cases with the same power from DG, the operation states based on the method proposed in this paper and the no-control strategy are shown in Figs. 4 and 5. The figures contain only three-phase node voltage and line current.

From Fig. 4, it can be seen that in the case of only DG participating in the operation, a large part of the node voltage exceed the rated voltage by ±5 %, which is very harmful to electrical insulation and equipment, even to the human safety. So in this case there is a big risk in the system operation, while after adopting the method proposed in this paper to optimize, all nodes are in the safe operating range, which reduces the risk.

As can be seen in Fig. 5, there exists excess current capacity at the head part of the feeders under the no-control condition. When the system load fluctuations, such as the startup of large power, protection equipment is likely to act to make the whole network lose load. Meanwhile, if the feeders operate in the overload condition over a long period, the line insulation will speed up aging, and will also bring great security risk to system. However, SOCP optimize and adjust the state of each feeder to ensure the feeders under rated current operation with a certain margin, and then the operation risk in the system can be reduced accordingly.

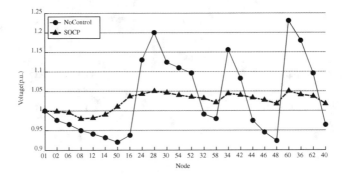

Fig. 4. Results of voltage optimization

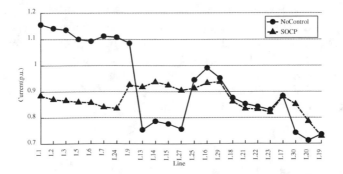

Fig. 5. Results of current optimization

In order to verify the accuracy of SOCR, namely the optimal solution in (16) whether can meet the requirements of the equation. An index is defined as follows:

$$D^\varphi = \left\| \tilde{U}^\varphi - \frac{(P^\varphi)^2 + (Q^\varphi)^2}{\tilde{I}^\varphi} \right\|_\infty \tag{17}$$

Where, D^φ is the infinite norm of all the feeders in the network, and it is calculated as: $D^A = 1.82 \times 10^{-7}$, $D^B = 3.17 \times 10^{-7}$, $D^C = 2.36 \times 10^{-7}$. It is easy to find the deviation after convex relaxation is very small, which indicates that the relaxation in this paper is strict and precise.

5 Conclusion

A large number of adjustable and controllable devices access to the traditional distribution network have significant impact on the power flow and control strategy. Therefore, how to coordinate these devices on the basis of three-phase model, improve resource utilization, guarantee grid security and economic operation, reduce the risk of distribution, is the optimization goal of this paper. This paper establishes Distflow model with the three-phase radial distribution network, as well as the model of ESS, DG, SVC and CB. According to the starting point of operation risk as the objective function, the quadratic equation in the Distflow power flow equivalently relaxes to the second-order cone form, making the original problem simpler and its solvability and optimization improved. Finally, the case study based on improved IEEE 34 nodes network verify the proposed method with high efficiency and good effect.

References

1. Li, Z.G., Wu, W.C., Zhang, B.M., et al.: A large-scale reactive power optimization method based on Gaussian penalty function with discrete control variables. Proc. CSEE **33**(4), 68–76 (2013). (in Chinese)
2. Farivar, M., Low, S.H.: Branch flow model: relaxations and convexification (part I). IEEE Trans. Power Sys. **28**(3), 2554–2564 (2013)
3. Taylor, J.A., Hover, F.S.: Convex models of distribution system reconfiguration. IEEE Trans. Power Syst. **27**(3), 1407–1413 (2012)
4. Liu, Y.B., Wu, W.C., Zhang, B.M., et al.: Reactive power optimization for three-phase distribution networks with distributed generators based on mixed integer second-order cone programming. Automat. Electr. Power Syst. **38**(15), 58–64 (2014). (in Chinese)
5. Quan, R., Wei, H., Jian, J.B.: Solution of large scale unit commitment by second-order cone programming. Proc. CSEE **30**(25), 01–107 (2010). (in Chinese)
6. Lofberg, J.: YALMIP: a toolbox for modeling and optimization in Matlab. In: 2004 IEEE International Symposium on Computer Aided Control Systems Design, pp. 284–289. IEEE, Taipei (2004)
7. Caramia, P., Carpinelli, G., Varilone, P.: Point estimate schemes for probabilistic three-phase load flow. J. Electr. Power Syst. Res. **80**(2), 168–175 (2010)

Rough-Set-Based Energy Consumption Model of Cutting Period in CNC Lathe

Binzi Xu, Yan Wang$^{(\boxtimes)}$, Zhicheng Ji, and Manfeng Hu

Engineering Research Center of Internet of Things Technology Applications
Ministry of Education, Jiangnan University, Wuxi 214122, China
wangyan88@jiangnan.edu.cn

Abstract. An energy consumption model of cutting period in CNC lathe is presented using rough set theory. Firstly, initial decision table is established from acquired data. Secondly, decision attribute is discretized according to its distribution. Furthermore, a novel continuous attribute discretization method is proposed to discretize condition attributes. Finally, output is calculated based on information space ratio. The experiment shows this method is viable and accurate.

Keywords: Rough set · Energy consumption · CNC lathe

1 Introduction

Discrete manufacturing is the foundation of mechanical products, which brings great economic benefits [1]. As productivity grows, energy consumed by machine tools also increases. Actually, manufacturing generates more than half of energy consumption in China. After decades of optimizing machining processes based on cost and productivity, a growing demand to increase energy efficiency of machine tools is widely acknowledged. Therefore, energy consumption analysis is fundamentally important in effectively mitigating the negative influences of machining and improving its energy efficiency.

Usually, energy consumption model seeks to find the relationship between machining parameters and input power of machine tools. Balogun et al. [2] divided the electrical energy requirements of a machining process into four parts: basic state energy, ready state energy, cutting state energy and non-cutting state energy. Peng et al. [3] proposed three types of function blocks to model the energy consumption of CNC machine tools. Guo et al. [4] divided the workpiece process into three parts and predicted energy consumption through an operation-mode based simulation approach.

Traditional approaches to model energy consumption of CNC machine tools are mainly based on analytical models, which requires clearly knowledge about machine tools. However, this is challenging now due to complex construction and varying parameters of CNC machine tools. Hence, there is a need to develop a novel modeling approach that could avoid these problems. Kant and Sangwan [5] used artificial neural network to predict the energy consumption. Garg et al. [6] proposed a multi-gene genetic programming approach combined with complexity and orthogonal basis functions to model the energy consumption of the milling process.

© Springer Science+Business Media Singapore 2016
L. Zhang et al. (Eds.): AsiaSim 2016/SCS AutumnSim 2016, Part III, CCIS 645, pp. 402–411, 2016.
DOI: 10.1007/978-981-10-2669-0_43

Typically, an operator could make favorable decisions based on production experience obtained from observing inputs and outputs. This process is similar to the main idea of Rough Set (RS). RS is a new mathematical technique in knowledge discovery. It aims to find the relationship between different data, but does not require a classical mathematical description of this process.

This paper applies knowledge modelling method based on RS to model the energy consumption of CNC lathe, and improves modelling method appropriately according to the specific application. It includes a novel approach to discretize decision attributes, a method based on Boolean logic and attribute importance to discretize continuous condition attributes, a computing method based on information space to obtain output. As the basis of sustainable production, this study has a focus on energy consumption model of cutting period in CNC lathe.

2   Methodology

This section presents basic definitions and knowledge of energy consumption and RS.

2.1   Energy Consumption Model of CNC Machine Tools

CNC machine tools are widely used in today's society. In this case, accurate energy consumption model is necessary for follow-up studies, like energy consumption optimization. Related researches [7] shown that operational state of CNC machine tools has a bearing on energy cost. Typically, the process of CNC machine tools includes four periods: startup period, standby period, idle period and cutting period. Each period has own characteristics, which are also shown in Fig. 1.

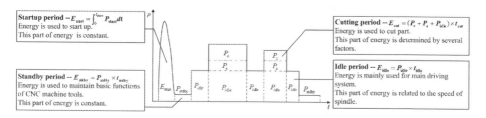

Fig. 1.   Input power curve of CNC machine tools

2.2   Rough Set Theory

Rough set is a soft computing approach that Pawlak Z presented in 1982 to deal with uncertain and incomplete problem [8]. An information system in RS is a rule-based knowledge, which is expressed in a decision table. That is to say, it does not require a specific description of process mechanism, but consists of sets of If-Then rules instead [9].

Decision Table.   In RS, information system is denoted as a nonempty finite set $S = (U, A, V, f)$. Here, $U = \{x_1, x_2, \ldots, x_n\}$ means a finite set of samples; $A = C \cup D$,

$C \cap D = \emptyset$, C and D denotes condition (C) and decision (D) attributes of samples, respectively; $V = \cup_{a \in A} V_a$ is the set of these attributes' range; $f : U \times A \to V$ is an information function that gives every attribute a value. Typically, this finite set is expressed in decision table, as shown in Fig. 1.

Indiscernibility Relation. According to RS, indiscernibility relation can be defined. Typically, the indiscernibility relation is:

$$ind(R) = \{(x, y) \in U \times U : f(x, a) = f(y, a), \forall a \in A\} \tag{1}$$

Where (x, y) is a pair of samples and $f(x, a)$ denotes the value of attribute a for sample x. Generally, sample set U could be divide into several elementary sets, such as U/R. If $(x, y) \in ind(R)$, then it is hard to distinguish x, y according to R.

3 Rough-Set Based Modeling Method

This section presents a novel RS-based modelling method, which is applied to cutting period in this paper.

3.1 Data Preprocessing

Decision table built from original sample mostly has many problems, like data redundancy, data incompatibility and data incompleteness [9]. This step is aim to clean sample set and improve data quality.

In this paper, cutting period of CNC lathe is seen as an information system $S = (U, C \cup D, V, f)$, where $U = \{x_1, x_2, \cdots, x_n\}$, $C = \{v_c, f, a_p\}$, $D = \{P_i\}$. Table 1 is an example with 12 groups of data that have been preprocessed.

Table 1. An example of the information system

U	v_c (m/min)	f (mm/s)	a_p (mm)	P_i (W)
x_1	100	0.14	1.1	2497
x_2	110	0.11	1.1	2505
x_3	110	0.14	1.1	2693
x_4	110	0.12	1.3	2725
x_5	120	0.13	1.2	2911
x_6	130	0.11	1.2	2949
x_7	130	0.14	1.1	3081
x_8	120	0.17	1.1	3083
x_9	130	0.14	1.2	3184
x_{10}	120	0.16	1.3	3234
x_{11}	120	0.14	1.5	3272
x_{12}	130	0.15	1.4	3479

*: These data have been collected from experiments in Sect. 4

3.2   Discretization of Continuous Decision Attribute

Current studies provide little information on how to discretize continuous decision attribute. Continuous decision attribute is discretized by domain experts in most studies [9]. Besides, it would be discretized into several equidistant intervals sometimes. However, the former method is subjective that may have potential problems; the latter method rarely considers data distribution. Therefore, a novel discretization method is urgently required. In this paper, input power of CNC lathe during cutting period is chosen as decision attribute, which is a continuous variable. Here presents a novel discretization method based on data distribution.

Algorithm 1. Discretization of decision attribute
(a)   Set a precision value Δ. Turn decision attribute values v_d (input power) into intervals $v_d \pm \Delta$.
(b)   If length of overlapping portion between two intervals is greater than threshold value k, then combine these two intervals into one.
(c)   If any two of these intervals have overlapping portion that less than threshold value k, then partition the overlapping portion to the interval with less length.
(d)   Divide all of intervals into round($length/2\Delta$) equal parts. Where, round ($\bullet$) returns rounded result.

Using the decision attribute value set in Table 1, $D = \{2497, 2505, 2693, 2725, 2911, 2949, 3081, 3083, 3184, 3234, 3272, 3479\}$. In this example, $\Delta=k= 50$. Then intervals formed from each decision attribute value are [2447, 2547), [2455, 2555), $\cdots$, [3429, 3529), respectively. According to step (b) and step (c), the range of this decision attribute value set is divided into six parts: [2447, 2555), [2643, 2775), [2861, 2999), [3031, 3133), [3134, 3322), [3429, 3529). Here, round((3322 − 3134)/100) = 2. So, interval [3134, 3322) needs to be divided into two parts: [3134, 3227), [3228, 3322). 1, 2, 3, 4, 5, 6, 7 is used to represent these intervals respectively. Hence, set $D^* = \{1, 1, 2, 2, 3, 3, 4, 4, 5, 6, 6, 7\}$ is the decision attribute value set after distribution.

In this novel method, distribution quality is directly determined by precision value and threshold value, which should be decided based on actual situation.

3.3   Discretization of Continuous Condition Attribute

After decision attribute being discretized, this section is aim to propose a novel discretization method based on Boolean logic and attribute importance.

A New Information System Based on Boolean Logic. Nguyen and Skowron [10] introduced Boolean logic into condition attribute discretization and proposed an effective discretization method. This method builds a new information system $S^* = (U^*, C^* \cup D^*, V^*, f^*)$ according to discernibility relation between two samples, whose decision attribute values are different. Besides, this new information system does not change indiscernibility relation of original system.

In this new information system, $U^* = \{(x_i, x_j) \in U \times U : d(x_i) \neq d(x_j)\}$, $C^* = \{c_i^a | i \in \{0, 1, \cdots, k_a\}, a \in C\}$, c_i^a is the cut point of attribute a,

$$f^*(u, c) = \begin{cases} 1 & \min[a(x_i), a(x_j)] < c < \max[a(x_i), a(x_j)] \\ 0 & \text{otherwise} \end{cases}.$$

Attribute Importance. Attribute importance is a crucial concept in RS. The more important the attribute is, the more attention it should get. In RS, attribute importance describes classification capacity of this attribute.

Let C, D be condition attributes set and decision attributes set respectively, $C' \subseteq C$. Then, the importance of attributes set C' is defined as:

$$\sigma_{CD}(C') = \gamma_C(D) - \gamma_{C-C'}(D) = \frac{|POS_C(D)|}{|U|} - \frac{|POS_{C-C'}(D)|}{|U|} \tag{2}$$

In particular, when $C' = \{a\}$, the importance of attribute $a \in C$ is

$$\sigma_{CD}(a) = \gamma_C(D) - \gamma_{C-\{a\}}(D) \tag{3}$$

In the information system shown in Table 1, the importance of v_c, f, a_p is 0.25, 0.33, 0.167, respectively.

A Novel Discretization Method Based on Boolean Logic and Attribute Importance. In this paper, a novel discretization method combined with Boolean logic and attribute importance is presented:

Algorithm 2. Discretization method based on Boolean logic and attribute importance
(a) Calculate attribute importance according to Eq. (3).
(b) Sort condition attributes in ascending order on the basis of attribute importance; Sort condition attributes with same importance in descending order according to the cut point numbers of these attributes.
(c) Built new information system S^* based on Boolean logic.
(d) Decide the cut point will stay or remove in turn. Observe all rows marked with 1 in the corresponding column. If there is one row that only have one 1, namely only the corresponding column is 1 in this row and others are 0, then keep this cut point and delete the corresponding column, together with all rows marked with 1 in it; otherwise, remove this cut point and delete the corresponding column.

According to step (a) and (b), the initial cut point set is:

$$CUT = C_{ap} \cup C_{vc} \cup C_f$$

Where,

$$C_{ap} = \{(a_p, 1.15), (a_p, 1.25), (a_p, 1.35), (a_p, 1.45)\}$$
$$C_{vc} = \{(v_c, 105), (v_c, 115), (v_c, 125)\}$$
$$C_f = \{(f, 0.115), (f, 0.125), (f, 0.135), (f, 0.145), (f, 0.155), (f, 0.165)\}$$

The new information system S^* based on Boolean logic is a 61×13 Boolean matrix. The part of it is shown in Table 2.

Table 2. Part of corresponding new information system

	1.15	1.25	1.35	1.45	105	115	125	0.115	0.125	0.135	0.145	0.55	0.165
(x_1, x_3)	0	0	0	0	1	0	0	0	0	0	0	0	0
(x_1, x_4)	1	1	0	0	1	0	0	0	1	1	0	0	0
(x_1, x_5)	1	0	0	0	1	1	0	0	0	1	0	0	0
(x_1, x_6)	1	0	0	0	1	1	1	1	1	1	0	0	0
(x_1, x_7)	0	0	0	0	1	1	1	0	0	0	0	0	0
(x_1, x_8)	0	0	0	0	1	1	0	0	0	0	1	1	1
(x_1, x_9)	1	0	0	0	1	1	1	0	0	0	0	0	0
(x_1, x_{10})	1	1	0	0	1	1	0	0	0	0	1	1	0
(x_1, x_{11})	1	1	1	1	1	1	0	0	0	0	0	0	0
(x_1, x_{12})	1	1	1	0	1	1	1	0	0	0	1	0	0
(x_2, x_3)	0	0	0	0	0	0	0	1	1	1	0	0	0
(x_2, x_4)	1	1	0	0	0	0	0	1	0	0	0	0	0

According to step (c), the final cut point is $CUT = \{(a_p, 1.15), (v_c, 105), (v_c, 125), (f, 0.125), (f, 0.135), (f, 0.145)\}$. Set $\{0, 1\}$ is used to represent interval set of attribute a_p, namely $\{(-\infty, 1.15), [1.15, +\infty)\}$. For attribute v_c, set $\{0, 1, 2\}$ is used to represent interval set $\{(-\infty, 105), [105, 125), [125, +\infty)\}$. For attribute f, set $\{0, 1, 2, 3\}$ is used to represent interval set $\{(-\infty, 0.125), [0.125, 0.135), [0.135, 0.145), [0.145, +\infty)\}$. The discretized information system is shown in Table 3.

Table 3. Discretized information system

U	v_c (m/min)	f (mm/s)	a_p (mm)	P_i (W)
x_1	0	2	0	1
x_2	1	0	0	1
x_3	1	2	0	2
x_4	1	0	1	2
x_5	1	1	1	3
x_6	2	0	1	3
x_7	2	2	0	4
x_8	1	3	0	4
x_9	2	2	1	5
x_{10}	1	3	1	6
x_{11}	1	2	1	6
x_{12}	2	3	1	7

Classical discrete method neither takes attribute importance into consideration, nor obtains minimal number of cut points. However, Algorithm 2 can find the most reasonable cut point set with fewest cut points.

So far, a feasible knowledge base has been obtained. In this knowledge base, each sample is seen as a rule. For a new sample, the decision attribute value could be predicted by matching every condition attribute.

3.4   A Novel Output Method of Knowledge Base

In the situation of continuous decision attribute, knowledge base only output an interval, not a value. Hence, a novel output method based on knowledge space is proposed.

When condition attributes all have upper and lower limit, knowledge system S becomes an enclosure space with $|C|$-dimension, namely knowledge space. Usually, this knowledge space is divided into several subspaces by cut points, in which samples have the same decision attribute value. These subspaces are called basic hypercube.

Typically, each basic hypercube corresponds to an interval when the decision attribute of this knowledge space is continuous. As shown in Fig. 2, sample x_1 and x_2 are in the same hypercube, but the output of x_1 should greater than x_2 when corresponding decision attribute value is an interval.

Let the corresponding decision attribute value be $[v_i^d, v_{i+1}^d)$, then the output of x_1 could be calculated by Eq. (4)

$$v^d = (v_{i+1}^d - v_i^d)\frac{V_t}{V} + v_i^d = (1 - \frac{V_t}{V})v_i^d + \frac{V_t}{V}v_{i+1}^d \qquad (4)$$

Where, V is the space volume of this basic hypercube; V_t is the volume of the space surrounded by this sample (Fig. 2).

Fig. 2. An example of basic hypercube

4   Case Study

In this paper, CK60 NC lathe, whose numerical control system is Hua-zhong NC system, is taken as an example and related data are collected from the model presented by Zhou [11]. The workpiece material is 45# HRS (Hot Rolled Steel). The diameter of workpiece is 50 mm, and cutting length is 100 mm.

Here, experiments are designed based on orthogonal experimental design, and related cutting parameters are shown in Table 4. 210 samples are recorded to build initial decision table.

In order to obtain a feasible knowledge base, continuous decision attribute is needed to be discretized first. The decision attribute value ranges from 1449 to 10234. In this case, precision value $\Delta = 50$, threshold value $k = 50$. So, the decision attribute is divided into 65 intervals.

Next step is condition attribute discretization. The calculating result shows that the importance of three cutting parameters are all 1. This result is generated because of orthogonal design and small precision value. Actually, no cut point will be deleted according to the calculating result. Finally, the knowledge base is obtained.

Tables 5, 6 and 7 shows the comparison of RS-based model and real value when cutting parameters change. The result indicates that this RS-based energy consumption model is precious enough to be applied to practical production.

Table 4. Values of cutting parameters

Parameters	Values
v_c (m/min)	70, 100, 130, 160, 190, 220, 250
f (mm/s)	0.1, 0.15, 0.2, 0.25, 0.3
a_p (mm)	0.5, 0.8, 1.1, 1.4, 1.7, 2.0

Table 5. Error analysis with different v_c

v_c (m/min)	RS (W)	Real value (W)	Error (%)
75	3903	3005	3.39
105	3898	3923	0.64
135	4792	4815	0.48
165	5699	5687	0.21
195	6565	6544	0.32
225	7457	7388	0.93

*: $f = 0.25$ mm/s, $a_p = 1.6$ mm

Table 6. Error analysis with different f

f (mm/s)	RS (W)	Real Value (W)	Error (%)
0.12	3201	3389	5.55
0.17	3798	3897	2.54
0.22	4275	4384	2.49
0.27	4794	4854	1.24

*: $v_c = 130$ m/min, $a_p = 1.6$ mm

Table 7. Error analysis with different a_p

a_p (mm)	RS (W)	Real Value (W)	Error (%)
0.7	3308	3143	5.25
1	3794	3654	3.83
1.3	4271	4162	2.62
1.6	4791	4668	2.63
1.9	5307	5172	2.61

*: $v_c = 130$ m/min, $f = 0.25$ mm/s

5 Conclusion

Energy consumption model is the foundation of the following research, like energy saving. This RS-based energy consumption model is proposed under the trend of manufacturing information, which makes it possible to record and store production data. Knowledge base used in this model could be built from real production data, and improved with the accumulation of data. Advantages of this RS-based model includes simplifying computing process of output and providing enough precision. The only problem of this RS-based modeling approach is that it requires mass data to find the mapping relationship between different data. Besides, this RS-based method solves the modeling problem of information system whose input and output are both continuous. Hence, it is viable to be generalized to other fields.

Acknowledgement. This work is supported by National Hi-tech Research and Development Program of China (863 Program, Grant No. 2014AA041505), the National Natural Science Foundation of China (Grant No. 61572238) and the Provincial Outstanding Youth Foundation of Jiangsu Province (Grant No. BK20160001).

References

1. Salonitis, K., Ball, P.: Energy efficient manufacturing from machine tools to manufacturing systems. Procedia CIRP **7**(12), 634–639 (2013)
2. Balogun, V.A., Mativenga, P.T.: Modelling of direct energy requirements in mechanical machining processes. J. Clean. Product. **41**(2), 179–186 (2013)
3. Peng, T., Xu, X., Wang, L.: A novel energy demand modelling approach for CNC machining based on function blocks. J. Manuf. Syst. **33**(1), 196–208 (2014)
4. Guo, Y., Duflou, J.R., Qian, J., et al.: An operation-mode based simulation approach to enhance the energy conservation of machine tools. J. Clean. Product. **101**, 348–359 (2015)
5. Kant, G., Sangwan, K.S.: Predictive modelling for energy consumption in machining using artificial neural network. Procedia CIRP **37**, 205–210 (2015)
6. Garg, A., Lam, J.S.L., Gao, L.: Energy conservation in manufacturing operations: modelling the milling process by a new complexity-based evolutionary approach. J. Clean. Product. **108**, 34–45 (2015)

7. Zhou, L., Li, J., Li, F., et al.: Energy consumption model and energy efficiency of machine tools: a comprehensive literature review. J. Clean. Product. **112**, 3721–3734 (2015)
8. Pawlak, Z.: Rough Sets: Theoretical Aspects of Reasoning About Data. Kluwer Academic Publishers, Dortrecht (1991)
9. Tan, T.: Rough Set-Based Process Modeling, Control and Fault Diagnosis. Zhejiang University, Zhejiang (2003)
10. Nguyen, S.H., Skowron, A.: Quantization of real value attributes-rough set and Boolean reasoning approach. In: Proceedings of the Second Joint Conference on Information Sciences, pp. 34–37 (1995)
11. Zhou, Z., Zhang, C., Xie, Y., et al.: Cutting parameters optimization for processing energy and efficiency in CNC lathe. Comput. Integr. Manuf. Syst. **21**(09), 2410–2418 (2015)

EOG Artifacts Reduction from EEG Based on Deep Network and Recursive Least Squares Adaptive Filter

Banghua Yang[1,2(✉)], Kaiwen Duan[1], Tao Zhang[1], and Yonghuai Zhang[2]

[1] Department of Automation, College of Mechatronics Engineering and Automation, Key Laboratory of Power Station Automation Technology, Shanghai University, Shanghai 200072, China
yangbanghua@shu.edu.cn, kaiwenduan@outlook.com, 1594270069@qq.com

[2] Shanghai Shenwei Electronic Technology Co., LTD., Shanghai 200444, China
yonghuaizhang@126.com

Abstract. We developed a cascade of deep network and recursive least squares adaptive filter (DN-RLS) for electrooculogram (EOG) artifacts removal. The proposed method can be divided into offline stage and online stage. During the offline stage, EOG signals are used to train an DN to learn features of EOG signals. During the online stage, the learned DN is used to extract EOG artifacts from electroencephalogram (EEG), then a RLS filter is used to further remove EOG artifacts. The proposed method not only just needs few number of EEG channels in removal process, but also doesn't need additional EOG recordings during online stage. We compared the proposed method to the independent component analysis (ICA) technique and a shallow network combined with RLS method. Experimental results show that the DN-RLS can learn features of EOG artifacts better and result in higher classification accuracy.

Keywords: Electrooculogram (EOG) · Electroencephalogram (EEG) · Deep Network (DN) · Recursive Least Squares adaptive (RLS) filtering

1 Introduction

An electroencephalogram (EEG) signal is the recording of neural electrical activities caused by nerve firings [1]. EEG can capture a fast dynamics of brain information processing at a high temporal resolution. One of the main applications for EEG is the research of motor imagery (MI) based brain computer interface (BCI) [2, 3]. However, it is easily influenced by noise especially the electrooculogram (EOG) artifacts, which is a problem for MI classification [4, 5].

This project is supported by National Natural Science Foundation of China (31100709), the Shanghai Pujiang Program, China (No. 14PJ1431300) and Natural Science Foundation of Shanghai (No. 16Z R1424200).

© Springer Science+Business Media Singapore 2016
L. Zhang et al. (Eds.): AsiaSim 2016/SCS AutumnSim 2016, Part III, CCIS 645, pp. 412–421, 2016.
DOI: 10.1007/978-981-10-2669-0_44

Estimating clean EEG signals from raw ones is very important for the further analysis of EEG. It's difficult to remove EOG artifacts from EEG, because EOG artifacts overlap in frequency and time domains with EEG signals. In recent years, there has been an increasing interest in applying various methods to remove EOG artifacts from EEG signals [6, 7]. In general, there are three common categories of removing EOG artifacts.

(i) Regression category: This category often assumes that the scalp potential is a linear combination of brain and ocular potentials. By subtracting propagated EOG artifacts from EEG recordings, EEG signals can be recovered [1, 8]. This category relies on EOG recordings, which are however, not always available.

(ii) Blind-source separation (BSS) category: This category employs a principal component analysis (PCA) and an independent component analysis (ICA) [5]. This category can separate raw EEG signals into a set of independent components (ICs) and EOG artifacts-related ICs will then be identified. This category relies on a large number of EEG channels to ensure that the ICs with distinct characteristics of EOG artifacts are identified.

(iii) Wavelet transformation category: This category usually uses wavelet transformation to extract features of EOG artifacts, which is effective. However, the threshold for wavelet transformation is difficult to determine. An unsuitable threshold may result in degradation of the EEG data [5, 9].

As we all know, deep network (DN) has already been used in image processing and other applications. Despite the success of DN, its application in EEG based BCI is still rare [10]. In this study, we proposed a novel method to remove EOG artifacts from raw EEG using a cascade of DN and recursive least squares (RLS) adaptive filter, which is called DN-RLS. The proposed method can be divided into offline stage and online stage (Fig. 1). A formal description is given in Table 1. During the offline stage, because EOG signals share many features with EOG artifacts [11, 12], the DN is trained to learn the features of EOG signals, which also are the features of EOG artifacts in a sense. Based on this principle, the DN is trained to only encode the information of the EOG artifacts. During the online stage, the trained DN model is used like an EEG filter to extract EOG artifacts, in which the denoising principle of autoencoder is skillfully applied [13]. Then an RLS adaptive filter is used to further remove EOG artifacts.

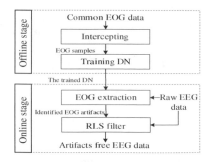

Fig. 1. Flowchart of the proposed method

Table 1. Component of the proposed method

Offline stage:
(i): provide common EOG data and intercept enough EOG samples.
(ii): use EOG samples to train an DN to learn the features of EOG signals.
Online stage:
(iii): apply the trained DN model to identify EOG artifacts from EEG signal. The raw EEG signal is used as input of DN.
(iv): apply RLS filter to remove EOG artifacts. The EOG artifacts identified by the trained DN are used as a reference signal.

2 Methods

2.1 Introduction of DN

DN is the new family of learning methods that can offer good representation of data using a multiple-layered structure, with each layer representing different degree of abstraction of data features [10] In this study, we apply the stacked sparse autoencoder [14] as an DN. Figure 2 shows an DN with 3 hidden layers of structure. Assuming that $\hat{x} = x$ are input data and output data of the DN. According to [14], it uses $\hat{x} = x$, where $x, \hat{x}$ are n dimensional column vectors, which correspond to n inputs of DN. Layer 1 is the input layer, layer 2, layer 3 and layer 4 are hidden layers, layer 5 is the output layer. The circles labeled "+1" are called bias units and correspond to the intercept terms. Two adjacent layers are connected by weights and intercept terms.

As shown in the Fig. 2, $W^{(i,j)}(j = i + 1; i = 1, 2, 3, 4)$ is the parameter (or weight) matrix associated with layer i and layer j. Also, $b^{(i)}$ denotes the bias associated with layer i and layer j. The structure of the DN can be seen as a deep neural network consisting of multiple layers of sparse autoencoders (SAE), in which the output of former SAE is wired to the input of successive SAE. Following the method of [14], a good way to obtain good parameters for an DN is to use greedy layer-wise training [15]. To do this, the first SAE is trained on raw input to obtain parameters accordingly.

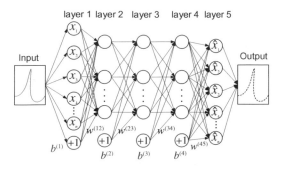

Fig. 2. The structure of DN

The first layer of the first SAE is used to transform the raw input into a vector consisting of activation of the hidden units. The second SAE on this vector is then trained to obtain parameters of the second SAE accordingly. All layers are repeated and the output of each layer is used as input for the subsequent layer. The approach about how to train an SAE can be seen in [16]. After this training is completed, fine-tuning using backpropagation can be used to improve the results by tuning the parameters of all layers at the same time.

2.2 Introduction of Adaptive Filter Using RLS

He et al. [17] used adaptive filtering to eliminate EOG artifacts in EEG. The method employs the raw EEG signal as input, and the EOG artifacts as reference signals. Clean EEG can be obtained by subtracting the filtered outputs. In order to guarantee that the reference signal has the most proper characteristics relative to the EOG artifacts, the filter coefficients need to be adjusted by using a RLS method.

In this study, the EOG artifacts identified by the DN serve as reference signal $r(n)$. An adaptive filter can be written as:

$$v(n) = \sum_{k=1}^{H} h(k)r(n - k + 1) \tag{1}$$

where $v(n)$ is the ocular activity, $h(k)$ is the kth coefficient of a finite impulse response filter with length H. The desired output from the noise canceller $e(n)$ is the corrected or clean EEG by subtracting the filtered reference signal from raw EEG signal $y(n)$.

$$e(n) = y(n) - v(n) = y(n) - \sum_{k=1}^{H} h(k)r(n - k + 1). \tag{2}$$

in order to obtain the best cancellation of the EOG artifacts, the filter coefficients $h(k)$ are adjusted using a RLS method by minimizing the target function ε_n:

$$\varepsilon_n = e^2(n) + \lambda e^2(n - 1) + \cdots + \lambda^{n-H} e^2(H) \tag{3}$$

where $0 < \lambda < 1$ is called forgetting factor [17]. In this paper, after a lot of experiments, $\lambda = 0.99$ was taken.

2.3 Cascade of DN and RLS Adaptive Filter

Figure 3 provides the block diagram of the proposed method. $y(n)$ is the raw EEG signal, $r(n)$ is the EOG artifacts identified by DN model. Clean EEG $e(n)$ can be obtained by subtracting the filtered outputs $v(n)$ from raw EEG $y(n)$. As shown in Fig. 1, the proposed method can be divided into offline stage and online stage. The offline stage includes EOG sample interception and DN learning for EOG artifacts features. The online stage includes EOG artifacts removal from raw EEG by RLS filter.

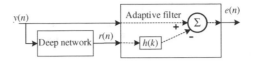

Fig. 3. Block diagram of the proposed method on one channel of EEG signal

2.3.1 EOG Feature Learning by DN Training During Offline Stage

The DN needs to be trained firstly before employing, which is one of the most important content of this method. A fixed training set of m training samples $\{x^{(1)}, \ldots, x^{(m)}\}$ is firstly intercepted from EOG signals. Where every sample $x^{(i)}, i <=m$ is n dimensional column vector (contains n sampling points), which corresponds to n inputs of DN. A formal description of the framework for 3 hidden layers is given in Table 2.

After the DN training described in Table 2, the learned optimal parameter set θ is computed. That is also to say that some features of EOG signals or EOG artifacts can be learned by these parameters. The next stage is online stage, when given one channel of raw EEG signal, the trained DN can be employed to identify the EOG artifacts $r(n)$ from the raw EEG signal $y(n)$.

Table 2. DN training algorithm

Input: A fixed training set of m training samples $\{x^{(1)}, \ldots, x^{(m)}\}$.

Output: The learnt optimal weight and bias θ, $\theta = (W^{(12)}, b^{(1)}, W^{(23)}, b^{(2)}, W^{(34)}, b^{(3)}, W^{(45)}, b^{(4)})$.

1: **for** $i = 1$ **to** 3 **do**

2:    Train the ith SAE model

3:    **if** $i < 3$

4:       Obtain optimal parameters $\hat{W}^{(ij)}, \hat{b}^{(i)}$.

5:       Obtain a vector consisting of activation of the hidden units.

6:       Use this vector as input for the subsequent SAE.

7:    **else**

8:       Obtain optimal parameters $\hat{W}^{(34)}, \hat{b}^{(3)}, \hat{W}^{(45)}, \hat{b}^{(4)}$.

9: **end for**

10: Learn an optimal parameter set $\hat{\theta} = (\hat{W}^{(12)}, \hat{b}^{(1)}, \hat{W}^{(23)}, \hat{b}^{(2)}, \hat{W}^{(34)}, \hat{b}^{(3)}, \hat{W}^{(45)}, \hat{b}^{(4)})$.

11: Obtain the optimal parameter set θ by fine-tuning.

12: **return** the learnt optimal parameter set θ.

2.3.2   EOG Artifacts Removal by RLS Filter During Online Stage

The procedure of online stage is summarized as follows:

- The trained DN is employed to identify the EOG artifacts $r(n)$ from the raw EEG signal $y(n)$ for one channel.
- The identified EOG artifacts $r(n)$ are served as reference signals for an adaptive filter.
- A RLS adaptive filter is used to estimate the ocular activity $v(n)$ using formula (1).
- Clean EEG signal $e(n)$ is obtained by subtracting the ocular activity $v(n)$ from $y(n)$.
- Change EEG channel and repeat the above steps.

According to above steps, clean EEG signals for a certain time from all EEG channels to be analyzed can be obtained. Then these signals can be used for EEG feature extraction and classification.

3   Data Description

The dataset used in this study is from "Graz data set B" for BCI Competition IV, which is launched on July 3rd 2008. This data set consists of EEG data from nine subjects of a study published in [18]. For each subject, two classes of motor imagery hand were selected: left hand and right hand. EEG signals were recorded from three channels (C3, Cz and C4), which positioned over sensorimotor areas densely. In addition to the EEG signals, the EOG was also recorded. In pretraining, only the EOG signals from Subject1 is selected to train DN. The signals were band-pass filtered between 0.5 and 100 Hz and then sampled at 250 Hz. More details were described in [19].

4   Experiments and Results

4.1   DN Training

In this study, as Table 2 shows, set $m = 10000$. Namely, 10000 training samples ($\{x^{(1)}, \ldots, x^{(10000)}\}$) are intercepted randomly from EOG signal of Subject1 to train DN. Also, there are 500 testing samples randomly intercepted to test the trained DN. The EOG signal is divided into two segments at first, one is used for training samples interception and the other is used for testing samples interception. In order to get enough samples, each segment is randomly intercepted into a number of samples. Set $n = 1000$, one is that each sample contains 1000 sampling points, which corresponds to 1000 units of the input layer. Let the number of hidden layers be 3 (based on lots of experimental results). Let numbers of units in hidden layers be 300, 1000, 300, respectively. The samples have been scaled to the range of 0 to 1. After training, the DN seems to have "learned" these waveforms adequately enough to be able to reconstruct them. In order to show stronger learning ability of DN, we have compared the reconstruction ability between DN and a shallow network called SAE. Figures 4 and 5 depict reconstructions of one testing sample drawn by the output of DN with 3

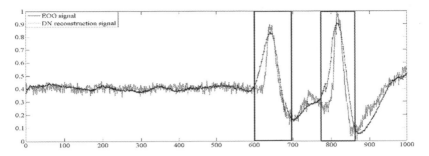

Fig. 4. The reconstruction of signals from DN

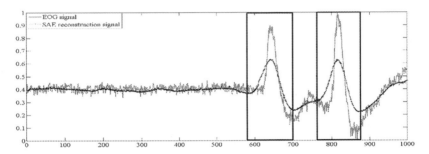

Fig. 5. The reconstruction of signals from SAE

hidden layers and SAE, respectively. Clearly, the DN performs better (details can be seen in the black boxes).

4.2   EOG Artifacts Removal

The EOG artifacts removal is processed during the online stage. In this stage, raw EEG signal is used as input of the trained DN. That is also to say 1000 input sampling points of one channel at a time. After calculation, the output $r(n)$ of DN is considered as EOG artifacts from the raw EEG signal. The raw EEG signal $y(n)$, together with the EOG artifacts $r(n)$ identified by the DN, is then used as input and reference input of RLS adaptive filter to remove EOG artifacts. In order to further show stronger learning ability of DN, we also have compared the removal ability between DN and the shallow network SAE. Figure 6 depicts raw EEG signal ($y(n)$) from single channel (Cz) of one random trial and the respectively processed one ($e(n)$). The left trials (119 trials) are also processed, and similar results are obtained. As shown in the Fig. 6, it is obvious that the most of the EOG artifacts in raw EEG data are removed. Moreover, it's also obvious that the DN-RLS performs better than the combination of SAE and RLS (SAE-RLS) (details can be seen in the black boxes).

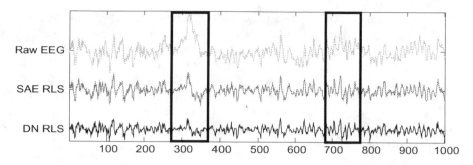

Fig. 6. Raw EEG signal and the respectively processed one

4.3 Classification Accuracy

In addition to the comparison of results showed in Sect. 4.2, classification accuracy is also used to evaluate the effect of the proposed method. Here, we compared the proposed method with other two methods. (1) ICA: it is widely accepted that the artifactual signals are independent from the ongoing cerebral activity, which provides the possibility of the application of ICA. In the last decade, ICA has had a crucial role in neuroscience research and it has taken great attention for artifacts rejection purpose [20]. Through ICA, the EEG data is decomposed into a set of independent components (ICs). Then EOG artifacts can be identified from the whole ICs. ICA can separate EOG artifacts efficiently. However, this method relies on a large number of EEG channels to ensure that the ICs with distinct characteristics of EOG artifacts are identified. (2) SAERLS: autoencoder was already used in image processing and other applications, particularly applied to extract robust feature of noisy for classification [13]. Despite the success of autoencoder, its application in EOG artifacts removal is still rare. We previously have applied the SAE-RLS method for EOG artifacts removal and achieved good results. However, the SAE is a kind of shallow network, whose study ability is limited.

In this study, the autoregressive (AR) model is used for feature extraction and the

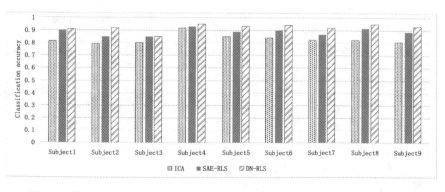

Fig. 7. Classification accuracy of different methods with three-channel signals

SVM for classification [21, 22]. In this experiment, a cross-subject testing scenario is applied to test the generalization ability of the proposed method: the training data (EOG signal) comes from Subject 1 and the test data (EEG signal) comes from all nine subjects. By the experiments, the proposed method is proven that it has a good generalization ability. The classification accuracies of EEG data from three channels (C3, Cz and C4) are calculated and showed in Fig. 7. The classification results show that the DN-RLS performs better than that of ICA and SAE-RLS. The DN-RLS leads to a higher 9.2 % and 3.4 % average classification accuracy than that of the ICA and SAE-RLS, respectively.

5 Conclusion and Discussion

In this paper, a method for removing EOG artifacts from EEG signal is presented, which joints use of DN with RLS filter to do cascade filtering. Compared with the three common categories above, the proposed method has the following properties: (i) theoretically, this method can effectively learn features of EOG artifacts offline. (ii) EOG artifacts can be automatically removed by using the learned network and RLS adaptive filter. (iii) This method does not need an additional EOG recordings in removal process, which is comfortable for the subject. (iv) this method is suitable for any small number of EEG electrodes, which is convenient for recording.

References

1. Nguyen, H.A.T., Musson, J., Li, F., et al.: EOG artifact removal using a wavelet neural network. Neurocomputing **97**(1), 374–389 (2012)
2. Nijboer, F., Broermann, U.: Brain-computer interfaces for communication and control in locked-in patients. In: Graimann, B., Pfurtscheller, G., Allison, B. (eds.) Brain-Computer Interfaces. The Frontiers Collection, pp. 185–201. Springer, Heidelberg (2010)
3. Chen, M., Liu, Y., Zhang, L.: Classification of stroke patients' motor imagery EEG with autoencoders in BCI-FES rehabilitation training system. In: Loo, C.K., Yap, K.S., Wong, K. W., Beng Jin, A.T., Huang, K. (eds.) ICONIP 2014, Part III. LNCS, vol. 8836, pp. 202–209. Springer, Heidelberg (2014)
4. Hassan, A., Song, X.: A study of kernel CSP-based motor imagery brain computer interface classification. In: Signal Processing in Medicine and Biology Symposium, pp. 1–4 (2012)
5. Jing, H., Wang, C.-S., Min, W.: Removal of EOG and EMG artifacts from EEG using combination of functional link neural network and adaptive neural fuzzy inference system. Neurocomputing **151**, 278–287 (2015)
6. Devuyst, S., Dutoit, T., Ravet, T., Stenuit, P., Kerkhofs, M., Stanus, E.: Automatic processing of EEG-EOG-EMG artifacts in sleep stage classification. In: Lim, C.T., Goh, J.C. H. (eds.) ICBME 2008. IFMBE Proceedings, vol. 23, pp. 146–150. Springer, Heidelberg (2009)
7. Ai, G., Sato, N., Singh, B., et al.: Direction and viewing area-sensitive influence of EOG artifacts revealed in the EEG topographic pattern analysis. Cogn. Neurodyn. **10**, 301–314 (2016)

8. Gratton, G., Coles, M.G.H., Donchin, E.: A new method for off-line removal of ocular artifact. Electroencephalogr. Clin. Neurophysiol. **55**(4), 468–484 (1983)
9. Ghandeharion, H., Erfanian, A.: A fully automatic ocular artifact suppression from EEG data using higher order statistics: improved performance by wavelet analysis. Med. Eng. Phys. **32** (7), 720–729 (2010)
10. Ahmed, S., Merino, L.M., Mao, Z., et al.: A deep learning method for classification of images RSVP events with EEG data. In: Global Conference on Signal and Information Processing, pp. 33–36. IEEE (2013)
11. Hagemann, D., Naumann, E.: The effects of ocular artifacts on (lateralized) broadband power in the EEG. Clin. Neurophysiol. Off. J. Int. Fed. Clin. Neurophysiol. **112**(2), 215–231 (2001)
12. Pizzagalli, D.A.: Electroencephalography and high-density electrophysiological source localization, pp. 56–84 (2007)
13. Vincent, P., Larochelle, H., Lajoie, I., et al.: Stacked denoising autoencoders: learning useful representations in a deep network with a local denoising criterion. J. Mach. Learn. Res. **11** (6), 3371–3408 (2010)
14. Stacked Autoencoders. http://ufldl.stanford.edu/wiki/index.php/Stacked_Autoencoders
15. Rueda-Plata, D., Ramos-Pollán, R., González, F.A.: Supervised greedy layer-wise training for deep convolutional networks with small datasets. In: Núñez, M., Nguyen, N.T., Camacho, D., Trawiński, B. (eds.) ICCCI 2015, Part I. LNCS, vol. 9329, pp. 275–284. Springer International Publishing, Switzerland (2015)
16. Ng, A.: Sparse autoencoder. CS294A Lecture Notes, vol. 72, pp. 1–19 (2011)
17. He, D.P., Wilson, G., Russell, C.: Removal of ocular artifacts from electro-encephalogram by adaptive filtering. Med. Biol. Eng. Comput. **42**(3), 407–412 (2004)
18. Leeb, R., Lee, F., Keinrath, C., et al.: Brain-computer communication: motivation, aim, and impact of exploring a virtual apartment. IEEE Trans. Neural Syst. Rehabil. Eng. **15**(4), 473–482 (2007)
19. Leeb, R., Brunner, C., Mller-Putz, G.R.: BCI Competition 2008-Graz dataset B. Graz University of Technology (2008)
20. Klados, M.A., Bratsas, C., Frantzidis, C., et al.: A kurtosis-based automatic system using Naïve Bayesian classifier to identify ICA components contaminated by EOG or ECG artifacts. In: XII Mediterranean Conference on Medical and Biological Engineering and Computing, vol. 29, pp. 49–52 (2010)
21. Schlögl, A., Flotzinger, D., Pfurtscheller, G.: Adaptive autoregressive modeling used for single-trial EEG classification. Biomed. Tech. **42**(6), 162–167 (1997)
22. Hortal, E., Iáñez, E., Úbeda, A., María Azorín, J., Fernández, E.: Training study approaches for a SVM-based BCI: adaptation to the model vs adaptation to the user. In: Manuel Ferrández Vicente, J., Ramón Álvarez Sánchez, J., de la Paz López, F., Toledo Moreo, F. (eds.) IWINAC 2013, Part I. LNCS, vol. 7930, pp. 131–140. Springer, Heidelberg (2013)

Application of the Multimodal Human-Computer Interaction Technology in Product Virtual Display

Xiaoling Li[✉], Lingyu Ji, Feng Han, and Xiuwen Sun

School of Mechanical Engineering, Xi'an Jiaotong University, Xi'an, China
xjtulxl@mail.xjtu.edu.cn, floriousfu@hotmail.com

Abstract. In the existing product virtual display system, the interactions are mainly operated by mouse and keyboard. Inevitably, the user experience is often interrupted and disturbed by the continually input and output actions. This paper proposes a multimodal virtual display system which is integrated with speech and gesture recognition technology. First, we established a digital automobile model and set the interactive actions of the automobile display in a Web3D platform. Next, the speech interaction was realized by the re-development of the Microsoft Speech SDK and the gesture recognition was accomplished by Leap Motion controller. At last, the whole system was achieved on a holographic experimental platform. The proposed system makes the interactions more intuitive, natural and comprehensive in product virtual display.

Keywords: Virtual display · Multimodal · Human-computer interaction · Speech · Gesture

1 Introduction

Over the past decades, Virtual Reality (VR) has been increasingly valued by American and European countries and has been widely researched in various fields. Web3D technology, based on VR, has also been widely applied in the fields of military [1, 2], architecture [3, 4], entertainment [5], etc. In the meantime, with the development of multimodal technology, which is integrated with eye tracking, speech recognition, gesture input, sensory feedback, users can simulate the interactive operations (motion, customization, assembly, etc.) of the products according to their needs in a natural, efficient and real-time parallel manner [6]. Multimodal interaction has become an important direction in the field of human computer interaction. Some technology companies have developed their multimodal interactive sensors and products and put them into market, such as Google's Project Glass, Microsoft's Kinect and HoloLens, and Leap Motion.

Applying multimodal interaction technology to virtual environment will be the mainstream form of VR interface in the future [7]. In recent years, a number of high-level institutions have carried out relevant researches on multimodal interaction, such as MIT's GALAXY project, CMU's INTERACT project, and the Amodeus project of the European Union's ESPRIT program [8]. Lozano-Quilis et al. [9] developed a Multiple Sclerosis rehabilitation system which created virtual environments to help patients do rehabilitation exercises using KINECT. Yecheng Gu et al. [10] introduced

© Springer Science+Business Media Singapore 2016
L. Zhang et al. (Eds.): AsiaSim 2016/SCS AutumnSim 2016, Part III, CCIS 645, pp. 422–430, 2016.
DOI: 10.1007/978-981-10-2669-0_45

a novel method for detecting and modeling intentions of students performing training tasks in a VR environment. However, there is no research about fusing multimodal interaction with product virtual display. Moreover, the interactions in the existing product virtual display system are mainly operated by mouse and keyboard, which are inefficient and not intuitive.

Therefore, in this paper a multimodal virtual display system which is integrated with speech and gesture recognition technology is proposed. The system is illustrated by using Leap Motion and Microsoft Speech SDK to achieve multimodal interaction in automobile virtual display. And a holographic experimental platform is established to improve user experience.

2 System Overview

According to the design objectives, the development process of the system is divided into four steps:

- **Modeling and conversion:** Build an automobile model and render in a 3D modeling software. Then optimize the model and import the model into Cult3D platform.
- **Setting the interactions in Cult3D:** According to the functional requirements, the interactions of automobile virtual display should not only include traditional operations (translation, rotation and scaling), but also show the automobile under dynamic state (moving forward, opening the door/trunk, etc.). In addition, the system should provide the capability of customization, including component customization and color customization. These can be realized in Cult3D by organizing different types of elements, including Actions, Events and Objects, in the proper way.
- **Achieving speech and gesture interaction:** The speech recognition is based on the secondary development of Microsoft Speech SDK. Call the SAPI interface and set the keyboard events. Then we can interact with the automobile model through voice. Gesture interaction is realized by using Leap Motion Controller and developing program based on Leap Motion SDK.
- **Publishing the system:** Automobile virtual display can be used as a sub module embedded in the network based interactive display platform, but also in a live demonstration at the actual scene like product launches or product seminar (Fig. 1).

3 Human-Computer Interaction in Virtual Display

3.1 Modeling and Dynamic Interactive Display

Modeling: First, we build an automobile model and render in 3ds Max. Next, a series of operations is done in order to facilitate the interactive settings in Cult3D, including streamline the volume of the model, reduce the surface numbers and set the rotation axis of the components. Then we import the model into Cult3D platform.

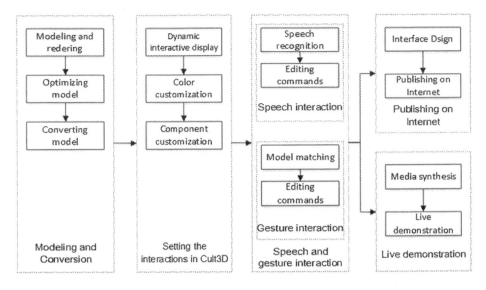

Fig. 1. System development process

Dynamic interactive display: The dynamic interactive display in automobile virtual display system includes four actions: open and close the doors (observe the interior of the car), open and close the trunk (know the space of the trunk), 360-degree rotating (observe the car without dragging the mouse) and move forward (know the state when the car's running). Wherein opening and closing the doors or trunk and 360-degree rotating is relatively simple. Link the Rotation XYZ action to the trigger event and the corresponding components of the automobile model, set the angle of the rotation and duration, and then an interaction is realized. For example, realizing the interaction of opening the left door contains three steps: first, drag a Rotation XYZ action, a Keyboard trigger event, and the group of all components of the left door onto the Event Map. Second, Link the Rotation XYZ action to the keyboard trigger and all components of

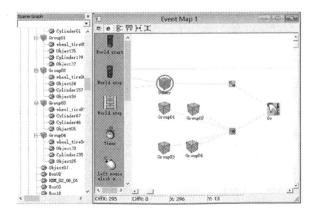

Fig. 2. The action setting of the automobile

the left door. Third, set Z axis as the center of rotation and the angle of the rotation to 40 °. The duration is 1.5 s. The action of moving forward contains two movements: the translation of the body and the rotation of the wheel. Link the Translation XYZ action to the whole body and the Rotation to the wheels. Set a Keyboard trigger and then the interaction is realized. When the users input a key which is preset, the automobile will simulate a real car's movements. The setting is shown in Fig. 2.

3.2 Color Customization

Color customization is achieved by toggling texture in Cult3D. First, we create body textures of different colors. We bake UV maps of all components of the body in 3ds Max, edit these maps in Photoshop and export textures of different colors. Next through different trigger events, we control the corresponding color textures explicit or implicit to achieve color switching. Open the Scene Graph window in Cult3D then click and open the Texture Node. Find the texture of a component of the body and double click on the texture. A window titled "Hotspots" is shown and we add the hotspots. There are four hotspots to be added corresponding to four different colors of body, including yellow, green, red and blue. Set the size of each hotspot the same as the original texture, and add textures of different colors which have been exported from Photoshop to the corresponding hotspots. Drag "Toggle Hotspot's Alter Ego" in the Action Window onto the Event Map and link to the keyboard triggers and textures. When the users input a key which is preset, the body switches to the corresponding color. Thus the color customization is achieved, as is shown in Fig. 3.

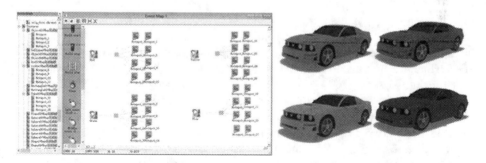

Fig. 3. Color customization of the automobile (Color figure online)

3.3 Component Customization

Component customization is a key demand when consumers are making purchase decisions. By selecting and combining different forms of components, the consumers are satisfied with customizing their own cars to meet their personal preferences. For automotive products, the components that can be customized include hub, tail, bumper, lights, etc. We can control the components explicit or implicit to achieve component customization in Cult3D.

For example, to achieve the customization of the hubs, first we build three sets of different styles of the hub models in 3ds Max export them to Cult3D. Then since only one set of hubs is shown at one time, link an Unhide Object to the set which is to be shown and link a Hide Object action to the other two sets. Next link keyboard triggers to the actions. When the users input a key which is preset, the corresponding set of hubs is shown and the other two are hidden, thus the component customization is achieved, as is shown in Fig. 4.

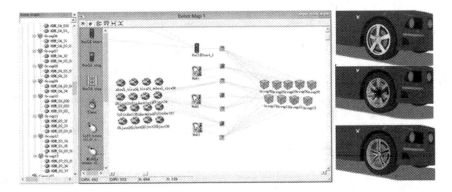

Fig. 4. Component customization of the automobile

4   Application of Multimodal Interaction Technology

4.1   Speech Interaction

In this study, we use Microsoft Speech SDK 5.1 as the secondary development platform. Speech interaction is achieved by calling the relevant speech program interface (SAPI) [11]. First initialize the COM port and create the speech recognition engine and context interface. Then we set the identification message to be addressed, create grammar files, load and activate different grammar rules for recognition. The grammar rules are written in XML files to identify the speech commands to be recognized.

When the recognition starts, the speech recognition engine obtains the recognition message and outputs the recognition result parameter through the ISpRecoResult interface. Then the recognition engine judges and executes the user's control command according to the grammar rule defined in the XML grammar file. Take the action "open the left door" in automobile virtual display as example, Press G on the keyboard is set

Table 1. The key code of speech recognition

1	if(b_Cmd_Grammar)
2	if(strcmp("Open the left door",lpszText2)==0)
3	keybd_event(VK_G,0,0,0)
4	keybd_event(VK_G,0,KEYEVENTF_KEYUP,0)

as the trigger event in Cult3D. When the speech engine recognizes the command of "open the left door", the keybd_event function is executed and the interaction is achieved. The key code is shown in Table 1.

4.2 Gesture Interaction

The Leap Motion controller uses infrared stereo cameras as tracking sensors, which can recognize and obtain the position, gesture or motion of the hands, fingers and tools in real time [12]. When detecting hands, fingers or tools, the sensors assign a ID value to them, query it in the new frame, and return a reference to the object. Leap Motion tracks various data including Hands, Pointables, Fingers, Tools and Gestures. The gestures that Leap Motion program can recognize includes Circle (a single finger tracing a circle), Swipe (a long, linear movement of a finger), Key Tap (a tapping movement by a finger as if tapping a keyboard key) and Screen Tap (a tapping movement by the finger as if tapping a vertical computer screen), as is shown in Fig. 5.

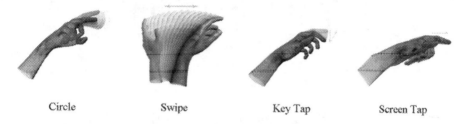

| Circle | Swipe | Key Tap | Screen Tap |

Fig. 5. Movement patterns definition

Before using the gestures to develop, we need to call enableGesture () function in the Controller classes to activate these gestures. Then link the certain gestures to the interactions in Chap. 3. Take the recognition of the Circle gesture as example, the corresponding interactive action is 360-degree rotating. And the trigger set in Cult3D is Keyboard Press 0. Thus we simulate the system input 0 when the sensors recognize the Circle gesture. A Sleep() function is used in order to avoid recognizing the same gesture

Table 2. The key code of gesture recognition

1	for (int g = 0; g < gestures.count();g++)
2	switch (gesture.type())
3	case Gesture::TYPE_CIRCLE:
4	CircleGesture circle = gesture
5	keybd_event(VK_0,0,0,0)
6	::Sleep(1000)
7	keybd_event(VK_0,0,KEYEVENTF_KEYUP,0)
8	break

too many times in a short time due to the equipment refreshing rate. The key code is shown in Table 2.

5   System Display on the Holographic Experimental Platform

The final interface design of the system is shown in Fig. 6(a). The system can be not only published online in html format, but also used in a live demonstration at the actual scene like product launches or product seminar. In addition, the system can be shown in holographic projection. We establish a holographic experimental platform which

(a) System interface design

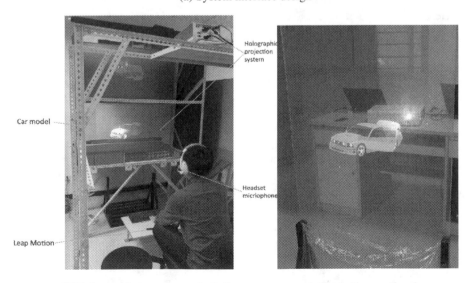

(b)Holographic experimental platform   (c)Projection on the glass

Fig. 6. Automobile virtual display under different scenarios

contains three parts: the holographic projection system, multimodal virtual display system and the host control system, as is shown in Fig. 6(b). The holographic projection system, which is used for naked-eye 3D display, includes a high-brightness, high-resolution projector and the holographic film. The multimodal virtual display system refers to the hardware and software that achieve speech and gesture interaction, including Leap Motion controller, a headset microphone and Cult3D software, etc. Host control system refers to the integration of hardware and software through the control of the host. Figure 6(c) shows projecting the system on a glass that is covered with holographic film. Since the interaction system is achieved by speech recognition and Leap Motion, we can operate the system from a long distance.

6   Conclusion

In this paper, we explore and study the interactive design method of speech and gesture in the product virtual display by taking the automobile display as an example. Based on the hardware and software platform, we designed the system development process. And according to the developing process, we established the automobile model, designed the interactions in Cult3D, and achieved speech and gesture interaction. Finally, the whole system was displayed on the holographic experimental platform. With the development of computer and internet technology in the future, the product virtual display integrated with multimodal interaction will have broad application prospects. Users can efficiently operate the 3D product model from a long distance in real time and have a more lifelike experience. In the meantime, the multimodal interaction system design method and implementation techniques can be further applied to other fields of virtual reality application researches, such as assembly simulation, scene roaming, remote education and rehabitation, etc. to help people use the interface in a more natural and efficient way and have access to enjoyable interactive experience. Our further research will focus on the gesture recognition algorithm, model matching and holographic algorithm to improve the recognition accuracy and achieve better display effects.

Acknowledgement.   This paper is supported by the National Natural Science Foundation of China (Grant No. 61472314).

References

1. da Silva Simões, P.D., Gabriel Inacio Ferreira, C.: Military war games edutainment. In: 2011 IEEE 1st International Conference on Serious Games and Applications for Health (SeGAH), vol. 7. IEEE (2011)
2. Rizo, A., Parsons, T.D., et al.: Virtual reality goes to war: a brief review of the future of military behavioral healthcare. J. Clin. Psychol. Med. Settings **18**(2), 176–187 (2011)
3. Wu, X., Gao, F.: Research of virtual reality technology in automotive engine assembly teaching. In: 2011 6th IEEE Joint International Information Technology and Artificial Intelligence Conference (ITAIC), vol. 1. IEEE (2011)
4. Barrett, M., Blackledge, J., Coyle, E.: Using virtual reality to enhance electrical safety and design in the built environment. ISAST Trans. Intell. Syst. **3**, 1 (2011)

5. Suma, E.A., Lange, B., Rizzo, A., et al.: FAAST: the flexible action and articulated skeleton toolkit. In: 2011 IEEE Virtual Reality Conference (VR), pp. 247–248 (2001)
6. Obrenovic, Z., Starcevic, D.: Modeling multimodal human-computer interaction. Computer **37**(9), 65–72 (2004)
7. Wang, L., Zhang, B., Dai, G.Z., et al.: PIP: a natural interaction interface based on multimodal interaction technology. In: Proceedings of the 3rd Joint Conference on Harmonious Human Machine Environment (HHME 2007), College of Computer and Science Technology, Shandong University, vol. 7 (2007)
8. Myers, B., Pausch, R., Pausch, R.: Past present and future of user interface software tools. ACM Trans. Comput. Hum. Interact. **7**(1), 1–28 (2000)
9. Lozano-Quilis, J.A., Gil-Gomez, H., Gil-Gomez, J.A., Albiol-Perez, S., et al.: Virtual reality system for multiple sclerosis rehabilitation using KINECT. In: Proceedings of the 2013 7th International Conference on Pervasive Computing Technologies for Healthcare and Workshops, PervasiveHealth, pp. 366–369 (2013)
10. Gu, Y., Sosnovsky, S., Ullrich, C.: Modeling children's pedestrian safety skills in an intelligent virtual reality learning environment. In: Conati, C., Heffernan, N., Mitrovic, A., Felisa Verdejo, M. (eds.) AIED 2015. LNCS, vol. 9112, pp. 604–607. Springer, Heidelberg (2015)
11. Muda, L., Begam, M., Elamvazuthi, I.: Voice recognition algorithms using mel frequency cepstral coefficient (mfcc) and dynamic time warping (dtw) techniques. arXiv preprint arXiv: 10034083 (2010)
12. Varas, A., Cornejo, M.D., Mainemer, D., et al.: Cellular automaton model for evacuation process with obstacles. Phys. Stat. Mech. Appl. **382**(2), 631–642 (2007)

Experimental Performance Analysis of Inverted Pendulum Platform

Dajun Du[1], Wangpei Li[1(✉)], Bin Zhan[1],
Minrui Fei[1], and Taicheng Yang[2]

[1] Shanghai Key Laboratory of Power Station Automation Technology,
School of Mechatronical Engineering and Automation, Shanghai University,
Shanghai 200072, People's Republic of China
lwp_shu@163.com
[2] Department of Engineering and Design, University of Sussex,
Brighton BN1 9QT, UK

Abstract. The focus of this paper is that the experimental design and performance analysis of inverted pendulum platform. Firstly, Different weighting matrices Q and R of LQR controller is set, and the effect on the cart-inverted pendulum system stability is analyzed. Different control cycles are then used to analyze their influence on the system stability. Finally, Time-delay impacts on the system performance are also validated. These experimental studies lay a solid foundation for future research of networked inverted pendulum system based on visual information.

Keywords: Inverted pendulum · LQR controller · Weighting matrices · Control cycle · Time-delay

1 Introduction

Due to the high-order, multivariable, nonlinear and instability of the inverted pendulum system, it is has been a classic representative of the control field. The control of a cart-inverted pendulum is able to effectively reflect in control of many of the typical issues such as nonlinear, robustness, follow-up, stabilization and tracking problems. The inverted pendulum system represents the basis of many complex systems such as biped robot upright walking balance control, rocket launch vertical control, spacecraft attitude control and offshore drilling platform stability control. Therefore, the inverted pendulum system has very important theoretical research value and the actual engineering application background [1–3].

Generally speaking, the control goal of a cart-inverted pendulum is that achieving the cart position quickly and accurately control and then keeping the pendulum always erecting in its inverted position during the process of movement. To realize the desired control response and performance of the system, the control laws or strategies need to be determined according to the deduced model of the inverted pendulum system.

This work is supported by National Science Foundation of China (61473182, 61533010), Science and Technology Commission of Shanghai Municipality (14JC1402200, 15JC1401900).

L. Zhang et al. (Eds.): AsiaSim 2016/SCS AutumnSim 2016, Part III, CCIS 645, pp. 431–440, 2016.
DOI: 10.1007/978-981-10-2669-0_46

The Linear Quadratic Regulator (LQR) is often employed to implement the stable control of an inverted pendulum system [4]. Further, a lot of improved LQRs have been studied by the previous works. A LQR controller is designed as the balancing controller for a rotary inverted pendulum [5]. The LQR gains are obtained based on the GA and GA-PSO optimization algorithms and fuzzy logic [6]. The improved artificial bee colony algorithm is used to design the LQR controller [7], and GA is applied to design weighting matrices of LQR [8].

Pervious works have shown that the weighting matrices Q and R of LQR controller greatly determine the control performance, which need to be adjusted and set through trial and error. However, it will be tedious and challenging to find a reasonable matrix Q or R if there is no a priori experience. In this paper, three kinds of real-time control experiments are designed to explore the effect of the weighting matrices Q and R on the system stability. Moreover, other experiments also are operated to analyse the influence of different control cycle on the system stability.

In the recent years, the inverted pendulum system is introduced into the visual servoing by using visual sensor to replace the traditional photoelectric encoders, i.e., it constitutes an inverted pendulum system based on vision feedback [9, 10]. Meanwhile, the network also has been added into inverted pendulum system, i.e., it constitutes a system with network feedback loop [11, 12]. However, time delay which induced by the image processing or network communication will affect the system stability and even cause instability.

To analyze the effect of the weighting matrices, control cycle and time delay on the system stability of the inverted pendulum system, the paper mainly focuses on experimental performance analysis of an inverted pendulum platform by designing some experiments.

2 Inverted Pendulum System

2.1 Introduction of Inverted Pendulum Experimental Platform

In this paper, a special inverted pendulum system named double-parallel inverted pendulum platform illustrated in Fig. 1 is employed to operate the real-time control experiments [2, 4, 13]. The inverted pendulum platform is consisted of the following parts:

Mechanical Equipment: The mechanical equipment has two identical inverted pendulums consisting of two straight lines rails of which the length is 0.6 m, and two carts side-to-side moving on the lines rails are driven by the motors through the belts and a spring coupling the two identical pendulums which can rotate freely around their own pivots. The special of this system is that the two pendulums are connected by the spring thus constituted a coupling system.

Controller: The controller is implemented on a computer including a motion control card where the version is GT- 400-SV-PCI. The computer receives the status information measured through the photoelectric encoders, calculating the control quantity according to the control law and then sending the corresponding pulse via the motion control card.

Actuator: The actuator is consisted of two dc servomotors and two servo drives. Two servo drives are installed in a control box which also includes some adapter plate. The version of servo drives is MSDA023A1A and the power is 200 W. Two servo drives are used to translate the pulse transmitted from the controller into a current and feed to the motors.

Using the inverted pendulum platform, there are many real-time control experiments including single inverted pendulum and double-parallel inverted pendulum experiments- the research of control algorithms such as PID and LQR. The external interferences such as adding a sine wave, a square wave or a sawtooth wave interference signal can be studied, and the remote control experiments are able to implement. Furthermore, this system can be extended to an inverted pendulum platform based on visual feedback by using visual sensor to replace the traditional photoelectric encoders.

In this paper, some real-time control experiments on single inverted pendulum are carried out.

Fig. 1. Double-parallel inverted pendulum set-up

2.2   Modeling of Single-Inverted Pendulum

The model of the cart-inverted pendulum as follows is deduced based on the Newton's Second Law and the model parameters are given in Table 1.

$$\dot{x}(t) = Ax(t) + Bu(t), x(t) \in R^4, u(t) \in R \tag{1}$$

where $x_1 = \alpha, x_3 = \dot{\alpha}$ denote the cart position and cart velocity, respectively; $x_2 = \theta$, $x_4 = \dot{\theta}$ denote the pendulum angular and angular velocity, respectively; u, which is the cart acceleration, denotes the control input signal; A and B shown as follows are constant matrices with appropriate.

$$A = \begin{bmatrix} 0 & 0 & 1 & 0 \\ 0 & 0 & 0 & 1 \\ 0 & 0 & 0 & 0 \\ 0 & \frac{lmg}{J} & 0 & 0 \end{bmatrix}, B = \begin{bmatrix} 0 \\ 0 \\ 1 \\ \frac{ml}{J} \end{bmatrix}.$$

Table 1. The detailed model parameters

Parameter	Physical meaning	Value/Unit
l	the length from the pivot to the center of mass of the pendulum	0.25 m
m	the mass of the pendulum	0.109 kg
J	the moment of inertia of the pendulum	0.009083 kg · m2
g	the acceleration of gravity	9.81 m/s2
α	the displacement of the cart	m
θ	the angular deviated from the vertical	rad

Remark 1. The input signal of the inverted pendulum state space model in previous works mostly is the force of the cart, but it is the acceleration of the cart in this paper.

2.3   Designing of the Controller

To keep the stabilization of the pendulum, full state feedback control method named LQR is used for the cart-inverted pendulum system [14, 15], i.e.,

$$u(t) = -Kx(t) \tag{2}$$

Substituting (2) into (1) yields

$$\dot{x}(t) = Ax(t) + (-BK)x(t) \tag{3}$$

where K is LQR gain vector derived from minimization of the cost function

$$J = \int_0^\infty \left[x^T(t)Qx(t) + u^T(t)Ru(t) \right] dt \tag{4}$$

where Q is positive semi-definite and R is positive definite symmetric constant diagonal matrices, respectively.

The control gain vector is given by

$$K = R^{-1}B^T P \tag{5}$$

where $P > 0$ is a symmetric constant matrix obtained from the solution of matrix equation

$$A^T P + PA - PBR^{-1}B^T P + Q = 0 \tag{6}$$

If the matrices Q and R are given, MATLAB function "LQR" is capable of performing this operation and computing the optimum gain vector.

From the cost function (4), it is know that Q is the weighting matrix corresponding to the state variables and R is the weighting matrix corresponding to the control variables. The variable or control quantity is more important in the performance function with a larger value of the corresponding diagonal elements.

3 Analysis of Experimental Performance

To test the effect of the weighting matrices, control cycle and time delay on the system stability of the inverted pendulum system, some experiments are designed and operated. This can lay a solid foundation for future networked inverted pendulum system or visual inverted pendulum system.

3.1 Effects of the Weighting Matrices Q and R

In order to analyze the effect of varying weight of matrices Q and R on the performance of inverted pendulum system, three groups of experiments are implemented. The first/second group of experiment is that the matrix R is invariant and the first/second diagonal element of the matrix Q is variant. The third group of experiment is that the matrix Q is invariant and the diagonal element of the matrix R is variant. The detail matrices Q and R are listed in Table 2. Figures 2, 3, and 4 show the cart position and pendulum angular, respectively.

Table 2. The detailed matrices Q and R

First group: Invariant $R=1$	
$Q = diag(400,230,0,0)$	$K_1 = [-20.0000 \quad 60.3198 \quad -14.3598 \quad 10.7673]$
$Q = diag(950,230,0,0)$	$K_2 = [-30.8221 \quad 72.3263 \quad -19.8319 \quad 13.0424]$
$Q = diag(3000,230,0,0)$	$K_3 = [-54.7723 \quad 96.7864 \quad -31.1823 \quad 17.6296]$
Second group: Invariant $R=1$	
$Q = diag(950,50,0,0)$	$K_4 = [-30.8221 \quad 71.0585 \quad -19.6298 \quad 12.9090]$
$Q = diag(950,230,0,0)$	$K_5 = [-30.8221 \quad 72.3263 \quad -19.8319 \quad 13.0424]$
$Q = diag(950,500,0,0)$	$K_6 = [-30.8221 \quad 88.1613 \quad -22.2016 \quad 14.6064]$
Third group: Invariant $Q = diag(950,230,0,0)$	
$R=1$	$K_7 = [-30.8221 \quad 72.3263 \quad -19.8319 \quad 13.0424]$
$R=50$	$K_8 = [-4.3589 \quad 33.3396 \quad -4.5760 \quad 6.1359]$
$R=100$	$K_9 = [-0.9747 \quad 25.3067 \quad -1.7563 \quad 4.6664]$

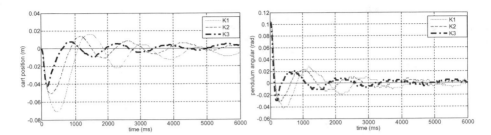

Fig. 2. The cart position and pendulum angular of the first group of experiment

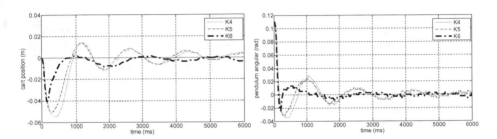

Fig. 3. The cart position and pendulum angular of the second group of experiment

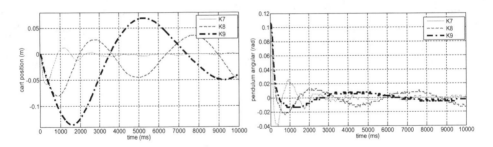

Fig. 4. The cart position and pendulum angular of the third group of experiment

From Figs. 2 and 3, it can be observed that the dynamic response process is improved and the response of system is obviously better with the corresponding diagonal element of the matrix Q increasing. Figure 4 shows that the dynamic response process becomes slowly and the amplitudes of state variables increase which cause oscillation phenomenon with the corresponding diagonal element of the matrix R increasing.

Noting that the control cycles of above experiments are all $T = 0.010s$ and the initial conditions are set as $x(0) = (0 \quad 0.1000 \quad 0 \quad 0)^T$.

3.2 Effect of the Control Cycle

In order to analyze the influence of different control cycles on the performance of the inverted pendulum system, three control laws, K_{10}, K_{11} and K_{12}, are selected to implement the real-time control experiments for the cart-inverted pendulum in different control cycle T, where

$$K_{10} = [-30.8221 \quad 72.3263 \quad -19.8319 \quad 13.0424], \quad K_{11} = [-17.3205 \quad 54.1335 \quad -12.5184 \quad 9.8508],$$
$$K_{12} = [-14.1421 \quad 53.7216 \quad -11.2590 \quad 9.4689], \quad T = 0.003/0.005/0.010/0.017/0.019s.$$

Figures 5, 6, and 7 show the pendulum angular of the experiments in different control laws with different control cycles, respectively. From Figs. 5, 6, and 7, the detail moments, which are given in Table 3 and shown in Fig. 8, of the inverted pendulum reaching steady state in different control cycle can be found.

Figure 8 illustrates that different control cycles correspond to different stable times. With increasing of control cycle, the stable time decrease firstly and then increase in the same control law, which presents a kind of shape similar as the letter "U". This shows that an appropriate control cycle contributes significantly to improve the performance of system and a too small or too large control cycle will result in seriously oscillatory and even instability.

Table 3. The detailed stable time in different control cycle

Control cycle(ms)	3	5	10	17	19
K_{10} Stable time (ms)	2950	1145	1095	1850	2845
K_{11} Stable time (ms)	2750	745	415	3600	3712
K_{12} Stable time (ms)	4300	700	145	3300	3920

Noting that when the pendulum angular is always in $[-0.02, +0.02]$ (rad), the cart-inverted pendulum system is in steady state.

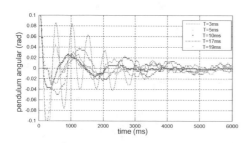

Fig. 5. The pendulum angular of the control law K_{10} with different control cycle (Left)

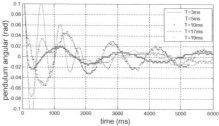

Fig. 6. The pendulum angular of the control law K_{11} with different control cycle (Right)

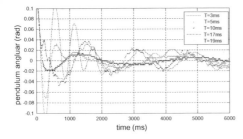 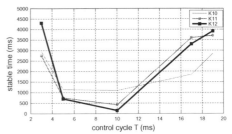

Fig. 7. The pendulum angular of the control law K_{12} with different control cycle (Left)

Fig. 8. The stable time with different control cycle (Right)

3.3 Effect of the Time-Delay

Time-delay affecting the system performance and even leading to uncontrollable is also studied. If time-delay h is induced by the image processing or network communication, then the control input signal will become

$$u(t) = -Kx(t - h) \tag{7}$$

Substituting (7) into (3) yields

$$\dot{x}(t) = Ax(t) + (-BK)x(t - h) \tag{8}$$

Obviously the system (8) is a typical time-delay system. In order to analyze the influence of time-delay h on the performance of the system (8), some real-time control experiments with different time-delays are implemented and the experimental results are shown in Fig. 9.

From Fig. 9, we can observe that compared with the case without time-delay, the cart is unable to return to the original position and the pendulum appears oscillation phenomenon with time-delay $h = 15$ ms, and the trajectories are emanative which is instable with time-delay $h = 30$ ms. It indicates that a important research for the inverted pendulum based on the visual feedback is to reduce the image processing time thus reduce time-delay.

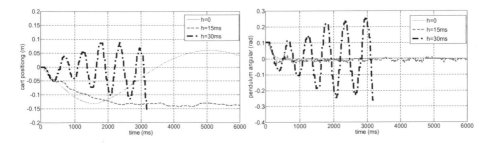

Fig. 9. The cart position and pendulum angular of the experiments with different time-delays

Noting that in these experiments, the control laws are all $K_{13} = [-1.000 \quad 25.5765 \quad -1.7944 \quad 4.7004]$ with the weighting matrices $Q = diag(50 \quad 230 \quad 0 \quad 0)$ and $R = 50$, and the control cycle is $T = 0.010$ s.

4 Conclusions

The paper has designed and analysed experimental performances of inverted pendulum. Three kinds of experiment (i.e., different weighting matrices Q and R of LQR controller, control cycle and time-delay) are operated, and their effect on the system stability are discussed and analysed. These works can provide a solid foundation for future research of networked inverted pendulum system fused visual information.

References

1. Tu, Y.W., Ho, M.T.: Design and implementation of robust visual servoing control of an inverted pendulum with an FPGA-based image co-processor. Mechatronics **21**(7), 1170–1182 (2011)
2. Lan, Y., Fei, M.: Design of state-feedback controller by pole placement for a coupled set of inverted pendulums. In: 2011 10th International Conference on Electronic Measurement & Instruments (ICEMI), vol. 3, pp. 69–73. IEEE (2011)
3. Li, Z., Zhang, Y.: Robust adaptive motion/force control for wheeled inverted pendulums. Automatica **46**(8), 1346–1353 (2010)
4. Wang, L., Ni, H., Zhou, W., et al.: MBPOA-based LQR controller and its application to the double-parallel inverted pendulum system. Eng. Appl. Artif. Intell. **36**, 262–268 (2014)
5. Teng Fong, T., Jamaludin, Z., Bani Hashim, A.Y., et al.: Design and analysis of linear quadratic regulator for a non-linear positioning system. Appl. Mech. Mater. **761**, 227–232 (2015)
6. Molazadeh, V.R., Banazadeh, A., Shafieenejad, I.: Design of the LQR controller and observer with fuzzy logic GA and GA-PSO algorithm for triple an inverted pendulum and cart system. In: 2014 International Conference on Advanced Mechatronic Systems (ICAMechS), pp. 295–300. IEEE (2014)
7. Yang, H.D.: Optimal design of LQR controller based on improved artificial bee colony optimization algorithm. Adv. Mater. Res. **971**, 1272–1275 (2014)
8. Wongsathan, C., Sirima, C.: Application of GA to design LQR controller for an inverted pendulum system. In: IEEE International Conference on Robotics and Biomimetics, ROBIO 2008, pp. 951–954. IEEE (2009)
9. Magana, M.E., Holzapfel, F.: Fuzzy-logic control of an inverted pendulum with vision feedback. IEEE Trans. Educ. **41**(2), 165–170 (1998)
10. Espinoza-Quesada, E.S., Ramos-Velasco, L.E.: Visual servoing for an inverted pendulum using a digital signal processor. In: 2006 IEEE International Symposium on Signal Processing and Information Technology, pp. 76–80. IEEE (2006)
11. Dajun, D., Qi, B., Fei, M., Peng, C.: Multiple event-triggered H2/H∞ filtering for hybrid networked systems with random network-induced delays. Inf. Sci. **325**, 393–408 (2015)
12. Du, D., Fei, M., Jia, T.: Modeling and stability analysis of MIMO networked control systems with multi-channel random packet losses. Trans. Inst. Measur. Control **35**(1), 66–74 (2013)

13. Fei, M.R., Zhao, W.Q., Yang, T.C., et al.: A new experimental set-up for control study. Trans. Inst. Measur. Control **32**(3), 319–330 (2010)
14. Kizir, S., Ocak, H., Bingul, Z., et al.: Time delay compensated vision based stabilization control of an inverted pendulum. Int. J. Innov. Comput. Inf. Control **8**(12), 8133–8145 (2012)
15. Prasad, L.B., Tyagi, B., Gupta, H.O.: Optimal control of nonlinear inverted pendulum system using PID controller and LQR: performance analysis without and with disturbance input. Int. J. Autom. Comput. **11**(6), 661–670 (2014)

Experimental Analysis of Visual Inverted Pendulum Servoing System

Dajun Du[1], Bin Zhan[1(✉)], Wangpei Li[1], Minrui Fei[1], and TaiCheng Yang[2]

[1] Shanghai Key Laboratory of Power Station Automation Technology,
School of Mechatronical Engineering and Automation, Shanghai University,
Shanghai 200072, People's Republic of China
rubin_zhan@163.com
[2] Department of Engineering and Design, University of Sussex, Brighton, BN1 9QT, UK

Abstract. This paper is concerned with experimental analysis of visual inverted pendulum servoing system. Firstly, visual inverted pendulum servoing system is introduced, and three typical image processing algorithms are described. These three algorithms are then employed to process the image of inverted pendulum captured by camera. Comparative experiments are operated, and the detection precision and real time performance are analyzed. This lays a solid foundation for future control research of visual inverted pendulum servoing system.

Keywords: Machine vision · Image processing · Inverted pendulum · Computational time · Computational error

1 Introduction

With the rapid development of industrial camera and image processing, machine vision has been widely used in some fields such as automatic inspection, process control, and robot guidance and so on [1–3]. It can improve importantly the level of intelligence and automation and enhance efficiency and reliability of equipment.

According to real-time requirement, the applications of machine vision are roughly classified into two categories. In the first case, real-time demand is not very high, e.g., we usually see the recognition system of vehicle license plate, where vehicle license is extracted and recognized from the background. In the second case, high real-time requirements and high accuracy of image processing are considered importantly, e.g., visual servo control system. Visual servoing is a kind of control framework that incorporates visual information in feedback control loops [4, 5].

As a typical representative of the control field, the inverted pendulum system becomes the visual servoing by using the visual sensor to replace the traditional photo-electric encoder, leading to visual inverted pendulum servoing system [6–8]. In the

This work is supported by National Science Foundation of China (61473182, 61533010), Science and Technology Commission of Shanghai Municipality (14JC1402200, 15JC1401900).

L. Zhang et al. (Eds.): AsiaSim 2016/SCS AutumnSim 2016, Part III, CCIS 645, pp. 441–450, 2016.
DOI: 10.1007/978-981-10-2669-0_47

system, it is a very important that the pendulum angular and the cart position are obtained from the images by the image processing. For example, the pendulum angular is acquired through the linear search algorithm from the visual images, which is then taken as a fuzzy state variable of the fuzzy-logic controller [9]. Further, the visual maker method is employed to improve the speed of image processing.

The above literatures mainly focus on the realization of image processing algorithms and don't analyze dentally the errors caused by the algorithms. The paper firstly introduce visual inverted pendulum servoing system. Several typical image processing algorithms are then described, which are employed to process the image of inverted pendulum. Comparative experiments are operated, and the detection precision and real time performance are analyzed. This lays a solid foundation for future control research of visual inverted pendulum servoing system.

2   Description of Experiment Platform

Single inverted pendulum experimental platform shown in Fig. 1 is employed to operate the image preprocessing experiments. The inverted pendulum platform is consisted of the following parts:

Fig. 1. The experiment platform   **Fig. 2.** Image captured by the camera

A. Mechanical Equipment

Single inverted pendulum system is composed of an inverted pendulum mounted on the mobile cart. Two incremental encoders are employed to measure the state variable: cart position and pendulum angle.

B. Vision Sensor

As for Euclidean and Manhattan algorithms, the traditional static floor field model is as follows, Vision sensor is key of the whole system, which consists of CCD cameras and lens. To implement image acquisition quickly and accurately, a camera (acA640-120 gm of Basler Corporation) is selected as vision sensor, which has a maximum resolution of 659×492 pixels and can capture a maximum of 120 frames per second.

C. Image Processing and Controller Unit

A computer is used as an image processing and controller unit, which receives the status information which measured from visual sensors and calculate the control signal according to the control law and then sending the corresponding pulse via the motion control card (i.e., GT-400-SV-PCI).

D. Actuator

The actuator is consisted of a dc servomotors and a servo drives. The servo drive is installed in a control box which also includes some adapter plates. The version of servo drive is MSDA023A1A and the power is 200 W is used to translate the pulse transmitted from the controller into a current and feed to the motors.

3   Image Processing

An original image is captured by the camera with a uniform background is shown in Fig. 2. To calculate accurately the angular displacement of pendulum, the image collected by camera needed be processed by a series of steps including image denoising, edge detection and threshold segmentation.

3.1   Image Denoising

Image denoising is a necessary step in digital image processing, because there exist always a large number of noises in an image. The image denoising methods can be roughly divided into two kinds: transform domain de-noising and spatial domain de-noising. We should choose different de-noising processing algorithms in different scenarios.

To reduce computational complexity, the local regions of the image from an acquired frame are used, leading to the resulting image shown in Fig. 3. Considering the obvious differences between background and foreground, Gaussian filter is applied to the image in Fig. 3, and the result shown in Fig. 4.

Fig. 3. Local regions of the image   **Fig. 4.** Image denoising

3.2 Edge Detecting

Edge characters are often used to segmentation and recognition. It is relatively effective for soble operator to realize digital image fringe detecting and picking up. The idea of computing image gradients is used in edge detection techniques. Let $f(x, y)$ denote the gray scale level of the pixel (x, y). The gradient of an image is given by

$$\nabla f(x, y) \equiv \begin{bmatrix} \dfrac{\partial f}{\partial x} \\ \dfrac{\partial f}{\partial y} \end{bmatrix} = \begin{bmatrix} f_x(x, y) \\ f_y(x, y) \end{bmatrix}$$

In the field of edge detection, we focus on the magnitude of the gradient of the image, which given by

$$|\nabla f| \triangleq \sqrt{f_x^2 + f_y^2}$$

Here, a sobel operator is used to calculate the image gradient, and the partial derivatives by a mask operation. A 3×3 mask operator is given by

$$f_x(x, y) = \sum_{j=-1}^{1} \sum_{i=-1}^{1} f(x + i, y + j) w_x(i, j)$$

$$f_y(x, y) = \sum_{j=-1}^{1} \sum_{i=-1}^{1} f(x + i, y + j) w_y(i, j)$$

Here, $w_x(i, j)$ is the coefficient of the horizontal operator, and $w_y(i, j)$ is the coefficient of the vertical operator. Sobel operator is applied to the image Fig. 4, and the result is shown by Fig. 5.

3.3 Threshold Segmentation

Threshold segmentation is more simple and efficient, and it is applied to gray images to differentiate the background and foreground in the image. Threshold converts a gray image into a binary image and includes all kinds of the feature information such as the position, shape, and numbers of objects. The global threshold is used and the threshold process is given by

$$f_T(x, y) = \begin{cases} 255 & f(x, y) \geq T \\ 0 & f(x, y) < T \end{cases}$$

Here T is the threshold value and T = 150 is applied to the image of Fig. 5, and the result image is shown in Fig. 6.

Fig. 5. Edge detection using Sobel masks.   **Fig. 6.** Thresholding

4   Location and Measurement

Feature location accuracy is directly related to the accuracy of the angular displacement. The selection of characteristic points is one of the critical steps during the image measurement. Modern image feature is composed of color features, texture features, shape features, spatial relations. As an important characteristic of image, edge is the important content of image vision information. After image edge is obtained, angular displacement is calculated by of the following three methods i.e., Linear Search Algorithm, Hough Transform Algorithm and Visual Maker Algorithm.

4.1   Linear Search Algorithm

To detect the feature point with the greatest black/white transition in a row, we use a linear search algorithm that compares the contrast of the pixels and returns the position with the greatest dark value. According to the coordinates shown in Fig. 7, we calculate the distances and obtain the angle by

$$\theta = \tan^{-1} \frac{\Delta c}{\Delta v}$$

Linear search algorithm is applied to the image in Fig. 6, leading to a feature location shown in Fig. 8.

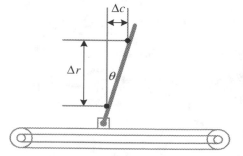

Fig. 7. Angle computation sketch   **Fig. 8.** Feature point location

To analyze the effect of the row space, different experiments with,100 and 200 are operated 150 times, and the measurement values obtained from the encoders are regarded as base values. Compared result between the values calculated by linear search algorithm and base values are illustrated in Figs. 9, 10, and 11. It is seen that the values calculated by linear search algorithm follows base values. With the increase of the row space, the errors decrease. It indicates that the larger row space should be selected.

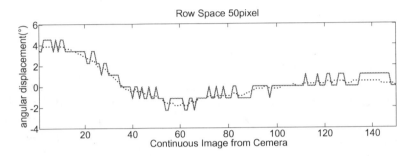

Fig. 9. $\Delta r = 50$

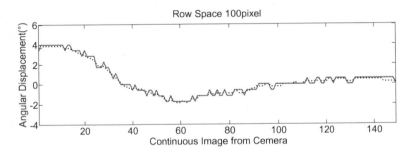

Fig. 10. $\Delta r = 100$

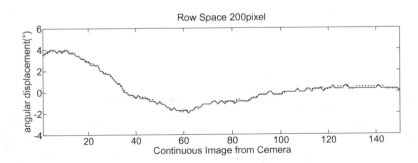

Fig. 11. $\Delta r = 200$

Computational time, error mean and error variance between the values calculated by linear search algorithm and base values with different row space were listed in Table 1.

Table 1. Computational Time, error mean and variance with different row space

Row space (pixel)	Time (ms)	Error
50	3	0.17 ± 0.13
100	3	0.06 ± 0.043
200	4	-0.02 ± 0.012

4.2 Hough Transform Algorithm

Hough transform is another algorithm of geometric features recognition for the image, which is mainly used for the separation of the certain characteristics of the same geometry from the image (such as straight line, circle, etc.). The basic application is line detection from binary image. Hough transform using the transformation between two coordinates to space will have the same shape in a space curve or straight line map to another space coordinates of a point on the peak.

An angle value is obtained when the measured subimage is processed by edge detection, thinning and Hough transformation, leading to the resulting image shown in Fig. 12.

Fig. 12. The result of hough transform

The effect of the angular precision, $\Delta = 0.5°, 0.25°, 0.125°$, in the experiments is analyzed. Experimental results are illustrated in Figs. 13, 14 and 15, respectively. It is found that the values calculated by hough transform algorithm follows base values. With the increase of the angular precision, the errors decrease. It indicates that the larger angular precision is better.

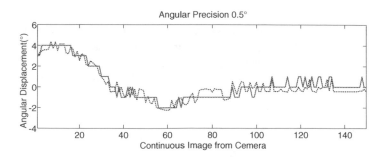

Fig. 13. Angular precision 0.5°

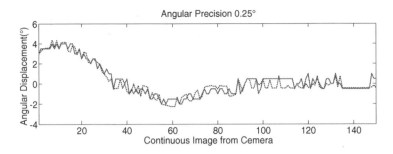

Fig. 14. Angular precision 0.25°

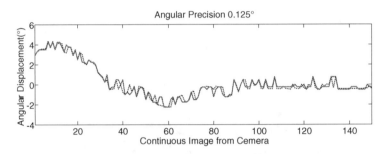

Fig. 15. Angular precision 0.125°

Computational time, error mean and error variance between the values calculated by hough transform algorithm and base values with different angular precision were listed in Table 2.

Table 2. Computational time, error mean and variance with different angular precision

Precision (degree)	Time(ms)	Error
0.50	13	0.12 ± 0.13
0.25	19	0.10 ± 0.11
0.125	32	0.06 ± 0.09

4.3 Visual Maker Algorithm

To improve the accuracy of visual measurements, a circular-shaped marker is placed on the top of the pendulum. Ideally, the threshold operation separates the edge of the marker from the background and the pendulum rod. As shown in Fig. 16, the white pixels correspond to the edge of the marker. Because the marker is symmetrical, the centroid of the edge is taken as its location. The centroid (X_c, Y_c) is given by.

$$x_c = \frac{\sum_x \sum_y x \cdot f_T(x, y)}{\sum_x \sum_y f_T(x, y)}$$

$$y_c = \frac{\sum_x \sum_y y \cdot f_T(x, y)}{\sum_x \sum_y f_T(x, y)}$$

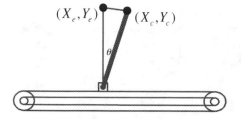

Fig. 16. Angle computation sketch.   **Fig. 17.** Gray-gravity to the masks

Considering the angular displacement of the pendulum rod shown in Fig. 17 (X_e, Y_e) are the $X - Y$ coordinates of the centroid of the marker for the pendulum rod in the upright position. (X_c, Y_c) are the $X - Y$ coordinates of the centroid of the marker when the angular dis-placement of the pendulum rod is θ. The angular displacement of the pendulum rod is given by

$$\theta = 2 \sin^{-1} \frac{\sqrt{(X_c - X_e)^2 + (Y_c - Y_e)^2}}{2L}$$

where L is the distance between the pivot joint and the center of the marker, and L is 0.365 m.

Figure 18 illustrates Experimental results for visual maker algorithm. It is seen that this algorithm can deal with the angular displacement detecting efficiently. But because it is needed to deal with large dataset, it will take long time to calculate gravity.

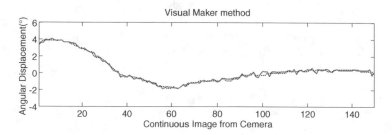

Fig. 18. Experimental result of the visual maker algorithm

5   Simulation Models Summary and Conclusion

This paper has investigated experimental analysis of visual inverted pendulum servoing system. Three typical image processing algorithms are described, which are then employed to process the image of inverted pendulum captured by camera. Comparative experiments are operated, and the detection precision and real time performance are analyzed. Experimental results show that hough transform algorithm and visual maker algorithm have strong robustness and high precision, but the image processing time is longer than the linear search algorithm. This lays a solid foundation for future control research of visual inverted pendulum servoing system.

References

1. Zheng, X., Wang, S., Zhang, Y.: The obstacle detection and measurement based on machine vision. Int. J. Intell. Syst. Appl. **2**(2), 17–24 (2010)
2. Keenan, S.J., Diamond, J., Mccluggage, W.G., et al.: An automated machine vision system for the histological grading of cervical intraepithelial neoplasia (CIN). J. Pathol. **192**(3), 351–362 (2000)
3. Bulanon, D.M., Kataoka, T., Okamoto, H., et al.: Development of a real-time machine vision system for the apple harvesting robot. In: SICE 2004 Annual Conference, vol. 1, pp. 595–598. IEEE (2004)
4. Hutchinson, S., Hager, G.D., Corke, P.: A tutorial on visual servo control. IEEE Trans. Robot. Autom. **12**(5), 651–670 (1996)
5. Xie, W.F., Li, Z., Tu, X.W., et al.: Switching control of image-based visual servoing with laser pointer in robotic manufacturing systems. IEEE Trans. Ind. Electr. **56**(2), 520–529 (2009)
6. Espinoza-Quesada, E.S., Ramos-Velasco, L.E.: Visual servoing for an inverted pendulum using a digital signal processor. In: International Symposium on Signal Processing and Information Technology, pp. 76–80. IEEE (2006)
7. Kizir, S., Ocak, H., Bingul, Z., et al.: Time delay compensated vision based stabilization control of an inverted pendulum. Int. J. Innov. Comput. Inf. Control **8**(12), 8133–8145 (2012)
8. Wang, H., Vasseur, C., Koncar, V., et al.: Design and implementation of robust hybrid control of vision based underactuated mechanical nonminimum phase systems. Stud. Inf. Control **19**(1), 35–44 (2010)
9. Magana, M.E., Holzapfel, F.: Fuzzy-logic control of an inverted pendulum with vision feedback. IEEE Trans. Educ. **41**(2), 165–170 (1998)

Utilizing Pre- and Postoperative CT to Validate an Instrument for Quantifying Pectus Excavatum Severity

Qi Zeng[1], Nahom Kidane[2], Mohammad F. Obeid[2(✉)], Chenghao Chen[1],
Ruofan Shen[3], Robert E. Kelly[4], and Frederic D. McKenzie[2]

[1] Pediatric Thoracic Surgery Beijing, Children's Hospital,
Capital Medical University, Beijing, China
zengqi-1@163.com, chenchenghao@hotmail.com
[2] Modeling, Simulation and Visualization Engineering,
Old Dominion University, Norfolk, USA
{nkida001,mobei001,rdmckenz}@odu.edu
[3] Ocean Lakes High School, Virginia Beach, USA
ruofanshen@yahoo.com
[4] Clinical Surgery/Pediatrics, Children's Hospital of The King's Daughters and EVMS,
Norfolk, USA
Robert.Kelly@chkd.org

Abstract. An instrument that objectively quantifies a condition's severity and its improvement after treatment is of great use. This is also the case for pectus excavatum (PE), a congenital chest wall deformity, for which several severity indices have been introduced. This work describes a system that utilizes chest surface scans generated from CT-data or optical scanning to provide a gauge and visualization of chest wall deviations. A validation experiment is conducted to evaluate the fidelity of such an instrument utilizing pre- and postoperative CT scans. Statistical analysis shows the ability of the instrument to accurately recognize changes in the chest surface profile.

Keywords: Pectus excavatum · Registration · Validation

1 Introduction

Pectus excavatum (PE), also called sunken or funnel chest, is a congenital chest wall deformity characterized by a deep depression of the sternum and accounts for about 90 % of congenital chest wall abnormalities in children [1]. PE occurs approximately once in every 400 births and is often accompanied by other problems such as scoliosis and breathing issues [2]. A surgical intervention is generally recommended for a patient with a Haller Index (HI) larger than 3.25. Haller index (HI), introduced in 1987 and considered a gold standard for assessing Pectus Excavatum (PE) severity, is evaluated with computed tomography (CT) [3]. For less severe cases, conservative treatments that involve gradual changes of the chest wall have been developed [4, 5].

© Springer Science+Business Media Singapore 2016
L. Zhang et al. (Eds.): AsiaSim 2016/SCS AutumnSim 2016, Part III, CCIS 645, pp. 451–456, 2016.
DOI: 10.1007/978-981-10-2669-0_48

In addition to HI, several indices have been introduced to quantify PE deformity and severity using chest CT scans [6]. However, such scans are not widely available postoperatively due to the intent to limit ionizing radiation exposure and avoid associated costs. This makes obtaining the aforementioned indices, including HI, very challenging for assessing post-treatment improvements for both surgical and conservative interventions.

While some have proposed the use of rudimentary techniques for external measurements of the chest such as chest cyrtometry with a metric tape [7] or simple linear measurements using cylindrical rulers, others explored the use of optical scanning for creating an external profile of the chest surface to quantify the deformation. While the optical scanning approach is very beneficial, the systems used were stationary and relatively expensive. Furthermore, a method for evaluating pre- versus post-treatment data was not identified [8, 9].

In this work, therefore, a validation experiment is conducted to evaluate a developed portable hardware/software system that uses an inexpensive method for creating 3-dimensional external profile of the thorax. The system then utilizes pre- and post-treatment models (generated using such scanning method or reconstructed from CT-data) and performs registration-based point comparisons to assess the change in chest shape over the course of the treatment. Results and statistical findings of the experiment are reported to quantify the error margin of the system.

2 Methods and Materials

2.1 Developed System

The hardware component of the system incorporates a 3-dimensional motion sensor (Microsoft Kinect) to capture depth and color information using infrared projection and construct a model of the thorax. The sensor is fixed on a curved platform that provides a stable horizontal motion which is mounted on a movable overhead frame as shown in Fig. 1 (left). The developed software receives models generated using the mentioned setup or from chest surface models reconstructed from CT scans [10]. In this work, the latter method is used to generate the models used for validation.

The first step in the pipeline is concerned with transforming the pre- and postoperative models into the same coordinate system and aligning overlapping anatomical landmarks (e.g. navel). Unwanted points far from the region of interest can affect the surface alignment/registration and are, therefore, discarded. For each patient's surface model, four landmark coordinates are selected and used for initial estimation Fig. 1 (right). Since producing an accurate measurement depends on proper registration, the iterative closest point (ICP) algorithm is subsequently applied for fine tuning. The algorithm attempts to find the best match between corresponding points by iteratively applying spatial transformation.

Registration parameters, such as the number of iterations, were selected based on initial assessment and root mean square error (RMS). Chest surface deformation values are computed by calculating the distance between aligned surface meshes; and the

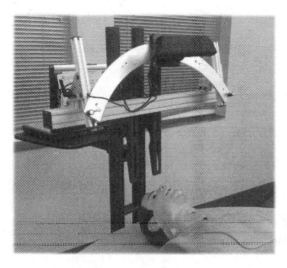
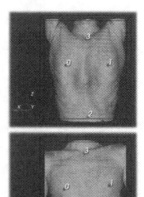

Fig. 1. Developed apparatus for capturing real-time 3D skin surface (left); and interface of software showing landmark selection for pre- (top right) and postoperative (bottom right) models of patient "PA 26".

distance map for the region of interest is generated to give both a quantitative and qualitative representation of the chest wall improvement.

2.2 Study Design

The conducted study aims to validate the developed system utilizing CT scans. Although postoperative CT scanning is not routinely performed at many institutions, pre- and postoperative CT data for six patients who underwent the Nuss procedure was obtained from the Beijing Children's Hospital. The study included 5 males and 1 female with a mean age of 13 ± 1.6 years at the time of surgery and the morphologies included 5 cups and 1 trench as classified by [11].

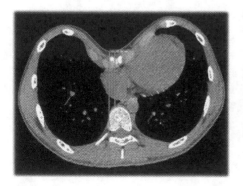
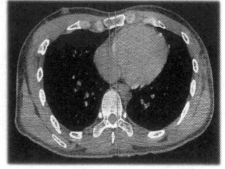

Fig. 2. Pre- (left) and postoperative (right) CT images showing ground truth measurements of *chest-to-spine* and *chest-to-back* distances for patient "PA26".

To obtain *ground truth*, each patient's CT was reviewed to measure: (i) the distance from the external skin of the front chest wall to the most anterior point of the spine (*chest-to-spine* distance) and (ii) that to the external skin of the back chest wall (*chest-to-back* distance) for pre- and postoperative CT at the slice that shows the deepest point of the deformation (Fig. 2).

For both datasets and for each patient, 3D segmentation was used to reconstruct a 3D model of the chest surface from CT. To investigate the validity of the instrument, 10 measurement points are drawn from each reconstructed model around the deepest point of the deformation and are averaged to produce a single value (*software-measured*) to be compared with its ground truth counterpart. A t-test was conducted on the mean error hypothesizing that the mean difference between the *software-measured* and *ground truth* values is equal to zero with $\alpha = 0.05$.

3   Results and Discussion

As described earlier, for each of the six patients, ground truth values were obtained from CT analysis, whereas experimental values were generated using the developed software from corresponding 3D meshes. Figure 3 shows the measurement produced by the software for one of the patients where the distance map visualizes an informative representation of the improvement. Furthermore, Table 1 shows ground-truth as well as experimental (software-measured) difference values for all patients.

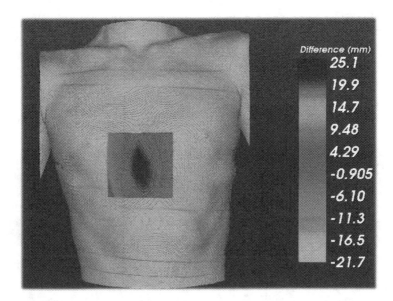

Fig. 3. Software-generated difference values visualized in a color map for patient "PA26".

Table 1. Subject characteristics and pectus deviation measurements.

No	Patient	Age	Pre- and postoperative improvement measurement (mm)		
			Ground Truth (CT)		[a]Software-measured
			Chest to Spine	Chest to Back	
1	PA15	11	20.1	23.03	26.41
2	PA16	11.25	9.56	14.55	12.52
3	PA21	13.25	21.44	23.36	20.37
4	PA22	14	28.87	30.97	27.91
5	PA23	14	22.78	21.54	23.66
6	PA26	14.75	28.14	27.96	25.53

[a]Mean of 10 randomly selected software measured points from around center of deformity.

Table 2 shows the results of a paired t-test with 95 % significance level ($p < 0.05$). For validation purposes, the two ground truth measurements were used to determine the accuracy of the developed software. Statistical analysis showed a mean difference between ground truth and software measured values (error margin) in the range -0.92 and 0.84 mm with 95 % confidence interval half-width of 1.21 and 1.05, respectively. Comparison of ground truth and software-measured values showed no statistically significant difference ($p = 0.52$ and 0.50) suggesting that the software can distinguish differences and improvements between provided surface meshes at least as sufficiently as traditional CT analysis.

Table 2. Paired t-test between CT and software measurements of pectus improvement.

[a]Ground truth vs. [b]Software-measurement (mm)	Statistical paired t-test ($p < 0.05$)	
	Difference mean and half-width (n = 7)	p-value
[b]Chest to Spine	-0.92 ± 1.21	0.52
[b]Chest to Back	0.84 ± 1.05	0.50

[a]Postoperative ground truth obtained from CT slice of deepest deformation.
[b]Mean of 10 randomly selected software measured points from around center of deformity.

4 Conclusion

This work described a study to investigate the extent to which our developed software is able to measure improvement in a patient's chest surface as well as could be obtained from a postoperative CT, but utilizing 3D optical scans with no ionizing radiation. Pre- and postoperative imaging was utilized to calculate a ground truth, against which the results from the developed software are compared. Results showed no significant difference between the CT-obtained measurements and the software-measured counter parts.

References

1. Pretorius, S.E., Haller, A.J., Fishman, E.K.: Spiral CT with 3D reconstruction in children requiring reoperation for failure of chest wall growth after pectus excavatum surgery. Clin. Imaging 22, 108–116 (1998)
2. Protopapas, A.D., Athanasiou, T.: Peri-operative data on the Nuss procedure in children with pectus excavatum: independent survey of the first 20 years' data. J. Cardiothorac. Surg. 3, 40 (2008)
3. Haller, J.A., Kramer, S.S., Lietman, S.: Use of CT scans in selection of patients for pectus excavatum surgery: a preliminary report. J. Pediatr. Surg. 22, 904–906 (1987)
4. Haecker, F.-M.: The vacuum bell for conservative treatment of pectus excavatum: the Basle experience. Pediatr. Surg. Int. 27, 623–627 (2011)
5. Harrison, M.R., Curran, P., Jamshidi, R., Christensen, D., Bratton, B., Fechter, R., Hirose, S.: Magnetic mini-mover procedure for pectus excavatum: initial findings of a Food and Drug administration–sponsored trial. J. Pediatr. Surg. 45, 185–192 (2010)
6. Martinez-Ferro, M.: Indexes for pectus deformities. In: Kolvekar, S., Pilegaard, H. (eds.) Chest Wall Deformities and Corrective Procedures, pp. 35–60. Springer International Publishing, New York (2016)
7. Brigato, R.R., Campos, J.R.M., Jatene, F.B., Moreira, L.F.P., Rebeis, E.B.: Pectus excavatum: evaluation of Nuss technique by objective methods. Interact. CardioVasc. Thorac. Surg. 7, 1084–1088 (2008)
8. Poncet, P., Kravarusic, D., Richart, T., Evison, R., Ronsky, J.L., Alassiri, A., Sigalet, D.: Clinical impact of optical imaging with 3-D reconstruction of torso topography in common anterior chest wall anomalies. J. Pediatr. Surg. 42, 898–903 (2007)
9. Glinkowski, W., Sitnik, R., Witkowski, M., Kocoń, H., Bolewicki, P., Górecki, A.: Method of pectus excavatum measurement based on structured light technique. J. Biomed. Opt. 14, 044041 (2009)
10. Obeid, M.F., Kidane, N., Rechowicz, K.J., Chemlal, S., Kelly, R.E., McKenzie, F.D.: Validation of an objective assessment instrument for non-surgical treatments of chest wall deformities. Stud. Health Technol. Inform. Med. Meets Virtual Reality 220, 273–280 (2016)
11. Cartoski, M.J., Nuss, D., Goretsky, M.J., Proud, V.K., Croitoru, D.P., Gustin, T., Mitchell, K., Vasser, E., Kelly Jr., R.E.: Classification of the dysmorphology of pectus excavatum. J. Pediatr. Surg. 41, 1573–1581 (2006)

An Extended DEVS Based Modeling and Simulation of Complex Information Systems

Xiaokai Xia[1,2(✉)], Luo Xu[1(✉)], Bing Su[2], and Chao Liu[2]

[1] North China Institute of Computing Technology, Beijing, China
xiaxiaokai@buaa.edu.cn, xuluo@sei.buaa.edu.cn
[2] School of Computer Science and Engineering, Beihang University, Beijing, China
{subing,liuchao}@buaa.edu.cn

Abstract. The complex information systems like military information systems have many complex characteristics, such as large-scale, complex interacted, dynamical changing of the structure, lots of concurrent events, and running in many different scenarios like jamming and damaging. DEVS and its extensions have been proven to be promising Modeling and Simulation tools for different systems, but the current DEVS extensions cannot perfectly support modeling and simulation of the complex characteristics of the information systems. So an extended DEVS formalism based on the current DEVS extensions is proposed for the purpose in this paper. The algorithms and the M&S environment of the extended DEVS are also proposed. And the case study in this paper shows the feasibility and effectiveness of the research.

Keywords: Extended DEVS formalism · Simulation algorithm · Complex information systems · M&S environment

1 Introduction

Along with the development and improvement of the computer and network technologies, the information systems like C4ISR have become more complex. Modeling and Simulation (M&S) are playing an important role in the development of the information systems. The information systems now have many characteristics, and each demands the M&S tool to satisfy some requirements: (1) The components constituted the information systems are large and their interactions are complex, which require the simulation model can be described in a structured manner; (2) The number of events in the system is very large, and many of them need to be processed concurrently, which require the simulation models can process the concurrent events; (3) There are many complex usage scenarios for information systems, such as Jamming and damaging, which require the simulation model can describe the normal behavior and exception handling behavior separately; (4) Some types of information systems can be adaptive, which means that the structure of the systems and the configuration of the systems can be changed to obtain the better effectiveness when the runtime environment or the mission has changed. This requires the simulation models' structure and parameters can be changed dynamically in the simulation run.

© Springer Science+Business Media Singapore 2016
L. Zhang et al. (Eds.): AsiaSim 2016/SCS AutumnSim 2016, Part III, CCIS 645, pp. 457–467, 2016.
DOI: 10.1007/978-981-10-2669-0_49

The DEVS, which is the abbreviation of the Discrete Event System Specification, was first proposed by Zeigler [1]. DEVS is a modular and hierarchical formalism for modeling and analyzing general systems that can be discrete event systems which might be described by state transition tables, and continuous state systems which might be described by differential equations, and hybrid continuous state and discrete event systems. DEVS has been proven to be a universal formalism to express any sub-class of discrete event systems, such as Cellular Automata, Petri Nets, and Generalized Markov Chains. DEVS can also be used to express more restricted formalism like workflow systems, state machines, and fuzzy logics [2, 3]. Because of the advantages of the DEVS, many extensions of DEVS have been proposed to satisfy users' different requirements. Parallel DEVS (PDEVS) is used to simulate the concurrent system by considering the concurrent transition events [4]. Port-DEVS (also called DEVS with ports) considers the transitions of events through input and output ports [5]. Fault DEVS (FDEVS) separates the fault behavior description from the normal behavior description by adding fault state and fault transition [6]. FDEVS is suitable for studying fault-sensitive systems. Dynamic Structure DEVS (DSDEVS) supports the structure change in the process of simulation run [7, 8]. There are more types of extensions, such as Real Time DEVS, Fuzzy DEVS, Cell DEVS, which can be found in [4, 9, 10].

By analyzing the abilities of the different DEVS extension, we find that some extensions of DEVS can satisfy one or two characteristics of the complex information systems, but none of them can satisfy all the characteristics. For example, the Port-DEVS can support modeling the system in a structured manner, but cannot support other requirements. PDEVS can only support the concurrent simulation. The FDEVS can support effectively modeling of the different excepting handling behavior, but cannot support other requirements. The DSDEVS can support dynamic structure change during simulation, but cannot support parameters dynamic change and other requirements. By absorbing the advantages of above DEVS extensions, this paper proposes an extended DEVS to support modeling and simulation of the complex adaptive information systems.

The remainder of the paper is organized as follows. Section 2 firstly shows the extended DEVS formalism for M&S of complex adaptive information systems, and then presents the algorithms of the proposed extended DEVS model. Finally Sect. 2 concludes the advantages of the extended DEVS. Section 3 shows the implementation of the M&S environment for complex information systems based on the extended DEVS proposed in Sect. 2. Section 4 uses a case study to show the feasibility of the proposed method. And Sect. 5 concludes the paper.

2   The Extended DEVS Formalism

The proposed extended DEVS includes two types of models like DSDEVS, which are basic model and network model. The basic model describes the behavior of a component which cannot be divided. The network model describes the structure of the system and the change of the structure. Their formalisms are introduced in the following section separately.

2.1 Formalism of Basic Model

The basic model of the extended DEVS, which fuses the characteristics of Port-DEVS, PDEVS, and FDEVS, can be defined as an 11-tuple:

$$BM = \langle X_n, Y, S, \delta_{int}, \delta_{ext}, \delta_{con}, \lambda, ta, X_f, F, \delta_{fault}, \delta_{ext \& fault}, P \rangle$$

- $X_n = \{(p, v) | p \in InPorts, v \in X_p\}$ specifies the set of normal input events.
  - p is the input port of the model
  - v is the discrete value of the corresponding port
  - X_p is the set of discrete inputs at port p
- $Y = \{(p, v) | p \in OutPorts, v \in Y_p\}$ specifies the set of output events.
- S specifies the normal internal states.
- $F = F' \cup \{\emptyset\}$ specifies the set of **faults**, where $\emptyset$ means that there is no fault.
- $X_f = \{(p, v) | p \in FInPorts, v \in X_{pf}\}$ specifies the set of fault input events. The definitions of F and X_f allows the model to define transient or permanent faults.
- P specifies the set of parameters of the model.
- $ta: S \times F \rightarrow \mathcal{R}_0^+$. The time advance function $ta(s, f)$ represents the time when the next internal event will arrive.
- $\delta_{int}: S \times F \rightarrow S \times F$. The internal transition function represents that when there is no external event (normal input event or fault input event) arriving, the current state (s, f) will become to $\delta_{int}(s, f)$ after the $ta(s, f)$ time.
- $\delta_{ext}: Q \times F \times \mathcal{R}_0^+ \times X_n^b \rightarrow S \times F$. The normal external transition function handles the normal external input event. When the event $x \in X_n^b$ arrives, the model's current state (s, f) becomes to $\delta_{ext}(s, f, e, x)$
  - $Q = \{(s, e) | s \in S, 0 < e < ta(s)\}$, where e is the elapsed time
  - $X_n^b = \{x_i | x_i = (p, v), p \in InPorts, v \in X_p\}$ is a bag covering elements of X_n
- $\delta_{fault}: S \times F \times \mathcal{R}_0^+ \times X_f^b \rightarrow S \times F$. The fault external transition function handles the fault input events. The difference between external transition function and fault transition function is the type of events they handle.
- $\delta_{ext \& fault}: S \times F \times \mathcal{R}_0^+ \times X_n^b \times X_f^b \rightarrow S \times F$. The external confluent transition function specifies the execution sequence when δ_{ext} and δ_{fault} occur at the same time.
- $\delta_{con}: S \times F \times X^b \rightarrow S \times F$. The confluent transition function specifies the execution sequence when δ_{int} and $\delta_{ext}/\delta_{fault}$ occur at the same time.
- $\lambda: S \times F \rightarrow Y^b$. The output function generates outputs depending on the current state (s, f).
  - $Y^b = \{y_i | y_i = (p, v), p \in OutPorts, v \in Y_p\}$ is a bag covering elements of Y.

2.2   Formalism of Network Model

The network model of the extended DEVS, which fuses the characteristics of DSFEVS, Port-DEVS and PDEVS, can be defined as follow:

$$NM = \langle X_\Delta, Y_\Delta, \chi, M_\chi \rangle$$

- Δ is the name of the model,
- X_Δ and Y_Δ are the sets of input and output events. Their definitions are similar to X and Y in the basic model.
- χ is the network executive of the model. The network executive controls the change of the network structure (describes the compostion of the model).
- M_χ is the model of the network executive χ.

  M_χ can be defined by a revised basic model defined above as follow:

$$M_\chi = \langle X_\chi, SF_\chi, Y_\chi, \delta_{int}, \delta_{ext}, \delta_{con}, \lambda_\chi, ta_\chi, X_{\chi\_f}, \delta_{fault}, \delta_{ext\,\&\,fault}, S_\chi, F_\chi, P_\chi \rangle$$

The definitions of $X_\chi, Y_\chi, \delta_{int}, \delta_{ext}, \delta_{con}, \lambda_\chi, ta_\chi, X_{\chi\_f}, \delta_{fault}, P_\chi$ and $\delta_{ext\,\&\,fault}$ are similar to the corresponding elements in the basic model. $SF_\chi = S_\chi \times F_\chi$ specifies the set of execute states. Each execute state $sf_\chi \in SF_\chi$ can be defined as a network structure as follow:

$$sf_\chi = (D^\chi, \{M_i^\chi\}, EIC, EOC, IC, \Theta^\chi)$$

- D^χ specifies the set of sub-components constituted the network structure
- M_i^χ is the model of sub-component i, where $i \in D^\chi \cup \chi$. M_i^χ can be basic model or network model. So the extended DEVS is hierarchical.
- $EIC = \{\langle in_p, i.in_p \rangle | in_p \in InPorts, i \in D^\chi \cup \chi, i.in_p \in M_i.Inports\}$ specifies   the external input couplings, where in_p and $i.in_p$ are the input ports of network model Δ and sub-component i respectively, $InPorts$ and $M_i.Inports$ are the sets of input ports respectively.
- $EOC = \{\langle i.out_p, out_p \rangle | out_p \in OutPorts, i \in D^\chi \cup \chi, i.out_p \in M_i.OutPorts\}$ specifies the external output couplings.
- $IC = \{\langle i.out_p, j.in_p \rangle | i, j \in D^\chi \cup \chi, i.out_p \in M_i.OutPorts, j.in_p \in M_j.InPorts\}$. specifies the internal couplings.
- Θ^χ specifies the set of parameters.

  From the above definition of the network model, we can find that each executive state corresponds to a network structure. When the executive state is changed, the structure of the network model is changed.

2.3 Simulation of the Extended DEVS

The simulation mechanism of the proposed extended DEVS is similar to the DEVS and PDEVS. The extended DEVS model can be transformed to an executable simulator model using simulator elements. Four types of simulator elements are needed for the simulation of the extended DEVS. The *Simulator* is responsible for the simulation of basic model. The *Executive Simulator* is responsible for the simulation of the executive of the network model. The *Coordinator* is responsible for the simulation of the network model. The *Root-Coordinator* controls the running process. The structure of the simulator model corresponds to the hierarchical extended DEVS model structure except the *Root-Coordinator* instance added as the topmost entity.

The transformation of an extended DEVS model to an executable simulation model using associated simulator elements is shown in Fig. 1. Two network models named *GPT* and *QPT* are mapped to two *Coordinator* instances respectively, and each one includes an *Executive Simulator instance as the child*. The other models such as *F1Generator, JobGenerator,* and *Queue,* are mapped to *Simulator* instances.

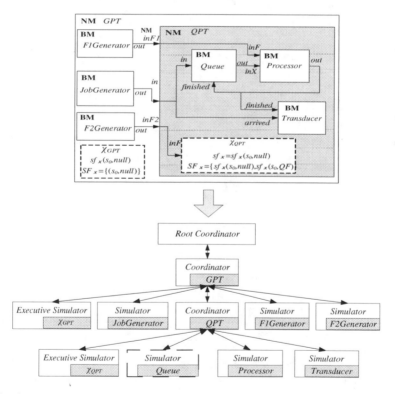

Fig. 1. An extended DEVS model and the corresponding executive simulator model

Several types of messages are used for the communications among the *Root-Coordinator, Coordinator, Simulator* and *Executive Simulator. init_message* is used to initialize the models. * *_message* is used to trigger the internal transition. *y_message* is used to represent the output message. *x_message* is used to trigger the external transition. *update_message* is used to inform the parent *Coordinator* instance to change the structure of the executive simulation model constituted by simulator elements according to the change of the network structure.

The algorithm of the *Executive Simulation* is similar to the algorithm of *Simulator* except that the *Executive Simulator* will send a message typed *update_message* to the parent *Coordinator* instance when it processes the messages of ∗_*message* or *x_message*. The algorithm of the *Executive Simulator* is shown in Fig. 2.

ExDEVS-Executive Simulator

tl, tn //tl—the last event, tn—the next internal event

bm //the executive model associated the Executive Simulator

when receive $init\_message(init, t)$ at t

    $bm.init(t)$ //initialization of the model

    $tl = t;\ \ tn = tl + bm.ta(s, f)$

when receive ∗_$message(∗, t)$ at t

    $y_{bag} = bm.\lambda(s, f)$ //send output to the parent Coordinator instance

    send $y\_message(y_{bag}, t, bm)$ to $parent$

    $(s, f) = \delta_{int}(s, f)$ //update the state of the model

    send $update\_message(sf_{x}(s, f), t)$ to $parent$

    $tl = t;\ \ tn = tl + bm.ta(s, f)$

when receive $x\_message(x_{bag}, t)$ at t

    $e = t - tl$

    if $t == tn$ //when internal event occurs

        $(s, f) = \delta_{con}(s, f, x_{bag})$

    else if $t <> tn\ \&\&\ x_{bag} \subseteq X_{n}^{b}$ //when normal external events occur

        $(s, f) = \delta_{ext}(s, f, e, x_{bag})$

    else if $t <> tn\ \&\&\ x_{bag} \subseteq X_{f}^{b}$ //when fault external events occur

        $(s, f) = \delta_{fault}(s, f, e, x_{bag})$

    else   //concurrent transitions occur

        $(s, f) = \delta_{ext\&fault}(s, f, e, xn_{bag}, xf_{bag})$ //$x_{bag} = \{xn_{bag}, xf_{bag}\}$

    end if

    send $update\_message(sf_{x}(s, f), t)$ to $parent$

    $tl = t;\ \ tn = tl + bm.ta(s, f)$

end ExDEVS-Executive Simulator

Fig. 2. Algorithm for the *Executive Simulator*

Compared to the *Coordinator* for classical DEVS or PDEVS, the *Coordinator* for the extended DEVS is not only responsible for transmitting messages between parent *Coordinator* instance and child simulator instances, but also is responsible for the structure changing of the executable simulator model of the corresponding network structure. The algorithm of the *Coordinator* for the extended DEVS is shown in Fig. 3.

```
ExDEVS-Coordinator
Variables:
    nm, M_χ          //the corresponding network model and the executive model
    M_χ.simu, M_i.simu  //the simulator instance of the executive and the sub-component i
when receive init_message(init, t) at t
    tl = t                    //transmit the init message to child simulator elements
    send init_message(init, t) to M_χ.simu
    for-each M_i in TM={M_i|i ∈ M_χ.sf_t.D^t}
        send init_message(init, t) to M_i.simu
    tl = t; tn = min ( {M_i.tn| i ∈ M_χ.sf_t.D^t ∪ nm.χ})
when receive *_message(*, t) at t
    TM={M_i|i ∈ M_χ.sf_t.D^t ∪ nm.χ ∧ M_i.tn == t}
    for-each M_i in TM        //transmit the *_message to the set of simulator instances which need
        send *_message(*, t) to M_i.simu
    tl = t; tn = min ( {M_i.tn| i ∈ nm.M_χ.sf_t.D^t ∪ nm.χ})
when receive x_message(x_{bag}, t) at t
    Receivers = {M_i|i ∈ (M_χ.sf_t.D^t ∪ χ) ∧ (nm.in_p, M_i.in_p) ∈ sf_t.EIC ∧ (nm.in_p ∈ x_{bag}.ports)}
    for-each M_i in Receivers  //transmit the x_{bag} to the set of simulators instances which need

        send x_message(x_{bag}^{M_i}, t) to M_i.simu  //x_{bag}^{M_i} is the value M_i needed

    tl = t; tn = min ( {M_i.tn| i ∈ nm.M_χ.sf_t.D^t ∪ nm.χ})
when receive y_message(y_{bag}, t, d) at t from d
    for-each coupling =< d.out_p, nm.out_p) > in M_χ.sf_t.EOC

        send y_message(y_{bag}, t, nm) to parent

    Receivers = {M_i|i ∈ M_χ.sf_t.D^t ∪ nm.χ ∧ (d.out_p, M_i.in_p) ∈ M_χ.sf_t.IC}
    for-each M_i in Receivers  //transimit y_{bag} to the set of simulator instances which need
        for-each coupling =< d, M_i.in_p) > in nm.M_χ.sf_t.IC
            send x_message(y_{bag} → x_{bag}, t, M_i.in_p) to M_i.simu
    tl = t; tn = min ( {M_i.tn| i ∈ nm.M_χ.sf_t.D^t ∪ nm.χ})
when receive update_message(sf_p, t) at t
    update()            //update the network model and the corrsponding simulator instances
    Receivers = {M_i|i is the new added component}
    for-each M_i in Receivers  //send init_message to the new added simulator instances
        send init_message(init, t) to M_i
    tl = t; tn = min ( {M_i.tn| i ∈ nm.M_χ.sf_t.D^t ∪ nm.χ})
end ExDEVS-Coordinator
```

Fig. 3. Algorithm for the *Coordinator*

The *Root Coordinator* initiates, controls and ends a simulation cycle with different messages. It holds the simulation clock. The algorithm of the *Root Coordinator* for the extended DEVS is similar to the classical DEVS and PDEVS, which can be referred in [4].

2.4   Advantages for M&S of Complex Information Systems

By fusing the advantages of the DEVS, PDEVS, FDEVS and DSDEVS, the proposed extended DEVS above has the following characteristics, which are suitable for the modeling and simulation of the complex information systems like C4ISR.

- The extended DEVS is modular, hierarchical, and the communications in the model are based ports, which make it suitable for describing the large-scale, complex interconnected information systems.
- The extended DEVS supports processing the concurrent events. While the nodes of the information system usually need to response to the arrived information at the same time.
- The extended DEVS can describe the component's normal behavior and abnormal behavior separately by defining the fault sets and fault transition function in the basic model or the executive model, which are very suitable for studying the influence of the sudden events. However, the information systems like C4ISR need to work in very complex environment, and many sudden events need to be processed correctly.
- The extended DEVS can change the structure of the network model dynamically. Complex information systems like C4ISR are dynamical or adaptive structure, which means the configuration of the system, the communication of the system, and the components constituted the system can change while running according to the change of the mission or the change of the environment (such as Jamming or damaging by the enemy). We can see that the extended DEVS can perfectly satisfy the requirement.
- The extended DEVS supports defining parameters for the model, which make the model can be easily reused. Many types of equipment in the information systems have the same mechanism, like the radars. By changing the values of the parameters of one radar's simulation model, we can get other radars' simulation models. Besides, the values of the parameters can be changed during the simulation just like the dynamical changing of the network structure.

3   M&S Environment Based on the Extended DEVS

Based on the proposed extended DEVS formalism (called ExDEVS for convenience) and the corresponding algorithms in the above section, the M&S environment for the complex information systems is developed. The architecture of the environment is shown in Fig. 4.

The modeling environment, simulation engine and the simulation database constitute the M&S environment. The simulation engine takes the model from the modeling environment as the input, and sends the simulation results to the simulation database by executing the model. The implementation of the simulation engine is based on the algorithms proposed in Sect. 2. The modeling environment provides ExDEVS abstract classes for users to implement ExDEVS models by inheriting them just like DEVSJava and xDEVS. One can also use the XML to describe the ExDEVS model based on the proposed ExDEVS schema just like DEVSML [11, 12]. Then the model described by

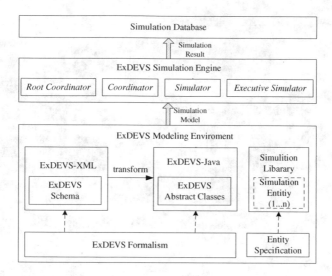

Fig. 4. M&S Environment based on the extended DEVS

XML can be transformed to model described by ExDEVS-Java automatically by the M&S Environment. More information about the ExDEVS schema and the abstract classes can be found in [13].

In order to support the M&S of the complex information systems, many reusable simulation entities related with the information systems are implemented, including the simulation entities of different sensors, different information process unit, and simulation entities of different weapons, and so on. Besides, some simulation entities are developed to record the output of other entities during the simulation, and the output data can be stored into the database for analyzing.

4 Case Study

The proposed M&S environment based on the extended DEVS has been used in studying the anti-missile systems, which is a typical complex information system. Three alternatives have been studied. Alternative I can perform better in the scenario of interference than Alternative I, while Alternative II can perform better in the scenario of nil interference. The detail information of Alternative I and II can be referred in our previous work [14]. The Alternative III adapts its structure between Alternative I and II, according to the circumstance.

Figure 5 shows the simulation results in a complex scenario based on the proposed M&S environment. It shows that Alternative III can obtain better performance by having the characteristic of adaptation. Due to the limit of the paper length, more information about the case study cannot be shown. But we will present it in the future study.

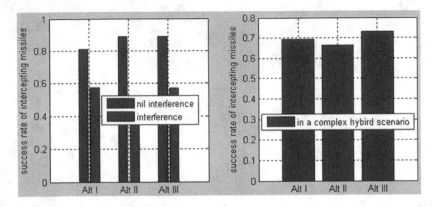

Fig. 5. Simulation result of the case study

5   Conclusion

An extended DEVS formalism based on the classical DEVS and its current extensions is proposed to model and simulate information systems with complex characteristics. The extended DEVS includes basic model and network model. The basic model describes the behavior of a component which cannot be divided. The network model describes the structure of the system and the change of the structure during runtime. The simulation algorithms and the M&S environment of the extended DEVS are proposed next. A ballistic missile defense system, a typical complex information system, is used to verify the feasibility and effectiveness of the proposed research. In the future, we will complete and optimize the M&S environment, and publish it as open source.

References

1. Zeigler, B.P., Kim, T.G., Praehofer, H.: Theory of Modeling and Simulation: Integrating Discrete Event and Continuous Complex Dynamic Systems, 2nd edn. Academic Press, San Diego (2000)
2. Vangheluwe, H.: Multi-Formalism Modeling and Simulation. Gent University, Gent (2000)
3. Sarjoughian, H.S., Cellier, F.E.: Discrete Event Modeling and Simulation Technologies: A Tapestry of Systems and AI-Based Theories and Methodologies. Spring-Verlag, New York (2001)
4. Chow, A.C.: Parallel DEVS: a parallel, hierarchical, modular modeling formalism and its distributed simulator. Trans. Soc. Comput. Simul. Int. **13**, 55–67 (1996)
5. Olaf, H.: Simulation Based Parameter and Structure Optimisation of Discrete Event Systems. Liverpool John Moores University, Liverpool (2009)
6. Kofman, E., Giambiasi, N., Junco, S.: FDEVS: a general devs-based formalism for fault modeling and simulation. In: 12th European Simulation Symposium, pp. 77–82. SOC Computer Simulation, San Diego(2000)
7. Barros, F.J.: Dynamic structure discrete event system specification: a new formalism for dynamic structure modeling and simulation. In: Proceedings of the 1995 Winter Simulation Conference (1995)

8. Barros, F.J.: Modeling and Simulation of Dynamic Structure Discrete Event Systems: A General Systems Theory Approach. University of Coimbra, Coimbra (1996)
9. Hae, S.S., Tag, G.K.: Application of real-time DEVS to analysis of safety-critical embedded control systems: railroad crossing control example. Simul. Trans. Soc. Model Simul. Int. **81**, 119–136 (2004)
10. Kwon, Y.W., Part, H.C.: Fuzzy-DEVS formalism: concepts, realization and applications. In: Proceedings of 1996 Conference on AI, Simulation and Planning in High Autonomy Systems, pp. 227–234. IEEE, New York (1996)
11. Martin, J.L.R., Mittal, S., Pena, M.A.P.: A W3C XML schema for DEVS scenarios. In: Proceedings of the 2007 Spring Simulation Multi-Conference, pp. 279–286. Society for Computer Simulation International, San Diego (2007)
12. Mittal, S., Douglass, S.A.: DEVSML 2.0: the language and the stack. In: Proceedings of the 2012 Symposium on Theory of Modeling and Simulation-DEVS Integrative M&S Symposium, pp. 1–12. Society for Computer Simulation International, San Diego (2012)
13. Xia, X.K.: Research on Effectiveness Evaluation Oriented System Architecture Simulation and Optimization Method. Beihang University, Beijing (2015)
14. Xia, X., Zhao, K., Xu, L., Liu, C.: To execute the C4ISR architecture based on DoDAF and simulink. In: Tan, G., Teo, Y.M., Turner, S.J., Yeo, G.K. (eds.) AsiaSim 2013. CCIS, vol. 402, pp. 25–36. Springer, Heidelberg (2013)

Modeling and Simulating of Atmospheric Turbulence in Flight Simulator

Weiting Cui[✉], Xiaoli Shi, and Yongqing Wang

Beijing Electro-Mechanical Engineering Institute, Beijing, China
565225676@qq.com

Abstract. Atmospheric turbulence is an atmospheric disturbance that frequently encountered during the course of the flight, which affects ride comfort and flight safety and one cause of fatigue damage of airplane structures. This article conducts a research on the modeling and simulating technology of the wind field, and analyzes Dryden model and Von Karman model which are existing at present, we used the better Von Karman model of atmospheric turbulence to simulate in high frequency range, to simplify the model and solve the time-domain decomposition problems, which satisfied the demands of real-time systems at last. Finally, we applied model application into flight simulator to validate the correctness of the model further, besides, to provide important reference for flight training and flight simulator design.

Keywords: Atmospheric turbulence · Wind field model · Von Karman model · Flight simulator

1 Introduction

Nowadays, with the development of computer simulation technology and aviation industry, the flight simulator has become a virtual reality (VR) technology which plays a very important role in aviation industry. The flight simulation systems used the key technique of modeling and simulating for the wind field, which one of the most important steps in achieving virtual reality simulation of flight dynamics [1]. The real-time capability and authenticity of the atmospheric wind model is an important performance indicator that ensures the pilot immersed in and man-machine interacted friendly and restricts each other with these two features [2]. Therefore, the establishment of efficient real-time atmospheric wind model will be of great importance to improve the performance of the flight simulator.

Turbulent motion is superposed by various scales of vertical continuous distribution which scale up to several hundred meters and minimum scale is about 1 mm. [3] A big incentive bumps occur when aircraft fly in turbulent field not only directly affects ride comfort and flight safety, [4] but also affects the structural fatigue. So it is very important to research atmospheric turbulence in the flight simulation system [5]. In this article, in order to improve the reality of flight dynamics system, [6] we intend to change the modeling approach which based on Dryden model and reasonably deal with Von Karman model which cannot be used in analogue simulation, we can directly come up

© Springer Science+Business Media Singapore 2016
L. Zhang et al. (Eds.): AsiaSim 2016/SCS AutumnSim 2016, Part III, CCIS 645, pp. 468–476, 2016.
DOI: 10.1007/978-981-10-2669-0_50

with a simplified model of Von Karman Von which trends closer to Karman model, thereby realizing three-dimensional numerical simulation in the turbulent model of Von Karman, which to meet the requirements of authenticity and real-time in simulation system for flight simulator. Finally, we made a brief introduction about design procedures and implementation results used in real-time emulation of flight simulator.

2   Modeling and Simulating of Atmospheric Turbulence

At present, the simulation methods of atmospheric turbulence in the three-dimensional space have some problems in huge computation, large memory occupation, and poor real-time capability of simulation, which cannot meet the needs of real-time flight simulator. We use recursive model to generate data in atmospheric turbulence with characteristics of low computational complexity and less memory occupation to carry out real-time simulation based on the atmospheric turbulence simulation methods of related functions. This article does a research on stochastic process models based on 3-D atmosphere turbulence of related functions to generate 3-D atmosphere turbulence.

2.1   The Modeling of Atmospheric Turbulent

We often use the related functions or frequency functions to describe atmospheric turbulence in the flight simulation. The frequency functions transform the related functions into Fourier, so two descriptive methods are equivalent.

Dryden and Von Karman counted and deduced the various theoretical systems based on measured data to check the related functions or frequency spectrum in flight simulation. These two models are the most important models in aerospace field, which recognized as the turbulent model used in flight simulation. We will briefly introduce two models below.

2.1.1   The Turbulent Model of Dryden
Dryden [8] puts forward longitudinal correlation functions and transverse correlation functions of exponential type based on a large number of measurements and statistical data, as follow:

$$f(\xi) = e^{-\frac{\xi}{L}} \tag{1}$$

$$g(\xi) = e^{-\frac{\xi}{L}}(1 - \frac{\xi}{2L}) = f(\xi)(1 - \frac{\xi}{2L}) \tag{2}$$

We set V (x, y, z) as turbulent speed in 3-D atmosphere turbulence, the turbulent speed has three components in coordinates of flight path, respectively setting the turbulent speed component u flowing forward direction of x-axis in flight direction, the turbulent speed component v flowing rightward direction of y-axis and the turbulent speed component w flowing vertical direction of z-axis.

According to Dryden model, the spatial frequency spectrum of its turbulent speed should be expressed as:

$$\left.\begin{array}{l} \Phi_{uu}(\Omega) = \sigma_u^2 \dfrac{L_u}{\pi} \dfrac{1}{1 + (L_u\Omega)^2} \\[3mm] \Phi_{vv}(\Omega) = \sigma_v^2 \dfrac{L_v}{\pi} \dfrac{1 + 12(L_v\Omega)^2}{\left[1 + 4(L_v\Omega)^2\right]^2} \\[3mm] \Phi_{ww}(\Omega) = \sigma_w^2 \dfrac{L_w}{\pi} \dfrac{1 + 12(L_w\Omega)^2}{\left[1 + 4(L_w\Omega)^2\right]^2} \end{array}\right\} \tag{3}$$

In the formula, the frequency Ω really exists in turbulence space along with x-axis of the spatial frequency, which dimension is (rad/m), we define the frequency as time-frequency ω when planes pass through the field of turbulence space, which dimension is (rad/m), for the aircraft that flying by true airspeed V, whose relationship between the spatial frequency and the temporal frequency as $\Omega = \dfrac{\omega}{V}$, σ_u, σ_v, σ_w is the turbulence intensity flowing upward in three directions; L_u, L_v, L_w are the turbulence scale in three directions; for every turbulence of same orientation, the formula has the connection as $\sigma_u = \sigma_v = \sigma_w$, $L_u = 2L_v = 2L_w$.

2.1.2 The Turbulent Model of Von Karman

Von Karman [9] deduce energy spectrum of energy in atmospheric turbulence according to the theory and measured data, as follows:

$$E(\Omega) = \sigma^2 \frac{55L}{9\pi} \frac{(aL\Omega)^4}{\left[1 + (aL\Omega)^2\right]^{17/6}} \tag{4}$$

a = 1.339 inside.

Von Karman put forward the longitudinal correlation functions and transverse correlation functions, respectively as:

$$f(\xi) = \frac{2^{2/3}}{\Gamma(1/3)} \zeta^{1/3} K_{1/3}(\zeta) \tag{5}$$

$$g(\xi) = \frac{2^{2/3}}{\Gamma(1/3)} \zeta^{1/3} [K_{1/3}(\zeta) - \frac{1}{2}\zeta K_{2/3}(\zeta)] \tag{6}$$

In formula, $\zeta = \xi(aL)$, Γ is function of Gamma, K is second kind of Bessel function to improve [10].

Thus, Von Karman obtains the function of spatial spectrum that have responded the atmospheric mathematical statistics characteristic in three directions, as follows:

$$\left.\begin{aligned}
\Phi_{uu}(\Omega) &= \sigma_u^2 \frac{L_u}{\pi} \frac{1}{\left[1 + (aL_u\Omega)^2\right]^{5/6}} \\[2ex]
\Phi_{vv}(\Omega) &= \sigma_v^2 \frac{L_v}{\pi} \frac{1 + \frac{8}{3}(2aL_v\Omega)^2}{\left[1 + 4(aL_v\Omega)^2\right]^{11/6}} \\[2ex]
\Phi_{ww}(\Omega) &= \sigma_w^2 \frac{L_w}{\pi} \frac{1 + \frac{8}{3}(2aL_w\Omega)^2}{\left[1 + 4(aL_w\Omega)^2\right]^{11/6}}
\end{aligned}\right\} \tag{7}$$

In the isotropic turbulence field, the current dimension is $L_u = 2L_v = 2L_w$.

2.1.3   Comparison of the Dryden Turbulence Model and the Von Karman Model

Dryden turbulence model and the Von Karman turbulence model is currently the most important turbulence model recognized aerospace, but Dryden model system is the opposite to Von Karman model. Dryden model established the correlation function of atmospheric turbulence based on experience, and then derived the spectral function, while The Von Karman model established a spectral function of atmospheric turbulence based on a number of measurements and statistical data, and then pushed the export-related functions.

It shows that they are different by comparing two models of correlation function and spectral function, as shown in Fig. 1. The Von Karman model established the energy of spectral function based on the measured data, and its spectral distribution is consistent with the actual situation of atmospheric turbulence, it is very practical for the spectral response characteristics of the aircraft in the frequency domain. It cannot be used in the process of real-time emulation because the Von Karman model of time spectrum function cannot be conjugated and decomposed, while Dryden model of time spectrum function can be used as rational expression to factorize, which emulated in the time domain, so we do the former study on Dryden model to conjugate and decompose atmospheric turbulence that has generated. But practice shows that wind turbulence generated by the model are different from the actual situation gap.

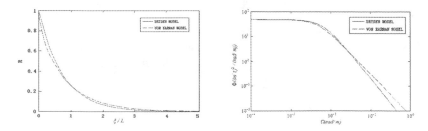

Fig. 1. Comparison on vertical correlation function and vertical space frequency function between Dryden model and Von Karman model.

According to the case of the turbulence intensity and turbulence scale, it shows that both two models almost coincide in the low-frequency range, but in the high-frequency range shows the difference, especially between the slopes whether in time domain or spatial domain by comparing with Vertical spectral function of two models. However, the aircraft structural modal frequencies usually happen in the high frequency range because turbulence in the high frequency range may stimulate its structural vibration. Compared to the Von Karman model, Dryden model cannot simulate the high-frequency response of aircraft turbulence, so using Dryden model will result in insufficient for large aircraft with apparently high-frequency vibrations.

In order to improve the reality of flight dynamics system, we intend to change the modeling approach which based on Dryden model and reasonably deal with Von Karman model which cannot be used in analogue simulation, we can directly come up with a simplified model of Von Karman which trends closer to Von Karman model, thereby realizing three-dimensional numerical simulation in the turbulent model of Von Karman.

2.2   The Simulating of Atmospheric Turbulent Model

2.2.1   The Basic Principles of the Simulation of Atmospheric Turbulence Model

The basic principles of the numerical simulation of turbulent flow is the general principles generated by random process which converted white noise of input into colored noise of output by shaping filter. In other words, first to use the pseudo random signal generated from computer which distributes with zero mean, then pass the shaping filter accord with the given design of spectral, finally, atmospheric turbulence signal Obtained by conforming to turbulence model spectrum and Gauss velocity distribution law of three-dimensional time history. Its principles are shown in Fig. 2.

Fig. 2.   The numerical simulation method in atmospheric turbulence

Among the white noise signal adopted mean value equal to 0 and standard deviation equal to 1 as pseudorandom sequence of distribution Gauss. The key was to confirm the transfer function G(s).

In the control process, the white noise could be converted into links of colored noise called the shaping filter. White noise spectrum is a constant set as the unit value, the white noise r(t) of unit strength pass through transfer function G(s) of the filter to generate a random process u(t), then spectral function of u(t) as:

$$\Phi(\omega) = G^*(i\omega)G(i\omega) = |G(i\omega)|^2 \tag{8}$$

The sign of $*$ means complex conjugate in formula. This is the method adopted from engineering to simulate the stationary random process. When the functions of time spectrum were decomposed as above, we could confirm the parameters of shaping filter, thus made simulation in time domain. In order to generate transfer functions G(s) of shaping filter required from frequency spectrum given, all the functions of time spectrum in turbulence would be decomposed according to (8).

2.2.2   The Numerical Simulation Based on Three-Dimensional Numerical Simulation in the Turbulent Model of Von Karman

In this article, in order to improve the reality of flight dynamics system, we intend to change the modeling approach which based on Dryden model and reasonably deal with Von Karman model which cannot be used in analogue simulation, we can directly come up with a simplified model of Von Karman Von which trends closer to Karman model, thereby realizing three-dimensional numerical simulation in the turbulent model of Von Karman.

To Confirm the Parameters of Shaping Filter. In order to make the model implemented in the time-domain simulation, the Von Karman model approached to rationalization and then simplified into first order, we get the formula as:

$$\left. \begin{array}{l} G_u(s) = \dfrac{K_u}{T_u s + 1} \\[2mm] K_u = \sigma_u \sqrt{\dfrac{L_u}{\pi V}}, T_u = \left(\dfrac{a L_u}{V} \right)^{5/6} \end{array} \right\} \tag{9}$$

$$\left. \begin{array}{l} G_v(s) = \dfrac{K_v}{T_v s + 1} \\[2mm] K_v = \sigma_v \sqrt{\dfrac{L_v}{\pi V}}, T_v = \sqrt{\dfrac{3}{8}} \left(\dfrac{2 a L_v}{V} \right)^{5/6} \end{array} \right\} \tag{10}$$

$$\left. \begin{array}{l} G_w(s) = \dfrac{K_w}{T_w s + 1} \\[2mm] K_w = \sigma_w \sqrt{\dfrac{L_w}{\pi V}}, T_w = \sqrt{\dfrac{3}{8}} \left(\dfrac{2 a L_w}{V} \right) \end{array} \right\} \tag{11}$$

As shown in Fig. 3, we designed the structural block diagram of generator model in atmospheric turbulence according to the above results. Of which WNG inputted signal for pseudo-random numbers to approach the white noise of Gauss, transferred the function G(s) to shaping-filter in the right side of textbox, outputted the signal of turbulence as three velocity components u, v, w.

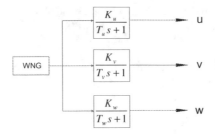

Fig. 3. The structural block diagram of generator model in atmospheric turbulence.

To Generate the Signal Sequence of Atmospheric Turbulence. We rewrite the transfer function G(s) of forming filter as follows:

$$G(s) = \frac{x(s)}{r(s)} = \frac{c}{s+a} \tag{12}$$

In formula, r(s) is input, that is Laplace transformation form of pseudo-random numbers. x(s) is output, that is Laplace transformation form required of pseudo-random numbers. $a = 1/T$, $c = K/T$.

We get the difference equation used in the simulation through the derivation, as follows:

$$x_{i+1} = e^{-aT}x_i + \frac{c}{a}(1 - e^{-aT})r_i \tag{13}$$

T is set as the sampling period, namely of time step in formula.

We continually generate the required random sequence in atmospheric turbulence from formula of (13).

2.3   The Simulation Result

We set $\sigma_u = \sigma_v = \sigma_w = 1.5$ m/s, $L_u = 2L_v = 2L_w = 750$ m, $V = 172$ m/s, $T = 0.05$ s to get fragments of turbulent velocity through the derivation above, as Fig. 4:

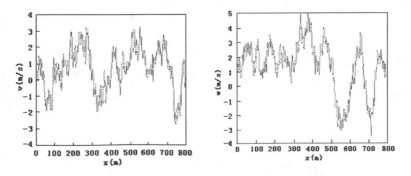

Fig. 4. To simplify the speed fragment v and w in sequence of turbulence Von Karman.

3 The Application of Flight Simulator Based on Improved Von Karman Model of Atmospheric Turbulence

The atmospheric turbulence movement is a major disturbance source interferes with aircraft movement, so establishment of an integrated model of atmospheric turbulence on a flight simulator is of great significance. In this article, FlightGear platform established the support platform for operation, and study could be targeted at a flight simulator, which simulated the response of the aircraft under various wind effects and provided an important basis for flight training, flight simulation, flight simulator.

Users can set the parameter information of various types of basic wind field in total control of the interface by the simulation interface. The above information was calculated by the incoming interface to an integrated wind field model and calculated the value of the current particles of aircraft's wind speed vector at each step in the real-time simulation, and then passed to the aircraft dynamics model. Figure 5 shows the comparison diagrams which encountered the changes of space velocity and kept away from them in the situation without any manipulation.

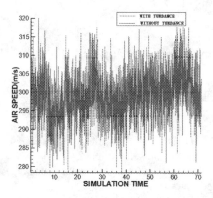

Fig. 5. The changes of space velocity encountering turbulence in plane.

4 Conclusions

The flight simulation systems use the key technique of modeling and simulating for the wind field, which one of the most important steps in achieving virtual reality simulation of flight dynamics. The real-time capability and authenticity of the atmospheric wind model is an important performance indicator that ensures the pilot immersed in and man-machine interacted friendly and restricts each other with these two features. This article started from the practical application and mainly researched on the modeling method of atmospheric turbulence model and its improvement to improve simulation fidelity in flight simulator, next to determine the atmospheric turbulence model and do the simulated test of flight dynamics in flight simulator. The specific job done in this paper is as follows:

(1) The article has introduced and analyzed the theory and method in building the atmospheric turbulent model, has introduced the atmospheric turbulent model of Dryden and Von Karman concretely, and then made a comparison between them.

(2) To better meet the requirements of authenticity and real-time in simulation system for flight simulator, we used the better atmospheric turbulent model of Von Karman to simulate in high frequency range and simplify the model, which satisfy the demands of real-time systems at last.

(3) Finally, the atmospheric turbulent model building was evaluated by simulation in this article, its results showed that the atmospheric turbulent model based on improved model of Von Karman can reflect the essential characteristic better in the atmospheric turbulence with good real -time performance, which met the basic requirements in real time flight simulation. The author would do the modeling research on disturbance wind field on mountains, the fields of windstorm and so forth in order to improve the fidelity in flight simulator further, we will establish a more comprehensive wind field model to improve and perfect the flight simulator in simulation systems.

References

1. Xiao, Y.L., Jin, C.J.: Atmospheric Disturbances in the Principles of Flight, pp. 11–18. Defense Industry Press, Beijing (1993)
2. Wu, Y.: Research on Modeling and Application Technologies of Wind Field in Virtual Test. Harbin Institute of Technology, Harbin (2011)
3. Sytsma, M.J., Lawrence, U.: Low order turbulence modeling methods for MAVs flight environment. In: AIAA Atmospheric Flight Mechanics Conference, pp. 1–20 (2010)
4. Xiao, X., McRae, D.S., Hassan, H.A.: Modeling atmospheric optical turbulence. In: 44th AIAA Aerospace Sciences Meeting and Exhibit (2006)
5. Morelli, E.A., Cunningham, K.: Aircraft dynamic modeling in turbulence. In: AIAA Atmospheric Flight Mechanics Conference (2012)
6. Liu, G., Wang, X.R., Jia, R.Z.: Engineering simulation method of variable wind field in synthetic natural environment. J. Syst. Simul. **18**, 297–300 (2006)
7. Lu, D.J.: Stochastic Process and its Applications. Tsinghua University Press, Beijing (2009)
8. Dryden, H.L.: A review of the statistical theory of turbulence. In: Friedlander, S.K., Topper, L. (eds.) Turbulence: Classical Papers on Statistical Theory, pp. 115–132. Interscience Publishers Inc., New York (1942)
9. Von Karman, T.: Progress in the statistical theory of turbulence. Proc. Nat. Acad. Sci. U. S. A. **34**(11), 530 (1948)
10. Zhang, F., Wang, P., Wang, C.: Simulation of three - dimensional atmospheric turbulence based on Von Karman model. Comput. Simul. **124**(1), 35–38 (2007)

Driving Performance Research in Foggy Conditions Based on Driving Simulator

Xiufeng Chen[✉], Jiabin Tian, and Xianghua Xu

Automobile and Transportation College, Qingdao University of Technology,
Qingdao, China
chenhill7765@163.com

Abstract. In order to reveal driving performance in different foggy conditions, the current study addressed the issue utilizing a driving simulator-based method to achieve vehicle operating in foggy conditions under driver-vehicle-environment closed system. A number of different instructions and speed feedback mechanisms were tested in order to determine how drivers react when driving in varying levels of fog. In view of combination of three influencing factors (speed indicator, speed meter and keeping lane), speed choice and driving behavior characteristics were analyzed in 500, 200, 80, 50 and 30 m visibilities. The results show that: With the visibility reducing, the vehicle speed is increased at first, then decreased trend, the actual speed and expect speed mismatch; reducing visibility has few effect on lane keep ability except when visibility is 30 m; when visibility is 80 m, there is highest average speed and lane maintain rate.

Keywords: Foggy conditions · Visibility · Speed choice · Land keeping

1 Introduction

Any driver are facing driving risk as driving in foggy days, the Federal Highway Administration statistics, every year traffic accidents due to fog caused about 600 people die and 16300 people injured. Many accidents in the fog day are multi vehicle accident, resulting in a large number of serious casualties. In our country, fog damage is becoming more and more serious with the development of social economy, the traffic accident rate caused by the thick fog is also increasing. Foggy weather is one of the most severe weather conditions, a sharp drop in the sight can cause the driver to hesitate, neglect and even delusion. The sharpness of the target profile will drop because the fog can absorb and scatter light, and then drivers are difficult to identify traffic signs, road facilities and pedestrians, and it will cause rear-end collision, therefore, it has important practical significance to ensure the safety of the driver's life and property by study the traffic influence in foggy conditions, discover the rule of traffic accident and put forward measures and countermeasures to reduce and prevent traffic accident in fog weather.

© Springer Science+Business Media Singapore 2016
L. Zhang et al. (Eds.): AsiaSim 2016/SCS AutumnSim 2016, Part III, CCIS 645, pp. 477–483, 2016.
DOI: 10.1007/978-981-10-2669-0_51

2   Research Survey

R.J. Snowden propose driver often driving at a higher speed in low visibility foggy conditions on the basis of the consumption that the contrast is uniform in the fog days. On the contrary, On the experiment study D.A. Owens thought the driver often travel at less than the speed because they often overestimate their own speed. P. Pretto proposed that the fog contrast uniform down assumption is not reasonable, fog vision contrast with distance change, away from the regional correlation of the driver is very low, close to the pilot area of high contrast. Pretto thought people will overestimate the driving speed because of the decrease of visibility in foggy conditions. Although he determined the perception and control of the vehicle speed. But on the one hand did not involve speed limits and speed to driving behavior study under the guidance of driving, without considering the influence of road marking on driving behavior, On the other hand, there is no in-depth research on the relationship between the reality in the process of running speed and lane keeping behavior.

The influence factor of driving behavior and driving ability in foggy conditions are far more complicated than driving speed in foggy conditions. Many researcher have done the research on car-following in foggy conditions by using observing sensors. Hawkins research shows that when the fog visibility is less than 150 m, the driving speed is reduced, when the fog visibility is less than 100 m, Speed decreased by 25 % to 30 %, at the same time the average headway distance is less than 60 m of the vehicle with an increase of 25 %. The usual way to study the change of driver's driving behavior is driving simulator. van Derhulst used driving simulator to simulate the driving behavior when the visibility is 150 m, experimental results show that the driver will increase headway at low visibility, but the reason is because the driver wants to know what is causing the visibility to fall rather than the driver's field of vision. Broughton studied the driver's reaction to the visibility reduction by using car-following simulation in foggy conditions, and the impact of changes in driving mode on vehicle speed, safety and accident risk. And then he put forward "lag" and "non-lag" two driving mode.

Domestic research on traffic safety in foggy days is relatively late, Pan Xiaodogn put forward traffic construction measures and Countermeasures by analyzing the reasons of the fog on the highway and its influence on the traffic safety. According to Liao Haifeng car parking sign recognition process and method of parking and traffic sign recognition technology based on the distance of the safe speed. Li Hongqiang and Shi Guifang made a calculation on fog day limit speed by means of mathematical formula derivation and site test method. Throughout the domestic researches, traffic safety research in foggy day mainly focuses on vehicle speed perception, if only study from the fog of speed limits and parking, diversity can not reflect the actual environment fog influence vehicle operation safety. For this, the author studied the vehicle speed selection and vehicle track characteristics under different visibility conditions to aim at the combination of the 3 kinds of instruction of the fog day minus acceleration prompt, the vehicle speed meter and the keeping lane. The research results can accurately reflect the actual driving characteristics of drivers in fog, fog and provide decision support for traffic safety management and decision-making.

3   Design of Driving Experiment in Foggy Weather

3.1   Test Sample

Choose 120 person (80 males and 40 females) to carry out the pilot test, between the ages of 25 to 55 years old, the average driving age is 2.9 year, all the driver's health checks are in line with the requirements of physical health, and no visual problems. There are 20 participants in each group and there are three instructions for each participant: (1) use or not use speed tips, (2) priority of driving tasks, (3) use or not use speedometers. Specific grouping and instruction combination see Table 1.

Table 1. Participant groups drove with speed indicator, task instructions, and a speedometer

Group	Speed indicator	Task priority	Speedometer availability
1	Decrease indicator	No priority	Speedometer
2	Decrease indicator	Task priority	speedometer
3	Decrease indicator	Task priority	No Speedometer
4	No indicator	No priority	Speedometer
5	No indicator	Task priority	Speedometer
6	No indicator	Task priority	No speedometer

Speed prompting device is used to provide speed feedback to the driver, when their speed is greater than or less than the requirements of the test speed, to remind the driver to reduce your speed or improve your speed. If a group uses a speed indicator, it will give the appropriate warning in all foggy weather conditions. Did not receive any speed prompt is known as no speed tips. Task priority is to require the driver to adjust the speed so that the vehicle can be kept safely. The test can provide theoretical support for the fog of vehicle active safety warning and roadside variable message application version.

3.2   Test Methods

The test platform is composed of the driving device, computer control, virtual simulation scene and vehicle operation information collection system and so on. The driver drives a fixed driving simulator and a two channel stereo display screen is connected with the driving simulator. The main control machine established a virtual road scene and the driver input information fusion simulation through the VCR technology. Interaction between the steering wheel and pedal operation and the simulator. In the whole experiment, the simulator uses the frequency of 100 Hz to collect vehicle speed and position data, and the effective data acquisition is not included in the former 30 s test data.

Road simulation environment for straight to the curve linear combination of secondary highway, two-way two lane, lane width by 3,75 m, design speed of 60 km/h. Lane with single edge of the white line and single yellow center line as a marker.

3.3   Fog Sense

Fog is a large number of fine droplets suspended in the air near the ground. Emergence of the fog resulted in a significant decrease in ground level visibility. In normal driving, the visibility 500 m, and visibility of the fog weather below 30 m. The driver in a straight line visibility gradually decreased along with the changes in the concentration of fog, the test take Fog Visibility for 500, 200, 80, 50 and 30 m.

4   Analysis of Test Results

In order to ensure the validity of the test data, the data obtained from the previous 30 s of the trial are not calculated. According to the 2.1 groups and requirements for driving simulation, the tester can continue to repeat the test link until they feel comfortable driving the simulator so far. Each link is tested for a short break after the test.

4.1   Vehicle Running Speed

The average speed of the test group changed with the change of visibility is shown in Fig. 1, different visibility of the average speed of different groups of vehicles is shown in Table 2.

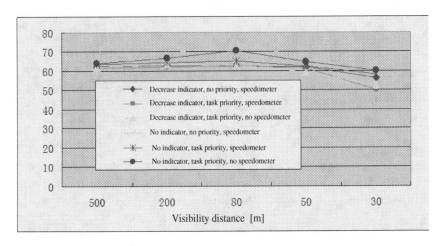

Fig. 1. Mean speed as a function of fog's visibility distance and driver group

From Table 2, From 500~50 m visibility, 6 sets of test driver's average speed in the 56.8~62.3 km/h changes, with the decrease of the visibility of the vehicle speed is not obvious, the vehicle speed and fog days do not match the expected speed, 80 m visibility of the highest average speed; Under the visibility of 30 m, the average speed of the vehicle is reduced significantly, which is 56.8 km/h. Using SPSS software for each group to do a single factor analysis of variance, fog visibility to reduce the first groups except for the other 5 groups were significantly affected by driving speed. With the decrease of visibility, the velocity increases first and then decreases. Draw a conclusion after single factor analysis of different visibility. 500 m visibility $F(5,71) = 2.9$ p < 0, 200 m visibility $F(5,71) = 3.1$, p < 0.5, 80 m visibility $F(5,70) = 4.2$ p < 0.001, 30 visibility $F(5,71) = 65$ p < 0.001. Under the visibility of 500200,80 and 50 m, the fourth groups of vehicles with the highest running speed, while the average running speed of the first 1 groups of the 30 m visibility was the highest.

Table 2. Mean speed as a function of fog's visibility distance and driver group[km/h] (standard errors)

Group	Visibility distance[m]					
	500	200	80	50	30	Mean
1	58.5(0.5)	59.6(0.6)	60.3(0.8)	59.7(0.8)	58.5(0.7)	60.94
2	59.3(0.6)	61.2(0.7)	62.5(0.7)	59.3(0.8)	50.8(0.7)	59.30
3	58.3(0.6)	57.8(0.6)	59.1(0.5)	56.9(0.9)	52.3(2.5)	59.78
4	60.2(1.7)	61.4(1.9)	62.2(1.7)	60.2(2.1)	57.6(2.7)	68.48
5	60.8(1.5)	60.3(1.6)	61.1(1.3)	59.2(1.8)	51.0(3.0)	62.56
6	63.2(2.5)	64.5(2.8)	68.7(2.5)	66.9(2.7)	58.3(3.8)	64.98
Mean	60.0	60.8	62.3	60.4	56.8	

4.2 Vehicle Lane Keeping

1. Lane keeping ability
   In the course of driving, the driver can adjust the vehicle speed according to the traffic condition and the characteristic of the road surface, so that the ability to maintain the correct lane position is known as the lane keeping ability. As shown in Fig. 2 is the vehicle's lane keeping capacity between a and b.
2. Lane keeping rate
   Lane keeping rate refers to the driving vehicle over 2 road marking running time and all the time the ratio formula, expressed as:

$$e = (t_1 + t_2) \times 100 / T$$

   Where e is the rate of lane keeping, t_1 is the time that vehicle drives across road markings a, t_2 is the time that vehicle drives across road markings b, T is the total driving time.
3. Experiment data analysis
   Under different fog visibility, lane keeping rate analysis is shown in Fig. 3 and Table 3. From Table 3, all the test subjects are able to keep the original lane in the top 3 of the highest visibility environment, lane retention rate was higher than that of the other 2 test groups, the average percentage of the 6 groups was 96.32 % when the visibility is 80 m, lane retention rate decreased significantly when the visibility is 30 m, and when the visibility decreased to 80 m, the driver will be very nervous due to the decrease of driving sight distance, road marking has become the main way of driving induction, at this time the lane retention rate has increased, but with the

reduce of the visibility, road marking gradually blurred and loss of driving induction, the driver of the Lane keep rate decreased. In summary, Lane keeping rate will increase after lower when in the change of visibility.

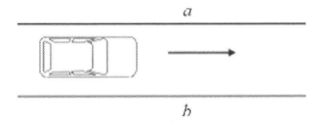

Fig. 2. Lane keeping of vehicle

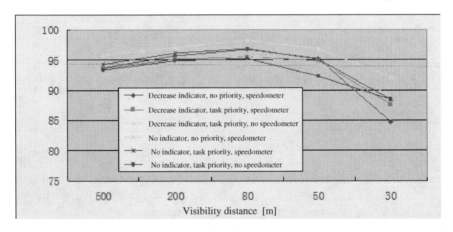

Fig. 3. Mean percentage of the trial in lane as a function of fog's visibility distance and driver group

Table 3. Mean percentage of the trial in lane as a function of fog's visibility distance and driver group[km/h] (standard errors)

Group	Visibility distance[m]					
	500	200	80	50	30	Mean
1	93.7(1.5)	95.7(1.4)	96.7(1.0)	95.2(1.5)	84.7(2.5)	93.20
2	93.6(1.4)	95.1(1.2)	95.4(0.9)	94.9(1.7)	87.6(2.4)	93.32
3	95.8(1.4)	97.1(1.6)	98.2(0.7)	96.9(1.0)	91.7(3.5)	96.04
4	91.5(1.6)	94.6(3.2)	95.5(2.2)	94.5(1.8)	89.1(4.7)	93.24
5	94.3(1.5)	96.2(3.5)	96.9(1.3)	95.1(1.7)	88.4(3.1)	94.18
6	93.3(1.6)	94.9(2.1)	95.2(1.6)	90.0(2.5)	88.4(4.5)	92.82
Mean	93.7	95.6	96.3	94.4	88.4	

Using SPSS statistical analysis of the main effects of fog visibility on the vehicle lane to maintain the impact of far greater than the impact of different groups. According to ANOVA, the foggy weather has a significant effect on the lane keeping rate of each group. Post Hoc multiple show that group 1, group 2 and group 6 were significantly lower in lane keeping rate than other visibility distance, and the group 3 is the highest in lane keeping rate, the average is 96.04 %. The effective way to control the path of the vehicle is to reduce the speed of the vehicle. But there are mainly two reason for driver in the fog day to driving at a significant lower speed: (1) Driver will pay more attention to drive in foggy conditions, (2) decreased road marking recognition ability in fog days.

5 Conclusions

This paper studied the driving behavior under the constraint conditions such as speed perception, speed feedback, driving behavior feedback and driving priority, the results of the study were better able to reflect actual driving behavior in fog days. The experiment indicates the drive can maintain a good lane keeping ability and has a trend to drive in high speed in fog days. But the driver visibility is too small, the vehicle can't avoid road danger effectively. In the future, investigation and analysis on the driver's driving behavior in the foggy conditions, study on different driver's driving characteristics of the psychological and physiological characteristics in foggy conditions, it will be more beneficial to the safety management of foggy conditions.

Acknowledgements. This work was financially supported by the Shandong Natural Science Foundation (ZR2012EEL28).

References

1. Shi, G.F., Yuan, H., Cheng, J.: Caculation of speed limit on foggy days. J. Southwest Jiaotong Univ. **45**, 136 (2010)
2. Snowden, R.J., Stimpson, N., Ruddle, R.A.: Speed perception fogs up as visibility drops. Nature **392**, 450 (1998)
3. Owens, D.A., Wood, J., Carberry, T.: Perceived speed and driving behavior in foggy conditions. J. Vis. **2**, 631 (2002)
4. Pretto, P.: The Perception and Production of Speed During Self-motion: Evidence for Non-optimal Compensation Mechanisms. Universita Degli Studi Di Padova, Padua (2008)
5. Hawkins, R.K.: Motorway traffic behavior in reduced visibility conditions. In: Freeman, M.H., Smith, P., Gale, A.G., Taylor, S.P., Haslegrave, C.M. (eds.) Vision in Vehicles II, vol. 2, p. 9. Elsevier Science Publishers B.V., North-Holland (1998)
6. Van Der Hulst, M., Rothengatter, T., Meijman, T.: Strategic adaptations to lack of preview in driving. Transp. Res. Part F **1**, 59 (1998)
7. Broughton, K.L., Switzer, F., Scott, D.: Car following decisions under three visibility conditions and two speeds tested with a driving simulator. Accid. Anal. Prev. **39**, 106 (2007)

The Research on Fault Diagnostic Technologies Based on Dynamic Simulation Test

Xinchi Dun[(✉)], Zhenghao Zhou, Yanlei Li, Wenhua Kong, and Chuanlin Jiang

Beijing Electro-mechanical Engineering Institute,
Yungang North No.40, Fengtai District, Beijing 100074, China
1060022877@qq.com

Abstract. As an important means for functionality, performance and reliability verification of guidance and control system, Dynamic Simulation Test has become an important part of equipment development. On the basis of analysis and establishment of simulation models for failure modes, the fault test cases can be generated automatically via the graphical modeling method put forward in this paper refer to the modeling principle of UML activity diagram. Failure modes online simulation is realized by injecting failure into the testing environment. Based on the features extraction of simulation test data under different fault conditions, an information fusion fault diagnosis method for feature level on continuous dynamic parameters based on support vector machines was proposed and preliminarily verified on actuators of the guidance and control system. The results demonstrate the feasibility of applying dynamic simulation test to fault diagnosis, but some issues need further study.

Keywords: Dynamic simulation test · Failure mode · Fault injection · Features extraction · Information fusion · Support vector machines

1 Preface

Based on dynamic simulation test, the fault diagnosis knowledge of one system can be obtained by adequate learning of simulation test data, which is available through fault simulation under different fault conditions.

Taking a guidance and control system for the study, this paper researched the feasibility and specific method of applying dynamic simulation test to fault diagnosis, including failure mode online simulation, fault features extraction, and fault diagnosis. Finally, a preliminary verification on the above method has been carried out on actuators in the guidance and control system.

2 Failure Mode Online Simulation

After building the target system's operating environment on the testing platform, the specific failure mode needs to be injected into this environment during the simulation run in order to obtain fault simulation test data. Here, two problems need to be solved: (1) How to generate the fault test case used for fault injection based on the failure

© Springer Science+Business Media Singapore 2016
L. Zhang et al. (Eds.): AsiaSim 2016/SCS AutumnSim 2016, Part III, CCIS 645, pp. 484–492, 2016.
DOI: 10.1007/978-981-10-2669-0_52

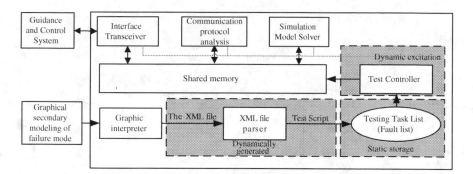

Fig. 1. Implementation process of failure mode online simulation

mode, namely the secondary modeling. (2) The manner to implement fault injection. This paper presents a method of failure mode online simulation. Figure 1 shows the implementation process, the main modules are as follows:

1. **Graphical secondary modeling of failure mode:** Part of failure simulation models can be obtained by Failure Mode Effects and Criticality Analysis (FMECA). Some basic drawing graphics were defined refer to the modeling elements of UML activity diagram. Based on the modeling principle of UML activity diagram [1], the flowchart of failure simulation model can be graphical built.
2. **Graphics interpreter and XML file parser:** The flowchart is converted to a specific XML structure and written into XML test file. XML file parser reads the elements and attributes in the XML test file, and converts them into test script, according to Python scripting language syntax.
3. **Test Controller:** During initialization, the test scripts were automatically converted by XML file parser, and added to the tasks testing list. After setting the handshake signal at the appropriate position (fault injection points) in simulation process, fault triggering condition was extracted from testing task list when handshake signal arrives, this determines whether to inject a fault.
4. **Shared memory:** Shared Memory Middleware enables centralized management of all data and provides interface to dynamically modify the data. When the fault condition is triggered, Test Controller will modify the corresponding data in shared memory to inject fault.

3 Fault Features Extraction

The fault features implicated in status parameters needs to be extracted. Various state parameters of guidance and control system can be divided into three categories according to the type, as shown in Table 1. Most of the parameters are continuous dynamic parameters, whose features extraction method is focused in this paper.

Table 1. Status parameters category of guidance and control system

Parameter type	Feature	Example
State identification parameters	Characterize the working status of each system, component, function modules, and interface	state flag of terrain match
Discrete state parameters	Parameter value have limited discrete states	Climbing, diving and other control instruction
Continuous dynamic parameters	Parameter value are dynamic continuous	Speed, location

Two following questions need to be considered when extracting the fault features.

(1) Which features should be extracted?
(2) What parameters should be selected?

The former is the method of features extraction; the latter is the redundancy of features or parameters. In this paper, the basic idea to solve those is as follows.

(1) For one continuous dynamic parameter, extract useful features as much as possible from the time domain, frequency domain, statistics and other aspects.
(2) Utilize the principal component analysis (PCA) to reduce the dimensionality and redundancy of fault features, just for using the least amount of features to achieve the purpose of fault diagnosis.

3.1 Features Extraction of Continuous Dynamic Parameter

For one continuous dynamic parameter, the signal sequence over time before and after the failure occurs were intercepted and processed following the steps in sequence, as shown in Fig. 2.

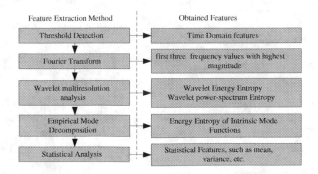

Fig. 2. Features extraction procedure of continuous dynamic parameter

- **Time Domain Features:** Taking signal amplitude and rate of change as features, the combined threshold detector has been applied.
- **Frequency Domain Features:** Taking flourier transform on angular acceleration, angular velocity, angle and other attitude parameters, the first three frequency values with highest magnitude were selected as frequency domain features.
- **Time-frequency Features:** The wavelet transform [2] and empirical mode decomposition [3] were both adopted to get time-frequency features. The wavelet energy entropy has been calculated according to the method described in literature [4] as well as the energy entropy according to the method described in literature [5].
- **Statistical Features:** Calculating some common statistical features [6], including maximum, minimum, mean, absolute mean, range, standard deviation, peak, RMS, root, etc.

According to the above steps, a plurality of features can be obtained from one parameter's signal sequence. For the Guidance Control System, the most basic continuous dynamic parameters are acceleration, velocity, displacement, angular acceleration, angular velocity and angle of six degrees of freedom, which describes the flight condition. Therefore, the above 18 parameters in geographic coordinate system were chosen and calculated to form a fault sample.

3.2 Features Reduction of Continuous Dynamic Parameters

Hundreds of features can be gained from the above 18 parameters. The principal component analysis (PCA) method has been applied for feature reduction, specifically principle see reference [7]. Among them, the threshold of cumulative contribution rate α_0 determines the number of feature after reduction.

For each failure mode, set different model parameters value, carry out multiple times of online simulation, gain certain number of fault samples, extract features sequentially from each sample, then apply feature reduction, thus get the fault failure sample set.

4 Information Fusion Diagnosis Method at Feature Level Based on Support Vector Machine (SVM)

Information Fusion is widely used in machinery monitoring, medical diagnostics, fault diagnosis and could be divided into data level fusion, feature level fusion and decision level fusion [8]. At the present stage, this paper focuses on the diagnosis method with continuous dynamic parameters at feature level.

In order to map and optimize the relationship between the failure mode (and fault location) and fault features based on the fault failure sample set, Support Vector Machine (SVM) has been carried out for classification on fault features. Since the standard SVM can only classify two-category samples, commonly used classification method of multi-category includes "decision tree", "one to one", etc. [9].

The steps of the diagnosis method with continuous dynamic parameters at feature level are as follows:

- First, build a fault diagnosis network according to the actual problem; determine the number of SVM classifier and the number of category that each classifier has to distinguish; use "one to one" method to construct multi-category SVM classifier.
- Then, according to the structure of the network, determine the composition and number of required samples; set the corresponding parameters of failure mode simulation model; get fault samples by on-line simulation; obtain a feature sample set by features extraction and reduction.
- Next, choose part of the sample from set as training and testing samples, train and optimize the network in order to improve the diagnostic accuracy rate.
- Thus, apply the network to fault diagnosis and analyze the results in order to provide the basis for the improvement of diagnostic method as well as the features extraction and reduction method.

5   Application Validation

5.1   Failure Mode Analysis and Modeling of Actuator System

Failure modes of actuator system generally include injury, stuck failure and deviation failure, whose fault model can be expressed as follows:

$$\mu_{ai}(t) = \beta_i \mu_{ci}(t) + \bar{\mu}_i(t), \forall t \geq t_{Fi}, i = \{0, 1, 2, 3\} \tag{1}$$

i refers to the serial number of actuators. $\mu_{ci}(t)$ refers to the output under normal circumstances; $\mu_{ai}(t)$ refers to the actual output of actuator; $\beta_i \in [0, 1]$, t_{Fi} refers to the time when fault occurred; $\bar{\mu}_i(t)$ has different physical meanings in different failure modes, the range of parameters in different failure modes are shown in Table 2.

Table 2. Range of parameters in different failure modes of one type of actuator system

Fault type	Parameters value
Injury	$\beta_i \in (0, 1)$, $\bar{\mu}_i(t) = 0°$
Stuck	$\beta_i = 0$, $\bar{\mu}_i(t) \in [-20°, +20°]$
Deviation failure	$\beta_i = 1$, $\bar{\mu}_i(t) \in [-20°, 0°) \cup (0°, +20°]$

5.2   Construction of Information Fusion Diagnostic Network Based on SVM

This paper focuses on two issues: (1) Which actuator malfunctioned? (2) Which type of fault has occurred? namely mapping relationship between the fault features and failure modes as well as fault location.

There are four actuators and three failure modes for each actuator, numbered as actuator 0 to actuator 3. Specially, under the same failure mode and parameters value,

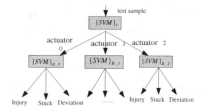

Fig. 3. Information Fusion diagnostic network based on SVM

the variations of above 18 continuous dynamic parameters when actuator 1 malfunctioned are exactly the same as actuator 3. Thus, actuator 1 and actuator 3 are temporarily classified as one actuator, namely issue (1) can be simplified as a 3-class classification problem.

Information Fusion diagnostic network based on SVM is shown in Fig. 3. $\{SVM\}_I$ (3-Class Classifier) identify the fault location, $\{SVM\}_{II\_i}(i = 0, 1, 2)$ judge the fault type.

5.3 Failure Mode Online-Simulation

The learning of above network requires fault sample data with three failure modes of three actuators. Set model parameters value of each fault sample in accordance with equal interval, as shown in Table 3. Assumed, all failures occurred at 30 s after the aircraft took off. A total of 162 fault samples can be obtained by testing each failure mode of each actuator 18 times with different model parameters value. After test, the corresponding fault sample data has been saved with a period of 20 ms.

5.4 Gaining Fault Features Sample Set

As it was assumed that all failures occurred at 30 s after the aircraft took off in this paper. For each parameter of above 18 continuous dynamic parameters, taking 1001 sampling points between 25 to 45 s, 33 features can be extracted according to the extraction procedure as shown in Fig. 4. Thus, one fault sample has a total of 594 features; features of 162 fault samples constitute a sample matrix of 162×594.

Table 3. Simulation model parameters value corresponding to each fault sample

Fault type	Parameter	Value ($\bar{\mu}_i(t)$ in degree)
Injury	β_i	0.1, 0.15, 0.2, 0.25, 0.3, 0.35, 0.4, 0.45, 0.5, 0.55, 0.6, 0.65, 0.7, 0.75, 0.8, 0.85, 0.9, 0.95
Stuck	$\bar{\mu}_i(t)$	±2, ±4, ±6, ±8, ±10, ±12, ±14, ±16, ±18
Deviation	$\bar{\mu}_i(t)$	±1, ±2, ±3, ±4, ±5, ±6, ±7, ±8, ±9

A sample matrix of 162×20 can be gained by applying principal component analysis (PCA) to the above sample matrix when taking $\alpha_0 = 90\%$, namely the features can be reduced to 20 from 594.

5.5 Training and Optimization of Diagnostic Network

The first layer of the diagnostic network is a 3-class classifier, while the second layer comprises 3 three-class classifiers, which are used to diagnose the fault location and failure modes. Each classifier has two parameters need to be optimized, namely variance σ and penalty coefficient C among SVM algorithm. The training and parameter optimization process of each SVM classifier is shown in Fig. 4.

N-fold cross-validation error and grid search algorithm were chosen as the optimization indicator and the optimization method which are widely used in engineering.

Taking the first layer 3-class classifier $\{SVM\}_1$ as an example, the 162×20 features sample matrix has been divided into three groups by fault location. Selecting one sample from each group, three sample compose a subset, then can get a total of 54 subsets, namely $n = 54$. The ranges of variance σ and penalty coefficient C were both

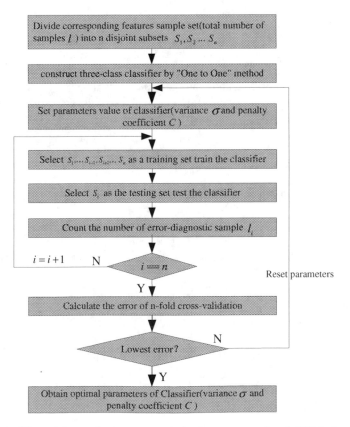

Fig. 4. The training and parameter optimization process of each SVM classifier

Table 4. Optimization results by grid search of each classifier in the SVM diagnostic network

Classifier	Optimized value		Number of samples l	N-fold	N-fold cross-validation error (%)	Estimate of diagnostic accuracy (%)
	σ	C				
$\{SVM\}_I$	3.3	2.5	162	54	3.0068	97.0
$\{SVM\}_{II\_0}$	2.9	1.6	54	18	5.0835	95.0
$\{SVM\}_{II\_1}$	1.4	1.7	54	18	3.7037	96.3
$\{SVM\}_{II\_2}$	3.0	2.3	54	18	2.7959	97.2

set to (0,5], while the grid search step is set to 0.1. Then, the optimal value of those two parameters can be obtained in accordance with the training and parameter optimization process shown in Fig. 4.

Similarly, the parameters optimization results of each classifier in the SVM diagnostic network were shown in Table 4.

5.6 Typical Application and Analysis

After parameters optimization, the information fusion diagnostic network based on SVM has been applied to the fault diagnosis of actuator system.

Providing a group of parameter values of actuator simulation model which is independent of the above fault sample set (assumed, actuator 0 is stuck at 7 ° 30 s after the aircraft took off, namely $t_{Fi} = 30$, $\sigma_i = 0$, $\bar{\mu}_i(t) = 7$), the fault data has been obtained and the corresponding fault feature vector X_{rudder} (20 features) has been gained by the same above features extraction procedure and PCA reduction method.

$$
X_{rudder} = \begin{bmatrix}
9.3170 & -2.9980 & 1.0185 & -2.6810 & 2.2629 \\
0.3116 & -1.0060 & -0.8053 & 0.3401 & -2.9757 \\
0.0972 & -3.0719 & -0.4598 & 1.5079 & 0.5044 \\
1.2873 & 1.7906 & 0.7278 & -0.5553 & -0.0377
\end{bmatrix} \tag{2}
$$

Take X_{rudder} into the diagnostic network, the output of the first layer 3-class classifier $\{SVM\}_I$ was 0, which represents the diagnosed fault location was actuator 0, while the output of the second layer 3-class classifier $\{SVM\}_{II\_0}$ was 1, which indicates the diagnosed fault mode was stuck fault.

6 Conclusion

Validation result demonstrates that the fault information hiding in the continuous dynamic parameters of Guidance and Control System can be well analyzed by information fusion diagnosis method based on Support Vector Machine (SVM). At the same time, validation procedure also shows the feasibility of applying dynamic simulation test to fault diagnosis.

But there are some issues that need further study, such as further improvement of information fusion diagnosis method, diagnosis of occurrence time point of fault, multiple subsystems, and multiple faults occur simultaneously or occur at regular intervals.

References

1. Xie, N.: An Automatic Test Cases Generation Method Based on UML activity diagrams. Xi'an Electronic Science and Technology University, Xi'an (2011)
2. Zhu, K., Wong, Y.S., Hong, G.S.: Wavelet analysis of sensor signals for tool condition monitoring: a review and some new results. Int. J. Mach. Tools Manuf. **49**, 7–8 (2009)
3. Rato, R.T., Ortigueira, M.D., Batista, A.G.: On the HHT, its problems, and some solutions. Mech. Syst. Sig. Process. **22**(6), 1374–1394 (2008)
4. Tian, B.: Information Theory. Posts and Telecommunications Press, Beijing (2008)
5. Yu, D., et al.: Hilbert-Huang Transformation Method of Mechanical Fault Diagnosis. The Science Publishing Company, Beijing (2007)
6. Wang, R.: Study on Rocket Engine Turbo Pumps Real-time Fault Detection Method. University of Electronic Science and Technology of China, Chengdu (2013)
7. Lin, J.: The Study on Statistical Feature Optimization and Patter Recognition of Partial Discharge in GIS. School of Electrical Engineering of Chongqing University, Chongqing (2013)
8. Shen, H.: Information Fusion Fault Diagnosis. Beijing Science and Technology Press, Beijing (2013)
9. He, X.: The Study on Theory and Method of Fault Intelligent Diagnosis Based on Support Vector Machine. Central South University, Changsha (2004)

Dynamics Model of Landing Process
for Parachute Simulator

Gai Li[(✉)], Jiang-yun Wang, and Liang Han

School of Automation Science and Electrical Engineering,
Beijing University of Aeronautics and Astronautics, Beijing 100191, China
li_gai@126.com

Abstract. The traditional way of training paratrooper has limited effect, due to lack of the feeling in the air. But we can solve this problem by using virtual reality technology to build a parachute simulator. And ensure to provide a true feeling, the work of modeling the landing process of the parachute is crucial. In this paper we divide the parachute landing process into four stages and model separately, and propose a model of the parachute landing process which can be used to parachute simulator.

Keywords: Parachute simulator · Circular parachute · Virtual reality · Parachute dynamics

1 Introduction

Parachute simulator is one of training simulation machines, it is used to help train paratroopers. It can simulate the parachute landing process, and generate real time image base on the simulate data. Then display the image on Head-mounted display (HMD). Paratrooper who puts HMD on will immerse in the virtual scene. By training in this way, paratrooper can train more effective and more secure, also can reduce the training cost. Parachute simulator usually consists of control frame, visual system, parachute dynamic model and management platform. The other parts all need the parachute dynamic model to support, and the parachute dynamic model is the key part to ensure the authenticity of simulation.

In the paper [1, 2], Hogue et al. present how virtual reality technology can be used in paratrooper training, and give the composition and overall structure of the simulator. But they only focus on the visual generation method, and didn't take parachute dynamics into account. And very few similar articles mentioned the dynamics part.

There are many scholar do research on the parachute dynamic problem. For example, In order to evaluate the feasibility of the AGAS(Affordable Guided Airdrop System), Scott et al. [3] divide the overall system into three parts, and in dynamics model part, they built a 3 DOF dynamics model of the G12 parachute. And Shen et al. [5] establish a 6DOF nonlinear mathematical model of the parachute and vehicle system in Mars. But the parachute model is control by the vehicle, it's not same as the man use parachute. Vladimir et al. [6] build a air-drop Six-Degree-of-Freedom model of the air drop system. And use the model to simulate the airdrop process. And Guglieri [7] use the general

© Springer Science+Business Media Singapore 2016
L. Zhang et al. (Eds.): AsiaSim 2016/SCS AutumnSim 2016, Part III, CCIS 645, pp. 493–502, 2016.
DOI: 10.1007/978-981-10-2669-0_53

procedure for the design of a flight simulation, build limited complexity simulation models to solve the dynamics problem. Cao [8] build a parachute's flying physical model, and give method to analyze and calculate the variations of canopy shape.

First, The model of parachute applied to parachute simulator must have control input, that's most articles didn't mention. Second, the model need to cover the total process. And the last, the asymmetry characteristics must take into account when build a paratrooper parachute, but most parachute models are ignore that, and this article is aim to these three problem.

2   Parachute Dynamics Models

2.1   Coordinate Systems Definition

Two coordinate system are used in the whole process, geographic coordinate system and parachute body-fixed coordinate system.

- geographic coordinate system

The ground coordinate system $OX_dY_dZ_d$ is fixed on the earth. O is at the airport, OZ_d axis is upward along the direction of gravity direction; OX_d to south, and OZ_d to east;

- Parachute coordinate system

Parachute coordinate system $OX_sY_sZ_s$ is fixed on the body of the parachute. O is at the parachute pressure center(assumes that the center of pressure is at the geometric center of the canopy), OZ_s is upward to the top of canopy, OX_s is to the front of the parachute,OY_s perpendicular to the plane of the OX_sZ_s.

2.2   Deployment Stage Model

When parachute package is opened, pilot chute will spring out. And then it will pull the canopy and rope out, finally the canopy and rope will be pulled straight, this process is named deployment stage. In this paper, we will use a continuous pull out model to

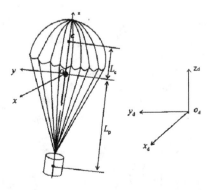

Fig. 1. Coordinate systems definition

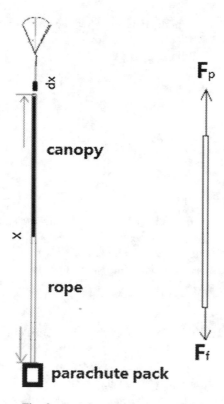

Fig. 2. Parachute deployment model

describe the process (as Fig. 1), this model is just like we are pulling a folded rope to straight. We regard the pulled out parts as a variable mass object, its length is X. And when X reached the total length of the canopy and the rope, the deployment stage come to an end.

Make the following assumptions for the model:

(1) The friction between canopy and canopy pack is constant, and the value is F_f;
(2) The mass of the canopy is evenly distributed, so the mass is proportional to the length, and the ratio is ρ;
(3) Pilot chute and the pulled out part are in the same plane, and the pulled out part's speed is same as the will be pulled out part (Fig. 2);

We can see that the pulled out part is under the action of two forces, F_p and F_f. According to Newton's second law, we can have this equation:

$$F_P - F_f = ma = \rho x \cdot \frac{d^2 x}{dt^2} \tag{1}$$

ρ is the mass per unit length of the canopy.

There is a spring inside the pilot chute, so when the package opened, the pilot chute will spring out immediately and full filled. So we can use resistance formula to calculate the resistance F_p, and the resistance of the pilot chute is the force which pull canopy out.

$$F_p = k_2 \rho_0 \left(\frac{dx}{dt}\right)^2 \tag{2}$$

ρ_0 is the density of air; k_2 is the resistance coefficient of the pilot chute.

2.3   Model of Inflatable Stage

Inflatable stage is the period from the end of the deployment stage to the moment when canopy full filled. And due to changes of parachute shape in Inflatable stage, the physical process of Inflatable stage is the most complex stage in the whole process of parachute landing. Two problems must be solved to solve the trajectory of inflation stage, they are parameter (CA) and added mass.

- Parameter (CA)

When an object is having relative motion in a fluid, the object is subjected to the resistance of the fluid. And the resistance Q is related to the speed and the characteristics of the object itself ($Q = \frac{1}{2} C_D \rho_0 \upsilon^2 A$). C_D is the resistance coefficient, and ρ_0 is air density, A is the windward area. In inflatable stage C_D and A are both variable, to Simplify the analysis process, the parameter (CA) is used to represents the product of C_D and A.

The inflatable stage can divide in two small period, Initial inflation period and main inflation period. In the empirical formula, (CA) is related to the distance parachute travelled. In Initial inflation period (CA) and S varied almost linearly, and in main inflation period (CA) is power function to S. The formula is:

$$(CA) = \begin{cases} KS & (0 \leq S \leq S_l) \\ (CA)_l + \beta(S - S_l)^4 & (S_l \leq S \leq S_m) \end{cases} \tag{3}$$

- The added mass method

An object effected by constant force motions in incompressible fluids have smaller acceleration than in vacuum. It is because that the object cause the surrounding fluid movement, and just like the object's mass has been added. So people use added mass (or Apparent mass) to describe this phenomenon.

Experimental results shows that the added mass is approximately equal to mass of the air inside canopy. On the assumption that the air inside canopy is a sphere, and its radius is same as the wind-ward area's radius ($m_f = \rho_0 4/3\pi r^3$). The windward area and the parameter (CA) have approximate linear relationship ($CA = C_{st} A = C_{st} \pi r^2$). So, we can have the equation, and $K_f \approx 0.41$.

$$m_f = K_f \rho_0 CA^{\frac{3}{2}} \tag{4}$$

Lamb [4] derives the apparent mass effects and identifies 15 independent terms. In this paper we consider 3 terms for three axis. a_{11}, a_{22}, a_{33} correspond to x-axis, y-axis, z-axis.

$$a_{11} = a_{22} = \frac{1}{2}a_{33} = \frac{1}{2}m_f \tag{5}$$

2.4 Landing Process Model

In the whole process, parachute system is mainly affected by the air resistance, gravity, horizontal push force, the Force developed by operation. Specific analysis is as follows:

- Air resistance

Before stable stage, attack angle (α_0) is approximately zero. And direction of Q is along the opposite direction of speed

$$
\begin{aligned}
Q_x &= \frac{1}{2}(CA)\rho_0 v^2 \frac{v_x}{v} \\
Q_y &= \frac{1}{2}(CA)\rho_0 v^2 \frac{v_y}{v}. \\
Q_z &= \frac{1}{2}(CA)\rho_0 v^2 \frac{v_z}{v}
\end{aligned}
\tag{6}
$$

In stable stage, The air resistance is complex, and we can divide it into two force, the axial force and radial force. The axial force coefficient(C_T) is a constant, the radial force coefficient (C_N) change with the attack angle (α_0). The relationship is as follows, $C_N = 0.51150\alpha_0^3 - 0.2652\alpha_0$. When inflatable stage ends, the parachute's track angle suddenly turn to 90, and the attack angle can be obtained by the formula:

$$\alpha_0 = \arctan\left(\frac{\sqrt{v_x^2 + v_y^2}}{v_z}\right) \tag{7}$$

$v = (v_x, v_y, v_z)$ are centroid speed of the parachute.

According to the resistance formula, resistance $(Q = (Q_x, Q_y, Q_z))$ can be obtained by:

$$
\begin{cases}
Q_x = -\frac{1}{2}A\rho v^2 C_N \frac{v_x}{\sqrt{v_x^2 + v_y^2}} \\
Q_y = -\frac{1}{2}A\rho v^2 C_N \frac{v_y}{\sqrt{v_x^2 + v_y^2}} \\
Q_z = -\frac{1}{2}A\rho v^2 C_T
\end{cases}
\tag{8}
$$

- Horizontal forward force

Parachute for people to use is usually asymmetry, because in order to make the parachute easy to control, several vent hole is set around the side of the canopy. and the vent hole in front is small then the back ones. The structure like this give the parachute a forward speed even without wind. So we should take the horizontal forward force into account.

In this paper, we use a horizontal forward constant force F to describe this phenomenon. The force is always to the front side, so we need to transfer F to geographic coordinate.

$$
\mathbf{F}_p = \begin{bmatrix} \mathrm{F}_x \\ \mathrm{F}_y \\ 0 \end{bmatrix} = \begin{bmatrix} \mathrm{F} \cdot \cos\beta_0 \\ \mathrm{F} \cdot \sin\beta_0 \\ 0 \end{bmatrix} \tag{9}
$$

β_0 is the heading angle (or yaw), and the F is a constant.

- Force produced by operation

Generally, the circular parachute have two operating bands, each bands have two kinds of operate mode, pull frontward or pull backward. and these four kind of control methods were recorded as the left frontward control with LF, the right frontward control with RF, the left backward control with LB, the right backward control with RB.

And from the parachute training guide, we know that pull the operating bands frontward will acceleration both vertical and horizontal velocity, and back ward will be the opposite. And if pull the left band frontward or right band backward, the parachute will turn right. On contrary, if pull the right band frontward or left band backward, the parachute will turn left. So we add three forces ($\Delta \mathrm{F}_{xs}$, $\Delta \mathrm{F}_{ys}$, $\Delta \mathrm{F}_{zs}$) and a moment (M_y) to the description. And use the parameter K_y, K_y, K_z, K_M to be the adjustable parameter of the operation. α_t is the combined operation gain.

$$
\begin{cases}
\Delta \mathrm{F}_{xs} = K_x \left[1 - e^{-\frac{\Delta t}{\tau_t}} \right] [(\mathrm{LF} + \mathrm{RF} + \alpha_t \cdot \mathrm{LF} \cdot \mathrm{RF}) - (\mathrm{LB} + \mathrm{RB} + \alpha_t \cdot \mathrm{LB} \cdot \mathrm{RB})] \\
\Delta \mathrm{F}_{ys} = K_y \left[1 - e^{-\frac{\Delta t}{\tau_t}} \right] [(\mathrm{LF} + \mathrm{RB} + \alpha_t \cdot \mathrm{LF} \cdot \mathrm{RB}) - (\mathrm{LB} + \mathrm{RF} + \alpha_t \cdot \mathrm{LB} \cdot \mathrm{RF})] \\
\Delta \mathrm{F}_{zs} = K_z \left[1 - e^{-\frac{\Delta t}{\tau_t}} \right] [(\mathrm{LF} + \mathrm{RF} + \alpha_t \cdot \mathrm{LF} \cdot \mathrm{RF}) - (\mathrm{LB} + \mathrm{RB} + \alpha_t \cdot \mathrm{LB} \cdot \mathrm{RB})]
\end{cases} \tag{10}
$$

Torque produced by operation

$$
\mathrm{M}_y = K_M \left[1 - e^{-\frac{\Delta t}{\tau_t}} \right] [(\mathrm{LF} + \mathrm{RB}) - (\mathrm{LB} + \mathrm{RF})] \tag{11}
$$

Transfer the force to geographic coordinate.

$$
\begin{bmatrix} F_{\delta x} \\ F_{\delta y} \\ F_{\delta z} \end{bmatrix} = \begin{bmatrix} \Delta \mathrm{F}_{xs} \cos\beta_0 + \Delta \mathrm{F}_{ys} \sin\beta_0 \\ \Delta \mathrm{F}_{ys} \cos\beta_0 - \Delta \mathrm{F}_{xs} \sin\beta_0 \\ \Delta \mathrm{F}_{zs} \end{bmatrix} \tag{12}
$$

- kinematical equation

Equation of motion of mass center:

$$
\dot{V}_G = \begin{bmatrix} \dot{v}_x \\ \dot{v}_y \\ \dot{v}_z \end{bmatrix}_G
$$
$$
= \begin{bmatrix} m+a_{11} & 0 & 0 \\ 0 & m+a_{22} & 0 \\ 0 & 0 & m+a_{33} \end{bmatrix}^{-1} \times \left\{ \begin{bmatrix} Q_x \\ Q_y \\ Q_z \end{bmatrix} + \begin{bmatrix} 0 \\ 0 \\ G \end{bmatrix} + \begin{bmatrix} F_x \\ F_y \\ 0 \end{bmatrix} + \begin{bmatrix} F_{\delta x} \\ F_{\delta y} \\ F_{\delta z} \end{bmatrix} \right\} \quad (13)
$$

And we suppose there is a resistance moment (ΔM) in the process of operation:

$$
\Delta M = 2 \times \frac{1}{R} \int_0^R r \cdot (kV)dr = 2 \times \frac{1}{R} \int_0^R r \cdot (k \cdot r\omega)dr = \frac{2}{3}k\omega R^2 \quad (14)
$$

Equation of horizontal rotation torque:

$$
\begin{cases} M_y - \Delta M = I_y \frac{dw}{dt} \\ \beta_0 = \beta + \omega \cdot \Delta t \end{cases} \quad (15)
$$

3   The Simulation and Analysis of Examples

- Simulation Approach

We divide the dynamic calculation process into four part, the manipulation input part is for transfer control methods to operation force and torque. Dynamic model part to calculates speed, displacement, heading and other information. Dynamic parameter part to provide the (CA) and added mass in different stage. The check stage work to determine what stage are staying in (Fig. 3).

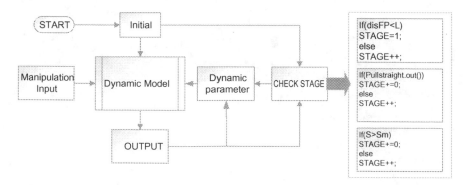

Fig. 3. Dynamic calculation process

- Result Analysis

We use the XLS-4 parachute, and set the plane height of 750 m, the speed of 150 km/h and direction of 45 degrees northeast. The parts of result are as fellow (Table 1):

Table 1. Time of each stage ends

	Stage one	Stage two	Stage three	Landing
Real training	0.46 s	1.85 s	2.93 s	143.03 s
Simulation	1 s	1.9 s	4.1 s	135.2 s

This table is the result of simulation and the real training, There is a certain error, but point of each stage ends are fundamentally coincide with the real training (Fig. 4).

The above is graph of the three axis velocity, the horizontal direction is basically stable in the 1.91 m/s. And the vertical velocity first increase, and then decrease, the final stable at −5.73 m/s. Satisfied with the description of the parachute, horizontal about 2 m/s and vertical velocity no more than 6 m/s (Fig. 5).

Above are the Trace with manipulate compare with the without manipulate trace. We can see when pull both band backward, there is a obvious acceleration process, and when pull both band frontward, there is a obvious reduction process. Same as the real parachuting (Fig. 6).

Shoulder dynamic load is the feeling of hypergravity and weightlessness, above are shoulder dynamic load curve of the 70 kg, 75 kg and 80 kg body weights. By the graph, we can see by the end of deployment stage and inflatable stage the load both reach to peak value, and the end of inflatable stage, the value reach to twice the weight. And when at the stable stage the value is basic is equal to the weight. Basic restore the original feeling of the shoulder in parachuting.

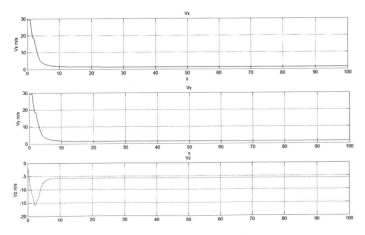

Fig. 4. Speed of three axis

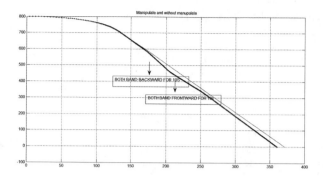

Fig. 5. Trace with manipulate and without manipulate

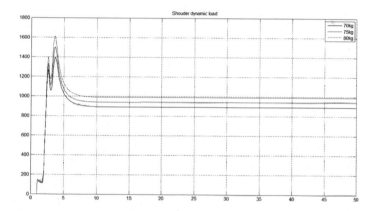

Fig. 6. Shoulder dynamic load

4   Conclusion

In this research, a mathematical model of paratrooper parachute is given. And the model can provide output the parachute simulator need. And the model has take the paratrooper parachute's asymmetry characteristics into account, also add four manipulate methods. And give analysis of some output. The result basically coincide with the real training.

References

1. Hogue, J.R., Pelz, C.A., et al.: Enhanced safety and effectiveness for parachute training and mission performance through virtual reality simulation. Virtual Reality (2008)
2. Hogue, J.R., Allen, R.W., Pelz, C.A., et al.: Methodology and improvements in aircrew parachute descent virtual reality simulation training (2000)

3. Dellicker, S., Benney, R., Brown, G.: Guidance and control for flat-circular parachutes. J. Aircr. **38**(5), 809–817 (2001)
4. Lamb, S.H.: Hydrodynamics, 6th edn. Dover, New York (1945)
5. Shen, G., Xia, Y., Sun, H.: A 6DOF mathematical model of parachute in mars EDL. Adv. Space Res. **55**(7), 1823–1831 (2015)
6. Dobrokhodov, V., Yakimenko, O., Junge, C.: Six-degree-of-freedom model of a controlled circular parachute. J. Aircr. **40**(3), 482–493 (2003)
7. Guglieri, G.: Parachute-payload system flight dynamics and trajectory simulation. Int. J. Aerosp. Eng. **2012**, 2012 (2012)
8. Cao, Y.: Parachute flying physical model and inflation simulation analysis. Aircr. Eng. Aerosp. Technol. **76**(2), 215–220 (2013)

Modeling and Simulation of Dynamic Effect of Micro-downburst on Aircraft

Li Jing[1,2(✉)], Xu Chang[2], and Zhang Shao-ning[1,2]

[1] Beijing Electromechanical Engineering Institute, Beijing, China
59183142@qq.com
[2] Beijing Institute of Technology, Beijing, China

Abstract. Low-Level wind shear is one kind of atmospheric disturbance which can bring the most serious damages for aircraft. This paper presents the physical characteristics, temporal and spatial scale, and air flow of the micro-downburst which is the most dangerous wind shear. Combined with characteristics of the flight environment and mission course, simplified fluid dynamic model of the micro-downburst was built by setting different intensity vortex pairs at a certain height, to simulate the flight control process when the aircraft encounters the micro-downburst during gliding and examine its dynamic performance. Thus it provides a reliable method for control design of aircraft which flying at the adverse atmospheric disturbances.

Keywords: Low-level wind shear · Micro-downburst · Modeling and simulation · Dynamic effect

1 Introduction

For researching influence of the variable wind field on the flight characteristics of an aircraft, low-level wind shear is a kind of atmospheric disturbances that cannot be ignored. It refers to the mean variation of wind at spatial and temporal, and can be defined as frontal wind shear, wind shear associated with ground strong wind, and wind shear associated with convective storm. The wind shear associated with convective storm is the most harmful for the flight of aircraft among them, and can be defined as macro-downburst and micro-downburst.

Combined with the flight task characteristics of an aircraft, this paper focus on modeling and simulation of the micro-downburst, and studies its dynamic effect on flight performance.

2 Mathematical Modeling

2.1 Introduction of the Micro-downburst

Micro-downburst is one manifestation of the most dangerous kind of low-level wind shear. In short time, it forms outward radiating flow when downdraft reach the ground, like as flying water flow when the water column sprayed to ground vertically.

© Springer Science+Business Media Singapore 2016
L. Zhang et al. (Eds.): AsiaSim 2016/SCS AutumnSim 2016, Part III, CCIS 645, pp. 503–510, 2016.
DOI: 10.1007/978-981-10-2669-0_54

When the aircraft flights through the micro-downburst, it will encounter head-wind first, and then the tailwind. This process leads to non-symmetry in the flow spectrum of shear flow, that means existing the difference in scale and magnitude between headwind and tailwind. Figure 1 shows the wind velocity profile of non-symmetric micro-downburst.

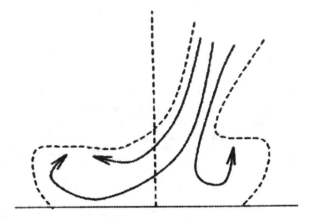

Fig. 1. The wind velocity profile of non-symmetric micro-downburst

The horizontal outflow diameter of micro-downburst is between 1 and 4 km, and the height is less than 10 km. According to the measurement data issued by JAWS (Joint Airport Weather Research Program) of United States, the velocity and velocity's varia-tion are gradually increased during the period after the micro-downburst first impact on the ground, and the peak value of velocity can reach more than 10 m/s in 5 to 10 min. Afterwards the wind shear begins to decay, and then begins to dissipate after 10 to 20 min.

2.2   Control Characteristics of the Aircraft Flying Through Micro-downburst

The horizontal whirlpool of micro-downburst includes downdrafts and strong updraft. In the process of flying through micro-downburst, the aircraft encounters headwind first, and then encounters tailwind after crossing the center of airflow, the change of wind's speed and direction can directly affect on its airspeed and angle of attack. When the aircraft flies into the upwind region of micro-downburst, its airspeed is increased, and flight control system will make the aircraft nose down to maintain the vertical attitude. With the aircraft closes to the center of airflow, the speed of headwind decreases, the speed of the lateral wind and longitudinal wind increase gradually. After flying through the center of airflow, the direction of horizontal wind turns into tailwind, the airspeed of aircraft decreases suddenly, the lift disappeares quickly, and the phenomenon of dropping flight altitude is appeared significantly. To get lift, the control system needs adjust the flying attitude to increase the angle of attack. However, the aircraft is still at keeping the bow state in headwind, it is extremely easy to cause stall and crash by executing rapid correction on longitudinal control loop in adverse situation.

2.3   Modeling of the Micro-downburst

- Selection of modeling method

    This research proposes three methods for modeling micro-downburst field as follow:
    1. Interpolation evaluation by using observed data. Storing measurement data of Doppler radar into computer in grid format or creating wind shear accident data-base, and use these data by interpolation method in simulation application. In this method, the wind field disturbance data is real, but the accuracy is limited by the size of data grid, and the data acquisition cost is high.
    2. According to the law of fluid mechanics or thermodynamics, establish and solve atmospheric dynamics equations. Due to numerical solving of nonlinear equation of the atmosphere usually occupies large amount of computation time, it not very suitable for the simulation in engineering application.
    3. Building a simplified fluid dynamics model which can describe the mechanism and movement process of low-level wind shear. This method is more applicable for engineering application, it has advantages such as lower modeling cost and less model solution calculation, and can reflect the motion characteristics of micro down burst, has good authenticity.

    In this paper, we use the third method to build the simplified fluid dynamics model of micro-downburst and carry out the numerical simulation based on the model.

- Modeling of the vortex ring of two-dimensional micro-downburst

    In the method of fluid dynamics modeling of micro-downburst, wind shear field is hypothesized as incompressible, non-viscous, non-rotating or non bit flow field, and the temperature change is not considered.

    Based on the above hypothesis, the principle model of vortex ring is widely used in the mathematical simulation of micro-downburst. The principle is that a series of vortex rings which strength is Γ_i are arranged on the longitudinal direction H_i and horizontal direction x_i, and a series of corresponding mirror vortex rings are arranged on $(-H_i, x_i)$ in order to meet the ground boundary conditions. Different assignments of Γ_i can induce the flow filed of micro-downburst by Γ_i and $-\Gamma_i$ according to the requirements.

    In the analysis of the impact of micro-downburst on missile motion characteristics, our major concern is the impact on the longitudinal motion characteristics. In this case, we can further simplify the model as the N vortex pair model of two-dimensional micro-downburst.

    The relationship between the induced velocity and the radius of a single linear vortex and the time is:

$$V(r,t) = \frac{\Gamma_0}{2\pi r}(1 - e^{\frac{-r^2}{4vt}}) \tag{1}$$

    In the equation, Γ_0 is the strength of vortex when $t = 0$, v is the dynamic viscosity coefficient. Horizontal and longitudinal wind components that induced by the n linear vortexes are:

$$V_x = \sum_{i=1}^{n} \frac{\Gamma_{0i} \Delta H_i}{2\pi r_i^2}(1 - e^{\frac{-r^2}{4\upsilon t}}) \qquad (2)$$

$$V_y = \sum_{i=1}^{n} \frac{\Gamma_{0i} \Delta x_i}{2\pi r_i^2}(1 - e^{\frac{-r^2}{4\upsilon t}}) \qquad (3)$$

Among them, $\Delta H_i = H - H_{i0}$, $\Delta x_i = x - x_{i0}$, $r_i^2 = x_i^2 + H_i^2$.

Figure 2 shows the superposition principle of linear vortex of two-demotion model of micro-downburst.

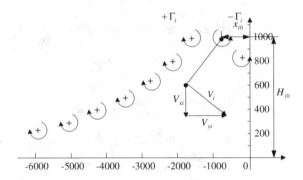

Fig. 2. Superposition principle of linear vortex of two-demotion model of micro-downburst

Note that the establishment of micro-downburst model requires a combination of some main features of wind shear:

- Wind shear magnitude: The change of wind speed is a function of flight distance.
- Change rate of wind speed: The change of wind speed within the prescribed range or within the time range.
- Wind shear scale: The spatial or temporal scale of wind shear events.
- The non-symmetry of wind shear field: Most of the observed wind shear fields are asymmetric, headwind and tailwind areas are different in scale and magnitude.

According to the statistics of radar measurements, micro-downburst has the scale space range of 1830 m to 3660 m from the strongest headwind to the strongest tailwind, so the horizontal distribution range of vortex pair is set to 5 km. Moreover, the spatial scale of wind shear and the aircraft speed determine the time scale of aircraft crossing the wind shear, so most severe wind shear encounter time is only 20 s ~ 30 s.

In addition, combined with flight altitude, 6 pair of vortex pairs are set at the height of 1000 m and in the horizontal direction range of (−5000, 0). The center of the micro-downburst is set at −2000 m to −1000 m. The 6 vortex pairs distribution model of is shown in Table 1.

Table 1. 6 vortex pairs distribution model

Vortex pair NO.	x_{i0}(m)	H_{i0}(m)	Γ_{i0}(m^2/s)
1	−5000	+− 1000	+− 18000
2	−4000	+− 1000	+− 30000
3	−3000	+− 1000	+− 30000
4	−2000	+− 1000	+− 45000
5	−1000	+− 1000	+− 45000
6	0	+− 1000	+− 30000
Surface dynamic viscosity coefficient v	$v = 15$ m^2/s		
Vortex duration t	$t = 900$ s		

2.4 Simulation Results of Micro-downburst Model

In order to verify the two-dimensional vortex model in Sect. 2.3, we calculate 16 horizontal and vertical wind components those are distributed at the 0 m, −1000 m, −2000 m, −3000 m, −4000 m and −5000 m on x direction, and at the height between 0 m and 1500 m. The 3D images are shown in Fig. 3.

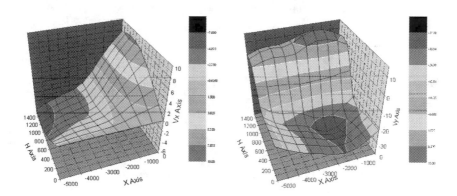

(a) Horizontal component wind speed   (b) Vertical component wind speed

Fig. 3. Numerical simulation of wind speed of two-dimension micro-downburst

In horizontal direction, wind shear field is headwind when located at −1000 m on x direction left to the center of downburst, while it is tailwind when located at the right to the center. In longitudinal direction, the undershoot speed reaches the maximum at the center of the air flow, also noted inversion phenomenon in the direction of airflow appears at high altitude.

The micro-downburst model fully reflects the essential mechanism and movement process of wind shear phenomenon, and can be used for the research on the dynamic effect of wind shear on flight performance of aircraft.

3   Simulation of Dynamic Effect of Micro-downburst on Flight Performance

3.1   Design of Simulation Conditions

Because it is relatively dangerous when the aircraft flies the micro-downburst region during the glide process, so researches aim at aircraft glide process, through modeling of glide motion and simulation, the attitude control and dynamic performance of aircraft in the process of longitudinal maneuver is evaluated.

Vortex pairs of micro-downburst are distributed according to Table 1. By adjusting the intensity of vortex, medium intensity and high intensity wind shears are simulated separately.

3.2   Influence Mechanism Analysis

When aircraft enters the setting micro-downburst area, it first encounters the disturbance of headwind, and receives an additional positive angle of attack, and then encounters the disturbance of tailwind and receives an additional negative angle of attack. This process is shown in Fig. 4. Accordingly, the additional aerodynamic force and aerodynamic torque are generated during this process, which influences some control variable, such as attitude, position and velocity etc.

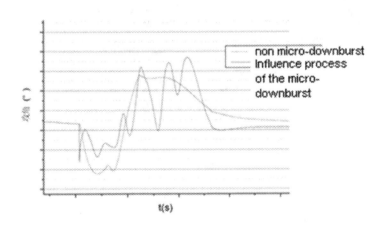

Fig. 4. Influence process of the micro-downburst on attack angle

Figure 5 shows the change process of roll angle when the aircraft influenced by the micro-downburst in glide process. As can be seen from the figure, when there is no micro-downburst, longitudinal attitude change has little influence on the roll channel. With the increase of micro-downburst strength, the change rate of roll angle increased. And roll angle can be returned to the normal control level after the aircraft flight through the micro-downburst disturbed field.

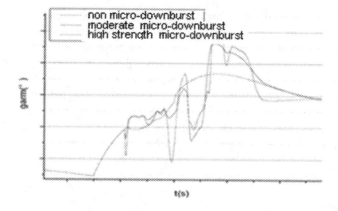

Fig. 5. Influence process of the micro-downburst on roll angle

For the glide process of aircraft, the effect time of micro-downburst is longer, and has asymmetry when in headwind and tailwind. Tailwind has longer effect time, it also has a certain influence on some long period variation parameter such as velocity and height. In altitude control, the aircraft attack angle is negative in most time in glide process because of the additional attack angle produced by micro-downburst. So if we adopt the same glide control process, the micro-downburst will make the aircraft generate height control overshoot, and lead to height control error as shown in Fig. 6.

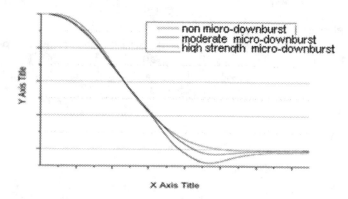

Fig. 6. Height change curve in micro-downburst

4   Conclusion

Low-Level wind shear is one kind of atmospheric disturbance which can bring the most serious damages for aircraft. This paper presents the physical characteristics, temporal and spatial scale, and air flow of the micro-downburst which is the most dangerous wind shear. By assuming characteristics as incompressible, non-viscous, non-rotating and non bit flow field of the wind shear, this paper build the two-dimensional micro-downburst model in horizontal and longitudinal direction without considering the temperature.

Besides, combined with the simulation model and flight mission characteristics of an aircraft, moderate intensity vortex pairs and high intensity vortex pairs is settled at a certain height and level to simulate flying through strength micro-downburst, and analyzes the dynamic effects of micro-downburst on aircraft flight performance.

This method is feasible even in the case of no wind shear site measurement data. It can reflect the process how the micro-downburst effect on the aircraft, and can be used to simulate different scales' wind shear by adjusting the energy and distribution mode of vortex pairs, as well as evaluate the design performance of the control low under various intensity atmospheric disturbance conditions.

References

1. Xiao, Y., Jin, C.: Flight Principle in Atmospheric Turbulence. National Defend Industry Press, Beijing (1993)
2. Huang, K., et al.: System Simulation Technology. National University of defence Technology Press, Beijing (1998)
3. Hu, M.: Advanced Atmospheric Flight Mechanics. Aviation Industrial Publishing House, Beijing (2007)
4. Lei, H.: Missile Guidance and Control Principle. National Defend Industry Press, Beijing (2006)
5. Ang, H., et al.: Micro Air Vehicle System Technology. Science Press, Beijing (2014)
6. Liu, X., et al.: Influence of micro-downburst on aircraft ski-jump takeoff. J. Naval Aeronaut. Eng. Inst. 22(5), 505–508 (2007)
7. Liu, F., et al.: Influence of micro-downburst on aircraft landing performance. J. Naval Aeronaut. Eng. Inst. 28(6), 639–642 (2013)
8. Cheng, M.: Characteristic analysis of airport surface wind and gale and its effect on the flight. Meteorol. Hydrol. Marine Instrum. 28(4), 44–46 (2011)
9. Yu, Z., Tao, Y., Sun, J.: Analysis of aircraft longitudinal mode under effect of wind shear. J. Naval Aeronaut. Astronaut. Univ. 25(4), 403–405 (2010)

Development and Credibility of Multi-disciplinary Virtual Prototype

Huiyang Qu[1(✉)], Guoqiang Shi[2], and Ruiying Pu[3]

[1] State Key Laboratory of Intelligent Manufacturing System Technology,
Beijing Institute of Electronic System Engineering, Beijing, China
quhuiyang@163.com
[2] Science and Technology on Space System Simulation Laboratory,
Beijing Simulation Center, Beijing, China
sunnyqiang737@163.com
[3] Beijing Complex Product Advanced Manufacturing Engineering Research Center,
Beijing Simulation Center, Beijing, China
windflowerpray@sohu.com

Abstract. The development of multi-disciplinary virtual prototype (MVP) is a system engineering which involves analysis, development, integration, testing and other activities. The credibility of MVP is important which decides whether or not the MVP could be applicable. The authors' team has developed a software development kit for MVP named collaborative simulation (COSIM). Based on the research work, firstly, the development and execution process of MVP engineering is illustrated. Secondly, verification, validation and accreditation (VV&A) across the whole MVP development process is introduced, and the indicator system of credibility evaluation is proposed. Finally, an application of VV&A for landing gear virtual prototype is given as an example.

Keywords: Multi-disciplinary virtual prototype · VV&A · Credibility

1 Introduction

Virtual prototype technology is a digitized product design approach based on computer simulation model, which utilizes the digital product model to provide visual, auditory, tactile, functionality, behavior and performance simulation of the real product. It uses a virtual prototype to replace the physical prototype while implementing innovative design, testing, evaluation and training for new product. It is becoming an important approach to shorten the product development cycles, reduce the costs, and improve the product design quality.

The federation development and execution process (FEDEP) was originally proposed for the high-level architecture (HLA) simulation. From 1997 to 1999 the Department of Modeling and Simulation Office (DMSO) released 5 versions of FEDEP [1]. In 2003, IEEE published updated FEDEP as standard of IEEE1516.3 [2]. As a generic method aiming at reuse of simulation, FEDEP includes several steps, and each step has its sub-goals and detailed activities, as well as preconditions and outputs.

L. Zhang et al. (Eds.): AsiaSim 2016/SCS AutumnSim 2016, Part III, CCIS 645, pp. 511–520, 2016.
DOI: 10.1007/978-981-10-2669-0_55

VV&A is developed from model verification. It gradually absorbed the thinking of software engineering and quality control, and developed into a set of solutions for the whole life cycle of simulation system [3]. It consists of verification, validation and accreditation. Verification usually analyzes the structural integrity of the model, and evaluates the extent to which it is consistent with the conceptual description of the developer. Validation is to compare the data of simulation experiments with real systems, and to determine whether the performance of the model is in accordance with the actual situation. Accreditation is to determine whether or not a model or simulation system can be applicable [4, 5].

Design and development of MVP involves developing simulation models of many disciplines. Based on the standard FEDEP, the design methodology of MVP engineering for COSIM is studied taking into consideration the features of MVP modeling and simulation. The credibility of MVP is affected by many factors because of the complexity. Therefore, VV&A and credibility evaluation, which includes activities with detailed plan and procedure, will be carried out across the FEDEP of MVP. Its purpose is to make sure that the credibility of simulation models and the system is measurable and controllable.

2   Design Methodology of Multi-disciplinary Virtual Prototype

The MVP system is characterized by a large number of models with variety and complex relationships between them, and it has multi-level structure and multi-functional behaviors. The top-down analysis method is adopted to decompose the system into element component models and composition component models. By defining the interfaces and couplings between the components, the developers can implement these components independently by using different design and analysis tools, and can integrate them to form high-level composition components. The collaborative simulation for a specific application will be completed by bottom-up integration of the composition components.

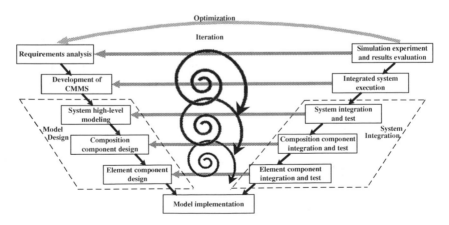

Fig. 1. The FEDEP of MVP

Based on the V-shaped development mode of concurrent engineering, the FEDEP of MVP is proposed as shown in Fig. 1. It includes requirement analysis, development of conceptual model of mission space (CMMS), model design, model implementation, system integration, integrated system execution, simulation experiment and results evaluation. The model design also includes system high-level modeling, composition components and element components design. The system integration includes integration and testing of element components, composition components and the system. It implements collaborative design, simulation and optimization of multiple disciplines in iterations of separately design for each disciplinary and system integration.

Step 1: Requirements Analysis. The purpose of requirements analysis is to understand the user's requirements about the application and functionality of the MVP system. It determines the objectives of the design and development. A comprehension of the requirements can correctly guide the FEDEP. Requirements analysis includes the activities of defining the user requirements and defining the design and development objective.

Step 2: Development of CMMS. The development of CMMS is a process of using domain knowledge to analyze and describe the simulation task space of the MVP, based on comprehension of the requirements and design objectives. Its purpose is to assist the analysis of the system structure and functionality by scenario deduction of the simulation task, and to transform the design objectives into concrete design indicators. The activities included in this step are scenario deduction, establishing the conceptual model and task decomposition.

Step 3: Model Design. The purpose of model design is to carry out a detailed design for MVP. It is also the foundation of the following step of model implementation. The activities of this step mainly focus on models of three levels: high-level model of the MVP, composition component model and element component model.

High-level modeling is to design structure and behaviors of the MVP, that is, the element components and/or composition components constructing the MVP, and the interfaces, couplings, interactions between them, as well as the model states and state transitions are identified. It is also needed to check whether these component models could meet the functionality and performance requirements.

Composition component design is to determine what sub-components (composition components or element components) are included in the composition component, and to check whether the sub-components derived from the decomposition could achieve the required functionalities.

Element component design is to determine the interfaces, mappings, simulation algorithms, the necessary computing resources and designing tools of the element components.

Step 4: Model Implementation. Model implementation aims at realizing the element components, composition components and the system of the MVP, using different analysis and design tools for different disciplines. It also provides basic environment for the next step of system integration and testing. Activities included in this step are implementing the simulation components, making the plan for system integration and testing, and preparing the running environment of system integration and testing.

Step 5: System Integration. The purpose of system integration is to combine the simulation components of various disciplines together to build the MVP system, and to carry out relevant tests. It mainly consists of three levels of integration and testing, which correspondingly are element component, composition component and system model.

Step 6: Execution of the Integrated System. The purpose of the integrated system execution is to check whether the system can achieve the design and development objectives and application scenarios defined in conceptual model through the running of the MVP system. Before executing the integrated system, an execution plan should be prepared firstly.

Step 7: Simulation Experiment and Results Evaluation. Simulation data are collected during the execution process of the MVP system, and also analyzed to evaluate the system. The activities included in this step are defining the simulation input data, configuring the experiment parameters, executing the simulation, recording simulation results, and evaluating the system according to the performance and functionality requirements. The simulation data should be preprocessed using some analysis tools. In this step, a series of documents will be saved for further improvement and system accreditation.

3   VV&A and Credibility of Multi-disciplinary Virtual Prototype

The process of development and execution of MVP includes a number of activities, and generates a series of products. At the end of development iteration, if the performance does not meet the user requirements, it often takes a long time to locate the problems. Therefore, verification and validation is effective to reduce the frequency of error occurrence, and to decrease the development risk, to improve the development efficiency and system credibility.

3.1   VV&A of Multi-disciplinary Virtual Prototype

VV&A of MVP should be throughout the entire life cycle of design and development, as shown in Fig. 2.

Phase 1: Verify the Requirements. The purpose of this phase is to verify the objectives of design and development of the MVP, at the same time to identify the targets of VV&A work. This phase includes the activities of supporting the developers to understand the user requirement, making plan of system accreditation, verifying the objectives of design and development, collecting the system evaluation reference data, defining the system acceptability criteria, supporting risk assessment and cost estimation, and drawing up V&V plan.

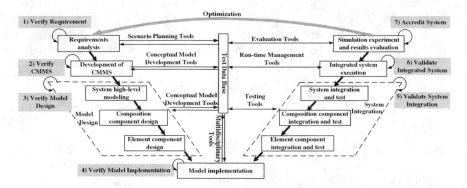

Fig. 2. The VV&A process of multi-disciplinary virtual prototype

Phase 2: Verify the Conceptual Model. The purpose of this phase is to make verification to the analysis and description of the simulation task space, to determine if it is in accordance with the user requirements and design objectives. The activities of this phase include assisting the scenario deduction, verifying conceptual model and verifying the design specifications.

Phase 3: Verify the Model Design. The purpose of this phase is to verify the design of the MVP system, which includes verification for the high-level modeling of the system, the design of composition components and element components. The activities include verifying the design of structure and behavior of the system high-level modeling, verifying the design of interfaces, couplings, interactions between the composition components and/or element components, as well as the model states and state transitions.

Phase 4: Verify the Model Implementation. The purpose of this phase is to make the verification for implementation of the simulation model of the MVP. The included activities are checking whether the model outputs are correct when given some inputs, verifying whether the algorithms used can meet the performance specifications, and supporting to make the system integration plan and the testing plan, to construct the system integration and testing environment, and verifying and validating testing datasets.

Phase 5: Validate the System Integration. The purpose of this phase is to validate the integrated MVP system and the testing results. The activities of this phase are ensuring the integration performed according to the plan, verifying whether the MVP system is integrated correctly, supporting the MVP system testing and validating the output data of system testing.

Phase 6: Validate the Execution of the Integrated MVP System. The purpose of this phase is to the execution result of the integrated MVP system. The activities included are supporting to make the execution plan of the integrated system and validating the execution data of the integrated system according to the reference specifications.

Phase 7: Accredit the MVP System. The purpose of this phase is to prove that the MVP system can meet the user requirements for a specific simulation application. The activities included are assisting the experiment on the MVP simulation system, assisting in analyzing and evaluating the simulation result, validating the simulation experiment data, accrediting the system and preparing the VV&A products.

3.2   Credibility of Multi-disciplinary Virtual Prototype

Multi-disciplinary virtual prototype is usually a complex system composed by heterogeneous components, and the credibility is affected by many factors. The purpose of conducting VV&A activities throughout the process of design and development of MVP is to minimize the effect of these factors and to improve the credibility. In this section the evaluation indicator system is proposed based on the analysis of the factors which may affect the credibility of MVP, as shown in Fig. 3.

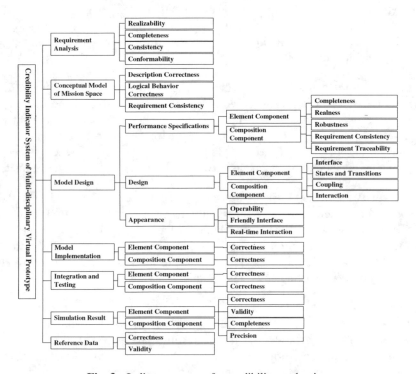

Fig. 3. Indicator system for credibility evaluation

Among the steps of design and development of MVP, requirements analysis, development of CMMS and simulation system design, which in the early or middle stage of development, will impact the design objectives and development direction of the MVP. They will also directly decide the success or failure of the later steps of the system implementation, integration execution, and simulation experiment.

Requirements analysis is to study and fully understand the functionality and performance requirements of MVP from the view of the users. It is the beginning of the whole project and also is the most important milestone to carry out the project. Evaluation of the requirements analysis needs to examine the completeness, consistency, confirmability and realizability. CMMS identifies the basic units in the task space based on requirements analysis, describes the properties, states and behaviors of these units and determines the couplings and interactions between them according to the information flow. In the evaluation of conceptual model, the correctness and its consistency with the user requirements of the logical behavior should be emphasized.

Simulation system design is to transform the functional requirements of MVP described by the user requirements and CMMS into the specific quantitative performance indicators of the composition components and element components, to design and optimize the structure, behavior and parameters of the system and the components. The evaluation objects of this step include the performance specifications and system design. The evaluation of performance specifications focuses on the completeness, realness, robustness, and consistency and traceability of the user requirements, and the evaluation of the designed model includes the design of the static structure and dynamic behavior, which can be specified as the interfaces of components, their states and state transitions, their couplings and interactive scenarios. In addition, the credibility also represents the user's confidence of the MVP system, that is, to what degree the MVP system can meet the application requirements. So the credibility evaluation should also consider the user experience of the MVP system, such as operability, user-friendly interface and real-time interactive capabilities.

In the later stage of design and development, it is mainly a process of transforming the model design into a specific simulation model, using design tools of different professional fields. So it focuses on correctly using various development tools, integration tools, testing tools and evaluation tools, to build the MVP system in accordance with the designs. Moreover, the correctness of simulation result is also one of the most important factors in credibility evaluation, and the corresponding indicators are correctness, validity, completeness and precision.

Reference data play another important role in FEDEP of MVP. It is necessary to use the validated historical data and empirical data to support the testing, evaluation and accreditation. The reference data with flaws or even mistakes may lead the designers, testers, and evaluation and accreditation personnel to a wrong judgment of the system.

Based on the above analysis, the indicator system for MVP credibility is proposed as the basis for the design and development process and VV&A activities, as shown in Fig. 3. (To keep the figure concise, using element component and composition component represents all the component models.) According to these indicators, verification, validation and accreditation should be carried out strictly to ensure the correct execution of each step during the design and development process, thus to improve the credibility of the MVP system.

4   Application of VV&A for Landing Gear Virtual Prototype System

The landing gear virtual prototype is taken as an example to illustrate the application of VV&A. The activities of VV&A are conducting throughout the whole process of the design and implementation of the landing gear MVP.

Step 1: Verify the Requirement. In this application, the user requirement is to develop a virtual prototype for landing gear system, which simulates the take-off and landing in various environments, such as different roads, atmospheric and overloads situations caused by rapid take-off and landing, so that the aircraft can take off and land safely and smoothly. According to this requirement, the design and development objective of the project is that the landing gear virtual prototype system can achieve the actions of folding, unfolding and emergency stopping, in a short time and with smooth velocity and acceleration. The above user requirement and design and development objective are verified on a reviewing session participated by domain experts, and are considered that they are realizable for the landing gear virtual prototype system.

Step 2: Verify the Conceptual Model. The VV&A personnel check the application scenarios of folding, unfolding and emergency stopping of the landing gear virtual prototype system, and the corresponding functionalities and interactions of the modules including the multi-body dynamic model, the hydraulic system model, the electric control model and the multi-disciplinary optimization model. They also determine that the internal information transfer and the behavior of the conceptual model are correct and consistent with the user requirement. The design specifications, that the landing gear virtual prototype system should achieve folding and unfolding quickly and smoothly, are also verified and taken as the system acceptability criteria.

Step 3: Verify the Design of Landing Gear Virtual Prototype System. The landing gear virtual prototype system is designed as four element components of the multi-body dynamic model, the hydraulic system model, the electric control model and the multi-disciplinary optimization model. The interfaces, mappings of the four element components, their states as well as state transitions, are verified in this phase.

Step 4: Verify the Implementation of Landing Gear Virtual Prototype System. The V&V personnel check the models of the multi-body dynamic model, the hydraulic system model and the electric control model, which are implemented using ADAMS, EASY5 and MATLAB respectively. The simulation algorithm of each model is also examined. In the verification, these models can generate correct outputs when given some inputs.

Step 5: Validate the Landing Gear Virtual Prototype System Integration. According to the system integration plan, the electronic control model, the hydraulic system model, the multi-body dynamics model and the multi-disciplinary optimization model are integrated in the predefined order to construct the landing gear virtual prototype system. These models are tested independently during execution of the integrated system and the results are collected to compare with validated testing datasets to verify whether the information can be correctly transferred between the models.

Step 6: Validate the Execution of Landing Gear Virtual Prototype System. During the execution of the integrated landing gear virtual prototype system, the V&V personnel use run-time management tool for simulation to check whether or not the system can run in accordance with the defined application scenarios. The outputs of all the four models corresponding to some given inputs are compared with reference data and basis to validate the behaviors of the landing gear virtual prototype.

Step 7: Accredit the Landing Gear Virtual Prototype System. The VV&A personnel organize domain experts to determine whether or not the landing gear virtual prototype can be accepted according to the results of simulation experiments and system testing. The folding and unfolding time of the landing gear virtual prototype is 1.76 s with smooth velocity and acceleration. The result is in accord with the user requirement and the design and development objective. In addition, with conduction of V&V activities throughout the whole design and development process, the landing gear virtual prototype has enough credibility to be accepted and used in simulation applications.

5   Conclusion

The design methodology covers the entire life cycle of the MVP which includes requirements analysis, development of CMMS, model design, model implementation, system integration, execution of the integrated system, simulation experiment and results evaluation.

VV&A is conducted throughout the whole development process of the MVP. It includes several phases as verifying the requirements, verifying the conceptual model, verifying the model design, verifying the model implementation, validating the system integration, validating the execution of the MVP system, and accrediting the system. The credibility indicator system is a basis of evaluating whether the virtual prototype can be applicable in practice.

Using the design methodology to guide the development of the MVP, conducting VV&A throughout the whole process and organizing the project participants, project process and products will achieve the integration and optimization of the personnel/organization, management and technology, thus to improve the efficiency and quality of the MVP engineering, to reduce the project risk and to enhance the user's confidence.

References

1. U.S. Department of Defense (DoD): High level architecture federation development and execution process (FEDEP) model (version 1.5) (1999)
2. The Institute of Electrical and Electronic Engineers, Inc.: IEEE Std1516.3, IEEE Recommended practice for high level architecture (HLA) federation development and execution process (FEDEP) (2003)

3. Yang, M., Zhang, B., Ma, P., Wang, Z.: Five key issues of the development of simulation systems VV&A. J. Syst. Simul. **15**, 1506–1508 (2003)
4. U.S. DoD, Defense Modeling and Simulation Office (DMSO): Verification, validation and accreditation recommended practice guides BUILD 2 (2000)
5. The Institute of Electrical and Electronic Engineers, Inc.: IEEE Recommended practice for verification, validation, and accreditation of a federation – an overlay to the high level architecture federation development and execution process (2007)

Management Methodology of Multi-disciplinary Virtual Prototype Engineering

Huiyang Qu[1(✉)], Guoqiang Shi[2], and Ruiying Pu[3]

[1] State Key Laboratory of Intelligent Manufacturing System Technology,
Beijing Institute of Electronic System Engineering, Beijing, China
quhuiyang@163.com
[2] Science and Technology on Space System Simulation Laboratory, Beijing Simulation Center,
Beijing, China
sunnyqiang737@163.com
[3] Beijing Complex Product Advanced Manufacturing Engineering Research Center,
Beijing Simulation Center, Beijing, China
windflowerpray@sohu.com

Abstract. The development of multi-disciplinary virtual prototype (MVP) for complex product is a system engineering, which involves integration and optimization of human/organization, management and technology during the whole process. In this paper, the comprehensive management methodology of the MVP is proposed. Firstly, the general MVP engineering management pattern is elaborated. Afterward, the exectuation methods of multi-disciplinary team/organization management, process management and product management are illustrated. Finally, the standard system for the MVP engineering is establised as the guidance of development, management and application.

Keywords: Virtual prototype · Management methodology · Standard system

1   Introduction

Complex products virtual prototype engineering technology aims at the optimization of 'three factors' (human/organization, management and technology) and 'three flows' (information flow, value flow and knowledge flow) during the development process in integrated enabling environment [1] as shown in Fig. 1.

The development of MVP is in a manner of spiral iteration, and VV&A runs through the whole process [2]. It involves information communication between subsystems, cooperation of multi-disciplinary personnel and coupling of sub-tasks. With the development of the MVP, the organization structure and the decomposed project/task tree of the engineering will increase in depth and breadth, and the resource needed will become more diverse [3, 4]. Therefore, a good management pattern is necessary to efficiently organize the developers and the managers in different departments, to share the information and engineering resources, and to optimize the resource allocation during the whole process.

© Springer Science+Business Media Singapore 2016
L. Zhang et al. (Eds.): AsiaSim 2016/SCS AutumnSim 2016, Part III, CCIS 645, pp. 521–529, 2016.
DOI: 10.1007/978-981-10-2669-0_56

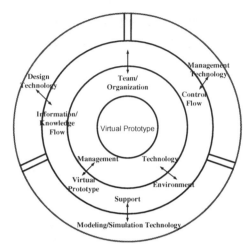

Fig. 1. Wheel process of complex products virtual prototype engineering

2 Virtual Prototype Engineering Management Pattern

Considering the key factors of MVP engineering, the management pattern mainly concentrates on engineering process management, team/organization management and product management, which are three dimensions as shown in Fig. 2.

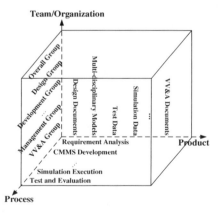

Fig. 2. Management pattern of multi-disciplinary virtual prototype

The process management involves task decomposition, workflow construction and reconfiguratinon optimization in the entire process of requirements analysis, the MVP design, development, integration, testing and evaluation. The team/organization management includes constituting the project team, defining the duties and privileges of the developers, the managers and the VV&A personnels. The product management mainly focuses on data, models and documents of the MVP and its external environment during the development process.

The development of the MVP depends on the engineering environment of collaborative design and simulation. Similarly, its management pattern relies on an infrastructure of cooperative management environment as shown in Fig. 3. The underlying layer is the enterprise resource platform which provides access to various resources. The top layer is a two-level structure, the inner one is project management (PM), and the outer level is the virtual prototype life-cycle management (VPLM) which includes product data management (PDM), test data management (TDM) and simulation data management (SDM).

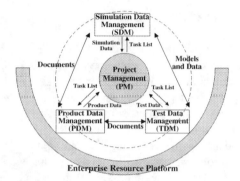

Fig. 3. Environment of cooperative management of the MVP

Project management covers the whole life cycle of the MVP engineering, which plans, organizes, guides and controls all the tasks in the project to achieve agile management, comprehensive coordination and optimization.

The VPLM is in charge of the products, data and resources involved in the development process. PDM stores and organizes the documents and models produced at each phase, according to the product's physical constitution. TDM stores the results of physical experiments. SDM is used for the data generated in executions of the simulation models and the MVP system.

The task list generated by PM is used as input of PDM, TDM and SDM. At the same time, the workflow in PDM will be started when the corresponding task executed in PM. At the end of the workflow, the task state will be returned to PM and used to supervise and analyze the project progress. TDM and SDM also return the state of data collection to PM for product verification and validation in every development stage.

3   Multi-disciplinary Team/Organization Management

For each project, the multi-disciplinary team is organized in the form of integrated project team (IPT). As shown in Fig. 4, in the horizontal direction is the multi-level team divided according to the project complexity, and in the vertical direction shows the group partitioned in accordance with its role in the engineering, which includes the synthesis group, design group, development group, testing group, VV&A group, and quality control group, configuration management group, training group, and so on.

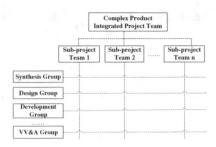

Fig. 4. IPT of multi-disciplinary team

According to the multi-layer structure in the horizontal direction, the team in the upper layer is responsible for task allocation to the lower-layer teams, leading and coordinating their work. The team leader of the lower layer is team member of the upper layer. The upper-layer team makes a preliminary or general schedule for the tasks of the lower layer and defines the interface between these tasks. The lower-layer team provides the upper layer with simulation component models.

The organization and management of multi-disciplinary team is according to the task decomposition. The sub-projects are divided according to the layered architecture corresponding to the multi-disciplinary team/organization respectively. Each IPT has a project leader, who is responsible for the overall management, including communicating with the outside world, allocating project resources, coordinating between sub-teams, and supervising the project progress, etc. The project leader also needs to define the participants' roles and duties, and set their access privileges on models and data, according to the related tasks. Any team member can not be assigned two mutually exclusive roles.

4 Process Management

4.1 Requirement Management

Requirement management goes through the entire MVP engineering. As shown in Fig. 5, it involves technical and non-technical requirements and includes requirement allocation, requirement tracing and requirement change management.

Requirement allocation must be documented and reviewed to ensure the feasibility. A requirement management plan will be made according to the project actual situation, which decomposes and specifies requirements from the perspective of multiple disciplines. The related personnel of requirement management, such as project leader, managers, developers, testers and so on, will also be appointed.

Requirement tracing is needed in each stage in order to guarantee the consistency of the schedule, product, task, and the requirement allocation. It supervises and controls the development process according to the requirement management plan. The activities, progress and results of the MVP development should be evaluated and reviewed to ensure the consistency with the requirements.

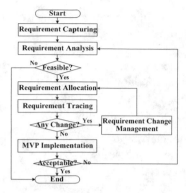

Fig. 5. The process of requirement management

Once the allocated requirement needs to be changed, requirement change management will be performed to evaluate the effect, to identify the inconsistency with the requirement, and to organize review session. If the requirement change is allowed, the related plans, products and tasks should be adjusted accordingly. The bidirectional traceability of the requirement should be maintained. On the other hand, it is necessary to record the requirement change, including change reasons, effect and countermeasures. Also the statistic of the ratio, the resulted work delay and the time of requirement change should be recorded, as the basis for further analysis and decision-making of requirement management.

4.2 Project Planning Management

A feasible project plan is important for the MVP engineering project. At the early stage, the project contract is made and reviewed according to the objective, scope, performance specification, technical capability, resources and other requirements. The workload is estimated using project management tools, as well as forecasting time limit for the project, cost estimation and potential risk assessment. The project plan is made according to resource constraints, requirement analysis and development capacity, as well as the estimated time limit, total cost and potentia risk. An appropriate project life-cycle model is determined by the project leader to partition the main stages. The project leader also needs to carry out task decomposition and scale estimation for main work according to its level and discipline, to measure workload and progress of each task. The project plan will be drawn up using management tools and the multi-disciplinary IPT will be organized. The leader of each disciplinary group will determine the goals of each sub-project, break down the development tasks into element components and composition components of the MVP, and allocate the tasks to team members.

4.3 Project Tracking and Supervision Management

The purpose of project tracking and supervision management is to provide appropriate visibility of the actual progress of the MVP engineering. So that the project managers can take effective measures when the project deviating from the plan. On the one hand, periodic examination is performed to supervise the project progress, and to ensure that any problems can be found and solved in time. On the other hand, several time points are settled in each development phase to check the progress. The managers have to collect the estimated development duration time of each discipline, as well as the estimated resource consumption in that time. It should be noticed to identify the following activities, and to set them as key events or milestones of the project.

- Activities requiring a long preparation time
- Activities lasting a long duration time
- Activities on critical path or with special events
- Activities requiring particular input or decision-making
- Activities having key output at a specific time point

The project tracking and supervision management plan is drawn up according to the time objectives, the relationship between the activities, duration time, and key events or milestones mentioned above. The tracking plan will be carried out so as to supervise the development process timely and effectively. The relevant data will be collected at the same time, including workload, key resources, cost, schedule and risk. These data will be analyzed and evaluated to determine whether the actual progress of each discipline and sub-project is consistent with the predefined objectives and requirements. If some change of the project plan happened, the tracking plan should also be adjusted accordingly, so that it could keep consistent with the updated project plan.

5   Product Management

Product management of the MVP engineering is to make an integral organization and management to the models, documentations and data generated in development process. It aims at improving the information sharing between disciplines and projects. Product management is performed using PDM, SDM and TDM, which establishes a structure tree of the MVP and classified the products to corresponding discipline. Version control and quality control are main concerns of product management.

During the development process of the MVP, version control maintains the old product version and updates the new version when the product switches from pre-release state or released state to working state. PDM receives the project plan and task list from PM. The developers of different disciplines carry out their design and development work concurrently, and release or update their products in PDM according to the project plan. The large number of data generated in the MVP system testing, simulation running, analysis and evaluation will be managed by SDM and TDM.

Quality control is to ensure the MVP products to meet the quality specifications. It includes determining the requirements, making plan and managing product states. There should be integral flows and unified standards for approval, publication, modification and archiving of all the products. The requirements which can change the development process should be identified, confirmed rationally and recorded in documentations. It can transfer to the next development stage when all the products meet the quality specifications.

6 Specification System of Multi-disciplinary Virtual Prototype Engineering

Considering the whole development process of the MVP, a specification system is proposed from a practical perspective, with reference to the related overseas standards. It covers all important aspects of the MVP engineering, as shown in Fig. 6.

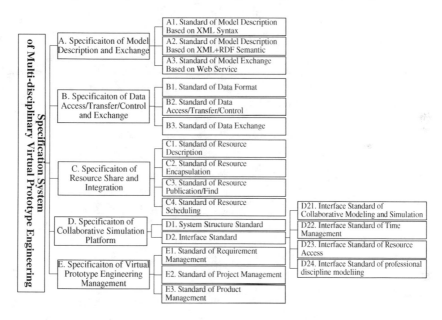

Fig. 6. Specification system of multi-disciplinary virtual prototype engineering

6.1 Specification of Model Description and Exchange

The MVP system usually contains control, dynamic, fluid, hydraulic and other disciplinary heterogeneous models. To improve interoperability and reusability of these models, a standard description is necessary. The model description and exchange specification defines the syntax and semantics of description and exchange of the mission space model (such as the demand model), conceptual space model and simulation space model (such as the simulation model).

Currently, the XML (Extensible Markup Language) specification has been widely used in many fields. XML uses tags and attributes to describe data, and takes advantage of the validation rules, such as DTD (Document Type Definitions) or XML Schema, to regulate the content and structure of XML documents. It is simple and easy to be parsed, which can not only be used to describe the models consistently, but also to facilitate the organization and extension of the file contents. Therefore, the description and exchange specification for the MVP models is proposed based on XML language. It includes the standard of model description based on XML syntax and XML + RDF (Resource Description Framework) semantics, the standard of model exchange based on

XML /Web Service. These standards provide description methods for the MVP models with the following standards: the syntax description specifications of port, event, element component and composition component; the semantic description specifications of data type, state, and behavior; the specification of information exchange between heterogeneous models.

6.2   Data Access, Transfer, Control and Exchange Specifications

Multi-disciplinary virtual prototype involves various disciplinary fields. There are mature specifications of data access, transfer, control and exchange in each disciplinary field or industry. While these specifications are applicable for development of single disciplinary virtual prototype, they are not suitable for data sharing and integration between different disciplinary fields.

Table 1. Specifications of data access, transfer, control and exchange

Category	Description
Data format specification	Rules and requirements of data representation
	Specification and standardization of the MVP engineering meta-data
	XML data format of the MVP engineering
Data access, transfer, control specification	Specification of heterogeneous database interface
	Standard data access interface for the MVP engineering
	XML data interface of database
	Platform interface based on EAI (Enterprise Application Integration) technology
Data exchange specification	Data exchange format based on XML
	Application rules of data exchange
	Guidance of data exchange syntax

To solve these problems, the data access, transfer, control and exchange specifications are set up to support the life cycle of design, development and execution of the MVP. It mainly contains the following contents as shown in Table 1.

6.3   Specifications of Resource Sharing and Integration

Resources used in the MVP engineering include software, computing resources and models, etc. These resources usually distribute in different locations or departments. The specifications of resource sharing and integration provide unified standards of resource description, encapsulation, publication/detection and scheduling, which describe the resources in the form of 'service' based on WSDL (Web Service Description Language) and GWSDL (Grid WSDL).

6.4   Collaborative Simulation Platform Specifications

Collaborative simulation platform mainly consists of the collaborative modeling and simulation platform, visualization environment, multi-disciplinary optimization platform, multi-disciplinary development tools and other accessories. To regulate their relationships and the architecture, the structure and interface specifications for the collaborative simulation platform are set up, to support connection and interaction of information and data during development, integration and execution of the MVP. The interface specification also includes interface specifications for collaborative modeling and simulation, time management, resource access and single disciplinary modeling.

6.5   Management Specifications of the MVP Engineering

Multi-disciplinary virtual prototype is designed and developed based on the thinking of concurrent engineering. Management of the research and development work is a systematic process, which should cover the whole life cycle. Thus the management specifications include requirement management specification, project management specification and product management specificatin. Requirement management specification regulates plan, execution and documentation of the activities of definition, allocation and change for technical and non-technical requirements. Project management specification regulates team/organization management, project planning, tracking and supervision. Product management specification regulates the management organization, version control, quality control and flow management for the products (models, data, documents, etc.) and resources in the MVP engieering.

7   Conclusion

The management methodology includes multi-disciplinary team/organization management, process management and product management. The process management mainly considers requirement management, project planning management and project tracking and supervision management. Product management involves version control and quality control. A specification system is proposed as guidance of the MVP engineering, which respectively defines the description and exchange of the model, data access, transfer, control and exchange, resource sharing and integration, collaborative simulation platform, and management standard.

References

1. Li, B., Chai, X.: Virtual prototyping engineering for complex product. Comput. Integr. Manuf. Syst. **8**(9), 678–683 (2002)
2. Li, B., Chai, X., Xiong, G., et al.: Research and primary practice on virtual prototyping engineering. J. Syst. Simul. **14**(3), 336–341 (2002)
3. Huang, S., Fan, Y.: Overview of product lifecycle management. Comput. Integr. Manuf. Syst. **10**(1), 1–9 (2004)
4. Xiao, S., Li, B., Chai, X.: Research of complex product virtual prototype lifecycle management system. J. Syst. Simul. **19**(11), 2484–2487 (2007)

The Numerical Simulation for Effect of Vibratory Stress Relief on Titanium Alloy Ti-6Al-4V Fatigue Life

Song Jing[1,2], Zhang Yidu[1,2(✉)], and Sun Ke[3]

[1] State Key Laboratory of Virtual Reality Technology and Systems,
Beihang University, Beijing 100191, China
{songjing,ydzhang}@buaa.edu.cn
[2] School of Mechanical Engineering and Automation, Beihang University,
Beijing 100191, China
[3] Beijing Xinli Machinery Co., Ltd., Beijing, China
630038480@qq.com

Abstract. Effect of vibratory stress relief on titanium alloy Ti-6Al-4V fatigue life was investigated by numerical simulation method in this paper. This paper aimed to determine whether vibratory stress relief can adversely affect fatigue life of titanium alloy Ti-6Al-4V or not. Firstly, the modal analysis for titanium alloy Ti-6Al-4V specimen was carried out by using finite element method, then, using transient dynamic analysis method simulated specimen dynamic stress in vibratory stress relief process. Secondly, the finite element model that contained initial stress for VSR simulation was established. Vibratory stress relief was simulated by using transient dynamic analysis method. Finally, we used FE-safe software for fatigue simulation. It is concluded that titanium alloy Ti-6Al-4V fatigue strength increased with amplitude, but the phenomenon "much vibration" appeared when amplitude continued to increase that led to decrease of fatigue life.

Keywords: Titanium alloy Ti-6Al-4V · Vibratory stress relief · Exciting force · Dynamic stresses · Residual stresses · Fatigue life

1 Introduction

Thin-walled parts produced by various methods are widely used in modern aircraft industry. The residual stress plays an important role in thin-walled parts processing. The residual stress is defined as the stress state which exists in a body after all external loads are removed. Depending on their natural (tensile or compressive stresses) stresses can either enhance or impair the ability of a component to withstand severe loading conditions in service such as stress corrosion cracking, creep, fatigue, etc. Furthermore, inhomogeneous residual stress field distribution on a component may also led to dimensional instability after mechanical processing. Therefore, the homogenized residual stress measures must be taken in the production of aluminum alloy components.

© Springer Science+Business Media Singapore 2016
L. Zhang et al. (Eds.): AsiaSim 2016/SCS AutumnSim 2016, Part III, CCIS 645, pp. 530–539, 2016.
DOI: 10.1007/978-981-10-2669-0_57

Vibratory Stress Relief (VSR) is a green and efficient aging technology. It prompted the workpiece vibrated under periodic external force, produces micro plastic deformation on component and makes residual stress relief that led to stable component size. Compared with the traditional natural stress relief (NSR) and thermal stress relief (TSR), VSR technology has advantages of short production cycle, ease of implementation in manufacturing process, low investment cost and so on [1], besides, VSR have high social and economic benefits. VSR as an important supplement for NSR and TSR has been widely used in the world [2, 3].

Researchers have been perplexed by the relationship between VSR load bearing and fatigue processes of component. Many researchers have studied the relationship between VSR and the fatigue life of components. Some investigators commented on an increase in fatigue life after VSR, whereas others have found quite opposite. Buhler [4] believed that VSR treatment can produce fatigue damage for cast iron. Song Tian Min [5] studied the influence of VSR on welded components fatigue lives, concluded that VSR can improve its fatigue life. Wozney [6] commented that VSR treatments have a bad effect on the fatigue life of steel. However, no particular experimental data were presented to support these views. Sonsino [7] reported that VSR decreased welded joint fatigue life significantly. Jesensky [8] found no damages in the fatigue life of the components because of VSR treatment. Fang Dexin [9] disclosed a higher fatigue life in vibrated welded components. Lu Yaping [10] analyzed dislocation and the dislocation pileup group-stress field through the use micromechanical methods and concluded that VSR can increase the fatigue life of the specimen. However, Most of the above investigations were conducted mainly targeting steel, cast iron and welded component, but the researches on titanium alloy are much less. In view of the conclusions, the uncertainty and the importance of titanium alloys in modern aircraft industrial applications and the components were vibrated at resonance frequency in a VSR process [11, 12]. The material for the research is titanium alloy Ti-6Al-4V, we use ANSYS software to finite element simulation. Determine the position that vibratory stress relief is middle section of specimen by modal analysis. The specimen was assigned initial stress in the middle section of specimen and conducted VSR simulation, the residual stress changed before and after VSR under the condition of first order frequency and various amplitude were studied. On the basis of above, fatigue lives of specimens were studied by fatigue simulation.

2 Titanium Alloy Ti-6Al-4V Specimen

The type of Ti-6Al-4V is a $\alpha + \beta$ type two-phase martensitic alloy, it was developed by institute of technology Illinois in 1954 and it has been used as an important structural titanium alloy due to its excellent mechanical properties. Ti-6Al-4V has been widely used in aeronautics, aerospace, ordnance, automotive, energy, mechanical and sport equipment fields. The amount of Ti-6Al-4V accounted for more than 50 % of total titanium alloy [13]. The chemical compositions and mechanical properties of titanium alloy Ti-6Al-4V are shown in Tables 1 and 2. Figure 1 is a schematic illustration of the

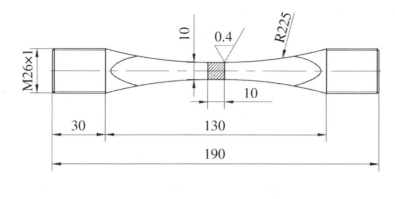

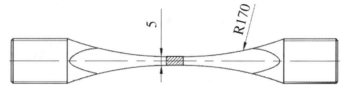

Fig. 1. Fatigue specimen of titanium alloy Ti-6Al-4V

Table 1. Chemical compositions of Ti-6Al-4V [14]

Main element wt. (%)								Other element	
Al	V	Fe	C	N	H	O	Ti	Single	Total
5.5-6.8	3.5-4.5	≤0.3	≤0.1	≤0.05	≤0.015	≤0.2	Balance	≤0.1	≤0.4

Table 2. Mechanical properties of Ti-6Al-4V [15]

Elastic modulus E (MPa)	Yield strength $\sigma_{0.2}$ (MPa)	Ultimate strength σ_b (MPa)	Elongation δ (%)	Hardness (HV)
110-140	800-1100	900-1200	13-16	300-400

fatigue specimen, which is designed according to China national standard GB/T 3075-2008, its length is 190 mm, and the middle section of specimen is 10 mm × 10 mm × 5 mm.

3   Finite Element Simulations

3.1   Modal Analysis

The modal analysis used to determine vibration characteristics of the structure, namely determine natural frequencies and vibration type of the structure, they are the important design parameters in structure that bearing dynamic loads. Determine the position of

Fig. 2. Finite element model titanium alloy Ti-6Al-4V specimen

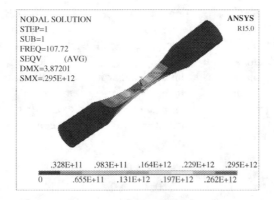

Fig. 3. The first order vibration type of titanium alloy Ti-6Al-4V specimen

specimen that residual stress need to relax by modal analysis method, and selected vibration type match to the position that need to residual stress relief according to the theory of orientational vibratory stress relief. The middle section of the specimen was the position that need to residual stress relief in this paper. Figure 2 is finite element model of titanium alloy Ti-6Al-4V specimen, solid185 solid element was used to grid model, the element size is 0.5 mm in middle section and else is 1 mm of the specimen, the total of the element for finite element model is 386729. The first order resonance frequency of fatigue specimen is 107.72 Hz by FEM modal analysis on the condition of constrained all DOF at one end of specimen and free to the other end. The first order modal of specimen corresponding to the vibration type is bending vibration mode, and the position that produced maximum dynamic stress was in the middle section of specimen. As can be seen in Fig. 3, the red part is maximum dynamic stress location. The value of the modal stress in Fig. 3 is meaningless because it reflects the magnitude of the stress and is not the true stress value under the first-order vibration mode. However, it can be used as a reference for judging the magnitude of stress.

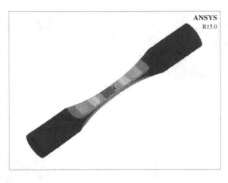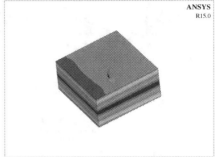

Fig. 4. The dynamic stress distribution of specimen when VSR

3.2   Dynamic Stress Simulation of Specimen

The dynamic stress depends on amplitude under the condition of certain geometry, vibration mode and vibration frequency, the dynamic stress increasing with the amplitude. One end of specimen was constrained all DOF except X axis and free to the other end, dynamic stress were simulated at first order frequency 107.72 Hz of specimen and various amplitudes in X direction according to results of modal analysis. The result of whole and middle section of specimen dynamic stress has been shown in Fig. 4 (The red part was the position of biggest dynamic stress). The results of various amplitudes corresponding to dynamic stress values have been shown in Table 3.

Table 3. Various amplitudes corresponding to dynamic stress values

Amplitude/mm	0	0.1	0.2	0.3	0.4	0.5
Dynamic stress/MPa	0	22.2	44.3	66.5	88.6	111

According to Table 3, fitting out the curve in Fig. 5 by using least square method with matlab software, it can be concluded that a linear relationship between amplitude and dynamic stress, as shown in Eq. (1):

$$\sigma_d = 136.8A - 1.9 \tag{1}$$

3.3   VSR Simulation of Specimen

The position that vibratory stress relief was the middle section of specimen, it was divided to 10 layers. The element shape was hexahedron, its length was 0.5 mm. We assigned residual stress in Y and Z directions for each layer, and assigned residual stress changed along with X direction according to the principle of force and torque balance, the residual stress value was assigned as 0 on rest of specimen. It is assumed that initial residual stress distribution along with thickness direction shown in Fig. 6

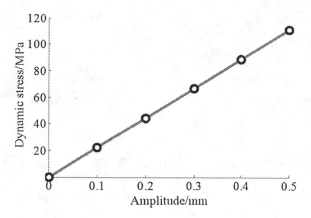

Fig. 5. The amplitude-dynamic curve

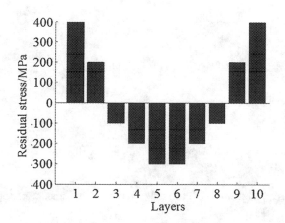

Fig. 6. The initial residual stress distribution along with thickness direction

according to the literature [16]. The finite element model that contained initial residual stress was build up, it has been shown in Fig. 7. On the basis of above, VSR process was simulated by using transient dynamic analysis method, the residual stress dropped after VSR, residual stress distribution after VSR has been shown in Fig. 8, the surface residual stress in middle section of specimen corresponding to various amplitudes has been shown in Table 4.

According to Table 4, fitting out the curve in Fig. 9 by using least square method, it can be concluded that a quadratic function relationship between amplitude and residual stress on surface in middle section of specimen, as shown in Eq. (2):

$$\sigma r = 712.5A^2 - 563.7A + 405.6 \tag{2}$$

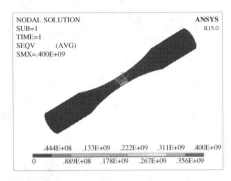

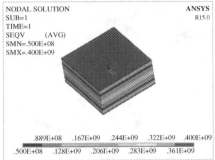

Fig. 7. The finite element model that contains initial residual stress

Fig. 8. The residual stress distribution in Z direction after VSR

Table 4. The surface residual stress in middle section of specimen corresponding to various amplitudes

Amplitude/mm	0	0.1	0.2	0.3	0.4	0.5
Surface residual stress/MPa	400	365	327	288	296	304

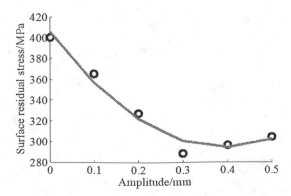

Fig. 9. The curve of amplitude and surface residual stress in middle section of specimen

It can be concluded that the surface residual stress decreasing with amplitude increased in a certain range, when amplitude reached to 0.3 mm, the surface residual stress was minimum 288 MPa in middle section, the residual stress can be rose again when amplitude continued to increased.

3.4 Fatigue Simulation of Specimen

The FE-safe software was adopted to fatigue simulation of specimen. FE-safe was developed by Safe Technology Company, and then acquired by Dassault Systems. A large number of materials and structures were test in the software development process. FE-safe is widely used in aerospace, automobile, shipbuilding industries, it is an excellent software for fatigue simulation.

On the basis of VSR, import result files to FE-safe after VSR from ANSYS, the fatigue simulation was conducted at stress ratio of -1 corresponding to 10^7 cycles, material was set to titanium alloy Ti-6Al-4V, surface roughness was set to $0.6 < Ra \leq 1.6\ \mu m$.

FE-safe will pop-up a result dialog box automatically when FE-safe analysis finished, and generate a suffix called .rst files, import the.rst files to ANSYS, the position of fatigue can be viewed, as shown in Fig. 10.

Figure 11 has been shown S-N curves that the results of fatigue simulation in initial and various amplitudes state. The fatigue limits have been shown in Table 5.

With the increase of amplitude, the fatigue strength of Ti-6Al-4V specimen also increased according to fatigue simulation. Fatigue strength reached maximum when amplitude was 0.3 mm, and fatigue limit increased from 380 MPa to 410 MPa. The fatigue strength and fatigue limit can be decreased when continue to increase the amplitude.

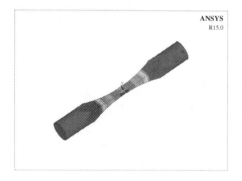

Fig. 10. The position of fatigue on specimen

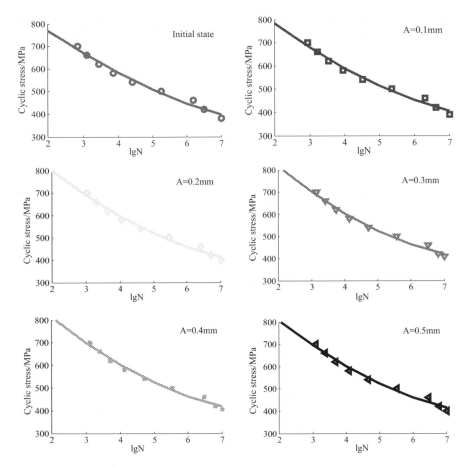

Fig. 11. Various amplitudes S-N curves

Table 5. The fatigue limits in the state of various amplitudes

Amplitude/mm	0	0.1	0.2	0.3	0.4	0.5
Fatigue limit/MPa	380	390	400	410	405	400

4 Conclusion

1. A linear relationship between amplitude and dynamic stress for titanium alloy Ti-6Al-4V, dynamic stress increased with amplitude increasing.
2. A quadratic function relationship between amplitude and residual stress on surface of specimen. The surface residual stress was minimum 288 MPa when amplitude was 0.3 mm. The residual stress can be rose again when amplitude continued to increase.

3. VSR can improve the fatigue life of Ti-6Al-4V in a certain range, and fatigue limit increased from 380 MPa to 410 MPa. The phenomenon of "much vibrated" can be occurred when continue to increase amplitude, which led to fatigue life dropped.

References

1. Zhang, Y.: The technology of high efficiency, energy saving and environment friendly in the 21st century. China Mech. Eng. **13**(19), 26–28 (2002)
2. Dawson, R., Moffat, D.G.: Vibratory stress relief—a fundamental study of its effectiveness. J. Eng. Mater. Technol. **102**(2), 169–176 (1980)
3. Gao, Y.Y., Lin, L.C.: Review of vibratory stress relief. J. Xiangtan Normal Univ. **15**(6), 23–26 (1994)
4. Buhler, H., Pfalzgraf, H.G.: Discussion on the reduction of residual stresses in work pieces made of cast iron. Werkstatt und Betreib **171**, 36–43 (1964)
5. Song, T.M.: Effect of vibration time-effect on fatigue life of welds and its mechanism. Acta Scientiarum Naturalium Universitatis Jilinensis (2), 55–58 (1997)
6. Wozney, G.P., Crawmer, G.R.: An investigation of vibration stress relief in steel. Weld. Res. Suppl. **23**, 411–419 (1968)
7. Sonsino, C.M., Muller, F., De Back, J., Gresnigt, A.M.: Influence of stress relieving by vibration on the fatigue behaviour of welded joints in comparison to post-weld heat treatment. Fatigue Fract. Eng. Mater. Struct. **19**(6), 703–708 (1996)
8. Jesensky, M.: Vibratory lowering of residual stresses in weldments. In: Proceedings of International Institute of Welding (IIW) Conference on Stress Relieving Heat Treatment of Welded Construction, Sofia, pp. 153–160 (1987)
9. Fang, D.X., Sun, F.H., Gong, Z.K., Jia, A.X., Qu, Y.A.: Improving fatigue life of welded components by vibratory stress relief technique. J. Exper. Mech. **6**(1), 89–95 (1991)
10. Lu, Y.P., Ma, Z.Y., Jia, Q.S., Gu, R.R.: Research on vibratory stress relief mechanism. Mech. Sci. Technol. **20**(4), 587–589 (2001)
11. Hu, Y.H., Wu, Y.X.: Interaction between residual stress and natural frequency in VSR. Mater. Res. Appl. **3**, 14–20 (2012)
12. Walker, C.A., Waddell, A.J., Johnston, D.J.: Vibratory stress relief—an investigation of the underlying processes. J. Process Mech. Eng. **1**, 51–58 (1995)
13. Liu, Y., Qu, Z.D., Wang, B.X.: Research development and application of titanium alloy TC4. Ordnance Mater. Sci. Eng. **28**(5), 47–50 (2005)
14. Wang, J.Y., Ge, Z.M., Zhou, Y.B.: Aeronautical Titanium Alloys. Shanghai Science and Technical Publishers, Shanghai (1985)
15. Leyens, C., Peters, M.: Titanium and Titanium Alloys. Wiley-VCH Verlag Gmbh & Co. KgaA, Weinheim (2003)
16. Wang, Q.C., Ke, Y.L., Zhang, Y.L.: Evaluation of residual stress depth profiling in 7075 aluminum alloy plates. Acta Aeronautica ET Astronautica Sinica **24**(4), 336–338 (2003)

Key Technique Research on Virtual Machine Management Based on KVM

Yue Li[1], Liqin Guo[2], Tingyu Lin[2], Hongyan Quan[1(✉)], and ShuangShuang Zhou[1]

[1] College of Computer Science and Software Engineering,
East China Normal University, Shanghai, China
hyquan@sei.ecnu.edu.cn
[2] State Key Laboratory of Intelligent Manufacturing System Technology,
Beijing Institute of Electronic System Engineering, Beijing, China

Abstract. One essential problem of cloud manufacturing is how to make full use of cloud resources,in order to meet the requirements of practical applications in the field of computer aided manufacturing. In this paper, we present an efficient virtualization solution for sharing resources, which is able to manage and monitor the performance of virtual machine (VM) under the common hardware environment with using the application program interface of *Libvirt*, machine management can be achieved efficiently. The kernel-based Virtual Machine (KVM) technique is an open source server virtualization and is employed for manipulating VMs. Better virtualization performance can also be acquired in the kernel mode of operating system. Especially, our method is based on web technique. User resources management and monitoring of VM are all achieved under the web environment. We demonstrate our results to show the validity of our scheme and provide qualitative evaluation to our method.

Keywords: Virtualization · Libvirt · KVM · VM

1 Introduction

Virtualization is one of key techniques for improving physical resources sharing and utilization in computing system for cloud manufacturing [1, 2]. In the past decades, virtualization technology has been studied systematically [3, 4]. According to the different fields of application, virtualization technology is divided into three types: server virtualization, network virtualization and storage virtualization.

Server virtualization is to improve the utilization of hardware resources, which aims to give full play to their functions and reduce economic costs [5]. In server virtualization, full virtualization including processors, memory, and I/O devices makes it possible to run multiple operating systems on a single physical platform [3].

In order to share these resources to multiple users more efficiently, hypervisor, also called VM monitor (VMM), is needed. Currently, hosted, bare-metal, and kernel-based virtual machine are the main types of hypervisor [6]: (1) *Hosted hypervisor*. VMware Workstation is the typical products of hosted hypervisor [7]. The hypervisor applications

© Springer Science+Business Media Singapore 2016
L. Zhang et al. (Eds.): AsiaSim 2016/SCS AutumnSim 2016, Part III, CCIS 645, pp. 540–546, 2016.
DOI: 10.1007/978-981-10-2669-0_58

like VMware Workstation and VMware Fusion provide functions like VM management [8]. (2) **Bare-metal hypervisor**. The typical products of bare-metal hypervisor include vSphere from VMware, Hyper-V from Microsoft, and XenServer from Citrix. It is unnecessary to install operating system since these products run directly on the bare metal and the client management software are located on the other computer [9]. (3) **Kernel-based virtual machine**. KVM is a full virtualization solution of kernel-based virtual machine for Linux on x86 hardware, which contains virtualization extensions. Intel VT and AMD-V are the virtualization technologies of Intel Company and AMD respectively. They are based on Linux kernel and regard the Linux host inside the kernel as hypervisor [8, 10]. Due to being a part of kernel, better performance of VM management can be gained.

Among the above hypervisors, vSphere solved the problem of virtualization effectively, but the application and promotion are limited by its commercialization [11]. On the other hand, Hyper-V provides free services, while it is short of GUI functions [10]. Compared to them, KVM offers strong and free virtualization services, while high performance management is also supported. XEN has a better performance than KVM in the CPU test, but KVM is better in disk I/O. Meanwhile, KVM has good performance isolation [12]. However, web services based tools have not been provided in KVM [6, 8]. Here, we present an efficient KVM based virtualization scheme to provide web services, which has three advantages:

1. **Free and efficient virtualization function.** Kernel based hypervisor is employed, which can keep high performance in resources sharing.
2. **Web service.** We set additional web layer between VM and KVM, which can supply convenient web services for efficient VM management. It is not just limited to the function of web services, manipulating and controlling VM conveniently in user browsers are also achieved without any additional client software.
3. **General template.** A general template is set up for constructing VM and employing the application program interface **Libvirt** provided by KVM, which provide convenient service for VM management. It has the advantage that users do not need to download operating system image files.

2   System Model

Our system model is made up of three layers [11]: VM level, control-manage level and hypervisor level, as shown in Fig. 1. In hypervisor level, VMM runs on physical machine. Being part of operating system kernel services, it provides better time performance and higher efficiency to access the physical machine. Hardware accessing in our system is achieved through the KVM, which is capable of separating physical machine into parts and allocating them to every VM user. As a result, for every VM user, the physical devices is occupied exclusively, which cannot be affected by others.

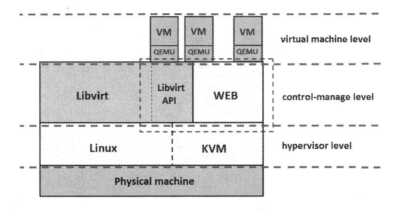

Fig. 1. Three-level schematic of our system model

2.1   Three-Level Structure Based on Web

Virtual machine level. KVM, virtualization of user PC simulation environment is achieved by QEMU [12, 13], which handles creating the context in user space and initializing the network and peripheral. For any user, if resources are shared in the cloud environment, application of creating VM can be sent to server at any time. After the authentication and permission validation, a customized VM can be created.

Control-manage level. In this level, web server checks the validity of customized parameter and record the VM information into database. In addition, this level provides the image of VM operating system (OS) and updates the VM information in database after system configuration files are set up by system,

Hypervisor level. This level handles allocating hardware resources in VM creation. In VM deletion, it recycles the allocated resources. Besides, it monitors the shared resources and deal with hardware exceptions.

Under the three-level structure, the VM creation and management includes the following steps:

1. Pre-processing.

Pre-processing includes the following work: (1) *libvirt* connecting, setting the server IP, port number and writing the parameters to the configuration file. (2) Database connecting. Under web structure, it is necessary to connect the database to manage VM and validate user information. (3) Authentication. To maintain security, the validity of any users must be checked.

2. Central section.

In VM creation, this section provides hardware allocation, creating OS image, and updating information in the database. In the VM management, it handles controlling the

VM starting up shutting down, OS installing, monitoring the resources usage and exceptions. Besides, VM management transmits and updates the run-time information of VM to server and records them into the database.

3. Exception handling and post-processing.

This section handles the exceptions and interruptions during VM running. When a user applies for VM deletion, it recycles the allocated resources, then updates the corresponding information and record into the database.

2.2 VM Creation and Management Algorithm

In this section, we will introduce VM creation and management using our three-level structures.

VM creation. Diagram of VM creation with three levels is shown in Fig. 2. The algorithm ***VM creation*** can be described as:

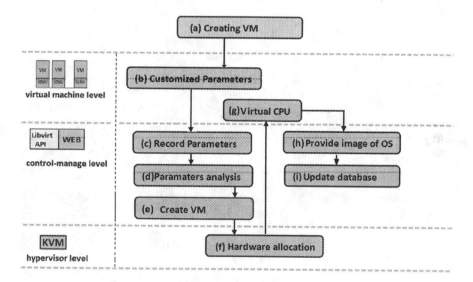

Fig. 2. Diagram of VM creation with three levels

Step 1: Customized parameters are inputted by users (see Fig. 2b).
Step 2: Our system records customized parameters into the XML data exchange file (see Fig. 2c), which will be detailed in the next section.
Step 3: Customized parameters are analyzed (see Fig. 2d).
Step 4: Create the customized VM using the function provided by ***Libvirt*** (see Fig. 2e).
Step 5: Cloud hardware is allocated to the VM by KVM (see Fig. 2f).
Step 6: QEMU emulates CPU on host (see Fig. 2g).
Step 7: Provide the image of OS for the customized VM (see Fig. 2h).
Step 8: Update the information of VM on the database (see Fig. 2i).
Step 9: End.

VM managing. Diagram of VM managing is shown in Fig. 3. We design function ***startup*** for starting up VM (see Fig. 3b–f), function ***Browsing*** for browsing VM (see Fig. 3g–h), function ***shutdown*** (see Fig. 3i–k) for turning off VM, function ***deleting*** for deleting VM (see Fig. 3l–o).

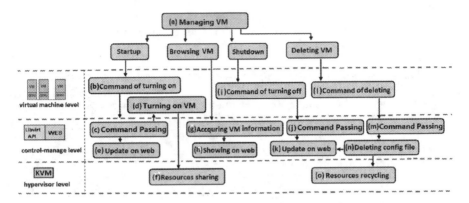

Fig. 3. Diagram of VM managing.

2.3   Data Exchange and General Template Scheme

Our method use XML files for data exchange. The inputted parameters from users are written into XML files for data exchange, while they are extracted and analyzed by the *domainDefineXML* function of ***Libvirt***

ServerInit.connect.domainDefineXML(docu.asXML());

The highlight of our work is providing a general template for VM creating. In the pre-process, a general template structure is written into the predefined XML file. When any user applies for VM creation, their requests can be met flexibly from coupling dynamic customized parameters to the predefined XML file.

3   Simulation and Discussion

Quantitative evaluations of the presented scheme are provided here. Our hardware platform is PC with Intel (R) Pentium (R) 2.67 GHz CPU, 6 GB memory. The memory and CPU performance under different conditions is tested in the experiment.

In order to test the memory and CPU performance, we employ the following ways. The first way uses VMware workstation, the second uses KVM on cloud service, and the last one takes the client browser to test.

We create different number of VMs and test the memory and CPU performance. We use the percentage of memory and CPU cost to evaluate. Figure 4(a) and (c) show an example with only one VM running. Figure 4(b) and (d) show an example with two VMs running.

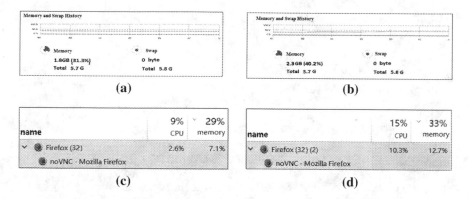

Fig. 4. Memory situation with different number VMs running

Meanwhile, performance of memory and CPU consumption is tested in the web environment. Memory and CPU utilization cost percentages are listed in Table 1. It can be easily seen that the KVM based method is better in memory and CPU cost performance, and the memory and CPU cost in the web environment is much better, which means the validation of our presented approach.

Table 1. Memory and CPU utilization rate of different methods

Number of VM	VMware workstation		KVM-visualized tools		KVM-Web	
	Memory	CPU	Memory	CPU	Memory	CPU
1	42 %	16 %	31.3 %	8.0 %	7.1 %	2.6 %
2	54 %	19 %	40.2 %	10 %	12.7 %	10.3 %
3	67 %	29 %	53.8 %	20 %	11.8 %	6.1 %
4	81 %	21 %	66.9 %	25 %	12.8 %	12.5 %

4   Conclusions and Future Work

In this work, we provide a solution of virtualization for resources sharing, which achieves free and efficient virtualization function. The highlight includes both web service and general template customized style. Our scheme can supply convenient web service for efficient VM management. Not just limited to the function of web service, manipulating and controlling VM conveniently in user browsers are also achieved without any additional client software. Hence, it will be rather significant to the practical application. Future work includes desktop transmission and virtualization based on VM management. Besides, memory management is another topic considered.

Acknowledgements. This work is supported and funded by the National High Technology Research and Development Program (2015AA042101), and special thanks to the reviewers for their valuable comments and suggestions.

References

1. Zhang, L., Luo, Y., Tao, F., et al.: Cloud manufacturing: a new manufacturing paradigm. Enterp. Inf. Syst. **8**(2), 1–21 (2012)
2. Wu, D., Greer, M.J., Rosen, D.W., et al.: Cloud manufacturing: strategic vision and state-of-the-art. J. Manuf. Syst. **32**(4), 564–579 (2013)
3. Uhlig, R., Neiger, G., Rodgers, D., Santoni, A.L., Martins, F.C.M., Anderson, A.V., et al.: Intel virtualization technology. Computer **38**(5), 48–56 (2005)
4. Song, X., Ma, Y., Teng, D.: A load balancing scheme using federate migration based on virtual machines for cloud simulation. Math. Probl. Eng. **2015** (2015)
5. Oguchi, Y., Yamamoto, T.: Server virtualization technology and its latest trends. Fujitsu Sci. Tech. J. **44**(1), 46–52 (2008)
6. Goto, Y.: Kernel-based virtual machine technology. Fujitsu Sci. Tech. J. **47**(3), 362–368 (2011)
7. King, S.T., Chen, P.M.: Operating system extensions to support host based virtual machines. Computing **23**, 19 (2002)
8. Ma, B.: VMware, Citrix and Microsoft Virtualization Technology Explanation and Application Practice. China Machine Press, Jiangsu (2013)
9. Kivity, A.: KVM: the Linux virtual machine monitor. In: Proceedings of Linux Symposium (2007)
10. Ren, Y.: Research on virtualised resources management platform based on VMware vSphere. Comput. Appl. Softw. **29**(5), 218–219 (2012)
11. Sun, L.: Virtual machine KVM and XEN performance analysis. Comput. Knowl. Technol. **10**, 2364–2366 (2013)
12. Bellard, F.: QEMU, a fast and portable dynamic translator. In: Conference on Usenix Technical Conference, pp. 41–46. USENIX Association (2005)
13. Yao, H.C., Wang, Z.Y.: Construction of virtualized resource pool based on KVM-QEMU with Libvirt. Comput. Modernization **1**(7), 26–29 (2013)

Flow Effect Simulation of River in Inland River Ship Simulator

Xiaoming Zhai, Yong Yin[⊠], and Helong Shen

Laboratory of Marine Simulation and Control, Dalian Maritime University,
Dalian 116026, China
{zhxml06, bushyin}@163.com, shenhelong@126.com

Abstract. To improve the reality of river visual in inland river ship simulator and meet real time of rendering, a method based on concept and property of steam function for solving velocity of river surface was introduced. The method generated values of stream function with real bank of river, and introduced the algorithm of inverse distance weighted (IDW). The velocity can be generated effectively, and the algorithm can be suitable to solve velocity of river branch channel. Simulation results show that this method can reflect the real distribution of river velocity, and satisfy the demand of real time and improve the environment reality of river visual in inland river ship simulator.

Keywords: Ship simulator · River · Stream function · Simulation

1   Introduction

Inland river ship simulator is one of navigation simulator, the research has made great progress in recent years. As one of import part of inland river ship simulator, river visual scene can effectively promote environment reality [1]. But river modeling is also based on the method of sea modeling in river visual of inland river ship simulator. Due to the difference of movement characteristics between seawater and river, the original method cannot reflect the flowing characteristics of river. Therefore, river scene which can improve the environmental sense of reality is an import research content in inland river ship simulator.

The motion of river is a complex phenomenon, which attract a lot of researchers in computer graphic field. River fluid simulation is mainly based on the physical-based method and procedural method. It can accurately construct velocity field of fluid with physical-based method, Shallow water equation (SWE) is mainly used to solve river velocity field [2]. Physically-based method is applied to fluid simulation, especially large scale river, which is difficult to achieve real-time rendering, it is reserved for off-line simulation or small domain real-time simulations. As simulating river and waterfall, it usually adopts procedural method which is on the basis of height field. Procedural method can compute velocity locally without doing simulation in a whole domain. Perlin extends Perlin noise for that purpose, but cannot handle boundaries nor global flowing [3]. Chenney proposes a tiling of velocity tiles, but this is not adapted to complex boundaries and obstacles [4]. Kniss and Hart demonstrate the idea of using the curl of Perlin noise for incompressible flow fields [5]; Robert extends to handle

L. Zhang et al. (Eds.): AsiaSim 2016/SCS AutumnSim 2016, Part III, CCIS 645, pp. 547–554, 2016.
DOI: 10.1007/978-981-10-2669-0_59

boundary conditions and other effects [6]. But this solution does not work with complex channel confined flows with branch and obstacles. At present, the representation is that Yu presents an algorithm baseing on procedural method for simulation of realistic flowing fluid in large virtual world [7]. The algorithm can compute velocity field of a steady flow given boundary conditions, such as river banks and obstacles. But they render river as flat surfaces with bump mapping using fake reflection and refraction in the implementation, like in most game engines. This very common technique has known limitations, especially at grazing view angles. Based on reference [7], Sena presents a new approach called SiviFlow for simulating watercourse in real time [8]. This improvement makes the algorithm much more flexible and adaptive for various river terrain. But the computation of algorithm is performed in CPU and the speed of algorithm need to be increased. Ran also introduces a novel river-simulating method which is familiar with reference [7, 8]. The method bases on Poisson disk distribution algorithm which can achieve a well-structured distribution pattern in screen space [9]. Rui uses GLSL to render flowing river fluid base on the above algorithm, and take advantage of parallel computing of GPU [10]. It can reduce CPU computation and helps to speed up the performance of the algorithm significantly.

In this paper, we adopt the curl of steam function to solve river velocity field base on above mentioned reference. The focus is on improving the algorithm of solving river velocity field, the new algorithm can adapt for river channel with branch and fixed obstacles. The velocity field be simulated in MATLAB, and can be used to render river surface.

2   Basis Theory for Solving River Velocity Field

Flow is one of main difference between sea model and river model, the theory and method of river model also differ from sea model. Figure 1 shows that the exiting river scene base on theory of sea model in inland river ship simulator. In this paper, we solve river velocity field base on the concept and property of stream function. Values of stream function in river channel are acquired by interpolating, and partial derivative of stream function is river velocity.

As we build mathematical model for solving river velocity, river fluid should meet: incompressible, boundary confined and flowing along certain direction. So we can introduce steam function for solving river velocity. The partial equation of streamline for 2D flowing fluid is as Eq. (1). The incompressibility of river field just is shown as Eq. (2).

$$-vdx + udy = 0 \tag{1}$$

$$\frac{\partial u}{\partial x} + \frac{\partial v}{\partial y} = 0 \tag{2}$$

This is necessary and sufficient conditions of $\psi(x, y)$, as following:

$$d\psi = \frac{\partial \psi}{\partial x} dx + \frac{\partial \psi}{\partial y} dy = -vdx + udy$$

ψ is called steam function, and the partial derivative of ψ is velocity vector component. We can obtain river velocity field as soon as computing the partial derivative of ψ in 2D river surface.

$$u = \frac{\partial \psi}{\partial x}, v = -\frac{\partial \psi}{\partial y} \tag{3}$$

Volume flow rate is related to the stream function values ψ placed on the channel boundaries. The volume flow rate is equal to the differences of stream function values respectively on the left and right boundary.

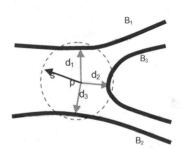

Fig. 1. River visual built on the basis of sea model

Fig. 2. Solve stream function of point P

3 Model Velocity Field in River Channel

3.1 Solving Velocity Field for Branching Channel

We introduce inverse distance weighted to build appropriate stream function. The reprehensive branching river channel is shown as Fig. 2. In order to calculate the stream function ψ, we use an interpolated scheme suggested by reference [7]. The following equations are used to obtain the steam function of point P.

$$\psi(p) = \frac{\sum_i w(d_i)\psi_i}{\sum_i w(d_i)} \tag{4}$$

B_i is the river boundary, d_i is the distance from point P to the each of the boundaries and the weighting factor W is:

$$W(d) = \begin{cases} d^{-p} \cdot f(1 - d/s), if & 0 < d < s \\ 0, & if \quad s < d \end{cases} \tag{5}$$

where s is the radius used to search for boundaries, p is a positive real number and f is defined as:

$$f(t) = 6t^5 - 15t^4 + 10t^3 \tag{6}$$

We must guarantee that at least two boundaries are inside every vertex search radius when we run the interpolated scheme. This guarantee is very important for effectiveness of algorithm.

3.2   Solving Velocity Field for Fixed Obstacle Region

Figure 3 shows that the basis situation of fixed obstacle in river channel. It is inappropriate to use the original method for calculating velocity field around fixed obstacle region. Therefore, we improve the algorithm to solve river velocity field on the basis of reference [7]. The boundary is just as the ordinary boundary of river channel. Velocity field around the region between river channel and fixed obstacle are calculated by using Eqs. (4) and (5). The only adjustment is to change search radius s for conforming to the algorithm. In order to obtain the values of steam function between river channel and fixed obstacle, the boundary values of obstacles need to be determined before interpolating.

At first, calculate the center value of obstacle based on Eqs. (4) and (5) suggested by reference [7], then use the center value as an estimation of the boundary value. Finally, river velocity field can be obtained by solving the derivative of steam function. In this paper, our method is similar to reference [7], but adopt precomputation to obtain d_i, in which d_i is the distance from point P to the each of the boundaries. Then the stream function can be calculated by Eqs. (4) and (5). In this paper, the improved method can be executed easily and the computation can be decreased.

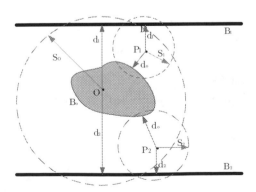

Fig. 3. Solve the stream function of point nearby obstacle

4 Simulation Results and Analysis

4.1 Simulate River Velocity Field

In this paper, the segment of Huangpu River in china is selected as study site for testing algorithm, the branching channel is added artificially for test, and the length of the simulated river is 15 km. The configuration of computer used in the simulation is: windows 7 system, Core 2 CPU, 2G RAM, NVIDIA Graphic card whose memory is 2G. MATLAB is used to simulated velocity field in river channel. The distribution of river velocity field generated in channels is shown as Figs. 4 and 5. The left figure is the whole distribution of river velocity in channel, and the right figure is local enlarge distribution of river velocity. As results shown, the distribution of velocity field can achieve the expected effect that the velocity field placed intermediate river channel is much more influenced by the boundaries. The velocity is faster and distribution is denser. The flowing trend of river fluid is obviously. The results accord with the IDW algorithm. The narrower the distance between river boundary and fixed obstacle, the speed of river is greater and the flowing effect is much more notable. On the contrary, the speed of river is smaller. The results can be met the conservation of volume flow between channels and there is no jump and break around fixed obstacle.

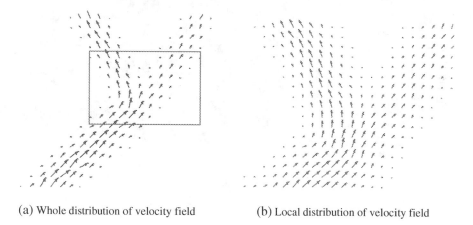

(a) Whole distribution of velocity field   (b) Local distribution of velocity field

Fig. 4. Velocity distribution branch channel

4.2 Render River Surface

After solved the river velocity field, the related technology and method are used to render surface in order to describe the river velocity field. In this paper, the focus is on modeling the river velocity field, it is to briefly introduce the process of rendering river surface. Sprite textures are utilized to implement the river fluid rendering. In order to

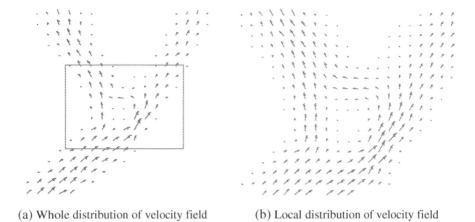

(a) Whole distribution of velocity field   (b) Local distribution of velocity field

Fig. 5. Distribution of velocity field around obstacle

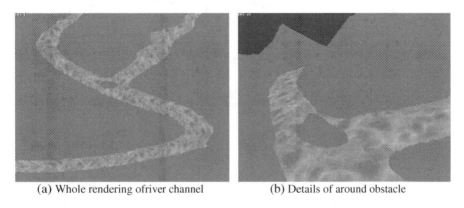

(a) Whole rendering of river channel   (b) Details of around obstacle

Fig. 6. Visualize river with fixed obstacle

reflect the river field effectively, the boundary sample algorithm is used to create the sample point onto the river velocity field. The rendering result is shown in the Figs. 6 and 7. Compared with the effect as Fig. 1 shown, dynamic flowing effects are obvious and accord with the water features. The poisson disk sample algorithm can be used to describe the river velocity field effectively, and the frame rate is greater than 40 fps which can satisfy the real time requirement.

Fig. 7. The whole visualization in Inland ship simulator

5 Conclusion

The flowing feature of river is one of important characteristic that can influence the environment reality of river scene. In this paper, we review the method on fluid simulation at home and abroad, and basing on the practical characteristics of inland river ship simulator, we introduce the stream function to solve velocity field of river surface during the river simulating, which can be much more realistically to simulate river fluid. In order to reflect the flow characteristics of river directly, we use particles generated by Poisson disk distribution to express river flow field, and superimpose river texture by Perlin noise disturbed. But we do not consider the situation of floatable obstacles in river channel, and the test results is just shown the current status not compare with the situation of exiting river scene. In future, the main research is focus on the interactive simulation between river fluid and floatable obstacles, and build similar river scene for testing the rendering result.

Acknowledgments. The authors would like to acknowledge the support from the National High Technology Research and Development Program of China ("863" Program) [No. 2015AA016404] and the Fundamental Research Funds for the Central Universities [No. 3132016310].

References

1. Zhai, X.-m., Yin, Y., Shen, H.-l., et al.: Review on methods of rendering of rivers in Inland river ship simulator. Navig. China **37**(3), 41–45 + 126 (2014). (in Chinese)
2. Tan, J., Yang, X.B.: Physically-based fluid animation: a survey. Sci. China Ser. F Inf. Sci. **52**(5), 723–740 (2009)
3. Perlin, K., Neyret, F.: Flow noise: textural synthesis of animated flow using enhanced Perlin noise. In: SIGGRAPH 2001 Technical Sketches and Applications (2001)
4. Chenney, S.: Flow tiles. In: ACM SIGGRAPH/Eurographics Symposium on Computer Animation, Grenoble, France, pp. 233–242 (2004)
5. Kniss, J., Hart, D.: Volume effects: modeling smoke, fire, and clouds. Section from ACM SIGGRAPH 2004 courses, Real-Time Volume Graphics [EB/OL] (2004). http://www.cs.unm.edu/~jmk/sig04_modeling.ppt
6. Bridson, R., Houriham, J., Nordenstam, M.: Curl-noise for procedural fluid flow. ACM Trans. Graph. (TOG) **26**(3), 46 (2007). ACM, USA
7. Yu, Q., Neyret, F., Bruneton, E., et al.: Scalable real-time animation of rivers. Comput. Graph. Forum **28**(2), 239–248 (2009). Blackwell Publishing Ltd.
8. Sena, D., Pereira, J., Costa,V.: Physics-based water interaction and shading: the SiViFlow algorithm. In: WSCG, pp. 49–60 (2013)
9. Jian, R., Ying, D.: River simulation based on Poisson disk distribution. J. Beijing Univ. Aeronaut. A **V38**(12), 1649–1652 (2012)
10. Rui, X.-p., Song, X.-f., Ju, Y.-w., et al.: Flow adaptive simulation of dynamic water body based on river velocity field. Przeglad Elektrotechniczny **89**(3b), 221–227 (2013)

Simulation and Big Data

An Approach to the Faster Than Real Time Distributed Interactive Simulation of Large Scale Systems

Yinghua Li[✉], Qian Wang, and Jiaxun Zhang

Institute of Spacecraft System Engineering, CAST, Postbox 5142-358,
Beijing 100094, China
liyinghua96@tsinghua.org.cn, wendy_letgo@163.com,
zhangjiaxun@yahoo.com

Abstract. The research is aimed at solving the problem of faster than real time distributed interactive simulation for large scale systems based on personal computer networks or workstation networks. The HLA services are integrated with the reflective memory networks and the sector minimization method are used in the study. An approach is proposed to solve the problem of faster than real time data transfer, ensuring the general speed of simulation and the speed of instantaneous synchronization for the large scale system simulation. A platform based on this approach provides interface services of which the call methods are the same as HLA. Using the platform, the existing HLA simulation systems can be conveniently migrated and new simulation systems can be developed and run in faster than real time.

Keywords: Large scale system · Faster than real time simulation · Distributed interactive simulation · High level architecture · Reflective memory network

1   The Background

A large scale system often contains thousands of systems of different kinds, such as terrestrial, oceanic, aeronautic, astronautic and cyberspacial etc. These member systems may interact with each other frequently. The general speed of simulation and the speed of instantaneous synchronization must be high for the simulation of large scale systems. The former high speed is needed for the multivariable/multi-parameter simulation and the comparison of simulation results of large samples. The latter high speed is needed for the join of the faster than real time simulation nodes and the cooperative simulation with them. If the large scale system simulation is run on one computer, the computer must be of great capabilities and will be very expensive, costing a lot to utilize, run and maintain it. Thus, the approach of running on one computer is not favorable to spreading applications. The fast distributed interactive simulation is the main approach to the large scale system simulation.

From 1990's, the development of HLA (High Level Architecture) technologies and high performance computers boosts the simulation and analysis work of complex systems. The exploration of the later technologies of grid simulation and cloud simulation et al. lays the foundations for sharing simulation resources widely and servicing a

© Springer Science+Business Media Singapore 2016
L. Zhang et al. (Eds.): AsiaSim 2016/SCS AutumnSim 2016, Part III, CCIS 645, pp. 557–565, 2016.
DOI: 10.1007/978-981-10-2669-0_60

great amount of users. But the existing technologies are difficult to implement the faster than real time simulation for the antagonism of large scale systems and the information flow of the space-air-ground integration systems, for the current simulation efficiency and speed are both low. Although high performance computers are used, it is still necessary to strike a balance between the model precision and the simulation speed. Therefore, the accurate simulation of these complex systems is still difficult to implement. It is necessary to develop the approaches and platforms of the faster than real time distributed interactive simulation for large scale systems.

2   The Situation

The HLA technologies are usually used to develop distributed interactive simulation systems for large scale systems. The HLA is a kind of high level architecture technologies of distributed interactive simulation, achieving the efficient interaction between simulation members. However, the synchronization speed of HLA is usually as slow as 100 ms per pace, for the foundation of HLA is ordinarily laid on the ethernet networks and TCP/IP protocols. Thus, the HLA technologies are far from the capability of the faster than real time simulation for large scale systems.

YAO Yiping et al. [1] established a high performance parallel simulation platform based on multi-kernel SMP computers or computer clusters. But its applications are restricted, because the platform depends on the expensive hardware and users need to be well qualified. Furthermore, the platform lacks a unified modeling framework to describe different kinds of equipments or systems. It cannot satisfy the requirements of the faster than real time simulation of large scale systems using workstation computer networks.

LI Bohu et al. [2] studied on the efficient simulation frameworks and algorithms for complex systems. They setup a cloud simulation platform of high compatibility and expansibility, using a cooperation mechanism to share different resources and to provide efficient simulation services. But this platform cannot satisfy the requirements of the faster than real time simulation of large scale systems either.

The grid simulation [3] and the cloud simulation [4, 5] technologies are based on the Web services. Their purposes are to provide simulation services to a large amount of users, not to model large scale systems and simulate them in faster than real time. They have superiority in expansibility and interaction (requesting services and providing services), sharing more resources of storage, computation, simulation etc. These technologies cannot implement the faster than real time distributed interactive simulation for large scale systems, because the fundamental communication protocols and hardware of them are based on internet or similar to internet.

The extensible modeling and simulation framework (XMSF) technology was introduced in 2002. Based on the Web technologies, it defines a group of standards, profiles, and rules for modeling and simulation [6]. The XMSF technology raises the expansibility and compatibility of the simulation framework, but cannot solve the problem of faster than real time.

HU Leshen et al. [9] developed a set of interface programs, such as communication service program, data service program and synchronization service program. These programs realize harmonious calling of reflective memory network services among a group of computers, and can be referenced by other applications of reflective memory networks. FENG An et al. [10] facilitated the data exchange of simulation models in the reflective memory network and raise the data exchange speed by 70 %–80 % relative to HLA-RTI (e.g., MAK-RTI) in Windows XP, using two kinds of technologies named encapsulator and capacitation program. But these technologies are some kinds of common combinations of the HLA technology and the reflective memory network technology. They also cannot satisfy the requirements of the faster than real time distributed interactive simulation for large scale systems.

There are many studies on the faster than real time distributed interactive simulation for large scale systems [12–21]. But by far, these efforts are still limited in the statistically high general speed, demanding high performance computers or hardware and restricting the computation time of simulation models. These studies cannot solve the kernel problems of the faster than real time simulation of large scale systems, and can only be fit for some specific cases, because their faster than real time speeds are not ensured in the simulation interface services and the data transfer mechanism of models.

To sum up, the problem of the faster than real time distributed interactive simulation for large scale systems is not solved at present. But the productions of many researches, such as the complex system simulation, the Advanced Distributed Simulation (ADS) etc., especially the advantages of the HLA distributed interactive simulation and the reflective memory network, favor our approach.

3 Problem Analysis

The main performance of the simulation system is decided by the running speed, the program flexibility and capacity. See Fig. 1. If the simulation programs are not flexible enough, the simulation entities or objects over a certain quantity cannot be modeled or loaded successfully. Thus the simulation system has a low capacity. If the large scale system can be modeled while the simulation system runs slowly, the real applications still cannot be implemented.

The flexibility and capacity of simulation programs are decided by the flexibility of the program framework, and the organization form and efficiency of the simulation models. These two factors affect each other to some extent, but the organization form and efficiency of the simulation models are more fundamental, for the upper level framework of the simulation programs is usually restricted by the organization form of simulation models of the lower levels. The simulation running speed is decided by the computation speed of simulation models and the information exchange speed (or the data transfer speed). Under the same hardware conditions of CPUs and networks, the simulation system runs faster if the model efficiency is higher. The models can be implemented by optimal algorithms and run parallel on CPUs and GPUs to raise the efficiency. The simulation speed is higher if the procedures of data

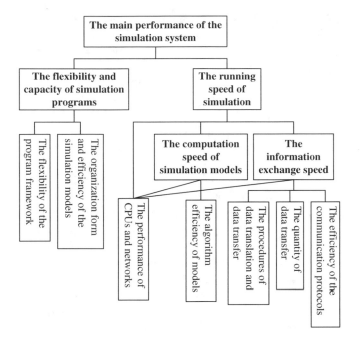

Fig. 1. The main performance of the simulation system

translation and data transfer are fewer, or if the quantity of data transfer is smaller, or if the efficiency of the communication protocols is better.

The key points of the faster than real time distributed interactive simulation for large scale systems are that the computation and data transfer of all procedures must be as fast as possible, that is, the models are carried out in optimal algorithms and the hardware is utilized as much as possible. The algorithms of simulation models are implemented differently in different application domains. As a research of universal methods, this paper focuses on the speed of information interaction and aims at solving the problem of faster than real time data transfer among simulation models or simulation members, especially solving the problem of data transfer among networks.

4   The Approach

4.1   The Basic Ideas

- The HLA services are closely integrated with the faster than real time networks, by a multiplication method, not by the popular addition method.

In the HLA technologies, there are advantages in the high level architecture, and disadvantages in fundamental communication usually based on the ethernet networks and TCP/IP protocols. Our approach makes use of the advantages of HLA, such as the publication/subscription of object/interaction classes, the group broadcast of messages and data, the simulation services of six classes. The disadvantages of low speed of fundamental communication in HLA are overcome by using high speed real time networks. The close integration of the HLA services and the faster than real time networks is made to setup a faster than real time simulation environment named F-RTI (Fast Run Time Infrastructure). See Fig. 2. This environment is a new platform which can be used to not only the faster than real time distributed interactive simulation of large scale systems, but also many other simulation applications. Based on the F-RTI, the HLA simulation systems already developed can run on this new platform at a high speed by only modifying the interface codes and replacing the fundamental programs of libRTI et al., obtaining a high general speed and a large scale simulation and avoiding wastes of simulation resources.

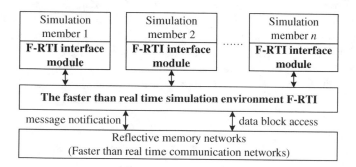

Fig. 2. The simulation framework

- The simulation models are organized by a uniform, space-air-ground framework of simulation objects, to improve the program efficiency of models as high as possible.

For a large scale system simulation, the development units are usually from different institutions or departments and the source codes of simulation models cannot be shared transparently because these codes are usually kernel technologies of the units. In the system integration of our approach, the models are organized by a uniform framework of simulation objects, to avoid adding information translation interfaces between models, and then to avoid reducing the efficiency of models. For detailed information of the framework of simulation objects, see References [13, 14].

4.2   The Key Points

- Key Point 1

The reflective memory network is used as the fundamental hardware and software of the HLA simulation. Based on the communication technology and synchronization technology of the reflective memory network, the RTI services of HLA are improved into F-RTI services, minimizing the bottom communication costs and making the simulation faster than real time.

The upper level programs of the F-RTI services are still the codes of HLA publication/subscription of classes, updating/reflection of objects, sending/receiving of interactions. The lower level programs of the F-RTI services are the message notification codes and the data block access codes of the reflective memory network. For example, when the reflective memory network products of GE Fanuc are used, the lower level programs are not the codes of calling the TCP/IP Socket of ethernet data transfer et al., but the codes of using RFM2gSendEvent to send messages, using RFM2gWrite to write data into the reflective memory, using the callback functions of RFM2gEnableEvent-Callback et al. to receive messages, using RFM2gRead to read data blocks from the reflective memory.

See Fig. 3. The interactive information in the distributed simulation is directly written into the data pool of the reflective memory. The receiver nodes also read data directly from the memory or perform some operations according to the message notifications received. The data blocks are accessed through the reflective memory, and the message notifications are also reflected on the memory. Thus the data transfer procedures are reduced the furthest. The data block access and message notification are both very fast, about 1 μs at a time, if 2Gbps reflective memory networks are used. This speed can satisfy the requirements of the faster than real time simulation. In Fig. 3, the solid state disks are used to increase the disk I/O speeds of the simulation nodes. The solid state disks and time synchronization hardware are utilized to ensure the performance of faster than real time.

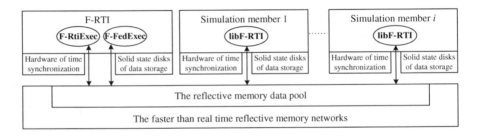

Fig. 3. The structure of the faster than real time simulation environment F-RTI

- Key Point 2

The basic simulation models, i.e. the behavior models of entities, are hooked on the uniform framework of simulation objects. See Fig. 4. The object classes defined in the framework are inherited by the interface object classes of distributed interactive simulation, e.g., the HLA object classes, and the HLA interaction classes. During the simulation run, the basic simulation models are called to update the attribute values of the simulation objects. Then the updated values are automatically assigned to the corresponding attributes of the interface objects.

The attributes of the interface objects use the names of the corresponding attributes of the uniform framework, but distinguished by a prefix "ms_". For example, when the *position* attribute of the *aircraft* class defined in the framework is updated by the object member function aircraftFlying(...), the corresponding attribute *ms_position* of the interface object is updated along with the state space of the *aircraft* object, using the automatic assignment mechanism *ms_position = position*.

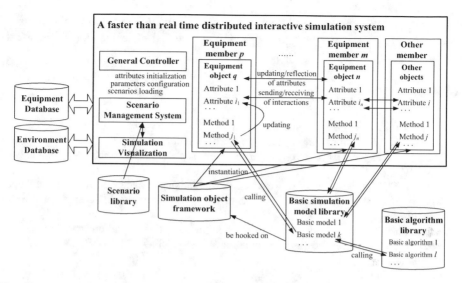

Fig. 4. The model integration of large scale simulation based on the simulation object framework

By this means, the basic simulation models and the HLA simulation interfaces are separated relatively and can be developed concurrently, thus the development efficiency and the degree of code inheritance of the programs are increased.

- Key Point 3

Two organization modes of the simulation system are provided. One is that all simulation members are in one federation (still using the terms of HLA). The other is that the more relative members are grouped into same federations and then federations are bridged together. In both modes, the foundation of simulation system is supported by the F-RTI and the reflective memory network. The bridge member is a special simulation member which is developed into a faster than real time simulation node by code modification of lower level programs similar to that described in Key Point 1, utilizing the interface functions of the reflective memory network and the current mature federation bridging technology.

5   Conclusions

In this paper, an approach is proposed to solve the problem of faster than real time transfer of simulation data and to ensure the general speed of simulation and the speed of instantaneous synchronization, based on an idea of close integration of the HLA services and the faster than real time networks. By this means, a faster than real time simulation environment F-RTI is described, in which the advantages of the high level architecture of HLA and the advantages of the reflective memory network hardware are combined sufficiently. Using this high speed platform of F-RTI, not only the simulation systems already developed can be inherited, but also new simulation applications of large scale systems can be promoted and implemented. The technology is worth spreading applications.

References

1. Yao, Y., Liu, G.: High-performance simulation computer for large-scale system-of-systems simulation. J. Syst. Simul. **23**(8), 1617–1623 (2011). (in Chinese)
2. Li, B., Chai, X., Li, T., et al.: Research on high-efficiency simulation technology of complex system. J. CAEIT **7**(3), 221–228 (2012)
3. Peng X., Li, N., Cai, Z., Xiao, Z.: Research on simulation grid and its applications. In: Super Forum of Global Manufacture and 21st Century Seminar of Simulation Technologies (2004) (in Chinese)
4. Li, B., Chai, X., Hou, B., et al.: Networked modeling & simulation platform based on concept of cloud computing "Cloud Simulation Platform". J. Syst. Simul. **21**(17), 5292–5299 (2009). (in Chinese)
5. Gao, W., Kang, F., Zhong, L., et al.: Cloud simulation technology based on HLA evolved. J. Syst. Simul. **23**(8), 1643–1647 (2011). (in Chinese)
6. Zhong, W., Hao, J., Huang, J., et al.: The integration and demonstration of emerging open standards on XMSF. J. Natl. Univ. Defense Technol. **32**(2), 146–151 (2010). (in Chinese)
7. Blais, C., Brutzman, D., Drake, D., Moen, D., Morse, K., Pullen, M., Tolk, A.: Extensible Modeling and Simulation Framework (XMSF 2004) Project Summary Report, ADA431159 (2005)
8. Li, H., Wu, S.: Hardware-in-the-loop simulation system of communication satellite countermeasure based on HLA and reflective memory network. J. Syst. Simul. **18**(6), 1520–1523 (2006). (in Chinese)
9. Hu, L.: Research on real time simulation environment and its applications. Master Dissertation of Northwestern Polytechnical University, March 2006 (in Chinese)
10. Feng, A., Du, C., You, T., et al.: A study of entity operating mechanism based on federate paradigm with VMIC. Comput. Measur. Control **18**(4), 912–915 (2010). (in Chinese)
11. Xiao, W., Er, L., Xie, T., et al.: Research on data communication real-time based on shared-memory mechanism micro-computer real-time network. J. Syst. Simul. **16**(8), 1717–1720 (2004). (in Chinese)
12. Wu, Y., Song, X., Gong, G.: Real-time load balancing scheduling algorithm for periodic simulation models. Simul. Model. Pract. Theory **52**(1), 123–134 (2015)
13. Li, Y., Li, Y., Liu, J.: An HLA based design of space system simulation environment. Acta Astronaut. **61**(1–6), 391–397 (2007)
14. LI, Y.: A design of the simulation framework of space systems SSSOTL V2.0a. Technical report of China Academy of Space Technology, WY-ZTSEJB445 (2013) (in Chinese)
15. Brunett, S., Gottschalk, T.: A large-scale metacomputing framework for the ModSAF real-time simulation. Parallel Comput. **24**(12), 1873–1900 (1998)
16. Li, Y., Li, Y., Yang, Y., Ge, X.: An HLA based design of collision simulation system for large-scale LEO objects. In: ICICTA 2009, pp. 3–6, July 2009
17. Chessa, M., Bianchi, V., Zampetti, M., et al.: Real-time simulation of large-scale neural architectures for visual features computation based on GPU. Comput. Neural Syst. **23**(1/4), 272–291 (2012)
18. Nicol, D.M., Liu, J., Liljenstam, M., Yan, G.: Simulation of large-scale networks using SSF. In: 2003 Winter Simulation Conference (WSC 2003), vol. 1, pp. 650–657 (2003)

19. Gong, W.-B., Cassandras, C.G.: Real-time simulation technologies for complex systems. ADA372150,AFRL-IF-RSTR-1999-245
20. Wehage, R.A., Petzold, L.R.: Real-time simulation of large-scale multibody systems using automated equation decoupling techniques. ADA281544,ARO30980.1-MA
21. Gonzalez, F.G.: Real-time simulation and control of large scale distributed discrete event systems. Procedia Comput. Sci. **16**, 177–186 (2013)

The Application of Big Data Technology in the Field of Combat Simulation Data Management

Li Guo[(✉)], Wenyuan Xu[(✉)], Hao Li, Shengxiao Zhang, and Dongmei Zhao

China Shipbuilding Industry Systems Engineering Research Institute, Beijing, China
guolicssc@163.com, xwy0987@sina.com

Abstract. The impact of big data technology in the field of traditional simulation is analyzed, an effective way to verify and develop the big data applications in the field of simulation within a small and controllable range is presented, and that is with the aid of big data technology to promote technological progress in the field of combat simulation data management. At the same time, the combat simulation data classification and big data characteristics are researched in depth, big data problems faced by the construction of combat simulation data engineering are summed up, the construction objectives and significance of combat simulation data management platform are defined. Based on big data technology, the research of combat simulation data management platform is carried out, which provides a feasible solution for the application of big data technology in the field of simulation.

Keywords: Big data technology · Combat simulation data · Data management platform

1 Introduction

Following the cloud computing and networking technology, big data is a disruptive change in the field of information technology. The arrival of the era of big data has brought great changes to human life, science and technology activities have also been an unprecedented challenge. Facing the big data from the field of science and engineering, the subject of modeling and simulation based on engineering is facing opportunities and challenges. In the traditional modeling and simulation field, data is only a basic condition for the simulation operation test of models, and in the era of big data, data can be the main body of discovery, as long as the data is large enough, scientific discovery can rely on the data to be completed. Scientific discovery is made possible without mathematical model, which is bound to impact the traditional simulation technology based on the precise and quantitative analysis. It can be predicted that the simulation technology and methods will develop along with the development of the science of big data. It will be an important direction to research the organic fusion of big data and existing simulation theory, experimental model, simulation calculation model in the field of simulation.

Combat simulation is an important application of the simulation technology in the field of defense. With the development of science and technology, combat simulation

© Springer Science+Business Media Singapore 2016
L. Zhang et al. (Eds.): AsiaSim 2016/SCS AutumnSim 2016, Part III, CCIS 645, pp. 566–573, 2016.
DOI: 10.1007/978-981-10-2669-0_61

gradually transforms from the independent small scale simulation to system, large-scale distributed collaborative simulation. In the traction of new military requirements, the throughput of military simulation data is increasing, the update speed is higher and higher, and the document data for data representation and message transmission has a large number, a variety of types and complex structure. Big data is with 4V features and emphasizes interdisciplinary, multiple types of data integration and utilization, big data technology can promote technology progress in the field of combat simulation data management, can also verifies and develops the big data application of simulation field in a smaller, controllable range.

2 The Overview of Combat Simulation Data

Combat simulation supports the combat research by simulating the combat process. Combat simulation data is the basis for combat simulation, which is the quantitative representation of the information of various objects in the war system. Because the war system has characteristics of complexity, including multi-level, multi-factor multi-domain, emergence and pathological, and the simulation data described the various entities, the operational activities of entities, and the interaction between entities also has the characteristic of complexity, mainly reflected in the extensive, multifocal and mutual relation.

Combat simulation data relates to the battlefield environment, weapons, combat theories, operations, scenario tasks and other types of data, before targeted data management, analysis and application, it is first necessary to analyze the composition of the combat simulation data. Through the analysis of the data requirements of the typical combat simulation tasks in the combat simulation system, the combat simulation data can be classified by different stages of the combat simulation process, mainly include: basic data, configuration data, scenario data, model data, situation data, and evaluation and analysis data, as shown in Fig. 1.

- Simulation basic data. The sort of data doesn't change with the changes in the specific simulation content, which is characterized by a large amount of data, involving a wide range, and the relative stability. Mainly including equipment technical and performance indexes, basic geographic information data, combat targets, various types of combat document template, military symbols, etc.
- Simulation configuration data. The sort of data is related to the organization and management of combat simulation activities, and the system operation configuration. Mainly including the configuration operation solutions, data collection program, hardware and software configuration information and a series of documents, as well as simulation step size, the operation control strategy, etc.
- Simulation scenario data. The sort of data changes with the changes of the simulation scenario and combat plan. Its essence is the information which describes the specific simulation training activities by text, charts and other forms of document, Including the battlefield environment data, combat purpose, combat plan, and combat group.
- Simulation model data. The sort of data is used to describe entities, equipments and the interaction between them in the combat simulation activities. Mainly includes the entity model, equipment model, behavior model, etc.

- Simulation situation data. The sort of data reflects the distribution and movement of the combat entities in the battlefield. Situation data mainly refers to the entity information and the interactive information between entities, which are produced during the simulation operation process.
- Evaluation and analysis data. The sort of data is the result that is generated by using the evaluation analysis system to analyze the simulation process data.

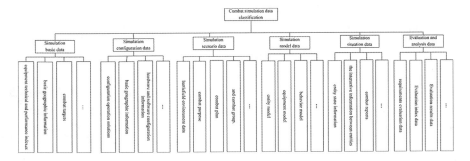

Fig. 1. Combat simulation data classification

The combat simulation data is derived from the analysis and understanding to the war and its related factors, which possesses the characteristics of various types, large quantity and wide range. The multi-source and heterogeneous characteristics of combat simulation data have brought great challenges to the overall management of data and the reuse of data assets.

3   The Analysis of Combat Simulation Big Data Problem

3.1   The Big Data Features of the Combat Simulation Data

With the development of information technology, combat simulation data has jumped out of the scope of the traditional relational data, more and more highlights the characteristics of big data, the specific performance in the following aspects:

- Feature 1: the source of data is wide; the amount of data is large.

Under the background of the era of big data, the sources of combat simulation data are increasingly diversified, the total amount of data is increasing as geometric series. Features: (1) command information system begins to pay attention to acquiring data from public media information, these types of data are complex and large volume, such as the history of wars, the military topography; (2) with the development of the information level of weapons and equipments, the weapon and equipment platform produce various types of technical and tactical data continuously, the total amount of this type of data increasing large; (3) with the development of the command mode based on information system, the commanding organization produces a variety of combat command original data and data products in the command process continuously, and the amount of this kind of data gradually increases;

(4) with the promoting of the storage technology, equipment test, simulation test and training exercises continue to accumulate more and more data.

- Feature 2: the data has so much variety; non-structured data has large proportion.

While the total amount of data is increasing, the type of combat simulation data is increasing continuously. Due to all kinds of combat simulation data derive mostly from different information systems and the data has so much variety, including structured data, such as DMP, rtcom, txt, also contains non-structured data, such as avi, m4v, MP3, BMP, non-structured data has large proportion.

- Feature 3: producing fast, requirements of the processing and analysis technology are high.

With the development of command information system, obtaining data and storing data quickly and accurately are possible, however, the increasing of the amount of data and the complexity of data structure and relationship puts forward very high requirements for the technology to filter, process and analysis data. To filter out the information which can be used as the combat simulation data from the mass information source, the technologies to deal with and analyze the data are needed.

3.2   The Problem Analysis for Combat Simulation Big Data

Obviously, the traditional IT infrastructure and data management and analysis methods already cannot adapt to the rapid growth of combat simulation data, the new data management mode and the processing and analyzing technologies for big data need to be used to solve the problem. After analysis, the problem faced by the combat simulation big data can be summarized as the 5 categories listed in Table 1:

Table 1. Problems faced by combat simulation big data

Problem categories	Problem description
facets of processing velocity	I/O
	Statistical analysis
	Search query
	Real time response
facets of categories and structure	Multiple sources
	Heterogeneous
	The underlying architecture of the original system
facets of value mining	Data analysis and data mining
	The actual efficiency of data mining
facets of storage and security	Structure and non-structured
	Data security
	Privacy security
facets of communication and data sharing	Data standards and interfaces
	Sharing protocols
	Access permission

- The problem of processing velocity. Combat Simulation provide the "battle lab" for military personnel, the data adopting from weapon equipment test, training exercises, simulation experiments, the history of wars, military topography, statistical calculation is the foundation and support for combat simulation. Big data era, with the increasing of the amount of data above, how to import the mass data to the laboratory and apply the data has become the main problem faced by combat simulation data management. Previous combat simulation data management most uses the relational database management system to centralized store and process data, without using distributed architecture. In the face of the import and export, statistical analysis, retrieval query of large amounts of data, due to the dependence on centralized data storage and index, system performances decline rapidly with the growth of data quantity. To real-time response statistics and query scenarios, this kind of system is powerless.
- The problem of categories and structure. Combat simulation data usually come from different information systems and different data sources, the data may contain text, pictures, video, vector map etc. For different types of combat simulation, the format of data is usually not fixed, if the use of structured storage model will be difficult to deal with the changing needs. For these different types of multi-source heterogeneous data, it is needed to use different storage and processing mode, which combine the structured and non-structured data storage methods. To the data management mode and the whole architecture, it is need to adopt new distributed file systems and distributed NoSQL database architecture in order to fit for the large data quantity and structure change.
- The problem of value mining. Currently, the construction of the combat simulation data engineering is still in the initial stage, how to manage combat simulation data assets effectively in order to sharing the data between the different departments and project groups, it is a key value embodiment to combat simulation data assets, and also an important objective of the construction of combat simulation data engineering. The traditional data mining algorithm usually is used to the situation of small amounts of data, the algorithm is relatively complex, and the convergence rate is slow. The amounts of combat simulation data is larger and larger, in order to realize effective value mining, the methods to store, clean, ETL (extraction, transformation, loading) data need to the requirements and challenges of coping with the large amount of data.
- The problem of storage and security. Combat simulation data are mostly classified data, requirements of the data storage and security are stricter, in addition to ensure that data is not lost, reasonable redundancy backup policy is necessary, but also the protection of data from unauthorized access and steal is needed, only the user who has the permission to access the database can query and use the data. At the same time, a large number of non-structured data may require different storage and access policy, so it is an immediate problem to solve that form a unified security access control policy for multi-source, heterogeneous data.
- The problem of data sharing. To realize the integration of data across systems, it is necessary to develop uniform data standards, exchange interface and sharing agreement, in order to the different formats data derived from different departments can

be access, exchanging and sharing based on a uniform rules. For data access, it is need to develop a detailed access rights based on confidentiality provisions.

4 Combat Simulation Data Management Platform Based on Big Data Technology

In order to solve problems faced by the combat simulation big data, combined with the requirements of the construction of combat simulation data engineering project to the systems engineering research institute (SERI), a Combat simulation data management platform is built based on big data technology. SERI is composed by several departments, each department focuses on different specialty and produces a large number of structured and non-structured data during the processes of the equipment test, training exercises, simulation experiment, in which the non-structured data including TXT, DAT, JPG and avi, MPEG and so on, these data is stored in different departments dispersedly, the data utilization rate is not high and the data cannot be sharing between different departments. To realize the data unified storage, centralized management, and more effective data accumulation and utilization, to provide a efficient, stable and secure data resource pool, dig data value deeply, and resolve big data problems that may be encountered during the construction process of the combat simulation data engineering project, the research and construction of the combat simulation data management platform is carried out.

By using enterprise-level, mature and stable distributed architecture, The platform provide an open and advanced distributed data management solution based on the idea of Share-Nothing; the data querying and retrieval operation is to accelerate by making full use of parallel computing, distributed query planning, multi-dimension index, multi-level partitioning technology; The platform uses the distributed memory processing framework to improve data retrieval and access speed. It achieves unified storage for structured, semi-structured and non-structured data by integrating several storage models, including Row-Storage, Volume- Storage and mixed storage model.

It integrates the data privacy protection, information security technology to solve the problem of privacy and security, and it solves the requirements of storing, managing and scheduling large-scale data by using data de-duplication technology, data storage redundancy technology, data scheduling technology, and data traceability technology. The platform architecture is shown in Fig. 2.

- Infrastructure layer. It contains servers, storage facilities, networks and other physical equipments.
- Data source layer. It contains the structured and non-structured data of all the departments in the experimental network, and the combat simulation data collected in the external network.
- Data collection layer. The processing methods Include ETL, manual entry, bulk load and special equipment import. The existing decentralized structured and non-structured data is bulk loaded by ETL, and that is operated automatically on-demand, the new obtained combat simulation data is imported the combat simulation data management platform by a set frequency. The manual entry function is provided

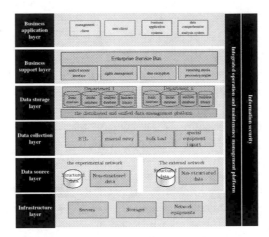

Fig. 2. The architecture of combat simulation data management platform

under the special security level. The bulk load function is required by user to provide a real-time combat simulation data load. The special equipment import is special to the combat simulation data which is collected in the external network and the amount of that is large.

- Data storage layer. It contains a distributed and unified data management platform and some virtual storage pools for the different departments. The distributed unified management data platform includes distributed data warehouse, distributed storage and distributed information retrieval modules, which adopts a unified, distributed, parallel architecture based on the memory calculation technology, manages all structured, semi-structured and non-structured data, and provides a unified access interface. Distributed information retrieval module is used to reverse index text files, word files, etc., to build a reverse index based on the contents of the file, to provide full text retrieval. Based on the distributed unified data management platform, the logic independent storage resource pool is provided to all the departments, the own basic database, theme database, analysis database, business library, and non-structured file storage space and capacity allocation can be built according to need to the departments.
- Business support layer. Includes unified access interface, rights management, data encryption, streaming media processing engine and ESB. The streaming media processing engine is used to process the image, audio and video, which provides the ability to retrieve the multimedia files.
- Business application layer. It includes the management client, the user client, all kinds of business application systems and data comprehensive analysis system. The management client achieves organizational maintenance, personnel maintenance, rights management, space allocation and other functions. The user client is use of importing, exporting, modifying, and searching of the data and files by users.
- Integrated operation and maintenance management platform. It is used to monitor, manage and alarm the operation status of the equipment of the storage center, and other maintenance management.

- Information security. It uses security management services and intelligent security card to achieve the double security.

5 Conclusions

By the analysis of the types and the big data characteristics of combat simulation data, this paper puts forward the problems of combat simulation big data, and defines the target and significance of the construction of the combat simulation data management platform. Based on the big data technology, the research of the combat simulation data management platform is carried out, which provides a feasible solution for solving the problem of combat simulation big data and the construction of the combat simulation data engineering.

References

1. Zhang, H.: Data Engineering for Combat Simulation. National Defense Industry Press, Beijing (2014)
2. Tang, J., Cha, Y.: Verification, Validation and Accreditation and Credibility Evaluation for Warfare Simulation System. National Defense Industry Press, Beijing (2013)
3. Hu, X.: The challenges and thoughts faced by simulation and modeling in the big data era. Mil. Oper. Res. Syst. Eng. 27(4), 5–12 (2013)
4. Li, J.: Big data science simulation theory, methods, platforms and technology. Syst. Simul. Technol. Appl. 15, 2–6 (2014)
5. Bi, C.: Modeling and simulation are geared to challenge in the age of big data. Comput. Simul. 31(1), 1–3 (2014)
6. Cai, Y.: Analysis of joint combat simulation data system. Syst. Simul. Technol. 9(1), 38–44 (2013)
7. Li, M.: Research on data for combat simulation. Command Control Simul. 32(4), 71–74 (2010)
8. Meng, X., Ci, X.: Big data management: concept, technology and challenge. J. Comput. Res. Dev. 50(1), 146–169 (2013)
9. Gong, J.: Construction and application of big data processing system for naval operations. Command Inf. Syst. Technol. 6(2), 22–26 (2015)
10. Xue, Q.: Study on data mining for combat simulation. J. Sichuan Ordnance 34(8), 93–95 (2013)
11. Gao, H., Zhang, H.: Research and implementation of military simulation data aggregation framework. Fire Control Command Control 34(2), 150–152 (2009)
12. Tao, W., Cui, T.: The design of combat simulation situation data model. J. Geomatics Sci. Technol. 35 (2010)
13. Xue, Q., Cao, B., Tang, Z., Pei, H.: Discussion on data mining for the M&S technique in armored equipment support. Syst. Simul. Technol. Appl. 13, 563–567 (2011)
14. Wei, J.: Data management in naval fleet battle simulation system. J. Syst. Simul. 20(8), 2011–2013 (2008)

A Public Safety Deduction Framework Based on Real-Time Big Data

Bin Chen[✉], Yuyu Luo, and Xiaogang Qiu

College of Information System and Management,
National University of Defense Technology, Changsha 410073, Hunan, China
nudtcb9372@gmail.com

Abstract. Under the instruction of Public Safety Network, the research on public safety management based on the big data of human space-time behavior has become the main work in academic field. The traditional researches only focus on the discovering of statistical laws from big data. The problems such as dynamic increasing of big data, the relationships between human behavior in micro view and public management in macro view, and the relationships between data perception in real world and scenario deduction in virtual artificial system are easily ignored. Therefore, the integration of big data for urban population distribution modeling is proposed to solve the problem of big data integration. Real-time big data driven public safety scenario deduction system framework is proposed to find the most optimal emergency decision plan. ACP approach based public safety emergency decision method is proposed to apply the game theory in real public safety scenarios. Two specific safety scenarios are chosen to study from evacuation in streets and park, chemical gas leak in ports and chemical industrial area. The computational experiments are designed according to the requirements of public safety scenario to apply real-time big data. The main work can be summarized as following: big data collection from internet of things for public safety, multi-paradigm modeling based urban population distribution modeling by big data integration, computational experiments of crowd in specific situations, the applications of emergency decision analysis is for public management. Based on iterations of interactions between micro and macro views, real world and virtual systems, the research can be used to solve the problems in real public management application.

Keywords: Big data · Public safety scenario · Safety scenario deduction system framework · Public safety emergency decision

1 Introduction

With the development of a series of emergencies, the academic fields and government pay more and more attention to the research of big data, public management and especially the fusion of them. Many tragedies give us lessons about the lack of public security management measures such as the oil pipeline explosion event of Qinghai in 2013, the stampede in shanghai Chenyi square in the eve of lunar in 2014, and Tianjin port 812 big explosion event in 2015. But because the emergency itself is complex and the

© Springer Science+Business Media Singapore 2016
L. Zhang et al. (Eds.): AsiaSim 2016/SCS AutumnSim 2016, Part III, CCIS 645, pp. 574–584, 2016.
DOI: 10.1007/978-981-10-2669-0_62

construction of emergency management system is independent, it is difficult to construct different events perception and processing system for all kinds of emergencies. According to this situation, academician Weicheng Fan suggest "the public safety network is a vertical and horizontal interconnection and virtuality and reality combination big-scale complex system, which regards emergency, hazard-affected carriers and emergency management as core research objects and the relationship between them as core factor. The public safety networks extend to every social cell, monitor every angel, cover all related information and interconnect the vertical and horizontal parts; the vertical part involves all government levels and the horizontal one includes all regions." in the "national public security science and technology development strategy research" academic conference on the 2015 big consulting project of Chinese academy of engineering. Following the public triangle theory, this is a new theory concluded by experts in emergency management region based on many years' study. As the research focus on the industry, the focus of public safety network includes the real-time big data collected by public safety Internet of Things (IOT), the data analysis is combined with public safety situation, as well as calculation and decision analysis service.

This paper puts forward a public safety deduction framework based on real-time big data under the guide of public safety network theory and ACP (Artificial Societies, Computational Experiments, Parallel Execution). The following parts include: in Sect. 2, we introduce the research of big data briefly, and point the problems and challenges existed; in Sect. 3, we discuss the reduction hierarchical relationship between big data and public safety situation; in Sect. 4, we put forward a public safety scenario deduction system framework which is driven by real-time big data; in Sect. 5, we give examples of public safety deduction system in streets, scenic spots, ports and chemical industry areas separately; in Sect. 6, we conclude the whole paper.

2 Problems and Challenges

There are plenty of fruits about big data, for example, the latent social law can be analyzed by the method, which include traditional space-time behavior analysis based on questionnaire survey data [1, 2], space-time behavior analysis based on GPS, LBS and GIS data [3, 4], and space-time behavior analysis based on social media data. But there are still many problems existed when we research on the public safety deduction problem:

(1) The start point of research focuses on big data of all industry, and does not regard basic urban population data as support, so it is difficult to research on the validity, reliability and integrality from global perspective.

(2) The exploration process between big data itself, statistical rules and mechanism is completed, and the model mechanism is extracted. But there is no multiple mechanism model to combine the macro regularity which is presented by micro big data together, and conclusions are still independent from each other.

(3) Just do one-way research, that is to say, the current research only explores the behavior from micro to macro, but ignore the reverse effect. Besides, they just

find the rules and analyze them, but do not study how to solve actual problems by using the rule.

(4) Put most emphasis on the mining and analysis on existing data, but do not consider the dynamic growth of big data, besides, the research on how to construct big data analysis mechanism driven by dynamic data is not sufficient.

(5) Most of current research is used in city planning, commercial activity, large gatherings, industry internal communication and so on. The research on how to use big data to support public management is relatively few.

Building the decision-making technologies which interact with the real world closely under the background of dynamic big data is the key issue for the problem of how to combine emergency decision with public safety scenarios. But as carrier of public safety scenario problem, the public safety scenario deduction system should not be a system based on static data. Traditional public safety scenario deduction system is supported by deduction model, such as multi-dimensional space method suggested by Yi Liu's team in Tsinghua University [7], scenario deduction system based on GERTS suggested by Sifeng Liu's team in Nanjing Aerospace University [8], the incident scene construction and inference method suggested by Xuping Wang's team in Dalian University of Technology [9]. Those traditional scenario deduction methods put emphasis on the effect of model methods in deduction, and the deduction is built in an abstract level, besides, the deduction process is relatively closed and does not interactive with actual factors in public safety scenario, so it can't support scenario deduction on dynamic data driven condition. In order to solve this problem, the public safety deduction system framework which can support dynamic data must get rid of the basic effect of deduction model in deduction process and use bottom-up deduction mode. Multi-agent simulation technology is a popular system developing method at present. ACP method suggested by Feiyue Wang in Automation of Chinese Academy of Science is a perfect deduction idea. Combining ACP method with big data analysis and digging methods, this paper puts forward a public safety scenario deduction framework based on real-time data, and starts from macro-micro interconnection and virtuality-reality interaction those two levels to construct a quantitative and reusable public management deduction system platform for urban public management.

3   The Status of Public Safety Scenario Deduction

Starting from urban population space-time big data, the public safety scenario deduction system based on real-time data provides emergency decisions for public safety. The deduction system builds a bridge between micro-macro combination level and virtuality-reality interconnection level. Big data fusion, public safety scenario deduction and public safety emergency decision based on ACP are three levels in which the data from real world are cleaned and abstracted firstly, then those data evolve and iterate repeatedly in artificial/virtual system, that is to say this is a process from real-time big data integration to scenarios and then to management decisions, and from micro level to macro level. The situation of public safety scenario deduction in macro and micro level, real world and artificial system is as in Fig. 1.

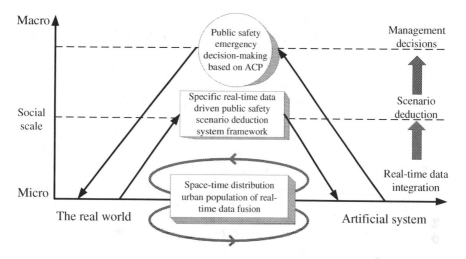

Fig. 1. The relationship between big data, scenario deduction and emergency decisions

4 Specific Real-Time Big Data Driven Public Safety Scenario Deduction System Framework

4.1 Scenario Deduction System Framework

Considering existing problem of scenario deduction research which is based on big data, the design of public safety scenario deduction system framework is as Fig. 2. From macro level, public safety scenario can divided into normal state and emergency state. Many social sensors and physical sensors are used in scenario deduction framework to monitor the real world, such as streets, ports, chemical industry areas, scenic spots and so on. When analyzing collected data, if we find the state monitored satisfies the condition on which the emergencies happen. On the one hand, warning signal should be provided in micro level, on the other hand, the public safety scenario should be switched into emergency state. Using artificial system which is mapped from the real world and

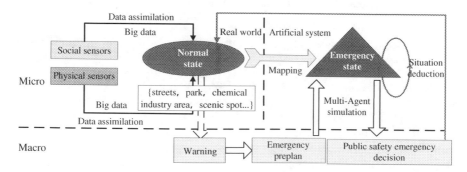

Fig. 2. The specific public safety situation deduction system framework with real-time data injection

multi-agent simulation technology to do repeated deduction for scenario deduction, thus the best emergency preplan is obtained, so we can achieve the purpose to provide emergency aid decision for public safety management.

In this scenario deduction system framework, the key technologies need to be solved are: the fusion technologies of urban population space-time distribution metadata and model, population space-time distribution model prediction based on data assimilation, dynamic urban population space-time distribution model framework, as well as quantitative risk analysis, warning analysis and emergency decision of public safety scenarios. In this section, we will discuss those related technologies.

4.2   Metadata and Model Fusion Methods of Urban Population Space-Time Distribution

Those technologies such as 3S technology, IOT and mobile Internet can be used to observe human behavior continuously and from full range, so the urban population behavior big data obtained are in a form of discrete, have different structure and describe complicated object. Starting from the perspective of global space-time behavior, and on the premise of restricting space (four scenarios), time (daily), object (urban active population) and behavior (urban population flow), the urban space-time distribution metadata describe meaning, form, data and action mechanism of all kinds of big data. By abstracting the general expression paradigm of population space-time big data, and constructing urban population space-time distribution metamodel based on urban population space-time distribution metadata, we can provide basic support for the fusion methods of multi-region population space-time models.

The fusion of population space-time distribution models is to solve the problem of comprehensive data fusion in macro level which can not be solved in micro level. The multi-paradigm modeling method can be introduced to solve the problem that the model abstracted from big data is in a form of discrete, and the core of this method is the design of model paradigm transition. Besides, the transition is bidirectional, that is to say, not only the transition from domain model paradigm to urban population space-time metadata is supported, but also the transition from urban population space-time metadata to domain model is supported. On the premiere of ensuring causality and consistency, the complete correction mechanism is provided for all domain models.

4.3   The Population Space-Time Distribution Model Prediction Methods Based on Data Assimilation

The population space-time distribution model prediction methods based on data assimilation build a complete set of model framework to couple dynamic injection data, macro and micro state transition, population distribution state equation and population distribution state estimation equation. Using the population distribution state at t−1, population distribution state estimation equation, and dynamic injection data, we can estimate population state at time t, as in Fig. 3. The core research of the method is the state transition of macro and micro population distribution as well as the designing of population distribution state estimation equation.

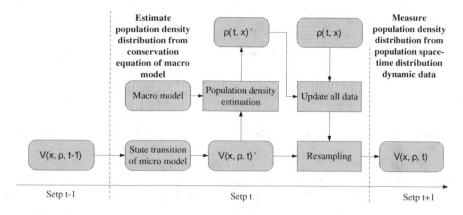

Fig. 3. The population space-time distribution model prediction methods based on data assimilation

4.4 Dynamic Space-Time Distribution Model Framework of Urban Population

Based on data assimilation method, dynamic urban population space-time distribution model framework injects the urban population space-time dynamic data which is obtained by the IOT of public safety into models, and get dyanmic space-time distribution model of urban population. In macro level, it abstracts population space-time distribution as state space of data assimilation system. And then, combining all of those and urban population distribution model, it designs population space-time distribution estimate equation. The model framework is as in Fig. 4.

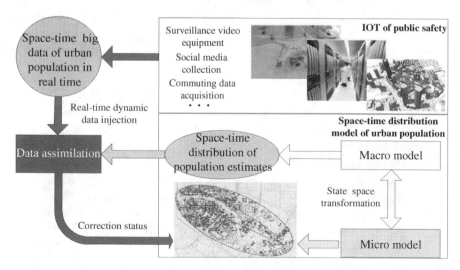

Fig. 4. The space-time distribution model framework of dynamic urban population

Based on the urban population space-time distribution of real-time big data fusion methods which use multi-paradigm modeling, many kinds of population behavior models can be build, such as netizen space-time distribution model, mobile phone user distribution model, mobile phone user behavior online model, taxi commuter model,public transport commuter model and so on. Based on population space-time distribution metadata and using the multi-paradigm modeling methods, we can design conversion methods for each of those big data model. By abatracting those data model to related level, we can get population space-time distribution model clusters. The basic idea of general system theory can be used in model clusters. According to principle of causality and consistent principles of time and space, the model clusters are fused, thus, the dynamic population space-time distribution model is produced. The obtaining of urban population space-time distribution data is as in Fig. 5.

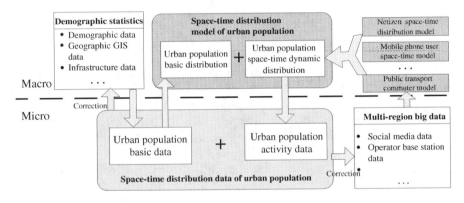

Fig. 5. Space-time data of urban population

4.5   The Quantitative Risk Analysis, Warning Analysis and Emergency Decision of Public Safety Scenarios

The quantitative risk analysis,warning analysis and emergency decision of public safety scenarios construct a bridge between artificial world and real world in public safety scenario deduction system framework. They are concentrated reflection of the part P idea in ACP method and are the basic basis of scenario deduction and the purpose for public safety problem. Taking typical public safety scenario—the crowd stampedes as an example, the key process of quantitative analysis is to design individual/crowd game model in evacuation process. In evacuation process, supported by limited information, individual/crowd will do the game to maximize his own survival probability. And the game can be cooperative or incooperative. So on the one hand, we have to obtain real-time population space-time distribution to predict possible game results, such as the total population in streets, the maximum population capacity of street, population, the population density distribution in street and street population flow; on the other hand, we need to arrange guiding persons properly, distribute appropriate evacuation information and guide the evacuation game from incooperative to cooperative to both guarantee individual's safety and minimize the risk of total crowd. The research emphases in this aspect is to design different guiding person arrangement plan, different evacuation information distribution plan. Under the support of dynamic real-time data, we can calculate the optimal decision based on individual/group basic behavior rules.

For quantitative warning analysis of public safety scenarios, the key lies at evaluating the probability and possible consequence or loss. Event tree, fault tree and bowknot model can be combined with expert opinion to evacuate this quantitatively, then by generating safety accident risk map for specific area, the safety situation can be very clear. The implementation of safety measures will change this map, then change the real system. The results of real system can be used to evacuate validity of related safety measures in turn.

The key of risk analysis for social safety emergencies such as Kunming terrorist attack is to construct offensive and defensive game model. This model is a two-person game consisting of public safety management part (e.g. the government emergency personnel) and potential enemies (terrorist attackers). It is generally believed that public safety management part will meet complete rational person hypothesis and the potential enemies just have limited ration. At the same time, in game process, information obtained by enemy is regarded as complete and perfect, but defender can only get incomplete and imperfect information. The policy sets of the two parts are described by discrete strategy model. The total profit of two parts is nonzero.

So we can conclude key points of emergency decision of social safety emergencies as follows:

(1) how to model enemy who is not entirely rational;
(2) how to describe the incomplete information of enemy;
(3) how to construct game policy set for those two parts;
(4) how to calculate their benefit matrix reasonably;
(5) how to design the algorithm which can slove the benefit matrix quickly so that real-time results can be obtained when rejecting dynamic data into model.

5   The Scene of Public Safety Scenario Deduction

On the basis of the public safety scenario deduction system framework above, and combining it with typical public safety scenarios, such as streets, scenic spots, ports and chemical areas, this paper puts forward corresponding system framework.

5.1   The Scenario of Population Evacuation in Streets and Scenic Spots

Population evacuation is a common public safety scenario for streets and scenic spots, if proper emergency preplan is not used in the crowded condition, the crowd stampede may happen. Figure 6 presents working process of public safety scenario deduction system of streets and scenic spots' population evacuation. For real streets and scenic spots, cameras can be used to collect video data. In dynamic surveillance process, dynamic poplation distribution information can be found through those data. At first, orginal public safety scenario data are used to initialize artificial streets system, then when dynamic data are injected into system to monitor real-time population distribution, the evaluation capacity can be used to judge whether normal state should be switched to emergency state, if it is switched into emergency state, the process will move to the calculation of population evacuation emergency preplan, the dynamic optimal preplan will be obtained after repeated iteration. Referring to this preplan, we can manage the process of population evacuation emergency management for streets and scenic spots.

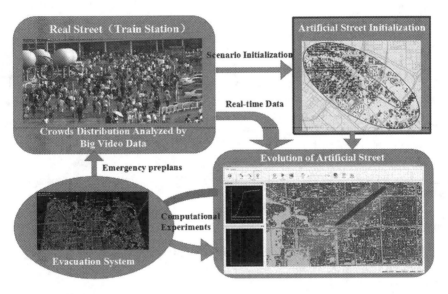

Fig. 6. The public safety scenario deduction system of streets and scenic spots' population evacuation

5.2   The Scenario of Toxic Gas Dispersion in Ports and Chemical Industry Areas

The common public safety scenarios in ports and chemical industry areas are the explosion of dangerous compound and toxic gas dispersion. The deduction system aiming at this kind of public safety scenario can be seen in Fig. 7. Fixed environment surveillance station and airborne toxic gas sensors are used to monitor environment gas in ports and chemical industrial areas, once the density of toxic gas exceeds standard, public safety scenario will be switched from normal state to emergency stata. At the same time, artificial chemical industrial area system starts to calculate the dispersion process and dispersion sources. The range of influence will be found after repeated computational experiments, then the emergency management system will be activated to form the optimal processing schemes. Those schemes can be consulted when dealing with emergency disposal problem in ports or chemical industrial areas.

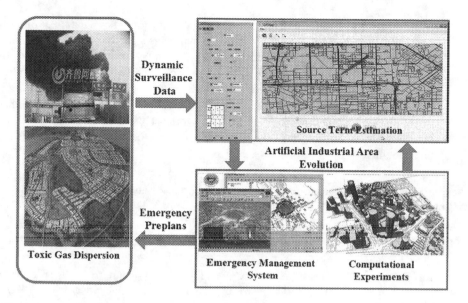

Fig. 7. The public safety scenario deduction system of ports and chemical industrial areas' toxic gas dispersion

6 Conclusion

The public safety scenario deduction framework based on real-time data in this paper starts from macro-micro interconnection and virtuality-reality combination those two levels, and sloves public safety problem by using mutual supporting and repeated iteration methods. The characters of this framework can be concluded as follows:

(1) Fuse multi-source big data by changing the macro and micro perspective constantly. At first, in order to find "common language" for different kinds of big data, it designs urban population space-time distribution metadata in macro level; then using model paradigm transition to make big data in different micro level get interactive capability; finally it fuses urban population space-time distribution metadata in macro level to form an union urban population space-time distribution model which is based on multi-source big data.

(2) Achieve models' mutual correction in macro and micro level. Because big data sets have a characteristic of multi-source and multi-region, micro data can be used correct macro model, and the macro model can be used to guarantee the correctness of big data, and even find errors in big data in turn. At the same time, this method can provide an approach to correct and verify risk decision methods. In this way, the defects of traditional risk analysis methods such as they can only explain results after events but can not predict and warn before events, and they can not be validated by experiment will be compensated.

(3) Under the joint action of specific public safety scenario deduction and emergency decision methods, emergence from micro level to macro level (the crowd early

warning), controls from macro level to micro level (the crowd evacuation guiding) will be achieved, besides, the micro behaviors will cause macro regulations and the macro regulations will guide micro behaviors. Equally, from the perspective of virtuality-reality combination, artificial system is constructed using the real world data collected by IOT and the emergence will cause emergency events warning, thus by doing emergency decision analysis in artificial/virtual system; control plan can be formed and then feedback to the real world. This iterative acting process between the real world and artificial system will achieve the purpose of public safety management.

Acknowledgement. The authors would like to thank National Nature and Science Foundation of China under Grant Nos. 71303252, 61503402, 61403402, 61374185, 91024032.

References

1. Zhang, W., Chai, Y.: Urban citizens' moving and activing system restricted by space and time. The Thesis and Model Development of Activity Analysis. Int. Urban Plann. **24**(4), 60–68 (2009)
2. Chai, Y., Shen, Y., Xiao, Z.: The research development and practical application prospect of space-time behavior. Geogr. Sci. Prog. **31**(6), 667–675 (2012)
3. Kwan, M.P., Lee, J.: Geo-visualization of Human Activity Patterns Using 3D GIS. A Time-geographic Approach, pp. 48–66. Oxford University Press, Oxford (2004)
4. Edwards, D., Griffin, T., Hayllar, B.: Using GPS to track tourists spatial behavior in urban destinations. SSRN (2009). http://dx.doi.org/10.2139/ssrn.1905286
5. Malleson, N., Birkin, M.: Analysis of crime patterns through the integration of an agent-based model and a population microsimulation. Comput. Environ. Urban Syst. **36**(6), 551–561 (2012)
6. Cranshaw, J., Schwartz, R., Hong, J.: The livehoods project: utilizing social media to understand the dynamics of a city. In: 6th International AAAI Conference on Weblogs and Social Media (ICWSM 2012), Dublin, Ireland vol. 6, pp. 4–7 (2012)
7. Qian, J., Liu, Y., Liu, C., Jiao, Y.: Multi-dimension scenario space-time methods and their application in scenario deduction. Syst. Eng. Theor. Pract. **35**(10), 2588–2595 (2015)
8. Bier, V.M., Azaiez, M.N. (eds.): Game Theoretic Risk Analysis of Security Threats. Springer Science and Business Media, Berlin (2008)
9. Wang, X., Yang, X., Fan, S., Ruan, J.: Research on construction and deduction methods of unconventional emergencies. J. Univ. Electron. Sci. Technol. **1**, 22–27 (2013)
10. Wang, F.: Artificial society, calculation experiment and parallel system—the discussion about complex social economy system calculation research. Complex Syst. Complex. Sci. **4**, 25–35 (2004)

Numerical Simulation and Optimization Analysis of Anti-/De-Icing Component of Helicopter Rotor Based on Big Data Analytics

Long Chen[1], Yidu Zhang[1], Qiong Wu[1(✉)], Zhengsheng Chen[2],
and Youyun Peng[2]

[1] State Key Laboratory of Virtual Reality Technology, School of Mechanical
Engineering and Automation, Beihang University, Beijing, China
wuqiong@buaa.edu.cn
[2] Department of Science and Technology, AVIC Changhe Aircraft Industry Co.,
Ltd., Jingdezhen, China

Abstract. A numerical optimization method of helicopter rotor composite material anti-/de-icing component based on big data analytics was proposed. Considering the uneven distribution problem of the temperature field on the iron surface of the rotor composite material anti-/de-icing component, the multi-parameter heat transfer numerical simulation model of the rotor composite material anti-/de-icing component was established based on big data analytics. The environment of the composite material anti-/de-icing component was simplified. Linear heat conduction temperature field optimization method was proposed. The optimization program was determined by using orthogonal test method combined with the composite material anti-/de-icing component multi-parameter model. The optimized temperature field distribution on the iron surface of the composite material anti-/de-icing component meets the anti-/de-icing requirements through the finite element numerical simulation based on big data analytics of the rotor composite material anti-/de-icing component. Thus, the temperature field numerical simulation of the rotor composite material anti-/de-icing component with multi-parameter under a big data environment is effectively achieved. Simulation results show that the optimization effect is more evident than the non-optimized temperature distribution with the optimized results of the proposed method. Results verify the effectiveness of the proposed method.

Keywords: Big data analytics · Composite material anti-/de-icing component · Temperature field · Finite element numerical simulation · Optimization method

1 Introduction

In recent years, the evolution of communication and digital storage technologies allowed the collection of a significant amount of information. Thus, the need for effective ways of maintaining, accessing, and processing data efficiently increased. In this context, the term "big data"has become widely used. The rapid development of big data resulted in new

© Springer Science+Business Media Singapore 2016
L. Zhang et al. (Eds.): AsiaSim 2016/SCS AutumnSim 2016, Part III, CCIS 645, pp. 585–601, 2016.
DOI: 10.1007/978-981-10-2669-0_63

opportunities and challenges to various disciplines in different fields. According to McKinsey, a well-known management consulting firm, data penetrated every area of industries and business functions, and the use of big data indicated a new increase in productivity growth and consumer surplus [1]. Big data are subject to analysis and content calculation. Deep learning and knowledge computing are the basis of data analysis, whereas visualization is the key technology for data analysis, and presentation of results [2]. The multi-variable factors that influence the mathematical model, the problems of big data analysis, and the subsequent big data information mining must be considered in conducting complex analysis of numerical simulation results under a big data environment, particularly for multi-field coupling to solve the model.

Big data analytics is an emerging field because massive storage and computing capabilities are made available by advanced electrical infrastructures [3]. Traditional statistical methods focus on small data and not suitable for big data analysis. Seung-Joo Lee et al. proposed efficient big data analysis using principal component analysis, a popular method in multivariate statistics [4]. Peter Baumann et al. suggested a solution for coverage-type datasets; this solution is based on an array of high-performance database technologies and involves the adoption and enhancement of standards for service interaction (OGC, WCS, and WCPS) [5]. Jean-Pierre Belaud et al. introduced a lightweight computing platform for scientific simulation, collaboration in engineering, 3D visualization, and big data management. The open platform is available for collaborative simulation and scientific big data analysis [6].

Ice protection systems, which are essential equipment of all transport category aircraft, are used to ensure compliance with airworthiness requirements in icing conditions [7]. Icing causes helicopter rotor lift decrease and instability, which could result in stalling or crash [8–11]. The primary means to preventing accreting ice is installing a composite material anti-/de-icing component on the rotor surface. The voltage and electric current of the heating wire are controlled in the composite material anti-/de-icing component to achieve anti-icing and deicing effect [12, 13]. The structure of the composite material anti-/de-icing component is shown in Fig. 1.

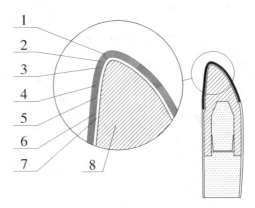

1. Iron Surface 2. Adhesive Film 3. Heat Transfer Layer 4. Heating Wire 5. Heat Insulation Layer
6. Adhesive Film 7. Skin of Rotor 8. Rotor

Fig. 1. Structure of composite material anti-/de-icing component.

The composite material anti-/de-icing component consist of multilayer composite components. The thermal performance of each composite material layer is complex. When the rotor functions in high-speed rotation and in a low-temperature environment, the heat transfer process of the rotor composite material anti-/de-icing component is related to the coupling effect of the external convection heat transfer of the flow field and internal heat conduction in the multilayer composite components. Heat transfer analysis of the rotor composite material anti-/de-icing component becomes highly complicated because of the effect of electric wire disposition in the rotor composite material anti-/de-icing component. Previous studies indicate that the iron surface temperature field distribution of the rotor composite material anti-/de-icing significantly affects the efficiency of eliminating ice. The uneven temperature field distribution of the iron surface leads to the failure of ice melting in some local areas on the rotor, and exacerbates the icing of these areas, which seriously threatens flight safety through the loss of maneuverability and controllability of a helicopter [14]. Therefore, this paper proposes a numerical simulation optimization method for rotor composite material anti-/de-icing component based on big data analytics considering the complexity of variable parameters in heat transfer analysis and multi-field coupling. The simulation results show that the optimization effect is more evident than that of the non-optimized temperature distribution based on the optimized results of the proposed. Thus, the effectiveness of the proposed method is verified.

2 Rotor Composite Material Anti-/De-Icing Component Information Management Simulation

Temperature field coupling optimization analysis that uses numerical simulation for rotor composite material anti-/de-icing component optimization analysis involves many variable parameters with multi-field coupling. The weighting factors of each interacting parameter are not identical, which complicates the temperature field coupling optimization analysis. Figure 2 shows the interrelations of multi-variable parameters in the multi-field coupling.

Figure 2 shows that the temperature field is mainly associated with multi-layer parameters such as heating wire, external flow field and anti-/de-icing component. The heating wire is involved in electric current, electric voltage, electrical resistivity, heating wire disposition and other parameters. The external flow field is involved in flow velocity, environment temperature, liquid water content (LWC), median volumetric diameter (MVD), and other parameters. The anti-/de-icing component is involved in rotor speed, thermal conductivity, thickness, layer angle, layer order, adhesive thickness, and other parameters.

2.1 Basic Assumptions

Based on the preceding analysis, the following assumptions are set in the information management of the numerical simulation analysis of the rotor composite material anti-/de-icing component:

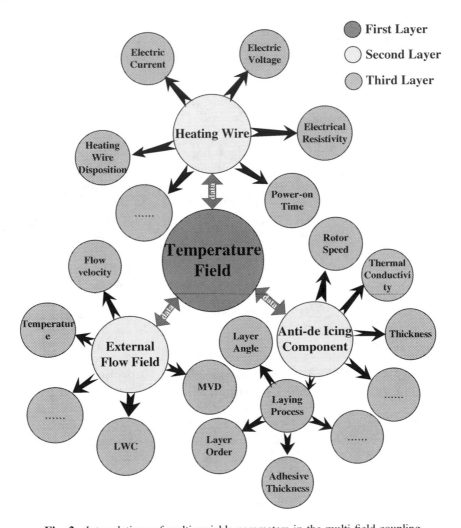

Fig. 2. Interrelations of multi-variable parameters in the multi-field coupling

- Internal heat transfer of rotor composite material anti-/de-icing component is assumed to be a 2D steady heat transfer problem.
- A minimum temperature of 2 °C of the iron surface is considered to achieving the desired effect in the process of anti-/de-icing.
- The droplet is spherical and does not break up before its impact on the iron surface.
- The forces acting on the droplets include drag, viscous resistance, gravity, and air lift.
- The droplets do not affect the flow field.
- The initial droplet velocity is equal to air velocity.

2.2   Thermodynamic Analysis Model of Flow Field Based on Big Data Analytics

The iron surface of the rotor composite material anti-/de-icing component is the research object, and the styles of its external ice are mainly divided into rime ice, glaze ice, and mixed ice. The types of heat transfers of the external flow field vary and correspond to different types of icing. In the ice-free state, heat convection is the heat transfer type of the external flow field of the iron surface. Convective heat transfer occurs between the iron surface and high-speed flow of air. Different shapes of ice exist on the iron surface during the icing state. Thus, heat conduction occurs. In the mixed icing state, and under the action of anti-/de-icing component, parts of the ice on the iron surface area melt into liquid water and parts of the liquid water on the surface evaporate and sublimate, forming a dry surface. Other parts of ice would still exist and exacerbate the icing of these areas. The thermodynamic analysis model of external flow field is established based on big data analytics through the preceding analysis.

A Flow Control Equations

The flow field is assumed to be incompressible and fully turbulent. The governing equations are continuity equations, momentum equations and energy equations. The standard k-ε turbulence model (Launder and Spalding [15]) is applied to estimate turbulence effects.

The continuity equations:

Air:

$$\frac{\partial \rho}{\partial t} + \frac{\partial (\rho u_j)}{\partial x_j} = 0 \tag{1}$$

Super cold droplet:

$$\frac{\partial (\alpha \rho_w)}{\partial t} + \frac{\partial (\alpha \rho_w u_{wj})}{\partial x_j} = 0 \tag{2}$$

The momentum equations:

Air:

$$\frac{\partial (\rho u_i)}{\partial t} + \frac{\partial (\rho u_j u_i)}{\partial x_j} = -\frac{\partial p}{\partial x_i} + \frac{\partial}{\partial x_j}\left[\mu\left(\frac{\partial u_i}{\partial x_j} + \frac{\partial u_j}{\partial x_i}\right)\right] - \frac{\partial}{\partial x_j}\left(\rho \overline{u_j' u_i'}\right) \tag{3}$$

Super cold droplet:

$$\frac{\partial (\alpha \rho_w u_{wi})}{\partial t} + \frac{\partial (\alpha \rho_w u_{wj} u_{wi})}{\partial x_j} = \frac{3}{4}\alpha \frac{C_D \mathrm{Re}_{wi}}{d_{eq}^2/\mu}(u_i - u_{wi}) + \alpha(\rho_w - \rho)g_i \tag{4}$$

Where d_{eq} is the mean effective diameter of a droplet based on big data, α is the volume factor, C_D is the drag coefficient.

The Energy Equations:

Using the standard k-ε equation model as the control equations turbulence model of air phase and combining the Reynolds stress with time average velocity gradient by the concept of Boussinesq eddy motion viscosity coefficient, the equation is given as follow:

$$-\rho \overline{u'_j u'_i} = -\frac{2}{3}\delta_{ij}\rho k + \mu_t \left(\frac{\partial u_j}{\partial x_i} + \frac{\partial u_i}{\partial x_j}\right) \tag{5}$$

$$\mu_t = c_\mu \rho \frac{k^2}{\varepsilon} \tag{6}$$

The turbulent kinetic energy equation and dissipation rate equation can be written:

$$\frac{\partial (\rho u_j k)}{\partial x_j} = \frac{\partial}{\partial x_j}\left[\left(\mu + \frac{\mu_t}{\sigma_k}\right)\frac{k}{\partial x_j}\right] - P_k - \rho\varepsilon \tag{7}$$

$$\frac{\partial (\rho u_j \varepsilon)}{\partial x_j} = \frac{\partial}{\partial x_j}\left[\left(\mu + \frac{\mu_t}{\sigma_\varepsilon}\right)\frac{\varepsilon}{\partial x_j}\right] + c_{\varepsilon 1}P_k - c_{\varepsilon 2}\rho\frac{\varepsilon^2}{k} \tag{8}$$

$$P_k = -\mu_t \left(\frac{\partial u_i}{\partial x_j} + \frac{\partial u_j}{\partial x_i}\right) \tag{9}$$

The values of parameters in the above equations are shown in the Table 1:

Table 1. Control equation values.

Parameters	$c_{\varepsilon 1}$	$c_{\varepsilon 2}$	c_μ	σ_k	σ_ε
Value	1.44	1.92	0.09	1	1.22

B The Thermodynamics Model

The thermodynamics model is the extend Messinger model [16], based on Stefan problem which is a generic method of phase change. The governing equations can be written as follows:

$$\frac{\partial T_i}{\partial t} = \frac{k_i}{\rho_i C_{pi}}\frac{\partial^2 T_i}{\partial y^2} \tag{10}$$

$$\frac{\partial T_w}{\partial t} = \frac{k_w}{\rho_w C_{pw}}\frac{\partial^2 T_w}{\partial y^2} \tag{11}$$

$$\rho_w \frac{\partial h_w}{\partial t} + \rho_i \frac{\partial h_i}{\partial t} = m_{im} + m_{in} - m_{e,s} \tag{12}$$

$$\rho_i L_F \frac{\partial h_i}{\partial t} = k_i \frac{\partial T_i}{\partial y} - k_w \frac{\partial T_w}{\partial y} \tag{13}$$

Where Eqs. (10) and (11) are the energy equations of ice and water layers respectively, Eq. (12) is the mass conservation, Eq. (13) is the phase change condition at ice-water interface. And ρ_i, T_i, k_i, C_{pi} and h_i denote the density, temperature, thermal conductivity, specific heat and thickness based on big data analytics respectively. The subscript i and w indicate ice and water respectively. t is the time, y is the normal direction to a wall. m_{im}, m_{in} and $m_{e,s}$ are the mass flow rate of impinged droplets, runback in and evaporate (or sublimation) based on big data analytics. L_F is the latent heat of water icing.

2.3   Heat Transfer Analysis Model of Composites Based on the Big Data Analytics

The internal heat transfer of rotor composite material anti-/de-icing component directly affects the temperature distribution of anti-/de-icing on the rotor surface. Considering the material anisotropy of composite material internal heat transfer and the diversity of main directions of conductivity of material in different layers, a heat transfer analysis model of composites based on the big data analytics is set up.

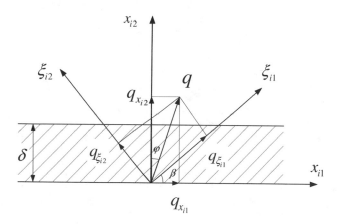

Fig. 3. Two-dimensional steady-state heat conduction of anisotropic material.

Set δ stands for the thickness of the ith layer of the composite material anti-/de-icing component. The ξ_{i1} and ξ_{i2} stand for the main direction of material thermal conductivity (see Fig. 3), and the Fourier law as follows:

$$q_{\xi_{i1}} = -\lambda_1 \frac{\partial t}{\partial \xi_{i1}}, \quad q_{\xi_{i2}} = -\lambda_2 \frac{\partial t}{\partial \xi_{i2}} \qquad (14)$$

Thus the heat flux density can be written:

$$q = -\lambda_1 \frac{\partial t}{\partial \xi_{i1}} - \lambda_2 \frac{\partial t}{\partial \xi_{i2}} \qquad (15)$$

Through the coordinates change, coordinate system (ξ_{i1}, ξ_{i2}) transforms to coordinate system (x_{i1}, x_{i2}). Due to simplifying as 2D steady heat conduction, we can get the following heat transfer coefficients:

$$q_{x_{i1}} = (\lambda_1 - \lambda_2)\sin\beta\cos\beta\frac{t_1 - t_2}{\delta} \tag{16}$$

$$q_{x_{i2}} = (\lambda_1\sin^2\beta + \lambda_2\cos^2\beta)\frac{t_1 - t_2}{\delta} \tag{17}$$

The angle φ between q and temperature gradient direction satisfies:

$$\tan\varphi = \frac{q_{x_{i1}}}{q_{x_{i2}}} = \frac{(\lambda_1 - \lambda_2)\sin\beta\cos\beta}{\lambda_1\sin^2\beta + \lambda_2\cos^2\beta} \tag{18}$$

Thus, the coefficient of thermal conductivity of the ith layer of anisotropic composite material is obtained in the coordinate system (x_{i1}, x_{i2}). By the multilayer composite material stable heat conduction theory, the contact surface temperature between the ith layer and the $(i - 1)$th layer can be written:

$$T_{wi} = T_{w1} - \phi\sum_{j=1}^{i-1}\frac{\delta_j}{A\lambda_j} = T_{w1} - \phi\sum_{j=1}^{i-1}R_{\lambda j} \tag{19}$$

Substitute Eq. (17) into Eq. (19) and obtain the following equation:

$$T_{wi} = T_{w1} - \phi\sum_{j=1}^{i-1}\frac{\delta_j}{A\lambda_j} = T_{w1} - \phi\sum_{j=1}^{i-1}\frac{\delta_j}{A(\lambda_{j1}\sin^2\beta + \lambda_{j2}\cos^2\beta)} \tag{20}$$

Where T_{w1} is the temperature of heating wire, T_{wi} is the temperature between the ith layer and the $(i - 1)$th layer of rotor composite material anti-/de-icing component based on big data, δ_j is the thickness of the $(i - 1)$th layer based on big data, A is the contact surface area between the ith layer and the $(i - 1)$th layer based on big data, λ_j is the heat conductivity coefficient of the $(i - 1)$th layer of rotor composite material anti-/de-icing component based on big data.

3 Rotor Composite Material Anti-/De-Icing Component Temperature Field Optimization Based on Big Data Analytics

3.1 Temperature Field Optimization Framework Based on Big Data Analytics

The temperature field optimization of rotor composite material anti-/de-icing component should consider many variable parameters. The traditional optimization method involves a large number of variable parameters. Optimizing control variables leads to repeated simulation analysis, and a significant amount of data are not used in the optimization. Thus, this paper proposes an optimization framework based on big data analytics using the orthogonal experiment optimization method as optimization kernel. The optimization framework is shown in Fig. 4.

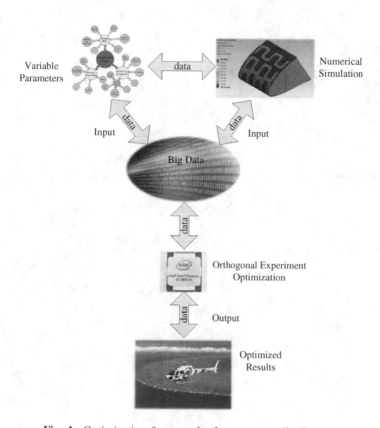

Fig. 4. Optimization framework of temperature distribution

Orthogonal experiment design and analysis is the most commonly used technique to optimize the design of the test and analysis method, which is the main method of partial factor design [17]. The orthogonal experiment is based on probability theory, mathematical statistics, and practical experience. By using the standard orthogonal table to arrange the experiment scheme, the orthogonal experiment can calculate and analyze the simulation results and quickly determine the optimization solutions. The orthogonal experiment is a kind of efficient scientific calculation method for multi-factor optimization problems [18].

3.2   Optimization Program Steps

A new orthogonal experiment to optimize multivariable parameters is established based on big data analytics because of the many variable parameters [19, 20]. The optimization process is shown in Fig. 5.

- An orthogonal test table is establish by using the orthogonal experiment.
- The optimization variables and levels are determined according to the multivariable parameter data structure.
- The orthogonal test table is designed and the test scheme is determined.
- The test is conducted, the test results are extracted, and the optimization analysis is performed.

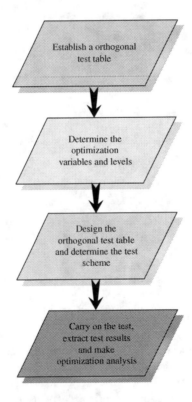

Fig. 5. Flow chart of orthogonal optimization experiment.

3.3   Result Analysis Based on Big Data Analytics

The finite element model of anti-/de-icing component and the orthogonal test table are established through the orthogonal optimization experiment and based on big data analytics. ANSYS Workbench software and orthogonal test scheme are adopted to conduct multi-field coupling analysis rotor composite material anti-deicing component

Table 2. Material thermal physical parameters of layers

Layer	Density (Kg/m³)	Specific heat (J/kg·K)	Coefficient of thermal expansion (1/K)	Thick (mm)
Iron Surface	7750	502	9e-6	0.3
Adhesive Film	1500	568	8e-5	0.47
Heat Transfer Layer	1760	964	4e-5	0.3
Heating Wire	8250	448	1.3e-5	0.3
Heat Insulation Layer	1760	964	4e-5	0.3
Skin of Rotor	2800	963	2e-5	0.3

according to multi-coupling finite element method and optimization scheme. The material thermal physical parameters of the layers are presented in Table 2.

The relevant variable parameters and the optimization parameters are selected and determined respectively as shown in Table 3, where V denotes flow velocity, T indicates environment temperature, W signifies rotor speed, λdenotes heat conductivity coefficient of heat transfer layer, H indicates the thickness of adhesive layer, U signifies electric voltage, and L denotes the distance of heating wire. By using iron surface temperature difference (ΔT) as the optimization index, orthogonal test analysis is conducted; the results are shown in Table 3.

Table 3. Analysis results of orthogonal optimization

Test	V (m/s)	T (°C)	LWC (g/m³)	MVD (um)	W (r/min)	λ (W/(m·K))	H (mm)	U (V)	L (mm)	ΔT(°C)
Test1	60	−10	0.8	10	300	5.8	0.2	50	10	44.31
Test2	60	−15	1.0	20	450	7.6	0.3	100	15	56.39
Test3	60	−20	1.5	25	600	11.9	0.4	150	20	67.86
Test4	60	−25	2.0	30	800	12.8	0.5	200	25	71.02
Test5	80	−10	0.8	20	450	11.9	0.4	200	25	60.70
Test6	80	−15	1.0	10	300	12.8	0.5	150	20	65.34
Test7	80	−20	1.5	30	800	5.8	0.2	100	15	56.16
Test8	80	−25	2.0	25	600	7.6	0.3	50	10	51.79
Test9	100	−10	1.0	25	800	5.8	0.3	150	25	52.44
Test10	100	−15	0.8	30	600	7.6	0.2	200	20	58.05
Test11	100	−20	2.0	10	450	11.9	0.5	50	15	53.52
Test12	100	−25	1.5	20	300	12.8	0.4	100	10	69.81
Test13	150	−10	1.0	30	600	11.9	0.5	100	10	58.41
Test14	150	−15	0.8	25	800	12.8	0.4	50	15	51.51
Test15	150	−20	2.0	20	300	5.8	0.3	200	20	56.28
Test16	150	−25	1.5	10	450	7.6	0.2	150	25	66.96
Test17	60	−10	2.0	10	800	7.6	0.4	100	20	49.29

(Continued)

Table 3. (*Continued*)

Test	V (m/s)	T (°C)	LWC (g/m³)	MVD (um)	W (r/min)	λ (W/(m·K))	H (mm)	U (V)	L (mm)	ΔT(°C)
Test18	60	−15	1.5	20	600	5.8	0.5	50	25	42.35
Test19	60	−20	1.0	25	450	12.8	0.2	200	10	67.93
Test20	60	−25	0.8	30	300	11.9	0.3	150	15	68.76
Test21	80	−10	2.0	20	600	12.8	0.2	150	15	62.67
Test22	80	−15	1.5	10	800	11.9	0.3	200	10	64.36
Test23	80	−20	1.0	30	300	7.6	0.4	50	25	48.51
Test24	80	−25	0.8	25	450	5.8	0.5	100	20	53.83
Test25	100	−10	1.5	25	300	7.6	0.5	200	15	55.37
Test26	100	−15	2.0	30	450	5.8	0.4	150	10	55.77
Test27	100	−20	0.8	10	600	12.8	0.3	100	25	61.10
Test28	100	−25	1.0	20	800	11.9	0.2	50	20	56.89
Test29	150	−10	1.5	30	450	12.8	0.3	50	20	48.80
Test30	150	−15	2.0	25	300	11.9	0.2	100	25	57.62
Test31	150	−20	0.8	20	800	7.6	0.5	150	10	62.96
Test32	150	−25	1.0	10	600	5.8	0.4	200	15	59.26
Mean Value1	58.48	53.73	54.67	53.26	58.25	52.55	53.57	49.71	53.62	
Mean Value2	57.92	55.38	54.23	52.97	57.89	56.16	54.24	57.82	52.41	
Mean Value3	57.87	54.37	54.03	52.61	57.68	61.01	55.13	62.84	51.86	
Mean Value4	57.25	54.49	53.96	52.28	58.07	62.27	55.97	61.62	50.94	
Range	1.23	1.65	0.71	0.98	0.57	9.72	2.40	11.91	2.68	

Table 4. Analysis results of orthogonal optimization

Test	V (m/s)	T (°C)	LWC (g/m³)	MVD (um)	W (r/min)	λ (W/(m·K))	H (mm)	U (V)	L (mm)
Test1	60	−10	0.8	10	300	5.8	0.2	50	10
Test2	80	−15	1.0	20	450	7.6	0.3	100	15
Test3	100	−20	1.5	25	600	11.9	0.4	150	20
Test4	150	−25	2.0	30	800	12.8	0.5	200	25

The parameters listed in Table 4 correspond to the mean values in Table 3. The table above shows that nine factors are ranked from large to small: range of electric voltage 11.91> range of heat conductivity coefficient of heat transfer layer 9.72> range of distance of heating wire 2.68> range of thickness of adhesive layer 2.40> range of temperature 1.65> range of flow velocity 1.23> range of median volumetric diameter 0.98> range of liquid water content 0.71> range of rotor speed 0.57. Therefore, the

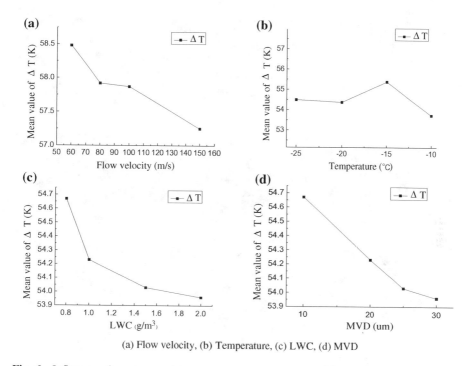

(a) Flow velocity, (b) Temperature, (c) LWC, (d) MVD

Fig. 6. Influence of environmental parameters on temperature difference of the iron surface.

most effective factor among the nine factors on the temperature field uniform distribution on the rotor iron surface is electric voltage, followed by heat conductivity coefficient of heat transfer layer. Rotor speed has the least influence among the factors.

Based on the results of the analysis of environment parameters of common working conditions(see Fig. 6), a high wind speed indicates a high content of super-cooled water droplets, a large droplet diameter of the super-cooled water, and a small temperature difference value of the iron surface. The minimum temperature difference of the iron surface is achieved when the temperature is −10 °C. Therefore, environmental parameters are as follows: V = 150 m/s, T = −10 °C, LWC = 2 g/m³, MVD = 30 um. At the same time, the controllable parameters are optimized and the optimized parameters are presented, as shown in Table 5.

Table 5. Optimization parameters

Test	V (m/s)	T (°C)	LWC (g/m³)	MVD (um)	W (r/min)	λ (W/(m·K))	H (mm)	U (V)	L (mm)
Test33	150	−10	2.0	30	550	5.8	0.15	40	35

The eight results from the smallest temperature difference tests are considered. Figure 7 shows the temperature distribution of the iron surface in the nine tests and the optimization test. The simulation results indicate that the temperature difference of the

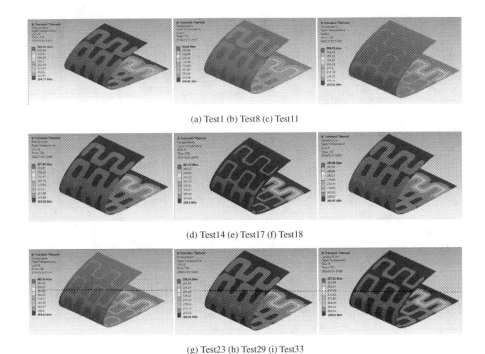

(a) Test1 (b) Test8 (c) Test11

(d) Test14 (e) Test17 (f) Test18

(g) Test23 (h) Test29 (i) Test33

Fig. 7. Temperature distribution of iron surface in the select tests and the optimization test.

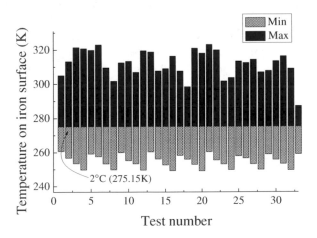

Fig. 8. Temperature extremes distribution of iron surface in Test1-Test33.

iron surface in the optimized Test33 is 23.48 K, which is substantially smaller than the temperature difference in other tests.

The iron surface temperature distribution of the preceding tests show that the temperatures of the heating areas are higher than 2 °C (275.15 K) and the iron surface temperature requirements of the composite material anti-/de-icing component are met. Figures 7 and 8 show that the temperature extremes in the optimizing group are substantially smaller than the original plans and those in the aforementioned tests in the heating area are larger than that in Test33, which increases power consumption.

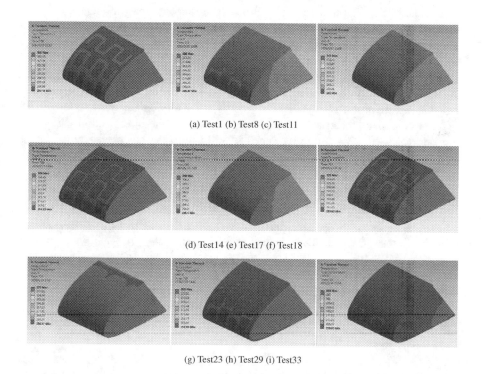

(a) Test1 (b) Test8 (c) Test11

(d) Test14 (e) Test17 (f) Test18

(g) Test23 (h) Test29 (i) Test33

Fig. 9. Temperature distribution inside the skin in selected tests and optimization test.

The temperature distribution inside the skin (see Fig. 9) shows that skin internal heating area is the minimum in Test33, whereas the skin internal heating areas in other tests are larger. Overheating can produce heating effect in the internal cementation structure of the skin, and the heating effect would result in cracking of the rubber and structural deformation, thereby adversely affecting the fatigue life of a helicopter rotor.

The ideal results in Test33 meet the requirement of heating temperature on the iron surface and reduce the energy consumption of power. Therefore, the optimized parameters are as follows: the rotor speed is 550 r/min, the layer heat transfer coefficient of thermal conductivity is 5.8 W/(m·K), the thickness of the adhesive layer is 0.15 mm, the power supply voltage is 40 V, and the distance of heating wire is 35 mm.

4   Conclusion

The numerical simulation model of the rotor composite material anti-/de-icing component is established based on big data analytics and numerical simulation method. The rotor composite material anti-/de-icing component temperature field distribution is optimized by employing orthogonal experiment. Based on the optimization, the following conclusions are presented:

- The factor that most significantly affects the uniform distribution of the temperature field on the rotor iron surface is electric voltage, followed by heat conductivity coefficient of the heat transfer layer. Rotor speed has the least influence.
- According to the orthogonal test, the environmental parameters that favor iron temperature homogenization are determined as follows: the flow velocity is 150 m/s, the environment temperature is −10 °C, the liquid water content is 2 g/m³, and the median volumetric diameter is 30 um.
- According to the minimum temperature difference on the rotor iron surface and considering the problems of electricity energy consumption and thermal fatigue life of rotor composite material anti-/de-icing component, the optimization parameters are selected as follows: the rotor speed is 550 r/min, the layer heat transfer coefficient of thermal conductivity is 5.8 W/(m·K), the thickness of adhesive layer is 0.15 mm, the power supply voltage is 40 V, and the distance of the heating wire is 35 mm.

Acknowledgements. This work is supported by Defense Industrial Technology Development Program (A0520110009), State Key Laboratory of Virtual Reality Technology Independent Subject (BUAA-VR-16ZZ-07), and National Science and Technology Major Project (2014ZX04001011). The authors thank the referees of this paper for their valuable and very helpful comments.

References

1. Manyika, J., Chui, M., Brown, B., et al.: Big data: the next frontier for innovation, competition, and productivity. Las Vegas: The McKinsey Global Institute, vol. 5, No. 33, p. 222 (2014)
2. Cheng, X., Jin, X., Wang, Y.: Review of big data system and analysis technology. J. Softw. **25**(9), 1889–1908 (2014)
3. Kambatla, K., Kollias, G., Kumar, V.: Trends in big data analytics. J. Parallel Distrib. Comput. **74**(7), 2561–2573 (2014)
4. Lee, S.J.: Big data analysis using principal component analysis. J. Korean Inst. Intell. Syst. **25**(6), 592–599 (2015)
5. Baumann, P., Mazzetti, P., Ungar, J.: Big data analytics for earth sciences: the earth server approach. Int. J. Digit. Earth **9**, 1–27 (2015)
6. Belaud, J.P., Negny, S., Dupros, F., et al.: Collaborative simulation and scientific big data analysis: illustration for sustainability in natural hazards management and chemical process engineering. Comput. Indus. **65**(3), 521–535 (2014)
7. Pourbagian, M., Habashi, W.G.: Aero-thermal optimization of in-flight electro-thermal ice protection systems in transient de-icing mode. Int. J. Heat Fluid Flow **54**, 167–182 (2015)
8. Coffman, H.J.: Helicopter rotor icing protection methods. J. Am. Helicopter Soc. **32**(2), 34–39 (1987)
9. Gent, R.W., Dart, N.P., Cansdale, J.T.: Aircraft icing. Philos. Trans. R. Soc. Lond. A Math. Phys. Eng. Sci. **358**(1776), 2873–2911 (2000)

10. Jang, W.H., Chan, D.K., Jae, S.J.: A study on the parameters for icing airworthiness flight tests of surion military helicopter. J. Korean Soc. Aeronaut. Space Sci. **43**(6), 526–532 (2015)
11. Cao, H.Y., Li, G.Z., Hess, R.A.: Helicopter flight characteristics in icing conditions. Aeronaut. J. **116**(116), 963–979 (2012)
12. Elangovan, R., Olsen, R.F.: Analysis of layered composite skin electro-thermal anti-icing system. In: Proceedings of the 46th AIAA Aerospace Sciences Meeting and Exhibit, pp. 1–15 (2008)
13. Coffman, H.J.: Review of helicopter icing protection systems. In: American Institute of Aeronautics and Astronautics, Aircraft Design, Systems and Technology Meeting, Fort Worth, TX, vol. 17, No: 19 (1983)
14. Liu, G.W., Gao, B.F., Zhang, G.H., et al.: Study on helicopter icing intensity design standard. Helicopter Technol. **2**, 30–33 (2011)
15. Veillard, X., Habashi, W.G., Aube, M.S., et al.: Fensap-ice: Ice accretion in multi-stage jet engines. AIAA **2009**, 4158 (2009)
16. Yee, H.C.: Upwind and symmetric shock-capturing schemes. NASA-TM-89464 (1987)
17. Üstün, B., Melssen, W.J., Oudenhuijzen, M., et al.: Determination of optimal support vector regression parameters by genetic algorithms and simplex optimization. Anal. Chim. Acta **544**(1), 292–305 (2005)
18. Liu, R., Zhang, Y., Wen, C., et al.: The orthogonal experiment design and analysis method study. Exp. Technol. Manage. **27**(9), 52–55 (2010)
19. Zhifei, W., Hua, W.: Inflatable wing design parameter optimization using orthogonal testing and support vector machines. Chin. J. Aeronaut. **25**(6), 887–895 (2012)
20. Su, P., Chen, W.: Orthogonal test analysis on the sensitivity of stability influence factors of Dao Guapai Perilous rock in Jiangyou. In: Lollino, G., Giordan, D., Crosta, G.B., Corominas, J., Azzam, R., Wasowski, J., Sciarra, N. (eds.) Engineering Geology for Society and Territory, vol. 2, pp. 1735–1739. Springer International Publishing, Switzerland (2015)

Prediction of Aero-engine Test Bed Performance Based on Big Data Technology

Gao Hanjun[1,2], Zhang Yidu[1,2], Wu Qiong[1,2(✉)], and Fu Guoxiang[1,2]

[1] School of Mechanical Engineering and Automation, Beihang University,
Beijing 100191, People's Republic of China
wuqlc@126.com
[2] State Key Laboratory of Virtual Reality Technology,
School of Mechanical Engineering and Automation,
Beihang University, Beijing 100191, People's Republic of China

Abstract. Traditional mechanical product design methods often rely on the experience of designers. With these methods, only a few mechanical properties can be checked, as a result, designers cannot comprehensively understand the product performance at the design stage, which causes a great increase of the research and development costs. With the arrival of the big data era, predicting product performances by simulations has become more and more important. In order to explore the influence of the circumferential deflection angle, the axial deflection angle, the thrust and other factors of the aircraft engine on the measurement accuracy of the test bench, FEM (Finite Element Method) model with 213530 finite elements of aero-engine test bed is built in ANSYS software. Through the calculation of 173 working conditions, the results, including the displacement, stress and strain, of all the elements can be obtained. According to a large number of analysis data, the performance of the test bench in the test process can be overall predicted, which makes the test bench measurement data more accurate and reliable.

Keywords: FEM · Aero-engine test bed · Big data · Static analysis

1 Introduction

Traditional mechanical product design usually depends on the designer's experience. In those cases, mechanical parts are simplified as beam, rod, shell and other elementary structures when the check work is conducted. Instead of comprehensively understanding the product performances, only a few mechanical properties can be obtained by these methods [1, 2].

With the continuous development of computer technology, the strength analysis, CFD (Computational Fluid Dynamics) analysis, mechanical system Dynamics analysis and thermal analysis have been widely used in aerospace, automotive, medical equipment and other manufacturing areas. Based on large amounts of simulation data, designers can not only acquire the overall performance rapidly and accurately and make adjustments according to the defects in the early stage of design, but also improve the original product by optimization technique. Thus, the cost and cycle will be greatly reduced.

© Springer Science+Business Media Singapore 2016
L. Zhang et al. (Eds.): AsiaSim 2016/SCS AutumnSim 2016, Part III, CCIS 645, pp. 602–614, 2016.
DOI: 10.1007/978-981-10-2669-0_64

Enrico Cestino uses the Msc/Patran/Nastran code to predict the static and dynamic behaviour of the UAV (Unmanned Air Vehicle) structure, and several profiles and wing plans are analyzed by CFD software Xfoil and Vsaero [3]. Paola Tamburini et al. [4] apply FEM static analysis to estimate the platforms calibration matrices based on least square fitting of each platform. In order to determine the optimal initial winding angle and lay-up, a FEM-based design procedure is developed by Hu et al. [5] taking into account the variations of the laminate thickness and winding angle. Aiming at reducing the weights and predicting the aerodynamic characteristics, E. Oktay et al. [6] carry out topology optimization of aircraft wing structures coupled with CFD analyses.

Aircraft engine test bed is a large test equipment for engine performance test, which plays a very important role in aero-engine factory testing and maintenance [7]. In the process of test, measured data is collected by force sensor installed on the movable frame, then ground thrust, which is an important indicator to the engine performance, is got after the vector operations [8].

Many studies on aero-engine thrust have been carried out [9–11]. The thrust measurement method and numerical simulation are two main research directions. Simulation model of test bed is proposed in the light of a new algorithm in literature [11]. Zhang et al. [12] calculate thrust measurement result by CFD software and calibrate thrust value. A new thrust estimation method is put forward by Li et al. [13], as a result, the estimation accuracy is improved. Besides, the influence of airflow disturbance and uneven distribution of temperature and pressure on the engine surface on stability of engine test and evaluation of engine performance also receive attention [14–16].

Although some simulation calculations on aero-engine test bed have been conducted by previous researchers, predicting the overall performances of test bed based on a large amounts of simulation data is hardly reported. For aero-engine test bed, whether the engine thrust can all be passed to the sensors under different circumstances and whether the measurement results will be affected by the existence of the deflection angle and offset of the engine axis are needed to be systematic verified in the design stage. In Sect. 2, the finite element model of engine test bed is established by ANSYS software. In order to explore the effect of nozzle deflection angle and the deflection angle and the offset of the engine axis on the measurement accuracy, 173 working conditions are calculated by FEM static analysis. The simulation results are comprehensively analyzed in Sect. 3, and the key factor affecting the test bench measurement accuracy is found. Finally conclusions are given in Sect. 4.

2   Modeling and Simulation

Aero-engine test bed can be divided into two parts: static and movable frame (as shown in Fig. 1(a)). Static frame can be regarded as rigid body providing constraints, and the movable frame is the main object of analysis. Movable frame is fixed by six flexible sensors on static frame. There are one senor in X direction, two sensors in Y direction and three in Z direction. The six sensors respectively named X1, Y1, Y2, Z1, Z2, Z3 (Fig. 1(b)). Moveable frame is consist of dozens of beams whose material is Q345 steel. The weight and thrust of aero-engine are passed to moveable frame through installation points, thus the value of thrust can be measured by the readings of the six sensors.

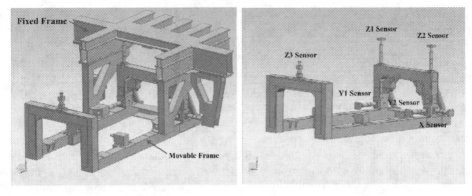

(a) Test bed structure   (b) Sensor position

Fig. 1. Test bench structure and sensor position

2.1   Modeling of Sensors and Flexible Parts

Sensors and the flexible parts are the key of the whole FEM model. The modeling strategy of flexible parts will directly affect the calculation results. In this paper, the sensor and flexible parts are substituted by three mutually perpendicular line spring element. The stiffness of the spring element is calculated by separate static analysis. FEM model of flexible assembly is built in ANSYS. Meshing of flexible part assembly is shown in Fig. 2 and the deformation contour under Z direction pressure is presented in Fig. 3.

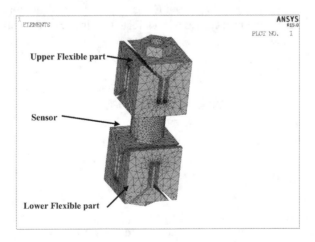

Fig. 2. Meshing of flexible parts and sensor assembly

According to the structure of the flexible parts, the flexible parts have the same stiffness in the two non-main load-bearing directions, which can also be verified by static analysis results (Table 1). By assigning the stiffness value to the springs, flexible

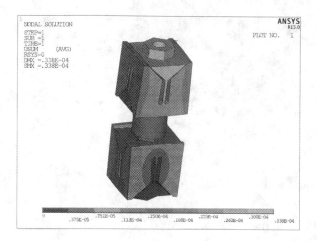

Fig. 3. Deformation Contour of flexible parts and senor assembly

Table 1. Stiffness in three directions of flexible parts

Installation position	Direction	Load (N)	Displacement (mm)	Stiffness (N/mm)
Z	principal direction	10000	0.0305	3.28E + 05
	non-principal	100	1.445	69.2
Y	principal direction	10000	0.0276	3.62E + 05
	non-principal	100	1.387	72.1
X	principal direction	10000	0.0338	2.96E + 05
	non-principal	100	1.608	62.19

parts can be well replaced by equivalent spring elements. One end of the three spring elements is intersecting at the same node, and the other end is constrained in six degrees of freedom, which is also the constraints of the whole test bed model.

2.2 Modeling of Movable Frame

Static frame, which has little effect on the measurement results, is treated as the basic. Therefore, no solid model is built in FEM analysis. The movable frame is consist of dozens of beams and also the main load-bearing components of the test bed. Taking the calculation accuracy and efficiency into consideration, shell elements, hexahedron solid elements, tetrahedral elements and line element are all applied to compose the FEM model. Eventually, the FEM model including 213530 elements and 92215 nodes is established (Fig. 4).

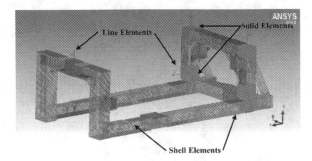

Fig. 4. Meshing of test bed movable parts

2.3 Boundary Conditions

Aero-engine is the thrust provider. It is unnecessary to analyze stress and deformation of the aero-engine when calculating the accuracy of test bed. Thus, aero-engine is simplified as several mass points, including inlet gravity center, main installation point, engine gravity center, auxiliary installation point and trust point. These mass points are connected to the test bed elements by multi point constraint at the main installation point and auxiliary installation point (Fig. 5).

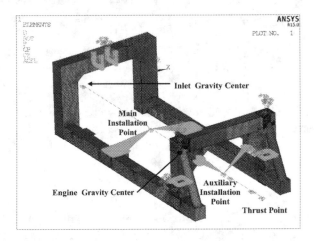

Fig. 5. Constraints and loads

As mentioned in Sect. 2.1, the constraints are added at the free end of the 18 spring elements. The movable frame is subjected to the thrust of the engine, the gravity of the engine, the gravity of the inlet and the gravity of the moving frame. The thrust is applied to the thrust point, and gravity of the engine and the inlet are applied to inlet gravity center and engine gravity center respectively. The gravity of the movable frame is defined through the inertia force.

2.4   Simulation

Under the actual situation, the sensor can only present the force value in main load-bearing direction. Theoretically, the thrust value of the engine can be obtained by calculating the vector sum of six sensor readings. Actually, however, the stiffness of the flexible part in the non-main load-bearing directions is not 0. Therefore, a part of the thrust force might be absorbed by the flexible parts in non-main load-bearing directions, and it cannot be measured by the sensors. This may be even worse when the engine nozzle is deflected in circumferential and axial direction or the engine installation error exists. It is quite difficult to obtain the thrust force that absorbed by the flexible parts in non-main load-bearing direction in experiment, but it can be got from FEM simulation results. The main target of the FEM analysis is to calculate the reaction force of all the spring elements in the three directions. By checking the reaction force in non-main load-bearing direction, measurement error of the test bed can be obtained.

Based on the FEM model of the test bed, the static analysis is carried out under the following conditions:

(1)   The thrust (F) equals 5, 10, 15 and 20 ton; engine nozzle axial deflection angle (α) equals 0°, 5°, 10°, 15°, 20°; engine nozzle circumferential deflection angle (θ) equals 0°, 45°, 90°, 135°, 180°, 225°, 270° and 315° (Fig. 6). To understand the effect of nozzle deflection angle on measurement error, permutation and combination of three factors above are chosen as 160 working conditions.

(2)   When the engine axis is deflected from 0° to 5° (Interval 1°), 6 working conditions are selected to research the effect of engine axis deflection angle on measurement error. (Fig. 7)

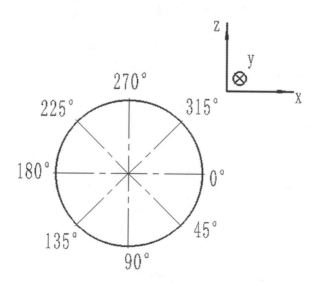

Fig. 6. Definition of circumferential angle(θ)

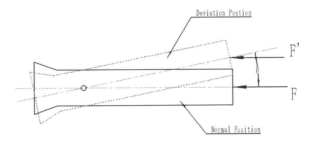

Fig. 7. Schematic diagram of the engine axis deviation

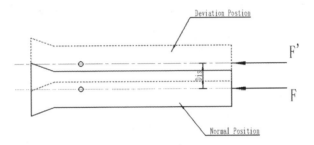

Fig. 8. Schematic diagram of the engine axis offset

(3) When the engine axis offset is 0.5 mm, 1 mm, 1.5 mm, 2 mm, 5 mm, 10 mm and 20 mm, 7 working conditions are selected to research the effect of engine axis offset on measurement error. (Fig. 8)

3   Results and Discussions

According to the force balance condition, the force of the test bed should satisfy the Eqs. (1), (2) and (3):

$$F_X + X_1 + \Delta x = 0 \tag{1}$$

$$F_Y + Y_1 + Y_2 + \Delta y = 0 \tag{2}$$

$$F_Z + (Z_1 + Z_2 + Z_3) + (G_E + G_J + G_D) + \Delta z = 0 \tag{3}$$

F_X, F_Y and F_Z are the thrust component in X, Y and Z direction respectively. X1, Y1, Y2, Z1 Z2 and Z3 are the reaction force value in main load-bearing direction of corresponding sensor position, and they also present the sensor readings in practice. Δx, Δy, Δz are respectively sum value of non-main load-bearing direction reaction force in X, Y and Z direction. G_E is the gravity of Engine. G_J is the gravity of Inlet. G_D is the gravity of the movable frame.

Thus, the relative error of the three directions δx, δy and δz can be expressed as:

$$\delta x = -\frac{\Delta x}{Fx} \tag{4}$$

$$\delta y = -\frac{\Delta y}{Fy} \tag{5}$$

$$\delta z = -\frac{\Delta z}{Fz} \tag{6}$$

3.1 Influence Analysis of Thrust and Engine Exhaust Gas Deflection

According to the simulation results of 160 working conditions, reaction force value at 6 sensor position can be got. After plugging these value into Eqs. (4), (5) and (6), measurement error of test bed under different thrust and nozzle deflection angle can be achieved. Due to limited space in this paper, only part of the results are shown below. Table 2 is the reaction force results under $F = 20T$, $\theta = 0°$, $\alpha = 0°–20°$, and Table 3 shows the results under $F = 20T$, $\theta = 225°$, $\alpha = 0°–20°$. The measured thrust relative error of five typical working conditions is collected in Table 4.

From Tables 2 to 4, it is not difficult to find that:

(1) When X component of thrust is 0, reaction force distributed symmetrically along the axis of the engine, which means that Y1 and Y2 suffer force equally.

Table 2. Reaction force results under $F = 20T$, $\theta = 0°$, $\alpha = 0°–20°$

Sensor position	Direction	0°	5°	10°	15°	20°
X1	**X**	**1.5785**	**17069**	**34006**	**50684**	**66976**
X1	Y	−17.959	−20.285	−22.457	−24.458	−26.273
X1	Z	5.2876	5.6617	6.0336	6.4006	6.7598
Y1	X	−1.3627	3.796	8.9227	13.979	18.925
Y1	**Y**	**−97984**	**−86154**	**−73668**	**−60622**	**−47114**
Y1	Z	6.2484	6.452	6.6635	6.8814	7.1038
Y2	X	0.54042	4.7319	8.8877	12.976	16.967
Y2	**Y**	**−97944**	**−109030**	**−119280**	**−128620**	**−136990**
Y2	Z	6.2707	6.1605	6.0604	5.9712	5.8935
Z1	X	−0.2758	6.4398	13.107	19.675	26.094
Z1	Y	−25.605	−23.617	−21.506	−19.287	−16.978
Z1	**Z**	**23422**	**23587**	**23749**	**23906**	**24058**
Z2	X	−0.5402	6.2505	12.991	19.629	26.114
Z2	Y	−26	−28.102	−30.046	−31.817	−33.403
Z2	**Z**	**23422**	**23257**	**23091**	**22926**	**22763**
Z3	X	0.05974	−7.2087	−14.423	−21.53	−28.474
Z3	Y	−1.8108	−1.7022	−1.3613	−0.7908	0.00498
Z3	**Z**	**26741**	**26741**	**26744**	**26751**	**26761**

Table 3. Reaction force results under F = 20T, θ = 225°, α = 0°–20°

Sensor position	Direction	0°	5°	10°	15°	20°
X1	**X**	**1.5785**	**−12066**	**−24042**	**−35835**	**−47355**
X1	Y	−17.959	−16.197	−14.311	−12.317	−10.228
X1	Z	5.2876	6.8488	8.3989	9.9259	11.418
Y1	X	−1.3627	−5.1958	−8.9924	−12.724	−16.361
Y1	**Y**	**−97984**	**−105710**	**−112640**	**−118700**	**−123860**
Y1	Z	6.2484	7.7577	9.265	10.759	12.228
Y2	X	0.54042	−2.4254	−5.3725	−8.2782	−11.121
Y2	**Y**	**−97944**	**−89472**	**−80318**	**−70554**	**−60252**
Y2	Z	6.2707	8.0029	9.7311	11.442	13.123
Z1	X	−0.2758	−4.9632	−9.6122	−14.187	−18.654
Z1	Y	−25.605	−23.64	−21.551	−19.354	−17.066
Z1	**Z**	**23422**	**31256**	**39028**	**46679**	**54152**
Z2	X	−0.5402	−5.5806	−10.582	−15.505	−20.314
Z2	Y	−26	−21.121	−16.139	−11.089	−6.0109
Z2	**Z**	**23422**	**31486**	**39486**	**47363**	**55055**
Z3	X	0.05974	5.0845	10.069	14.976	19.768
Z3	Y	−1.8108	−9.2413	−16.382	−23.179	−29.58
Z3	**Z**	**26741**	**22918**	**19128**	**15399**	**11760**

Table 4. Relative error of measured thrust value under typical working conditions

Load	Direction	Theoretical value	Measured value	Relative error
F = 20T, θ = 0°, α = 20°	X	−67035.96	−66976	−0.09 %
	Y	184179.76	184104	−0.04 %
	Z	0	39.28	/
F = 20T, θ = 45°, α = 5°	X	−12079.17	−12069	−0.08 %
	Y	195254.16	195181	−0.04 %
	Z	12079.17	12111.28	**0.27 %**
F = 15T, θ = 315°, α = 10°	X	−18049.81	−18035	−0.08 %
	Y	144766.74	144713	−0.04 %
	Z	−18049.81	−18004.72	−0.25 %
F = 10T, θ = 180°, α = 15°	X	25364.26	25340	−0.10 %
	Y	94660.74	94637	−0.03 %
	Z	0	37.28	/
F = 5T, θ = 135°, α = 0°	X	0	−1.03	/
	Y	49000	48993	−0.01 %
	Z	0	39.28	/

(2) When X component of thrust exists, the test bed will twist around the Z axis. Positive X component will reduce Y2 reading and increase Y1 reading, while negative X component will reduce Y1 reading and increase Y2 reading. And it has no obvious effect on Z readings.

(3) When Z component of thrust exists, the test bed will twist around the X axis. Positive Z component will reduce Z1 and Z2 readings (even decrease to negative value) and increase Z3 reading, while negative Z component will reduce Z3 readings and increase Z1 and Z2 readings.

(4) Measurement relative errors of the thrust component under different conditions, if the component does not equal 0, are all quite small. The maximum error among five typical conditions is 0.27 %. For the case of 0 component in one direction, the absolute error is less than 40 N. These errors can be neglected in the actual measurement.

3.2   Influence Analysis of Engine Axis Deflection and Deviation

Figure 9 shows the change trend of the sensor readings with the engine axis deflection angle. The measurement relative errors of sensors in Z direction with the change of engine axis deflection angle are presented in Table 5.

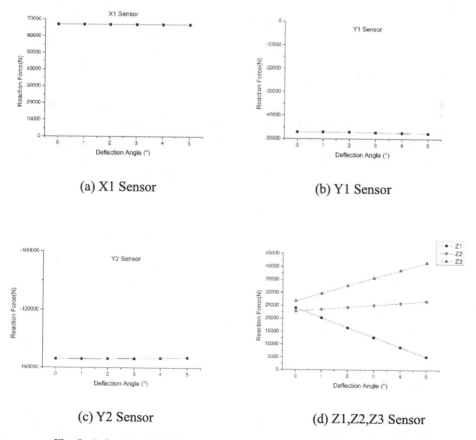

(a) X1 Sensor

(b) Y1 Sensor

(c) Y2 Sensor

(d) Z1,Z2,Z3 Sensor

Fig. 9. Influence of Engine axis deflection angle on measured thrust value

Table 5. Relative error of measured thrust value of Z direction sensors under different Engine axis deflection angle

Sensor position	1°	2°	3°	4°	5°
Z1	−15.72 %	−31.44 %	−47.16 %	−62.87 %	−78.56 %
Z2	3.58 %	7.15 %	10.71 %	14.26 %	17.81 %
Z3	11.09 %	22.19 %	33.29 %	44.39 %	55.47 %

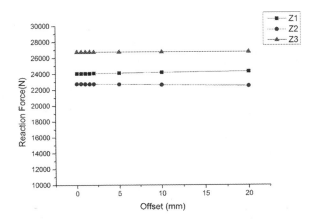

Fig. 10. Influence of Engine axis offset on measured thrust value in Z direction

As seen in Fig. 9(a), (b) and (c), the engine axis deflection angle has not obvious influence on the X1, Y1 and Y2 readings. However, the deflection angle will have a great impact on the sensor readings in Z direction. As the angle grows, the relative error will increase. The maximum relative error will reach −78.56 %, which would be quite unacceptable in actual measurement. Even one degree deflection for the engine axis will lead to 15.72 % relative error for Z1 sensor reading (Table 5).

Figure 10 shows the change trend of Z sensor readings with the engine axis offset. As is illustrated in Fig. 10, the readings remain almost unchanged while the offset increases. Hence, the engine axis offset is not the key factor to the measurement accuracy.

4   Conclusions

Based on three dimensional geometric model, FEM model of aero-engine test bed is established. In order to research the effect of nozzle deflection angle and the deflection angle and offset of the engine axis on the measurement accuracy, 173 working conditions are calculated by FEM static analysis. By analyzing the calculation results, several conclusions can be drawn:

(1)   When X component of thrust is 0, reaction force distributed symmetrically along the axis of the engine, which means that Y1 and Y2 suffer force equally.

(2) When X component of thrust exists, the test bed will twist around the Z axis. Positive X component will reduce Y2 reading and increase Y1 reading, while negative X component will reduce Y1 reading and increase Y2 reading. And it has no obvious effect on Z readings.

(3) When Z component of thrust exists, the test bed will twist around the X axis. Positive Z component will reduce Z1 and Z2 readings (even decrease to negative value) and increase Z3 reading, while negative Z component will reduce Z3 readings and increase Z1 and Z2 readings.

(4) Under different nozzle deflection angles, the measurement relative error can be limited to a very small value.

(5) The engine axis deflection angle has not obvious influence on the X1, Y1 and Y2 readings. However, the deflection angle will have a great impact on the sensor readings in Z direction. As the angle grows, the relative error will increase. The maximum relative error will reach -78.56 %, which would be quite unacceptable in actual measurement. Therefore, controlling the deflection angle of the engine axis is the key to ensure the accuracy of the measurement.

(6) The readings of sensor remain almost unchanged while the offset increase.

(7) Based on a large number of analysis results, the overall performance of the aero-engine test bed can be obtained in the early stage of the design. Then, the most significant factor to measurement accuracy can be found. Thus, the simulation data can provide a comprehensive basis for the whole research and development process including design, manufacture, assembly, debugging and optimization, which will definitely reduce the costs and the design cycle.

Acknowledgments. This work is supported by Defense Industrial Technology Development Program (A0520110009), State Key Laboratory of Virtual Reality Technology Independent Subject (BUAA-VR-16ZZ-07), and National Science and Technology Major Project (2014ZX04001011). The authors thank the referees of this paper for their valuable and very helpful comments.

References

1. Liu, S., Ye, W., Lou, P., Chen, W., Huang, J., Xiao, L.: Bionic design for column of gantry machining center to improve the static and dynamic performance. Shock Vibr. **18**, 1–12 (2011)

2. Zhao, L., Chen, W., Ma, J., Yang, Y.: Structural bionic design and experimental verification of a machine tool column. J. Bionic Eng. **5**(08), 46–52 (2008)

3. Cestino, E.: Design of solar high altitude long endurance aircraft for multi payload & operations. Aerosp. Sci. Technol. **10**, 541–550 (2006)

4. Tamburini, P., Stagni, R., Cappello, A.: Design of a novel force platform for gait analysis: fem analysis. J. Mech. Med. Biol. **15**(2), 6 pages (2015). 1540007

5. Hu, H., Li, S., Wang, J., Zu, L.: Structural design and experimental investigation on filament wound toroidal pressure vessels. Compos. Struct. **121**(10), 114–120 (2015)

6. Oktay, E., Akay, H.U., Merttopcuoglu, O.: Parallelized structural topology optimization and CFD coupling for design of aircraft wing structures. Comput. Fluids **49**(1), 141–145 (2011)

7. Jiao, X.: Measuring error of thrust. Aviat. Metrol. Meas. Technol. **15**(2), 20–22 (1995)

8. Lian, X., Wu, H.: Principle of Aviation Gas Turbine. National Defend Industry Press, BeiJing (2001)
9. Gullia, A., Laskaridis, P., Ramsden, K.W.: A preliminary investigation of thrust measurement correction in an enclosed engine test facility. AIAA-2005-1128 (2005)
10. Robert, N.P., Colin, A.W., Martin, R.T.: Method of determining thrust. United States 6851303B2, 8 February 2005
11. Song, J., et al.: Research on simulation test-bed thrust of aero-engine. Comput. Simul. **29**(1), 67–69 (2012)
12. Zhang, Z., et al.: Numerical simulation on thrust correction of an aero-engine in indoor engine test cell. Eng. Mech. **29**(6), 308–313 (2012)
13. Li, Q., et al.: A new method for estimating the thrust of aircraft engines. Control Theor. Appl. **28**(2), 85–191 (2011)
14. Runyan, R.B., Rynd, Jr., J.P., Seely, J.F.: Thrust stand design principles. AIAA-92-3976 (1992)
15. Hu, M.H., Lin, W., Duan, S.Y.: Developing a neural network and real genetic algorithm combined tool for an engine test bed. Automob. Eng. **220**, 1737–1752 (2006)
16. Perez, F., Moulin, P., Del Mastro, A.: Vehicle simulation on an engine test bed. In: SIA International Conference, pp. 1–8 (2008)

Revenue-Aware Request Admission Control in Distributed Simulation Data Centers

Haitao Yuan[1], Jing Bi[2,3(✉)], Xiao Song[4], Bo Hu Li[4], Tingyu Lin[5],
Jian Zhang[2,3], and Changshun Yan[2,3]

[1] School of Software Engineering, Beijing Jiaotong University, Beijing 100044, China
[2] School of Software Engineering, Beijing University of Technology,
Beijing 100124, China
bijing@bjut.edu.cn
[3] Beijing Engineering Research Center for IoT Software and Systems,
Beijing 100124, China
[4] School of Automation Science and Electrical Engineering,
Beihang University, Beijing, China
[5] Beijing Simulation Center, Beijing 100854, China

Abstract. For lower cost and better performance, different applications concurrently run in distributed simulation data centers (SDCs). Requests arrive in a highly dynamic way, and they are difficult to accurately predict. This work presents the Revenue-Aware Request Admission Control (RARAC) approach to intelligently accept arriving requests by incorporating priority, response time, and revenue, etc. Experiments based on realistic requests in Google data centers demonstrate the proposed RARAC can greatly improve the revenue of SDCs provider.

Keywords: Simulation data center · Request scheduling · Admission control · Genetic algorithm

1 Introduction

Cloud simulation is proposed based on several technologies including high-performance computing, pervasive computing, virtualization, simulation grid, etc. [1–5]. Cloud simulation supports complex system modeling, virtual reality, distributed simulation, etc. As a service-oriented and network-based simulation model, cloud simulation is increasingly implemented and deployed in distributed simulation data centers (SDCs) [6]. Multiple heterogeneous simulation applications concurrently run in SDCs, and present applications to users. Global users can send requests to SDCs, and utilize simulation services to fulfill their requirement. Typically, users' requests arrive in distributed SDCs through multiple Internet service providers (ISPs). Recently emerging software-defined networking (SDN) can realize centralized control by scheduling requests through multiple ISPs [7].

The arrival of applications' requests in distributed SDCs is proven to be unstable and highly dynamic [8]. Therefore, it is difficult or nearly impossible to accurately predict future arriving rates of requests. Therefore, it is highly essential and critically

L. Zhang et al. (Eds.): AsiaSim 2016/SCS AutumnSim 2016, Part III, CCIS 645, pp. 615–623, 2016.
DOI: 10.1007/978-981-10-2669-0_65

important to provide the admission control for requests of different applications in distributed SDCs. The admission control can avoid the overload of servers and guarantee applications' performance. Recently, there are an increasing number of existing works on the admission control problem. The work in [9] proposes an admission control method based on which the energy cost can be optimized using intelligent request scheduling. However, these studies ignore the competition of bandwidth of ISP among requests of different applications. The work in [10] presents a coordinated approach to intelligently admit requests by scheduling resources in a data center. However, it is only suitable to one data center. This paper provides a Revenue-Aware Request Admission Control (RARAC) method to maximize the SDCs provider's revenue by considering response time, and priority of each request, and provide performance assurance in distributed SDCs.

The organization of this paper is shown here. Admission control problem is formulated in Sect. 2. Besides, the RARAC method is also proposed. Simulation results based on rea-life data are shown in Sect. 3. The conclusion is provided in Sect. 4.

2 Problem Formulation

The problem of the request admission control is first formulated here. Then, we adopt the typical genetic algorithm (GA) to solve this problem. To ensure the response time constraint, the SDCs provider typically needs to selectively admit some requests due to the limited servers in distributed SDCs. Therefore, too few or excessive requests may be refused due to the poor request admission control mechanism.

RARAC judiciously admits some of arriving requests by considering several factors including priority, the predicted response time, and revenue of requests corresponding to each application. Typically, more revenue is brought to the SDCs provider by requests of high-priority applications. Therefore, RARAC inclines to admit requests with more revenue while satisfying the ISP bandwidth constraint. Nevertheless, low-priority requests may be also admitted even if high-priority requests have not been totally admitted. A typical scenario is described as follows. If the number of servers that can execute high-priority requests is insufficient, the response time of these requests may be extremely long. In this case, the SDCs provider can only obtain less revenue. Then, it is more sensible for RARAC to judiciously admit some low-priority requests and to refuse some of high-priority requests. In this way, the SDCs provider can achieve the revenue maximization.

It is assumed that requests corresponding to application a $(1 \leqslant a \leqslant A)$ arrive based on the Poisson distribution. Let λ_a^* denote the request arriving rate of application a. Then, the admitted request arriving rate of application a is denoted as λ_a. Similar to [11], distributed SDCs are modeled as an $M/M/c$ queue. To maintain the stability of the queueing system, each application's traffic intensity should be no more than 1. The average service rate of a physical server corresponding to application a is then calculated as the average one of all physical servers. Besides, it is assumed that there are always requests in each switched on server, and therefore each server can keep busy all the time.

Then, according to the characteristics of the $M/M/c$ queueing system, the average response time of requests corresponding to application a, T_a can be obtained as follows.

$$t_a = \frac{1}{\left(\sum\limits_{s=1}^{S} N_{s,a}\mu_{s,a}\right) - \lambda_a} + \frac{\sum\limits_{s=1}^{S} N_{s,a}}{\sum\limits_{s=1}^{S} N_{s,a}\mu_{s,a}} \tag{1}$$

Then, this paper adopts the time-fluctuating utility function described in [12] to calculate the predicted revenue brought by the execution of requests corresponding to application a. The specific definition of the utility function is further given in Eq. (2). The revenue brought by each request whose response time is t_a is denoted as $u_a(t_a)$. In Eq. (2), the maximum revenue that each request corresponding to application a can bring is denoted by V_a. V_a corresponding to high-priority requests is larger, and therefore these requests bring more revenue to the SDCs provider. In addition, T^a_{max} and T^a_{min} denote the maximum and minimum acceptable response time, respectively. Let R_a denote the specified response time constraint of requests corresponding to application a. Here, T^a_{min} is set to R_a, i.e., $T^a_{min} = R_a$. Besides, γ_a denotes the decay rate of revenue. Therefore, the revenue of each request is proportional to its actual response time.

$$u_a(t_a) = \begin{cases} V_a, & t_a \leq T^a_{min} \\ V_a - \gamma_a(t_a - T^a_{min}), & T^a_{min} < t_a \leq T^a_{max} \\ 0, & t_a > T^a_{max} \end{cases} \tag{2}$$

As is shown, if $t_a \leq T^a_{min}$, requests of application a bring the maximum revenue V_a to the SDCs provider. However, if $T^a_{min} < t_a \leq T^a_{max}$, each request' revenue brought to the SDCs provider decreases with the increase of response time. Then, if $t_a > T^a_{max}$, the actual response time is too large and unacceptable. Thus, requests bring no revenue to the SDCs provider. It is further defined that $V_a - \gamma_a(t_a - T^a_{min}) = 0$ if $t_a = T^a_{max}$. Therefore, $V_a - \gamma_a(T^a_{max} - T^a_{min}) = 0$, i.e. $\gamma_a = \dfrac{V_a}{T^a_{max} - T^a_{min}}$. Then,

$$u_a(t_a) = \begin{cases} V_a, & t_a \leq T^a_{min} \\ V_a - \dfrac{V_a}{T^a_{max} - T^a_{min}}(t_a - T^a_{min}), & T^a_{min} < t_a \leq T^a_{max} \\ 0, & t_a > T^a_{max} \end{cases} \tag{3}$$

Then, the Request Admission Control Problem (RACP) is formulated as follows. Its objective function is the total revenue brought by requests of all applications.

$$\underset{\lambda_a}{Max} \sum_{a=1}^{A} (\lambda_a \cdot u_a(t_a))$$

$$\lambda_a \leq \lambda_a^* \tag{4}$$

$$\sum_{a=1}^{A} (d_a \cdot \lambda_a) \leq \sum_{c=1}^{C} \Omega_c \tag{5}$$

$$\lambda_a < \sum_{s=1}^{S} N_{s,a} \cdot \mu_{s,a} \tag{6}$$

Constraint (4) guarantees that λ_a should be less than λ_a^*. Besides, the size of every application a's request is denoted by d_a. ISP c's bandwidth capacity is denoted by Ω_c. Then, constraint (5) guarantees the bandwidth required by all accepted requests should not exceed to all ISPs' bandwidth. Constraint (6) guarantees the stability of an $M/M/c$ queueing system.

In this problem, λ_a ($a \in \{1, \cdots, A\}$) are decision variables. Constraints (4), (5), and (6) are linear with respective to λ_a. Besides, the objective function in the problem is nonlinear with respect to λ_a. Thus, the formulated problem is a constrained nonlinear optimization one. Several deterministic methods (e.g., dynamic programming [13], branch and bound [14]) can be adopted to solve this problem. However, these methods often need mathematical structures of constrained optimization problems. It may be difficult or impossible to analyze the mathematical structure due to the complexity of optimization problems. What's more, their execution cost is typically large because they usually need relatively long execution time to finally converge to the optimal solution.

Currently, meta-heuristic algorithms are adopted to tackle nonlinear constrained optimization problems. These algorithms are robust and can be easily implemented. In addition, they can still work without mathematical relations of constrained optimization problems. Therefore, they are widely used to solve different types of constrained linear and nonlinear problems. Then, the method of penalty function is used to convert a nonlinear constrained optimization problem. The value of the penalty function is denoted by Pnt. The violation of each inequality or equality constraint in the original optimization problem brings a corresponding penalty to the objective function in RACP. The transformed problem is shown as follows.

$$\underset{\lambda_a}{Min} \left(-\sum_{a=1}^{A} (\lambda_a \cdot u_a(t_a)) + \theta \cdot Pnt \right)$$

In the unconstrained problem, θ is a relatively large positive number that denotes the effect of Pnt. Each invalid solution brings a large penalty. Thus, the minimization of the new objective function can find a valid solution, and maximize the original objective function in RACP.

GA is an effective algorithm to obtain globally optimal solutions for constrained optimization problems [15]. GA can efficiently find a close-to-optimal solution from potential candidate solutions. GA begins with a population that consists of a certain number of solutions or chromosomes. Then, new populations are produced based on existing chromosomes in old populations. Chromosomes are chosen to reproduce new offspring according to their fitness values. GA repeats this process until its termination condition is met. GA's basic elements include selection based on fitness values, crossover for new offspring reproduction, and potential mutation of new offspring. Therefore, this paper applies GA to solve RACP.

In this paper, GA is implemented by integrating the roulette-wheel selection, and the elitism mechanism. Roulette-wheel is a widely adopted approach that supports selection proportionate to fitness values. The elitism mechanism can preserve some best chromosomes by coping several chromosomes with larger fitness values in the old population into the new population. Besides, the binary encoding is adopted in GA's implementation where each solution is designed as a bit string consisting of 0 or 1. Besides, GA's implementation adopts single point crossover that is executed with a specified probability. Mutation is integrated to prevent GA from trapping into locally optimal solutions. The bit in each position of a chromosome is mutated with a certain probability. GA's pseudo code is shown as follows.

Algorithm 1 GA

1: Randonly initialize the first population

2: **while** $g \leq \xi$ or $\omega \leq 90\%$ **do**

3:   rank(ψ, ζ)

4:   select(ψ, ζ)

5:   crossover(ψ, ζ)

6:   mutation(ψ, ζ)

7:   Update current population with new population

8:   $g = g + 1$

9: **end while**

10: **return** the optimal solution

Let ψ denote the size of a population. In Algorithm 1, Line 1 initializes the first population by randomly initializing a population of ψ chromosomes. Let ζ denote the length of each chromosome. Let ξ denote the number of GA's total generations. Let ω denote the percentage of chromosomes whose fitness values are the same in current population. Line 2 shows that if $g \leq \xi$ or $\omega \leq 90\%$, the **while** loop continues. Line 3 ranks all chromosomes in current population based on their fitness values. Line 4 randomly chooses old chromosomes to reproduce new chromosomes using roulette-wheel selection and the elitism mechanism. Line 5 performs the crossover operation by randomly choosing a position and exchanging subsequences after it between two different chromosomes. New offspring is produced to create the next population. Line 6 performs the mutation operation based on a specified probability. Line 7 replaces current population with new population. The optimal chromosome is transformed into the optimal solution according to the typical decoding strategy in Line 10.

3   Evaluation

This section evaluates RARAC with real-life requests in Google clusters [16]. Figure 1 shows arriving requests of 4 applications for about 380 min. Each time slot lasts for five minutes. Besides, priority values of requests corresponding to different applications (types 4, 3, 2, and 1) are 4, 3, 2, and 1. Requests with larger priority contribute more revenue and they are preferred to be admitted.

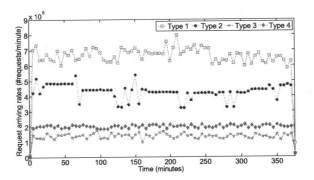

Fig. 1. Arriving requests in Google data centers

The parameter setting in the experiment is shown as follows. $A = 4$. $S = 3$. d_1, d_2, d_3, d_4 are set to 1 MB, 2.5 MB, 4 MB, 5 MB, respectively. $\theta = 10^{15}$. $T^a_{max} = 1.5 \, T^a_{min}$. Ω_1, Ω_2, and Ω_3 are set to $0.5 * 10^9$, $0.4 * 10^9$, and $0.3 * 10^9$, respectively. Besides, R_1, R_2, and R_3 are set to 1 ms, 1.25 ms, 2 ms, and 2.5 ms, respectively. V_1, V_2, V_3, and V_4 are set to 0.24\$, 0.32\$, 0.4\$, 0.48\$. Besides, the setting of $N_{s,a}$ and $\mu_{s,a}$ are shown in Table 1.

Table 1. Parameter setting of SDCs

s	n	$N_{s,a}$	$\mu_{s,a}$ (10^3reqs./s)
$s = 1$	$n = 1$	1200	3.6
	$n = 2$	1000	3
	$n = 3$	1000	1.2
	$n = 4$	1500	0.6
$s = 2$	$n = 1$	2200	1.8
	$n = 2$	2200	1.5
	$n = 3$	1500	0.64
	$n = 4$	3000	0.4
$s = 3$	$n = 1$	1200	4.2
	$n = 2$	1200	2.4
	$n = 3$	1500	1.2
	$n = 4$	2400	0.64

Figure 2 shows the admitted request rates of different applications using RARAC. As is shown, almost all application 3's requests are directly admitted while many requests of applications 1, 2 and 4 are refused. The result shows that RARAC can achieve revenue maximization by judiciously admitting requests. RARAC tries to accept higher-priority requests. Nevertheless, there are only limited servers to serve application 4's requests. Thus, requests' response time of application 4 might be long, and less revenue is brought. Therefore, though priority of application 4 is larger than that of application 3, application 3's requests are preferred to be accepted. RARAC's effectiveness is demonstrated with this result.

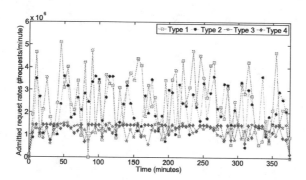

Fig. 2. Admitted request rates

Then, RARAC is further compared with the typical Priority-Based Admission Control (PBAC) [17]. In PBAC, higher-priority requests are always preferred to be admitted. Figure 3 illustrates the revenue comparison between RARAC and PBAC. It can be observed that RARAC's revenue is more than PBAC's revenue. This is because RARAC first evaluates the predicted revenue of all admitted requests, and inclines to admit arriving requests that can realize the revenue maximization for the SDCs provider.

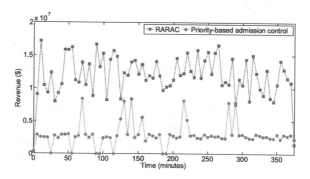

Fig. 3. Revenue comparison

4 Conclusion

Distributed simulation data centers currently support the concurrent running of multiple heterogeneous applications. Arriving requests are highly dynamic and hard to accurately predict. Different from existing works, to guarantee application performance and to realize the revenue maximization for the SDCs provider, this paper presents the Revenue-Aware Request Admission Control (RARAC) approach to judiciously admit requests of different applications by comprehensively considering the response time, priority, and revenue. The evaluation based on realistic requests demonstrates that RARAC can significantly increase the revenue brought by the admitted requests in comparison with the priority-based admission control method.

References

1. Li, B.H., Chai, X., Zhang, L., et al.: New advances of the research on cloud simulation. In: Proceedings of the Asia Simulation Conference 2011, Seoul, Korea, pp. 144–163 (2012)
2. Yuan, H., Bi, J., Tan, W., et al.: TTSA: an effective scheduling approach for delay bounded tasks in hybrid clouds. IEEE Trans. Cybern. **PP**, 1–11 (2016). doi:10.1109/TCYB.2016.2574766
3. Bi, J., Yuan, H., Tie, M., et al.: Heuristic virtual machine allocation for multi-tier ambient assisted living applications in a cloud data center. China Commun. **13**(5), 56–65 (2016)
4. Yuan, H., Bi, J., Tan, W., et al.: Temporal task scheduling with constrained service delay for profit maximization in hybrid clouds. IEEE Trans. Autom. Sci. Eng. **PP**, 1–12 (2016). doi:10.1109/TASE.2016.2526781
5. Bi, J., Yuan, H., Tan, W., et al.: Application-aware dynamic fine-grained resource provisioning in a virtualized cloud data center. IEEE Trans. Autom. Sci. Eng. **PP**, 1–13 (2016). doi:10.1109/TASE.2015.2503325
6. Li, B.H., Chai, X., Hou, B., Zhu, W., Zhang, Y., Tang, Z., Song C., Mu, S.: Cloud simulation platform. In: Proceedings of the 2009 Grand Challenges in Modeling and Simulation Conference, Istanbul, Turkey, pp. 303–307 (2009)
7. Kim, H., Feamster, N.: Improving network management with software defined networking. IEEE Commun. Mag. **51**(2), 114–119 (2013)
8. Wu, L., Garg, S.K., Buyya, R.: SLA-based admission control for a Software-as-a-Service provider in cloud computing environments. J. Comput. Syst. Sci. **78**(5), 1280–1299 (2012)
9. Luo, J., Rao, L., Liu, X.: Temporal load balancing with service delay guarantees for data center energy cost optimization. IEEE Trans. Parallel Distrib. Syst. **25**(3), 775–784 (2014)
10. Muppala, S., Chen, G., Zhou, X.: Multi-tier service differentiation by coordinated learning-based resource provisioning and admission control. J. Parallel Distrib. Comput. **74**(5), 2351–2364 (2014)
11. Bi, J., Zhu, Z.L., Tian, R.X., Wang, Q.B.: Dynamic provisioning modeling for virtualized multi-tier applications in cloud data center. In: Proceedings of the IEEE 3rd International Conference on Cloud Computing, Miami, USA, pp. 370–377 (2010)
12. Lee, Y.C., Wang, C., Zomaya, A.Y., Zhou, B.B.: Profit-driven scheduling for cloud services with data access awareness. J. Parallel Distrib. Comput. **72**(4), 591–602 (2012)
13. Liu, D., Wei, Q.: Policy iteration adaptive dynamic programming algorithm for discrete-time nonlinear systems. IEEE Trans. Neural Netw. Learn. Syst. **25**(3), 621–634 (2014)

14. Yin, Y., Wu, W.H., Wu, W.H., Wu, C.C.: A branch-and-bound algorithm for a single machine sequencing to minimize the total tardiness with arbitrary release dates and position-dependent learning effects. Inform. Sci. **256**, 91–108 (2014)
15. Roberge, V., Tarbouchi, M., Labonté, G.: Comparison of parallel genetic algorithm and particle swarm optimization for real-time UAV path planning. IEEE Trans. Ind. Inform. **9**(1), 132–141 (2013)
16. Di, S., Cappello, F.: Gloudsim: Google trace based cloud simulator with virtual machines. Softw. Pract. Experience **45**(11), 1571–1590 (2015)
17. Nafea, I., Younas, M., Holton, R., Awan, I.: A priority-based admission control scheme for commercial web servers. Int. J. Parallel Program. **42**(5), 776–797 (2014)

The Application and Management of Big Data in Quality Engineering

Taotao Liu[✉], Shuyuan Song, and Guijiang Duan

School of Mechanical Engineering and Automation, Beihang University, Beijing, China
hbliutaotao@126.com

Abstract. Big data has become an important issue in academia and industry and offers the potential value for quality engineering. Some technology of big data in quality engineering is given in this paper. Moreover, some applications of big data in the quality engineering are proposed. The big data is used in the quality improvement and quality problem prevention. This study indicates that the big data play an increasingly important role in quality engineering.

Keywords: Big data · Quality engineering · MapReduce

1 Introduction

The big data is widely researched and used in academia and industry. Thanos Papadopoulos proposed a theoretical framework to explain resilience in supply chain networks for sustainability using unstructured big data [1]. Based on relevant sets of big data, Hualin Xie explored the factors influencing ecological land change during the period of 2000–2005 in China's Beijing-Tianjin-Hebei Region [2]. Aisha Siddiqa investigated feasible techniques of managing big data by emphasizing on storage, pre-processing, processing and security [3]. The rapid development of the advanced engineering and industrial technology has led to the rapid growth of data. These data are very important to the quality of the products and the data scale is very large. So these data is called quality big data.

Figure 1 illustrates the landscape of the technology of big data in quality engineering, in which various sensor devices and other devices get large amounts of data. These large amounts of data are collected and stored in the big data center. The big data center is composed of many modules, such as the collection of big data module, the storage of big data module, the analysis of big data module and so on.

The technology of big data has played a key role in quality engineering, for example, identifying and obtaining valuable information from large amounts of design and development data can be extremely beneficial in terms of the plan of the process. Analytics of the design data could inform the processors to optimize the process plan. Cloud manufacturing is emerging as a new manufacturing paradigm as well as an integrated technology [4–5]. Some cloud manufacturing companies have begun to build smart workshops for collection of big data and analysis these big data. The target of these companies is to improve the quality by the technology of big data.

L. Zhang et al. (Eds.): AsiaSim 2016/SCS AutumnSim 2016, Part III, CCIS 645, pp. 624–631, 2016.
DOI: 10.1007/978-981-10-2669-0_66

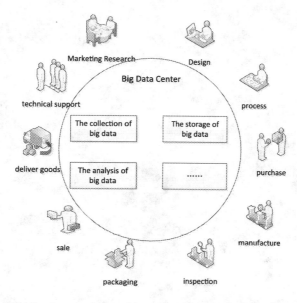

Fig. 1. The landscape of the technology of big data in quality engineering

The rest of the paper is organized as follows. Section 2 discusses the technology of big data in quality engineering. Section 3 presents the applications of big data in the quality engineering. Section 4 gives the conclusion of this paper.

2   The Technology of Big Data in Quality Engineering

2.1   The Technology of Quality Big Data Collection

The data could be collected from the man, machines, products and other enterprise resources. These data is transferred to the management information systems by the RFID or other devices (Fig. 2).

1. RFID

RFID operates based on electromagnetic fields to automatically identify and track tags attached to objects [6]. RFID can be applied in the workshops, the machine tools could identify the operator by the RFID. The RFID microchips embedded in the parts, products, measuring and cutting tools etc. for identifying. Such an identification method enables the realization of traceability with these parts, products, measuring tools and cutting tools.

2. Barcode and two-dimensional code

The parts, products, measuring tools and cutting tools could be identified by the barcode or the two-dimensional code. The cost of the barcode or the two-dimensional

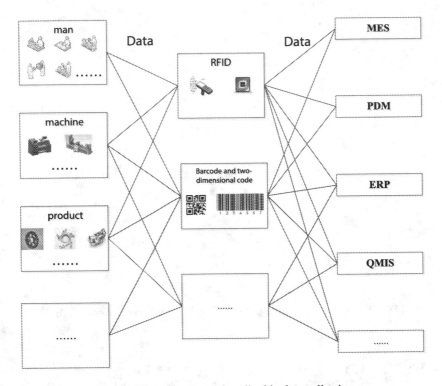

Fig. 2. The technology of quality big data collection

code is lower than the RFID, but they could not be put inside and the reader could not read the signal when the tag is invisible.

3. Management information system

There are many management information systems in a workshop, for example, the MES, PDM, ERP, QMIS (quality management information system) etc. Much information in these management information systems is valuable but isolate form others. These management information systems could provide much information to the big data center.

2.2 The Source of the Quality Big Data

The quality data should be collected from a variety of dimensions (Fig. 3):

1. The product tree

    Usually, a product is composed by some assemblies, an assembly is composed by some subassembly or parts, the structure of a product is just like a tree. The quality data of the parts contains the geometry characteristic, physicochemical characteristic etc. The assembly data can be derived from the assembly process and this data contains the worker, the assembly machines, the assembly methods etc. The quality data of the products contains performance data, test data etc. All of the quality data from the products, assemblies, parts would be transferred to the big data center.

2. Departments of the manufacture enterprise

   The manufacture enterprise contains design department, manufacture department, inspection department etc. Each department would provide the quality data according to its functions.

3. Granularity

   The quality data comes from in different granularity, the companies, the factories, the workshops, the workbenches and so on. The quality data which from a company may be quality objectives, quality plan etc. In the factories, the quality data contains train of the quality staff, the quality cost, etc. The products are manufactured in the workshops, so the quality data of the workshops may be the analysis of the product quality, trend of the product quality etc. In the workbench, the quality data comes from the machining, part inspection etc.

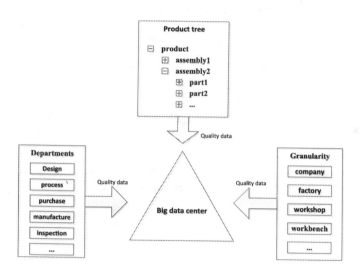

Fig. 3. The source of the quality big data

2.3 The Storage of Big Data

HDFS is designed to reliably store very large files across machines in a large cluster. It stores each file as a sequence of blocks [7]; The general data in the quality engineering not only contains the special data, but also the quality files, in any format. The files could be generated in any steps of the quality loop. The HDFS is used for storing these quality files (Fig. 4).

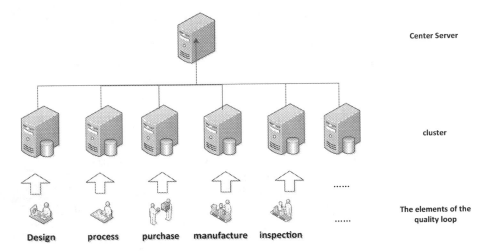

Fig. 4. The storage of big data

2.4   The Analysis of Big Data

MapReduce is presented as one of the most efficient big data solutions [8]. The programming model implemented by MapReduce is based on the definition of two basic elements: mappers and reducers [9]. The mappers could generate a set of intermediate key/value pairs and the reducers merge all of the intermediate values that are associated with the same intermediate key.

1. Data input: The MapReduce system designates map processors with a value K1, then the input data is associated with that K1 to each processor;
2. Map: The key values K2 are generated by the Map() function;

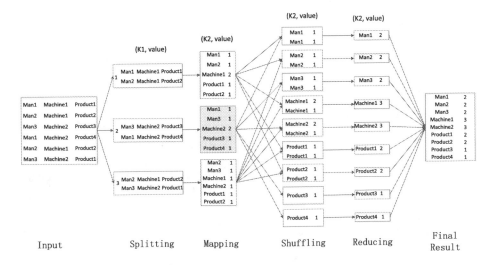

Fig. 5. MapReduce processes for manufacture

3. Shuffle: The data belonging to one key are located on the same worker node;
4. Reduce: Worker nodes execute the Reduce() function with each K2;
5. Final Result: All of the reduce outputs are collected by the MapReduce system based on the value K2.

An example is given to show the steps of the MapReduce system, shown in Fig. 5.

As Fig. 5 shown, in this example, the manufacture resources are man, machines and products. The man could be the designer, the operator, the inspector etc. The machines could be the lathe, the milling machine the CNC etc. The products could be wheel gears, nuts, bolts etc. In this example, They are numbered man1, man2, man3, machine1, machine2, product1, product2, product3, product4. The manufacture resources are split into a subset that will later be processed by the mappers. When the key/values are generated by mappers, the keys of K1 are 1, 2, 3, the values are shown in the Fig. 5. The shuffling process is used to combine the same keys in the same worker node. Finally, the numbers of the manufacture resources are generated.

3   Applications of Big Data in the Quality Engineering

3.1   Quality Improvement

PDCA is a cycle for continuous quality improvement. Using of the PDCA cycle means continuously looking for better methods of improvement [10]. The PDCA is composed of 4 stages in a cycle (Fig. 6).

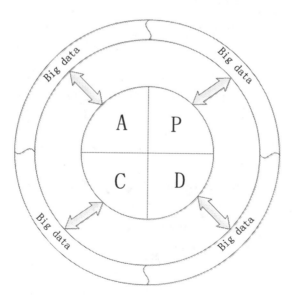

Fig. 6. The big data and the PDCA

Stage1: Plan, the quality objectives should be made in this stage. The big data is used for providing decision information to the decision-maker. New data could be generated in this stage.

Stage2: Do, in this stage, the quality activities may contains procurement, just-in-time supplies, process capability, product reliability, materials handling etc. The using of the big data could optimize these quality activities. Likewise, new data may be generated in this stage. For example, in the materials handling, the information of the materials, the workers, the storehouse etc. should be recorded in the data center.

Stage3: Check, in this stage, the quality activities may involve control charts, the inspection, the functional testing, the metrology etc. The plans of the inspection could be guided by the big data. Lots of new data will be put into the data center in this stage.

Stage4: Action, the ISO 9001 certification, the total quality management and the improvement are implemented in this stage. These quality activities also need big data to optimize and generate new data.

The application of big data technologies for the PDCA enables efficient quality improvement.

3.2 Quality Problem Prevention

The similarity of the different enterprise resources could help the quality control staff to prevent the quality problems. There are many resources in an enterprise, the quality of the products depends on these resources. Some of the resources are similar to others. The quality problem could be prevented by the resources similarity (Fig. 7).

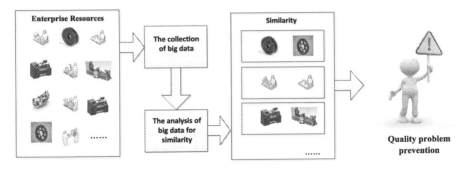

Fig. 7. The analysis of big data for quality problem prevention based on similarity

4   Conclusions and Future Work

In this context, we discussed the technologies used in the industry, the RFID, Barcode and two-dimensional code are used to collect the big data. The HDFS is designed for storing these big data, including the quality files. An example is given to show the steps of the MapReduce system in manufacturing.

Finally, we conclude that big data can play an important role in terms of the quality improvement and the quality problem prevention. However, the big data research in quality engineering is very valuable in the future.

Acknowledgement. This research is funded by the National High Technology Research and Development Program of China (863 Program) No (2015AA042101).

References

1. Papadopoulos, T., et al.: The role of Big Data in explaining disaster resilience in supply chains for sustainability. J. Cleaner Prod. (2016)
2. Xie, H., He, Y., Xie, X.: Exploring the factors influencing ecological land change for China's Beijing–Tianjin–Hebei Region using big data. J. Cleaner Prod. (2016)
3. Siddiqa, A., et al.: A survey of big data management: taxonomy and state-of-the-art. J. Netw. Comput. Appl. (2016)
4. Ren, L., Zhang, L., Wang, L., Tao, F., Chai, X.: Cloud manufacturing: key characteristics and applications. Int. J. Comput. Integr. Manuf. (2014)
5. Ren, L., Zhang, L., Tao, F., Zhao, C., Chai, X., Zhao, X.: Cloud manufacturing: from concept to practice. Enterp. Inf. Syst. 9(2), 186–209 (2015). Taylor & Francis
6. Hashem, I.A.T., et al.: The role of big data in smart city. Int. J. Inf. Manag. 36(5), 748–758 (2016)
7. Liu, K., Xu, G., Yuan, J.E.: An improved hadoop data load balancing algorithm. J. Netw. 8(12), 2816–2822 (2013)
8. Dean, J., Ghemawat, S.: MapReduce: simplified data processing on large clusters. In: Proceedings of the 6th Conference on Symposium on Operating Systems Design and Implementation, OSDI 2004. USENIX Association (2004)
9. Bello-Orgaz, G., Jung, J.J., Camacho, D.: Social big data: recent achievements and new challenges. Inf. Fusion 28, 45–59 (2016)
10. Sokovic, M., Pavletic, D., Pipan, K.K.: Quality improvement methodologies-PDCA cycle, RADAR matrix, DMAIC and DFSS. J. Achievements Mater. Manuf. Eng. 43(1), 476 (2010)

Resource Allocation and Optimization of Simulation Models Based on Improved Genetic Algorithm in High-Throughput Simulation

Wei Zhao[1], Yanlong Zhai[1(✉)], Han Zhang[2], and Duzheng Qing[2]

[1] School of Computer Science,
Beijing Institute of Technology, Beijing, China
ylzhai@bit.edu.cn
[2] Science and Technology on Special System Simulation Laboratory,
Beijing Simulation Center, Beijing, China

Abstract. For the resource allocation and optimization problem of simulation model in high-throughput simulation, an extended genetic algorithm was proposed to improve the throughput of the simulation application. New coding approach and fitness function were designed to satisfy the model dependency. Corresponding algorithm for generating the initial population was also investigated. The experimental results showed that the extended GA can optimize the resource allocation and achieve better performance and reduce the execution time of simulation applications.

Keywords: High-throughput simulation · Resource allocation · Genetic algorithm

1 Introduction

High performance computing and high-throughput computing technology is one of the most used in computational science, and is also considered to solve complex system simulation technology of the most effective way.

The study of high flux simulation is still in the initial stage, in high-throughput simulation modeling, invoking, and data processing also needs further study, make full use of the distributed and parallel computer technology to improve the concurrency of simulation application, throughput, parallelism and reliability. In this paper, using the genetic algorithm, it has simulation characteristics about allocation and optimization between model and resource by improving genetic algorithm.

© Springer Science+Business Media Singapore 2016
L. Zhang et al. (Eds.): AsiaSim 2016/SCS AutumnSim 2016, Part III, CCIS 645, pp. 632–641, 2016.
DOI: 10.1007/978-981-10-2669-0_67

2   Model and Resource Mapping Problem in Simulation System

2.1   The Analysis of Simulation Model and System Resource On-Demand Mapping

Simulation model with on-demand mapping aspects of system resources is refers to the simulation application running early static resource allocation. Because of the particularity of the simulation, the running time of model could not be determined. So in this paper, based on the static scheduling in the case of unknown operating time, we considered computation and communication cost. The following is the precondition:

All nodes in the cluster are heterogeneous. They are full connection, and communication ability is a fixed value. The running time of each model on each node is unknown. The computational cost and communication cost of model is known.

To sum up, this is a combination optimization problem in multidimensional constraint [1, 2].

2.2   The Representation of Simulation Model and Resource

Simulation model using DAG Model $= (M, E)$ figure show the preference constraint relations between models, using two-dimensional matrix Comp[MCount, NCount] to show the amount of calculation about each model in different nodes, Comm[MCount, MCount] represents the communication relationship between the models, and the expected bandwidth.

$M = \{M_i | i \in MCount\}$: Represents a collection of nodes, each node represents a model. MCount represents amount of model.

$$M_i = \{i , Pre(M_i), Suf(M_i), H(M_i)\}$$

i: Represents model number. $Pre(M_i)$: Represents direct forerunners of model M_i. $Suf(M_i)$: Represents direct successors of model M_i. $H(M_i)$: Represents height of model in the DAG, and reflect priority of model in the scheduling. In the DAG figure, calculation formula of model height is as follows:

$$H(M_i) = \begin{cases} 0, & Pre(M_i) = \emptyset \\ 1 + MAX_{M_j \in Pre(M_i)}\{H(M_j)\}, & Pre(M_i) \neq \emptyset \end{cases}$$

$E = \{E_i(M_i, M_j) i \in MCount, j \in MCount\}$: Represents the set of edge, and reflect the sequence of model operation.

$E_i(M_i, M_j)$: Represents an edge in E, and reflect must run M_i first, and then run M_j, we call the model M_i is direct forerunner of M_j.

Comp[MCount, NCount]: Represents model calculation consumption. MCount represents amount of model. NCount represents amount of node. Comm[MCount, MCount]: Represents communication overhead between models.

2.3   System Resources

In this paper, system resources are heterogeneous resources of full connectivity, and they have the same bandwidth. The system can use DAG to represent Resources = (R, E, BW), recorded the resources calculation ability and communication ability between the nodes. $R = \{R_i \mid i \in NCount\}$: Represents a collection of nodes, and each node represents a resource. NCount is amount of resources. $R_i = \{i, W(R_i)\}$. i: Represents resources number. $W(R_i)$: Represents computing power of resource R. $E = \{E_i(R_i, R_j) \mid i \in NCount, j \in Ncount\}$: Represents collection of edges. BW: Represents actual bandwidth between resources.

3   Mapping Method Based on Genetic Algorithm

3.1   Efficient Encoding Method with Model Dependence

Model resource mapping can be divided into two steps, allocating these models and the running order of models. The first step is called the distribution of the model, the second step is called scheduling model. So the generated encoding solution would also reflect these two steps. Based on the resource mapping of model and analysis of the genetic code related knowledge, this paper uses the two-dimensional floating-point encoding. Assume that there are nine models, three resources. Encoding is as follows:

1	2	3	7	4	5	6	8	9
1	2	1	1	3	2	2	1	3

In first dimension, each value in the gene represents model number, and represents resource number in second dimension. Coding meaning is as follows:

Model： (M1, M2) (M3, M7) (M4, M5) (M6, M8) (M9)
Resource：R1   R2   R1   R1   R3   R2   R2   R1   R3

In this paper, before encoding we need to calculate the height of each model according to the above mentioned model DAG, and according to the height of each model to generate a model number sequence: (M1,M2)(M3,M7)(M4,M5)(M6,M8) (M9). Model in the same bracket represents that these models can perform at the same time. In bracket, the latter must be implemented only after the former finished. The model number of the same brackets can swap places, but the order can't exchange between parentheses. Encoding of resource number needs to be generated in the 1 to NCount.

According to the encoding above, Decoding is as follows:

R1 : M1, M3, M7, M8; **R2** : M2, M5, M6; **R3** : M4, M9;

Therefore, the encoding method determines which model assigned to which resources, and determines the running order of each model.

3.2   Algorithm of Initial Population

This article when generating the initial population, is not completely random, besides considering the dependent relationships between models, also hope that through optimizing operation generates better initial population, reducing evolution time of the genetic algorithm [3]. Optimized the following three aspects:

1. When generating the initial population, the same height as far as possible, the model of huge computation is assigned to the resources of the high computing power.
2. When generating the initial population, the same height model will be assigned to different resources as far as possible, in order to achieve maximum parallelization.
3. When generating the initial population, the combination of random distribution and optimization works best.

3.3   The Fitness Function

According to resource mapping target, the amount of calculation in each resources and traffic between models, the paper decided to use load unbalance to represent the fitness function. Load balancing technology is considering the computing performance, communication performance and so on in heterogeneous distributed system to ensure that all the nodes work effectively [4]. As far as possible to ensure the resource load balancing, promote faster simulation clock and the simulation process. So the fitness function of load unbalance is very appropriate.

$$F = \frac{1}{L} \tag{1}$$

$$L = \frac{1}{\bar{L}} \times \sqrt{\frac{\sum_{i=1}^{NCount}(L_i - \bar{L})^2}{NCount}} \tag{2}$$

$$\bar{L} = \frac{1}{NCount} \times \sum_{i=1}^{NCount} L_i \tag{3}$$

$$L_i = A \times CompLoad_i + B \times CommLoad_i \tag{4}$$

$$CompLoad_i = \sum_{j=1}^{Task_i} Comp_j \tag{5}$$

$$CommLoad_i = \sum_{j=1}^{Task_i} Comm_j \tag{6}$$

$$Comm_j = \begin{cases} 0, & \text{on the same resource} \\ comm_j, & \text{on the different resource} \end{cases} \tag{7}$$

F represents individual fitness value, *NCount* represents amount of resources, L represents amount of unbalance in the whole simulation system, L_i represents load of resource i, $\bar{L}$ represents average load, CommLoad$_i$ represents computing load of resource i, CommLoad$_i$ represents communication-load of resource i, Task$_i$ represents amount of models in resource i, Comp$_j$ represents calculated amount of j model in resource i, Comm$_j$ represents communication traffic of j model in resource i, Comm$_j$ represents communication traffic of j model. If communicating models are on the same resources, the communication overhead is negligible. This paper argues that the smaller load unbalance, the higher the throughput of the system simulation. Due to the smaller amount of unbalance with the better fitness, we used the reciprocal of the load unbalance to represent fitness function.

3.4   The Improved Selection Operator

Fitness proportion method is one of the most basic selection method. In this method, the probability of each individual selected and its fitness value are proportional. Assumed group size of M, individual fitness value of F_i, the probability is selected as:

$$P_i = \frac{F_i}{\sum_{i=1}^{M} F_i} \tag{8}$$

In order to solve the problem about the optimal chromosome damaged, the paper takes Elitism Strategy. Theoretically, the introduction of Elitism Strategy a fitness proportion method improve the fitness of the individual, faster tend to be the optimal solution, and make evolutionary process easily approach the optimal solution.

But in practice, we found evolution processes easily fall into a local optimal solution. To avoid falling into local optimal solution, this paper introduces a new concept "catastrophe". It will be presented in this Sect. 3.7. By using fitness proportion, the Elitism Strategy and catastrophe, will effectively avoid into local optimal solution.

3.5   The Improved Crossover Operator

This paper uses the single point crossover method. Individual which have higher fitness value should have lower crossover probability, so as to make excellent individual to enter the next generation. Based on the above consideration, the single point crossover method has the following optimization:

- Individuals of high fitness value select model sequences or resource sequences by equal probability to cross operation, and the whole model and resource do crossover operation in individuals of low fitness. Judgment of fitness value is that if high fitness individual in two parent individuals is greater than average fitness of population, we argue that the fitness is well. On the contrary, the fitness is low.
- Model and resource sequence of coding use different ways to cross. Resource sequence uses single-point crossover. Cross method of model sequence is as follows:
  - According to the height of each model group models.
  - Randomly generated an integer Num in the [1, MCount], determine which group should put this number. If Num is the last one in the group i, exchange model sequence of two parents from next group i + 1. If Num is the first or the middle model, exchange model sequence of two parents from this group i.

3.6   The Improved Mutation Operator

This paper uses gene variation method. Individual which have higher fitness value should have lower variation probability, can enter the next generation easily. Based on the above consideration, the gene variation method has the following optimization:

- Individuals of high fitness value select model sequences or resource sequences by equal probability to variation operation, and the whole model and resource do variation operation in individuals of low fitness.
- Resource sequence uses the traditional gene variation method. Method is as follows:
  - According to the height of each model group models.
  - Randomly generated an integer Num in the [1, MCount], determine which group should put this number, and then randomly selected a model to swap their places.

3.7   The Cataclysm Operator

Catastrophe is a geology theory. When devastating disasters happened, many living thing species extermination are caused by this way, but there are exceptions. This has a great enlightening [5] on the genetic algorithm. When obtained an optimal solution, in addition to the solution retained, other individuals randomly generated again, into the next phase of evolution. Algorithm process is as follows:

Input: Evo: predefined value of trigger catastrophe,
1: **if** evolutional generation==*Evo* **And** the best fitness remains the same **then**
2:    Retain the chromosome of the best fitness and generation the rest of the chromosomes again. Finally, evolve to the next generation.
3: **end if**

---

4   Experimental Evaluation

4.1   Experimental Environment

In genetic algorithm, the selection of related parameters effect performance [6]. Due to the focus of this paper is not on the determination of related parameters, so the experimental data is according to the rules defined in Table 1 randomly generated. Assuming the number of resource is set to 3, randomly generated 10 groups of model, and changes in 10–100 DAG figure. In Tables 2 and 3 defines the related parameters.

4.2   Experimental Results and Analysis of Improved Crossover Operator

Firstly, comparing the time between improved crossover and ordinary single point operator, the method is that, based on the same population, respectively, run two

Table 1. Relevant parameter and figure DAG

DAG	1	3	5	7	9	2	4	6	8	10
The number of models	10	30	50	70	90	20	40	60	80	100
The range of computation	50 ~ 100					100 ~ 150				
The range of communication	0 ~ 10									

Table 2. Relevant parameter about genetic operation

Operating data	Value
Population scale	2*(model amount)
Evolutionary algebra	30
Crossover probability	0.8
Mutation probability	0.15

(a)

Operating data	Value
Population scale	2*(model amount)
Evolutionary algebra	500
Crossover probability	0.8
Mutation probability	0.15

(b)

Table 3. Parameters of the ten groups

Group Id	1	2	3	4	5	6	7	8	9	10
The number of models	20	20	20	20	20	50	50	50	50	50
The range of computation	50 ~ 100									
The range of communication	10 ~ 20									
Running time	40 ~ 60									
Time delay	1 ~ 5									

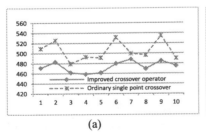

(a)

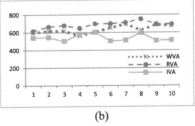

(b)

Fig. 1. (a): DAG1 time comparison of crossover (b): DAG3 time comparison of variation

different crossover operator each 10 times (parameters as shown in Table 2(a)). Experiment records the average time of each crossover operator (in ms). Here select representative figure DAG1 as test data, the result is shown in Fig. 1(a). We can see that the average time of the improved crossover operation is shorter from Fig. 1(a).

4.3   Experimental Results and Analysis of Improved Variation Operator

In the experiment, three kinds of mutation operators are used to compare performance. The first variation operation is that randomly select a model and corresponding resource, called WVA. The second variation operation is models and resources randomly select variation point. They will not interfere with each other, called RVA. The third variation is improved mutation operation. We called IVA operation.

First of all, we compared running time of three kinds of variation operation. The experimental method is that run three different mutation operation each 10 times (each operation parameters as shown in Table 2(a)). We record average running time of mutation operation when every genetic operation is completed (in ms). We selected representative figure DAG3 as test data, the result is shown in Fig. 1(b).

From Fig. 1(b), we can found that the average running time of improved mutation operation IVA is lower than other two kinds of mutation operation.

Secondly, this article puts forward further performance verification about three kinds of mutation operation. Experimental method is that each kind of mutation operation runs 10 times respectively, each time parameter of the genetic operation as shown in Table 2(b). We recorded the change of optimal fitness situation. We selected representative figure DAG3 as test data, the result is as follows.

From Fig. 2(a), we can found that WVA mutation operation can find the best fitness of chromosomes after 160 generations, and IVA mutation operation is about 200 generations. But RVA mutation operation began to close to the optimal fitness about 320 generation. According to the result, if in the increased models and more complex DAG, WVA and IVA will have greater advantages.

In WVA and IVA, owing to randomness of the evolution process, we can learn that the performance of WVA and IVA can be considered approximately equal. But, from the perspective of execution time, the improved mutation operation had more advantages. Especially in a large number of models, it is more obvious advantage. So, we must admit that the improved mutation operation has an advantage.

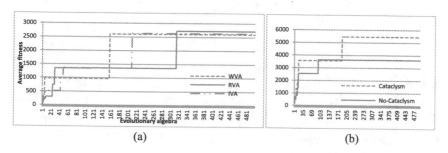

Fig. 2.   (a): Fitness comparison of mutation. (b): Optimal fitness influence about catastrophe

4.4   Experimental Results and Analysis of Improved Catastrophe Operator

Using DAG6 as experimental samples, Table 2(b) as the experimental parameters, we recorded the optimal fitness in the process of evolution. In the process of the concrete experiment, recorded result 20 times, and then calculate its average.

From Fig. 2(b), we found that the biggest fitness remains at 3630 from 85 generations in No-cataclysm. It shows the genetic operation has entered local optimal solution. After cataclysm operation introduced, although the genetic operation also found fitness 3630, the evolution did not stop, finally, fond the largest fitness from 190 generation. At that time, corresponding chromosome was the optimal solution. So, the introduction of cataclysm operation is to avoid the population into local solution.

4.5   Experimental Results and Analysis of Simulation

Simulation experiment need the calculation of each model, the traffic of model, the constraint relationship between models and calculation of system resource, also need running time and communication delay to evaluate optimal solution. The three resources of computing power are respectively 90–100, 80–90, 70–80. The following introduce the basic information of the model and resources used in the experiment.

Improved Initialization Population Experiment. This section contrasts the random algorithm of generating population and optimizing algorithm proposed. In ten groups of model, two methods are used to generate the initial population with 50 models, and then compare the best individual simulation time in initial population. The result is shown in Fig. 3(a).

Simulation time of optimal solution based on the optimized initial population is better than randomly generated population. So, considering parallelism and computing power of resource in the same set of model, not only can increase the parallelism of the same set of model, but also the subsequent model can perform much earlier, and increase simulation throughput. Meanwhile, we can make full use of the characteristics of heterogeneous resources which have different computing power, and makes the large amount of calculation model can be run to finish as soon as possible.

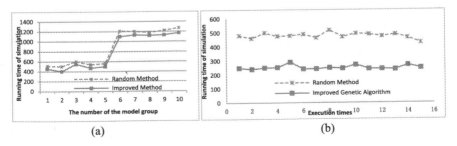

Fig. 3. (a): Simulation time comparison. (b): Simulation efficiency comparison.

The Experimental Results of Simulation Using Improved Genetic Algorithm. This section compares running time of simulation between random distribution method and improved genetic algorithm. For the same model group, we conduct respectively experiment 15 times using random distribution method and improved method. The situation of the model group: 20 models and 3 resources. The population size of improved genetic algorithm: 50, Evolutionary algebra: 200. The experimental result is shown in Fig. 3(b). In Fig. 3(b), time of random allocation method is more dispersed. By the improved genetic algorithm to get running time of optimal solution is relatively stable, and the simulation running time is shorter. Therefore, improved genetic algorithm can effectively reduce time, and increase the throughput.

5   Summary

According to the demand of high-throughput simulation, use the improved algorithm to solve resource allocation in high-throughput simulation. The paper proposed efficient coding method, accordingly genetic operation was improved. Meanwhile, we put forward the optimization of the initial population, crossover operation and mutation operation. Finally, catastrophe operation is well integrated with genetic algorithm. Through a series of experimental operation, we found that model and resource allocation method based on genetic algorithm in this paper can effectively improve the efficiency of the simulation running and reduce running time of simulation.

References

1. Tan, Y.L., Jiong, Y.U., Deng, D.L., et al.: Grid task scheduling algorithm based on multi-dimensional quality of service constraints. Comput. Eng. **36**(12), 75–77 (2010). (in Chinese)
2. Ma, T., Yan, Q., Liu, W., et al.: Grid task scheduling: algorithm review. IETE Techn. Rev. **28**(2), 158–167 (2014)
3. Abdulal, W., Jadaan, O.A., Jabas, A., et al.: Rank-based genetic algorithm with limited iteration for grid scheduling. In: First International Conference on Computational Intelligence, Communication Systems and Networks, CICSYN 2009, pp. 29–34. IEEE (2009)
4. Han, Y., Jiong, Y.U., Zhang, W., et al.: An task scheduling algorithm based on load balance. Microelectr. Comput. **27**(8), 200–201 (2010). (in Chinese)
5. Zhang, Y., Ren, Z., Zhong, H., et al.: Cataclysmic genetic algorithms based optimal reactive power planning. Autom. Electr. Power Syst. **26**(23), 29–32 (2002). (in Chinese)
6. Cheng, S.T., Hsieh, M.T., Chen, B.F.: Fairness-based scheduling algorithm for time division duplex mode IEEE 802.16 broadband wireless access systems. IET Commun. **4**(9), 1065–1072 (2010)

Author Index